To my wife, Rebecca, for her love, patience, and support, and to Sammy and Miriam, for bringing joy to all the days.

M.S.

To my husband, Barry Lotenberg, and my children, Sienna, Lucas and Eliana, for giving up the time I needed to prepare this second edition.

L.D.L.

SECOND EDITION

MARKETING
PUBLIC HEALTH

STRATEGIES TO PROMOTE SOCIAL CHANGE

Michael Siegel, MD, MPH
Professor
Boston University School of Public Health
Boston, Massachusetts

Lynne Doner Lotenberg, MA
Social Marketing Consultant
Arlington, Virginia

JONES AND BARTLETT PUBLISHERS
Sudbury, Massachusetts
N   TORONTO   LONDON   SINGAPORE

World Headquarters
Jones and Bartlett Publishers
40 Tall Pine Drive
Sudbury, MA 01776
978-443-5000
info@jbpub.com
www.jbpub.com

Jones and Bartlett Publishers
Canada
6339 Ormindale Way
Mississauga, Ontario
L5V 1J2
CANADA

Jones and Bartlett Publishers
International
Barb House, Barb Mews
London W6 7PA
UK

Substantial discounts on bulk quantities of Jones and Bartlett's publications are available to corporations, professional associations, and other qualified organizations. For details and specific discount information, contact the special sales department at Jones and Bartlett via the above contact information or send an email to specialsales@jbpub.com.

Jones and Bartlett's books and products are available through most bookstores and online booksellers. To contact Jones and Bartlett Publishers directly, call 800-832-0034, fax 978-443-8000, or visit our website www.jbpub.com.

Library of Congress Cataloging-in-Publication Data

Siegel, Michael, M.D.
  Marketing public health : strategies to promote social change / Michael Siegel and Lynne Doner.
  — 2nd ed.
    p. ; cm.
  ISBN-13: 978-0-7637-3891-4
  ISBN-10: 0-7637-3891-3
  1. Public health—Marketing. I. Doner, Lynne. II. Title.
  [DNLM: 1. Public Health. 2. Marketing of Health Services. 3. Social Change.
  WA 100 S571m 2007]
  RA427.S53 2007
  362.1068'8—dc22
                                              2006022680
    6048

Production Credits

Publisher: Michael Brown
Associate Editors: Kylah Goodfellow McNeill
  and Katey Birtcher
Associate Production Editor: Daniel Stone
Marketing Manager: Sophie Fleck
V.P. of Manufacturing and Inventory Control:
  Therese Connell
Composition: Jason Miranda, Spoke & Wheel
Cover Design: Eve Siegel
Cover Printing: Malloy, Inc.
Printing and Binding: Malloy, Inc.

Cover Credits

Cover photos: © iStockphotos.com
Top left (runner): Oleg Prikhodko
Top right (vaccine): Mikhail Tolstoy
Middle left (vegetables): Slawomir Fajer
Middle right (no smoking sign): Stefan Klein
Lower left (newspaper stack): Kyle Maass
Lower right (classroom): Bonnie Jacobs
Bottom left (dollars): Mecaleha
Bottom right (smokestacks): Greg Nicholas

Printed in the United States of America
11 10 09 08 07   10 9 8 7 6 5 4 3 2

CONTENTS

FOREWORD

In the nineteenth and twentieth centuries the most important improvements in the public's health may have come from innovations in plumbing and general sanitation, and in inoculation against disease. These environmental changes may have had more impact than the curative work of doctors. Many other successes in public health have contributed to increasing the life span of the average American by about 30 years over the past century. We can see some of these successes, for example, through decreases in infant mortality, the management of AIDS, the increasing use of seat belts, and the decrease in smoking rates from about 50% of the adult population in 1970 to about 20% today.

But all is not positive. The state of the public's health is not as good as it could be. As some changes have led to longer and healthier lives, others have led to a diminution of health. Labor saving devices, leisure products, and easily-accessible, good-tasting, unhealthy food have led to a new class of health issues. For example, about 65% of the U.S. population now is overweight or obese.

Clearly there is a relationship between positive and negative developments in public health. As one set of problems was conquered, leading to a longer and potentially healthier life, new issues arose that threatened the previous gains.

We can attribute the successes to a variety of public health practices in law enforcement, message campaigns, and environmental changes. While social marketing has had some impact in each of these three strategic categories, it has been underutilized as a way to manage behavior. It is possible that future environmental breakthroughs may come from social marketing, wherein strategies can be developed, for example, to make it easier for people to eat well and put more physical activity into their lives.

Marketers generally believe that almost everybody does almost everything out of immediate self-interest. Many public health message campaigns tell people what they should be doing to achieve long-term good health, when these people are merely seeking a nice appearance, less hassle in their lives, or a quick sugar fix to pick them up in the afternoon. This has led to disconnects where people tend to know what they should be doing to improve their health and are motivated to do so but aren't following through. For example, while 78% of adults feel that obesity is a serious problem, only 38% consume the proper level of produce; while 58% want to lose weight, only 27% are seriously trying to do so. Perhaps we need a better understanding of self interest.

Social marketing offers a planning tool based on the use of marketing research to define targets, specific desired behavioral outcomes, an increase in benefits that reinforce self interest, and a way to decrease the barriers that inhibit behavior. Commercial marketers are adamant about focusing on behavior, on setting specific goals, and on measuring results. These foci can offer potentially major contributions to a public health practice, which often neglects each of these. Marketing works as a result of listening carefully to what consumers say, but too often public health efforts are paternalistic in telling consumers what they ought to do, rather than first listening to what people want for themselves.

The marketing model can work well in combination with the epidemiologic model of public health. While epidemiologic research is well suited to defining health problems and broad classes of affected people, marketing research provides insights on how the environment needs to be changed so that behavior can follow. While epidemiologic research gives insight to a top-down model of soliciting behavior, marketing research gives insights for a bottom-up participative perspective.

The current definition of marketing is based on creating, communicating, and delivering value to the target while developing long-term relationships. Creating deals with the development of desired benefits; delivering concerns the reduction of the barriers that keep people from behaving; communicating concerns informing and persuading in the interests of motivating behavior.

So we have three important questions before us: Why are people behaving poorly with respect to their own health? Why has the field of public health not had more consistent successes? What can we do about these problems? *Marketing Public Health* tries to answer these questions by considering both the pitfalls currently existing in public health practice and the potential for moving forward using social marketing. This combination of analyzing pitfalls and recommending practice gives *Marketing Public Health* its strength.

One of the disconnects of health practice concerns preventative care versus curative care. In the United States, vastly more money is spent on curing, while a vastly greater impact is made through preventive practice. Perhaps this is because curative medicine shows immediate response at a visible individual level, while the impact of preventive medicine is much more difficult to observe. *Marketing Public Health* tries to show how marketing can be used to move the field of public health forward, in addition to showing how to use marketing to remedy specific public health problems.

In order to solve public health problems, there needs to be a proper understanding of the issues that led to today's problems before strategic solutions can be proposed. *Marketing Public Health* begins with a cogent layout of the underlying issues before moving on to a discussion of strategic and tactical contributions from social marketing. Without having a clear understanding of the state of the government and its health policies, the potential solutions would have less context and less value. Readers will benefit from the careful exposition of current public health practice (as put forth in the first half of the text), as a base for understanding the strategic and tactical practice of social marketing (as described in the second half).

Michael L. Rothschild
University of Wisconsin

ACKOWLEDGMENTS

This book draws on the work of scholars and practitioners in a range of disciplines. Their inspiration, ideas, and experiences were invaluable to us. We especially thank those who allowed us to share some of their work through examples and case studies included in this volume.

Our editor at Jones and Bartlett, Mike Brown, was the driving force behind both the original and the second edition of this book. The staff of Health Unlimited and Health Unlimited Rwanda, particularly the contributing authors for Chapter 7—Narcisse Kalisa, Prudence Uwabakurikiza, Samuel Kyagambiddwa, Jeannette Wijnants, and Stephen Collens—were kind enough to take time from their vital health promotion work to share their experiences for the benefit of our readers. Erin Fortunato spent months researching and preparing Chapter 8. Our special thanks to Eve Siegel for the cover design for this second edition.

Finally, we are indebted to the many family members who put up with our distractions and mumblings during the year we spent preparing this second edition.

INTRODUCTION

The events of September 11, 2001 changed the nation in many ways. One of those changes, unfortunately, has been a diversion of public health focus to the threat of bioterrorism and a resulting decrease of attention to, and resources for, public health epidemics that are real and ongoing threats representing the major causes of death in the nation.

In 2001, an anthrax scare prompted a large-scale smallpox vaccination campaign that was implemented in response to a completely unproven threat (Dowling & Lipton, 2005). The campaign cost more than $0.6 billion and resulted in the deaths of three healthcare workers. On August 29, 2005, Hurricane Katrina made landfall along the Central Gulf Coast and caused massive devastation along the coastlines of Louisiana, Mississippi, and Alabama. Literally thousands of vulnerable and helpless Americans were left to die in the streets due to lack of medical attention and a dismal failure of the nation's ability to respond appropriately and effectively to a very real and imminent health threat (Dowling & Lupton, 2005). These events have only highlighted the complete mismatch between the most pressing health threats our nation faces and the areas of focus for allocation of public health resources and preparedness.

In 2006, while the nation may be prepared for an imagined and theoretical smallpox attack against the country, there is little question that we are ill-prepared to prevent, monitor, and respond to the real and possibly imminent threat of an avian ("bird") flu pandemic. The diversion of resources to bioterrorism preparedness in the wake of September 11 represents a disaster for public health in the United States (Cohen, Gould, & Sidel, 2004). Chronic disease epidemics are raging, newly emerging infectious disease threats await, and yet funding for public health programs is being cut in order to secure short-term financial savings and allow politicians to boast that they are not raising taxes.

On February 6, 2006, President George W. Bush announced his proposed budget for fiscal year 2007. As the nation braced for a potential bird flu pandemic, its President cut funding for the Centers for Disease Control and Prevention (CDC)—the nation's leading public health and prevention agency—by 2% (American Public Health Association, 2006). Accounting for new spending for flu preparedness and response, however, the proposed CDC budget for its vital and existing chronic and infectious disease prevention and control programs was cut by 4.5%. Proposed funding for the CDC's Preventive Health and Health Services Block Grants was eliminated, as was proposed funding for the universal newborn hearing screening program and the urban American Indian health program. The proposed budget also cut, although did not completely eliminate, funding for the Children's Health Insurance Program, which provides insurance to millions of low-income children. Fiscal year 2006 had already seen the elimination of CDC's Verb campaign, an effective effort to promote physical activity in order to address the nation's burgeoning obesity epidemic, as well as severe cuts to Medicaid.

As we enter the new millennium, the public health community faces unprecedented threats to its funding, its ability to appropriately and effectively respond to existing and imminent crises, and its very existence at the national, state, and local levels. It is no longer enough for public health professionals to work to protect the health of the public. Public health practitioners must work to protect the survival of public health as an institution.

Changes in the social, political, and economic environments in which health care is delivered present a direct threat to the survival of public health. Public health programs must now compete vigorously for public attention and resources. Even within the category of public health funding, practitioners must convince policy makers and the public that bioterrorism and other emerging threats require supplemental funding, and not simply a shift in funding from critical existing programs to the threat of the month. Strengthening the public health infrastructure so that it can respond to any threat has been overlooked for far too long.

This threat to the survival of public health comes at the same time as these changes in the social, political, and economic environments also present a direct threat to the public's health itself. Unhealthy lifestyles and behaviors and deteriorating social and environmental conditions threaten the public's health. As the chief causes of death in the United States have gradually shifted from communicable illnesses to chronic diseases, lifestyle and behavioral risk factors, as well as social and environmental conditions, have become the key determinants of the public's health. In contrast to its successes in controlling infectious diseases, the public health movement has been ineffective in controlling the emerging chronic disease epidemic. Programs intended to change individual behaviors and lifestyles have often been ineffective, and public health professionals have not fully accepted the role of advocating for changes in social conditions and social policies. As a result, the public health community is equipped neither to confront existing public health crises, nor to prevent new ones.

Despite these threats, there are tools available to help the public health profession save itself and enable it to confront existing and emerging public health crises. There are public health initiatives that have successfully changed societal behaviors, improved social conditions, reformed social policies, and retained and even increased funding for public health programs and departments.

The common feature of many of these initiatives is public health practitioners' strategic use of marketing principles to promote social change. Understanding and applying marketing principles is essential for public health practitioners to successfully confront the imposing challenges they face—challenges to both the public's health and to the survival of the public health profession. However, public health practitioners are not typically trained in the principles of marketing.

Marketing Public Health: Strategies to Promote Social Change (Second Edition) is designed to help public health practitioners understand basic marketing principles and strategically apply these principles in planning, implementing, and evaluating public health initiatives. We hope that this book will provide public health practitioners at all levels of government and in the private sector with a valuable tool to create and deliver more effective initiatives to change individual behavior, improve social and economic conditions, advance social policies, and compete successfully for public attention and resources.

We argue that the key to creating and running effective public health programs is to abandon the traditional practice of deciding what policy makers, or the public, ought to want, and then trying to sell it to them in the absence of significant demand. Instead, public health practitioners must first learn the needs and wants of their target audience (policy makers or the public) and understand their motivation, opportunity, and ability to engage in our desired behavior (changes in individual health behavior or the adoption of public health programs and policies). We must then create product offerings that increase opportunities to engage in the behavior, increase skills, and/or increase motivation. Often this means addressing the social, economic, and policy environments. Successful product offerings provide compelling benefits, increase convenience or access, and, when necessary, reduce barriers. Rather than appealing exclusively to the benefits of improved health, public health practitioners must learn to identify benefits that are salient and compelling to the target audience and then create and deliver product offerings that provide these benefits. Compelling benefits often are tangible and immediate and/or connected to powerful and influential core values: freedom, independence, autonomy, control, fairness, democracy, and free enterprise.

In this *Second Edition*, we have not only brought the material up to date, but have tried to make it come alive in a more meaningful way for current public health students and practitioners. Examples from areas of public health interest that have arisen only in the past few years (e.g., bioterrorism, SARS, West Nile virus) are included throughout. A new case study from the field of international health aims to give this edition more relevance to the global practice of public health and to widen its scope beyond the borders of the United States. All-new case studies from front-line programs help illustrate the principles and strategies discussed in the book in a way that makes it immediately apparent to readers how the material can be used in modern, real-life public health marketing efforts.

This edition has been influenced both by changes in the marketing environment and also by the latest thinking among marketing and social marketing researchers and practitioners. Discussion of current emphases, such as building relationships with audiences rather than managing individual transactions, using the power of branding, and ensuring that audience self-interest is considered and addressed, have been incorporated into the book in both its narrative and its case studies and examples.

The book is organized into two parts. Part I explains the reasons why the understanding of marketing principles is necessary for the public health practitioner to effectively confront these challenges. It outlines the major marketing principles that public health practitioners need to understand and illustrates the application of these principles to public health problems through examples within the chapters and two case studies presented separately.

Part I is divided into three sections. The first section (Chapters 1–3) describes threats to the public's health and establishes that changing individual behavior, social and economic conditions, and social policy are important to successfully confront the chronic disease epidemic (Chapter 1). It illustrates the difficulties of promoting these social changes discussed in Chapter 2 and also demonstrates how public health practitioners can use basic marketing principles to structure interventions that will facilitate social change (Chapter 3).

The second section (Chapters 4–6) describes threats to the survival of public health as an institution. It establishes that learning how to effectively market public health programs and policies, and the idea of public health itself, is essential to confront challenges to public health's survival. It shows why marketing public health programs and policies is profoundly difficult (Chapter 5), but demonstrates how public health practitioners can strategically apply basic marketing principles to promote public health programs and policies (Chapter 6).

The third section (Chapters 7 and 8) presents two case studies. In Chapter 7, guest contributors Narcisse Kalisa, Prudence Uwabakurikiza, Samuel Kyagambiddwa, and Jeannette Wijnants illustrate the innovative use of marketing principles to promote healthier sexual behaviors among women in Rwanda. In Chapter 8, guest contributor Erin Fortunato examines the framing of public health as an institution. She uses the Congressional debate over funding for CDC's budget to identify the current strategies that are used to frame public health, analyzes and evaluates these strategies in light of the principles outlined in Chapters 1–6, and then recommends ways to more effectively frame public health in the future.

Part II discusses how to apply the principles presented in Part I in planning, developing, implementing, evaluating, and refining public health efforts to change individual behavior or to promote the adoption of public health programs and policies. Examples within chapters, and case studies at chapter ends illustrate key points.

Part II is divided into three sections that correspond to the stages of a marketing effort (planning; development, testing, and implementation; and assessment). Section I (Chapters 9–12) provides background on the basic marketing principles that a public health practitioner must understand and presents a process for planning public health efforts based on these principles. It begins by presenting key marketing concepts and discussing how they apply to individual and policy changes (Chapter 9). It then presents a strategic planning process (Chapter 10) and describes how some commonly used formative research techniques can be used to support the strategic planning process (Chapter 11). The final chapter in the section (Chapter 12) discusses how to frame and deliver messages about the social change so that they are relevant, compelling, and actionable for target audiences.

Section II of Part II (Chapters 13–15) covers the process of developing and implementing the tactics, or components, involved in an initiative. Chapter 13 discusses translating the strategic plan into specific tactics and a carefully timed implementation. Because public health marketing efforts often involve working with other organizations, Chapter 14 describes the various roles that partners, allies, and intermediaries can play in an initiative and provides suggestions for developing and managing productive relationships. Chapter 15 provides guidance on developing and assessing mass media and other promotional activities and materials.

The third section of Part II (Chapters 16–18) discusses tracking, evaluating, and refining social change efforts. Chapter 16 discusses approaches to tracking and monitoring implementation of marketing efforts and discusses how to use the information to make improvements. Chapter 17 discusses issues in assessing the outcomes of marketing-based efforts using traditional approaches to summative evaluation and presents some techniques for assessing outcomes and using the results to make program refinements. The final chapter in the section (Chapter 18) discusses a number of theories of behavior change as well as common marketing research methodologies-focus groups, in-depth interviews, observational techniques, surveys, and quasi- and true experiments-and details how to plan, conduct and report on studies using these methods.

Although marketing principles have been applied to some efforts to change health-related behaviors for many years, the integration of marketing principles into day-to-day public health practice is a new concept, and one that has not yet been fully developed. These principles can provide powerful tools for influencing all the factors that contribute to social change: the individual, the environment, and social policy.

This book is a first attempt to describe how marketing principles might become part of public health practice and be used to develop and implement more effective public health initiatives. If our ideas stimulate further thought, research, and, most important, experimentation among public health practitioners, we will have achieved our goal. It is our hope that the efforts that come from practitioners who read this book will provide far more answers to the difficult questions we pose here than does the book itself. For in the final analysis, the experience of public health practitioners will teach us to develop and implement more effective programs to promote social change and improve the quality of life today and tomorrow.

References

American Public Health Association. (2006, March). 2007 budget proposal paints dire picture for public health. *The Nation's Health*. Washington, DC: American Public Health Association.

Cohen H.W., Gould R.M., & Sidel, V.W. (2004). The pitfalls of bioterrorism preparedness: The anthrax and smallpox experiences. *American Journal of Public Health*, 94, 1667–1671.

Dowling K.C., & Lipton, R.I. (2005). Bioterrorism preparedness expenditures may compromise public health. *American Journal of Public Health*, 95, 1672.

I

Marketing Principles for Public Health Practice

I

Marketing Social Change

To confront the chronic disease epidemic that threatens to dominate human health in the twenty-first century, public health practice must begin to focus on far more than providing basic medical care. To establish a favorable environment for human well-being, public health practitioners must concentrate on effecting social change by helping to modify individual behaviors and lifestyles, improve social and economic conditions, and reform social policies.

This section demonstrates that social change is essential to protecting the public's health and why creating social change presents a formidable task for public health practitioners. The ways that practitioners can use basic marketing principles to effectively confront this challenge are also explained.

This section focuses mainly on how to employ marketing principles to accomplish the first task: modifying individual behavior. Using marketing principles to improve social and economic conditions and reform social policy is discussed in Part I, Section II.

CHAPTER

1

Emerging Threats to the Public's Health—The Need for Social Change

An epidemic of chronic disease threatens the public's health. Fueling this epidemic are unhealthy lifestyles and behaviors, deteriorating social conditions, and an increasingly hazardous environment, coupled with a crisis in access to quality health care. The emerging chronic disease epidemic poses both a threat to the public's health and a challenge to public health practice. Public health practice must focus on far more than the provision of medical care. It must, first and foremost, dedicate its efforts to modifying individual lifestyle and behavior, improving social and economic conditions, and reforming social policy to establish an environment that fosters optimal human health. In other words, the business of public health must focus on creating social change.

The United States is experiencing an epidemic unlike any in its history. Chronic disease is now responsible for three out of every four deaths in the country each year—1.9 million deaths in all—and carries an annual financial burden of $325 billion. The impact extends beyond mortality rates: Approximately 100 million Americans—more than one-third of the U.S. population—experience disability or severe limitation of their daily activities due to chronic disease. It is projected to afflict 120 million Americans by the year 2010, and up to 134 million by the year 2020. By then, the costs associated with the epidemic will approach $1 trillion per year.

Unlike previous epidemics, the historic proportions associated with chronic disease today are not reported as front-page news; efforts to confront the issues are not among the priority program activities of most local health departments; and policy makers allocate precious few resources to eliminate the epidemic or even to slow its spread. Improving sanitation and hygiene will do little to stem the tide. Even the medical profession is nearly powerless against it.

The primary and most urgent challenge to public health today is to find a way to halt the epidemic of chronic disease that threatens to dominate the population in the twenty-first century. Chronic diseases—heart disease, cancer, stroke, injuries, chronic obstructive lung disease, diabetes, and liver disease—are the chief causes of death among Americans as we enter the twenty-first century (**Figure 1-1**).

By far, the leading causes of death in the United States are heart disease, cancer, and stroke, which account for about 1.4 million (58%) of the nation's 2.4 million deaths each year (National Center for Health Statistics [NCHS], 2004). Injuries, including motor vehicle accidents, suicides, homicides, falls, and drownings, account for an additional 140,000 deaths annually (5.7% of all deaths). Violence, in particular, is an alarming part of the chronic disease epidemic. Homicide alone is the leading cause of death among Blacks ages 15 to 24, and is the second leading cause of death among all persons in this age group (NCHS, 2004; Rosenberg, Powell, & Hammond, 1997; Satcher, 1996). Chronic obstructive lung disease causes an additional 125,000 deaths annually (5.1% of all deaths). Combined, chronic disease and injuries account for nearly 1.9 million annual deaths, about 77% of all deaths in the nation (NCHS, 2004).

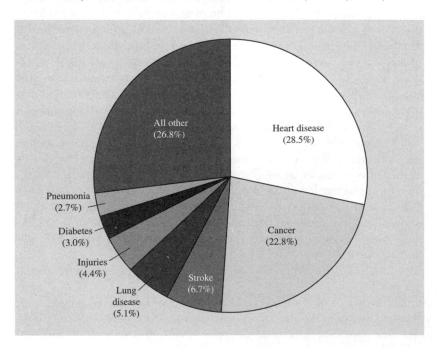

Figure 1-1 Causes of Death—United States. 2002.
Source: NCHS, 2004.

Chronic diseases also cause a substantial amount of disability and suffering among Americans. Approximately 100 million people in the United States have one or more chronic medical conditions, such as heart disease, stroke, cancer, arthritis, diabetes, lung disease, osteoporosis, multiple sclerosis, and mental retardation; about 40% of this population has more than one chronic condition (Hoffman, Rice, & Sung, 1996). The direct medical costs associated with chronic diseases accounted for about 76% of all direct medical expenditures in the nation (Hoffman et al., 1996). And chronic diseases resulted in 12.4% of all individuals, and 34.4% of those ages 65 years and over, having limitation of activity (i.e., limitation of their ability to perform activities usual for their age group) in 2002 (NCHS, 2004).

Despite advances in medical knowledge and treatment, little progress has been made in stemming the epidemic. Although stroke mortality rates declined by 62% and heart disease mortality rates declined by 51% from 1970 to 2002 (NCHS, 2004), only about one-third of the decline in mortality was due to a reduction in the incidence of cardiovascular disease (Sytkowski, Kannel, & D'Agostino, 1990), and the burden of disease morbidity is expected to increase, especially among the elderly (Bonneux et al., 1994). Although fewer people are dying of their disease, nearly the same proportion has cardiovascular disease and suffers from their chronic conditions (Bonneux et al., 1994; Centers for Disease Control and Prevention [CDC], 1993). The death rate from chronic lung disease increased by 54% between 1980 and 2002, with a more than doubling (150% increase) of the age-adjusted death rate among women (NCHS, 2004).

Thus, the overall health status among the American population seems to be worsening, not improving. Between 1993 and 2001, the proportion of adults who self-rated their health status as being poor increased from 3.5% to 4.1% (Zahran et al., 2005). The proportion of adults who reported more than 13 days of activity limitation due to ill health increased from 4.8% to 6.2%. And the proportion who reported more than 13 unhealthy days due to poor physical health increased from 8.6% to 10.4%.

Overall cancer death rates have remained essentially unchanged for the past 50 years (NCHS, 2004). There has been a modest decline in mortality from colorectal cancer, stomach cancer, uterine cancer, and liver cancer, but these changes have been more than offset by the striking increase in lung cancer mortality (American Cancer Society, 1994; NCHS, 2004). Although lung cancer death rates among men peaked in the early 1990s, rates are still increasing among women (NCHS, 2004).

The rate of suicide among U.S. teenagers is nearly three times as high as it was in 1950, and the homicide rate among teenagers is more than twice as high, mostly due to the widespread availability of firearms (NCHS, 2004; Satcher, 1996). The incidence of diabetes, which increased by 48% between 1980 and 1994 (CDC, 1997a), remained stable through 2000 (NCHS, 2004).

In 1994, the age-adjusted incidence of diabetes reached its highest level in underserved populations, and the nation has failed dismally in its efforts to reduce chronic disease mortality among these populations. While cancer death rates among White males decreased from 1970 to 2002 and rates among White females remained relatively stable, rates among Black males and Black females increased by 10% (NCHS, 2004). Ischemic heart disease death rates, which were higher among Whites than Blacks in 1980, have declined in both groups, but more rapidly among Whites, so that rates are now higher among Blacks than Whites (NCHS, 2004).

The disparity in overall mortality between higher and lower socio-economic groups continues to increase in the United States (Pappas et al., 1993). Between 1960 and 1986, overall mortality declined in all socioeconomic groups, but declines were significantly greater among persons with higher income and higher levels of education (Pappas et al., 1993). In communities that are particularly poor, death rates among Blacks have changed little since 1960 (Jenkins et al., 1977; McCord & Freeman, 1990; Pappas et al., 1993).

A striking disparity between higher and lower socioeconomic groups is evident not only in mortality, but in morbidity as well. While only 9.5% of non-poor individuals (those with incomes at least 200% of the poverty level) reported limitation of activity due to chronic disease in 2002, 22.9% of poor individuals (below the poverty threshold) reported limitation of activity (NCHS, 2004). While only 6.4% of non-poor individuals reported fair or poor health in 2002 (compared to good or excellent health), 20.4% of poor persons did (NCHS, 2004).

The contrast in health status between higher and lower socioeconomic class groups is itself a component of the chronic disease epidemic. Several studies have shown that the persistence of social class differences in health status is a stronger determinant of overall poor health than the level of poverty and disadvantage in a community (Henig, 1997; Kennedy, Kawachi, & Prothrow-Stith, 1995; Marmot, Bobak, & Smith, 1995; McCord & Freeman, 1990; Navarro, 1997; Townsend & Davidson, 1982; Wilkinson, 1990, 1992, 1997). As Johns Hopkins University professor Vincente Navarro (1997) pointed out,

> A poor person in Harlem, New York City, is likely to have worse health status than a middle-class person in Bangladesh (one of the poorest countries in the world), even though the former has, in absolute terms, more resources (monetary resources and goods and services) than the latter. Still, to be poor in Harlem is far more difficult (because of the social and psychological distance from the rest of society) than to be middle class in Bangladesh. It is not class structure but class relations that affect the levels of health of our populations. (p. 335)

The chronic disease epidemic must be viewed with no less urgency and concern than traditional infectious disease "epidemics" that have plagued society for centuries. As Dr. David Satcher, former director of the CDC noted, chronic disease (violence, in particular) "can erode the well-being of neighborhoods and destroy communities with the same deadly impact as the outbreak of a fatal disease" (Satcher, 1996, p. 1707). And an editorial in *American Journal of Public Health* asserted, "We should be as much concerned about the thousands of people who are homeless in American cities and the thousands of children in residentially unstable families as we are when there is an epidemic of an infectious disease affecting a few hundred people, and we should respond with the same urgency" (Breakey, 1997, p. 153).

To understand why medical and traditional public health efforts have been virtually powerless in confronting chronic disease, we must understand the factors that are fueling the chronic disease epidemic: (1) unhealthy lifestyles and behaviors, (2) deteriorating social and economic conditions, and (3) a crisis in access to quality health care.

■ UNHEALTHY LIFESTYLES AND BEHAVIORS

A large body of medical and public health literature documents the role of individual behavior in disease, especially chronic disease. A series of large, population-based, cohort studies has identified behavioral risk factors for a variety of chronic diseases, most notably heart disease, stroke, and cancer (Slater & Carlton, 1985). The Harvard Report on Cancer Prevention concluded that two-thirds of cancer deaths alone could be prevented by changes in individual behavior (Colditz et al., 1996).

Researchers from the CDC have estimated that of the 2.4 million annual deaths in the United States, more than 400,000 could be prevented by eliminating tobacco use; approximately 365,000 could be prevented through improved diet and physical activity; another 85,000 could be prevented by eliminating excess alcohol consumption; and an additional 20,000 could be prevented by eliminating unsafe sexual practices (Mokdad et al., 2004, 2005). Other behavior-related, preventable causes of death include workplace, home, recreational, and roadway injuries; firearms-related injuries; high blood pressure and high cholesterol levels (which are related to diet and physical activity); illicit drug use; and breast and cervical cancer (where early screening could impact prognosis) (Mokdad et al., 2004; CDC, 1995; U.S. Department of Health and Human Services [USDHHS], 1995).

In total, about 1.1 million American lives, or nearly one-half of all deaths, could be saved each year by changes in individual health-related behaviors (**Figure 1-2**).

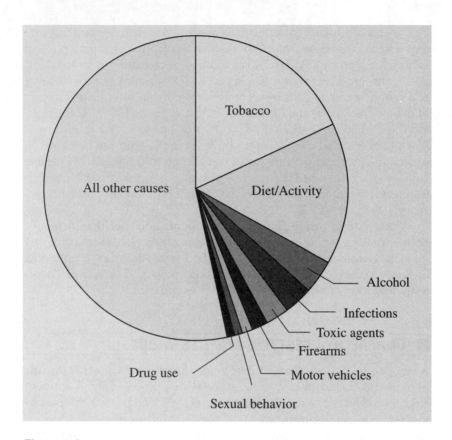

Figure 1-2 Behavior-Related Causes of Death—United States, 2000.
Source: Data from Mokdad et al., 2004, 2005.

■ DETERIORATING SOCIAL AND ECONOMIC CONDITIONS

Poverty

The single best predictor of a person's health status is his or her socio-economic status (Adler et al., 1997; Antonovsky, 1967; Gregorio, Walsh, & Paturzo, 1997; Hemingway et al., 1997; Kaplan & Lynch, 1997; Kawachi et al., 1997; Kitagawa & Hauser, 1973; Lynch, Kaplan, & Shema, 1997: Marmot et al., 1995; McDonough et al., 1997; Moss, 1997; Pappas et al., 1993; Patrick & Wickizer, 1995; Power et al., 1997; Satcher, 1996; Susser, Watson, & Hopper, 1985; Syme & Berkman, 1976; Yeracaris & Kim, 1978). Age-adjusted death rates for White males in 1986 ranged from 2.4 per thousand among men with an income greater than $25,000 to 16.0 per thousand among those with an income below $9,000 (Pappas et al., 1993). A similar pattern held for White females (1.6 versus 6.5 per thousand); Black males (3.6 versus 19.5 per thousand); and Black females (2.3 versus 7.6 per thousand).

Even after controlling for differences in unhealthy behaviors and lifestyles (e.g., smoking, alcohol use, drug use) and for access to health care, poverty remains a strong, independent predictor of poor health (Haan, Kaplan, & Camacho, 1987; Lantz et al., 1998). Controlling for baseline health status, race, income, employment status, access to medical care, health insurance coverage, smoking, alcohol consumption, physical activity, body mass index, and several other factors, persons living in poverty-stricken areas still have about a two to three times higher mortality rate as those who do not (Haan, Kaplan, & Camacho, 1987; Lantz et al., 1998). As Henig (1997) concluded, "the very fact of being poor is itself an independent risk factor for getting sick" (p. 103).

Poverty is a particularly strong risk factor for disease and death among children. Children who grow up in poverty are eight times more likely to die from homicide; five times more likely to have a physical or mental disability; five times more likely to be subject to child abuse; three times more likely to die in childhood; and twice as likely to be killed in an accident (Children's Defense Fund, 1994).

Lisbeth Schorr (1989) summarized the problem succinctly: "Poverty is the greatest risk factor of all. Family poverty is relentlessly correlated with high rates of school-age childbearing, school failure, and violent crime—and with all their antecedents. Low income is an important risk factor in itself, and so is relative poverty—having significantly less income than the norm, especially in a society that places a high value on economic success" (p. xxii).

Efforts to improve the public's health must therefore address the problem of poverty. Not only is poverty a social and economic problem, but it is also a fundamental threat to public health.

Despite the importance of poverty as a public health problem and in spite of the so-called War on Poverty during the Great Society reforms of the 1960s and President Lyndon Johnson's expressed national "commitment to eradicate poverty," poverty remains nearly as widespread as it was during the late 1960s and has become more prevalent in recent years (Bok, 1996; NCHS, 2004). The proportion of the population living below the official poverty line dropped from 22.4% in 1959 to 11.2% in 1974; however, it has increased overall since then, reaching 15.1% in 1993, the highest rate of poverty in the United States since the mid-1960s (Bok, 1996; NCHS, 1997). While the proportion of persons living below the poverty level declined during the 1990s, it increased from 11.3% to 12.1% between 2000 and 2002 (NCHS, 2004). Thus, the rate of poverty in the United States in 2002 was actually higher than it was 28 years earlier, in 1974.

The proportion of people living in extreme poverty (income less than half the official poverty line) also has increased, rising from 30% of those below the poverty line in 1975 to 40% in the late 1980s (Bok, 1996) and reaching 45% in the 2000 Census (U.S. Bureau of the Census, 2000b).

Not only have rates of abject poverty increased, but the mean family income for the lowest 40% income segment in the country has declined since 1972 (Bok, 1996). Family income for the highest 40% income segment during the same period has increased, widening the gap in income disparity between the middle and upper class and the poor. Mean family income among the lowest 20% income segment decreased from $10,769 in 1972 (in constant 1992 dollars) to $9,708 in 1992, and among the second lowest 20% income segment from $23,725 to $23,337 (Bok, 1996). At the same time, mean family income among the highest 20% income segment increased from $82,534 to $99,252 and among the second highest 20% income segment from $47,588 to $53,365.

Hunger

The health consequences of hunger go beyond medical conditions associated with nutritional deficiencies and include inability to concentrate in school, feelings of worthlessness, and other psychological problems (Meyers et al., 1989; Pollitt, Gersovitz, & Garginlo, 1978; Rose and Oliveira, 1997; Sidel, 1997). Thus, hunger can significantly affect a person's physical and mental well-being. Recent estimates suggest that at least four million children under age 12 in the United States experience hunger daily and an additional 9.6 million may experience hunger at some point during the year (Sidel, 1997; Wehler et al., 1995).

Educational Attainment

Education is one of the most important determinants of health status. Age-adjusted death rates for White males in 1986 ranged from 2.8 per thousand among those with at least four years of college to 7.6 per thousand among those without a high school diploma (Pappas et al., 1993). Similarly, death rates for these educational groups ranged from 1.8 to 3.4 per thousand among White females; 6.0 to 13.4 per thousand among Black males; and 2.2 to 6.2 per thousand among Black females. Education is strongly related to unhealthy behaviors. For example, educational attainment is one of the best predictors of smoking status. In 1994, adult smoking prevalence ranged from 12.3% among adults with 16 or more years of education to 38.2% among those with only 9 to 11 years of education (CDC, 1996). More recently (in 2002), age-adjusted adult smoking prevalence was 30.9% among those with no high school diploma, but only 10.0% among those with a college degree (NCHS, 2004). Independent of its relation to behavior, education influences a person's ability to access and understand health information. For example, people who are illiterate will not be helped by written educational materials produced by public health practitioners.

The United States has made little progress in improving the educational attainment of its population during the past two decades. The proportion of Americans ages 25 to 29 who have graduated from high school is approximately 83% and has remained stable at that level since the mid-1970s (Bok, 1996). The overall proportion of adults ages 25 and older with a high school diploma (or equivalency) increased only slightly from 75.2% in 1990 to 81.1% in 2000 (U.S. Bureau of the Census, 1990, 2000a). Perhaps of even more concern, the Department of Education estimates that about 35% of 18-year-olds in the nation are functionally illiterate (Harris, 1996; U.S. Department of Education, 1994). In 1992, more than one-fifth of all adults in the United States (representing more than 38 million individuals) scored in the lowest level of literacy measured in the National Adult Literacy Survey (U.S. Department of Education, 2002).

Housing

The lack of adequate and stable housing is associated with a number of chronic and severe health problems. Homelessness is associated with tuberculosis, trauma, depression and other mental illnesses, alcoholism, drug abuse, sexually transmitted diseases, and poor nutrition (Breakey, 1997, Breakey & Fischer, 1995, Dellon, 1995; Greene, Ennett, & Ringwalt, 1997, Robertson, Zlotnick, & Westerfelt, 1997). The lifetime prevalence of homelessness (the percentage of persons who report having been homeless at some time in their lives) in the United States is about 7.4%, and the five-year prevalence of homelessness is 3.1% (Breakey, 1997; Link et al., 1994). In any given year, nearly 1% of the population experiences homelessness, as do 6.3% of people living in poverty (Burt & Aron, 2000). Although accurate estimates of trends in homelessness are not available, there is no evidence that the extent of homelessness is decreasing (Breakey, 1997) and available evidence suggests that the number of homeless persons has markedly increased over the past two decades (Urban Institute, 2002).

Even among those who do have housing, the quality of housing conditions is a significant concern. In 1991, 6.7% of all housing units had a leaking roof, 5.1% had open cracks in the ceiling or walls; and 5.0% had unusable toilets (Bok, 1996). The percentage of families eligible for federal assistance through public housing, subsidized housing, and rent supplements who receive such aid is only 30% (Bok, 1996). Although the federal government provides about $90 million in housing subsidies each year, $70 million of it is in the form of tax deductions for homeowners (Bok, 1996). For families not receiving subsidies or living in public housing, 77% pay more than half their income for rent (Bok, 1996).

The health consequences of poor-quality housing can be substantial. A study published in the *New England Journal of Medicine* found that exposure to cockroach debris may be the leading cause of asthma among inner-city children (Rosenstreich et al., 1997). Children who were exposed to higher levels of cockroach allergen not only had higher rates of hospitalization for asthma, but had more symptoms of wheezing, more physician visits, and more days of school absence than other asthmatic children. The high exposure to cockroaches in the inner city may explain both the high prevalence of asthma in the inner city and the increase in the incidence of asthma among inner-city children over the past 30 years (Platts-Mills & Carter, 1997).

Another example of important health consequences caused by poor housing is lead poisoning among children. Peeling lead-paint chips in older housing is still the chief cause of lead poisoning. Children living in houses built before 1946 are at greatest risk. From 1991 to 1994, about 16% of poor children living in such housing had elevated blood lead levels, putting them at risk for significant neurological and psychological impairment, including decreased school performance and IQ (CDC, 1997b).

Unemployment

Unemployment is recognized as a major predictor of morbidity and mortality in the population. Catalano (1991) has shown that for every 1% increase in unemployment during the 1980s, there was a 5% increase in mortality from heart disease and stroke and a 6% increase in homicide deaths. Economic strains associated with unemployment pose especially large health risks to disadvantaged people (Smith, 1987).

Overall unemployment rates in the United States fell slightly during the latter part of the twentieth century, decreasing from 8.5% in 1975 to 4.9% in 1997 (U.S. Department of Labor, 1997). Since then unemployment rates have remained relatively stable and were still at 5.0% in July 2005 (U.S. Department of Labor, 2005). Among African-American men and women, however, unemployment rates have remained twice as high, at about 10%, during the past 10 years (U.S. Department of Labor, 2005).

Environmental Hazards

Exposure to environmental toxins is associated with a wide range of chronic health problems. Among the environmental hazards that cause the greatest disease burden are secondhand smoke (53,000 deaths per year) (Glantz & Parmley, 1991; Wells, 1988); indoor radon (7,000 to 30,000 deaths per year) (Environmental Protection Agency, 1992; National Research Council, 1998); and arsenic in drinking water (about 4,700 deaths per year) (Smith et al., 1992). The CDC estimated that approximately 17% of all deaths in the United States could be prevented by reducing exposure to environmental hazards (CDC, 1995; USDHHS, 1995).

Despite improvements in environmental quality for the advantaged segment of the population, disadvantaged segments of the population still suffer from the adverse health effects of an unhealthy environment. A classic example of the disproportionate burden of environmental risk on the disadvantaged is the problem of childhood lead poisoning. Although the problem has been recognized for decades, the lead content in paint and gasoline has been regulated for many years, and the federal and state governments have spent millions of dollars on lead abatement programs, lead poisoning is still a significant health problem for poor, inner-city children (CDC, 1997b). From 1991 to 1994, more than 16% of low-income children who lived in houses built before 1946 had elevated blood lead levels, compared with 4.1% and 0.9% of middle- and high-income children, respectively (CDC, 1997b).

A report by the Pew Environmental Health Commission at Johns Hopkins University reported that the ability of public health professionals to prevent health problems due to environmental hazards is being severely impaired by the nation's lack of adequate surveillance of environmental factors contributing to human disease. The panel's chairman, former Senator Lowell Weicker, Jr., noted that an epidemic of environmentally-caused diseases should be addressed with no less urgency and no less comprehensiveness than infectious disease threats that affect far fewer people: "We responded quickly to the threat of West Nile virus, tracking and monitoring every report of infected birds and people, but 20 years into the asthma epidemic, this country is still unable to track where and when attacks occur and what environmental links may trigger them" (Reuters Health, 2000).

Crime and Violence

In 1984, former Surgeon General C. Everett Koop declared violence to be an epidemic and a public health problem: "Violence is as much a public health issue for me and my successors in this country as smallpox, tuberculosis, and syphilis were for my predecessors in the last two centuries" (Henig, 1997, p. 110). In 1988, CDC researchers Mercy and Houk called for a similar approach to the problem of violence: "The time has come for us to address this problem in the manner in which we have addressed and dealt successfully with other threats to the public health" (p. 1284). And most recently, CDC director David Satcher said, "If you look at the major cause of death today it's not smallpox or polio or even infectious diseases. Violence is the leading cause of lost life in this country today. If it's not a public health problem, why are all those people dying from it?" (Applebome, 1993, p. A7).

The disadvantaged communities in the United States have been ravaged by violence. Despite a decrease in the rate of firearm-related deaths over the past decade (NCHS, 2004), homicide remains the second leading cause of death among young people, ages 15 to 24, and the homicide death rate remains six times higher among African-American males than among the general population, as it was 10 years ago (NCHS, 2004). There are more than 200 million guns in private ownership throughout the United States and 5.5 million new ones introduced each year, of which 100,000 are carried by children to school each day (Bok, 1996). These firearms cause an estimated 30,000 deaths each year (NCHS, 2004), and the link between the availability of firearms and the increasing homicide rate is "every bit as strong as the studies that linked cigarettes to lung cancer" (Taubes, 1992, p. 215). In addition, child abuse rates have increased from 10 per thousand children in 1976 to 45 per thousand in 1992; some of this increase may be attributable to increased reporting of abuse, but at least a portion is due to a real increase in incidence (Bok, 1996).

In 2004, there were 1.4 million violent crimes in the United States, including more than 16,000 murders, 95,000 cases of forcible rape, and 855,000 cases of aggravated assault (U.S. Department of Justice, 2004). Despite an 8.1% decline in the rate of violent crime between 2000 and 2004, there is still one murder every 33 minutes, one forcible rape every six minutes, and one aggravated assault every 37 seconds in this country (U.S. Department of Justice, 2004).

Social Support

The availability of a social support network—family, friends, and community programs to which an individual can turn for help, advice, reassurance, and consolation—is a strong determinant of health status (Berkman, 1984; Berkman & Breslow, 1983; Berkman & Syme, 1979; Broadhead et al., 1983; Cassel, 1976; Corin, 1995; Patrick & Wickizer, 1995; Pilisuk & Minkler, 1985; Schorr, 1989). Even after controlling for most other known determinants of health—socioeconomic status, access to health care, and individual behaviors and lifestyle factors—the absence of social support remains a strong, independent predictor of disease (Berkman & Syme, 1979). As Schorr (1989) argued, "Formal social supports protect people from an amazing variety of pathological states, including destructive family functioning, low birthweight, depression, arthritis, tuberculosis, and even premature death" (p. 155).

The focus on what policy makers have termed "welfare reform" has taken a devastating toll on the availability and quality of social support networks in American communities. By reducing the level of government provision of basic needs—food, housing, transportation, child care, and health care—welfare "reform" has forced traditional social support networks, such as community support programs, to abandon their supportive tasks and instead scramble to find ways to meet the basic needs of their clients (Pilisuk & Minkler, 1985). As Pilisuk and Minkler (1985) argue, the primary value of welfare benefits is that it allows alternative support systems (families, friends, and community programs) to provide exactly the kind of support needed to keep people healthy.

> Family and community effectiveness in the provision of social support is heavily dependent upon the broader economic and social environment. . . . To build and maintain strong supportive ties, we must provide those programs, services, and policies on a societal level, which can help meet basic human needs. For it is only within this broader context of system-level support and commitment to people of all ages and places that social support on the individual and community levels can fulfill its potential. (p. 11)

The real threat that "welfare reform" poses to the public's health is that it renders ineffective the systems of social support in the family and community that are so closely tied to health status (Broadhead et al., 1983; Cassel, 1976; Cobb, 1976; Cohen & Syme, 1985; Pilisuk & Minkler, 1985). By forcing social support networks to concentrate on filling gaps in the basic needs of the poor rather than on providing a true social support system for those in distress, "welfare reform" as it is currently crafted makes it increasingly more difficult to achieve within communities the social conditions in which people can be healthy. Lisbeth Schorr (1989) summarized the problem:

> For those living in persistent and concentrated poverty, it is reformed services and institutions that will furnish the essential footholds for the climb out of poverty. Yet in the legislative, academic, and political forums where antipoverty strategies and welfare reform are debated, the spotlight is only on short-term measures to reduce the numbers now on welfare, now unable to work productively. The shocking deficiencies in the health, welfare, and education of poor children, the long-term investments that could help the vulnerable children of today to become the productive and contributing adults of tomorrow, are rarely on the agenda . . . Children and families have needs that cannot be met by economic measures alone, and that cannot be met by individual families alone. (pp. xxiii, xxiv)

■ A CRISIS IN ACCESS TO QUALITY HEALTH CARE

Inadequate access to health care services is associated with increased burdens of economic hardship, poor health, and increased mortality (Blendon et al., 1994; Donelan et al., 1997; Franks, Clancy, & Gold, 1993; Henry J. Kaiser Family Foundation, 1994; Lurie et al., 1984; Lurie et al., 1986; Weissman & Epstein, 1994). The CDC estimated that about 11% of all deaths could be prevented by improving the population's access to quality medical treatment (CDC, 1995; USDHHS, 1995). Approximately 17% of the population—more than 40 million people—lack health insurance (NCHS, 2004). In spite of the widespread recognition of this problem and the rhetoric about the importance of ensuring all citizens access to health care, the proportion of uninsured Americans increased from 13.6% in 1970 to 15.4% in 1995 (Bok, 1996; NCHS, 1997), and is even higher now—16.5% in 2002 (NCHS, 2004). As of 2002, 11% of all children (under age 18) lacked any health insurance coverage (NCHS, 2004). Lack of insurance tends to be a problem of the poor. While only 10.9% of non-poor individuals lacked health insurance coverage in 2002, 31.4% of poor individuals had no health insurance coverage (NCHS, 2004).

The problem of access to quality health care among the poor is not limited to lack of insurance. Several studies have shown that disadvantaged populations tend to receive inferior health care, regardless of whether they have health insurance (Burstin, Lipsitz, & Brennan, 1992; Dalen & Santiago, 1991; Diehr et al., 1991; Goldberg et al., 1992; Kahn et al., 1994; Kasiske et al., 1991; Wenneker & Epstein, 1989; Yergan et al., 1987). For example, even among those who are insured by Medicaid, access to high-quality health care is limited. Several studies have shown that Medicaid patients are less likely to receive preventive care and that their physical health fares worse under Medicaid managed care than under fee-for-service payment (Ware et al., 1996). Ware and associates (1997) found that during a four-year follow-up period poor patients treated under Medicaid managed care suffered greater declines in physical health status than those treated under traditional, fee-for-service Medicaid. Even without managed care, Medicaid patients have less access to continuing care and preventive care than patients who are privately insured (Davidson et al., 1994; Kerr & Siu, 1993).

Similarly, poor elderly patients who are enrolled in Medicare managed care may be less likely to have access to the intensive rehabilitation and support services that are necessary to keep them self-sufficient and avoid institutionalization. Retchin 2nd associates (1997) found that compared with fee-for-service Medicare patients, Medicare managed care patients who suffer a stroke are more likely to be discharged to nursing homes and less likely to be placed in rehabilitative settings or discharged to home. Access to home health care and outcomes under Medicare managed care have also been shown to be worse than under traditional, fee-for-service Medicare (Experton et al., 1997; Shaugnessy, Schlenker, & Hittle, 1994). And Ware and colleagues (1996) reported that elderly patients in health maintenance organizations (HMOs) had more significant declines in physical health compared with those who remained in fee-for-service settings over a four-year follow-up period.

The problem of inadequate access to health care has been exacerbated by policy initiatives, such as California's Proposition 187 (approved in 1994), which deny health care benefits (Medicaid) to children of illegal immigrants.

■ IMPLICATIONS OF THE CHRONIC DISEASE EPIDEMIC FOR PUBLIC HEALTH PRACTICE

During the nineteenth and early twentieth centuries, when the chief causes of preventable death were infectious diseases spread by contaminated water and food, the focus of public health practice was building a societal infrastructure for proper sanitation and hygiene and for the delivery of vaccines and treatments to the population. The chronic disease epidemic of the early twenty-first century, however, is largely related to individual lifestyle and behavior, deteriorating economic and social conditions, and the failure of social policy to address problems such as affordable and accessible health care of high quality for all Americans. Thus, public health practice must now focus on modifying individual lifestyle and behavior, improving social and economic conditions, and reforming social policy.

To start, at least 1.1 million American lives, or nearly one half of all deaths, could be saved each year by changes in individual health-related behaviors (see **Figure 1-2**; Mokdad et al., 2004, 2005).

Although public health practice clearly has to focus on modifying individual lifestyle and behavior, it is important to note that personal behavior does not take place in a vacuum. Rather, it takes place within the context of a historical, cultural, and political environment and within communities with varying economic and social conditions. To effectively change individual behavior, one cannot ignore the conditions and environment in which that behavior takes place. In fact, some argue that focusing on the economic and social conditions that give rise to unhealthy behaviors is essential to changing those behaviors. Because behavior is a product of the social conditions and social norms of the community in which a person lives (Tesh, 1994), "discussing changes in lifestyles without first discussing the changes in the social conditions which give rise to them, without recognizing that the lifestyle is derivative, is misleading" (Berliner, 1977, p. 119).

Not only do social and economic factors influence health behaviors and individual lifestyle, but these factors are themselves independently related to health status. Several decades of research have demonstrated that lower social class, social deprivation, and lack of social support are among the most important determinants of health (Antonovsky, 1967; Berkman, 1984; Bright, 1967; Cassel, 1976; Conrad, 1994; Frey, 1982; Haan et al., 1987; Kitagawa & Hauser, 1973; Marmot, 1982; Morris, 1979, 1982; Rose & Marmot, 1981; Salonen, 1982; Stockwell, 1961; Syme & Berkman, 1976; Yeracaris & Kim, 1978). Moreover, the strong association between these socioeconomic factors and health is not entirely explained by differences in individual lifestyle and health behaviors between members of higher and lower social class groups (Haan et al., 1987; Lantz et al., 1998; Rose & Marmot, 1981; Salonen, 1982: Slater & Carlton, 1985; Slater, Lorimor, & Lairson, 1985; Wiley & Camacho, 1980). Link and Phelan (1996) proposed a novel view of the relationship between socioeconomic status and disease, asserting that socioeconomic status must be viewed as a "fundamental cause" of disease.

Lantz et al., writing in the *Journal of the American Medical Association*, noted that "Although reducing the prevalence of health risk behaviors in low-income populations is an important public health goal, socioeconomic differences in mortality are due to a wider array of factors and, therefore, would persist even with improved health behaviors among the disadvantaged" (1998, p. 1703). "We must look to a broader range of explanatory risk factors, including structural elements of inequality in our society" (p. 1708). The Institute of Medicine report (1988) on the future of public health, noting the importance of social and economic factors as determinants of health status, suggested that public health must take a much wider view of disease than in the past: "Public health programs, to be effective, should move beyond programs targeted on the immediate problem, such as teen pregnancy, to health promotion and prevention by dealing with underlying factors in the social environment. To deal with these factors, the scope of public health will need to encompass relationships with other social programs in education, social services, housing, and income maintenance" (p. 113).

The late Sol Levine noted that social factors "mean not only poverty but also social class, family, community, gender, ethnicity, racism, political economy, and culture. We have to learn how these interact with health, how, for example, culture, political economy, and racism may affect the community and family environment, which, in turn, may influence people's health. We have to look not only at individual characteristics but at the features of the society as well" (Henig, 1997, p. 102).

Because social and economic conditions are themselves a product of social policy, public health practice must also focus on changing social policy. Poverty is not a consequence of individual frailty, lack of responsibility, and lack of motivation, as some have argued. Rather, it is the product of social and economic conditions created and maintained by the historical, political, and cultural environment in which society has developed (Zaidi, 1988). Social policy contributes, at least in part, to the environment that determines social and economic conditions in the community. The availability of adequate food, housing, and jobs; the quality of the physical environment; access to medical services; the extent of social support in the community; and the amount of economic, employment, and educational opportunity are all influenced strongly by social policies. Former Harvard University president Derek Bok (1996) has argued that "current levels of poverty are not immutable but are the result of policy choices, choices that seem at odds with the stated desire of most Americans to do more for the deserving poor" (p. 35).

For example, government assistance for single mothers with no earned income is only 27% of the median family income in the United States, compared with 38% in France, 47% in Germany, 60% in Britain, and 64% in Sweden (Bok, 1996). The rate of poverty among single mothers in the United States is more than twice the rate in each of the other countries (Bok, 1996). Quite simply, social policy has a direct and understandable effect on social conditions.

To effectively confront threats to the public's health, the three major functions of public health must be (1) modifying individual behavior and lifestyle, (2) improving social and economic conditions, and (3) reforming social policies. All of these represent fundamental aspects of social change. Ultimately, then, public health is in the business of creating or facilitating social change (**Figure 1-3**).

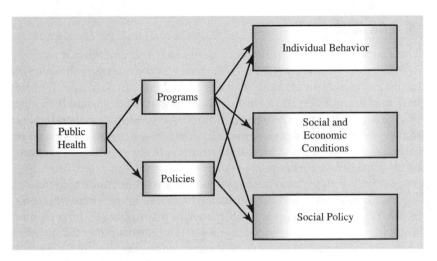

Figure 1-3 An Overview of the Functions of Public Health: Creating Social Change

It should be noted that although chronic diseases have replaced infectious diseases as the chief causes of death in the United States, the nation has experienced a reemergence of infectious diseases, primarily due to the emergence of the acquired immunodeficiency syndrome (AIDS), which accounted for an estimated 14,000 deaths in 2002 (NCHS, 2004). Although mortality from AIDS has decreased (from 43,000 deaths in 1995 [NCHS, 1997]), its incidence has remained relatively stable during the past 13 years, with 41,000 reported cases in 1990 and 44,000 cases in 2003 (NCHS, 2004). In addition, influenza and pneumonia caused nearly 66,000 deaths in 2002 (NCHS, 2004), bringing the total death toll from infectious diseases to no less than 80,000 and making it the sixth leading cause of death in 2002. With the rise of AIDS has come increased risk for other infectious diseases, such as drug-resistant tuberculosis.

The threat of emerging infectious diseases also remains a critical public health concern because of the potential for a worldwide avian flu epidemic (Parry, 2005), and because of already established threats, such as West Nile virus (Gorsche & Tilley, 2005) and SARS (Lu et al., 2005).

Infectious diseases, like chronic diseases, are strongly related to individual lifestyles and behaviors, social and economic conditions, and social policy. Infection with the human immunodeficiency virus (HIV), for example, is commonlyprecipitated by intravenous drug use. The spread of tuberculosis infection, especially multi-drug-resistant strains, is promoted by crowded and unsanitary living conditions. And the failure of society to develop rational policies to control the spread of HIV infection—such as needle exchange programs—that have been shown to be among the most highly effective interventions available has contributed to the AIDS epidemic (Lurie & Drucker, 1997).

■ CONCLUSION

The major implication of the chronic disease and emerging infectious disease epidemics for public health policy and practice is that public health must focus on far more than the provision of medical care. It must, first and foremost, focus on modifying individual lifestyle and behavior, improving social and economic conditions, and reforming social policy that contributes to an environment in which it is difficult for people to be healthy. Ultimately, then, public health is in the business of creating or facilitating social change.

The three-pronged attack that is necessary to control the epidemic of chronic disease and emerging infectious diseases in the United States— modifying individual lifestyle and behavior, improving social and economic conditions, and reforming social policy—is not one that public health practitioners have traditionally been well equipped to conduct. And it has not been one at which public health has been particularly successful. Chapter 2 explores the reasons that modifying individual lifestyle and behavior, improving social conditions, and reforming social policy represent a unique and formidable challenge to the public health practitioner.

References

Adler, N.E., Boyce, W.T., Chesney, M.A. Folkman, S., Syme, S.L. (1997). Socioeconomic inequalities in health: No easy solution. In P.R. Lee & C.L. Estes (Eds.), *The nation's health* (5th ed., pp. 18–31). Sudbury, MA: Jones and Bartlett.

American Cancer Society. (1994). *Cancer facts & figures—1994*. New York: Author.

Antonovsky, A. (1967). Social class, life expentancy, and overall mortality. *Milbank Memorial Fund Quarterly, 45*, 31–73.

Applebome, P. (1993, September 26). CDC's new chief worries as much about bullets as about bacteria. *The New York Times*, p. A7.

Berkman, L.F. (1984). Assessing the physical health effects of social networks and social support. *Annual Reviews of Public Health, 5*, 413–432.

Berkman, L.F., & Breslow, L. (Eds.). (1983). *Health and ways of living: The Alameda County Study*. New York: Oxford University Press.

Berkman, L.F., & Syme, S.L. (1979). Social networks, host resistance, and mortality: A nine-year follow-up study of Alameda County residents. *American Journal of Epidemiology, 109*, 186–204.

Berliner, H. (1977). Emerging ideologies in medicine. *Review of Radical Political Economics, 9*, 116–124.

Blendon, R.J., Donelan, K. Hill, C.A. Carter, W., Beatrice, D., & Altman, D (1994). Paying medical bills in the United States: Why health insurance isn't enough. *Journal of the American Medical Association, 271*, 949–951.

Bok, D. (1996). *The state of the nation*. Cambridge, MA: Harvard University Press.

Bonneux, L., Barendregt, J.J., Meeter, K., Bonsel, G.J., & van der Maas, P.J. (1994). Estimating clinical morbidity due to ischemic heart disease on congestive heart failure: The future rise of heart failure. *American Journal of Public Health, 84*, 20–28.

Breakey, W.R. (1997). Editorial: It's time for the public health community to declare war on homelessness. *American Journal of Public Health,* 87, 153–155.

Breakey, W.R. & Fischer, P.J. (1995). Mental illness and the continuum of residential stability. *Social Psychiatry and Psychiatric Epidemiology,* 30, 147–151.

Bright, M. (1967). A follow-up study of the Commission on Cultural Illness Morbidity Survey in Baltimore, IL. Race and sex differences in mortality. *Journal of Chronic Diseases,* 20, 717–729.

Broadhead, W.E., Kaplan, B.H., James, S.A., Wagner, E.H., Shoenbach, V.J., Grimson, R., Heyden, S. Tibblin, G. & Gehlbach, S.H. (1983). The epidemiological evidence for a relationship between social support and health. *American Journal of Epidemiology,* 117, 521–537.

Burstin, H.R., Lipsitz, S.R., & Brennan, T.A. (1992). Socioeconomic status and risk for substandard medical care. *Journal of the American Medical Association,* 268, 2383–2387.

Burt, M., & Aron, L. (2000). *America's homeless II: Populations and services.* Washington, DC: The Urban Institute.

Cassel, J. (1976). The contribution of the social environment to host resistance. *American Journal of Epidemiology,* 104, 107–123.

Catalano, R. (1991). The health effects of economic insecurity. *American Journal of Public Health,* 81, 1148–1152.

Centers for Disease Control and Prevention. (1993). *Cardiovascular disease surveillance: Ischemic heart disease,* 1980–1989. Atlanta, GA: Centers for Disease Control and Prevention, National Center for Chronic Disease Prevention and Health Promotion, Division of Chronic Disease Con trol and Community Intervention.

———. (1995). 1994: *Ten leading causes of death in the United States.* Atlanta, GA: Centers for Disease Control, National Center for Injury Prevention and Control.

———. (1996). Cigarette smoking among adults—United States, 1994. *Morbidity and Mortality Weekly Report,* 45, 588–590.

———. Trends in the prevalence and incidence of self-reported diabetes mellitus—United States, 1980–1994. *Morbidity and Mortality Weekly Report,* 46, 1014–1018.

———. (1997b). Update: Blood lead levels—United States, 1991–1994. *Morbidity and Mortality Weekly Report,* 46, 141–146.

Children's Defense Fund. (1994). *Wasting America's future.* Washington, DC: Author.

Cobb, S. (1976). Social support as a moderator of life stress. *Journal of Psychosomatic Medicine,* 38, 300–314.

Cohen, S., & Syme, S.L. (Eds.). (1985). *Social support and health.* New York: Academic Press.

Colditz, G.A., DeJong, D., Hunter, D.J., Trichopoulos, D., & Willett, W.C. (1996). Harvard report on cancer prevention, vol. 1: Causes of human cancer. *Cancer Causes and Control,* 7(Suppl. 1).

Conrad, P. (1994). Wellness in the workplace: Potentials and pitfalls of work-site health promotion. In H.D. Schwartz (Ed.), *Dominant issues in medical sociology* (3rd ed., pp. 556–567). New York: McGraw-Hill.

Corin, E. (1995). The cultural frame: Context and meaning in the construction on health. In B. C. Amick, III, S. Levine, A.R. Tarlov, & D.C. Walsh (Eds.), *Society and health* (pp. 272–304) New York: Oxford University Press.

Dalen, J.E., & Santiago, J. (1991). Insuring the uninsured is not enough. *Archives of Internal Medicine,* 151, 860–862.

Davidson, A.E., Klein, D.E., Settipane, G.A., & Alario, A.J. (1994). Access to care among children visiting the emergency room with acute exacerbations of asthma. *Annals of Allergy,* 72, 469–473.

Dellon, E.S. (1995). The health status of the Providence-area homeless population. *Rhode Island Medicine,* 10, 989–999.

Diehr, P.K. Richardson, W.C., Shortell, S.M., & LoGerfo, J.P. (1991). Increased access to medical care. *Medical Care,* 10, 989–999.

Donelan, K. Blendon, R. J., Hill, C.A., Hoffman, C., Rowland, D., Frankel, M. & Altman D. (1997). Whatever happened to the health insurance crises in the United States? Voices from a national survey. In P.R. Lee, & C.L. Estes (Eds.), *The nation's health* (5th ed., pp. 283–291). Sudbury, MA: Jones and Bartlett.

Environmental Protection Agency. (1992). *A citizen's guide to radon* (2nd ed.). Washington, DC: Author.

Experton, B., Li, Z., Branch, L.G., Ozminkowski, R.J., & Mellon-Lacey, D.M. (1997). Impact of payor-provider type on health care use and expenditures among the frail elderly. *American Journal of Public Health,* 87, 210–216.

Franks, P., Clancy, C.M. & Gold, M.R. (1993). Health insurance and mortality: Evidence from a national cohort. *Journal of the American Medical Association,* 270, 737–741.

Frey, R.S. (1982). The socioeconomic distribution of mortality rates in Des Moines, Iowa *Public Health Reports,* 97, 545–549.

Glantz, S.A., & Parmley, W.W. (1991). Passive smoking and heart disease: Epidemiology, physiology, and biochemistry. *Circulation,* 83, 1–12.

Goldberg, K.C. Hartz, A.J., Jacobsen, S.J., Krakauer, H., & Rimm, A.A. (1992). Racial and community factors influencing coronary artery bypass graft surgery rates for all 1986 Medicare patients. *Journal of the American Medical Association,* 267, 1473–1477.

Gorsche, R., & Tilley, P. (2005). The rash of West Nile virus infection. *Canadian Medical Association Journal,* 172:1440.

Greene, J.M. Ennett, S.T., & Ringwalt, C.L. (1997). Substance use among runaway and homeless youth in three national samples. *American Journal of Public Health,* 87, 229–235.

Gregorio, D.I., Walsh, S.J., & Paturzo, D. (1997). The effects of occupation-based social position on mortality in a large American cohort. *American Journal of Public Health,* 87, 1472–1475.

Haan, M., Kaplan, G.A., & Camacho, T. (1987). Poverty and health: Prospective evidence from the Alameda County Study. *American Journal of Epidemiology,* 125, 989–998.

Harris, I.B. (1996). *Children in jeopardy: Can we break the cycle of poverty?* New Haven, CT: Yale University Press.

Hemingway, H., Nicholson, A., Stafford, M., Roberts, R., & Marmot, M. (1997). The impact of socioeconomic status on health functioning as assessed by the SF-36 questionnaire: The Whitehall II Study. *American Journal of Public Health,* 87, 1484–1490.

Henig, R.M. (1997). *The people's health: A memoir of public health and its evolution at Harvard.* Washington, DC: Joseph Henry Press.

Henry J. Kaiser Family Foundation (1994). Project LEAN idea kit for state and community programs to reduce dietary fat. Menlo Park, CA: Author.

Hoffman, C., Rice, D., & Sung, H.Y. (1996). Persons with chronic conditions: Their prevalence and costs. *Journal of the American Medical Association, 276,* 1473–1479.

Institute of Medicine, Committee for the Study of the Future of Public Health (1988). *The future of public health.* Washington, DC: National Academy Press.

Jenkins, C.D. Tuthill, R.W., Tannenbaum, S.I., & Kirby, C.R. (1977). Zones of excess mortality in Massachusetts. *New England Journal of Medicine, 296,* 1354–1356.

Kahn, K.L., Pearson, M.L., Harrison, E.R., Desmond, K.A., Rogers, W.H., Rubenstein, L.V., Brook, R.H., & Keeler, E.B. (1994). Health care for Black and poor hospitalized Medicare patients. *Journal of the American Medical Association, 271,* 1169–1174.

Kaplan, G.A. & Lynch, J.W. (1997). Editorial: Whither studies on the socioeconomic foundations of population health? *American Journal of Public Health, 87,* 1409–1411.

Kasiske, B.L., Neylan, J.F., Riggio, R.R., Danovitch, G.M., Kahana, L., Alexander, S.R., & White, M.G. (1991). The effect of race on access and outcome in transplantation. *New England Journal of Medicine, 324,* 302–307.

Kawachi, I., Kennedy, B.P., Lochner, K., & Prothrow-Stith, D. (1997). Social capital, income inequality, and mortality. *American Journal of Public Health, 87,* 1491–1498.

Kennedy, B., Kawachi, I., & Prothrow-Stith, D. (1995). Income distribution and mortality: cross-sectional ecological study of the Robin Hood Index in the United States. *British Medical Journal, 312,* 1004–1007.

Kerr, E.A., & Siu, A.L. (1993). Follow-up after hospital discharge: Does insurance make a difference? *Journal of Health Care for the Poor & Underserved, 4,* 133–142.

Kitagawa, E.M., & Hauser, P.M. (1973). *Differential mortality in the United States: A study in socioeconomic epidemiology.* Cambridge, MA: Harvard University Press.

Lantz, P.M., House, J.S., Lepkowski, J.M., Williams, D.R., Mero, R.P., & Chen, J. (1998). Socioeconomic factors, health behaviors, and mortality: Results from a nationally representative prospective study of US adults. *Journal of the American Medical Association, 297,* 1703–1708.

Link, B.G., & Phelan, J.C. (1996). Review: Why are some people healthy and others not? The determinants of health of populations. *American Journal of Public Health, 86,* 598–599.

Link, B.C., Susser, E., Stueve, A., Phelan, J., Moore, R.E., & Struening, E. (1994). Lifetime and five-year prevalence of homelessness in the United States. *American Journal of Public Health, 84,* 1907–1912.

Lu, S.N., Jiang D.D., Liu, J.W., Lin, M.C., Chen, C.L., Su, I.J., & Chen, S.S. (2005). Outbreak of severe acute respiratory syndrome in southern Taiwan, 2003. *American Journal of Tropical Medicine & Hygiene, 73,* 423–427.

Lurie, N., Ward, N.B., Shapiro, M.F., & Brook, R.H. (1984). Termination from Medi-Cal: Does it affect health? *New England Journal of Medicine, 311,* 480–484.

Lurie, N. Ward, N.B., Shapiro, M.F., Gallego, C., Vaghaiwalla, R., & Brook, R.H. (1986). Termination of medical benefits: A follow-up study one year later. *New England Journal of Medicine, 314,* 1266–1268.

Lurie, P., & Drucker, E. (1997). An opportunity lost: HIV infections associated with lack of a national needle-exchange programme in the USA. *The Lancet, 349*, 604–608.

Lynch, J.W., Kaplan, G.A., & Shema, S.J. (1997). Cumulative impact of sustained economic hardship on physical, cognitive, psychological, and social functioning. *New England Journal of Medicine, 337*, 1889–1895.

Marmot, M., Bobak, M., & Smith, G.D. (1995). Explanations for social inequalities in health. In B.C. Amick, III, S. Levine, A.R. Tarlov, & D.C. Walsh (Eds.), *Society and health* (pp.172–210). New York: Oxford University Press.

Marmot, M.G. (1982). Socioeconomic and cultural factors in ischemic heart disease. *Advances in Cardiology, 29*, 68–76.

McCord, C., & Freeman, H.P. (1990). Excess mortality in Harlem. *New England Journal of Medicine, 332*, 173–178.

McDonough, P., Duncan, G.J. William, D., & House, J. (1997). Income dynamics and adult mortality in the United States, 1972 through 1898. *American Journal of Public Health, 87*, 1476–1483.

Mercy, J.A., & Houk, V.N. (1988). Firearm injuries: A call for science. *New England Journal of Medicine, 319*, 1283–1285.

Meyers, A.F., Sampson, A.E., Weitzman, M., Rogers, B.L., & Kayne, H. (1989). School Breakfast Program and school performance. *American Journal of Diseases of Children, 143*, 1234–1239.

Mokdad, A.H., Marks, J.S., Stroup D.F., & Gerberding, J.L. (2004). Actual causes of death in the United States, 2000. *JAMA, 291*, 1238–1245.

———. (2005). Correction: actual causes of death in the United States, 2000. *JAMA, 293*, 293–294.

Morris, J.N. (1979). Social inequalities undiminished. *The Lancet, 1*, 87–90.

———. (1982). Epidemiology and prevention. *Milbank Memorial Fund Quarterly/Health and Society, 60*, 1–16.

Moss, N. (1997). Editorial: The body politic and the power of socioeconomic status. *American Journal of Public Health, 87*, 1411–1413.

———. (1997). *Health United States, 1996–97, and injury chartbook* (DHHS Publication No. PHS 97–1232). Hyattsville, MD: Author.

National Center for Health Statistics (2004). *Health United States, 2004, with chartbook on trends in the health of Americans* (DHHS Publication No. 2004–1232). Hyattsville, MD: Author.

National Research Council. (1998). *Health effects of exposure to radon: BEIR VI*. Washington, DC: National Academy of Sciences, National Research Council, Committee on the Biological Effects of Ionizing Radiation (BEIR VI), Committee on Health Risks of Exposure to Radon.

Navarro, V. (1997). Topics for our times: The "Black Report" of Spain—The Commission of Social Inequalities in Health. *American Journal of Public Health, 87*, 334–335.

Pappas, G., Queen, S. Hadden, W., & Fisher, G. (1993). The increasing disparity in mortality between socioeconomic groups in the United States, 1960 and 1986. *New England Journal of Medicine, 329*, 103–109.

Parry, J. (2005). WHO launches "plan of war" to tackle avian flu. *BMJ, 331*, 70.

Patrick, D.L., & Wickizer, T.M. (1995). Community and health. In C.C. Amick, III, S. Levine, A.R. Tarlov, & D.C. Walsh (Eds.). *Society and health* (pp.46–92). New York: Oxford University Press.

Pilisuk, M., & Minkler, M. (1985, Winter). Social support: Economic and political considerations. *Social Policy,* 6–11.

Platts-Mills, T.A.E., & Carter, M.C. (1997). Asthma and indoor exposure to allergens. *New England Journal of Medicine,* 336, 1382–1384.

Pollitt, E., Gersovitz, M., & Garginlo, M. (1978). Educational benefits of the United States school feeding program: A critical review of the literature. *American Journal of Public Health,* 68, 477–481.

Power, C., Hertzman, C., Matthews, S., & Manor, O. (1997). Social differences in health: Life cycle effects between ages 23 and 33 in the 1958 British birth cohort. *American Journal of Public Health,* 87, 1499–1503.

Retchin, S.M., Brown, R.S., Yeh, S.J., Chu, D., & Moreno, L. (1997). Outcomes of stroke patients in Medicare fee for service and managed care. *Journal of the American Medical Association,* 278, 119–124.

Reuters Health (2000, September 7). Nation faces an environmental health gap. New York: Reuters Health.

Robertson, M.J., Zlotnick, C., & Westerfelt, A. (1997). Drug use disorders and treatment contact among homeless adults in Alameda County. *American Journal of Public Health,* 87, 221–228.

Rose, D., & Oliveira, V. (1997). Nutrient intakes of individuals from food-insufficient households in the United States. *American Journal of Public Health,* 87, 1956–1961.

Rose, G., & Marmot, M.G. (1981). Social class and coronary heart disease. *British Heart Journal,* 45, 13–19.

Rosenberg, M.L., Powell, K.E., & Hammond, R. (1997). Applying science to violence prevention. *Journal of the American Medical Association,* 277, 1641–1642.

Rosenstreich, D.L., Eggleston, P., Kattan, M., Baker, D., Slavin, R.G., Gergen, P., Mitchell, H., McNiff-Mortimer, K., Lynn, H., Ownby, D., & Malveaux, F. (1997). The role of cockroach allergy and exposure to cockroach allergen in causing morbidity among inner-city children with asthma. *New England Journal of Medicine,* 336, 1356–1363.

Salonen, J.T. (1982). Socioeconomic status and risk of cancer, cerebral stroke, and death due to coronary heart disease and any disease: A longitudinal study in eastern Finland. *Journal of Epidemiology and Community Health,* 36, 294–297.

Satcher, D. (1996). CDC's first 50 years: Lessons learned and relearned. *American Journal of Public Health,* 86, 1705–1708.

Schorr, L.B. (1989). *Within our reach: Breaking the cycle of disadvantage.* New York: Anchor Books.

Shaugnessy, P., Schlenker, R.E., & Hittle, D.F. (1994). Home health care outcomes under capitated and fee-for-service payment. *Health Care Financing Review,* 16, 187–222.

Sidel, V.W. (1997). Annotation: The public health impact of hunger. *American Journal of Public Health,* 87, 1921–1922.

Slater, C., & Carlton, B. (1985). Behavior, lifestyle, and socioeconomic variables as determinants of health status: Implications for health policy development. *American Journal of Preventive Medicine,* 14, 372–378.

Slater, C.H., Lorimor, R.J., & Lairson, D.R. (1985). The independent contributions of socioeconomic status and health practices to health status. *Preventive Medicine,* 14, 372–378.

Smith, A.H., Hopenhayn-Rich, C., Bates, M.N., Goeden, H.M., Hert-Picciotto, I., Duggan, M.H., Wood, R., Kosnett, N.J., & Smith, M.T. (1992). Cancer risks from arsenic in drinking water. *Environmental Health Perspectives, 97,* 259–267.

Smith, R. (1987). *Unemployment and health.* London: Oxford University Press.

Stockwell, E.G. (1961). Socioeconomic status and mortality in the United States. *Public Health Reports, 76,* 1081–1086.

Sunstein, C.R. (1997). *Free markets and social justice.* New York: Oxford University Press.

Susser, M., Watson, W., & Hopper, K. (1985). *Sociology in Medicine* (3rd ed.). Oxford, England: Oxford University Press.

Syme, S.L., & Berkman, L.F. (1976). Social class, susceptibility and sickness. *American Journal of Epidemiology, 104,* 1–8.

Sythowski, P.A., Kannel, W.B., & D'Agostino, R.B. (1990). Changes in risk factors and the decline in mortality from cardiovascular disease: The Framingham Heart Study. *New England Journal of Medicine, 332,* 1635–1641.

Taubes, G. (1992). Violence eqidemiologists test the hazards of gun ownership. *Science, 258,* 215.

Tesh, S.N. (1994). Hidden arguments: Political ideology and disease prevention policy. In H.D. Schwartz (Ed.). *Dominant issues in medical sociology* 3rd ed., pp. 519–529). New York: McGraw-Hill.

Townsend, P., & Davidson, N. (1982). *Inequalities in health: The Black Report.* Hamondsworth, England: Penguin.

Urban Institute. (2002). *Preventing homelessness: Meeting the challenge.* Washington, DC: The Urban Institute. Available at http://www.urban.org/url.cfm?ID=900475.

U.S. Bureau of the Census. (1990). *1990 Census of population and housing.* Table P57. Educational attainment, persons 25 years and over. 1990 Summary Tape File 3 (STF 3).

———. (2000a). *Census 2000.* Table P37. Sex by educational attainment for the population 25 years and over. Census 2000 Summary File 3 (SF 3).

———. (2000b). *Census 2000.* Table P88. Ratio of income in 1999 to poverty level. Census 2000 Summary File 3 (SF 3).

U.S. Department of Education. (1994, April). *The reading report card. 1971–88.* Washington, DC: U.S. Department of Education, National Center for Education Statistics, National Assessment of Educational Progress.

———. (2002, April). *Adult literacy in America: A first look at the findings of the National Adult Literacy Survey.* Washington, DC: U.S. Department of Education, National Center for Education Statistics. Available at: http://nces.ed.gov/pubs93/93275.pdf.

U.S. Department of Health and Human Services. (1995). *Healthy people 2000: Midcourse review and 1995 revisions.* Washington, DC: U. S. Department of Health and Human Services, Public Health Service.

U.S. Department of Justice. (2004). *Crime in the United States 2004: Uniform crime reports.* Washington, DC: U.S. Department of Justice, Federal Bureau of Investigation. Available at: http://www.fbi.gov/ucr/cius_04/documents/CIUS2004.pdf.

U.S. Department of Labor. (1997). *Employment and earnings.* Washington, DC: U.S. Department of Labor, Bureau of Labor Statistics.

————. (2005). *Labor force statistics from the Current Population Survey.* Washington, DC: U. S. Department of Labor, Bureau of Labor Statistics. Available at http://data.bls.gov/cgi-bin/surveymost.

Ware, J.E., Jr., Bayliss, M.S., Rogers, W.H., Kosinski, M., & Tarlov, A.R. (1996). Differences in 4-year health outcomes for elderly and poor, chronically ill patients treated in HMO and fee-for-service systems. Results from the Medical Outcomes Study. *Journal of the American Medical Association, 276,* 1039–1047.

Wehler, C.A., Scott, R.I., Anderson, J.J., Summer, L., & Parker, L. (1995). *Community childhood hunger identification project: A survey of childhood hunger in the United States.* Washington, DC: Food Research and Action Center.

Weissman, J.S., & Epstein, A.M. (1994). *Falling through the safety net: The impact of insurance on access to care.* Baltimore: Johns Hopkins University Press.

Wells, A.J. (1988). An estimate of adult mortality in the United States from passive smoking. *Environment International, 14,* 249–265.

Wenneker, M.B., & Epstein, A.M. (1989). Racial inequalities in the use of procedures for patients with ischemic heart disease in Massachusetts. *Journal of the American Medical Association, 261,* 253–257.

Wiley, J.A., & Camacho, T.C. (1980). Life-style and future health: Evidence from the Alameda County Study. *Preventive Medicine, 9,* 1–21.

Wilkinson, R.G. (1990). Income distribution and mortality: A "natural" experiment. *Sociology of Health and illness, 12,* 391–412.

————. (1992). Income distribution and life expectancy. *British Medical Journal, 304,* 163–168.

————. (1997). Comment: Income, inequality, and social cohesion. *American Journal of Public Health, 87,* 1504–1506.

Yeracaris, C.A., & Kim, J.H. (1978). Socioeconomic differentials in selected causes of death. *American Journal of Public Health, 68,* 432–451.

Yergan, J., Flood, A.N., LoGerfo, J.P. , & Diehr, P. (1987). Relationship between patient race and the intensity of hospital services. *Medical Care, 25,* 592–603.

Zahran, H.S., Kobau, R., Moriarty, D.G., Zack, M.M., Holt, J., & Donehoo, R. (2005). Health-related quality of life surveillance—United States, 1993–2002. MMWR Surveillance Summaries, 54(SS-4):1–36.

Zaidi, S.A. (1988). Poverty and disease: Need for structural change. *Social Science and Medicine, 27,* 119–127.

CHAPTER

2

Marketing Social Change— A Challenge for the Public Health Practitioner

Public health aims to satisfy the human need for health by facilitating a series of individual and societal exchange processes. These exchanges include the adoption of individual behavior and lifestyle changes and the adoption of societal programs to improve social and economic conditions. Marketing is defined as "human activity directed at satisfying needs and wants through exchange processes" (Kotler, 1976, p. 5) Thus, whether they realize it or not, public health practitioners are in the business of marketing.

The basic public health product is social change, and the fundamental mission of the public health practitioner is to market social change. Unlike most traditional products, however, those which public health must market tend to have negative demand, no demand, or unwholesome demand. People do not want the product, do not care about the product, or they desire an alternative product whose use is counterproductive to the goal of improving health. In addition, the environment is hostile to public efforts to stimulate demand for social change. Not only is the state of demand for social change unfavorable and the environment for marketing social change hostile, but the public health practitioner is not generally trained in the skills necessary to be an effective marketer.

Thus, the need to market social change represents a formidable challenge to the public health practitioner.

Marketing involves an exchange processes, which is simply the transfer, between two parties, of something that has value to each party. The marketer's task is to facilitate exchanges so that customers can fulfill their needs and wants. Usually, the marketer benefits from the exchange by obtaining money, while the customers benefit by obtaining a good or service that satisfies a need or desire. Public sector and nonprofit marketers may, however, benefit in non-monetary ways, through the fulfillment of their institutional mission, desires, and goals.

Health is certainly something that people need and want. It, however, is not something that comes without paying a price. To achieve health, people must give up something of value: time, convenience, money, pleasure. For example, to achieve cardiovascular health, a person may have to give up the pleasure associated with smoking; pay for physician visits and blood pressure medication; accept the inconvenience of having to read food nutrition labels; and put in the time necessary to exercise and lose weight.

Similarly, on a societal level, a healthy population simply cannot be created without paying a price. We have to be willing to give up something of value—usually, public resources—to achieve a healthy society. For example, government may have to pay for health care for the uninsured, food and shelter for the poor, and public education programs to teach people the benefits of quitting smoking. Sometimes, the cost to society is not in dollars, but in something else of value, such as the desire to interfere as little as possible with the marketplace. To improve societal health, government may have to impose environmental health regulations on corporations, consumer product safety rules on manufacturers, or even professional practice guidelines on physicians.

In any case, achieving health, whether individual or societal, requires an exchange. And the role of the public health practitioner can be viewed as facilitating the individual and societal-level exchanges necessary to satisfy the human need and desire for health. Public health activity is directed at satisfying the human desire and need for health by promoting or facilitating the exchange of behaviors and lifestyles at the individual level and the exchange of social programs and policies at the societal level. Thus, public health, by its very nature, is in the business of marketing.

An exchange is necessary in order for the individual or society at large to obtain its need and desire for health because alternative methods of obtaining these wants are not readily available. Kotler (1976) described the three potential alternatives to an exchange as self-production, coercion, and supplication. For example, an individual is unable to create health for himself or herself (self-production), cannot forcibly obtain health from others (coercion), and cannot effectively plead for others to provide health to him or her (supplication). However, the individual can obtain health through an exchange. The individual can give up something valued in order to obtain health. He or she may give up cigarettes to improve cardiovascular health or may start exercising or reducing fat intake. He or she may trade the freedom of unprotected sex to obtain the promise of freedom from acquired immunodeficiency syndrome (AIDS).

Similarly, society cannot simply create healthy individuals, cannot somehow steal health for its people, and cannot effectively plead with individuals or business to provide for a healthy public. Instead, society can give up something of value—in this case, fiscal resources—to adopt a public health program that is designed to improve the health of its citizens.

In both examples, something of value is being exchanged for the promise of health. In the first case, the individual forfeits a valued behavior, like smoking, or a valued experience, like the pleasure of unprotected sex, in exchange for the prospect of improved health. In the second case, society exchanges fiscal resources for the prospect of improved population health.

Chapter 1 detailed the types of exchanges that public health practitioners must promote: the adoption of individual behaviors (or elimination of unhealthy behaviors) and the adoption of programs to improve social and economic conditions. The overall task is to create or facilitate social change. In other words, the primary challenge of the public health practitioner is to market social change.

Social change, then, can be viewed as the product public health is trying to sell. A product is simply "something that is viewed as capable of satisfying a want. . . . Anything capable of rendering a service, that is, satisfying a need, can be called a product" (Kotler, 1976, p. 5). And in the eyes of the public health practitioner, changes in behavior, social conditions, and social policy can help to satisfy the public's desire for health. That is, social change is a product because the public health practitioner views it as something that is capable of satisfying the individual and societal desire for healthy citizens and healthy communities.

Public health can be considered marketing because it involves a set of core activities directed at satisfying an important need and desire of the public—health—through a variety of individual and societal-level exchanges that take place continually. The product of public health—social change—may not be tangible, but it can be considered a product in a marketing sense because it is perceived by the public health practitioner as capable of satisfying the human desire for health.

■ A UNIQUE MARKETING CHALLENGE

The public health practitioner's fundamental task of marketing social change is a unique challenge for three reasons: (1) the unfavorable state of individual and societal demand for social change, (2) the hostile environment in which social change must be marketed, and (3) the limited training of public health practitioners in the skills necessary to market social change.

An Unfavorable State of Demand for Social Change

Protecting and promoting the public's health is a unique marketing challenge because of the special nature of the products that public health practitioners are asked to promote. These products fall into a particular niche in the marketing world that, although not exclusive to public health products, poses especially difficult barriers that must be overcome. Specifically, the products of public health—changes in behavior, social conditions, and social policy—tend to be unwanted, considered unimportant, or directly opposed to alternative products that people desire. The public and the policy makers generally do not want social change, do not care about social change, or are committed to social norms that directly oppose social change. This places public health in the initial stages of the product life cycle and creates a special challenge faced by marketers of traditional products only when they are first being introduced into the marketplace.

Kotler described eight states of the demand level for a product that require differing marketing tasks (Kotler, 1976). Most traditional products are in a state of full, overfull, faltering, irregular, or latent demand. Products in a state of full demand, where demand is at the desired level, simply require maintenance marketing. Products in a state of overfull demand, where demand is higher than the level at which the marketer is able to supply it, require demarketing: temporarily or permanently discouraging customers from using the product. Products in a state of faltering demand, where demand is less than its former level, require remarketing: altering the product, the target audience, or the marketing effort. Products in a state of irregular demand, where demand is seasonal or fluctuates widely, require synchromarketing: efforts to synchronize the fluctuations in demand and supply. Finally, products in a state of latent demand, where people share a strong need for a product that does not yet exist, require developmental marketing: creating and marketing a product to satisfy the existing demand. In all five cases, there is preexisting demand for the product; the marketer's task is simply to maintain, enhance, reform, or re-time marketing efforts, or in the case of latent demand, to create a product to satisfy high levels of existing public demand.

Under these five demand states, it is reasonably possible to achieve significant changes in individual brand choices, product choices, and product use in the market. For example, within 3 years of introducing its Joe Camel marketing campaign in 1986, the youth market share for Camel cigarettes increased from less than 3% to 8%; after an additional 3 years, Camel's youth market share was up to 16% (Pollay et al., 1996; U.S. Department of Health and Human Services [USDHHS], 1994). Within 1 year of introducing a new 64-bit television video game system, Nintendo achieved a commanding 50% share of the market (Jensen, 1997). Within 4 years of an intensified marketing effort, Clorox increased its market share from 29% in 1992 to 40% in 1996 (Neff, 1997). And within 2 years of the initiation of the products in 1995, 17% of users of skin cream were buying Revitalist Plentitude antiaging cream (Zbar, 1997) and nearly 48% of Internet search engine users were using the Excite search engine (Heath, 1997).

In contrast, the public health product—social change—is generally in one of three demand states: negative demand, no demand, or unwholesome demand. Most commonly, public health products are in a state of negative demand, where the public dislikes the product, does not want the product, and is not willing to pay a price to obtain the product, regardless of its promised benefits. For example, people generally have a negative demand for low-fat foods. We enjoy the taste of high-fat foods and the convenience associated with their availability and easy access, and we would prefer not to give up the taste and convenience for the more distant promise of long-term health benefits. The high public demand for fast-food restaurants is a testament to the negative demand for healthy, low-fat diets. On a societal level, the adoption of programs to help people living in poverty by way of income redistribution is in negative demand. Policy makers stringently avoid the adoption of programs that would significantly redistribute income away from the wealthy and toward the poor. Policy makers often are more willing to pay the price of higher crime rates, more drug use, and higher rates of uncompensated medical care than to jeopardize their chances for reelection by increasing taxes on the wealthy and powerful.

Some public health products are in a state of no demand. People are simply uninterested in the product. For example, programs to provide job training for the homeless are not in great demand by policy makers. Officials are not necessarily making a conscious decision to avoid such programs—there simply is not a great deal of political pressure to address the needs of the homeless in the first place.

Other public health products must be marketed in an environment of unwholesome demand. These are products for which there are alternatives, under high demand by the public, that are considered unhealthy and undesirable by public health practitioners. On an individual level, tobacco, alcohol, and drugs are products for which there is unwholesome demand. On a societal level, there is an unwholesome demand among policy makers for "welfare reform" policies that cut social support for individuals without providing adequate job training, child care, and other support services. These programs are undesirable by public health standards because, as discussed in Chapter 1, they lead to adverse health outcomes. To reduce tobacco, alcohol, or drug use or to promote the adoption of programs that provide social support for poor individuals, public health practitioners must "de-market" popular alternative behaviors or social programs that run counter to the goals of improving health.

Unlike the traditional marketer, then, the public health marketer is almost always faced with a market in which there is no demand for his or her product, negative demand for his or her product, or an unwholesome demand for an alternative product whose use runs counter to the desires of the public health practitioner and the goals of improving health. All three of the public health practitioner's products—changes in lifestyle, changes in social and economic conditions, and changes in social policy—face this problem of an unfavorable state of preexisting demand.

Lifestyle Change

The most striking examples of the unfavorable state of demand for lifestyle change are the addictive behaviors. These unhealthy behaviors are, by definition, highly resistant to change. They represent an extreme example of unwholesome demand: They are behaviors that severely harm individual health but that are highly desired by those who are addicted to them. For example, demand for heroin among heroin addicts is extremely high. Despite the devastating effects of heroin on all aspects of the addict's life, the behavior is sustained at a high rate. Even among addicts who are successfully maintained on methadone for long periods of time, the overall relapse rate among patients who discontinue methadone is at least 50% (Weddington, 1990/1991). Similarly, despite the serious health consequences of smoking and the availability of a wide range of cessation programs ranging from hypnosis to acupuncture, the overall relapse rate for smokers who successfully graduate from cessation programs, even with nicotine replacement therapy, is about 80% (Fiore et al., 1994; Orleans et al., 1994; Silagy et al., 1994).

As a result of the unwholesome demand that exists for addictive behaviors, the public health movement has been relatively unsuccessful in reducing tobacco, alcohol, and illicit drug use. The decline in adult smoking prevalence from 42% in 1965 to 25% in 1990 was a result of 25 years of persistent antismoking messages (Giovino et al., 1995; Susser, 1995). Even so, smoking prevalence among adults has declined only slightly since then, reaching just under 21% in 2004, a decline of only 4 percentage points in 13 years (Centers for Disease Control [CDC], 2005; National Center for Health Statistics [NCHS], 2004). While past-month smoking among high school seniors is declining, nearly one-quarter of these young people smoke—a proportion higher than in their adult counterparts—and past-month smoking prevalence among these youths is only 6 percentage points lower than it was in 1980 (NCHS, 2004). The 40% reduction in alcohol-related traffic fatalities between 1980 and 1994 was the result of an intensive, 15-year public health campaign (Wald, 1996). However, there has been no further progress, with annual alcohol-related traffic deaths remaining at about 17,000 in both 1995 and 2004 (National Highway Traffic Safety Administration, 1997, 2005). And despite the adverse consequences of drug use and the highly publicized "Just Say No" campaigns, rates of cocaine and marijuana use among high school seniors have increased since 1990; past-month use of cocaine increased from 1.9% in 1990 to 2.1% in 2003; past-month use of marijuana increased from 14.0% in 1990 to 21.2% in 2003 (NCHS, 2004).

Public health interventions also have met with limited success in reducing high blood pressure, high cholesterol levels, and obesity. Several large-scale interventions conducted during the 1970s and 1980s to reduce heart disease risk factors failed to produce substantial differences in mortality rates in treated and comparison communities (Farquhar et al., 1990; Lefebvre et al., 1987; Luepker et al., 1994; Multiple Risk Factor Intervention Trial Research Group, 1982; Schwab & Syme, 1997). More recently, health indicators have revealed little progress in addressing these problems. The proportion of adults with high cholesterol has decreased only slightly, from 19.7% during the period 1988–1994 to 17.0% during the period 1999–2002 (NCHS, 2004). Obesity has actually increased in prevalence, rising from 23.3% in 1988–1994 to 31.1% in 1999–2002 (NCHS, 2004). And the proportion of adults with high blood pressure also increased, from 21.7% to 25.5% between these same time periods (NCHS, 2004).

Changes in Social and Economic Conditions

Changing the social and economic infrastructure of society to create conditions that will facilitate healthy individual behavior is a reform that tends to be under negative demand or no demand by the public and policy makers. Social and economic conditions are difficult to change, and investing the resources and effort to overcome barriers to change is not a priority for the general public or for most policy makers. Many politicians simply do not care about improving conditions for a segment of the population whose welfare will not affect their reelection chances (no demand). Among other policy makers, there has been a declining interest in providing support and resources to improve social and economic conditions for individuals living in poverty (negative demand).

For example, the maximum level of AFDC (Aid for Families with Dependent Children) benefits for poor families fell by more than 17% between 1970 and 1996, after adjustment for inflation, in all 50 states (Kilborn, 1996). Nonwelfare human service benefits were also reduced sharply. During the period 1994 to 1996 alone, federal subsidies for public housing declined by 11.1%; funding for programs to assist the homeless in finding and retaining housing was reduced by 31.3%; funding for food stamps dropped by 32.2%; emergency assistance to provide shelter for homeless families declined by 44.1%; and federal fuel assistance fell by 49.2% (John W. McCormack Institute of Public Affairs, 1997). Between 1990 and 1996, federal funding for the prevention of homelessness among families fell by 64.0%. There is clearly a negative demand among the public and policy makers for public investment in sincere efforts to improve social and economic conditions. If anything, demand for such an investment in society's social and economic infrastructure is declining.

Changes in Social Policy

The negative demand among the public and policy makers for the social policy reforms needed to create conditions in which people can be healthy is perhaps best illustrated by the 1995 Food and Drug Administration (FDA) regulations on the sale and promotion of tobacco products (FDA, 1996). The Clinton Administration's willingness, and the FDA's determination, to take on the tobacco industry by regulating tobacco for the first time in history represented the most positive political environment ever for social policy reform in the area of tobacco control. In asserting jurisdiction over tobacco products, the FDA found that nicotine is addictive, that cigarettes are a drug-delivery device, and that tobacco products kill more than 400,000 Americans each year (FDA, 1996). In spite of these findings, the FDA regulations did very little to change social policy regarding tobacco sale, marketing, and use in the nation. Given the magnitude of this public health problem and the finding that cigarettes represented a drug-delivery device not unlike others the FDA regulates, the most appropriate action, at least from a public health perspective, would have been to regulate the safety of the product. This might have taken the form of regulating the production, sale, and marketing of tobacco: for example, making cigarettes and smokeless tobacco a prescription product, requiring a reduction or elimination in the level of nicotine in tobacco products, or eliminating the marketing of these deadly products. Any of these actions would have represented a significant and profound change in social policy regarding tobacco.

However, due to perceived public and political opposition to meaningful social policy reform, President Clinton and the FDA decided to propose regulations that would confront only the sale and marketing of tobacco to minors, which were already either illegal or widely recognized as violating accepted social policy norms. The proposed FDA regulations left the production, sale, and marketing of tobacco essentially intact. They merely required enforcement of preexisting laws that restricted the sale of tobacco to minors and placed modest restrictions on forms of tobacco advertising and promotion that appeal to youth. In this way, the FDA regulations did not represent a true change in social policy. They simply strengthened the enforcement of the existing policy: that tobacco should not be sold or marketed to persons under the age of 18.

The FDA's failure to provide a rational, public health justification for the decision to regulate tobacco only insofar as it represents an addictive threat to adolescents highlights the intensity of our policy makers' resolve not to alter deeply ingrained norms of social policy.

As the FDA example demonstrated, changing social policy is under negative demand in our society: Policy makers are willing to pay a price to avoid having to tamper with longstanding social policy norms.

A Hostile Public Health Marketing Environment

Few marketers have to compete with high-intensity, well-financed campaigns that aim to reduce demand for their products. There is no industry dedicated to reducing the demand for Beanie Babies or to convincing people to avoid eating in restaurants or to stop wearing shoes.

In contrast, public health practitioners often face high-intensity campaigns conducted specifically to counteract their marketing efforts. The marketer of public health products must compete with industries whose prime objective is the promotion of unhealthy behaviors. At the same time that public health practitioners try to convince people not to smoke and not to drink, the tobacco and alcohol industries are spending $15 billion and $2–3 billion each year, respectively, for the sole purpose of trying to get people to smoke cigarettes and drink alcohol (Federal Trade Commission, 1999, 2005). At the same time public health officials are trying to convince Congress and state legislators that firearms are a leading cause of death among young Americans, the National Rifle Association is spending approximately $8 million each year to influence legislators to vote against any proposals that would restrict the production, sale, or use of firearms (Burchfield, 2000).

In addition to opposition to public health efforts by major industries and lobbying groups, the social environment itself, with its deeply ingrained social norms, often contributes to a hostile environment in which to market social change. For example, despite a vigorous campaign to increase physical activity among the population, and despite a high level of public demand for ways to increase physical activity, the social and occupational environments are hostile to this type of change. Workplace schedules generally are not designed to allow for a sufficient period of physical activity during the work day. Public transportation systems and urban planning are not developed well enough to allow large numbers of people to walk or bike to work. Intense marketing of and easy access to beer, fast food, and high-fat products undermine individual attempts to improve diet and reduce weight. In 2002, about 38% of adults reported having no leisure-time physical activity, and between 1999 and 2002, about 65% reported being overweight (NCHS, 2004).

The Limited Capacity of Public Health Practitioners to Market Social Change

The capacity of public health practitioners to market social change is limited by three factors: (1) inadequate emphasis on the advocacy role in public health, (2) limited expertise in advocacy skills among current public health practitioners, and (3) lack of training of public health students and practitioners in advocacy skills.

Inadequate Emphasis on Advocacy in Public Health Practice

The public health practitioner is, first and foremost, an advocate for social change. The historical roots of the public health movement lie in the efforts of visionaries whose lives were dedicated to advocating for social change. (See Chapter 4 for a more thorough discussion.) It was the social reforms advocated by these figures that gave public health its source, its mission, its foundation, and its original vision.

In recent years, the public health movement has lost its appreciation of advocacy as its primary tool and its sense of a common, unifying social mission that can serve as a rallying cry for the movement (Institute of Medicine, Committee for the Study of the Future of Public Health, 1988; Stevens, 1996). As discussed in Chapter 4, many public health officials have confused advocacy and lobbying, and in an effort not to violate federal laws that restrict lobbying by government and nonprofit agencies, they have completely renounced any semblance of a role in social advocacy. As the Institute of Medicine (1988) report on the future of public health showed, "although public health professionals have traditionally recognized influences of the physical environment on health status, they have been less adept at recognizing health-related influences in the business, economic, and social environment and in fashioning and advocating strategies to control these factors" (p. 113). The report later concludes that "too frequently, public health professionals view politics as a contaminant rather than as a central attribute of democratic governance" (p. 154).

Public health practitioners need a new job description: one that lists advocacy as the chief role and responsibility of the job and that calls on the public health practitioner to mobilize community support for societal efforts to produce social change. As Turnock (1997) concluded in his book, *Public Health: What It Is and How It Works*, "the public health system, from national to state and local levels, must recognize these circumstances and move beyond capably providing services to aggressively advocating and building constituencies for efforts that target the most important of the traditional health risk factors and that promote social policies that both minimize and equalize risks throughout the population. These represent a new job description for public health in the United States, but one that is both necessary and feasible" (pp. 355–356).

Limited Expertise in Advocacy among Current Public
  Health Practitioners

Even among public health agencies that still retain an advocacy role, few of the individual practitioners have been thoroughly trained in advocacy, and many of the skills necessary to advocate effectively are incompletely developed. As the Institute of Medicine (1988) noted, "effective public health action for many problems requires organizing the interest groups, not just assessing a problem and determining a line of action based on top-down authority" (p. 122). The Institute of Medicine found, however, that most public health workers have not received formal education in public health itself, much less in other critical areas needed for effective advocacy, including political science, community organizing, and management. Public health workers tend to lack skills that derive from education in these areas, including skills in media advocacy, political activity, community organizing, and coalition building.

Inadequate Training in Advocacy for Public Health Students and Practitioners

A convention of public health practitioners and academicians met in 1992 to develop a set of "universal competencies for public health professionals" (Sorenson & Bialek, 1992; Turnock, 1997). One of the competencies developed was "advocating for public health programs and resources" (Sorenson & Bialik, 1992). The Institute of Medicine (1988) recommended a set of political skills and capacities that should be essential components of training for all public health students and practitioners: "public health agencies should be able to mobilize the support of important constituencies, including the general public, to compete successfully for scarce resources, to handle conflict over policy priorities and choices, to establish linkages with other organizations, and to develop a positive public image" (p. 154). These are essentially skills in advocacy.

Dr. Barry Levy, a former president of the American Public Health Association (APHA) wrote of the need for public health leaders who

> educate and inform, who facilitate grassroots advocacy to shape public policy. . . . Leaders with a holistic vision of public health, who appreciate the relevance of education, employment and housing to public health, who create horizontal integration of programs and services. . . . Leaders who do not fight to get a seat at the table, but who figuratively are the table—who set the stage, frame the issues, pose the questions and engage a wide range of people and organizations in the issues that affect them and their communities. Leaders who work for social justice. Leaders who empower the disadvantaged. (Levy, 1996, p. 2)

As a discipline, advocacy generally is not taught and certainly is not emphasized in schools of public health. For example, in 1997–98 less than one-third of accredited schools of public health in the United States offered a course in public health advocacy, and less than half offered a course in media advocacy or mass communication.

■ CONCLUSION

The combination of the unfavorable state of public demand for social change, the hostile environment in which public health practitioners must market social change, and the limited training of public health practitioners in marketing and advocacy makes confronting the emerging threats to the public's health a formidable marketing challenge for the public health practitioner. But the same marketing principles that help explain why social change is so difficult to create also can be used to redefine and reposition the public health product so that it is in demand by the public and by policy makers. Chapter 3 shows why marketing social change is both a challenge and an opportunity for the public health practitioner.

References

Burchfield, B. (2000, April 5). *Statement of Bobby R. Burchfield before the Senate Committee on Rules and Administration*. Washington, DC: United States Senate. Available at: http://rules.senate.gov/hearings/2000/04500burchfield.htm.

Centers for Disease Control and Prevention. (2005). Cigarette smoking among adults—United States, 2004. *Morbidity and Mortality Weekly Report, 54*, 1121–1124.

Farquhar, J. W. Fortmann, S.P., Flora, J.A., Taylor, D.B. Haskell, W.L. Williams, P.T. Maccoby, N, & Wood, P.D. (1990). Effects of community-wide education on cardiovascular disease risk factors. *Journal of the American Medical Association, 264*, 359–365.

Federal Trade Commission. (1999, September). *Self-regulation in the alcohol industry: A review of industry efforts to avoid promoting alcohol to underage consumers*. Washington, DC: Author. Available at: http://www.ftc.gov/reports/alcohol/alcoholreport.htm.

———. (2005). *Federal Trade Commission cigarette report for 2003*. Washington, DC: Author. Available at: http://www.ftc.gov/reports/cigarette05/050809cigrpt.pdf.

Fiore, M.C., Smith, S.S., Jorenby, D.E., & Baker, T.B. (1994). The effectiveness of the nicotine patch for smoking cessation: A meta-analysis. *Journal of the American Medical Association, 271*, 1940–1947.

Food and Drug Administration. (1996, August 28). *Regulations restricting the sale and distribution of cigarettes and smokeless tobacco to protect children and adolescents: Final rule* (Fed. Reg., 21 C.F.R. Parts 801, 803, 804, 807, 820, and 897, pp. 44396–45318). Washington, DC: U.S. Department of Health and Human Services, Food and Drug Administration.

Giovino, G.A., Schooley, M.W., Zhu, B., Chrismon, J.H., Tomar, S.L., Peddicord, J.P. Merritt, R.K., Husten, C.G., & Eriksen, M.P. (1995). Surveillance for selected tobacco use behaviors—United States, 1900–1994. *Morbidity and Mortality Weekly Report (CDC Surveillance Summaries), 43*(SS-3), 1–43.

Heath, R.P. (1997, June 30). The marketing 100: Excite. *Advertising Age, 68*(26), p. s10.

Institute of Medicine, Committee for the Study of the Future of Public Health. (1988). *The future of public health*. Washington, DC: National Academy Press.

Jensen, J. (1997, July 14). Nintendo plots fall ad campaign for its 64 system: Branding efforts for software, hardware will share message. *Advertising Age,* 68(28), pp. 3, 36.

John W. McCormack Institute of Public Affairs. (1997, January 10). *Over the edge: Cuts and changes in housing, income support, and homeless assistance programs in Massachusetts.* Boston: University of Massachusetts-Boston, John W. McCormack Institute of Public Affairs.

Kilborn, P.T. (1996, December 6). Welfare all over the map. *The New York Times,* p. 3E.

Kotler, P. (1976). *Marketing management: Analysis, planning, and control* (3rd ed.). Englewood Cliffs, NJ: Prentice-Hall.

Lefebvre, R.C., T.M., Carleton, R.A., & Peterson, G. (1987). Theory and delivery of health programming in the community: The Pawtucket Heart Health Program. *Preventive Medicine,* 16, 80–95.

Levy, B.S. (1996, December). Putting the public back in public health. *The Nation's Health,* p. 2.

Luepker, R.V., Murray, D.M., Jacobs, D.R., Mittelmark, M.B., Bracht, N., Carlaw, R., Crow, R., Elmer, P., Finnegan, J., Folsom, A.R., Grimm, R., Hannan, P.J., Jeffrey, R., Lando, II., McGovern, P., Mullis, R., Perry, C.L., Pechacek, T., Pirie, P., Sprafka, J.M., Weisbrod, R., & Blackburn, H. (1994). Community education for cardiovascular disease prevention: Risk factor changes in the Minnesota Heart Health Program. *American Journal of Public Health,* 84, 1383–1393.

Multiple Risk Factor Intervention Trial Research Group. (1982). Multiple Risk Factor Intervention Trial: Risk factor changes and mortality results. *Journal of the American Medical Association,* 248, 1465–1477.

National Center for Health Statistics (2004). *Health United States, 2004, with chartbook on trends in the health of Americans* (DHHS Publication No. 2004-1232). Hyattsville, MD: Author.

National Highway Traffic Safety Administration. (1997, March). *Alcohol involvement in fatal traffic crashes 1995* (Tech. Rep. DOT HS 808-547). Washington, DC: Author.

———. (2005, August). *Traffic safety facts: Alcohol-related fatalities in 2004.* Washington, DC: National Highway Traffic Safety Administration, National Center for Statistics and Analysis. Available at: http://www-nrd.nhtsa.dot.gov/pdf/nrd-30/NCSA/RNotes/2005/809904.pdf.

Neff, J. (1997, June 30). The marketing 100: Clorox. *Advertising Age,* 68(26), p. 218.

Orleans, C.T., Resch, N., Noll, E., Keintz, M.K., Rimer, B.K., Brown, T.V., & Snedden, T.M. (1994). Use of transdermal nicotine in a state-level prescription plan for the elderly—A first look at "real-world" patch users. *Journal of the American Medical Association,* 271, 601–607.

Pollay, R.W., Siddarth, S., Siegel, M., Haddix, A., Merritt, R.K., Giovino, G.A., & Eriksen, M.P. (1996). The last straw? Cigarette advertising and realized market shares among youths and adults, 1979–1993. *Journal of Marketing,* 60, 1–16.

Schwab, M., & Syme, S.L. (1997). On paradigms, community participation, and the future of public health. *American Journal of Public Health,* 87, 2049–2051.

Silagy, C., Mant, D., Fowler, G., & Lodge, M. (1994). Meta-analysis on efficacy of nicotine replacement therapies in smoking cessation. *The Lancet, 343*(1), 139–142.

Sorenson, A.A., & Bialek, R.G. (Eds.). (1992). *The public health faculty/agency forum.* Gainesville, FL: University of Florida Press.

Stevens, R. (1996). Editorial: Public health history and advocacy in the money-driven 1990s. *American Journal of Public Health, 86,* 1522–1523.

Susser, M. (1995). Editorial: The tribulations of trials—Interventions in communities. *American Journal of Public Health, 85,* 156–158.

Turnock, B.J. (1997). *Public health: What it is and how it works.* Gaithersburg, MD: Aspen.

U.S. Department of Health and Human Services. (1994). *Preventing tobacco use among young people: A report of the Surgeon General.* Atlanta, GA: U.S. Department of Health and Human Services, Centers for Disease Control and Prevention, National Center for Chronic Disease Prevention and Health Promotion, Office on Smoking and Health.

Wald, M.L. (1996, December 15). A fading drumbeat against drunk driving. *The New York Times,* p. E5.

Weddington, W.W. (1990/1991). Towards a rehabilitation of methadone maintenance: Integration of relapse prevention and aftercare. *International Journal of the Addictions, 25,* 1201–1224.

Zbar, J.D. (1997, June 30). The marketing 100: Revitalift. *Advertising Age, 68*(26), p. s16.

CHAPTER

3

Marketing Social Change—An Opportunity for the Public Health Practitioner

The primary challenge facing public health practitioners is the need to market changes in behavior, societal conditions, and social policy in the absence of significant public demand for these changes. Through the strategic use of marketing principles, the public health practitioner can effectively confront these challenges. The key is for public health practitioners to abandon the traditional approach of deciding what they want the target audience to buy and then attempting to sell this product to an audience that has little demand for it. Instead, public health professionals must first find out what the consumer wants and then redefine, repackage, reposition, and reframe the product in such a way that it satisfies an existing demand among the target audience. The public health official must be able to offer a benefit that the audience appreciates and demands, to back up this offer with support, and to communicate an image of the product and its benefit that reinforces the most influential core values of the target audience.

Chapter 2 demonstrated that the public health practitioner must market changes in behavior, social conditions, and policies under an unfavorable state of public demand for social change and in an environment that is hostile to social change. Fortunately, the same marketing principles that help explain why social change is so difficult to create can also provide the public health practitioner with powerful tools to facilitate social change.

This chapter examines how the strategic application of marketing principles can provide the public health practitioner with a unique opportunity to effect changes in individual behavior, social conditions, and social policies.

To see how the public health practitioner can use the principles of marketing to effect social change, we must return to the definition of *marketing*: "human activity directed at satisfying needs and wants through exchange processes" (Kotler, 1976, p. 5). At the very heart of marketing is the task of identifying and understanding the needs and wants of consumers. And at the very heart of public health is the task of identifying and understanding the individual's need for, and desire for, health.

What does it mean to people to be healthy? Why is it that people want to be healthy? How do people perceive health as a personal benefit? What about health makes it desirable? Is it the mere absence of disease that people desire, or does health have positive values that drive people's wants?

Perhaps the best way to find out what health means to people is to study what people miss most in the absence of health. To answer this question, we must turn to the field of medical sociology—the sociology of health and illness. And the first thing we must understand is the fundamental distinction between disease and illness.

As Conrad and Kern (1994) pointed out, disease and illness are not the same. Whereas disease is "the biophysiological phenomena that manifest themselves as changes in and malfunctions of the human body," illness is "the experience of being sick or diseased" (Conrad & Kern, 1994, p. 7). People might feel ill in the absence of disease, and they may be diseased without experiencing illness (Enthoven, 1980; Turnock, 1997). Because people experience illness, or the subjective experience of being sick, it is the illness experience rather than disease itself that best defines the nature of the value that individuals place on their health. Research on the illness experience can perhaps best tell us what it means to people to be healthy.

In her classic ethnographic study of the experience of illness among gay and bisexual men with acquired immunodeficiency syndrome (AIDS), Rose Weitz (1994) found that the feeling of lack of control over one's life is the single most important and widely shared aspect of the illness experience. Weitz describes the critical importance to these men of learning to cope with uncertainty, to inject some degree of control over their lives. The great challenge to these men is dealing with the loss of control over their futures: Despite taking all the proper actions, they cannot control "what will happen to them, when it will happen, and why" (p. 138).

Perhaps the centrality of the concept of control to the illness experience was described best by one of the participants in the study by Weitz, who stressed the importance of "being active about this disease, whether it involves drinking a certain kind of tea or standing on your head twice a day or doing something. Something that gives the patient a feeling of control over his own life that if you do these things, this might help you a little bit. . . . It's a sense of being in control, of being actively involved in your own health, which in itself produces health" (p. 145).

In fact, uncertainty is recognized as a central and common characteristic of all illness experiences (Conrad, 1987; Glaser & Strauss, 1968; Mishel, 1984; Mishel et al., 1984; Molleman et al., 1984; Weitz, 1994). In contrast to the uncertainty that accompanies other types of life crises, ill persons cannot necessarily alter the eventual outcomes of their situations (Weitz, 1994).

Weitz (1994) described the basic mechanism of coping with uncertainty in ill persons as constructing a framework to explain their situations that gives them some sense of control over their lives:

> These frameworks give people the sense that they understand what has happened and will happen to them. By making the world seem predictable, these frameworks help individuals to choose (albeit sometimes from among limited options) how they will live their lives. Thus . . . these frameworks reduce the stresses of uncertainty by enabling people to feel at least minimally in control of their lives . . . . In the final analysis, it is this sense of control that enables people to tolerate uncertainty. (p. 139)

Thus, not the intrinsic presence of disease itself, but the loss of control associated with the illness experience brought on by that disease best characterizes the nature of the value people place on health. Weitz, for example, described one man with AIDS who lamented not being able to take a small trip for fear of having diarrhea while he was driving. Another man summarized his experience similarly: "AIDS has become my life. I live for AIDS. I don't live for me anymore, I live for AIDS. I'm at its beck and call and I'll do what it tells me when it tells me" (Weitz, 1994, p. 144). These examples illustrate the critical importance of values such as freedom, independence, autonomy, and control over one's life, above and beyond any value of health itself.

In *The Illness Narratives: Suffering, Healing, and the Human Condition*, psychiatrist Arthur Kleinman (1988) discussed the personal and social meaning of illness through the eyes of his patients. The themes of loss of control, loss of independence, and loss of freedom are repeatedly mentioned as the central source of personal suffering in the illness experience. For example, describing one severely disabled diabetic patient, Kleinman wrote, "It was not death that she feared, she would tell me, but the seemingly relentless march toward becoming an invalid. Loss of her leg forced the realization that she was now partially dependent and that one day she would be more completely so" (p. 35). And as the patient herself explains, "I began to see how terrible it would be to be incapacitated—to give up even the semblance of my independence, my control, my role in the family and in the community" (p. 37).

A large body of sociological research has revealed that health is of value to the individual not intrinsically, but because it assures a certain degree of personal freedom, independence, autonomy, and control.

The diseased individual suffers mainly because of the loss of control over his or her life. Depending on the severity of the disease, a person may lose control over basic bodily functions (e.g., eating, breathing, urination), basic activities of daily life (walking, sitting, washing), or more advanced functions that contribute to emotional and occupational fulfillment (speaking, typing, running). Disability is most troubling because of the loss of personal freedom that comes with it. Individuals who are disabled may also lose a degree of independence; they may have to rely on others to help them with complex or even basic activities. Placing a loved one in a nursing home, for example, is difficult not because it represents the loss of some ideal healthy state, but because it represents a loss of the individual's ability to live independently and often, of the family's ability to adequately care for the individual.

As these examples show, it is not really health itself that people value most. Rather, it is the freedom, independence, autonomy, and control over their lives that come with being healthy for which people have the most fundamental need and desire. Therefore, the first lesson that the public health practitioner can learn by applying basic marketing principles to the fundamental task of marketing social change is that health itself is not the most effective product that the public health practitioner has to offer. The most compelling product of the public health practitioner is the freedom, independence, autonomy, and control over life that comes with health.

If public health practitioners fail to make this subtle, yet critical, distinction in how they define and then market their product, they are unlikely to be successful. Why? Because it is not a disregard of health, but a desire for freedom, independence, autonomy, and control that leads to and sustains unhealthy behaviors and lifestyles in the first place. And if the public health practitioner ignores the role of the behavior in supporting these widely held core values, he or she can be sure that the industries promoting these unhealthy behaviors are fully aware of these core values and are using them to their advantage.

Although Americans certainly value health, they also hold other values that tend to be more important, more salient, and more influential on individual behavior. Often, these values are supported by maintaining, rather than changing, an unhealthy behavior. If an individual has firmly established a behavior in the first place, it must fulfill some core value for the individual. If the individual is aware that the behavior has undesirable health consequences, that awareness is less potent than the pull of the other values. The traditional public health approach to behavior change simply tries to reinforce the value of health, but in the process it conflicts with other deeply held values that are stronger and more influential.

The public health practitioner must realize that, as Andreasen (1995) described it, "target consumers in most behavior-change situations have very good reasons for maintaining the behavior patterns they have held— often for a lifetime" (p. 48). And as Salmon (1989) noted, public health campaigns "represent only one social force among many driving and re- straining forces. For every campaign message intending to dissuade con- sumers from illegal drug use or cigarette smoking, there are literally dozens of forces . . . espousing competing philosophies, similarly at work" (pp. 44, 45).

For example, although public health practitioners try to convince ado- lescents not to smoke by appealing to their desire for health, other mes- sages in the adolescent's world appeal to more salient and influential core values. Marlboro ads tell kids that smoking will make them free and in- dependent, like a cowboy. Seeing adults smoking in bars and other places where kids are not allowed tells teenagers that smoking is a symbol of maturity and autonomy. The cigarette companies themselves, through campaigns that portray smoking as an adult decision and encourage youths to listen to their parents, tell kids that smoking is a way to exert independence from their parents and to give them—not adult authority figures—control over their own lives.

The public health practitioner faces a similar challenge confronting al- cohol consumption. As Winett and Wallack (1996) suggested, "given the social value placed upon recreational alcohol consumption, the avail- ability and accessibility of alcoholic beverages, the environmental cues encouraging social drinking, and the pleasurable physical effects people often experience while drinking—the social marketing campaign designed to dissuade people from excessive drinking by teaching them of the health risks faces a profoundly difficult task" (p. 179).

Although public health practitioners have not traditionally conducted marketing research to identify and understand the needs and desires of their target audiences, their opponents—for example, the cigarette industry—have long used marketing research to find out what consumers want, what is important to them, and what values are most salient, in- fluential, and held most deeply by consumers. And although public health practitioners traditionally have relied solely on the individual's inherent value for health, their opposition has taken advantage of more com- pelling core values to sell their harmful products.

The tobacco industry, for example, conducted extensive research into the desires, needs and values of adolescents and young adults. The con- sistent finding of this research was the importance of the themes of in- dependence, freedom, autonomy, control, self-reliance, and rugged individualism. These themes have formed the basis for many of the to- bacco industry's promotional campaigns during this century. As Surgeon General Joycelyn Elders concluded, "United States advertisers, too, have long thought that individualism and the stimulating notions of independence, self-reliance, and autonomy are important strategic concepts in ad development" (U.S. Department of Health and Human Services [USDHHS], 1994, p. 177).

As early as 1929, Edward Bernays, a public relations consultant for the American Tobacco Company, organized a group of women to smoke publicly in the New York Easter Parade and to carry placards identifying their cigarettes as "torches of liberty" (Bernays, 1965; Schudson, 1984; USDHHS, 1994). This strategy was based on the work of consulting psychoanalyst A.A. Brill, who advised the company to promote cigarettes as "symbols of freedom" (Bernays, 1965; USDHHS, 1994, p. 165).

Young and Rubicam conducted a series of motivational interviews of smokers in the 1950s (Smith, 1954; USDHHS, 1994). These studies revealed the importance of the themes of freedom and escape to smokers (USDHHS, 1994). They suggested that appeals based on health claims would offer only transient results, but to increase the cigarette market, companies would have to "tap the driving force of the real psychological satisfactions of smoking" (USDHHS, 1994, p. 171).

Imperial Tobacco Limited of Canada conducted research on adolescents that revealed that "the adolescent seeks to display his new urge for independence with a symbol, and cigarettes are such a symbol" (USDHHS, 1994, p. 175). The research also found that young males in particular are "going through a stage where they are seeking to express their independence and individuality under constant pressure of being accepted by their peers" (USDHHS, 1994). Another Imperial Tobacco Limited study provided guidelines "for the effective display of freedom and independence in advertising imagery" (USDHHS, 1994, p. 177) and recommended that cigarette brands designed for youth show someone "free to choose friends, music, clothes, own activities, to be alone if he wishes," who "can manage alone" with "nobody to interfere, no boss/parents" (USDHHS, 1994, p. 177). The research described the importance of developing imagery to tap into four core adolescent values: independence, self-reliance, autonomy, and freedom from authority (USDHHS, 1994).

Indeed, the Surgeon General noted that "the brands most successful with teenagers seem to be those that offer adult imagery rich with connotations of independence, freedom and authority, and/or self-reliance" (USDHHS, 1994, p. 176). Marlboro, the most popular brand among adolescents, epitomizes the stereotype of American independence. As the Surgeon General noted, the Marlboro man is "usually depicted alone, he interacts with no one; he is strikingly free of interference from authority figures such as parents, older brothers, bosses, and bullies. Indeed, the Marlboro man is burdened by no one whose authority he must respect or even consider" (USDHHS, 1994, p. 177). R. W. Murray, former president and chief executive officer of Philip Morris, observed that "the cowboy has appeal to people as a personality. There are elements of adventure, freedom, being in charge of your destiny" (as cited in Trachtenberg, 1987, p. 109). Jack Landry, a key advertising executive behind the Marlboro Man campaign, described the cowboy as "a perfect symbol of independence and individualistic rebellion" (as cited in Meyers, 1984, p. 70).

Unfortunately, the core values that tobacco and other corporate marketers are reinforcing with their advertising messages—freedom, independence, autonomy, and self-control—are precisely those most deeply ingrained in American society. Once a person has recognized how an unhealthy behavior supports one or more of these core values, it will be most difficult to change the behavior, especially if one must rely solely on an appeal to the desire for health.

The importance of the core values of freedom, independence, autonomy, and control is apparent in the marketing campaigns of highly successful corporations. Nike, for example, has based its marketing of athletic footwear on the slogans "Just do it," and "I can." Nike is selling sneakers by telling people, essentially, that they can have control over their lives, they can be free, they can be independent. They can have control over their lives in much the same way as Michael Jordan has control over his body as he soars high over defenders to dunk the basketball while wearing Nike apparel. They can be independent, just as Michael Jordan is not dependent on others when making a spin move and body fake to break free and drive to the basket. And they can be autonomous, just as Bo Jackson has the ability to excel in any sport he chooses.

It is also instructive to note that when corporate marketers sell health products, they do not generally rely on the benefit of health to sell their products. Health clubs and exercise equipment are marketed to consumers not based on their ability to improve long-term health outcomes and prevent disease, but based on their ability to give people a feeling of control over how they look, how they feel, and how attractive they are to others. One doesn't usually see ads for health clubs that cite medical evidence about the benefits of physical activity in preventing chronic illness. More likely, one sees ads that show attractive people who seem to be in control of how they look, how they feel, and how others think about them.

Conrad and Kern (1994) conclude that "to understand the effects of disease in society, it is also necessary to understand the impact of illness" (p. 108). Perhaps it is the failure of the medical and public health professions to adequately understand the subjective meaning, experience, and impact of illness in addition to merely the objective phenomenon of disease that best explains the epidemic of unhealthy behaviors and lifestyles in the population. The advertisers of unhealthy products such as alcohol and tobacco have listened to the people, understood their feelings and experiences, and provided them with products to satisfy their subjective desires and needs. On the other hand, medical and public health professionals have tended to ignore the subjective meaning and experience of illness and to provide the public with what health professionals view as the needs of individuals. A public health practitioner's call for an individual to change his or her behavior may not be as compelling if it relies solely on the individual's intrinsic value of health as if it also feeds into the value that the individual places on personal freedom, independence, autonomy, and control over his or her life.

How can the public health practitioner begin to rely on these more influential core values to promote individual behavior change? The key is to redefine the public health product and its benefits in a way that appeals to the most compelling core values of the target audience. The public health practitioner must first abandon the traditional approach of deciding for himself or herself what product he or she wants the target audience to buy and then attempting to sell this product to an audience that has little demand for it. Instead, the public health practitioner must first find out what the consumer wants and then redefine, repackage, reposition, and reframe the product in such a way that it satisfies an existing demand among the target audience. All aspects of the marketing of the product must work together to reinforce, rather than conflict with, the most influential core values of the target audience.

In the remaining sections of this chapter, we review each of these steps in marketing individual behavior change to the public: (1) determining what the consumer wants; (2) redefining the public health product; and (3) repackaging, repositioning, and reframing the public health product.

■ FINDING OUT WHAT THE CONSUMER WANTS: THE ROLE OF FORMATIVE RESEARCH

What we are calling the "formative research" process in public health is not really a specific discipline, but a more general concept. The goal of "formative research" in public health is essentially to understand the consumer—in this case, the target audience for behavior change. Charlotte Vogel defined the purpose of formative research simply as "understanding consumers and what makes them tick" (Vogel, 1987, p. 31). Andreasen summarized the task as getting "inside the heads" of the target consumers (Andreasen, 1995, p. 47). Or as Marlboro Man creator Leo Burnett explains, "We have been able to get under (the consumers') skins a bit and find out what they really think about a product or the presentation of it and can't or won't express in words" (Burnett, 1961, p. 63).

There are many research fields that could potentially be used to help the public health practitioner accomplish this goal, including traditional marketing, political science, psychology, sociology, and anthropology. And there are many research methods that could help the public health practitioner understand what drives consumers' behavior. These methods include traditional marketing research methods, public opinion polling and surveys, clinical studies, behavioral research, cognitive and psychodynamic psychology research, focus groups, and ethnographic and other qualitative research methods.

It is not the method that is important, but the fact that some attempt is made to understand the consumer's needs, desires, and values before the public health program is designed and implemented. Andreasen emphasized the importance of this point by noting that John Sculley, former executive at Pepsi-Cola, had for years "been convincing consumers to buy his brand of colored sugar water over a competitor's colored sugar water with great success, mainly because he understood 'the Pepsi Generation' and how to speak to them" (Andreasen, 1995, p. 54).

While there is an abundance of quantitative articles in the medical and public health literature that consider why people do or do not engage in unhealthy behaviors, there is little qualitative research that allows the public health practitioner to learn "what makes them tick." For example, Weitz (1994) points out that "few published research studies have analyzed the experiences of persons with AIDS, and none has looked specifically at the issue of uncertainty. Instead, the social science literature on AIDS largely consists of quantitative studies regarding why people do or do not change their sexual behavior to protect themselves against infection" (p. 139).

Before public health practitioners can design programs that will be successful in changing individual behavior, they must attempt to get under the skin of their target audience and to explore core values such as freedom, autonomy, and control, and how they relate to the audience's perceptions of health, disease, behaviors, behavior change, and the experience of illness.

The existing biomedical paradigm for the practice of medicine and public health will not suffice for individual lifestyles to be changed in any significant way. Research that incorporates other models of behavioral and social change and provides a deeper understanding of the nature of illness and suffering—and not merely the presence or absence of disease—must become a central part of public health practice. "Whereas virtually all healing perspectives across cultures, like religious and moral perspectives, orient sick persons and their circle to the problem of bafflement, the narrow biomedical model eschews this aspect of suffering much as it turns its back on illness (as opposed to disease)" (Kleinman, 1988, p. 29).

The formative research is so essential to marketing in public health that Andreasen (2006) has listed "listening" to the audience as the first step in the social marketing process and describes this process as being "fanatically audience centered":

Because social marketing is fanatically audience centered, it is essential that campaigns begin with a thorough understanding of the target audience they seek to influence. Campaign planners must know "where the audience is coming from"—what do audience members think of the offer implicit in the campaign, what do they see as the benefits and costs, what do their friends think, and do they think they can actually carry out the behavior that is being recommended? Marketers must also know as much as they can about the competition the campaign faces from the target audience's point of view. What are the alternatives, and why are they attractive? Where are their weak points? This type of research is often called *formative* research. One of the most common causes of failure in social marketing campaigns is inadequate attention to the "listening" stage. (pp. 97–97)

One further essential element of the formative research process deserves emphasis. Even among a narrowly defined target group, such as gay men, there is a diversity of attitudes, beliefs, and values (see Appendix 3-A). Cultural differences between population groups make it imperative to conduct formative research among all the cultural subgroups that one is trying to reach. The values that are most important to gay White men, for example, may be quite different from those that are important to gay Black men, or to gay Latinos. When we speak about identifying the needs, desires, and values of the target audience, we are not assuming that these will be the same for all subgroups within the overall target audience. Depending on the extent of cultural differences within the audience, it may be necessary to intensively study various segments within the overall target population to identify their unique needs, desires, and culturally influenced values.

Flora, Schooler, and Pierson (1997) describe the importance of market segmentation, or breaking the target audience down into the smallest possible homogeneous groups, in formative research:

A fundamental tenet of social marketing is that health promotion programs must be designed in response to audience needs, implemented to meet those needs, effective in satisfying those needs, and monitored both to ensure that the program continues to meet these needs and to discover new or changing needs. Because a group's history, language, values, and beliefs influence group members' health-related knowledge, attitudes, and behavior, the values of a culture must be used as the foundation or building blocks of health promotion programs. Interventions or strategies that do not conform to cultural values (e.g., emphasizing long-term gains to a culture that prefers a present orientation) or worse, that actually challenge a group's values (e.g., assertive techniques in a society that values cooperative and fluid social relations) can be expected to fail. (p. 356)

■ REDEFINING THE PUBLIC HEALTH PRODUCT

In *Marketing Social Change: Changing Behavior To Promote Health, Social Development, and Environment,* Alan Andreasen (1995) summarizes the importance of redefining the marketing product based on actual consumer needs and wants, rather than on the beliefs, wishes, or intuitions of the marketer. Andreasen (1995) explains that good marketers

> do not seek to persuade target audiences to do what the marketer believes they ought to do. They do not try to make the audience accept the marketer's values and beliefs. Rather, they recognize that customers only take action when they believe that it is in their interests. Social marketing persuasion strategies therefore always start with an understanding of the target audience's needs and wants, their values, their perceptions. Social marketers do not start out with an assumption that their job is to change the customer to conform with the marketer. They recognize that they must often change their social marketing offerings and the way these are presented to meet target customer needs and wants. (pp. 14, 15)

Listening to the audience and changing the offering to meet its needs and wants means developing a new product based on the results of a formative research process. The marketer cannot decide in advance the product that he or she thinks the public will want and they try to sell it. Instead, the marketer must find out from the public what product it is seeking, and then design and present such a product to the public in a way that allows them to see how it will indeed provide the benefits being sought. As Andreasen (1995) explained it, "marketers know that they must understand where customers are coming from before they decide just what to try to sell" (p 16.)

Perhaps the key element of being able to adopt the marketing perspective is to understand that, as Rothschild (1999) points out:

> In most situations, people act primarily out of self-interest; in commercial marketing, this self-interest clearly and consistently is acknowledged and pursued. . . . In public health and social issues, managers often ask members of the target market to behave in ways that appear to be opposite of that member's perception of self-interest and are often the opposite of the current manifestation of that self-interest as observed through the member's current behavior. People choose to eat junk food, not exercise, smoke and drink to excess, or engage in unsafe sex because they have evaluated their own situation and environment and made a self-interested decision to behave as they do. (p. 26)

This means that the typical public health approach of trying to sell healthy behavior to the public based on the core value of health is not going to work. Clearly, if the person is already engaged in the unhealthy behavior, then he or she already perceives that it is in his or her self-interest to do so; usually, the individual has made this determination even with the awareness of the potential health risks associated with the behavior. An appeal based on health is likely going to be rejected because it does not alter the relationship between the perception of the behavior and the perception of what is in an individual's self-interest.

The challenge to the public health practitioner is to redefine the product so that it is now perceived as being in the individual's self-interest. The most effective way of doing that is to demonstrate that the product will help the individual fulfill some very salient and powerful need or desire. The practitioner can take advantage of, rather than be unsuccessful because of, the individual's self-interest if she is able to find values or ideals to which an individual aspires and then sell the product as meeting those values or ideals that are in the individual's self-interest, not opposed to it (see chapter 9 for a more detailed discussion of the concept of self-interest in public health marketing).

The central task of redefining the public health product is to clearly identify the benefits that the public health practitioner has to offer the target audience. This task is so important to the ultimate success of a public health campaign that it must not depend only on the intuition of the practitioner. Formative research is essential to identify the needs and wants of the target audience. Only then can the practitioner decide what product benefits will be most likely to satisfy these needs and wants. David Ogilvy, the advertising wizard who founded the advertising agency known later as Ogilvy and Mather, told his agency staff, "your most important job is to decide what you are going to say about your product, what benefit you are going to promise. . . . The selection of the right promise is so vitally important that you should never rely on guesswork to decide it" (Ogilvy, 1964, p. 93).

For public health practitioners, this may mean a drastic change in the way the public health product is defined. For the most part, practitioners will no longer be able to sell health. Instead, they will have to sell the more compelling, salient, and deep core values that are widely held by their target audiences. This concept, although new to many public health professionals, is basic to marketers of many traditional products.

For example, at the most basic level, Philip Morris is not selling Marlboro cigarettes to youth. Instead, it is selling freedom and independence, control over one's life, risk and adventure. R.J. Reynolds is not selling Camel cigarettes to youth. It is selling style and character, coolness and slyness. Crompton and Lamb (1986) explain that marketers are not only selling a tangible product, but they are selling a meaning as well: "People buy things not only for what they do, but also for what they mean" (p. 403). The meaning, the image, the theme—everything that a product symbolizes and stands for—is what defines the product more than anything.

In a similar way, Nike is not selling sneakers. It is selling control over one's life, a feeling of self-efficacy, a sense that you can do all the things you always wanted to do. The benefit—the promise that Nike is offering—is far more than a superior foot product or even superior athletic performance. The promise is control over your life and the fulfillment of your desires.

Public health practitioners must learn to redefine the public health product so as to offer a promise that appeals to people's core values. For example, the public health practitioner might try to prevent smoking initiation not by selling the idea of being a nonsmoker, but by selling freedom from nicotine addiction, independence from tobacco industry manipulation and victimization, and rebellion against an industry that is trying to trick you, seduce you, addict you, and ultimately, to kill you (**Table 3-1**). Instead of selling safe sex, the public health practitioner might redefine the product as freedom from AIDS, independence from the virus that is afflicting your friends and communities, and control over your destiny. And instead of selling exercise, the public health practitioner might sell control over your appearance, control over how you feel about yourself, control over how others think about you, and rebellion against feelings of unattractiveness.

Table 3-1   Product, Benefit, and Core Values for the Desired Action (Behavior Change) among the Target Audience—A Strategic Marketing Approach

Desired Action	Product/Benefits	Core Values
Prevent smoking initiation	Freedom from nicotine addiction	Freedom
	Independence from tobacco industry manipulation	Independence
		Control
	Rebellion against an industry that is trying to trick you, seduce you, addict you, and kill you	Rebellion
Practice safe sex	Freedom from AIDS	Freedom
	Independence from the virus that is afflicting your friends and communities	Independence
		Control
	Control over your destiny	Rebellion
Exercise more often	Identity as a physically strong and attractive person in control of your appearance	Freedom
		Independence
		Control
	Rebellion against feelings of unattractiveness and lack of control over your appearance	Rebellion

■ REPACKAGING, REPOSITIONING, AND REFRAMING THE PUBLIC HEALTH PRODUCT

Once the product is defined, the public health practitioner must begin the process of packaging it, positioning it, and framing it in such a way that it offers the benefits the target audience is seeking in a way that reinforces the audience's core values. At this stage, the process of developing an image for the product is central. This process involves the search for appropriate metaphors, symbols, words and phrases, visual images, and themes. All must work together to convince the consumer that the product will indeed fulfill his or her needs and desires, and in a way that is consistent with and reinforces his or her most salient core values.

Lauffer (1984) explains the significance of this task of framing, or image-building, as part of the strategic marketing process:

> In image building, symbols can be very important. In the United States, "welfare" tends to take on a negative connotation. To many, it means "cheating," "dependency," or a "drain on the taxpayers' resources." But no one is against the "deserving poor." In a recessionary economy, who can be against "laid-off" workers, in contrast with the "unemployed," some of whom, at least, are blamed for their situation. Some people may be turned off by the term "runaway kids" but not by "troubled teens." People may be against the high cost of Medicare or Medicaid, but they won't be against serving crippled children or good health care for impoverished senior citizens. They may be against welfare, but they are not against feeding hungry children. (p. 305)

For example, repackaging, repositioning, and reframing the product in a youth antismoking campaign might focus on the adolescent core values of freedom, independence, control, identity, and rebellion (**Table 3-2**). Focus group research conducted by the Centers for Disease Control and Prevention's (CDC's) Office on Smoking and Health has revealed that "the desire of teenagers to gain control over their lives would make them responsive to a counteradvertising strategy aimed at exposing the predatory marketing techniques of the tobacco industry" (McKenna & Williams, 1993, p. 85). The CDC research found that teens place a high value on "self-determination and being in control" (p. 87) and concluded that "teenagers' rebellion can be viewed as a manifestation of asserting their independence from adults' influence and control" (p. 87). The CDC researchers suggested that the important adolescent values of independence and control could be used to frame an antismoking message: "If you smoke, you are not in control; you are being manipulated by the tobacco industry" (p. 87).

Table 3-2 Repackaging, Repositioning, and Reframing the Public Health Product: Strategic Use of Marketing in a Smoking Prevention Campaign

Core Value	Message
Freedom	By not smoking, you can remain free of captivation by the addictive power of nicotine.
Independence	By not smoking, you can remain independent of the tobacco industry, which is trying to control you by fooling you into becoming a nicotine addict.
Control	By not smoking, you can maintain control over your social image, preventing being made a fool of by the tobacco industry.
Identity	Only the most mature youth are able to resist the tobacco industry's attempt to capture them; smoking is something that kids do because they are not mature enough to understand.
Rebellion	Rebel against an industry that is trying to deceive you, lie to you, manipulate you, seduce you, addict you, and kill you.

The results of formative research like this was used to develop a successful youth smoking prevention campaign in Florida (Hicks, 2001). The campaign, which emphasized to youths how they were being manipulated by the tobacco companies to start smoking, aimed to reframe the issue of independence and autonomy from something provided by smoking to something conferred to a youth by rejecting tobacco industry influence to attempt to get them to smoke. The campaign was successful in reducing thirty-day smoking prevalence among middle-school students from 18.5% to 11.1% and among high school students from 27.4% to 22.6% in just the first two years of the program (Bauer et al., 2000).

The potential effectiveness of such a reframing of the antismoking message can be seen in the success of tobacco prevention initiatives among Black youth. In 1992, the percentage of Black high school seniors who smoked was 8.2%, four times lower than the percentage who smoked two decades earlier (33.7% in 1974), while smoking prevalence among White youth during this period remained essentially unchanged at 30% to 34% (USDHHS, 1994). One explanation for this difference is the development, in the Black community, of social norms that view smoking as an infringement of individual freedom and view promotion of tobacco as an effort to control and enslave Blacks. Several campaigns in the Black community, including successful efforts to end the tobacco industry's marketing of X cigarettes and Uptown cigarettes, both directed specifically at young Black people, infused the community with a spirit of rebellion against an industry that was portrayed as trying to enslave it. As Cass Sunstein (1997) describes it, the antismoking campaign was "symbolized most dramatically by posters in Harlem subways showing a skeleton resembling the Marlboro man lighting a cigarette for a black child. The caption reads, 'They used to make us pick it. Now they want us to smoke it'" (p. 33).

Similar techniques could be used to reposition other public health "products" in ways that make their benefits to the audience more compelling (see **Table 3-1**). Fred Kroger, former director of CDC's Office of Health Communication, summarizes: "Just as athletic footwear is sold as aids to 'soar through the air, slam dunk, in your face' feats of athleticism, rather than as canvas covers for the feet, such prevention products as condoms, monogamy, or abstinence still lack similar, consumer-oriented positioning" (Kroger, 1995, p. 46).

In reframing the public health product, public health practitioners must recognize that the most deeply ingrained core value—freedom— represents not only the absence of something, but the presence of something as well. Frances Moore Lappe (1989) asks, "Aren't there really two basic aspects of freedom—freedom *from* interference and freedom to do what we want?" (p. 21) Freedom includes both negative liberty, or the absence of interference and infringement of one's privacy, and positive liberty, or the presence of an individual's ability to control his or her own life (Gaylin & Jennings, 1996).

This distinction has profound implications for framing behavior change as a public health product. Sometimes, the pursuit of positive liberty— helping people to be able to gain control over their lives—requires placing some limitations on negative liberty. For example, men may perceive wearing a condom as an infringement on their personal lives and their privacy. But the behavior itself may help to ensure positive liberty for the individual by keeping him in control of his future and allowing him, not AIDS, to make his decisions.

Public health efforts to change individual behavior tend to run up against opposition because they are perceived as conflicting with the core value of freedom. Usually, though, this is because they conflict with the concept of negative liberty. Public health practitioners may be able to show individuals that the desired behavior change actually reinforces the core value of freedom by emphasizing the aspects of positive liberty that will be conferred to the individual by adopting the behavior.

Public health practitioners must demonstrate that people's behavior choices are not really free, that these decisions are strongly influenced by economic, social, and environmental constraints that do not allow the full expression of individual autonomy. By providing people with healthy alternatives, the public health marketer is actually providing people with a degree of autonomy and freedom that they may not have previously experienced. "Individuals may not be able to make the healthy choices, such as lower cost but less nutritious foods at the local supermarket, unavailable exercise sites, or nonsupportive attitudes among their peers. Individuals have little or no control over their surroundings and so are dependent on their communities to maintain healthful conditions and choices" (Milio, 1995, p. 96).

Not only must public health practitioners demonstrate to the audience how the behavior change will fulfill basic needs and desires, but they must also show that the alternative (maintaining the behavior) will conflict with basic needs and desires. Thus, it is not enough merely to promote the behavior change in isolation. The public health practitioner must research the reasons for the maintenance of the behavior in the population, the alternative messages being communicated, the sources of these messages, and the core values to which these messages appeal. Part of the process of packaging, positioning, and framing the public health product is finding a way to demonstrate to the target audience that the desired behavior change will fulfill important core values, while maintaining the behavior is actually conflicting with these values. "Any program seeking to moderate or eliminate this destructive behavior must recognize that it meets important needs and wants of the target audience. To effectively change the behavior, the social marketer must understand those needs and wants and show how the proposed behavior can either also meet those needs and wants or can meet other needs and wants that are subordinate" (Andreasen, 1995, p. 80).

For example, to promote increased physical activity, public health professionals must not only show why being physically active will fulfill some important needs and desires, but how remaining inactive will conflict with important needs. Not only must public health professionals offer benefits for adopting the desired behavior change, but they must identify and understand contradicting messages and confront them directly. Andreasen (1995) explains that marketers "recognize that every choice of action on the consumer's part involves giving up some other action. Thus campaigns must keep in mind not only what the marketer is trying to get across but also what the customer sees as the major alternatives. Many times social marketers can bring about change as much by showing the deficiencies of an alternative as they can by emphasizing the benefits of the approach the marketer favors" (pp. 17, 18).

Part of demonstrating that a behavior will reinforce core target audience values is providing support to back up the promise. Traditionally, public health practitioners have relied on scientific evidence of the health benefits of a behavior change to support the promise of improved health from the behavior change. In contrast, successful corporate marketers tend to rely on much more compelling support for their promises. Nike, for example, backs up its offer of control over one's life with solid documentation: video footage of Michael Jordan—perhaps the most talented and successful athlete ever—in action. Ads for a health club might support their offer by showing a highly attractive, muscular, and self-confident individual using its facility.

Public health practitioners, too, must learn to provide equally compelling documentation or support for their promises. The increased use of peer as well as celebrity spokespersons is one approach that may be helpful. The source of the support is perhaps more important than the support message itself. People may be less likely to be convinced by documentation that comes from perceived public health authority, especially when there is now public skepticism about all the many public health messages that people are bombarded with, many of which present conflicting messages (e.g., fat is bad, some fat is good, polyunsaturated fat is good, trans-fat is bad, alcohol is bad, some alcohol is good, etc.).

The components of the process of defining, positioning, packaging, and framing the public health product, then, are (1) defining the product; (2) determining the promise or the benefit that the product should offer; (3) developing an image for the product that is consistent with the promise; and (4) providing support for the promise (**Figure 3-1**).

One way to put together the repositioning, repackaging, and reframing of the public health product is through the concept of branding. The

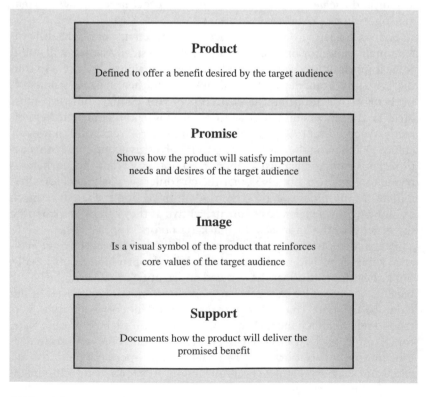

Figure 3-1 Components of the Strategic Marketing Process for a Public Health Product

concept of branding has been introduced recently into public health marketing (Andreasen, 2006) and has served as a useful framework for the development of a number of effective public health communication campaigns (see Hicks, 2001 for an excellent example and Chapter 9 for a detailed discussion).

Public health practitioners need to think of their product offering as a brand, similar in many ways to the brands that are offered to consumers by marketers of consumer products. As such, brands need to convey almost a personality of a product. The idea is to build a relationship with the customer, not merely to promote a one-time transaction: "In recent years, marketers have come to realize that the best way to influence behavior is not through one-time transactions, but by building ongoing relationships with their customers" (Hastings, 2003, p. 15).

By focusing on developing their brand "personality" for their public health product offering, public health practitioners can unify their promotional campaign around a single brand "identity," which can ensure that all aspects of the public health communication—the object, the promise, the benefit, the support, and the image—work together to convey an identity to which the target audience can relate, and to which it aspires. In this way, branding can serve as an ideal concept around which to incorporate the repackaging, repositioning, and reframing of the public health product.

After all, a brand not only forms the relationship between the organization or product and its consumer, but it has also been characterized as a repository, not merely of functional characteristics, but of meaning and value (Mark & Pearson, 2001; McDivitt et al, 2003). And it is that meaning and value (such as standing for freedom, independence, and autonomy), not merely the functional characteristics of the desired public health action (such as improving health and reducing disease or death) which is most closely tied to individual behavior.

Hicks (2001) describes how branding was used in the *truth*^{SM} youth smoking prevention campaign in Florida to make not smoking an identity to which youth would aspire: "In a search to define one's identity, brands (like piercing, haircuts, and even tobacco use) serve as a shorthand way for youth to identify themselves to the world. If we wanted youth to really embrace our anti-tobacco effort, it made sense that we should deliver it just like other successful U.S. youth products, such as Adidas, Fubu or Abercrombie—in a branded form they understood" (p. 5).

■ MARKETING PUBLIC HEALTH PROGRAMS AND POLICIES

Over the past 10 years, it has become increasingly recognized that traditional efforts to introduce marketing into public health ("social marketing") tended to focus too much on changing individual behavior and not enough on creating social change. Andreasen (2006), in his 2006 book on social marketing—Social Marketing in the 21st Century—calls this the difference between a "downstream" and "upstream" focus and his book devotes extensive attention to how basic principles of social marketing can be applied to changing not only individual behavior, but also the social determinants of that behavior, including programs that influence public opinion and social norms and policies that regulate the physical and social environment.

Marketing programs and policies for social change is in fact similar to marketing behavior change, except that the target audience is not the individual but the public in general and policy makers in particular. The public health practitioner must market the policy to the policy makers who have the power to implement it, or in the case of initiatives or referenda, to the voters who will decide the fate of the ballot proposal. In either case, the public health practitioner must market the policy to the public at large, because public attitudes toward the policy will affect legislators' voting behavior, regardless of their personal opinions on the proposal.

The steps in marketing policies are identical to those in marketing behavior change: (1) find out what the target audience wants; (2) define the product to fulfill these needs and wants; and (3) package, position, and frame the product so as to reinforce the most important core values of the target audience. These steps are described in some detail in Chapter 6, which focuses on the strategic application of marketing principles to market public health programs and policies. As shown in Chapter 6, branding can serve as an effective way to develop and convey to the public an identity for public health programs and policies, and even for public health organizations themselves.

For now, it is important to point out that the needs and wants of policy makers regarding health and a healthy society are different from those of the individual. But as we will see in Chapter 6, the core values underlying policy makers' needs and wants regarding a healthy society are the same as those underlying the need for health among individuals. Policy makers desire a healthy population not because of a primary concern for the health of individuals, but because of a desire for autonomy, economic livelihood, and control over their destinies.

The case of Mothers Against Drunk Driving (MADD) and its campaign to advance policies to lower the legal blood alcohol limit for driving demonstrate the effective use of basic marketing principles to advance public health policy goals. Formed in 1980 by Candy Lightner, whose 13-year-old daughter was killed by a drunk driver, MADD has learned how to generate media coverage and how to use that coverage to not only inspire public sentiment, but to define and frame the issue of drunk driving in a way that advances policies to address the problem. MADD has helped to define drunk driving as an important social problem, to place the problem on the national agenda, and to successfully promote policies that regulate drinking and driving.

Defining the Product

MADD has consistently defined its public health policy product as far more than simply the reduction of alcohol-related motor vehicle fatalities. While saving lives is certainly an important benefit that MADD offers to policy makers through its proposed policies, a benefit that offers something even more compelling to policy makers is the creation of a society in which children and young adults are free to live their lives without being needlessly brought to their deaths by irresponsible behavior of others—behavior that is entirely preventable. By killing innocent victims, drunk driving interferes with the ability of individuals to have control over their lives, even if they themselves make wise and prudent choices. By defining the problem of drunk driving in this way, it can be seen to interfere with the powerful ethic of individualism and self-determination that lies at the very core of American culture. By focusing not only on reducing the number of fatalities, but on the nature of the fatalities that can and must be prevented, MADD has been able to define a product that truly offers to the policy maker a benefit that resonates deeply with his or her core values as a public official.

As the U.S. Department of Transportation explained in its analysis of the role of the media in drunk driving interventions (Luckey et al., 1985), "when a person is killed or seriously injured as a result of someone else's drunken driving, the tragedy constitutes an obvious injustice as well. Such a clear affront to Americans' sense of fair play will sustain public attention longer than problems that appear more complex and ambiguous" (p. II-28). MADD has defined the problem of drunk driving in a way that appeals not merely to the policy maker's concern for the health of society's members, but to the widely shared principles of freedom, autonomy, fairness, and justice in society as a whole.

It is instructive to note that while public health efforts to reduce drunk-driving deaths have been quite successful (Ayres, 1994), efforts to address the problem of alcohol abuse itself have met with less success (DeJong & Wallack, 1992). To a large extent, this is due to the public health community's ability to define the problem of drunk driving in a way that offers a benefit that is highly important to policy makers—ensuring a society in which people, and especially children, have control over their lives. While reducing drunk-driving deaths is viewed as helping to ensure that parents can raise their children without the risk of having them taken away needlessly, reducing alcohol-related morbidity and mortality in its own right has not been defined in an equally compelling way. The public health product is still defined primarily as disease prevention. In light of the major public health successes observed in the area of policy regarding drunk driving, the lack of adequate prevention and treatment of alcohol abuse in society is a failure.

Positioning, Packaging, and Framing the Product

Not only has MADD been successful in defining its product in a way that offers a compelling benefit to policy makers, but the organization has been very effective in developing an overall campaign that packages the product such that it consistently reinforces the core values of policy makers. All components of MADD's marketing strategy—the product, the promise, the image, and the support—work together to reinforce these core values. The product is a society in which parents can raise their children free of the risk of having them taken away needlessly by other people's irresponsible behavior. The promise is that advancing MADD's policy goals—lowering the legal blood alcohol limit for driving, for example—will help policy makers to fulfill their need to ensure a society that provides freedom, independence, and autonomy to their constituents. The image that MADD has been able to consistently create is one of bereaved mothers mourning for a child who was killed by a drunk driver. This image has been created and reinforced by MADD's incredible ability to put a human face, an identified victim, to the policy issue. In this way, the support for MADD's promise is not merely scientific data about the reduction of alcohol-related traffic fatalities that result from lowering the legal blood alcohol limit, but documentation of the human suffering that results when a child is killed by a drunk driver.

An event staged by the Florida MADD chapter demonstrates these points vividly. To promote the creation of a state law that would reduce the legal blood alcohol limit for driving from 0.10 to 0.08 mg/dL, a candlelight vigil was held in the rotunda of the Florida Capitol building in Tallahassee. Hundreds of pairs of empty sneakers were placed in a circle around the rotunda, and the vigil participants joined hands around the sneakers. The sneakers represented children and adolescents whose lives were taken away by drunk drivers in Florida, and the number of pairs of sneakers corresponded with the statistics on drunk driving fatalities in the state. In addition to being a moving experience for all the participants and creating an effective visual image for television cameras, the event successfully framed MADD's public health product in a way that reinforced the core values of freedom, independence, and autonomy. The product, promise, image, and support were all working together to market the public health policy.

Another effective image used in the campaign to promote stricter drunk driving policies is the "red ribbon of memory," a collection of ribbons created by family members and friends of individuals killed by drunk drivers (National Highway Traffic Safety Administration [NHTSA], 1996). The ribbons are tied together to commemorate all victims of drunk driving in a community. A media event is organized around the ribbon ceremony that helps frame the issue of drunk driving as a threat to the safety, independence, and autonomy of the entire community (NHTSA, 1996).

The importance of using the identified victim, telling personal stories, and creating vivid images of the human suffering caused by drunk driving is emphasized in MADD's *How To Compendium*, a policy manual for public health advocates (Mothers Against Drunk Driving, 1991). The manual instructs advocates to "never underestimate your power or the power of a tragic true story to illustrate why the legislation is needed" (p. 138). The manual also instructs advocates to "utilize existing networks of victim service and victim rights organizations in your state. Be sure former victims who want to be involved and can make good presentations are given leading roles" (p. 138).

MADD's approach is effective not only because it appeals to the core values of policy makers, but because opponents of drunk-driving legislation are also trying to frame the issue as one of freedom and autonomy. The alcohol industry attempts to show policy makers that by tampering with the blood alcohol limit they will be imposing on the freedom of citizens to enjoy responsible, social drinking. Industry representatives have testified that lowering the blood alcohol limit to 0.08 will mean than an average-size woman can no longer drink two modest size glasses of wine if she is planning to drive. John Doyle of the American Beverage Institute, for example, argued that "they're trying to make .08 sound like some demonic level of consumption," when in fact "a 120-pound woman could reach .08 by drinking a couple of glasses of wine. . . . If you drop the legal limit to .08, that makes it illegal for a 120-pound woman to have two glasses of wine. You'll throw that 120-pound woman into jail, when she's not the problem" (McPhillips, 1997, p. A-22). The industry argues that the drunk driving problem is one of a few individuals who drink extremely heavily and irresponsibly, and that by lowering the blood alcohol limit, society is imposing on the freedoms of the rest of our citizens, who are responsible people. If MADD were to frame the issue only as one of health and saving lives, then the alcohol industry would carry the theme of individual freedom to victory. By showing policy makers how failing to adopt 0.08 laws is what really represents an infringement of individual freedom, MADD has been able to effectively counter this argument and to win the marketing battle for the most important core needs, desires, and values of the policy makers. After all, the ultimate unfairness is not arresting people for drunk driving, but having innocent people killed by irresponsible drunk drivers.

■ CONCLUSION

If one looks at the major events that have led to the adoption of basic behavior change in the population, one finds that individual concern over one's health has rarely been the driving force. Instead, it has generally been the perception of lack of control over important aspects of one's life, loss of freedom, dependence, or striving for a certain identity that has prompted the most substantial health behavior changes. The significant declines in smoking prevalence observed during the 1970s and 1980s have been attributed largely to changes in societal norms that made the image of the smoker less socially desirable. The increased use of the designated driver was probably attributable more to the establishment of a social norm of behavior and the individual need to fit into this social pattern than any increased concern over the health impact of drunk driving. Changes in dietary habits and physical activity are most likely due more to the establishment of a desirable social image and identity associated with dieting, exercise, and slim and trim physical appearance than to people's increased concern about their long-term health and their desire to avoid chronic disease.

Public health practitioners must begin to sell something other than health itself, or health behavior change itself, if they are ever to be effective in addressing the chronic disease epidemic. First, they must begin to sell freedom, independence, control, identity, and rebellion. In other words, they have to redefine their product so that it offers benefits that will fulfill a clearly identified need or desire among their target audience. Second, they must package the product, position it, and frame it in a way that appeals to their audience's core values. This means they must place and promote the product in a way that will demonstrate to their audience how the product will fulfill their desires or needs. The perception that the unhealthy behavior in question is fulfilling or will fulfill basic needs and desires of the audience must be transformed into a realization that changing or not performing the behavior will actually satisfy these needs and desires to a far greater degree. The practitioner must define the product so that it offers a benefit desired by the target audience; offer a promise for how the product will satisfy important needs and desires of the target audience; present a visual image of the product that reinforces the audience's core values; and provide support or documentation that the product will indeed deliver the promised benefit. Each of these components of the marketing strategy must work together to reinforce the most important and compelling core values of the target audience.

In this new view of public health, epidemiologic surveillance and formative research (broadly defined as research to understand the consumer) will combine to form a basic foundation (**Figure 3-2**).

Surveillance identifies the most critical public health problems, the source of these problems, and the interventions that will be effective in solving the problems. These interventions can be translated into a specific set of behavior changes, changes in social and environmental conditions, and policy changes that are desired. Then, based on the findings of formative research, the most important needs, desires, and values of the target audience can be identified. Next, the public health practitioner must define the product so that it will offer as a benefit the fulfillment of

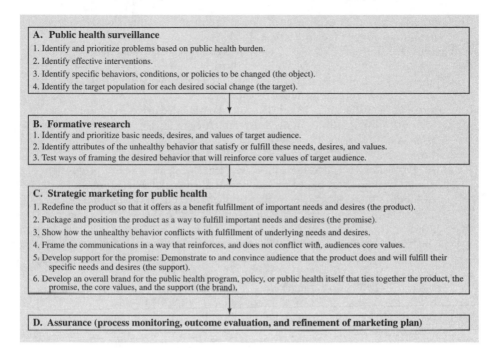

A. Public health surveillance
1. Identify and prioritize problems based on public health burden.
2. Identify effective interventions.
3. Identify specific behaviors, conditions, or policies to be changed (the object).
4. Identify the target population for each desired social change (the target).

B. Formative research
1. Identify and prioritize basic needs, desires, and values of target audience.
2. Identify attributes of the unhealthy behavior that satisfy or fulfill these needs, desires, and values.
3. Test ways of framing the desired behavior that will reinforce core values of target audience.

C. Strategic marketing for public health
1. Redefine the product so that it offers as a benefit fulfillment of important needs and desires (the product).
2. Package and position the product as a way to fulfill important needs and desires (the promise).
3. Show how the unhealthy behavior conflicts with fulfillment of underlying needs and desires.
4. Frame the communications in a way that reinforces, and does not conflict with, audiences core values.
5. Develop support for the promise: Demonstrate to and convince audience that the product does and will fulfill their specific needs and desires (the support).
6. Develop an overall brand for the public health program, policy, or public health itself that ties together the product, the promise, the core values, and the support (the brand).

D. Assurance (process monitoring, outcome evaluation, and refinement of marketing plan)

Figure 3-2 A New Marketing Strategy for Public Health: Confronting Threats to the Public's Health

these desires and needs. Finally, the practitioner can package, position, and frame the product in an effort to demonstrate to the audience how it will indeed fulfill these desires and needs. The strategic marketing plan should be continuously assessed and refined based on the results of process and outcome evaluation.

References

Andreasen, A.R. (1995). Marketing social change: Changing behavior to promote health, social development, and the environment. San Francisco: Jossey Bass.
———. (2006). *Social marketing in the 21ˢᵗ century.* Thousand Oaks, CA: SAGE Publications, Inc.

Ayres, B.D., Jr. (1994, May 22). Big gains are seen in battle to stem drunken driving. *The New York Times,* p. A1.

Bauer, U.E., Johnson, T.M., Hopkins, R.S., & Brooks, R.G. (2000). Changes in youth cigarette use and intentions following implementation of a tobacco control program: Findings from the Florida Youth Tobacco Survey, 1998–2000. *JAMA,* 284(6), 723–28.

Bernays, E.L. (1965). *Biography of an idea: Memoirs of public relations counsel Edward L. Bernays.* New York: Simon & Schuster.

Burnett, L. (1961). *Communications of an advertising man.* Chicago: Burnett.

Conrad, P. (1987). The experience of illness: Recent and new directions. *Research in the Sociology of Health Care,* 6, 1–31.

Conrad, P., & Kern, R. (EDS.). (1994). *The sociology of health & illness: Critical perspectives* (4th ed.). New York: St. Martin's Press.

Crompton, J.L. & Lamb, C.W., Jr. (1986). *Marketing government and social services.* New York: John Wiley & Sons.

DeJong, W., & Wallack, L. (1992). The role of designated driver programs in the prevention of alcohol-impaired driving: A critical reassessment. *Health Education Quarterly,* 19, 429–442.

Enthoven, A. (1980). *Health plan.* New York: Addison-Wesley.

Flora, J.A. Schooler, C., & Pierson, R.M. (1997). Effective health promotion among communities of color: The potential of social marketing. In M.E. Goldberg, M. Fishbein, & S.E. Middlestadt (Eds.), *Social marketing: Theorectical and practical perspectives* (pp. 353–377). Mahwah, NJ: Lawrence Erlbaum Associates.

Gaylin, W., & Jennings, B. (1996). *The perversion of autonomy: The proper uses of coercion and constraints in a liberal soceity.* New York: The Free Press.

Glaser, B.G., & Strauss, A.L. (1968). *Time for dying.* Chicago: Aldine.

Hastings, G. (2003). Social marketers of the world unite, you have nothing to lose but your shame. *Social Marketing Quarterly,* 9(4), 14–21.

Hicks, J.J. (2001). The strategy behind Florida's 'truth' campaign. *Tobacco Control,* 10, 3–5.

Kleinman, A. (1988). *The illness narratives: Suffering healing, and the human condition.* New York: Basic Books.

Kotler, P. (1976). *Marketing management: Analysis, planning, and control* (3rd ed.). Englewood Cliffs, NJ: Prentice-Hall.

Kroger, F. (1995). Exhibit 1.1: Fred Kroger on HIV prevention: Communications success, marketing failure. In A.R. Andreasen (Ed.), *Marketing social change: Changing behavior to promote health, social development, and environment* (pp.45–46). San Francisco: Jossey-Bass.

Lappe, F.M. (1989). *Rediscovering America's values.* New York: Ballantine Books.

Lauffer, A. (1984). *Strategic marketing for not-for-profit organizations: Program and resource development.* New York: The Free Press.

Luckey, J. W., Jolly, D., Mills, K.C., McGaughey,, K., Horn, D., & Richichi, E. (1985, December). *Role of media and public attention in drinking driver countermeasures* (Rep. No. DOT/OST/P-34/86/038). Washington, DC: U.S. Department of Transportation, Office of the Secretary of Transportation.

Mark, M., & Pearson, C.S. (2001). *The hero and the outlaw: Building extraordinary brands through the power of archetypes.* New York: McGraw-Hill.

McDivitt, J., et al. (2003). Innovations in social marketing conference proceedings. Session II: Is there a role for branding in social marketing? *Social Marketing Quarterly,* 9(3), 11–17.

McKenna, J.W., & Williams, K.N. (1993). I. Crafting effective tobacco counter-advertisements: Lessons from a failed campaign directed at teenagers. *Public Health Reports.* 108, 85–89.

McPhillips, J. (1997, December 21). Fight looms over effort to toughen drunken-driving law. *The Providence Sunday Journal,* pp. A-1, A-22.

Meyers, W. (1984). *The image-makers: Power and persuasion on Madison Avenue.* New York: New York Times Books.

Milio, N. (1995). Health, health care reform, and the care of health. In M. Blunden & M. Dando (Eds.), *Rethinking public policy-making: Questioning assumptions, challenging beliefs* (pp. 92–107). Thousand Oaks, CA: Sage Publications.

Mishel, M.H. (1984). Perceived uncertainty and stress in illness. *Research in Nursing and Health, 7,* 163–171.

Mishel, M.H., Hostetter, T., King, B., & Graham, V. (1984). Predictors of psychosocial adjustment in patients newly diagnosed with gynecological cancer. *Cancer Nursing, 7,* 291–299.

Molleman, E., Krabbendam, P.J., Annyas, A.A., Koops, H.S., Sleijfer, D.T., & Vemey, A. (1984). The significance of the doctor-patient relationship in coping with cancer. *Social Science and Medicine, 18,* 745–480.

Mothers Against Drunk Driving. (1991, April 1). *How to compendium.* Irving, TX: Author.

National Highway Traffic Safety Administration. (1996, September). *National drunk and drugged driving prevention month program planner* (Rep. No. DOT HS 808–455). Washington, DC: U.S. Department of Transportation, National Highway Traffic Safety Administration.

Ogilvy, D. (1964). *Confessions of an advertising man.* New York: Atheneum.

Rothschild, M.L. (1999). Carrots, sticks and promises: A conceptual framework for the management of public health and social issue behaviors. *Journal of Marketing, 63,* 24–37.

Salmon, C.T. (1989). Campaigns for social improvement: An overview of values, rationales, and impacts. In C. Salmon (ED.), *Information campaigns* (pp. 19–53), Newbury Park, CA: Sage Publications.

Schudson, M. (1984). *Advertising, the uneasy persuasion: Its dubious impact on American society.* New York: Basic Books.

Smith, G.H. (1954). *Motivation research in advertising and marketing.* New York: McGraw-Hill.

Sunstein, C.R. (1997). *Free markets and social justice.* New York: Oxford University Press.

Trachtenberg, J.A. (1987). Here's one tough cowboy. *Forbes.* 139(3), 108–110.

Turnock, B.J. (1997). *Public health: What it is and how it works.* Gaithersburg, MD: Aspen.

U. S. Department of Health and Human Services. (1994). *Preventing tobacco use among young people: A report of the Surgeon General.* U. S. Department of Health and Human Services, Centers for Disease Control and Prevention, National Center for Chronic Disease Prevention and Health Promotion, Office on Smoking and Health.

Vogel, C.M. (1987). Putting research to work. In C. Degen (Ed.), *Communicators' guide to marketing* (pp. 31–42). New York: Longman.

Weitz, R. (1994). Uncertainty and the lives of persons with AIDS. In P. Conrad & R. Kern (Eds.), *The sociology of health & illness: Critical perspectives* (4th ed., pp. 138–149), New York: St. Martin's Press.

Winett, L.B. & Wallack, L. 1996. Advancing public health goals through the mass media. *Journal of Health Communication, 1,* 173–196.

APPENDIX

3-A

The Importance of Formative Research in Public Health Campaigns: An Example from The Area of HIV Prevention Among Gay Men

The public health effort to promote safe sex among gay men to prevent human immunodeficiency virus (HIV) infection illustrates the type of research and the type of understanding of the target audience that could provide meaningful insight to guide the development of more effective strategies to change individual behavior to improve health. It also shows how our current efforts to understand the target audience are woefully inadequate and often lead to prevention programs that conflict with the audience's core values.

The failure of public health programs to prevent AIDS is demonstrated by the increase, rather than decrease, in the number of AIDS cases over the past decade and a half. Although mortality from AIDS has decreased (from 43,000 deaths in 1995 [NCHS, 1997] to 14,000 in 2002 [NCHS, 2004]), its incidence has remained relatively stable during the past 13 years, with 41,000 reported cases in 1990 and 44,000 cases in 2003 (NCHS, 2004).

Perhaps a part of the failure of current public health prevention programs is that they have not adequately used formative research to inform their development. In particular, most public health interventions have not been informed by a fundamental understanding of the community on the one hand, and of male sexuality and sex between men on the other. Few published research studies have delved into the lives, the minds, and the hearts of gay and bisexual men to try to understand what love, relationships, and sex mean to them and how this is affected by the threat of AIDS and by public health admonitions to practice safe sex. As Weitz (1994) pointed out, most of the existing social science literature on AIDS consists of quantitative studies that examine factors related to sexual behavior practices. Complicating this problem is the fact that many AIDS prevention initiatives are based on the medical model, and, being viewed as medical interventions, fail to take the time and effort necessary to do formative research and find out the inner workings of the minds of the target audience. As Green explained in a 1996 article in *The New York Times Magazine*, "understandably eager to ingratiate themselves with the mainstream medical establishment on which they depend for funds, they have gravitated toward purely 'medical' interventions" (p. 54).

As a result of the shallow understanding of the feelings, attitudes, experiences, and values of gay men and the dynamics of the gay men's community, public health programs to prevent AIDS have often been at odds with some of the deepest core values of their target audience.

One example of a shortcoming of most HIV prevention programs that stems from a lack of insight into the lives, feelings, and experiences of gay men is the virtual disregard for risk reduction as opposed to risk elimination strategies, and the reluctance to candidly discuss, rather than merely dismiss as deviant, unsafe sex. Public health programs have been characterized by what Green (1996) called "the unwavering focus of safe-sex campaigns on eternal condom use," (pp. 43–44) and what Rotello (1997) called "the condom code." As Odets (1995) pointed out, public health practitioners would never deliver this message—that people must use a condom every time they have sex for the rest of their lives—to the heterosexual community. Practitioners have respected the value heterosexuals place on long-term relationships, commitment, love, and marriage by acknowledging that heterosexuals do not need to use condoms to prevent AIDS after entering into a faithful marriage or monogamous relationship with a person who is free of infection. The same understanding and respect for individual values has not been afforded to homosexuals. Many gay men interpret this as a dismissal of the value of sex between men (Green, 1996). Internalized homonegativity has been shown to be an important factor in the sexual health behaviors of men who have sex with men (Rosser, 1991a). And fear induced by these types of public health messages has been shown to have adverse effects on the behavior of homosexually active men (Rosser, 1991b).

As a consequence of this public health program failure, a sense of hopelessness and complete lack of control has arisen among gay men. Because they do not really believe that they will use a condom every time, many men assume that they are destined to become infected and therefore see no point in using condoms at all (Green, 1996). As Odets explained, "there's a difference between going out with a guy you've never met whose status you don't ask about, and a friend you've known 10 years who tells you he's negative. Education has refused to allow gay men even to think about that difference. It's like telling people that if they want to be safe drivers, they must always drive 35 miles per hour without regard to when, where or road conditions, which any sane person will instantly reject" (Green, 1996, p. 45). Some men also feel that if the risk is so great that they cannot trust anyone, then there is no hope of obtaining a stable, long-term relationship. "If you can't trust, you can't love, so why even bother having a relationship?" (Green, 1996, p. 44).

Trust of the source of delivery of health messages is also important. Public health messages that do not take account of the realities of gay men's lives and the role of sex and sexuality in their lives will not be taken seriously. As Rofes stated: "A population with a long history of victimization by government, medicine, scientific research, and the media will not easily and quickly see these sectors as trustworthy partners in prevention. Our communities must have ownership of prevention in word as well as deed. We must lead it. Sex is a core part of most gay male identities and cultures and telling men not to have sex will not work. Programs that judge men with multiple partners or a taste for kinky sex will rapidly lose the confidence of much of the community" (Rofes, 1998, p. 215).

A second failure of public health programs has been the inability to understand and acknowledge that for some gay men, it is the destructive nature of unprotected sex that motivates and supports the behavior in the first place. "For some—guilty, depressed, anxious, and living a life that often seems not worth living—the self-destructive aspects of unprotected sex are important incentives to practice it. This has nothing to do with complacency, nor will traditional AIDS education address it" (Odets, 1995, p. 47). As Odets added, "while our education and public policy continue to assume that unsafe sex is practiced despite its dangers, some men engage in it for precisely that reason" (p. 188).

Public health programs have failed, explains Odets, because they "have been guilty of ignoring the deepest root of gay men's unsafety: the psychological root, what they feel" (Green, 1996, p. 42). As Green's interviews with gay men revealed, at the deepest level of a gay man's psyche is a hole, a void, a loneliness, a feeling of guilt, and for those who have recently come out, a feeling of newfound freedom. Often, those men have experienced hatred, abuse, and lack of acceptance by their families, friends, communities, and society in general. And as Green (1996) concluded, "ignoring the role that homophobia plays in the psychology of AIDS means ignoring an element of disease at least as powerful as biology. If we care about public health, there is little choice but to care about people's feelings too" (p. 84).

Ultimately, the consequence of public health programs' failure to seek a deeper understanding of the reality of life for gay men in the "shadow of the epidemic," Odets (1995) argued, is that gay men feel a lack of control over their lives, a sense of being told what to do by people who do not understand what it is like to be gay in today's society, and of being told not only what to do, but who they are supposed to be. As Odets explained, gay men have "allowed [their] lives to once again slip from [their] grasp into the hands of those who too often believe, if quietly, that [they] should not even be what [they] are (p. 264). And the public health practice of "simply instructing men in behaviors—'a condom every time'—actively obstructs the development of a capacity for informed judgment and perpetuates society's homophobic desire to simply dictate behaviors to gay men" (p. 194).

As Rofes noted: "Prevention for gay men is at a turbulent crossroads. We can continue fine-tuning traditional interventions focused on providing individual gay men with information, motivation, and skills. Or we can acknowledge the complexity of sexuality and trust and support gay men truly to manage their own risk" (Rofes, 1998, p. 216).

Instead of rendering gay men helpless, feeling a loss of independence, autonomy, and control, public health programs must find a way to offer gay men control over their lives. And rather than prescribing a course of action and even a lifestyle for these men and telling them how they should feel and what they should want, programs must help them to understand the epidemic and provide them with a realistic interpretation of the risks of HIV transmission, and must empower them to take control over their lives—lives that are respected, supported, and accepted and can therefore be meaningful and worthy of protecting and cherishing. The gay man can then discover and express the truth of his own feelings and develop new and independent desires.

Understanding the lack of control that many gay men feel may lead to prevention programs that place more control in the hands of the individual rather than the public health establishment. People must feel that their decisions are being left to them, that they are being given all the options and all the information, but that the final decision, and therefore the control of their future, is in their own hands. This means acknowledging, accepting, and even celebrating the meaning of love, relationships, and sex among gay men. It means discussing openly the differences in risk associated with sexual activities in different kinds of relationships. It means acknowledging the legitimacy of long-term relationships between men. Robinson et al. (2002) have incorporated many of these concepts into a model for HIV prevention that includes a focus on intimacy and relationships, positive sexuality, and spirituality, and which addresses institutionalized homonegativity, harassment, and discrimination.

Rofes has suggested that "Prevention workers might commit themselves to creating projects that respect individual men's decisions regarding how they situate themselves in relation to sex and gay male sex cultures. The job is not to judge or moralize, but support, affirm, and assist. The tasks at hand are to provide the information and resources needed for men to make their own sexual choices and manage their own risk, and work with the overseers of community institutions, including public sex venues, to help them critically consider their sites' relationships to gay men's health. AIDS education too often has given lip service to respecting gay men's diverse sexual strategies while failing to fully value men's varied options" (Rofes, 1998, p. 219).

Properly addressing the lack of control that many gay men feel also means providing true support, including counseling and other psychological services and benefits, to gay men and especially to gay youth. Instead of constantly telling these men what they should or should not be doing, public health practitioners must begin to tell them that they care, that they understand, that they accept gay men for who they are, and that they are available to help. As Green (1996) asked, "in a world where financing for AIDS research keeps increasing but agencies that serve gay youths go begging for pennies, should we be surprised if gay men wonder whether the disease is more important than they are?" (p. 85).

Finally, public health efforts to change gay men's sexual behavior must include efforts to change the way society treats homosexuals and views homosexual relationships. Unless gay and lesbian relationships are acknowledged, celebrated, and respected in the same way that heterosexual relationships are, we cannot expect gay men to take messages about safe sex, stable relationships, and decreased promiscuity seriously.

Ultimately, public health practitioners must realize that "there is an epidemic beneath the epidemic we know about. Beneath and beyond. It predates AIDS and will probably outlast it and comes not from a virus but a vacancy. Like most minorities in America, gay men grow up feeling different, but uniquely they grow up both different and alone" (Green, 1996, p. 84). Only if public health practitioners take the time to go a little deeper beneath the surface of the gay man, to do the formative research necessary to understand his world, will they be able to design effective programs to confront the spread of AIDS among the gay population.

References

Green, J. (1996, September 15). Flirting with suicide. *The New York Times Magazine,* pp. 39–45, 54–55, 84–85.

National Center for Health Statistics. (1997). *Health United States, 1996–97, and injury chartbook* (DHHS Publication No. PHS 97-1232). Hyattsville, MD: Author.

National Center for Health Statistics. (2004). *Health United States, 2004, with chartbook on trends in the health of Americans* (DHHS Publication No. 2004–1232). Hyattsville, MD: Author.

Odets, W. (1995). *In the shadow of the epidemic: Being HIV-negative in the age of AIDS.* Durham, NC: Duke University Press.

Robinson, B.B.E., Bockting, W.O., Rosser, B.R.S., Miner, M., & Coleman, E. (2002). The sexual health model: application of a sexological approach to HIV prevention. *Health Education Research,* 17(1), 43–57.

Rofes, E. (1998). *Dry bones breathe: gay men creating post-AIDS identities and cultures.* New York: Harrington Park Press.

Rosser, B.R.S. (1991a). *Male homosexual behavior and the effects of AIDS education: A study of behavior and safer sex in New Zealand and South Australia.* New York: Praeger.

———. (1991b). The effects of using fear in public AIDS education on the behaviour of homosexually active men. *Journal of Psychology and Human Sexuality,* 4(3), 123–134.

Rotello, G. (1997). *Sexual ecology: AIDS and the destiny of gay men.* New York: Penguin Books USA.

Weitz, R. (1994). Uncertainty and the lives of persons with AIDS. In P. Conrad & R. Kern (Eds.), *The sociology of health & illness: Critical perspectives* (4th ed., pp. 138–149). New York: St. Martin's Press.

SECTION

II

Marketing Public Health

To confront the threats to the survival of public health in the twenty-first century, public health practitioners must extend their focus beyond the effort to protect the health of the public. They must now learn how to promote themselves and their institutions. In other words, public health practitioners must enter the business of marketing public health.

This section shows why the survival of public health is threatened, why the task of marketing public health programs and policies is a formidable challenge for public health practitioners, and, finally, how practitioners can use basic marketing principles to confront this challenge effectively.

Section II also shows the public health practitioner how to strategically apply marketing principles to promote public health programs, public health policies, and the institution of public health itself.

CHAPTER

4

Emerging Threats to the Survival of Public Health

The survival of public health as a societal institution is threatened by emerging changes in the health care delivery system, the economy, the political climate, the public sentiment regarding public health and government in general, and the public health community itself. First, a misunderstanding of the relative importance of individual medical treatment compared with population-based prevention programs has led to a health system in which individual treatment rather than societal prevention is the dominant focus. This misunderstanding has fostered the illusion that health care reform is the solution to the nation's public health crises and that integration of public health into managed care represents an important area of focus for public health. As a consequence, public health practitioners have been sidetracked from their mission as agents for social change. Also, political and economic forces directly threaten funding for public health departments and their policies and programs. These factors include budget cuts, a misplaced emphasis on bioterrorism preparedness, the increasing influence of special interest groups, and the increasing antiregulatory sentiment in the nation. The greatest threat to the survival of the public's health, however, comes from within the public health movement itself. The public health community has lost a unified vision of its fundamental role and mission. To overcome these threats the public health movement must rediscover a strong, unifying model with a common vision, mission, and values to which the public and policy makers can relate. It will not be enough to promote the health of its constituents: the public health movement must now promote its own survival.

Part 1, Section 1 examined the factors that are responsible for the epidemic of chronic disease and emerging infectious diseases that threaten the health of the public. The key to confronting this epidemic is social change: changes in individual behavior, social conditions, and social policy. Public health practitioners are in the business of marketing social change, and the section demonstrated the ways they can use basic marketing principles to promote behavior and lifestyle change to the public.

Unfortunately, the attention of the public health practitioner cannot be focused entirely on improving the health of the public because the public's health is only one thing that the public health practitioner must save. Emerging changes in the health care delivery system, the economy, the political climate, public sentiment regarding government, and changes in the public health community itself now threaten the very survival of public health as a societal institution. In addition to promoting the health of constituents, public health must now find a way to promote its own survival.

Part I, Section II broadens our perspective and considers not merely the need to protect the public's health, but also the need to ensure the survival of public health. The reasons that the survival of public health is threatened (Chapter 4), the challenge this threat poses to the public health practitioner (Chapter 5), and the potential role that the strategic application of basic marketing principles could play in helping the public health practitioner to confront this challenge (Chapter 6) are examined.

The survival of public health as a societal institution is threatened because of the adverse consequences of three major factors: (1) the persistent emphasis on individual rather than societal health and on treatment rather than prevention, (2) economic and political factors that directly threaten public health funding, and (3) the loss, among public health practitioners, of a unified vision of the role and mission of public health.

■ MISUNDERSTANDING OF THE IMPORTANCE OF MEDICAL TREATMENT COMPARED WITH POPULATION-BASED PREVENTION

Despite the widely held perception that recent advances in medical treatment have resulted in a dramatic decline in mortality, there is substantial evidence that the observed decline in mortality in the developed world during the eighteenth to twentieth centuries was attributable largely to public health and not medical interventions (Evans, Barer, & Marmor, 1994; Lee & Estes, 1997; Levine, Feldman, & Elison, 1983; Turnock, 1997). The most extensive research into this hypothesis was conducted by Thomas McKeown, a physician and historical demographer who, over the course of more than 20 years, developed a convincing analysis of the reasons for mortality declines observed in England and Wales during the past three centuries (McKeown, 1971, 1976, 1978; McKeown, Record, & Turner, 1975).

McKeown concluded that declines in mortality observed during the eighteenth century were due to environmental changes, such as purification of water, efficient sewage disposal, and improved food, hygiene, and nutrition (McKeown, 1978). During the nineteenth century, McKeown argued, the declines in mortality were due only to a reduction in infectious diseases; chronic disease rates remained stable (McKeown et al, 1975). According to McKeown, the three major factors that contributed to the decline were (1) rising standards of living, (2) improved hygiene, and (3) improved nutrition (McKeown et al., 1975). Although the smallpox vaccination campaign was effective, McKeown attributes only 5% of the decline in mortality in the latter half of the nineteenth century to immunization. McKeown argues that declines in infectious disease rates account for about 75% of the mortality reductions observed during the twentieth century (through 1971). Although immunization played a limited role, the dominant factors in the control of infectious disease were improved nutrition and hygiene.

In research on the reasons for the dramatic decline in mortality in the United States during the twentieth century, John and Sonja McKinlay (1977, 1994) found that no more than 4% of the observed decline was due to medical treatment for infectious diseases. This conclusion is supported by the work of Rene Dubos (1959) and others (Cassel, 1976; Kass, 1971; Leavitt & Numbers, 1994; Lee & Estes, 1997; Magill, 1955; Powles, 1973; Weinstein, 1974). The U.S. Public Health Service (1995) estimated that of the 30 years that have been added to life expectancy since 1900, only 5 years are due to improvements in clinical medicine, while 25 years are attributable to population-based, public health programs. McKinlay and McKinlay (1994) also demonstrated that the steep decline in mortality between 1900 and 1950 slowed during the 1950s and leveled off during the 1960s. This was the precise period in which medical care expenditures skyrocketed. Increased spending for medical care does not necessarily translate into reduced mortality (Hingson et al., 1981; Kim & Moody, 1992).

The work of McKeown, McKinlay and McKinlay, and others helped to reveal a shift in the twentieth century in the type of diseases most responsible for mortality. The shift—known as the epidemiologic transition—was from infectious diseases to chronic diseases as the dominant cause of death in the developed countries (Omran, 1971). Whereas infectious diseases accounted for 40% of total mortality in the United States in 1900, they accounted for only 6% of mortality in 1973 (McKinlay & McKinlay, 1994). The proportion of total mortality attributable to chronic diseases (including injuries) increased form 20% to 67% during the same period.

The U.S. Department of Health and Human Services (USDHHS) estimated that approximately 75% of all premature deaths in the nation are preventable (Centers for Disease Control [CDC], 1995; USDHHS, 1995). Of these, about 63% could have been avoided by changes in individual behavior and another 23% by changes in social and environmental conditions. Only 15% of these deaths were deemed preventable through improved access to medical care.

As McKinlay and McKinlay (1994) pointed out, the policy implications of the hypothesis that public health measures, not medical treatment, are the dominant reason for improvements in the health of the population are profound. If this perspective is accurate, then the critical strategy to achieve meaningful health reform is not the better provision of more organized, higher quality, lower cost medical services, but the societal commitment to social change. Preventing disease and illness requires changing the conditions in which people live, improving the quality of the environment, and reforming public policy. As Tesh argued, "it appears that social and political events that affect the standard of living, rather than microorganisms, are the salient determinants of health and disease" (Tesh, 1994, p. 520). Nevertheless, the current view of disease prevention continues to rely on germ theory and lifestyle theory as the explanation for illness. The most prominent public health programs aim to control infectious disease and change individual behavior. "Changing the physical environment is, from this perspective a third choice, and to attack poverty as a way to reduce disease becomes a last resort" (Tesh, 1994, p. 521).

The observed shift in causes of mortality from infectious to chronic diseases has similar implications for the improvement of the public's health. Because chronic disease is largely related to individual and societal behavior, social conditions, and social policy, public health must inherently be committed to social change. Medical care is certainly important, and recent evidence suggests that some of the modern medical interventions for atherosclerotic heart disease may explain declines in heart disease mortality during the past five decades. However, the most substantial gains in human health will be achieved only through public health—that is, the societal institution whose mission is the promotion of social change.

Even if the ultimate aim of prevention programs is to change individual behavior, the physical, social, and political environment in which people live must be the primary level of intervention. Because behavior is a product of the social conditions and social norms of the community in which a person lives (Tesh, 1994), discussing lifestyle changes without discussing the social conditions that give rise to them is misleading (Berliner, 1977). Public health practitioners cannot ignore the decades of research demonstrating that lower social class, social deprivation, and lack of social support are among the most important determinants of health (Conrad, 1987; Morris, 1982; Syme & Berkman, 1976). Substantial and sustained improvement in public health will require, first and foremost, social change.

The challenge to public health is presented clearly in a 1994 article by David Mechanic, who wrote, "The determinants of health risks are far too complex and forceful to succumb to ordinary efforts to inform the public and change its practices. Effective health promotion requires a deeper scrutiny of the structure of communities and the routine activities of everyday life, as well as stronger interventions than those characteristic of much that goes on. Current efforts still function largely at the margins" (Mechanic, 1994, p. 569).

An additional reason that prevention rather than treatment of illness must form the core of a national public health strategy is that advances in medical treatment tend to disproportionately benefit the socioeconomically advantaged and, consequently, to increase the disparity in health status between rich and poor Americans. Dutton argues that the gap between health status of higher and lower socioeconomic classes is only partly due to differences in access to medical care (Dutton, 1994).

> But much of the gap undoubtedly stems from a variety of non-medical factors, including a hazardous environment, unsafe and unrewarding work, poor nutrition, lack of social support, and, perhaps most important of all, the psychological and emotional stress of being poor and feeling powerless to do anything about it. . . . To be efficient as well as effective, health care must remedy not only the consequences of poverty, but must aid in efforts to change the underlying circumstances that perpetuate it. This is the most fundamental form of disease prevention, and perhaps ultimately the only truly effective one (p. 479).

Foege, Amler, and White (1985) also emphasized the importance of disease prevention in closing the gap in health disparity between rich and poor.

The government's spending priorities, however, do not reflect the importance of preventive public health measures compared with the limited effect of medical treatment on the health status of the population (CDC, 1997; Eilbert et al., 1996; Eilbert et al., 1997; McGinnis, 1997; Public Health Foundation, 1994). In 2002, national health care expenditures totaled $1.56 trillion, or approximately $5,400 per person (National Center for Health Statistics [NCHS], 2004). In the same year, total public health expenditures were estimated to be $51.2 billion, or just $178 per person (NCHS, 2004). Public health expenditures thus accounted for only 3.3% of all national health expenditures. This means that as a nation, we spend about $30 for medical treatment for each $1 spent on the primary prevention of disease. And these figures include individual medical services provided by public health agencies; the actual investment in preventive, population-based public health programs is substantially lower.

And although health care spending continues to skyrocket, funding for preventive public health measures is barely keeping pace with inflation. The U.S. Public Health Service (1995) estimated that although total

U.S. health expenditures increased by more than 210% between 1981 and 1993, the proportion of these expenditures used for population-based public health measures declined by 25%. Between 1999 and 2002, the proportion of total national health expenditures devoted to public health programs declined from 3.6% to 3.3% (NCHS, 2004).

The societal focus on individual-level treatment rather than population-based prevention interventions is reflected not only by the nation's spending priorities, but by the issues that dominate the national health agenda. Perhaps the two best examples of this are the inappropriate attention given to health care reform and to integration of public health into managed care as potential solutions to the nation's public health crisis. It is a widespread fallacy that health care reform can solve many of the nation's public health problems. An equal inaccuracy holds that managed care organizations present a great opportunity for public health advancement. Each of these fallacies represents a direct threat to public health practice in this country because they are sidetracking the public, policy makers, and, most importantly, public health practitioners, from the vital need to focus on social change as the vehicle to achieve societal improvement in health.

■ THE ILLUSION OF HEALTH CARE REFORM AS A SOLUTION TO THE PUBLIC HEALTH CRISIS

The health care reform debate in the United States is dominated by arguments over health care delivery and reimbursement methods for medical care, not by arguments about how to deliver adequate, population-based prevention programs and policies to the American people. Therefore, the debate is hardly pertinent when determining how to improve the public's health. "In spite of the evidence pointing to deficiencies in health-supporting milieus, resulting in damage that had to be remedied by health care, by the 1990s the health policy debate—in the United States and other countries—had moved to an almost exclusively economic argument about health care services, as though these considerations alone were pertinent to better health" (Milio, 1995, p. 98). Addressing the implications of the health care reform discussion, Miller (1995) suggested the following: "The most disturbing conclusion is that current proposals are about financing, not about health care. . . . Consequently, health 'reform' is mainly about money and somewhat less about the organization of health services, and is not about broad, preventive measures that would reduce illness and injury and improve health functioning" (p. 356).

This country's failure to consider the real health care crisis, and its inappropriate focus on one small aspect of the problem as the solution to the whole problem, could spell doom for public health. If public and legislative debate continues to dwell on reforming the method of reimbursing physicians and hospitals, rather than on the method for ensuring the societal conditions in which people can be healthy, then the field of public health will be lost amid the complexities and conflicts of public debate.

■ THE ILLUSION OF MANAGED CARE AS AN OPPORTUNITY FOR PUBLIC HEALTH

Since the emergence of managed care, the field of public health has become preoccupied with it and its implications for the public's health. Managed care has dominated the agendas of major public health conferences, scientific journals, and policy debates. The emphasis on managed care's implications for the public's health is appropriate, given the research indicating the adverse consequences of managed care on medical services and outcomes, especially for the poor, the disadvantaged, the elderly, and the chronically ill (Anders, 1996; Bickman, 1996; Brown et al., 1993; Clement et al., 1994; Experton et al., 1997; Miller & Luft, 1994, Retchin & Brown, 1991; Retchin et al., 1997; Retchin & Preston, 1991; Shaughnessy et al., 1994; Ware et al., 1996; Webster & Feinglass, 1997; Wickizer et al., 1996).

However, some public health practitioners have suggested that managed care presents tremendous opportunities for the advancement of public health goals. While efforts to integrate some aspects of public health into managed care systems certainly are important, they cannot and should not substitute for the basic effort to strengthen and preserve public health's independent role and independent infrastructure. The practitioner should not mistakenly think that managed care can be changed in a way that will allow public health to be practiced correctly. Why? Because public health and managed care are fundamentally different in their overall mission, their underlying values, and their primary goals and incentives.

Overall Mission

Managed care is simply a system of sick care delivery. But the delivery of sick care is only a small subset of public health practice. As the Institute of Medicine (1988) defined it, the mission of public health is to fulfill "society's interest in assuring conditions in which people can be healthy" (p. 7). Access to quality health care certainly is necessary to assure conditions in which people can be healthy, but it takes more than medical care to ensure that people are truly healthy.

Creating conditions in which people can be healthy requires social change: improving the infrastructure of our communities, restructuring the physical and social environments to promote health behaviors, and establishing social norms that support, rather than undermine, healthy behaviors. Ensuring that people are truly healthy requires the elimination of social, economic, and political barriers to an individual's ability to achieve fulfillment in his or her personal development, education, occupation, and family well-being. None of these requirements can be achieved solely through a health care system, even under ideal conditions. The best managed care could assure only the public's access to quality health care, not the quality of the public's health.

As Keck (1992) explained, there is a basic philosophical difference in the fundamental questions that managed care and public health seek to answer. While managed care asks "how do we pay for services?" public health asks "how do we maintain and restore health?" (p. 1208).

Underlying Values

The underlying values of managed care are inconsistent with those of public health. Public health is based on the principle of social justice: the assertion that society has an inherent interest in assuring a basic level of well-being for all people, regardless of their age, race, income, social status, or health status. Managed care, especially when practiced in a for-profit environment, tends toward social injustice. While the system works well for people who are healthy, it is relatively unfair to the sickest and poorest individuals, who are generally those who need the most intensive intervention. The system of market justice, on which managed care is based, tends to produce inequalities in social, economic, and health status.

Managed care plans step back from the individual patient and allocate resources among their patient pool. The role of public health, however, is to step back even further and allocate public health resources among the entire population. Because of the disparities in health status, risk factors, and social and environmental conditions between different population subgroups, this means spending large amounts of money for people who are living in poverty, in the inner city, and in disadvantaged communities. This public health reality is incompatible with the mission of managed care: to reduce and control health care costs. Under managed care, people living in poverty cannot possibly receive the intensive intervention that is required.

The U.S. Department of Health and Human Services (2000), in its *Healthy People 2010* goals for the nation, called for public health efforts to "eliminate health disparities among segments of the population, including differences that occur by gender, race or ethnicity, education or income, disability, geographic location, or sexual orientation." However, the managed care system tends to increase the disparity in health status between low- and high-income groups. Because managed care was developed to reduce health care spending and the groups that require the most expensive health care are the poor, the elderly, the disabled, and the chronically, terminally, and mentally ill, it is these groups that tend to face a disproportionate burden of the reduction in health care spending.

Primary Goals and Incentives

The bottom line for managed care organizations is controlling medical costs for their overall patient pool, not providing the services that are in the best interests of individual patients. This is a basic, practical dilemma that cannot be overcome in a for-profit, managed care environment. Dr. Jerome Kassirer (1995b), editor of the *New England Journal of Medicine*, noted in a 1995 editorial that "although many see this as an abstract dilemma, I believe that increasingly the struggle will be more concrete and stark: physicians will be forced to choose between the best interests of their patients and their own economic survival" (p. 50). The best interests of the public's health cannot be served under a system in which quarterly earnings and shareholder value are critical concerns.

The conflict between the need to control costs and maintain corporate profit and the goal of improving the public's health is illustrated by the way in which HMOs use the cost savings generated by their practices. In 1994, publicly traded HMOs spent only about 75% of their patients' premiums on direct patient care (Anders, 1996). The remainder was used for executive salaries, marketing, administrative costs, retained earnings, stockholder payouts, and acquisition of other HMOs. In for-profit HMOs, the health of the public is not, and will not ever be, the chief concern. Government and nonprofit health agencies and organizations are unique in having improvement of public health as their primary charge.

Managed care and public health also conflict in terms of their inherent incentives to offer expensive prevention initiatives. Attempts to encourage HMOs to enhance and expand prevention programs have generally been unsuccessful; HMOs do not appear to be interested in long-term benefits to their patients because those patients remain in a specific health plan for only a few years. Denying treatment—i.e., not expanding prevention programs is the most effective way to increase short-term profits (Mallozzi, 1996). In contrast, prevention initiatives offer public health agencies and organizations the most effective strategies to achieve their goals of improving the societal conditions that affect health.

As long as HMOs are accountable primarily to their shareholders rather than to their patients, their providers, and their communities as a whole, the best interests of the public's health cannot be served. Investors generally want to see a return on their investments in a relatively short time period. For this reason, for-profit HMOs will always weigh short-term gains more heavily than intensive and costly preventive interventions whose payoff is in the distant future. For example, paying for intensive psychotherapy for youths with severe emotional problems might destroy an HMO's profit margin in the short term; the fact that this early intervention may prevent severe psychopathology many years in the future is of little interest to most investors. These types of interventions, however, are essential if we are to be effective in promoting public health.

The public health view is long term; social change takes many years, sometimes even decades. Programs must be administered repeatedly, consistently, and over a long period of time before the necessary changes in social conditions, norms, behavior, and policy can take place. The quarterly report framework that managed care uses for program evaluation and decision making is inappropriate for practicing public health.

Why an Emphasis on Managed Care Is Dangerous for Public Health

Because public health and managed care differ fundamentally in almost every basic premise, it is unrealistic to think that major public health achievements can be attained through the managed care system. Managed care is simply a method for the delivery and reimbursement of sick care; it cannot ever be a societal effort to create and facilitate social change. Managed care represents a threat to the survival of public health precisely because practitioners believe they can integrate public health initiatives into the managed care system. The institution that is charged with marketing social change—public health—must remain independent of managed care and must retain its focus on its fundamental mission.

While there is pressure for public health agencies to become involved in efforts to add a more preventive focus to managed care, public health practitioners must not become so sidetracked by managed care that they lose sight of the real area in which the health of the population depends— stimulating social change for the population, not simply improving health care for the individual. To survive, public health must find, claim, and maintain its place as a societal institution outside of the managed care system. Only external to this system of health care delivery can the mission of public health be accomplished. And by sidetracking public health practitioners from the real issue at hand—the need to create and facilitate social change—the present preoccupation with finding ways to realize some marginal benefits from convincing managed care corporations to incorporate some public health programs is threatening to erode the practice of public health.

■ POLITICAL AND ECONOMIC FACTORS THAT DIRECTLY THREATEN PUBLIC HEALTH FUNDING

Budget Crises

Although funding cuts for public health programs have plagued government agencies for at least two decades, unprecedented measures to reduce or eliminate many of the critical public health functions of government have emerged due to federal and state budget crises during the past five years. Funding for statewide tobacco control programs provides an excellent illustration of this dangerous trend. Despite tremendous success in reducing cigarette smoking as well as public exposure to secondhand smoke (Siegel, 2002), funding for a state tobacco prevention program in Massachusetts was cut by 95%, from a high of approximately $54 million per year to just $2.5 million in fiscal year 2004 (Campaign for Tobacco-Free Kids, 2005b). In spite of unprecedented declines in youth smoking attributable to an aggressive anti-smoking media campaign in Florida (Bauer et al., 2000; Siegel, 2002), the Florida legislature and governor cut funding for the program in every year since 1998 (the program's inception) and essentially eliminated the program in 2003 (Campaign for Tobacco-Free Kids, 2005b). And in Minnesota, a successful youth-directed smoking prevention marketing campaign was eliminated completely in 2003, accompanied by an 81% cut in overall state tobacco control program funding (Campaign for Tobacco-Free Kids, 2005b). The elimination of the Target Market program in Minnesota was demonstrated to have resulted in a significant increase in youth susceptibility to cigarette smoking (CDC, 2004).

In November 1998, the signing of a multi-state settlement between Attorneys General in 46 states and the major tobacco companies resulted in the availability of $246 billion to these states over 25 years, sufficient to adequately fund smoking prevention programs in every state. However, largely due to state budget crises, as of fiscal year 2006, only four states were using this money to fund tobacco prevention programs at the minimum level recommended by the Centers for Disease Control and Prevention (Campaign for Tobacco-Free Kids, 2005a). Overall, states were allocating only 2.6% of their tobacco revenue in fiscal year 2006 to tobacco prevention and cessation programs (Campaign for Tobacco-Free Kids, 2005a).

Overall state spending for public health has been an equally dismal failure, especially in light of the infusion of $1.8 billion of federal money into state public health preparedness following the bioterrorism fears instilled by the September 11, 2001 tragedy and subsequent anthrax attacks (Trust for America's Health, 2003). Despite this infusion of federal funding, nearly two-thirds of states cut funds to public health programs from fiscal year 2002 to 2003 (Trust for America's Health, 2003). During 2003, states reportedly faced a collective budget deficit of $66.6 billion; this may help explain why only 18 states were able to maintain their funding of public health services from 2002 to 2003 (Trust for America's Health, 2003).

These decreases in public health funding call into question both the ability of states to fight the chronic disease epidemic and their ability to prepare for bioterrorism, emerging infectious diseases, or other public health emergencies. A review of the preparedness of state health departments after the receipt of $1.8 billion of federal funds (Trust for America's Health, 2003) revealed that states were not only ill-prepared for a public health emergency, but for routine disease prevention activities as well:

Many state health departments are losing resources, and, therefore, capacity. Yet health departments are being called upon to expand their traditional scope to include preventing and preparing for bioterrorism, as well as responding to emerging infectious diseases, such as West Nile virus. The technical capabilities of many state and local health departments are being stretched to the point that emergency response and disease prevention services are in jeopardy. Although the states have received $1.8 billion in federal preparedness funds, many have cut their own spending on public health services. Consequently, there is evidence that the impact of the federal funds to help states has been diluted." (p. 13)

It is clear that a substantial number of states have used the availability of increased federal funding for public health as an excuse to cut their own funding for public health and divert that money to meet other budget needs, resulting in a net decrease, not increase, in overall public health funding. To make matters worse, much of the existing funding has been earmarked for the newly-needed programs in bioterrorism and emergency preparedness, meaning that basic chronic disease prevention programs are being sacrificed.

Despite an initial increase in funding for public health after September 11, largely due to spending on bioterrorism preparedness (not on chronic disease prevention), overall federal public health spending is now decreasing, even accounting for the influx of funds into bioterrorism-related programs. On February 6, 2006, President George W. Bush announced his proposed budget for fiscal year 2007. As the nation braced for a potential bird flu pandemic, its president cut funding for the Centers for Disease Control and Prevention (CDC)—the nation's leading public health and prevention agency—by 2% (American Public Health Association [APHA], 2006). Accounting for new spending for flu preparedness and response, however, the proposed CDC budget for its vital and existing chronic and infectious disease prevention and control programs was cut by 4.5% (APHA, 2006). Proposed funding for the CDC's Preventive Health and Health Services Block Grants was eliminated, as was proposed funding for the universal newborn hearing screening program and the urban American Indian health program. The proposed budget also cut, although did not completely eliminate, funding for the Children's Health Insurance Program, which provides insurance to millions of low-income children. Fiscal year 2006 had already seen the elimination of CDC's Verb campaign, an effective effort to promote physical activity in order to address the nation's burgeoning obesity epidemic, as well as severe cuts to Medicaid.

New and Perceived Public Health Threats: Bioterrorism and Emerging Infectious Diseases

The threat of bioterrorism and emerging infectious diseases has certainly increased attention to public health preparedness. However, there has also been a negative impact of this shift in focus: namely, some degree of decreased attention to existing chronic disease threats. As discussed above, despite the federal infusion of $1.8 billion into state public health funding in fiscal years 2002 and 2003 in response to bioterrorism threats, nearly two-thirds of states cut overall funding for public health programs. With much of the money earmarked for bioterrorism and other aspects of public health preparedness, funding for existing public health threats—largely, chronic diseases—has actually declined.

According to the Trust for America's Health (2003), the focus on bioterrorism, and especially on a possible smallpox terrorist threat, diverted resources away from other critical public health services: "achieving a battle-ready public health defense at the federal, state and local levels will take many years of sustained commitment, funding and oversight, especially because 'over the past two decades, the nation's public health infrastructure has greatly deteriorated. Initially, Congress, HHS and CDC narrowly focused the federal preparedness investment on bioterrorism concerns. Last year's controversial smallpox vaccination initiative, which pulled valuable time, resources and staffing away from other critical public health functions, illustrates the pitfalls of over-emphasizing a single threat" (p. 27).

A number of researchers have written that bioterrorism preparedness itself has wasted public health resources without benefit and has diverted funding from essential public health needs (Cohen, Gould, & Sidel, 2004; Dowling & Lipton, 2005; Sidel, Cohen, & Gould, 2005). While many predicted that bioterrorism funding would strengthen public health infrastructure by bringing funding not only for bioterrorism but for other functions of public health, this has not come to fruition. Instead, bioterrorism preparedness has shifted priorities and weakened the public health infrastructure and its ability to deal with real and existing threats (Cohen, Gould, & Sidel, 2004). In fact, Cohen et al. (2004) go so far as to suggest that bioterrorism preparedness has been a disaster for public health, squandering public health resources and diverting them away from real public health needs.

Cohen et al. (2004) concluded that "Massive campaigns focusing on 'bioterrorism preparedness' have had adverse health consequences and have resulted in the diversion of essential public health personnel, facilities, and other resources from urgent, real public health needs" (p. 1667). "In short, bioterrorism preparedness programs have been a disaster for public health. Instead of leading to more resources for dealing with natural disease as had been promised, there are now fewer such resources. Worse, in response to bioterrorism preparedness, public health institutions and procedures are being reorganized along a military or police model that subverts the relationships between public health providers and the communities they serve" (p. 1669). Thus, not only has the perceived need for bioterrorism preparedness diverted public health resources, it has also adversely affected the organization of the public health infrastructure and the relationship between public health institutions and the communities they are supposed to serve.

Cohen et al. (2004) conclude with a clear message on the dangers of the current focus on bioterrorism preparedness for public health: "In light of the daily toll of thousands of deaths from illnesses and accidents that could be prevented with even modest increases in public health resources here and around the world, we believe that the huge spending on bioterrorism preparedness programs constitutes a reversal of any reasonable sense of priorities. . . . these programs represent a catastrophe for American public health, and we hope it is not too late to change this dangerous direction" (p. 1670).

Even with the infusion of funding for bioterrorism and other public health emergency preparedness, a recent review found that states are woefully prepared for a public health emergency, especially a potential pandemic flu outbreak (Trust for America's Health, 2003). The overwhelming majority of states, as of 2003, did not have a plan for confronting a pandemic flu outbreak, were not prepared to communicate with health care practitioners and the public about any emerging health threats, and did not have sufficient laboratory facilities.

Decreased spending on state public health programs translates into reduced funding for local programs as well. And local public health programs are already funded at very low levels. Using data derived from a survey of more than 2,000 local health departments throughout the country, CDC estimated that the median per capita expenditure by local health departments in 1995 was just $20, and the mean per capita expenditure was $26 (Gordon et al., 1997). This amounts to just under a dime per day. The Trust for America's Health report revealed that most of the funding to state health departments for better public health emergency preparedness was not filtering down to the local level (Trust for America's Health, 2003). Only 17 states, as of 2003, had allocated at least 50% of their received federal public health capacity-building funds directly to local health departments. Not surprisingly, "a recent U.S. Conference of Mayors report found that in almost half of the states, major cities feel shut out of the state planning process for public health preparedness and claim state priorities do not reflect local concerns" (Trust for America's Health, 2003, p. 11).

The Influence of Special-Interest Groups

The continued influence of powerful special-interest groups, especially at the federal level, threatens many public health programs. An excellent case in point is federal funding for research on firearms-related injuries. In 1995, the National Rifle Association (NRA) lobbied Congress to eliminate all funding for the National Center for Injury Prevention and Control (NCIPC), a $46 million center that serves as the nation's leading agency dedicated to the prevention and control of intentional and unintentional injuries ("Gun Violence Remains," 1996; "House Cuts $2.6m," 1996; Kassirer, 1995a; Kent, 1996). Because gun-related deaths are a significant part of injury mortality, research on firearms control is a central part of the center's mission. The NRA was successful in getting Congress to consider a bill that would have eliminated the NCIPC completely. The bill failed, but 1 year later the NRA returned with a less ambitious objective: to eliminate funding for the firearms injury research at the center, which amounted to $2.6 million in 1995. In 1996, both the House of Representatives and the Senate approved a $2.6 million cut in the NCIPC budget to eliminate firearms injury research at CDC (HR3755: Health and Human Services FY97 Appropriations Bill). Ultimately, a Congressional compromise worked out in the last days of the legislative session restored the $2.6 million to the NCIPC budget but diverted most of it to study traumatic brain injury (Kong, 1997). In addition, a clause in the appropriations bill prohibited any of the NCIPC funds from being used to advocate or promote gun control ("Gun Violence Remains," 1996; Kong, 1997).

Since fiscal year 1997, Congress has included in its appropriations to the CDC language indicating that "none of the funds made available for injury prevention and control at the Centers for Disease Control and Prevention may be used to advocate or promote gun control" (NCIPC, 2005). In addition, language added in the fiscal year 2003 appropriations legislation included a detailed and burdensome requirement to ensure that CDC was not using any funds in any way that could be construed as trying to influence the development of responsible gun control policy (NCIPC, 2005). First, the legislation indicated that none of the funds for injury prevention and control could be used, **in whole or in part**, to advocate or promote gun control. Second, the Conference Report added a proviso "to prohibit Federal funds from being used to lobby for or against the passage of specific Federal, State or local legislation intended to advocate or promote gun control. The conferees understand that the CDC's responsibility in this area is primarily data collection and the dissemination of information and expect research in this area to be objective and grants to be awarded through an impartial, scientific peer review process. The conferees instruct the CDC to provide a detailed report, within

90 days of enactment, on the steps the CDC has taken to ensure this restriction is being followed" (NCIPC, 2005).

These severe and purely politically-motivated restrictions on the practice of public health are present in large part thanks to the efforts of the National Rifle Association, which is spending approximately $8 million each year to influence legislators to vote against any proposals that would restrict the production, sale, or use of firearms (Burchfield, 2000). Of note, 75% of the 263 House members who voted to cut the NCIPS's funding accepted contributions from the NRA during the prior 3 years and only six recipients of NRA funding voted against the funding cut (Montgomery & Infield, 1996). The NRA's influence was also instrumental in the 1995 House passage of a bill to repeal the ban on assault weapons (HR125: Gun Ban Repeal Act of 1995), which passed 239 to 173 but was not approved by the Senate. The NRA's influence on both bills is highlighted by the fact that 366 of the 421 members who voted on the NCIPC funding cut voted in a consistent manner on the repeal of the assault weapons ban ("How Members of Congress Voted," 1997). Ultimately, the 1994 federal assault weapons ban was allowed to expire in 2004, allowing 19 types of military-style assault weapons back into the hands of civilians. Failure of the effort to renew the assault weapons ban was attributed to a lobbying campaign by the NRA (Associated Press, 2004).

The magnitude of the extent to which special-interest lobbying attempts to influence federal policy making is demonstrated by an examination of the nature and amount of the top federal lobbying spenders. Between 1998 and 2004, Altria Group Inc., parent to Philip Morris—the nation's largest cigarette manufacturer—spent $101.2 million on federal lobbying, making it the second highest spender (The Center for Public Integrity, 2005). Eleven of the remaining top 20 lobbying spenders represented manufacturing, defense, electrical, oil, telecommunications, or pharmaceutical interests and combined to spend nearly $750 million on federal lobbying during this seven-year period.

Increasing Antiregulatory Sentiment

The practice of public health relies on a sense of public trust in government's ability to protect societal interests and a shared sense that the government has the responsibility to fund and conduct programs to accomplish this. However, recent public opinion polls have documented low levels of public trust in government and public acknowledgment of a central role and responsibility in protecting societal interests.

A 2005 poll by the Pew Research Center for the People & the Press (2005) found that favorable ratings of the federal government dropped to just 45%, having reached a high of 82% in 2001. Favorable ratings of Congress itself also dropped to 45%, after reaching a high of 74% in 1987. These ratings are not much better than a decade earlier, when a 1994 poll found that 70% of Americans were dissatisfied with the overall performance of the federal government, 70% believed that government programs are inefficient and wasteful, and 69% believed that the federal government creates more problems than it solves (Weisberg, 1996).

Perhaps more threatening than the public's lack of trust in government is the public's disinterest in the responsibility of government to promote the common good. The Progressive movement, which launched large-scale government programs to address public health issues and social problems, was based on the assertion "that social evils will not remedy themselves, and that it is wrong to sit by passively and wait for time to take care of them . . . that the people of the country should be stimulated to work energetically to bring about social progress, that the positive powers of government must be used to achieve this end" (Weisberg, 1996, p. 157).

As Weisberg argued in his 1996 book *In Defense of Government*, the values that underlie government's charge to promote social justice have not disappeared, but they need to be restored to prominence in the public, political, and media agendas: "Building a workable public activism is not a matter of starting from scratch but rather of recovering and renewing lost principles" (p. 158). What needs to be restored, according to Weisberg (1996), is the assertion of "the national government's responsibility for the welfare of the entire polity" (p. 159).

In a 1997 *American Journal of Public Health* editorial, Dr. Fitzhugh Mullan of the journal *Health Affairs* emphasized the same point, but referred specifically to the restoration of the public health movement:

> An acute hazard for the reinvention workers of our movement is that the pendulum of national life is swinging so far in the direction of proprietary and individual interests . . . a tougher and ultimately more central job is to retain public and communitarian principles, no small task when the rhetoric of this 'post-health-care-reform' era, both inside and outside the government, is so strongly oriented to the private sector. Yet it will be the response to this challenge—the stewardship of the public trust despite the siren calls of devolution and privatization—that will render the ultimate commentary on the leadership of federal public health. . . . (Mullan, 1997, p. 24).An acute hazard for the reinvention workers of our movement is that the pendulum of national life is swinging so far in the direction of proprietary and individual interests . . . a tougher and ultimately more central job is to retain public and communitarian principles, no small task when the rhetoric of this 'post-health-care-reform' era, both inside and outside the government, is so strongly oriented to the private sector. Yet it will be the response to this challenge—the stewardship of the public trust

despite the siren calls of devolution and privatization—that will render the ultimate commentary on the leadership of federal public health. . . . (p. 24)

■ THE LOST VISION OF PUBLIC HEALTH

In recent years, the public health community has lost a unified vision of its role and mission (Brown, 1997). The vision of public health as a form of social justice and of the mission of the public health practitioner as advocating for social justice and social change no longer guides the public health movement. To see how this has occurred, we must briefly review the historical roots of public health.

Public health has deep historical roots in what Beauchamp (1976) termed the "egalitarian tradition." Beauchamp proclaimed that "public health should be a way of doing justice, a way of asserting the value and priority of all human life" (p. 8). Turnock (1997) also explained that the underlying philosophy of public health is social justice: "In the case of public health, the goal of extending the potential benefits of the physical and behavioral sciences to all groups in the society, especially when the burden of disease and ill health within that is unequally distributed, is largely based on principles of social justice" (pp. 15–16).

Public health was founded on three basic principles: (1) the principles of social justice; (2) the notion of an inherent public responsibility for social health and welfare; and (3) the responsibility of the public health practitioner to advocate for social justice and collective, societal action.

The first principle—social justice—is based on the view that health is not an individual privilege but a social good that should be equally available to all individuals: "While many forces influenced the development of public health, the historic dream of public health that preventable death and disability ought to be minimized is a dream of social justice" (Beauchamp, 1976, p. 6).

The second principle—public responsibility for social health and welfare—is based on the assertion that government is responsible for achieving and preserving social justice. There is a collective, societal burden to ensure equal health protection and basic standards of living for all people: "Another principle of the public health ethic is that the control of hazards cannot be achieved through voluntary mechanisms but must be undertaken by governmental or non-governmental agencies through planned, organized and collective action that is obligatory or nonvoluntary in nature" (Beauchamp, 1976, p. 8). Burris (1997) explained: "While much of the most important public health work is done in the private sector and the work of the state must take a wide variety of forms beyond direct regulation, 'public health' without the dynamic leadership of government in deploying the nation's wealth against the ills arising from individual choices in the market is a contradiction in terms" (p. 1608).

The third principle—advocacy—is based on the view that the public health practitioner is, first and foremost, an advocate for social change: "Doing public health involves more than merely elaborating a new social ethic, doing public health involves the political process and the challenging of some very important and powerful interests in society. . . . While professional prestige is an important attribute in the modern day public policy process, public health is ultimately better understood as a broad social movement. . . . The political potential of public health goes beyond professionalism; at its very heart is advocacy of an explosive and radical ethic" (Beauchamp, 1976, p. 10).

The idea that public health's role is to promote social change dates back at least 150 years. Public health arose out of the establishment of healthy social conditions as a societal goal and recognition of public institutions as responsible for achieving this social goal (Institute of Medicine, 1988). Public health is not just about studying problems and proposing solutions. It is about organizing the community to support and implement those solutions. And organizing the community requires social and political intervention. As the Institute of Medicine (1988) explained, "the history of public health has been one of identifying health problems, developing knowledge and expertise to solve problems, and rallying political and social support around the solutions" (p. 70).

Public health cannot be separated from the political process. In fact, politics is at the heart of public health. As Dr. Gro Harlem Brundtland, chief of the World Health Organization, stated, "you cannot implement it [public health] without making it a political issue" (Altman, 1998, p. C3).

Rosemary Stevens (1996) outlined these fundamental principles of public health in an *American Journal of Public Health* editorial reviewing the vision of Dr. Henry Sigerist (1891–1957), a medical historian and public health advocate: "For Sigerist, as for many of us who were socialized into public health in the 20th century, health is quite simply a social good. The role of the state is to enhance and protect that good for all members of the population; indeed, in his view, the state has a public duty to do so" (p. 1522). Further, it is the role of the public health practitioner to advocate for the necessary social reforms. For Sigerist, advocacy was a responsibility for the individual as well as for the public health institution. Sigerist "threw his own energy, commitment, and enthusiasm on the side of what he perceived to be social equity and justice" (Fee, 1996, p. 1644).

The principles of social justice, societal responsibility for public health and welfare, and advocacy for social change remain the three pillars of public health today. As expressed in a 1996 American Public Health Association policy statement, "long-standing principles of the APHA establish a commitment to the right of all people to attain and maintain good health, through population based public health services and through access to personal health care services. . . . Further, it is the responsibility of society at large, and the public health system in particular, to safeguard the public interest in achieving these objectives" (APHA, 1997, p. 511).

Public health has begun to lose sight of its historical foundation and fundamental principles. No longer united by a common vision of its mission and role, public health has come to be viewed by many in the field more as an elite profession rather than a broad, social movement. In recent years, the "advocacy of an explosive and radical ethic" is all but lost. This, more than anything else, threatens the survival of public health as an institution.

Perhaps the most poignant illustration of the loss of the vision of public health as a broad social movement and its takeover by elite professionalism is the efforts of three national public health organizations—the National Center for Tobacco-Free Kids, the American Cancer Society (ACS), and the American Heart Association (AHA)—to promote a Congressionally mediated, "global" settlement to all but a strictly defined subset of past, present, and future lawsuits by citizens, businesses, and public bodies against the tobacco industry (Califano, 1998; "Koop Opposes Immunity in Tobacco Deal," 1997; LoPucki, 1998; McGinley & Harwood, 1997; Schwartz, 1998; Shackelford, 1997; Siegel, 1996, 1997; "The Reynolds Papers," 1998; "Tobacco Talk," 1998; Torry, 1998; Weinstein & Levin, 1997). The process by which the settlement was pursued and promoted violated the core principles of public health; eschewed social justice; and co-opted a broad, social movement, wresting it from the hands of community public health practitioners across the nation and into the hands of a few powerful individuals and organizations (McGinley & Harwood, 1997; Shackelford, 1997; Siegel, 1996, 1997; Weinstein & Levin, 1997). The very organizations that claimed to represent the interests of cancer and heart disease victims were willing to trade away the legal rights of these victims. And the leadership of these organizations remained willing to consider a deal that would grant the tobacco industry immunity for its wrongdoing, even after the grassroots membership of these organizations made it clear that they opposed the concept of using the legal rights of American citizens as a bargaining chip.

A more recent example is the effort of the American Legacy Foundation, arguably the nation's most heavily funded anti-smoking organization, to forge corporate partnerships with conglomerates and companies that are the leading reasons for youth exposure to cigarette advertising in magazines and to portrayals of smoking in movies (Siegel, 2005a), both of which have been shown to be strong factors in smoking initiation (Pucci & Siegel, 1999; Sargent et al., 2005). As of 2005, the American Legacy Foundation maintained corporate partnerships with Time Warner (Siegel, 2005a), whose Warner Brothers movie division is the leading source of youth exposure to smoking in movies (Polansky & Glantz, 2004) and whose Time Inc. magazine division publishes magazines such as *Sports Illustrated*, *People Weekly*, *Entertainment Weekly*, and *TIME Magazine*, which collectively exposed over four million adolescents to a total of 219 tobacco advertisements in 2004 (Siegel, 2005a). The American Legacy Foundation also partners with the Hearst Corporation (Siegel, 2005b), which at the same time bombards youths with ads for Kool and Camel cigarettes and for Skoal (smokeless tobacco) through its *Cosmopolitan*, *Esquire*, and *Popular Mechanics* publications, and with Condé Nast Publications (Siegel, 2005c), which heavily exposes youths to cigarette ads for Camel and Kool through its *Vogue*, *Glamour*, and *GQ* magazines.

The American Legacy Foundation went so far as to honor Time Inc. with an award for "reaching millions with an anti-tobacco message" at a $500-per-plate fundraiser, expressing gratification that "a selection of Time, Inc.'s magazines . . . do not accept any tobacco product advertising" (Siegel, 2005a). It turns out that only five of the more than 125 Time Inc. publications do not accept tobacco advertising and the top four Time Inc. magazines alone reach millions of youths with pro-tobacco messages, carrying more than 100 cigarette ads per year (Siegel, 2005a). This represents a troubling example of the loss of the vision of public health as a broad social movement and its takeover by elite professionalism. The efforts of the American Legacy Foundation undermined years of work by public health advocates to attempt to eliminate cigarette advertising in Time Inc. publications, and without their knowledge or consultation.

An article in the *American Journal of Public Health* illustrates another way in which health advocates have compromised public health values. Many health advocacy groups, such as professional medical and nursing associations, the AHA, the American Lung Association, and the ACS have hired lobbyists who also represent the tobacco industry (Goldstein & Bearman, 1996). For example, in 1994 more than 300 health organizations employed one or more tobacco lobbyists (Goldstein & Bearman, 1996).

Perhaps the most egregious example is the appointment of former tobacco industry lobbyist Kim Belshe as director of the California Department of Health Services in 1994. Belshe had been a lobbyist for the tobacco industry and had lobbied against Proposition 99, an initiative to establish a comprehensive, statewide tobacco control program funded by an increase in the state cigarette excise tax. There could hardly be a more inappropriate person to serve as director of a state health department than a former tobacco industry lobbyist who opposed one of the most important public health interventions in the state.

While some public health organizations have turned to professional lobbyists with dubious associations, many other public health groups have gone so far as to halt all advocacy in order to prevent the appearance of improper lobbying activity. The widely held perception that education is the only appropriate role for public health agencies and that advocacy is illegal or inappropriate for public health officials has arisen largely because of a widespread misunderstanding of the difference between advocacy and lobbying.

Many public health practitioners are under the impression that advocacy is synonymous with lobbying and therefore is restricted by federal law. Lobbying, however, is a very specific and legally defined term. As defined in the Internal Revenue Service Code, lobbying refers to an attempt to influence the outcome of legislation through communication with a legislator, government official, or the public (26 U.S.C.S. 4911). Generally, a communication is considered lobbying only if it (1) refers to specific legislation and (2) promotes a specific vote on that legislation (National Cancer Institute [NCI], 1993). Policy advocacy activities, such as researching, developing, planning, implementing, enforcing, and evaluating public health policy, are not lobbying, unless they involve the promotion of a specific vote on specific legislation.

Even when public health practitioners are convinced that their activities are legal, they often are scared into inaction by pressure from special-interest groups. A prime example is the use of federal funds to advocate for the control of tobacco use. The tobacco industry has used the Freedom of Information Act (FOIA) to intimidate tobacco control practitioners, often scaring them to inaction by forcing them to copy hundreds or even thousands of documents and accusing them of illegal activity (Levin, 1996; Mintz, 1997). For example, the Association for Non-smokers—Minnesota was hit with such a request. A spokesperson for the group explained: "They wanted people such as myself to be intimidated and fearful and confused—and at least to some extent they succeeded. Truly, we did almost nothing in the way of tobacco control for about three months" (Levin, 1996). Similar FOIA requests were made to state health departments in California, Massachusetts, Indiana, Colorado, and Washington (Levin, 1996; Mintz, 1997). According to an article in the journal *Tobacco Control*, the tobacco control section of the California Department of Health Services, which administers Proposition 99, received 59 FOIA requests from 1991 to 1993 (Aguinaga & Glantz, 1995). Although the tobacco industry's statements and actions imply that there is something wrong with the way tobacco control funds were being used, ethics board reviews cleared all the groups whose activities were challenged (Levin, 1996). Nevertheless, the tobacco industry's objective was accomplished: Many tobacco control groups have been scared into inaction or into a state of reserved action.

■ CONCLUSION

The public health movement is involved in a fight not only to protect the public from the emerging epidemic of chronic disease that threatens to dominate life in the 21st century, but to save itself as a vital and integral part of the societal infrastructure. A continuing societal focus on health care reform as the solution to the nation's public health crisis, and on individual medical treatment rather than population-based prevention, threaten to obscure the need for public health. The emergence of managed care and the perception, even among public health practitioners, that public health can somehow be integrated into a managed care system threaten to erode the independent role of the public health professional. Budget cuts, the emergence of bioterrorism and infectious disease threats, special-interest group influence, and increasing antigovernment sentiment are each contributing to unprecedented threats to public health infrastructure and programs. Finally, the failure of public health practitioners to assert their primary role as advocates for social change and the loss of a common vision for public health represent internal, yet critical, threats to the viability of the public health movement.

This is no longer a fight to protect people's health. It is now a life and death struggle for public health as a societal institution.

References

Aguinaga, S., & Glantz, S.A. (1995). The use of public records acts to interfere with tobacco control. *Tobacco Control, 4*, 222–230.

Altman, L.K. (1998, February 3). Next W.H.O. chief will have politics in name of science. *The New York Times*, p. C3.

American Public Health Association. (2006, March). 2007 budget proposal paints dire picture for public health. *The Nation's Health*. Washington, DC: American Public Health Association.

———. (1997). Policy statements adopted by the governing council of the American Public Health Association, November 20, 1996. *American Journal of Public Health, 87*, 495–518.

Anders, G. (1996). *Health against wealth: HMOs and the breakdown of medical trust*. New York: Houghton Mifflin.

Associated Press. (2004, September 13). Congress lets assault weapons ban expire: Gun dealers say it never worked; many police wanted it, though. Available at: http://msnbc.msn.com/id/5946127/.

Bauer, U.E., Johnson, T.M., Hopkins, R.S., & Brooks, R.G. (2000). Changes in youth cigarette use and intentions following implementation of a tobacco control program: Findings from the Florida Youth Tobacco Survey, 1998–2000. *JAMA, 284*(6), 723–28.

Beauchamp, D. (1976). Public health as social justice. *Inquiry, 13*, 3–14.

Berliner, H. (1977). Emerging ideologies in medicine. *Review of Radical Political Economics, 9*, 116–124.

Bickman, L. (1996). A continuum of care: More is not always better. *American Psychologist, 51,* 689–701.

Brown, E.R. (1997). Leadership to meet the challenges to the public's health. *American Journal of Public Health, 87,* 554–557.

Brown, R.S., Clement, D.G., Hill, J.W., Retchin, S.M., & Bergeron, J.W. (1993). Do health maintenance organizations work for Medicare? *Health Care Financing Review, 15,* 7–23.

Burchfield, B. (2000, April 5). *Statement of Bobby R. Burchfield before the Senate Committee on Rules and Administration.* Washington, DC: United States Senate. Available at: http://rules.senate.gov/hearings/2000/04500burchfield.htm.

Burris, S. (1997). The invisibility of public health: Population-level measures in a politics of market individualism. *American Journal of Public Health, 87,* 1607–1601.

Califano, J.A., Jr. (1998, January 9). Sellout to big tobacco. *The Washington Post,* p. A21.

Campaign for Tobacco-Free Kids. (2005a, November 30). *A broken promise to our children: The 1998 state tobacco settlement seven years later.* Washington, DC; Author. Available at http://www.tobaccofreekids.org/reports/settlements/2006/fullreport.pdf.

———. (2005b, November 10). *The impact of reductions to state tobacco control program funding.* Washington, DC: Author. Available at http://tobaccofreekids.org/research/factsheets/pdf/0270.pdf.

Cassel, J. (1976). The contribution of the social environment to host resistance. *American Journal of Epidemiology, 104,* 107–123.

Centers for Disease Control and Prevention. (1995). *1994: Ten leading causes of death in the United States.* Atlanta, GA: Centers for Disease Control and Prevention, National Center for Injury Prevention and Control.

———. (1997). Estimated expenditures for essential public health services—Selected states, fiscal year 1995. *Morbidity and Mortality Weekly Report, 46,* 150–152.

———. (2004). Effect of ending an antitobacco youth campaign on adolescent susceptibility to cigarette smoking—Minnesota, 2002–2003. *Morbidity and Mortality Weekly Report, 53,* 301–304.

Clement, D.G., Retchin, S.M., Brown, R.S., & Steagall, M.H. (1994). Access and outcomes of elderly patients enrolled in managed care. *Journal of the American Medical Association, 271,* 1487–1492.

Cohen, H.W., Gould, R.M., & Sidel, V.W. (2004). The pitfalls of bioterrorism preparedness: The anthrax and smallpox experiences. *American Journal of Public Health, 94,* 1667–1671.

Conrad, P. (1987). The experience of illness: Recent and new directions. *Research in the Sociology of Health Care, 6,* 1–31.

Dowling, K.C., & Lipton, R.I. (2005). Bioterrorism preparedness expenditures may compromise public health. *American Journal of Public Health, 95,* 1672.

Dubos, R. (1959). *Mirage of health.* New York: Harper & Row.

Dutton, D.B. (1994). Social class, health, and illness. In H.D. Schwartz (Ed), *Dominant issues in medical sociology* (3rd ed., pp. 470–482). New York: McGraw-Hill.

Eilbert, K.W., Barry, M., Bialek, R., & Garufi, M. (1996). *Measuring expenditures for essential public health services.* Washington, DC: Public Health Foundation.

Eilbert, K.W., Barry, M., Bialek, R., Garufi, M., Maiese, D., Gebbie, K., & Fox, C.E. (1997). Public health expenditures: Developing estimates for improved policy making. *Journal of Public Health Management and Practice, 3,* 1–9.

Evans, R.G., Barer, M., & Marmor, T.R. (Eds.). (1994). *Why are some people healthy and others not? The determinants of health of populations.* New York: Aldine DeGruyter.

Experton, B., Li, Z., Branch, L.G., Ozminkowski, R.J., & Mellon-Lacey, D.M. (1997). The impact of payor/provider type on health care use and expenditures among the frail elderly. *American Journal of Public Health, 87,* 210–216.

Fee, E. (1996). The pleasures and perils of prophetic advocacy: Henry E. Sigerist and the politics of medical reform. *American Journal of Public Health, 86,* 1637–1647.

Foege, W.H., Amler R.W., & White, C.C. (1985). Closing the gap: Report of the Carter Center health policy consultation. *Journal of the American Medical Association, 254,* 1355–1358.

Goldstein, A.O. & Bearman, N.S. (1996). State tobacco lobbyists and organizations in the United States: Crossed lines. *American Journal of Public Health, 86,* 1137–1142.

Gordon, R.L., Gerzoff, R.B., & Richards, T.B. (1997). Determinants of US local health department expenditures, 1992 through 1993. *American Journal of Public Health, 87,* 91–95.

Gun violence remains a public health risk that's still hard to track. (1996, November). *In the Nation's health* (p. 24). Washington, DC: American Public Health Association.

Hingson, R., Scotch, N.A., Sorenson, J., & Swazey, J.P. (1981). *In sickness and in health: Social dimensions of medical care.* St. Louis: C.V. Mosby.

House cuts $2.6m for CDC gun study: Critics, including NRA, say injury research based toward firearms control. (1996, July 14). *The Boston Globe,* p. A19.

How members of Congress voted on issues affecting public health. (1997, February). In *The nation's health* (pp. 8–16). Washington, DC: American Public Health Association.

Institute of Medicine, Committee for the Study of the Future of Public Health. (1988) *The future of public health.* Washington, DC: National Academy Press.

Kass, E.H. (1971). Infectious diseases and social change. *Journal of Infectious Diseases. 123,* 110–114.

Kassirer, J.P. (1995a). A partisan assault on science: The threat to the CDC *New England Journal of Medicine, 333,* 793–794.

———. (1995b). Managed care and the morality of the marketplace. *New England Journal of Medicine. 332,* 50–52.

Keck, C.W. (1992). Creating a healthy public. *American Journal of Public Health, 82,* 1206–1209.

Kent, C. (1996, August 5). Fight over federal agency pits medicine vs. NRA: Funding for research on firearms injuries at issue. *American Medical News,* pp. 3, 52.

Kim, K., & Moody, P. (1992). More resources, better health? A cross-national perspective. *Social Science and Medicine, 34,* 837–842.

Kong, D. (1997, September 25). State loses funds to track gun injuries. *The Boston Globe,* p. B2.

Koop opposes immunity on tobacco deal (1997, December 23). *The Los Angeles Times,* p. D12.

Leavitt, J.W., & Numbers, R.L. (1994). Sickness and health in America: The role of public health in the prevention of disease. In H.D. Schwartz (ed), *Dominant issues in medical sociology* (3rd ed., pp. 529–537). New York: McGraw-Hill.

Lee, P.R., & Estes, C.L. (Eds). (1997). *The nation's health* (5th ed). Sudbury, MA: Jones and Bartlett.

Levin, M. (1996, April 21). Legal weapon: Tobacco companies, facing increasingly strong opposition, have turned to open-records laws to fight back, inundating state offices with requests for documents. *The Los Angeles Times,* pp. D1, D4.

Levine, S., Feldman, J.J., & Elison, J. (1983). Does medical care do any good? In D. Mechanic (Ed.), *Handbook of health, health care, and the health professions* (pp. 394–404). New York: Free Press.

LoPucki, L.M. (1998, January 20). Some settlement (op-ed column). *The Washington Post,* p. A15.

Magill, T.P. (1995). The immunologist and the evil spirits. *Journal of Immunology,* 74, 1–8.

Mallozzi, J. (1996, December). Consumer advocacy in Medicare HMOs. *States of Health,* 6(8), pp. 1–9.

McGinley, L., & Harwood, J. (1997, August 1). Grass-roots activists try to derail tobacco settlement. *The Wall Street Journal,* p. A16.

McGinnis, J.M. (1997). What do we pay for good health? *Journal of Public Health Management and Practice,* 3, viii-ix.

McKeown, T. (1971). A historical appraisal of the medical task. In G. McLachlan & T. McKeown (Eds.), *Medical history and medical care: A symposium of perspectives* (pp. 29–55). New York: Oxford University Press.

———. (1976). *The modern rise of population.* New York: Academic Press.

———. (1978, April). Determinants of health. *Human Nature,* 60–67.

———., Record, R.G., & Turner, R.D. (1975). An interpretation of the decline of mortality in England and Wales during the twentieth century. *Population Studies,* 29, 391–422.

McKinlay, J.B., & McKinlay, S.M. (1977). The questionable contribution of medical measures to the decline of mortality in the United States in the twentieth century. *Milbank Memorial Fund Quarterly/Health and Society,* 55, 405–428.

———. (1994) Medical measures and the decline of mortality. In P. Conrad & R. Kern (Eds.), *The sociology of health & illness: Critical perspectives* (4th ed., pp. 10–23). New York: St. Martin's Press.

Mechanic, D. (1994). Promoting health. In H.D. Schwartz (Ed.), *Dominant issues in medical sociology,* 3rd ed., pp. 569–575. New York: McGraw-Hill.

Milio, N. (1995). Health, health care reform, and the care of health. In M. Blunden & M. Dando (Eds.), *Rethinking public policy-making: Questioning assumptions, challenging beliefs,* pp.92–107. Thousand Oaks, CA: Sage Publications.

Miller, R.H., & Luft, H.S. (1994). Managed care plan performance since 1980: A literature analysis. *Journal of the American Medical Association,* 271, 1512–1519.

Miller, S.M. (1995). Thinking strategically about society and health. In B.C. Amick, III, S. Levine, A.R. Tarlov, & D.C. Walsh (Eds.), *Society and health* (pp. 342–358). New York: Oxford University Press.

Mintz, J. (1997, April 19). 3-year-old U.S. program cuts smoking, draws fire. *The Washington Post,* p. A1.

Montgomery, L., & Infield, T. (1996, July 12). House votes to cut gun studies. The $2.6 million for the CDC was put to political use, critics said the vote was "very important," said the NRA *Philadelphia Inquirer,* p. A1.

Morris, J.N. (1982), Epidemiology and prevention. *Milbank Memorial Fund Quarterly/Health and Society,* 60, 1–16.

Mullan, F. (1997). Federal public health, semi-reinvented. *American Journal of Public Health,* 87, 21–24.

National Center for Injury Prevention and Control. (2005). Letter to grantees: Restriction of funding. Atlanta, GA: Centers for Disease Control and Prevention, National Center for Injury Prevention and Control. Available at: http://www.cdc.gov/ncipc/res-opps/restrictions.htm.

National Cancer Institute. (1993, March 11). *Restrictions on lobbying and public policy advocacy by government contractors: The ASSIST contract.* Bethesda, MD: U.S. Department of Health and Human Services, National Institutes of Health, National Cancer Institute.

National Center for Health Statistics. (2004). *Health United States, 2004, with chartbook on trends in the health of Americans* (DHHS Publication No. 2004-1232). Hyattsville, MD: Author.

Omran, A.R. (1971). The epidemiologic transition: A theory of the epidemiology of population change. *Milbank Quarterly,* 49, 509–538.

Polansky, J.R., & Glantz, S.A. (2004). *First-run smoking presentations in U.S. movies 1999–2003.* San Francisco, CA: Center for Tobacco Control Research and Education, University of California, San Francisco. Available at: http://repositories.cdlib.org/ctcre/tcpmus/Movies2004.

Powles, J. (1973). On the limitations of modern medicine. *Science, Medicine, and Man,* 1, 1–30.

Public Health Foundation. (1994). *Measuring state expenditures for core public health functions.* Washington, DC: Author.

Pucci, L.G., & Siegel, M. (1999). Exposure to brand-specific cigarette advertising in magazines and its impact on youth smoking. *Preventive Medicine,* 29, 313–320.

Retchin, S.M., & Brown, B. (1991). Elderly patients with congestive heart failure under prepaid care. *American Journal of Medicine,* 90, 236–242.

Retchin, S.M., Brown, R.S., Yeh, S.J., Chu, D., & Moreno, L. (1997). Outcomes of stroke patients in Medicare fee for service and managed care. *Journal of the American Medical Association,* 278, 119–124.

Retchin, S.M., & Preston, J.A. (1991). The effects of cost containment on the care of elderly diabetics. *Archives of Internal Medicine,* 151, 2244–2248.

The Reynolds papers. (1988, January 16). *The Washington Post,* p. A20.

Sargent, J.D., Beach, M.L., Adachi-Mejia, A.M., Gibson, J.J., Titus-Ernstoff, L.T., Carusi, C.P., Swain, S.D., Heatherton, T.F., & Dalton, M.A. (2005). Exposure to movie smoking: Its relation to smoking initiation among US adolescents. *Pediatrics,* 116(5), 1183–1191.

Schwartz, J. (1998, January 22). Anti-tobacco activists may heal rift: Koop works to unite public health groups. *The Washington Post,* p. A10.

Shackelford, L. (1997, December 29). AMA leaders have betrayed doctors to protect big tobacco. *The Louisville Courier-Journal,* p. D2.

Shaughnessy, P., Schlenker, R.E., & Hittle, D.F. (1994). Home health care outcomes under capitated and fee-for-service payment. *Health Care Financing Review,* 16, 187–222.

Sidel, V.W., Cohen, H.W., & Gould, R.M. (2005). Sidel et al. respond. *American Journal of Public Health,* 95, 1672–1673.

Siegel, M. (1996, December 22). Tobacco: The $10 billion dollar debate. *The Washington Post,* p. C7.

———. (1997, May 4). What sort of tobacco settlement? *The Washington Post,* p. C7.

———. (2002). The effectiveness of state-level tobacco control interventions: A review of program implementation and behavioral outcomes. *Annual Review of Public Health,* 23, 45–71.

———. (2005a, March 6). *American Legacy Foundation honors top tobacco ad publisher.* Boston, MA: Author. Available at: http://tobaccoanalysis.blogspot.com/2005/03/american-legacy-foundation-honors-top.html.

———. (2005b, August 23). *Weekly update on leader in tobacco control movement: The Hearst Corporation.* Boston, MA: Author. Available at: http://tobaccoanalysis.blogspot.com/2005/08/weekly-update-on-leader-in-tobacco_23.html.

———. (2005c, August 30). *Weekly update on leader in tobacco control movement: Condé Nast Publications.* Boston, MA: Author. Available at: http://tobaccoanalysis.blogspot.com/2005/08/weekly-update-on-leader-in-tobacco_30.html.

Stevens, R. (1996) Editorial: Public health history and advocacy in the money-driven 1990s. *American Journal of Public Health,* 86, 1522–1523.

Syme, S.L., & Berkman, L.F. (1976). Social class susceptibility and sickness. *American Journal of Epidemiology,* 104, 1–8.

Tesh, S.N. (1994). Hidden arguments: Political ideology and disease prevention policy. In H. D. Schwartz (Ed.). *Dominant issues in medical sociology* (3rd ed), pp. 519–529. New York: McGraw-Hill.

The Center for Public Integrity. (2005). *Top 100 companies and organizations.* Washington, DC: Author. Available at: http://www.publicintegrity.org/lobby/top.aspx?act=topcompanies.

The Pew Research Center for the People & The Press. (2005, October 25). *Public sours on government and business.* Washington, DC: Author. Available at: http://www.pewtrusts.com/pdf/PRC_gov_1005.pdf.

Tobacco talk. (1998, January 30). *The Washington Post,* p. A22.

Tony, S. (1998, February 6). Signals change on tobacco deal: White House bends on industry protection. *The Washington Post,* p. A18.

Trust for America's Health. (2003, September). *Ready or not? Protecting the public's health in the age of bioterrorism.* Washington, DC: Author. Available at: http://healthyamericans.org/state/bioterror/Bioterror.pdf.

Turnock, B.J. (1997). *Public health: What it is and how it works.* Gaithersburg, MD: Aspen.

U.S. Department of Health and Human Services. (1995). *Health people 2000: Midcourse review and 1995 revisions.* Washington, DC: U.S. Department of Health and Human Services, Public Health Service.

————. (2000). *Healthy people 2010: Understanding and improving health* (2nd ed.). Washington, DC: U.S. Government Printing Office. Available at: http://www.healthypeople.gov/document.

U. S. Public Health Service. (1995). *For a healthy nation: Returns on investment in public health*. Washington, DC: U.S. Department of Health and Human Services, Public Health Service.

Ware, J.E., Jr., Bayliss, M.S., Rogers, W.H., Kosinski, M., & Tarlov, A.R. (1996). Differences in 4-year health outcomes for elderly and poor, chronically ill patients treated in HMO and fee-for-service systems. Results from the Medical Outcomes Study. *Journal of the American Medical Association, 276,* 1039–1047.

Webster, J.R., & Feinglass, J. (1997). Stroke patients, "managed care," and distributive justice. *Journal of the American Medical Association, 278,* 161–162.

Weinstein, H., & Levin, M. (1997, December 15). Smoking foes split as factions oppose industry immunity. Health: As Congressional battle looms, groups struggle over how to gain passage of proposed $368.5 billion settlement. Fissure may threaten the deal, some say. *The Los Angeles Times,* p. A1.

Weinstein, L. (1974). Infectious disease: Retrospect and reminiscence. *The Journal of Infectious Diseases, 129,* 480–492.

Weisberg, J. (1996). *In defense of government: The fall and rise of public trust.* New York: Scribner.

Wickizer, T.M., Lessler, D., & Travis, D.M. (1996). Controlling inpatient psychiatric utilization through managed care. *American Journal of Psychiatry, 153,* 339–345.

5

Marketing Public Health— A Challenge for the Public Health Practitioner

The challenge for the public health practitioner is to market the need for specific public health programs and the need for public health itself in light of diminishing resources; tight budgets; a diversion of potential public health resources to bioterrorism preparedness; and a growing antiregulatory, antigovernment sentiment. The demand for population-based, preventive public health programs among the public and policy makers is low because the perceived benefit (reduction in morbidity and mortality) might not be realized for many years. Programs that can demonstrate an immediate and visible impact are more attractive to policy makers and to the public. Also, the most influential political and economic sectors—business, industry, and powerful special-interest groups—are able to convince policy makers of the immediate costs of public health programs. Not only is the demand for public health programs low, but public health practitioners have not traditionally had to compete for public attention and resources. Public health practitioners have not been in the business of self-promotion. Thus, the challenge to public health professionals includes both redefining the product that public health aims to provide and stimulating demand for this product in a somewhat hostile environment.

Understanding and applying marketing principles can provide public health professionals with the power and ability to compete successfully for the survival of public health programs and for public health as an institution.

Chapter 4 showed that the practice of public health itself is threatened and that public health practitioners must compete for public attention and resources. This chapter explains the reasons why selling the need for public health institutions and public health programs to policy makers and to the public is such a profound challenge for public health practitioners.

From its inception, public health has had to overcome great obstacles to convince policy makers and the public to invest resources and intervene on behalf of society's interest in preserving health. A brief review of some highlights in public health history reveals the many significant barriers to government adoption of public health programs and institutions.

As early as the eighteenth century, public health reforms faced fierce, organized opposition. For example, despite the availability of a safe and effective vaccine against smallpox, inoculation efforts in Europe were widely criticized as interfering with God's will and spreading the disease among healthy people (McNeill, 1989). In France, the widespread resistance to inoculation did not crumble until 1774, when Louis XV died from smallpox (McNeill, 1989).

For 42 years after Dr. James Lind's 1753 paper demonstrated the effectiveness of oranges and lemons in preventing and curing scurvy, the British naval administration failed to commit the resources necessary to provide this preventive intervention to its sailors (McNeill, 1989). Even when the British Navy decided to purchase supplies of citrus juice for all sailors, it chose West Indian limes, which contained a much lower dose of vitamin C than the more expensive Mediterranean lemons. As a result, outbreaks of scurvy on British vessels occurred as late as 1875, 122 years after Lind's discovery (McNeill, 1989).

Modern public health arose as a social reform of the nineteenth century. Society began to recognize illness not only as a sign of spiritual or moral weakness, but also of poor social and environmental conditions (Amick et al., 1995; Institute of Medicine, 1998; McNeill, 1989; Rosen, 1958, 1972; Turnock, 1997; Winslow, 1923). "In the absence of specific etiological concepts, the social and physical conditions which accompanied urbanization were considered equally responsible for the impairment of vital bodily functions and premature death" (Institute of Medicine, 1988, p. 59). Sanitation, and therefore disease control, was then seen as a public responsibility. The control of disease shifted from simply responding to outbreaks of illness to proactively instituting preventive measures. Thus, public health arose out of the establishment of healthy social conditions as a societal goal and the recognition of public institutions as responsible for achieving this social goal (Institute of Medicine, 1988).

In 1842, Edwin Chadwick documented the high prevalence of infectious disease in England and recommended the establishment of national and local boards of health to develop, implement, and maintain a system of sewage and waste disposal (Amick et al., 1995; Chadwick, [1842]

1965; Chave, 1984; Turnock, 1997). Chadwick charged the public with creating the infrastructure necessary to control and prevent the spread of infectious diseases; the public role was accepted and institutionalized in the Public Health Act of 1848. Similar reports published around 1850 by Lemuel Shattuck and John Griscom in the United States laid the foundation for the establishment of a government-directed system of public health surveillance and regulation in this country (Amick et al., 1995; Griscom, [1845] 1970; Institute of Medicine, 1988; Rosenkrantz, 1972; Shattuck, 1850; Winslow, 1923). In 1866, New York became the first large city to establish a permanent Metropolitan Board of Health (Duffy, 1992; Institute of Medicine, 1988; McNeill, 1989; Starr, 1982).

Notably, government action to establish new sanitation systems followed more than a decade of advocacy for such changes by groups of reformers (McNeill, 1989; Turnock, 1997). England's Public Health Act of 1848 was enacted a full 6 years after Chadwick's report. New York City's Metropolitan Board of Health was established 16 years after the Shattuck and Griscom reports.

The initial outbreaks of cholera in the United States in 1832 were met with limited interventions, such as cleaning the streets, caring for the sick, and disposing of the dead (Duffy, 1992). Duffy (1992) noted that "although the cholera epidemic of 1832 shocked the country and literally panicked many citizens, insofar as public health was concerned, its impact was fleeting. . . . Cities and towns, particularly those affected by the outbreak, temporarily remedied the worst sanitary abuses, but within a year or two sanitary conditions were even worse than before. None of the health agencies that came into existence as a result of the epidemic continued to function once the danger was past" (pp. 84, 91).

A reemergence of widespread cholera outbreaks in the United States between 1849 and 1854 led public health advocates to call for sanitary reforms, but their protests were largely ignored. State and local governments did not invest in major changes in societal infrastructure until the mid-1860s, when the nation was threatened by yet another epidemic of cholera. "In almost every American city the cholera outbreaks of the mid-nineteenth century occasioned sanitary surveys and reports. And in almost every case these reports recommended the building of water and sewer systems, the institution of street-cleaning and garbage-collection programs, the creation of strong sanitary measures" (Duffy, 1992, p. 100).

Ultimately, it took the threat of a reemergence of a cholera epidemic in England to precipitate Parliamentary action in 1848 (McNeill, 1989) and the threat of a third wave of approaching cholera to prompt the establishment of a formal and permanent Metropolitan Board of Health in New York City in 1866 (Duffy, 1992; McNeill, 1989; Rosenberg, 1962; Starr, 1982), almost 25 years after Chadwick's report and 15 years after similar reports by Shattuck and Griscom.

One reason for delayed implementation of sanitary reforms was that the early cholera epidemics largely affected the poor and were perceived as a scourge on their filthy living conditions. As Duffy (1992) pointed out, "in New Orleans, where civic leaders insisted that only strangers and the intemperate poor fell prey to pestilential disorders, the city's experience with cholera merely reinforced their belief" (p. 84). Further, the large capital expenditures required to build water and sewage systems would increase taxes for the wealthy. Duffy explained that "the upper classes in general had no desire to tax themselves for the welfare of the poor" (p. 100).

The necessary reforms were finally adopted only when the impending cholera outbreaks threatened to affect all segments of society. During the urbanization and industrialization of the nineteenth century, infectious diseases began to ravage the entire population, rich and poor alike. In New York City, for example, an 1865 field survey found more than 1,200 cases of smallpox and more than 2,000 cases of typhus in a single tenement district (Institute of Medicine, 1988; Winslow, 1923). Moreover, persons of all social classes were susceptible to these contagious diseases. "Increasingly, it dawned upon the rich that they could not ignore the plight of the poor; the proximity of gold coast and slum was too close" (Institute of Medicine, 1988, p. 59). Whereas disease had previously been viewed as a problem of the underclass, the poor, and the morally flawed, contagion throughout communities of rich and poor alike fostered the view of disease as a societal, not a personal, problem. "Poverty and disease could no longer be treated simply as individual failings" (Institute of Medicine, 1988, p. 59). The implication of this change in the disease paradigm was profound: Disease was a societal problem, thus prevention and control were societal responsibilities. Social reform gave rise to the establishment of public health agencies (Institute of Medicine, 1988). And because unhealthy social and environmental conditions threatened not only the poor but the entire community, public health came to be seen as a public responsibility (McNeill, 1989; Rosenkrantz, 1972).

Other governments were even slower to respond to the need for sanitary reforms. For example, Hamburg, Germany, held back the necessary expenditures to establish a clean water supply until 1892 when a widespread cholera epidemic affected all social classes in the city (McNeill, 1989).

The public in general, and government in particular, were relatively apathetic to the welfare of the poor. Public health advocates countered this sentiment in order to secure funding for many of their programs. "Health and social reformers inveighed against the prevailing social injustices and unsanitary conditions of the times, but the propertied classes had little concern for the welfare of the poor, and without their support little could be done" (Duffy, 1992, p. 118).

The delay in implementing sanitary reforms also was due, in part, to political opposition, especially the firmly held principle of individual freedom and control over one's property (McNeill, 1989). Installation of water and sewer pipes required intrusion onto private property as well as huge capital expenditures. The challenge to public health reformers at the time was not one of finding effective solutions, but of convincing policy makers to adopt these solutions. As McNeill (1989) explained, "The problem as it presented itself to sanitary reformers of the 1830s and 1840s was less one of technique than of organization. . . . a libertarian prejudice against regulation, infringing the individual's right to do what he chose with his own property was deeply rooted" (p. 239). Duffy (1992) argued that government did not respond more aggressively to the first wave of cholera because it was hesitant to infringe on "individual liberty and private property rights" (p. 84).

Public health measures were perceived as treading not only on individual rights but also on the rights and opportunities of business owners. The development of water and sewer systems was very costly. Other public health measures, such as quarantines, were perceived as interfering with free enterprise and harmful to business and economic development. For example, in 1866 the city of Memphis rejected its Board of Health's recommendations for preventing a cholera epidemic (Duffy, 1992). "The dominant commercial interests in Memphis reflected the prevailing view in the urban South that the only functions of government were to protect property and preserve the existing social order. That quarantines hindered trade and that sanitary programs cost money only reinforced this assumption" (p. 115).

Paul Starr (1982), in *The Social Transformation of American Medicine*, reinforced Duffy's point:

> The economic boundaries of public health were determined partly by constraints of cost—not simply the direct cost of public health programs to taxpayers, but the indirect cost of such measures to business and to society at large. In the first half of the nineteenth century, some authorities attributed epidemics to contagion and recommended quarantines—an economically damaging measure because of the disruption of commerce. Others ascribed epidemics to miasmas and advised general cleanups of the environment. The environmental approach may have been favored by commercial interest because it was less disruptive than the closing of markets. But wholesale cleanups and quarantines were both costly responses to disease. (p. 189)

Public health measures often have been perceived as interfering not with individual or business rights, but with individual behavior. As the Institute of Medicine (1988) explained, "repeatedly, the role of the government in regulating individual behavior has been challenged" (p. 71). Soon after it was formed, Britian's Board of Health was disbanded because Chadwick, its director, "claimed a wide scope for state intervention in an age when laissez-faire was the doctrine of the day" (Chave, 1984, p. 7).

A fourth reason for the delay in implementing sanitary reforms was that the public seemed interested in public health only during an outbreak—there was little interest in instituting preventive measures. For example, Duffy (1992) explained that despite the widespread second wave of cholera in the United States in the mid-nineteenth century, recommendations of public health reformers were ignored because citizens quickly lost interest after the epidemic disappeared: "Carrying out these recommendations would have required relatively huge capital expenditures and large increases in annual government budgets, but once cholera had disappeared, the average citizen had little interest in public health" (p. 100).

The routine nature of endemic infectious diseases also might explain why government officials did not respond with greater urgency (Duffy, 1971; Leavitt, 1982; Rosenberg, 1962). "The endemic disorders responsible for the high morbidity and mortality rates were all too familiar, and without the stimulus provided by a strange and highly fatal pestilence, the average citizen had little interest in—and even less inclination to spend money for—public health" (Duffy, 1992, p. 179). During the late 1800s, tuberculosis, diphtheria, scarlet fever, and typhoid were the chief killers, but newspapers and the public paid little attention (Duffy, 1992). Instead, "the press and the public worried about Asiatic cholera, which was of no consequence after 1873, and smallpox, which was relatively minor compared to the other epidemic disorders" (p. 179). Why the lack of public concern? According to Duffy, all of these endemic disorders "were familiar ones" (p. 179).

Leavitt (1982), discussing the history of Milwaukee's public health system, made a similar point:

> The frightening and dramatic quality of the unexpected provided the first impetus to health reform. . . . When smallpox or cholera threatened Milwaukee, citizens reacted vigorously. Not only were these diseases infrequent visitors, and therefore possibly preventable, they also carried ghastly symptoms and produced perilous outcomes. . . . Because of the fear generated at times of acute distress, epidemics frequently increased the power and authority of the health department. Conversely, chronic diseases, which killed more people than the epidemics, did not easily win the attention of citizen groups or health officials. (pp. 241, 242)

Leavitt (1982) explained: "The Milwaukee experience abounds with other examples that support the contention that unusual and acute disasters encouraged health reforms more than did the typical endemic problems. Tuberculosis, the city's major killer, received almost no attention until the turn of the twentieth century, in part because it was familiar, its symptoms lacked drama, and the disease took many years to kill its victims" (p. 243).

Even during colonial times, disease was viewed as a burden on society only when it represented something that was not well understood, something mysterious, or something unfamiliar—all conditions that evoke societal fear. As Duffy (1992) noted, malaria was by far the greatest threat to health and life in colonial times, but the epidemics that aroused the most attention during this period were smallpox and yellow fever. Although malaria was far more significant in terms of its public health burden on society, smallpox and yellow fever were less predictable, less well understood, more mysterious, and brought about quicker, more visible, and more graphic death:

> They appeared mysteriously, swept through the community with deadly force, struck down old and young alike, and brought a ghastly death to many of their victims. . . . The constant references in colonial letters, diaries, journals, newspapers, and official records to the two great killer diseases, smallpox and yellow fever, speak more for their dramatic nature than for their actual impact upon colonial health. People have always feared strange and unknown dangers far more than familiar ones, and this holds true for diseases. (Duffy, 1992, p. 23)

A final reason for the delay in implementing public health reforms was organized opposition from the medical profession, which historically has viewed many public health programs as intrusions on its autonomy. As Starr (1982) explained, "extending the boundaries of public health to incorporate more of medicine seemed necessary and desirable to some public health officials, but as one might imagine, private practitioners regarded such extensions as a usurpation. Doctors fought against public treatment of the sick, requirements for reporting cases of tuberculosis and venereal disease, and attempts by public health authorities to establish health centers to coordinate preventive and curative medical services" (p. 181).

Perhaps the most striking example of medical opposition to public health measures was the medical profession's opposition to the proposal for a series of rural health centers in New York State in the 1920s. "When the bill came before the state legislature, it had the backing of public health, social welfare, labor, and farming groups, but was opposed by the medical profession. The doctors' opposition, according to C.E.A. Winslow's account, proved fatal" (Starr, 1982, p. 196).

Starr (1982) summarized public health's perpetual struggle against social forces that oppose government intervention into personal or societal interests: "Much of the history of public health is a record of struggles over the limits of its mandate. On one frontier, public health authorities have met opposition from religious groups and others with moral objections to state intervention on behalf of the officially sponsored conceptions of health and hygiene. On another frontier, public health has met opposition from business and commerce, anxious to protect their economic interests" (pp. 180–181).

The lessons of public health history have three important implications in terms of the marketing environment that public health practitioners face. First, the nature of the public health product puts it in an unfavorable state of demand by the public and by policy makers. Second, the environment in which public health must be marketed is hostile. Third, the type of effort required to market public health involves skills that many public health practitioners have not developed and that are rarely taught to public health students. The reasons that marketing public health is a formidable challenge for the public health practitioner are explored in the following sections.

■ AN UNFAVORABLE STATE OF DEMAND FOR PUBLIC HEALTH PROGRAMS

As was just described, the public and policy makers have not demanded public health programs and policies and public health as an institution. The great public health reforms of the nineteenth century, for example, took many years of persistent advocacy by public health practitioners before they were adopted. From the foregoing discussion, several major reasons for the low level of public and political demand for public health interventions can be identified. The common denominator is that the benefits of public health programs are remote in time and remote in the mind of the consumer. In contrast, the benefits of medical interventions are usually immediate, both in time and in the mind of the patient. This point is illustrated by comparing characteristics of the benefits of medical interventions and public health programs.

The benefits of medical treatment are usually immediate. A patient with appendicitis, for example, entered the hospital in severe pain and with her life in jeopardy. Within hours of surgery, the patient's condition was stabilized and her pain was relieved. On the other hand, the very nature of prevention implies that benefits will not be seen for a long time after intervention, sometimes for many years. For example, cities that invested in new water and sewer systems did not benefit for many years.

Although improved sanitation might prevent an epidemic from occurring in the future, it cannot alleviate the epidemic conditions that already exist. Similarly, the benefits of programs that prevent smoking among adolescents, decrease fat intake, or increase physical activity might not be seen until many years later.

Because of the immediate benefits of medical treatment and interventions to control communicable diseases, it is easy to convince policy makers of the need for medical treatment and for infectious disease control programs. When Ebola virus attacks, people die within days and the immediate survival of a community is imminently threatened. It is easy to see the benefit of intervening to treat victims of Ebola infection. When an epidemic of smoking affects youth in a community, there is no immediate threat to survival or even to health. The benefits of intervention are not as readily apparent, not as immediate, and not nearly as compelling.

The benefits of public health interventions are remote in time as well as in the mind of the consumer, while the connection between a medical intervention and its benefits is much more apparent to the observer. For example, the benefits of instituting sanitary reforms were not visible when New York City's Metropolitan Board of Health was established in 1866, although it resulted in far better control of the subsequent cholera outbreak. In the public's perception, there simply were fewer victims after the implementation of the reforms.

The remote connection between public health programs and their benefits makes it more difficult to market public health programs to policy makers. Few, if any, policy makers question whether treatment of heart attack victims has a positive impact on their health and survival or whether treatment of victims of infectious diseases is beneficial. Even without scientific demonstration of a positive impact of treatment, a strong and unquestioned link between treatment and outcome is present, leading, for example, to the expenditure of billions of health care dollars on increasing the quantity, but not the quality, of the later years of life. In contrast, the relation between public health interventions and effects is often questioned seriously, even when scientific evidence clearly demonstrates a significant effect of the public health program on both longevity and quality of life. Despite a wealth of evidence that public assistance helps alleviate poverty and make life more tolerable for the impoverished, policy makers continue to question this link, even suggesting that public assistance causes the poverty. Mikhail et al. (1997) noted that "curative services often have been judged by their perceived value, while preventive services have been held to a more rigorous standard of documentation" (p. 37).

Because the results of public health programs often are invisible, it is much more difficult to develop vocal constituencies around public health issues than around medical treatment issues. As Turnock (1997) explained, "prevention efforts often lack a clear constituency because success results in unseen consequences. Because these consequences are unseen, people are less likely to develop an attachment for or to support the efforts preventing them. Advocates for mental health services, care for individuals with development disabilities, organ transplants, and end-stage renal disease often make their presence felt. But few state capitols have seen candlelight demonstrations by thousands of people who did not get diphtheria" (p. 20).

A major reason for the obscurity of the impact of public health programs, especially those that address chronic disease, is that the outcomes are neither visible nor graphic. The effect of medical treatment (or its absence), however, is highly visible and pervasive in our culture, especially through the media. Movies such as *Outbreak* and *Twelve Monkeys* show the immediate and vividly disturbing consequences of infection with "killer' viruses. Television portrays the immediate impact of treatment in medical emergencies weekly on shows like *ER* and *Trauma: Life in the ER*. Television news stories show vivid images of Hurricane Katrina victims on New Orleans rooftops, prompting an outpouring of concern and money for medical aid. No equally compelling images exist for most public health problems and interventions.

Harvard University researcher Graham Colditz explained: "One of the things we can't get away from is that if you're in a clinic treating patients with cancer, you can count the number treated and the successes. But if you have 10,000 people who increase their physical activity and 10 fewer of them get colon cancer in 10 years, well, those people are not identifiable. That's particularly frustrating when you're trying to lobby for dollars for prevention" (Lauerman, 1997, p. 14).

Mikhail and colleagues (1997) made the distinction between "identified" lives and "statistical" lives and argued that society favors treatment programs over prevention programs because they address the needs of identifiable individuals. "The clear social preference is to provide health care resources to respond to specific and immediate needs of identified individuals. By its very nature, prevention generally deals with amorphous populations; curative care deals with identified personalized lives and thus seems to carry a greater societal ethical imperative for committing resources in response to specific health care needs" (p. 38).

The nature of the demand for public health compared with medical intervention also is different in terms of its urgency. Physicians do not typically go out into the community trying to stimulate demand for medical treatment: When people become sick, they demand medical treatment. This is not the case with public health. The presence of public health problems does not itself imply an immediate demand for intervention. Usually, the demand for public health attention is dormant until a crisis arises. The nature of demand for public health interventions during the nineteenth century largely followed such a pattern. While temporary public health programs were established with each of the three waves of the cholera epidemic, demand dissipated when the outbreaks subsided.

Medical interventions often involve technological problems and solutions, while public health problems usually require social, economic, and political solutions. Americans tend to view technological challenges as a true test of the nation's strength. Atwood, Colditz, and Kawachi (1997) compared U.S. investment in sequencing the human genome with the limited effort in controlling tobacco use: "Tobacco is responsible for 30% of all cancer deaths, while 5% to 10% can be linked to inherited genetic causes. Yet the tobacco control budget of the National Cancer Institute (NCI) amounted to $60 million in 1996, as compared with the multibillion-dollar research project under way to sequence the human genome" (p. 1604).

■ A HOSTILE ENVIRONMENT FOR MARKETING PUBLIC HEALTH PROGRAMS

Because public health interventions often interfere with individual rights or behavior, or the conduct and livelihood of business, marketing public health programs often is done in a hostile environment. By their very nature, public health programs tend to interfere with personal behaviors and might well be interpreted as interfering with individual rights. As John Duffy (1992) noted in *The Sanitarians: A History of American Public Health*, "unfortunately, sanitary and health regulations inevitably infringe on individual rights, a situation compounded by the general American distrust of all laws and regulations. . . . The zealous guarding of individual rights creates major problems for health officials in a democracy" (p. 3).

For this reason, public health measures often run up against fierce opposition by many stakeholders, including the public. Regulations against public smoking are criticized on the grounds that individuals have the right to decide when and where to smoke and that infringing on this freedom will lead to regulating other aspects of personal behavior, including eating, drinking, and exercising. In such an environment, public health advocates aiming to reduce tobacco-related mortality are considered zealots seeking prohibition.

Not only do population-based, preventive, public health programs tend to intrude into the lives of individuals, they also often interfere with the autonomy of business and the perceived integrity of the free enterprise system. Public health programs often are seen as intruding into the free market system and placing undue economic burdens on business owners. The debate over public health regulations often is framed in terms of health versus wealth, implying that public health programs are, by definition, economically harmful.

In contrast, medical treatment programs are viewed as providing the individual with personal freedoms and individual rights. Efforts to limit the provision of medical care are attacked as being unfair encroachments on the health care system. Even when medical treatment does affect personal freedom, society often sanctions the treatment on the grounds that it safeguards the rights of other individuals. For example, several states have enacted laws that require pregnant women who are infected with the human immunodeficiency virus (HIV) to be treated with AZT. Although this interferes far more with individual freedom than do most public health programs, society still views forced treatment as a mechanism to ensure the rights of others—in this case, the unborn child.

The appropriateness of medical treatment interventions also tends to be unquestioned from an economic perspective. Even when their potential cost-effectiveness is not clear, treatment interventions generally are acceptable (Mikhail et al., 1997). Treatment programs are rarely challenged on the grounds that they will adversely affect the nation's economy in spite of the tremendous burden placed on the national economy by the increasing costs of medical treatment.

In addition to interfering with individual rights and business autonomy, public health programs often run up against firmly held social and economic norms. Because the central goal of effective public health interventions is to change social and economic conditions or policies, these interventions must in some way challenge existing norms. In contrast, medical treatment programs tend to support the established economic norms of the health care system. The more specialists, specialized equipment, and specialized procedures there are, the more deeply entrenched the health care industry becomes as an economic force in society. On the other hand, poorly funded public health agencies have been accused of promoting programs simply to ensure their continued personal livelihood. "Implications for life-style and resource allocation inherent in the modern definition of public health are often in conflict with prevailing social policy or perceived feasibility in an age of growing awareness of scarcity and debate regarding the limits of government" (Ellencweig & Yoshpe, 1984, p. 75).

The presence of opposition groups that fight public health measures that they perceive will harm their economic livelihood make for a hostile environment for marketing public health. In contrast, no established industry opposes medical treatment programs because they perceive them as threats to economic viability. For example, there is no anti-liver transplant industry opposing the extreme medical interventions required to treat liver disease. However, as soon as one proposes regulations on the advertising or sale of alcohol to prevent the need for some liver transplants, one runs into well-funded and well-organized opposition from the alcoholic beverage industry.

Often, public health programs run up against industries whose financial interests would be directly affected by the implementation of the program. Public health interventions to reduce alcohol and tobacco use, for example, can be successful only if they reduce alcohol and tobacco sales and therefore the profits of these industries. In contrast, there are no major special-interest groups whose primary purpose is to oppose medical treatment programs. There is no pro-hypertension industry, for example, that opposes treatment of hypertension. However, if public health officials were to propose a federal program to prevent hypertension in the population by regulating the sodium content of foods, a large and powerful food industry would be waiting for them at the Capitol steps. As Ellencweig and Yoshpe (1984) explained, "emphasis upon preventive medicine and environment threatens most prevailing systems of medical care organization and entrenched industrial and professional lobbies" (p. 75).

■ LIMITED CAPACITY OF PUBLIC HEALTH PRACTITIONERS TO COMPETE FOR PUBLIC ATTENTION AND RESOURCES

Because public health practitioners generally are not trained in marketing, communications, political science, and public relations, it might be difficult for them to compete in the battle to secure scarce resources to fund their programs. To gain attention and resources, public health practitioners must be able to work with lawmakers in the legislative process, build constituencies and coalitions, and form collaborative relations with other organizations. And to generate public understanding, appreciation, and support, they must employ public relations techniques and marketing and communications principles. The lack of training of public health practitioners in these areas makes the marketing challenge particularly difficult.

Fred Kroger, former director of the Centers for Disease Control and Prevention's Office of Health Communications, summarized:

> When colleagues at the state and local levels try to sell city councils, their boards of supervisors, or their state legislators on the merits of public health, folks are not buying. Some in public health have even admitted publicly that public health has done a singularly poor job of marketing. (Kroger et al., p. 273)

In addition, public health practitioners generally have not played the same kind of prominent leadership and advocacy roles for themselves, their programs, and their institutions that they have played for the health of their constituents. To promote the continued survival and growth of public health as an institution, public health practitioners must take more prominent leadership and advocacy roles, guided by improved competence in political advocacy.

■ CONCLUSION

Stimulating demand for public health programs is a formidable challenge for the public health practitioner because public health programs (1) tend to have delayed benefits that are not easily recognized and are not visible, (2) are perceived as intruding into individual autonomy and the free enterprise system or as conflicting with established social and economic norms, and (3) face heavy opposition by powerful special-interest groups.

Fortunately, the strategic application of marketing principles can be a powerful tool in redefining and repositioning public health as a product that is in demand by the public and by policy makers. Chapter 6 demonstrates that marketing public health is both a challenge and an opportunity for the public health practitioner.

References

Amick, B.C., III, Levine, S., Tarlov, A.R., & Walsh, D.C. (1995). Introduction. In B.C. Amick, III, S. Levine, A.R. Tarlov, & D.C. Walsh (Eds.), *Society and health* (pp. 3–17). New York: Oxford University Press.

Atwood, K., Colditz, G.A., & Kawachi, I. (1997). From public health science to prevention policy: Placing science in its social and political contexts. *American Journal of Public Health, 87,* 1603–1606.

Chadwick, E. ([1842] 1965). *Report on the sanitary condition of the labouring population of Great Britain.* Edinburgh, Scotland: Edinburgh University Press.

Chave, S.P.W. (1984). The origins and development of public health. In W.W. Holland, R. Detels, & G. Knox (Eds.), *Oxford textbook of public health: Vol 1. History, determinants, scope and strategies.* New York: Oxford University Press.

Duffy, J. (1971). Social impact of disease in the late 19th century. *Bulletin of the New York Academy of Medicine, 47,* 797–811.

———. (1992). *The sanitarians: A history of American public health.* Urbana, IL: University of Illinois Press.

Ellencweig, A., & Yoshpe, R. (1984). Definition of public health. *Public Health Review, 12,* 65–78.

Griscom, J.H. ([1845] 1970). *The sanitary condition of the laboring population of New York,* New York: Arno.

Institute of Medicine, Committee for the Study of the Future of Public Health. (1988). *The future of public health.* Washington, DC: National Academy Press.

Kroger, F., McKenna, J.W., Shepherd, M., Howze, E.H., & Knight, D.S. (1997). Marketing public health: The CDC experience. In M.E. Goldberg, M. Fishbein, & S.E. Middlestadt (Eds.). *Social marketing: Theoretical and practical perspectives* (pp. 267–290). Mahwah, NJ: Lawrence Erlbaum Associates.

Lauerman, J.F. (1997). Combating cancer: The power of prevention has scarcely been tapped. *Harvard Magazine, 99,* 11–14.

Leavitt, J.W. (1982). *The healthiest city. Milwaukee and the politics of health reform.* Princeton, NJ: Princeton University Press.

McNeill, W.H. (1989). *Plagues and peoples.* New York: Anchor Books.

Mikhail, O.I., Swint, J.M., Casperson, P.R., & Spitz, M.R. (1997). Health care's double standard: The prevention dilemma. *Journal of Public Health Management and Practice, 3,* 37–42.

Rosen, G. (1958). *A history of public health*. New York: MD Publications.
———. (1972). The evolution of social medicine. In H.E. Freeman, S. Levine, & L.G. Reeder (Eds.), *Handbook of medical sociology*, 2nd ed., pp. 30–60. Englewood Cliffs, NJ: Prentice-Hall.
Rosenberg, C.E. (1962). *The cholera years: The United States in 1832, 1849, and 1866*. Chicago: University of Chicago Press.
Rosenkrantz, B.G. (1972). *Public health and the state*. Cambridge, MA: Harvard University Press.
Shattuck, L. (1850). *Report of the Sanitary Commission of Massachusetts, 1850*. Boston: Dutton & Wentworth: State Printers.
Starr, P. (1982). *The social transformation of American medicine*. New York: Basic Books.
Turnock, B.J. (1997). *Public health: What it is and how it works*. Gaithersburg, MD: Aspen.
Winslow, C-E.A. (1923). *The evolution and significance of the modern public health campaign*. New Haven, CT: Yale University Press.

CHAPTER 6

Marketing Public Health— An Opportunity for the Public Health Practitioner

Public health practitioners must market population-based, preventive public health programs in the absence of significant demand among the public and policy makers for these programs. They must also market the need for public health itself in hostile and competitive political and social environments. The strategic use of marketing principles can help public health practitioners effectively confront these challenges. The key is to abandon the traditional approach of deciding what they want the public and policy makers to buy and then attempting to sell this product to an audience that has little demand for it. Instead, public health practitioners must first identify the needs and desires of the audience and then redefine, package, position, and frame the product in such a way that it satisfies an existing demand among the target audience.

The public health practitioner must be able to offer programs with a benefit that the audience appreciates and demands, to back up this offer, and to communicate an image of public health programs or the public health institution that reinforces core values of the target audience.

Chapter 5 demonstrated that public health practitioners must sell the need for specific public health programs and for public health itself to a public and to policy makers for whom the demand is low. Fortunately, the strategic application of basic marketing principles can provide the public health practitioner with a powerful tool to promote public health programs and policies and to establish public health as a highly regarded societal institution.

This chapter discusses the two major steps in marketing a public health program or policy: (1) identifying the needs, wants, and core values of the target audience to define the product as beneficial to that audience; and (2) packaging and positioning the program or policy so that it reinforces the core values of the target audience.

■ DEFINING THE PRODUCT: THE IMPORTANCE OF FORMATIVE RESEARCH IN MARKETING PUBLIC HEALTH POLICIES AND PROGRAMS

The first marketing principle that the public health practitioner must apply is the importance of identifying and understanding the needs and wants of the target audience and defining the product so that it offers a benefit that is desired by the target audience. Two major audiences for promoting a public health program or policy are policy makers and the public. Too often, public health practitioners determine the benefits that policy makers and the public ought to want and then attempt to sell these benefits even when there is low, or no, demand. Often, for example, practitioners try to sell a program or a policy based solely on the benefit of improving the health of individual members of society.

However, as described in Chapter 5, the intrinsic presence of disease among the population was not the policy makers' motivation for adopting major public health programs, policies, and reforms over the past two centuries. It was fear of the political and economic consequences of losing control over the spread of disease. The prospect of disease is dreaded not because it signifies that individuals are sick or suffering, but because it represents a threat to a society's freedom, independence, autonomy, and control. Just as freedom, independence, autonomy, and control form the individual's core values and underscore the value he or she places on health, the policy maker holds these same values, which explains his or her desire to exert some control over the spread of disease in society (see Appendix 6-A).

Therefore, in defining the public health product in a campaign to promote a public health program or policy, the practitioner may need to go beyond simply offering health as the benefit to society. The public health practitioner must redefine the product and its benefits. The product is not health for society's members, but something more basic, more compelling, and more at the core of the American policy makers' values system. The product is the preservation of freedom, independence, autonomy, and control for society.

While public health practitioners traditionally have based their public health campaigns solely on what they think should be important— health—their opponents have used marketing principles to define their campaign themes. They determine what the consumer (the public or policy makers) wants and then design, package, and position the product so that it satisfies the need. Often this leads to campaigns based on themes that have little to do with health. The marketing research process is used not only in consumer product campaigns to influence individual behavior, but it also is used in political campaigns to promote or oppose a specific legislative policy or program.

An example of the use of marketing research to defeat a public health campaign was the insurance industry's effort to defeat President Clinton's proposed health care reform initiative in 1994. The Coalition for Health Insurance Choices, an insurance industry front, conducted a carefully crafted media and grassroots lobbying campaign based on extensive research (Stauber & Rampton, 1995). Stauber and Rampton (1995) described how the coalition used formative research to identify campaign themes that would resonate with voters: "Instead of forming a single coalition, health reform opponents used opinion polling to develop a point-by-point list of vulnerabilities in the Clinton administration proposal and organized more than 20 separate coalitions to hammer away at each point" (p. 96). Campaign organizer Blair Childs emphasized the importance of formative research: "in naming your coalition . . . use words that you've identified in your research. There are certain words that . . . have a general positive reaction. That's where focus group and survey work can be very beneficial. 'Fairness,' 'balance,' 'choice,' 'coalition,' and 'alliance' are all words that resonate very positively" (Stauber & Rampton, 1995, pp. 96, 97).

Using careful, formative research, the coalition framed Clinton's health reform proposal in a way that conflicted with the core values of American voters, generating subsequent opposition to the proposal. The coalition identified a fear among Americans that government-sponsored health care would "bankrupt the country, reduce the quality of care, and lead to jail terms for people who wanted to stick with their family doctor" (Stauber & Rampton, 1995, p. 97). Clinton's proposal was framed as the archetypal example of government-sponsored health care, which would take away all individual choice, put health care into a helpless bureaucracy, hurt small businesses, and eliminate America's position as the international leader in quality of medical care. These messages appealed to the American core values of independence, autonomy, self-determination, free choice, free enterprise, capitalism, economic stability, and the democratic principle. With these core values at the heart of its arguments, it is no surprise that the insurance coalition's campaign was so effective.

A now-legendary television spot vividly illustrated to the public how the Clinton plan would affect them personally. In it, a middle-class couple named Harry and Louise lamented "the complexity of Clinton's plan and the menace of a new 'billion-dollar bureaucracy,' . . . 'Harry and Louise' symbolized everything that went wrong with the great health care struggle of 1994" (Stauber & Rampton, 1995, p. 97). Harry and

Louise became a symbol for the entire campaign and effectively suggested that the Clinton plan represented the opposite of everything for which America is supposed to stand. A pro-health-care reform campaign that relied primarily on the arguments that millions of Americans lacked health insurance, that the costs of health care were increasing, and that the insurance and pharmaceutical industries were acting irresponsibly (White House Domestic Policy Council, 1993) simply could not stand up against a campaign for the hearts and minds of the American people.

Another excellent example of the use of marketing research to defeat a public health campaign is the tobacco industry's successful effort to defeat a proposed Montana ballot initiative to raise the state cigarette excise tax in 1990. The tobacco industry did not restrict itself to the health-oriented aspects of the proposed cigarette tax in fighting this initiative. Nor did it design its campaign based on the public health community's definition and packaging of the product (Moon, Males, & Nelson, 1993). Instead, the tobacco industry conducted marketing research to identify the basic needs and desires of the Montana voters, messages that would and would not appeal to the voters, and the core values influencing their voting intentions. The industry then redefined the product and reframed the discussion over the product's benefits and costs such that voting against the initiative would be perceived as fulfilling the identified needs and desires and as reinforcing the most influential core values of Montana voters. Specifically, freedom, security, and fairness were targeted by tobacco interests as campaign messages to discourage voters from supporting the tax increase.

First the tobacco industry argued that the ballot initiative would interfere with the core value of security by causing cigarette smuggling problems: Gang members would bootleg cigarettes from nearby states with lower taxes. Second, the industry showed how the proposal conflicted with the core values of fairness and equality: Poor families would be harder hit by the cigarette tax than wealthier families. Third, the industry explained that the initiative would take control away from the voters: Bureaucrats would take the taxpayers' money and use it however they saw fit. Fourth, the proposed cigarette tax interfered with the core values of freedom and autonomy: The proposal represented an effort on the part of special-interest groups to override the concerns of the people of Montana and to manipulate voters into establishing programs favored by these special-interest groups. At the most basic level, the tobacco industry was not selling opposition to the initiative; it was selling freedom and independence, fairness, security, control over one's life, individual rights, and the democratic ideal.

In contrast, the public health coalition in Montana did not conduct extensive marketing research studies. Because of the lack of adequate resources, only one poll was conducted during the campaign. The coalition defined and positioned the initiative based on its health content alone and on speculation about the health benefits that would be most important to the voters: reducing the number of smokers, preventing children from starting to smoke, reducing exposure to secondhand smoke, and establishing better prenatal care programs for poor families.

A third example of how opponents of public health policies use marketing principles to fight reform comes from the environmental health movement. Stauber and Rampton (1995) explained how corporations that pollute the environment also use marketing principles to prevent significant policy reforms that could hurt their profits. Many corporations hire sophisticated public relations, marketing, and advertising firms to determine what the public thinks about them and about environmental policy issues. In this way, they learn how to frame environmental policy issues so that citizens perceive increased environmental regulation as conflicting with their core values. Joanna Underwood, president of one environmental research firm, explained the importance of talking to people to find out how they think: "Companies must have some vehicle for knowing what the intelligent public thinks about their products and processes. If they want to understand sophisticated outside views of environmental issues affecting their companies, they would do well to have someone in the room" (Stauber & Rampton, 1995, pp. 127, 128). Too often, public health practitioners attempt to design policy campaigns without having anyone else "in the room."

The key strategy of corporate polluters, according to Stauber and Rampton (1995), is to frame environmental issues so that the blame is shifted from corporations to the individual. In other words, these corporations rely on the core American value of rugged individualism, convincing people that individual actions are at the root of environmental problems. "In place of systemic analysis and systemic solutions to social problems, they offer an individualistic and deeply hypocritical analysis in which 'all of us' are to blame for our collective 'irresponsibility.' If we would all just pick up after ourselves . . . the problems would go away" (Stauber & Rampton, 1995, p. 132).

About 200 companies funded an organization called Keep America Beautiful, the "industry's most organized proponent of the belief that individual irresponsibility is at the root of the pollution" (Stauber & Rampton, 1995, p. 133). Although these companies produce products that are estimated to account for about a third of the material in U.S. landfills, Keep America Beautiful's message to consumers is that they are responsible for the trash problem in this country. Although Keep America Beautiful has used more than half a billion dollars of donated advertising time and space to encourage guilty consumers to "put litter in its place," the organization's leadership "opposes a national bottle bill that would place a deposit on glass and metal drink containers" (Stauber & Rampton, 1995, p. 133). These companies are strategically applying basic marketing principles to reframe the issue of environmental pollution so that responsibility for the problem shifts from the corporation to the individual.

Just as the industries that oppose public health programs and policies use marketing principles to convince the public that these policies are detrimental, public health practitioners must begin to use marketing principles to promote them. The key is to redefine the public health product and its benefits in a way that appeals to the most compelling core values of the target audience. To do this, the public health practitioner must first abandon the traditional approach of deciding for himself or herself what product he or she wants the target audience to buy and then attempting to sell this product to an audience that has little demand for it. Instead, the public health practitioner must begin to use formative research to determine what the public wants and to identify the arguments, messages, themes, and values that are highly salient and influential among these target groups. Case studies that demonstrate how practitioners can accomplish this are reviewed in Chapters 7 and 8, and the process is detailed in Chapters 11 and 12.

■ PACKAGING AND POSITIONING THE PRODUCT: FRAMING PUBLIC HEALTH PROGRAMS AND POLICIES

We have just explained that the first step in marketing a public health program or policy is to define the product such that it offers benefits that will satisfy the needs and desires of the public, and that formative research is an essential tool to identify these basic needs and desires. The second step is to package and position the program or policy so that it communicates these benefits in a way that reinforces the core values of the public—both general citizens and policy makers. The public health practitioner must provide support for the promised benefits and must communicate a compelling image for the product. The process of packaging and positioning a public health program or policy so that it reinforces the public's core values is called framing.

In the remainder of this chapter, we explain the process of framing public health programs and policies in order to tap into core values of policy makers and the public. We illustrate how opposition marketers (e.g., the tobacco industry) frame public health programs in a way that leads the public to perceive the program as conflicting with basic core values. We then demonstrate how issues can be reframed in such a way that the desired public health policy or program is actually perceived as reinforcing these same core values.

Framing—Definition and Examples

A *frame* is a way of packaging and positioning an issue to convey a certain meaning (Andreasen, 2006; Chapman & Lupton, 1994; Entman, 1993; Gamson & Lasch, 1983; Gamson & Modigliani, 1989; Iyengar,

1991; Kaniss, 1991; Ryan, 1991; Schon & Rein, 1994; Wallack & Dorfman, 1996; Wallack et al., 1993). Framing has been described as the emphasis placed around particular issues "that seeks to define 'what this issue is really about'" (Chapman & Lupton, 1994, p. 12) and as "the process by which someone packages a group of facts to create a story" (Wallack et al., 1993, p. 68). Schon and Rein (1994) defined frames as "the broadly shared beliefs, values, and perspectives familiar to the members of a societal culture and likely to endure in that culture over long periods of time, on which individuals and institutions draw in order to give meaning, sense, and normative direction to their thinking and action in policy matters" (p. xiii).

In 1922, political pundit and author Walter Lippmann wrote that people see the world through certain frameworks and that these frameworks affect what a person sees. Lippmann wrote, "We do not first see, and then define, we define first and then see" (Steel, 1981, p. 181). Steel (1981) expanded on the point: "We define, not at random, but according to 'stereotypes' demanded by our culture. The stereotypes, while limiting, are essential. . . . But if stereotypes determine not only how we see but what we see, clearly our opinions are only partial truths. What we assume to be 'facts' are often really judgments" (p. 181).

The concept of framing was formally introduced as early as 1954 (Tannen, 1993). Gregory Bateson theorized that "no communicative move, verbal or nonverbal, could be understood without reference to a metacommunicative message, or metamessage, about what is going on— that is, what frame of interpretation applies to the move" (Tannen, 1993, p. 3). Tversky and Kahneman (1982) showed that minor changes in the way decision problems are framed may influence people's decisions: "Systematic reversals of preference are observed when a decision problem is framed in different ways" (p. 3). The concept of framing has important implications for individuals' opinions and attitudes. On the most basic level, the framing of questions influences responses to attitude surveys and public opinion polls (Krosnick & Alwin, 1988).

On a broader level, the framing of an issue forms "the basis by which public policy decisions are made" (Wallack et al., 1993, p. 68; see also Nelkin, 1987). Framing not only defines the issue, it also suggests the solution: "If we alter the definition of problems, then the response also changes" (Wallack et al., 1993, p. 82; see also Ryan, 1991; Watzlawick, Weakland, & Fisch, 1974). As Wagenaar and Streff (1980) pointed out, "how questions are worded is related to how policy advocates and opponents shape and present policy options to legislators and other opinion leaders, as well as to the general public" (p. 203).

The effect of framing has been demonstrated in studies of public opinion on alcohol policies (Wagenaar & Streff, 1990), mandatory seat belt laws (Slovic, Fischoof & Lichtenstein, 1982), affirmative action (Fine,

1992), environmental policy (Vaughan & Seifert, 1992), and welfare policy (Smith, 1987). Message framing has been shown to influence not only public opinion, but individual behavior as well (Meyerowitz & Chaiken, 1987; Rothman et al., 1993; Vookles & Carr, 1993; Wilson, Purdon, & Wallston, 1988; Wilson, Wallston, & King, 1990).

Ryan (1991), one of the developers of framing theory and its applications in public policy advocacy, argued that a frame is defined by a core value or principle that underlies it. Ryan, adapting previous work done by Gamson & Lasch (1983), further characterized frames by their core positions, metaphors, images, catch phrases, attribution of responsibility for the problem, and the solution implied by the frame. Ryan and Gamson, through the work of their Media Research and Action Project (MRAP) in the Sociology Department at Boston College, adapted a useful framing matrix that can be used by public health practitioners to identify and outline the frames used by supporters and opponents of public health policy issues (see Ryan, 1991; also see Gamson & Lasch, 1983; Gamson & Modigliani, 1989).

For example, one frame used in debates over citywide smoking restrictions in restaurants is the "level playing field" frame (**Table 6-1**). The core position of this frame is that restricting smoking in restaurants in one city creates an unlevel playing field—customers will shift their business to restaurants in nearby cities that allow smoking, resulting in a loss

Table 6-1 The Level Playing Field Frame Used by the Tobacco Industry to Fight Local Smoke-free Restaurant Ordinances

Frame	Level Playing Field
Core position	Restricting smoking in restaurants in one city creates a selective advantage for restaurants in nearby cities.
Metaphor	An unlevel playing field in a sports event, favoring one team over another
Images	An unlevel playing field in a sports event
Catch phrases	"Level playing field"; "unfair advantage"; "discrimination"
Attribution of responsibility	The government, which is creating a selective advantage for some businesses
Implied solution	Maintain a level playing field by banning smoking in all restaurants nationwide, or do nothing
Core values	Fairness Equality Justice Economic opportunity

Note: This framing matrix model was adapted from Ryan (1991), following the work of Gamson & Lasch (1983) and Gamson & Modigliani (1989).

of business for restaurants in the affected city. The metaphor suggested by this frame is that of an unlevel playing field that favors one team over another. The core values, or principles, to which this frame appeals are fairness, equality, justice, and economic opportunity. It is simply unfair for the government to create an advantage for restaurants in one city over those in another city.

The Importance of Framing in Public Policy Debates

In their case studies of antismoking legislation in six states, Jacobson, Wasserman, and Raube (1993) found that the tobacco industry "attempted to shift the nature of the debate from the credibility of the scientific evidence to personal freedoms" (p. 800). Moreover, they observed that "antismoking forces fare better when public health issues dominate and that the tobacco industry benefits when personal freedoms arguments are predominant. . . . [L]egislative outcomes favored antismoking advocates during the time that public health dominated the debate. Once the debate shifted to personal freedoms, statewide antismoking legislation stalled" (p. 801).

As Jacobson and colleagues (1993) described it, the tobacco industry

> shifted its opposition to smoking restrictions to a broadly conceived argument equating smoking behavior with other personal liberties, such as freedom of speech and protection against racial discrimination. This argument involves three interconnected concepts; first, governmental interference—that smoking restrictions should be determined by private economic arrangements, not by governmental fiat; second, smokers' rights—that smokers have certain rights and autonomy in pursing personal social behavior; and third—nondiscrimination—that smokers cannot be discriminated against for their smoking behavior, particularly in employment, for smoking during nonworking hours. (p. 802)

In the late 1980s the tobacco industry shifted its strategy from a focus on challenging the scientific evidence about the health effects of tobacco to a focus on discussing non-health-related frames: civil liberties, government interference, individual rights, and discrimination. This was not a lucky guess but the result of public opinion research showing that these frames resonated well with American voters. For example, in 1988 a Tobacco Institute poll appraised the strength of various core values as well as alternative campaign messages and arguments. This poll assessed the extent of anti-regulatory sentiment among American voters to determine whether an antigovernment interference theme might be effective in generating opposition to tobacco policy proposals (Roper Center at University of Connecticut, 1989). In addition to assessing voter attitudes concerning specific tobacco policies, the poll also asked questions about government regulation of the use, transportation, and disposal of toxic chemicals (Roper Center at University of Connecticut, 1980; **Exhibit 6-1**).The tobacco industry's strategy has been quite successful because of the extent to which the core values of its messages are an inherent part of American thinking:

> The concept and symbolic importance of individual freedoms are deeply ingrained in American myth, culture, and law. Antismoking advocates may have underestimated how powerfully the idea of personal autonomy for life-style choices resonates among legislators, especially when used creatively to obscure the tobacco industry's goals. As the tobacco industry has correctly calculated, the individual liberties arguments are seductive when framed as unfair restrictions on private social behavior, even in the presence of compelling scientific evidence on the adverse health effects from smoking. (Jacobson et al., 1993, p. 807)

The findings of Jacobson and colleagues (1993) suggest that although health is an important core value, personal freedoms, civil liberties, and individual rights may be even more compelling values for the public. When the debate is framed in a way such that antismoking legislation is seen as conflicting with these values, smoking advocates must directly confront the opposition frames. They must develop their own frames that appeal to the same compelling core values being tapped into by the opposition. The development of these frames should be guided by market research, not by mere conjecture.

Exhibit 6-1   Sample Questions from a 1988 Tobacco Institute Public Opinion Poll

1. The U. S. Agriculture Department currently inspects food processing plants to make sure that they are sanitary. Do you think that these inspections should be made more strict than they are now, made less strict than they are now, or should they be left about as they are now?

2. The Federal Aviation Administration now places restrictions on the number of Commercial flights that can be scheduled in and out of major airports. Do you think that these restrictions should be made more strict than they are now, made less strict than they are now, or should they be left about as they are now?

3. The Environmental Protection Agency now requires companies using toxic chemicals to follow certain procedures in the use, transportation, and disposal of those chemicals. Do you think that those procedures should be made more strict than they are now, made less strict then they are now, or should they be left about as they are now?

Source: Data from Roper Center at University of Connecticut, 1989.

Wallack and associates (1993) have argued that, in a sense, debates over public health policy issues represent a battle for framing the issue in the eyes of the public. It is not necessarily the relative merits of various arguments for and against a proposal that most influence its legislative fate. Rather, it is the relative success of proponents and opponents in framing the overall terms of the debate. For example, in tobacco control, "the battle for framing is evident in how the tobacco industry uses symbols and images to promote itself as a good corporate citizen, defender of the First Amendment, protector of free choice, and friend of the family farmer. The industry paints antitobacco people, on the other hand, as zealots, health fascists, paternalists, and government interventionists" (Wallack et al., 1993, p. 71). As Jacobson and associates (1993) argued, "how the issue of smoking restrictions is framed is an important component of the legislative debate and outcome" (p. 806).

Similarly, Schon and Rein (1994) explained that in a policy controversy, "two or more parties contend with one another over the definition of a problematic policy situation and vie for control of the policy-making process. Their struggles over the naming and framing of a policy situation are symbolic contests over the social meaning of an issue domain, where meaning implies not only what is at issue but what is to be done" (pp. 28, 29).

The public's perception of how an issue relates to its needs, wants, and values most influences public opinion. The way in which a debate is framed has important implications for how the public relates the issue to its needs and core values. The battle over public health programs and policy initiatives, then, can be viewed not only as a battle over specific facts and arguments, but as a battle over the framing of the overall issue; not solely as a battle over policy, but as a battle over the packaging of that policy into symbols, images, and themes.

In their discussion of "the framing of debate," Chapman and Lupton (1994) emphasized the need to understand "how issues need to be reframed in order to steer public and political support in the desired directions" (p. 18). The authors stated that "political battles are seldom won only on the elegance of logic or by those who can best assemble rational arguments. These are mere strategies within a wider battle front. The real issue is which are the overall framings of debates that best succeed in capturing public opinion and political will" (p. 125).

Similarly, Schon and Rein (1994) saw policy controversies as "disputes in which the contending parties hold conflicting frames. Such disputes are resistant to resolution by appeal to facts or reasoned argumentation because the parties' conflicting frames determine what counts as a fact and what arguments are taken to be relevant and compelling" (p. 23).

Kaniss (1991), too, emphasized the importance of the "symbolic framing of the proposal," concluding that "the way in which new initiatives are presented and framed for the media is particularly important" (pp. 182, 183). She stressed that symbols play a critical role in the framing of policies and showed how the battle for the symbolic framing of a policy issue in a way that best appeals to the media is the central battle over a public health policy.

Framing can be viewed as the packaging and positioning of a public health policy or program so that it appeals to deeply ingrained, widely shared principles held by the target audience. Framing is an integral part of developing a strategy to market public health programs and policies.

Developing Public Health Frames

In developing frames, public health practitioners must identify how to define, position, and package an issue in ways that (1) present a unified, coherent core position; (2) evoke desired visual images; (3) employ recognizable "catch phrases"; (4) suggest appropriate metaphors; (5) attribute responsibility for the problem to society, rather than merely to the individual; and (6) imply as a solution the program or policy being marketed by the practitioner (**Exhibit 6-2**). All of these individual objectives must work together effectively to reinforce the deeply ingrained, widely held principles and values of the target audience.

For example, consider the framing of a local ordinance to protect the health of restaurant workers by eliminating smoking in restaurants. To market such a policy, one might develop four frames based on widely held core values; freedom, independence, control, and fairness. Instead of defining the product of an antismoking ordinance campaign as a law to protect the health of nonsmokers and offering health for restaurant customers as a benefit, the product and benefits can be redefined as the freedom to work in an environment free of health hazards, the right to

---

Exhibit 6-2 Key Objectives in Development of Framing Strategy for Public Health Programs and Policies

1. Present unified, coherent core position on the policy or program that is consistent with the core values of target audience.
2. Evoke visual images that appeal to the core values.
3. Develop catch phrases (verbal images) that appeal to the core values.
4. Suggest appropriate metaphors that evoke themes and images that appeal to the core values.
5. Attribute responsibility for the public health problem to society (including government), not merely to individuals.
6. Imply as a solution the program or policy being marketed.

make a living without being involuntarily exposed to carcinogens, creating a level playing field for all workers by affording restaurant workers the same protection that is provided to almost all other workers, helping business by preventing huge liability risks for damages caused by secondhand smoke, preventing discrimination against blue-collar workers by extending to all workers the protection that almost all white-collar workers have from secondhand smoke, and protecting the livelihood of workers in small restaurants by ending the suffering they endure from exposure to a hazardous working environment (**Table 6-2**).

Table 6-2 Core Values and Messages That Appeal to These Values for Several Public Health Policies

Public Health Policy	Core Value	Message
Eliminate smoking in restaurants	Freedom/Free enterprise	What could possibly be a more basic freedom to Americans than the freedom to make a living and support one's children without having to be exposed to dangerous working conditions?
		What is a more basic civil liberty than the right to work in a safe environment? Forcing employees to breathe carcinogens in order to make a living is a violation of the free enterprise principle.
	Independence/ economic opportunity	Liability risks posed by allowing employees to be exposed to secondhand smoke (workers' compensation, disability, etc.) could hurt business owners. Illnesses and deaths will cause a loss of jobs, productivity, and sales.
	Control	How can workers pursue a livelihood and support children if they are too sick to work or suffer (can't breathe) at work?
	Fairness/Equality	Excluding restaurant workers from health protection that all other workers take for granted is not fair; it represents discrimination against a certain class of workers; this is a class issue.

(continues)

Table 6-2 Core Values and Messages That Appeal to These Values for Several Public Health Policies (continued)

Public Health Policy	Core Value	Message
Increase cigarette tax	Freedom	Voting for the tax is a way to assert freedom from tobacco industry influence. Rejecting the tax is just playing into the hands of the industry and letting it dictate state policies.
	Independence	Without a higher tax, parents cannot effectively keep children from smoking, cannot effectively fight the tobacco industry's pressure on their children to smoke.
	Control	Voting for the tax allows you, not the tobacco industry, to decide the fate of your children's health.
	Democracy	Voting for the tax preserves the democratic ideal by keeping government in the hands of the people, not in the hands of a powerful, greedy, special-interest group that has intruded into our state.
Adopt stricter environmental regulations	Control	Regulations will allow society to retain control over the unknown consequences of environmental destruction.
	Economic opportunity	Regulations will help preserve livelihoods and economic opportunity by protecting tourism; rejecting the regulations will lead to economic devastation of the community.
Adopt needle exchange	Freedom	The program will allow society to remain free of the scourge of acquired immunodeficiency syndrome (AIDS); without it, AIDS may spread from the drug-using population to the general population.
	Control	If AIDS spreads to the general population, the epidemic may soon be out of control.
Adopt mandatory seat belt law	Fairness	It is not fair for taxpayers to have to pay medical bills for people seriously injured because they were irresponsible and failed to wear seat belts.

(continues)

Public Health Policy	Core Value	Message
Table 6-2 Core Values and Messages That Appeal to These Values for Several Public Health Policies (continued)		
Adopt mandatory seat belt law (continued)	Economic livelihood	The medical costs of accidents involving individuals not wearing seat belts are wreaking havoc on the budget and the economy and increasing taxes for everyone. The law will create savings that will translate into lower taxes and increased economic livelihood.
Adopt tuberculosis (TB) screening and treatment program in drug treatment clinics	Freedom	The program will prevent the epidemic scourge of TB that threatens to affect all of us, as TB spreads from drug users into the general population.
	Control	The program will allow society to retain control over the unknown consequences of the spread of multidrug-resistant TB into the general population. The consequences are unknown, but could be devastating to society.

Note: This framing matrix model was adapted from Ryan (1991), following the work of Gamson & Lasch (1983) and Gamson & Modigliani (1989).

Similarly, instead of framing an initiative to increase the cigarette tax simply as a measure to reduce cigarette consumption and improve health, supporting the initiative could be framed as a way for voters to remain free of the tobacco industry's influence, raise their children independent of the pressure being placed on their children to smoke, maintain control of the health of their communities, and preserve the principles of democracy (see **Table 6-2**).

Programs to adopt such measures as stricter environmental regulations, needle exchange programs, mandatory seat belt laws, and screening and treatment programs also could be framed to appeal to the core values of freedom, independence, economic opportunity, autonomy, control, fairness, and equality (see **Table 6-2**).

Reframing Public Health Issues

In addition to developing their own frames, public health practitioners must also learn to confront directly the frames developed by opponents of their proposed policies and programs.

How can public health advocates confront opposition framing? Two approaches are possible. Take, for example, the level playing field frame

used in fighting local smoking regulations (see **Table 6-1**). First, advocates can simply ignore the opposition frame and emphasize that this is
a health issue. The success of this approach depends on policy makers
perceiving the policy's conflict with the value they place on fairness and
equality. As Jacobson and colleagues (1993) noted, this approach may
be successful, but only if advocates are able to make the public health frame
the dominant one.

An alternative approach is to reframe the issue so that supporting the
policy reinforces rather than conflicts with the core values being tapped
by the opposition frame. In other words, public health advocates must
develop a new frame that shows policy makers how a local restaurant
smoking ordinance is necessary to preserve fairness and equality for the
city's residents.

One way the issue could be reframed is to demonstrate how denying
restaurant workers from the protection from secondhand smoke that we
afford most other workers is unfair (**Table 6-3**). The real unlevel playing
field is the singling out of restaurant workers as the one occupational
group not deserving of basic public health protections that most other
workers take for granted and consider to be their right.

A second way to reframe the issue might be to show how the failure
to protect citizens in the city would perpetuate an unlevel playing field
by denying citizens in that city a basic right guaranteed to the citizens of
more than 200 cities throughout the country—the right to work in an environment free of hazards (**Table 6-3**).

In both frames, the core values are the same: fairness and equality.
However, in the opposition frame, voting for the ordinance would conflict with these values, while in the proponent frame, voting for the ordinance would reinforce these values. (See Appendix 6-B.)

Another excellent example of the technique of redefining public health
issues so that the desired program reinforces rather than opposes core values was provided by former Surgeon General Joycelyn Elders. In 1994,
public health practitioners in Baltimore proposed a program to offer
Norplant—a system of long-term contraception that involves the surgi-
cal insertion of a slow-release hormone delivery device under the skin of
the upper arm—to teenage girls at a city health department clinic. The
plan was condemned on the grounds that it would interfere with the autonomy and freedom of the young women and restrict their reproductive rights. In response, Dr. Elders redefined the Norplant program as a
method to free young women from the enslaving grip of unwanted pregnancies: "If you're poor and ignorant, with a child, you're a slave. Meaning
that you're never going to get out of it. These women are in bondage to
a kind of slavery that the Thirteenth Amendment just didn't deal with"
(Gaylin & Jennings, 1996, p. 16). As Gaylin and Jennings (1996) explained, Surgeon General Elders framed the use of Norplant as "a liber-
ating factor from the veritable 'slavery' of teenage pregnancy" (p. 16).

Table 6-3 The Level Playing Field Frame: Reframing for Use by Public Health Advocates in Promoting Local Smoke-free Restaurant Ordinances

Frame	Level Playing Field— Reframe 1	Level Playing Field— Reframe 2
Core position	Singling out restaurant workers as the one occupational group not deserving basic health protection afforded to nearly all other workers creates an unlevel playing field for these workers.	Failing to protect citizens in this city from secondhand smoke when more than 200 cities nationwide more already afforded these protectionsto their workers creates an unlevelplaying field for our residents.
Metaphor	An unlevel playing field in a sports event, favoring one team over another	An unlevel playing field in a sports event, favoring one team over another
Images	An unlevel playing field in a sports event	An unlevel playing field in a sports event
Catch phrases	"Level playing field"; "unfair"; "disadvantage"; "discrimination"	"Level playing field"; "unfair"; "disadvantage"; "discrimination"
Attribution of responsibility for problem	Government, which is selectively protecting workers in typical offices, but excluding restaurant workers from protection	Government, which is selectively excluding our city's residents from protection that many residents in other cities have
Implied solution	Extend smoke-free working environment protections to all workers	Extend smoke-free working environment protections to workers in our city
Core values	Fairness Equality Justice Economic opportunity	Fairness Equality Justice Economic opportunity

Note: This framing matrix model was adapted from Ryan (1991), following the work of Gamson & Lasch (1983) and Gamson & Modigliani (1989).

Beauchamp (1976) discussed how public health practitioners can use the core value of justice to redefine public health problems in ways that will gain public support and motivate the public and policy makers to collective action: "In building these collective redefinitions of health problems, however, public health must take care to do more than merely shed light on specific public health problems. . . . This means that the function of each different redefinition of a specific problem must be to raise the common and recurrent issue of justice by exposing the aggressive and powerful structures implicated in all instances of preventable death and disability, and further to point to the necessity for collective measures to confront and resist these structures" (p. 10).

The process of reframing public health programs and policies effectively can be aided by considering the nature of societal core values. In particular, two characteristics of these core values are most salient. First, as discussed in Chapter 3, the deeply ingrained core value of freedom represents both the absence of interference from others (negative liberty) and the presence of control over one's life and destiny (positive liberty). Special-interest groups that oppose public health programs tend to emphasize their infringement on negative liberty. Public health practitioners can often reframe the debate by pointing out how the program or policy will actually enhance positive liberties. Thus, while a law that limits individuals' ability to drink and drive may be perceived as interfering with personal freedom, public health practitioners can market such a law by pointing out that it actually preserves individual autonomy by protecting society's members from being killed by drunk drivers and therefore preserves their ability to control their lives.

Second, core values such as freedom, independence, autonomy, and even justice have tended to be interpreted with an individualistic perspective. Civil rights laws, for example, usually have been interpreted as protecting the rights of individuals. But Gaylin and Jennings (1996) argued that "nothing inherent in civil rights laws . . . requires that they be interpreted in individualistic terms; their meaning could easily be construed in terms of nondiscrimination or equality" (p. 53). In other words, public health practitioners may be able to reframe public health programs and policies in a way that highlights how they will promote a communitarian or societal advancement of civil rights. For example, a law that eliminates smoking in bars could be promoted as a necessary measure to ensure equality of occupational safety protections for all workers. A smoke-free ordinance is simply an expression of a societal interpretation of civil rights.

Gaylin and Jennings (1996) suggested that in America, civil rights have become "a framework for individual claims against others," but that they could just as easily become "a framework for social solidarity" and a means of "building a moral community of equal citizens" (p. 53). Etzioni (1993) even claimed that a communitarian perspective of rights is not only consistent with, but is necessary for, the preservation of individual liberty: "Neither human existence nor individual liberty can be sustained for long outside the interdependent and overlapping communities to which all of us belong. . . . The exclusive pursuit of private interest erodes the network of social environments on which we all depend and is destructive to our shared experiment in democratic self-government. For these reasons, we hold that the rights of individuals cannot long be preserved without a Communitarian perspective" (pp. 253, 254).

Sunstein (1997) wrote that the government effort to change social norms is often necessary to advance individual autonomy:

In fact, there are many reasons why a legal system might seek to alter norms, meanings, and roles. The most important reason is that the resulting reforms might enhance autonomy. . . . Obstacles to autonomy and to good lives can also come from bad roles, norms, and meaning. . . . In some cases, existing norms undermine people's autonomy, by discouraging them from being exposed to diverse conceptions of the good and from giving critical scrutiny to their own conceptions, in such a way as to make it impossible for them to be, in any sense, masters of the narratives of their own lives (pp. 37, 55, 59).

Thus, in reframing public health programs and policies, public health practitioners can confront antiregulatory sentiment by positioning these reforms as necessary to eliminate obstacles to individual freedom and autonomy. "It should be clear that social norms, meanings, and roles may undermine individual autonomy. Above all, this is because norms can compromise autonomy itself, by stigmatizing it. . . . In such cases, autonomy cannot exist without collective assistance, people are able to produce the norms, meanings, and roles that they reflectively endorse only with governmental involvement. Something must be done collectively if the situation is to be changed" (Sunstein, 1997, p. 62).

In general, public health practitioners can confront the antiregulatory sentiment in the nation by reframing public health issues to show that government action is necessary precisely to preserve the societal interest in individual freedom and autonomy. As Sunstein (1997) wrote,

more broadly, a democratic government should sometimes take private preferences as an object of deliberation, evaluation, and even control—an inevitable task in light of the need to define initial entitlements—and precisely in the interest of welfare and autonomy. . . . The interest in liberty or autonomy does not call for government inaction, even if that were an intelligible category. Indeed, in many or perhaps all of the cases, regulation removes a kind of coercion. . . . The view that freedom requires an opportunity to choose among alternatives finds a natural supplement in the view that people should not face unjustifiable constraints on the free development of their preferences and beliefs. . . . Liberalism does not forbid citizens, operating through democratic channels, from enacting their considered judgments into law, or from counteracting, through the provision of opportunities and information, preferences and beliefs that have adjusted to an unjust status quo. Ironically, a system that forecloses these routes—and that claims to do so in the name of liberalism or democracy—will defeat many of the aspirations that gave both liberalism and democracy their original appeal, and that continue to fuel them in so many parts of the world (pp. 20, 30, 31).

Perhaps the best example of reframing social policy so as to reinforce the core values of freedom and autonomy is the description offered by Sunstein (1997) of the rationale for government programs to address poverty:

> Poverty itself is perhaps the most severe obstacle to the free development of preferences and beliefs. Programs that attempt to respond to the deprivation faced by poor people—most obviously by eliminating poverty, but also through broad public education and regulatory efforts designed to make cultural resources generally available regardless of wealth—are fully justified in this light. They should hardly be seen as objectionable paternalism or an unsupportable redistribution. Indeed, antipoverty efforts are tightly linked with traditional efforts to promote security and independence in the interest of creating the conditions for full and equal citizenship (p. 28).

The strategic use of issue framing to redefine the public health product and package and position it so that it supports the most compelling core values of the public and policy makers can play an important role in helping public health practitioners deal with the unique marketing challenge they face. Evidence suggests that issue-framing strategies derived from marketing and public opinion research can help promote support for public health policies. For example, a 1988 survey funded by the Coalition for a Healthy California explored the effectiveness of various issue-framing strategies for a state cigarette tax initiative and was used in developing the campaign that led to the passage of Proposition 99 (Marr, 1990; Traynor & Glantz, 1996). A 1991 survey funded by the Massachusetts division of the American Cancer Society played a key role in developing the campaign that led to the passage of a cigarette tax initiative in 1992 (Marttila & Kiley, Inc., 1991). Similar marketing research helped a public health coalition in Arizona promote the passage of a cigarette tax initiative in 1994 (Ross, 1996).

Despite the promise of issue framing in marketing public health programs and policies, more research must be done in this area. Chapman and Lupton (1994) suggested four specific questions to address in such research:

> (1) Are there important differences in the framings favored by those working in public health, and those that hold most public and political appeal?; (2) Are there methodologies that are sufficiently sensitive to be reliably used in pretesting different framings used in advocacy?; (3) What examples are there, where dominant framings that run against the interests of public health appear to have been successfully reversed?; (4) Are there principles that characterize such reversals, which can be applied in practical ways in future debates? (p. 12)

Providing Support for the Public Health Promise

In marketing terms, the message that a particular public health program or policy will provide a set of benefits as defined by a frame is called the "promise," just as the message that engaging in a particular behavior will reinforce certain core values is the "promise" of public health campaigns aimed at changing individual behavior (see Chapter 3).

Part of demonstrating that a behavior will reinforce core target audience values is providing support to back up the promise. But it is no different with promoting a public health program or policy. Public health practitioners must still offer support for their contention that the program or policy will indeed offer the promised benefits. Traditionally, public health practitioners have relied on scientific evidence of the health benefits of a policy or program to support the promise of improved health from the intervention. In contrast, successful corporate marketers tend to rely on much more compelling support for their promises. Nike, for example, backs up its offer of control over one's life with solid documentation: video footage of Michael Jordan—perhaps the most talented and successful athlete ever—in action, or images of everyday people (wearing Nike gear of course) reaching personal fulfillment through physical activity. Almost never does one see a corporate marketer offer statistics and data to support the promise of particular benefits from the use of a product.

Public health practitioners, too, must learn to provide equally compelling documentation or support for their promises. And while it is natural for public health practitioners to tend to rely on data and statistics to accomplish this, it is unlikely to be effective. Statistics and data are not terribly effective at influencing policy makers. But frames, images, and emotional appeals to core values are.

One way to bring frames, images, and core value appeals together in an emotional and compelling way is through the use of stories. In many ways, the successful telling of a story of one affected individual can be far more compelling than providing data and statistics that document the thousands of people affected by a particular health condition or disease. Public health practitioners need to learn how to tell and deliver effective and emotional stories to provide support for their promised benefits, rather than to simply rely on data and statistics.

Branding

One way to put together the repositioning, repackaging, and reframing of the public health program or policy product is through the concept of branding. The concept of branding has been introduced recently into public health marketing (Andreasen, 2006) and has served as a useful framework for the development of a number of effective public health communication campaigns (see Hicks, 2001 for an excellent example and chapter 9 for a detailed discussion).

Public health practitioners need to think of the policy or program they are promoting (or even of public health itself) as a brand, similar in many ways to the brands that are offered to consumers by marketers of consumer products. As such, brands need to convey almost a personality of a program or policy. The idea is to build a relationship with the policy maker, not merely to promote a one-time transaction: "In recent years, marketers have come to realize that the best way to influence behavior is not through one-time transactions, but by building ongoing relationships with their customers" (Hastings, 2003, p. 15).

By focusing on developing their brand "personality" for their public health policy or program product offering, public health practitioners can unify their promotional campaign around a single brand "identity," which can ensure that all aspects of the public health communication— the object, the promise, the benefit, the support, and the image—work together to convey an identity to which the target audience can relate, and to which it aspires. In this way, branding can serve as an ideal concept around which to incorporate the repackaging, repositioning, and reframing of a public health program or policy.

After all, a brand not only forms the relationship between the organization or product and its consumer, but it has also been characterized as a repository, not merely of functional characteristics, but of meaning and value (Mark & Pearson, 2001; McDivitt et al, 2003). And it is that meaning and value (such as standing for freedom, independence, and autonomy), not merely the functional characteristics of the desired public health program or policy (such as improving health and reducing disease or death) which is most closely tied to individual behavior.

■ CONCLUSION

To advocate successfully for public health policies and programs and to promote the survival of public health as a societal institution, public health practitioners must adopt two basic marketing principles.

1. The first step in developing campaigns to promote a public health policy or program is *not* to decide how to convince the public or policy makers to support the program, but to use market research to identify the basic needs, desires, and core values of the target audience.

2. When referring to public health, practitioners must define the product they are selling based on the results of formative research. Public health practitioners must acknowledge that they cannot always effectively sell public health programs. They must begin to sell basic values such as freedom, independence, control, and the democratic way. Public health must be positioned, packaged, and framed in such a way that it will be perceived as fulfilling the needs, desires, and

values of the target audience. And then the message must be reinforced and supported by compelling, emotional stories and images, not merely by statistics and data.

In the new view of public health presented in this chapter, epidemiologic research and formative research combine to form a basic foundation. Epidemiologic research helps identify the most effective programs and policies to solve public health problems. Then, based on the findings of formative research, the most important needs, desires, and values of the target audience (policy makers and/or the public) can be identified. Next, the public health practitioner must define the product so that it offers as a benefit the fulfillment of these desires and needs. Finally, the practitioner can package, position, and frame the product in an effort to demonstrate to the audience how it will indeed fulfill these desires and needs (**Figure 6-1**).

This model differs from traditional models of public health practice because it includes two intermediate steps not generally included in other models. Most models begin with step A and jump immediately to the final step D, running the campaign. In our model, before the actual planning, implementation, and evaluation of the public health campaign, we

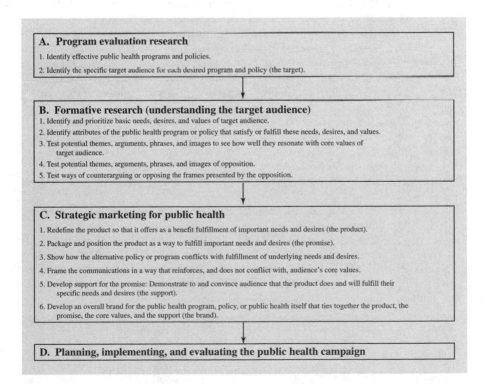

Figure 6-1 A New Marketing Strategy for Public Health: Confronting Threats to the Survival of Public Health

add two steps: formative research (understanding the consumer's needs, desires, and values) and strategic marketing for public health (using the results of formative research to effectively define, package, position, and frame the public health program or policy being promoted).

The next two chapters present case studies to illustrate the most important points of the first part of the book. Chapter 7 presents a case study of the use of marketing principles to market health behavior change to women in Rwanda. Chapter 8 presents a case study of the use of framing principles to market public health as an institution itself.

References

Andreasen, A.R. (2006). *Social marketing in the 21st century.* Thousand Oaks, CA: SAGE Publications, Inc.

Beauchamp, D. (1976). Public health as social justice. *Inquiry.* 13, 3–14.

Champman, S., & Lupton, D. (1994). *The fight for public health: Principles and practice of media advocacy.* London: BMJ Publishing Group.

Entman, R. (1993). Framing: Toward clarification of a fractured paradigm. *Journal of Communication, 43,* 51–58.

Etzioni, A. (1993). *The spirit of community: Rights, responsibilities, and the communitarian agenda.* New York: Crown.

Fine, T.S. (1992). The impact of issue framing on public opinion toward affirmative action programs. *The Social Science Journal, 29,* 323–334.

Gamson, W.A., & Lasch, K.E. (1983). The political culture of social welfare policy (pp. 397–415). In: Spiro, S.E. & Yuchtman-Yaar, E. (Eds.) *Evaluating the welfare state: Social and political perspectives.* New York: Academic Press.

Gamson, W.A. & Modigliani, A. (1989). Media discourse and public opinion on nuclear power: A constructionist approach. *American Journal of Sociology,* 95(1), 1–37.

Gaylin, W., & Jennings, B. (1996). *The perversion of autonomy: The proper uses of coercion and constraints in a liberal society.* New York: The Free Press.

Hastings, G. (2003). Social marketers of the world unite, you have nothing to lose but your shame. *Social Marketing Quarterly,* 9(4):14–21.

Hicks, J.J. (2001). The strategy behind Florida's 'truth' campaign. *Tobacco Control,* 10, 3–5.

Iyengar, S. (1991). *Is anyone responsible? How television frames political issues.* Chicago: University of Chicago Press.

Jacobson, P.D., Wasserman, J., & Raube, K. (1993). The politics of antismoking legislation. *Journal of Health Politics, Policy and Law,* 18, 787–819.

Kaniss, P. (1991). *Making local news.*Chicago: University of Chicago Press.

Krosnick, J., & Alwin, D. (1988). A test of the form-resistant correlation hypothesis: Ratings, rankings and the measurement of values. *Public Opinion Quarterly.* 32, 526–538.

Mark, M., & Pearson, C.S. (2001). *The hero and the outlaw: Building extraordinary brands through the power of archetypes.* New York: McGraw-Hill.

Marr, M. (1990, April). *Proposition 99: The California tobacco tax initiative, a case study.* Berkeley, CA: Western Consortium for Public Health.

Marttila & Kiley, Inc. (1991). *A survey of voter attitudes in Massachusetts: Benchmark survey.* Boston: Author.

McDivitt, J. et al. (2003). Innovations in social marketing conference proceedings. Session II: Is there a role for branding in social marketing? *Social Marketing Quarterly,* 9(3), 11–17.

Meyerowitz, B.E. & Chaiken, S. (1987). The effect of message framing on breast self-examination attitudes, intentions, and behavior. *Journal of Personality and Social Psychology,* 52, 500–510.

Moon, R. W., Males, M.A., & Nelson, D.E. (1993). The 1990 Montana initiative to increase cigarette taxes: Lessons for other states and localities. *Journal of Public Health Policy.* 14, 19–33.

Nelkin, D. (1987). Selling science: How the press covers science and technology. *New York: Freeman.*

Roper Center at University of Connecticut. (1989). *Public opinion online.* Tobacco Institute sponsored survey conducted by Hamilton, Frederick, and Schneiders, November 23-December 6, 1988.

Ross, M. (1996). *Tobacco tax campaigns: A case study of two states.* Washington, DC: Advocacy Institute.

Rothman, A.J., Salovey, P., Antone, C., Kcough, K., & Martin, C. D. (1993). The influence of message framing on intentions to perform health behaviors. *Journal of Experimental and Social Psychology,* 29, 408–433.

Ryan, C. (1991). *Prime time activism: Media strategies for grassroots organizing.* Boston: South End Press.

Schon, D.A., & Rein, M. (1994). *Frame reflection: Toward the resolution of intractable policy controversies.* New York: Basic Books.

Slovic, P., Fischoff, B., & Lichtenstein, S. (1982). Response mode, framing, and information-processing effects in risk assessment. In R.M. Hogarth (Ed.), *Question framing and response consistency* (pp. 21–36). San Francisco: Jossey-Bass.

Smith, T. (1987). That which we call welfare by any other name would smell sweeter: An analysis of the impact of question wording on response patterns. *Public Opinion Quarterly,* 51, 75–83.

Stauber, J., & Rampton, S. (1995). *Toxic sludge is good for you! Lies, damn lies and the public relations industry.* Monroe, ME: Common Courage Press.

Steel, R. (1981). *Walter Lippmann and the American century.* New York: Vintage Books.

Sunstein, C.R. (1997). *Free markets and social justice.* New York: Oxford University Press.

Tannen, D. (Ed.). (1993). *Framing in discourse.* New York: Oxford University Press.

Traynor, M.P., & Glantz, S.A. (1996). California's tobacco tax initiative: The development and passage of Proposition 99. *Journal of Health Politics, Policy and Law,* 21(3), 543–585.

Tversky, A. & Kahneman, D. (1982). The framing of decisions and the psychology of choice. In R.M. Hogarth (Ed.), *Question framing and response consistency* (pp. 3–20). San Francisco: Jossey-Bass.

Vaughan, E., & Seifert, M. (1992). Variability in the framing of risk issues. *Journal of Social Issues.* 48, 119–135.

Vookles, J., & Carr, J. (1993). The effects of message framing manipulations on AIDS preventive behavior. *AIDS Weekly,* 16.

Wagenaar, A.C., & Streff, F.M. (1990). Public opinion on alcohol policies. *Journal of Public Health Policy,* 11, 189–205.

Wallack L, Dorfman L, Jernigan D, & Thomba M. (1993). *Media advocacy and public health: power for prevention.* Newbury Park, CA: Saga Publications.

Wallack, L., & Dorfman, L. (1996). Media advocacy: A strategy for advancing policy and promoting health. *Health Education Quarterly,* 23, 293–317.

Watzlawick, P., Weakland, J., & Fisch, R. (1974). *Change: Principles of problem formation and problem resolution.* New York: Norton.

White House Domestic Policy Council, (1993). *Health security: The President's report to the American people.* New York: Touchstone.

Wilson, D.K., Purdon, S.E., & Wallston, K.A. (1988). Compliance to health recommendations: A theoretical overview of message framing. *Health Education Research: Theory and Practice,* 3, 161–171.

Wilson, D.K., Wallston, K.A., & King, J.E. (1990). Effect of contract framing, motivation to quit, and self-efficacy on smoking reduction. *Journal of Applied Social Psychology,* 20, 531–547.

6-A

Exploring the Core Values of Policy Makers: Lessons from Public Health History

To see how the public health practitioner can use the principles of marketing to promote the institution of public health, we must return to the importance of identifying and understanding the needs and wants of the target audience. In this case, we must identify what it is that policy makers need and want to support specific health programs and policies and to fund public health agencies.

What does public health mean to the policy maker? Why is it that policy makers want to protect the health of their constituents? What are the values associated with having healthy individuals in society that lead policy makers to allocate funds for public health protection?

Perhaps the best way to find out what public health means to policy makers is to study the conditions under which the institution of public health was created. What were the conditions that have led to the funding of major public health interventions during the past two centuries? To answer this question, we must turn to our review of major highlights in public health history presented in Chapter 5.

If one looks at the major events that have led to the adoption and funding of public health programs and institutions throughout history, one finds that a governmental concern over the health of the public has rarely been the driving force. Instead, it has generally been one factor or the combination of two factors that has led to government action: (1) the perception of broad, societal susceptibility to a disease and

(2) the perception of societal lack of control over the spread and consequences of a disease.

The perception that all persons—rich and poor alike—were susceptible to a disease has been a powerful stimulus for organized government action. Often, public policy-making bodies ignored diseases when they affected only the poorer classes, and acted only when a disease penetrated into the higher classes of society.

As was described in Chapter 5, it was because unhealthy social and environmental conditions threatened not only the poor but also the entire community that public health first came to be seen as a public responsibility. Government action to establish new sanitation systems followed more than a decade of advocacy for such changes by groups of reformers. It took the "lively fear" that cholera provoked among policy makers themselves to overcome entrenched opposition to public health action. The visible and widespread threat of cholera was the "catalyst" to action (McNeill, 1989). "To do nothing was no longer sufficient; old debates and stubborn clashes had to be quickly resolved by public bodies acting literally under fear of death" (McNeill, 1989, pp. 239, 240).

It has always been more difficult to motivate policy makers to allocate funds to improve social conditions in impoverished areas than in areas inhabited by the wealthy and politically powerful. As Duffy (1992) noted, referring to the late 1800s, "generally, accumulated piles of garbage and refuse characterized most urban areas. The one exception was the neighborhoods occupied by the well-to-do, which usually received special attention from the city authorities" (p. 175).

However, the penetration of disease across the boundaries of social class changed policy makers' views. The rapid changes in transportation that occurred in the nineteenth century helped bring infectious disease within the confines of all neighborhoods, regardless of socioeconomic level:

> One of the obvious lessons of this period, drawn from experiences with contagious disease, was that no community was an island. With yellow fever striking the southern coastal states and spreading up the Mississippi Valley, and with recurrent outbreaks of smallpox and Asiatic cholera plaguing the entire country, state officials took it upon themselves to proclaim statewide quarantines. The sanitary movement also demonstrated the interdependence of communities. Water pollution, for example, affected not only the community responsible for the pollution but also other communities dependent upon the polluted water source. (Duffy, 1992, p. 148)

Policy makers acted because it was no longer possible to ignore the afflictions of the poor. Diseases whose spread was initiated among the poor would sooner or later affect the upper classes as well: "In earlier centuries, disease was more readily identified as only the plight of the impoverished and immoral. The plague had been regarded as a disease of the poor; the wealthy could retreat to country estates and, in essence, quarantine themselves. In the urbanized nineteenth century, it became obvious that the wealthy could not escape contact with the poor" (Institute of Medicine, 1988, p. 39).

The broadened susceptibility to disease also changed the way policy makers came to view the reasons for disease, When it was only the poor who were affected, disease could be attributed to poor personal hygiene. But as soon as the wealthy were affected as well, disease had to be seen as a societal problem. "Almost all families lost children to diptheria, smallpox, or other infectious diseases. Because of the deplorable social and environmental conditions and the constant threat of disease spread, diseases came to be considered an indicator of a societal problem as well as a personal problem" (Institute of Medicine, 1988, p. 59).

Even when government action did occur in response to hazards within impoverished communities, the stimulus for action was the fear that the hazard could spread outside poor neighborhoods and affect everyone in the community. As Starr (1982) writes about the evolution of public health in the nineteenth century, "earlier in the century, cholera and yellow fever epidemics and concern about the squalid living conditions of the 'dangerous classes' had stimulated the organization of citizens' sanitary or hygiene associations to clean up the cities" (p. 184). It was not the suffering of the poor that precipitated action, but the fact that they were perceived as being dangerous to others.

The perception that a disease is out of control of societal effort, that it represents a threat to the economic and political fabric of society, and that it is unfamiliar, mysterious, unexplained, or graphically destructive of human life has also been a powerful stimulus for government action. Policy makers have not tended to take action when they perceived a disease as controlled, familiar, or explained, even if it was taking a huge toll on human life. But a new disease that is unfamiliar, mysterious, or out of society's control brings prompt government action to control it even if its mortality toll is relatively low.

Throughout public health history, the fear of the unknown, the ghastly, and the mysterious—not the actual public health impact of a disease—has determined the speed and extent of organized government action against the disease. It was these characteristics of cholera, for example, that prompted many of the sanitary reforms of the mid-nineteenth century. As McNeill (1989) explained,

> the speed with which cholera killed was profoundly alarming, since perfectly healthy people could never feel safe from sudden death when the infection was anywhere near. In addition, the symptoms were particularly horrible: radical dehydration meant that a victim shrank into a wizened caricature of his former self within a few hours, while ruptured capillaries discolored the skin, turning it black and blue. The effect was to make mortality uniquely visible: patterns of

bodily decay were exacerbated and accelerated, as in a time-lapse motion picture, to remind all who saw it of death's ugly horror and utter inevitability. (p. 231)

Not only did cholera produce graphic demonstrations of the impact of a disease on human victims, but it also represented a threat to society's sense of control over its own existence and viability. McNeill (1989) spoke of "the unique psychological impact of the approach of such a killer. . . . Cholera seemed capable of penetrating any quarantine, of bypassing any man-made obstacle: it chose its victims erratically" (p. 231).

Society also tended to take action against public health hazards when it perceived those hazards as a threat to its economic stability. As Duffy (1992) explained, the institutionalization of public health in many American cities occurred only when policy makers realized that having an unhealthy population was a threat to the economic viability of the population as a whole: "In Memphis and other southern cities, it would be some years before enlightened businessmen finally realized that a healthy population was necessary for a healthy economy" (p. 115). As Leavitt (1982) explained, competition between cities for economic progress was often the stimulus for investment in the public health infrastructure: "Local pride and inter-city competition provided an economic dimension of support for health campaigns to clean the streets and to eradicate epidemic diseases. Milwaukeeans believed that Chicago and Minneapolis-St. Paul threatened their own economic progress and, trying to surpass their rivals, became intolerant of serious sanitation problems. A prosperous Milwaukee could not rise from the piles of rotting garbage that supposedly caused high death rates" (p. 247).

And as Dr. James Howard Means, former president of the American College of Physicians, wrote in 1953,

when he is sick the individual creates a social vacuum which affects others than his immediate family. . . . The cost of his illness must be paid for somehow. . . . Illness of the individual, therefore, like fire, flood, or other destructive processes, is always an economic loss to the community. . . . Ill health subordinates other values, both on the part of the patient and of those immediately affected by his illness. Illness may even be said to be a political loss through the deterioration it causes in the sense of public responsibility. . . . Communities with many cases of chronic illness suffer economically, socially, and politically. (pp. 4, 5)

The factors that influence government funding of public health programs and institutions are little different today. For example, it was the threat of the uncontrolled and indiscriminate spread of acquired immunodeficiency syndrome (AIDS) that led to increased government funding of AIDS prevention programs in 1985, several years after the disease was first identified among homosexual men in San Francisco. It was not until AIDS affected a celebrity—Rock Hudson—in 1985, that the issue finally reached the media agenda, the public agenda, and the public policy agenda. When AIDS was perceived as being confined to the general homosexual population, it was viewed neither as a national newsworthy public health problem, nor as a funding priority. As Randy Shilts (1987) explained in *And the Band Played On*, "there was something about Hudson's diagnosis that seemed to strike an archetypal chord in the American consciousness. For decades, Hudson had been among the handful of screen actors who personified wholesome American masculinity; now, in one stroke, he was revealed as both gay and suffering from the affliction of pariahs" (pp. 578, 579). Hudson's announcement is viewed as "the single most important event in the history of the epidemic" (Shilts, 1987, p. 579). Even after Hudson's announcement and subsequent death, funding for AIDS prevention continued to be determined largely by its affecting celebrities. Odets (1995) noted that American society "more or less ignores AIDS between sporadic public concern about celebrities who contract it" (p. 24).

Reports of AIDS among heterosexuals also helped unleash the funding that, if released several years earlier, could have done much to prevent the epidemic from reaching the level it did. As Shilts (1987) explained,

> the outpouring of official attention to the handful of heterosexual AIDS cases in early 1985 proved a crucial event in determining the direction of the AIDS debate in the next two years. It instructed health officials and AIDS researchers, who had had such a difficult time seizing government and media interest in the epidemic, that nothing captured the attention of editors and news directors like the talk of widespread heterosexual transmission of AIDS. Such talk could be guaranteed air time and news space, which, in the AIDS business, quickly translated into funds and resources. (p. 513)

Indeed, funding for AIDS prevention, education, and research programs at the Centers for Disease Control and Prevention (CDC) increased from just $2 million in 1982, $6.2 million in 1983, and $13.8 million in 1984 to $33.3 million in 1985, $62.1 million in 1986, and $136.1 million in 1987.

As Duffy (1992) noted, "The appearance of a few cases of Legionnaire's disease or bubonic plague in the twentieth century has been enough to cause newspaper headlines and bring demands for action by the federal government. . . . By contrast, the thousands of deaths caused by smoking or drunken driving are familiar and hence acceptable. We may deplore them, but they arouse no fear or consternation among us" (pp. 23, 24).

From a societal perspective, disease is viewed as a burden not so much because of the individual suffering or loss that is causes, but because it impinges upon, ultimately, the freedom of other individuals and societal institutions. For example, disease places a burden on society because it imposes significant costs: for medical care, lost productivity, increased health insurance premiums, increased taxes, and strained public budgets. The government tends to respond to the threat of disease not when individual suffering reaches a certain level, but when the magnitude of the perceived threat to the freedom and autonomy of the rest of society's members reaches a level that demands public attention.

Disease has important societal meanings that go beyond the value society places on the absence of diseased individuals. In a sense, society as a whole has an "illness experience," a way in which it experiences, perceives, interprets, and acts to the presence of disease. And similar to the experience of individuals, it is not the existence of diseased individuals itself, but the threats to the freedom, independence, autonomy, and control of the members of society at large that most accurately characterize the salience of the experience to society.

References

Duffy, J. (1992). *The sanitarians: A history of American public health*. Urbana, IL: University of Illinois Press.

Institute of Medicine, Committee for the Study of the Future of Public Health. (1988). *The future of public health*. Washington, DC: National Academy Press.

Leavitt, J.W. (1982). *The healthiest city: Milwaukee and the politics of health reform*. Princeton, NJ: Princeton University Press.

McNeill, W.H. (1989). *Plagues and peoples*. New York: Anchor Books.

Means, J.H. (1953). *Doctors, people, and government*. Boston: Little, Brown.

Odets, W. (1995). *In the shadow of the epidemic: Being HIV-negative in the age of AIDS*. Durham, NC: Duke University Press.

Shilts, R. (1987). *And the band played on: Politics, people, and the AIDS epidemic*. New York: St. Martin's Press.

Starr, P. (1982). *The social transformation of American medicine*. New York: Basic Books.

6-B

An Example of Reframing a Public Health Policy Issue: Antismoking Ordinances

In 1995, the Ontario legislature considered a law to eliminate smoking in restaurants. The Ontario Restaurant Association (ORA) lobbied against the proposal, arguing that it would harm business; result in job losses for workers, and create hardship and suffering for restaurant owners, employees, and their families.

In an April 5, 1995, letter to the Ontario Campaign for Action on Tobacco, the ORA outlined its position. In response, Michael Siegel prepared a letter that was sent to Ontario government officials, attempting to reframe the issues. Excerpts from the two statements follow.

ORA:

The ORA believes that it is important to understand that any negative impact, if it is experienced by 1 restaurant or 1,000 restaurants, is a very serious situation to a restaurant owner, and depending on the degree and length of the negative impact, a foodservice operator could be forced to go out of business.

Response:

We believe that it is important to understand that any adverse health effects of secondhand smoke, if they are experienced by 1 restaurant worker or 1,000 restaurant workers, are a very serious situation for a restaurant owner, and depending on the degree and duration of the health effects, a restaurant worker could be forced to suffer, to have to stop working, or even to die.

ORA:

I do not believe that we can make light of a situation in which a negative impact on business is experienced, as it is both very serious and frightening for business owners who have placed their savings into their business and rely on their business for their livelihood. Nor can we ignore the fact that businesses employ people who will also be forced out of employment, if a severe negative impact is experienced as a result of a smoking by-law.

Response:

I do not believe that we can make light of a situation in which devastating health effects on restaurant workers are experienced, as it is both very serious and frightening for restaurant workers who have placed their careers into the food service business and rely on their work for their livelihood. Nor can we ignore the fact that businesses employ people who will be forced out of employment if they become sick due to a severe negative impact of secondhand smoke.

ORA:

No one knows the true impact of smoking bans on foodservice establishments in Ontario, except for foodservice operators who have the most direct contact with their customers and therefore know what percentage smoke.

Response:

No one knows the true impact of smoking in restaurants on foodservice workers in Ontario, except for the workers themselves, who have the most direct contact with secondhand smoke in their workplace, and therefore know the devastating impact that secondhand smoke has on their health and their lives.

III

Marketing Public Health— Case Studies

This section presents two case studies. The first case study illustrates the strategic application of marketing principles to develop and implement a novel intervention to reform health behavior among rural women of reproductive age in Rwanda: a radio soap opera. The second case study examines the role of issue framing in promoting public health as an institution.

7

Urunana— Radio Health Communication: A Case Study from Rwanda

Narcisse Kalisa
Prudence Uwabakurikiza
Samuel Kyagambiddwa
Jeannette Wijnants
Stephen Collens

Health Unlimited, Rwanda

This chapter describes how basic marketing principles were used to develop an innovative radio health communications project in Rwanda—*Urunana*—which has contributed to changes in awareness and attitudes to reproductive health, sexuality, and relationships of women, men and youth of Rwanda. It explains how a locally produced radio soap opera addresses culturally sensitive issues in an educational and entertaining manner, involving the target audience (rural women of reproductive age and youth) and a cross-section of stakeholders in its design and implementation. It also highlights the use of basic marketing principles used to research and understand the needs of impoverished, mainly rural listeners to inform the design and implementation of the *Urunana* radio program in a largely conservative and rural society. Although behavior change associated with mass media interventions remains difficult to measure, indirect and anecdotal evidence suggests that *Urunana's* "all-inclusive" approach has made substantial impact, not only on the target audience, but also on policy making in sexual and reproductive health in Rwanda.

Rwanda is a small landlocked country located in Central Africa with a total surface area of 26,338 sq. km. According to the national census conducted in 2002, the population of Rwanda was estimated at 8,128,553 inhabitants. About 90.2% of the population lives in rural areas and women make up more than half of the population, with disproportionately high levels of widow-headed households (Ministry of Finance and Economic Planning, 2002b). Population growth rate is 2.8%. UNICEF's State of World's Children report in 2005 indicates that 50% of its population is under the age of 18 and over 30% of these children are orphans, due to the 1994 genocide and its aftermath and to the high prevalence of HIV/AIDS.

Health status and overall socioeconomic status in Rwanda are poor. The under-five and infant mortality rates are 196 and 107 per 1000, respectively (Ministry of Health, 2001). The maternal mortality rate rose from 500 per 100,000 in 1992 to an average of 1,071 per 100,000 in 1995–2000. In 2005, the Treatment and Research on HIV/AIDS Centre survey revealed that HIV/AIDS prevalence was 4%. The Rwanda Ministry of Health indicates that malaria remains the main cause of morbidity, accounting for 41% of all consultations in health facilities (Ministry of Health, 2004).

The Demographic and Health Survey carried out in 2000 showed that almost all women were aware of at least one family planning method. However, the use of family planning methods is hampered by the lack of availability and/or utilization of these methods and misconceptions regarding the side effects of modern family planning methods (Institute for Reproductive Health, 2004). Furthermore, the lack of open discussions around sexual and reproductive health issues remains another obstacle, which fosters unwanted pregnancies, the spread of HIV/AIDS, and other sexually transmitted diseases. In addition, talking openly about sexual and reproductive health has been considered taboo.

Regarding health services, before 1994, Rwanda had 34 hospitals and 188 health centers. During the war, many of these facilities were looted and the majority of their staff were killed or exiled. The loss of health professionals had serious consequences on the country's ability to attend to the population in dire need of moral and medical support.

During the immediate aftermath of the war, the country saw an influx of international NGOs (non-governmental organizations) providing post-emergency services in various fields, but only a few seemed interested in long-term interventions to help rebuild the country.

This chapter is a case study of a successful health communication project in Rwanda: the "Well Women Media Project—Africa Great Lakes Region" (WWMP-AGLR). This public health intervention uses radio to provide primary health care information to the most vulnerable parts of the Rwandan population: rural women of reproductive age and young people. The chapter outlines the use of formative research in the development and implementation of the project, focusing on how it works with the target audience to formulate ideas and to make sure that the intervention appeals to the audience's core values. It also demonstrates how a brand was created for its main communication channel: the *Urunana* radio soap opera.

■ HEALTH UNLIMITED RWANDA: WELL WOMEN MEDIA PROJECT—AFRICA GREAT LAKES REGION

Founded in 1984, Health Unlimited, a British NGO, aims to "work with communities, service providers, policy makers and donors in difficult environments in Africa, Asia and Latin America to secure access to effective primary health care for marginalised people affected by conflict, instability or discrimination." Currently, Health Unlimited is established in 15 countries in sub-Saharan Africa, Asia, and Latin America. In 1997, Health Unlimited established its first project in Rwanda, the Well Women Media Project—Africa Great Lakes Region (WWMP-AGLR). The WWMP-AGLR has as its main purpose: to "increase public awareness and discussion of women's sexual and reproductive health issues leading to positive changes in knowledge, belief, attitude, and behaviour in the target group." This continues to be a very challenging task in a society where most sexual and reproductive health issues are considered taboo, hence not addressed. Such sexual and reproductive health "taboos" include sexuality, condom use, and family planning. In Africa, sociocultural taboos such as these are often not adequately addressed, resulting in additional barriers to achieving positive changes in sexual and reproductive health knowledge, attitude, beliefs, and reported practices and to addressing sexual and reproductive health-related topics. Therefore, the WWMP was set up to raise awareness of these health problems by providing relevant and accurate information via radio and encouraging discussions on sexual and reproductive health issues.

Since February 1999, the WWMP has broadcast two radio programs: *Urunana* (meaning "hand in hand" in Kinyarwanda, the national language of Rwanda), a soap opera, and *Umuhoza* ("the consoler"), a radio magazine. The *Urunana* radio soap opera has been broadcast on the Great Lakes Service of the British Broadcasting Corporation (BBC) and on Radio Rwanda and the fifteen-minute stand-alone radio magazine is exclusively broadcast on Radio Rwanda. *Urunana* is broadcast on Tuesdays and Thursdays at 6:45 P.M. on BBC Great Lakes and an omnibus edition is broadcast on Sundays at 7:30 A.M. and 5:00 P.M.

Urunana combines humor and health messages. This method is called "edutainment," a blend of "education" and "entertainment." By using the edutainment strategy in *Urunana*, the audience is motivated to listen with full attention to storylines that include everyday village life, while addressing more sensitive issues that are often considered taboo such as youth sexuality, condom use, and family planning. Since the beginning of the program on radio, *Urunana* has attracted many listeners; more than 74% of the Rwandan population regularly listens to the program (Health Unlimited Rwanda Well Women Media Project, 2005). Furthermore, feedback from the audience suggests that the *Urunana* serial drama also has a large audience in the entire Kinyarwanda-Kirundi speaking area of the Africa Great Lakes Region, including the whole of Burundi, the eastern part of the Democratic Republic of Congo, the western part of Tanzania, and the southern part of Uganda, where the program can be heard on BBC radio.

■ TARGET AUDIENCE

The main target group of the program is rural women of reproductive age and youth. The reason for choosing rural women of reproductive age and youth as the main target groups was the fact that they are the most vulnerable part of the population; they live in extreme poverty, desperately need sexual and reproductive health information to avoid unwanted pregnancies, HIV/AIDS, and other sexually transmitted diseases (STDs) and are in critical need of information on family planning methods.

After the genocide, there was a need to give this population information on their sexual and reproductive health in order to fight against HIV/AIDS, which was drastically devastating the country, to raise awareness on other prevailing diseases like malaria and tuberculosis, and to enhance awareness of the use of family planning methods, which were no longer valued. Only 7% of all women surveyed indicated that they used a family planning method, while this percentage was at 14% in 1992 (Institute for Reproductive Health, 2004). There was also a large need to lay strategies to adequately address youth sexuality and sex education and to curb the spread of HIV/AIDS and other sexually transmitted diseases among youth, who are the most vulnerable population.

It is worth noting that any project targeting women and youth must also involve those who are the main partners in behavior change. Therefore, the project targeted men as a secondary audience. This is why, for instance, while talking about family planning and the fight against HIV/AIDS, it is also very important to design messages targeting men; one must also stress the importance of their involvement and responsibilities. In order to help control the growth of the population, but also to improve maternal and child health, men need to be informed about the importance of family planning as well.

■ USING RADIO TO COMMUNICATE HEALTH INFORMATION

Within the specific context of Rwanda, producing a radio program with a large following for educational and entertainment purposes is quite a difficult task. During and leading up to the 1994 genocide, radio was effectively used to spread hate propaganda against part of its population. In the aftermath of the war and genocide, many Rwandans were suspicious of radio as a medium to pass on anything positive and educational. Yet Health Unlimited chose radio as a medium of communication in order to pass health messages to the target group, rural women of reproductive age and youth, as it has proven to be a powerful tool of communication that can be used effectively to change people's behavior, attitudes, beliefs, and practices (Adam & Harford, 1998; Crook, 1999).

In Rwanda, radio reaches a wider audience than any other medium. According to the national census (Ministry of Finance and Economic Planning, 2002a), only 61% of the population is literate. In this context, it is especially valuable to use radio to communicate health messages, knowing that other forms of communication, such as print media, are not appropriate for a primarily rural and illiterate population, and acknowledging that only 0.1% of the population owns a television set. The same census indicated that 41.7% of ordinary households own a radio set, but other research suggests that radio ownership differs very much from radio listenership, as people in rural areas come together to listen to their favorite radio programs, either at home, in the local bar, at the workplace, or on the bus (Health Unlimited Rwanda, 2005).

Another advantage of using radio is the fact that "Radio is based in oral tradition. Every culture has traditions of storytelling, and the fascination of listening to a good tale well told has never been lost. . . . A successful radio serial writer knows how to use this tradition to create an intriguing story that attracts and holds a listening audience" (DeFossard, 1997).

■ THE USE OF FORMATIVE RESEARCH IN URUNANA PLANNING AND IMPLEMENTATION

This section focuses on how the WWMP uses formative research in the development and implementation of *Urunana*, its main output, and the way that knowledge gained from intensive study of the audience is used in designing the program.

Research has been at the heart of every stage of development and production of *Urunana*. This health communication project started in the specific post-genocide context of 1994, when the country was emerging from the terrible turmoil which had put ablaze not only its social and economic status, but also claimed up to one million lives. People were still haunted by the horror of four years earlier and cases of trauma commonly occurred in villages around Rwanda. Scores of orphans and widows were still unattended to in terms of their shelter and basic health necessities. "The war and genocide affected men and women differently. It is estimated that more than 200,000 Rwandan women and girls were victims of some form of sexual violence. . . . Thus, many war widows and other single women survived to care for families alone, to take in orphans, and to assume duties traditionally carried out in patriarchal Rwanda by men" (USAID, 2000).

Furthermore, up to two million Rwandans who had fled the country as a result of war and genocide were being repatriated from neighboring countries and among returnees, scores were suspected of having perpetrated the 1994 genocide. This massive influx of returnees heightened a climate of suspicion in communities and villages. The precarious situation meant that needs of the population had shifted from long-term development into ad hoc, tangible interventions to solve problems immediately at hand, such as the need for shelter, security, food, clothing, etc.

With the peculiarities involved in post-genocide Rwanda, research was necessary in order to design and implement programs that were understandable, acceptable, relevant, attractive, and persuasive enough for the target audience to attend to and act on the information they receive.

Initial Needs Assessment

Before the actual start of any project, a media project needs to find answers to fundamental questions such as "Who is the program for?" (defining the target audience), "What are their needs and concerns?" and "How can we best address these concerns?" These questions serve as benchmarks throughout the project life and are an integral part of planning and implementing programs.

Before *Urunana* was created, initial research was carried out in 1998 and consisted of reviewing relevant literature on which the formulation of a hypothesis could be based. This consisted mainly of reviewing secondary source documents from government institutions, international NGOs, and United Nations agencies.

Initial KAPB Research

In 1998, the first research questionnaire into knowledge, attitudes, practices, and behavior (KAPB) was administered to a sample of 698 people comprised of 411 women (59%) and 287 men (41%). This sample was randomly drawn from rural areas of Rwanda and interviewees were met in their homesteads during their typical daily activities (farms, markets, schools, etc.). After the analysis of the results, a list of lessons learned was compiled and recommendations were made.

The following table highlights major lessons learned, gaps, and strategies to answer the remaining questions after the initial needs assessment.

Qualitative research techniques, especially the focus group discussions and interviews with key informants, helped to shed light on gaps identified.

This involved going back into the communities and organizing separate discussions with young boys, young girls, and men and women. In the process of engaging project staff with the community, ideas on characters and setting of the soap opera were developed. Stories collected from the various focus group discussions were used to portray the real day-to-day life in a typical village of Rwanda. The name of the soap opera, *Urunana*, also was drawn from the aspirations expressed during various encounters with the audience.

Table 7-1 Summary of Formative Research

What we learned	What we need to find out	What we need to do
Age: only 9% of the sample are over 50 years old	What is the life expectancy in Rwanda?	Check the secondary source review
Religion: 77% of the sample are Catholics	Is the Catholic church in Rwanda against modern contraceptive methods? This could affect the potential of birth spacing messages.	Talk to church leaders
Education: 42% of the sample cannot read or write	What are the factors that influence literacy?	Check during focus group discussions
Radio ownership: 32% of the female sample owns a radio against 58% of men	How many people will be listening to the radio programme?	Check with secondary sources or conduct a mini survey
Twice the number of men than women do not seek health information	What are the factors that influence this?	Focus group discussion
31% of the sample said that condom use protects people from HIV/AIDS. Twice as many men than women knew this	Which age group knows this?	Re-check KAPB
Attitudes toward people living with HIV/AIDS vary from individual to individual	Why do people in the community feel afraid or want to discriminate against people living with HIV/AIDS?	Secondary sources, Focus group discussion
Parents do not talk with their children about body changes and developments	Where do children get sexual and reproductive health information ?	Focus group discussion, key informants

Source: Health Unlimited Rwanda Well Women Media Project, 1999.

Stakeholders' Meetings

After the write-up of all the research accounts, organizations in the social and health sectors were invited to participate in the first stakeholder meeting. This included a host of government institutions, national, and international organizations whose actions may complement or impact the project interventions. The main objective was to present the projects and research findings and solicit the partners for their contributions in terms of information and message formulation. Subsequently, these meetings are held annually and participants are clustered according to their areas of interventions: sexual and reproductive health, health education, maternal and infant health, HIV/AIDS, people living with HIV/ADS, religious leaders, malaria, tuberculosis, etc. Participants exchange information on the latest developments in their various fields of interest and suggest priority health messages. The value of the stakeholders' meetings is that partners promote and advocate for *Urunana* in their different field activities and to their own partners. The stakeholders' workshop also considers a draft project document of health messages prepared by the project staff based on both internal and external sources. The internal sources include data gathered during regular KAPB surveys, monthly audience surveillance visits, as well as issues from letters of listeners. External sources consist of research publications of other partners and national health policies and strategies. The final health messages document guides *Urunana* stories over the whole year.

Audience Surveillance

Each month, the head writer suggests an outline of stories and messages with possible options to the production team during a monthly script meeting. The latter choose and suggest other courses stories may take. But the final direction is decided by the audience during audience surveillance visits.

Since 2001, project staff, especially a team of writers and producers, have conducted monthly audience surveillance visits to various provinces of Rwanda. These visits aim at engaging with the communities in discussions on the past episodes that have been broadcast, including past storylines, acting, and the language. A cross section of both listeners and non-listeners are gathered by a local volunteer in the open air, mostly under a tree. The project staff facilitates the discussions and a note-taker records the proceedings.

For gender- or culturally-sensitive issues, participants are divided into groups, i.e. youth (boys and girls separated) and women and men in their respective corners. In a patriarchal society like Rwanda, the presence of men in discussion could hamper the openness of women about issues that may be perceived as offensive to male self-esteem. Dividing the groups by gender helps prevent any possible inhibition or influence, especially of boys and men over girls and women respectively. Homogeneity of groups increases a free flow of ideas in "normal words and emotions" about specific issues appropriate to a specific group. For instance, how would a woman talk about how her husband fails her in bed in the presence of a host of men, or how would a young girl feel comfortable talking about her first menstruation in front of boys? What about men cheating on their wives? The facilitators are gender matched to the groups.

Below is a sample of audience surveillance questions:

1. What do you make of the last week's episodes? What did you like/dislike?
2. How do you think x, y, z (characters' names) will continue?
3. What do you think of x, y, z (characters' names) behavior?
4. In x, y, z's (characters' names) place what would you have done differently?
5. Are x, y, z (characters' names) behaviors of common occurrence in this area? Give us examples?
6. After x and y have protected sex; what may trigger x to go for an HIV/AIDS test?
7. In which instances can y agree to have sex with x without a condom?
8. What does a dowry consist of in this area?
9. Who decides about the dowry?
10. What are the necessary preparations for receiving a dowry on the girl's family side?

The writers' team meticulously reviews the information gathered during the audience surveillance sessions and uses it to further develop plots and stories.

Involvement of the target audience in the production increases the ownership of the program as its contributions are truly valued and taken into account. The interaction with the audience allows the production team to stay abreast of current events in the target audience's private lives that lends itself to a true-to-life product. Listeners identify with soap characters, following their trials and tribulations, and emulate the heroism of their models. According to the social learning theory, involvement of listeners in characters' emotions, i.e., their actions and personality, has the potential to inspire listeners and lead to vicarious learning (Bandura, 1986).

The monthly audience surveillance is coupled with the KAPB survey. The same team visits villages other than those chosen for the audience surveillance sessions and administers a standard questionnaire to community members. Filled questionnaires are compiled and tabulated regularly to monitor the "barometer" of responsiveness of the audience in terms of program awareness and content.

Table 7-2   Formative Research Results

Preliminary results from the analysis of the Knowledge, Attitudes and Practice (KAPB) survey conducted between September 2002 and July 2005 show that:

1. Listeners to the *Urunana* radio drama largely find the health messages relevant (91%), practical (76%) and acceptable (94%), but rates of understanding (54%) are somewhat lower and can be improved;

2. Large proportions of listeners to the *Urunana* radio drama report that they engage in discussions of the sexual and reproductive health messages (55%–81%); and

3. Large proportions of listeners to the *Urunana* radio drama report that they advise others on the sexual reproductive health messages they have learned from the program (59%–81%).

Source: Health Unlimited Rwanda Well Women Media Project: September 2005

The *Urunana* soap opera target audience is diverse in terms of social and demographic characteristics. Therefore it proved hard to maintain a good balance between reaching women and reaching youth with specifically-tailored health messages. In order to assess how youth might be more effectively reached, an action research study was conducted in 2002. About 200 questionnaires were administered and six focus group discussions, three with boys and three with girls, were held. The outcome helped re-shape *Urunana's* plots, providing ideas for storylines featuring young people and guidance in the use of appropriate language to better communicate the issues.

Rural Familiarization

Once a year, the team of writers engages for four days with the population in their daily activities and interactions and spends its days and nights with them in their homes. This activity helps the team to "live the life" of rural people in order to observe what people do and how they live rather than relying on what they say they do. The endeavor helps establish the general family interactions; i.e., gender roles, health-related behaviors, and how things happen on a typical day. For example, who is involved in what at what time?

It would be otherwise difficult for an urban-based production team to imagine what happens in the villages where the target audience lives. Although team members may have been born in different rural places, having left their villages early for schools and worked in cities has often influenced them. They may have lost touch with the village life of the target audience. These short opportunities to participate in village life strengthen still further the bond between the production team and the audience.

Behavior change communication strategies and interventions need to be "a two-way talk," rather than a patronizing top-down approach. Research informs the best ways to bolster the involvement of the target audience in the process of developing a product that has the potential to reflect their own needs. People respond positively to communications whose messages they can easily identify with and which portray them in a good light.

The Setting of Urunana

Everything happens in Nyarurembo, a typical rural village in Rwanda with schools, a church, banana plantations, a river and houses, and roads and streets in bad condition to reflect the reality in the Rwandan rural villages. This enables us to develop realistic and believable stories.

The name of Nyarurembo was randomly chosen, as far as we know there is no place in Rwanda called Nyarurembo, but it gives a picture of a typical rural village and the target groups consider Nyarurembo as their own village. The language used in the program is the one used in the villages with proverbs and idioms appropriate to the rural population.

Priority health messages addressed in the program are related to the most prevalent diseases and health topics in rural areas. These include malaria, STDs, HIV/AIDS, tuberculosis, safe motherhood, and youth sexuality. Other more social issues such as gender equality, domestic violence, and girls' education are also addressed. This is supported by the use of characters to reflect the reality on the ground in order to provide to the listeners the needed health information.

Urunana Characters

One of the most important aspects of a successful radio soap opera are convincing and credible characters. These characters reflect different attitudes in relation to the main theme of the soap and the population it is targeting. Listeners will follow characters they like in their daily endeavors in life, through their ups and downs. The *Urunana* soap opera has developed three types of characters with quite distinct behaviors and perceptions toward its educational messages.

a. Positive role model characters

These characters uphold and reflect values promoted in *Urunana*. They are role models in treatment seeking, in avoiding HIV/AIDS and other infections, and in advising their peers about bad attitudes that need to be changed.

The late Munyakazi and his wife Mariana are a good example of this kind of character. This couple is a reference for marital problem solving and communication over and above the basic primary health issues in the village. The couple played an important role in communication around HIV/AIDS and sexual and reproductive health issues. When Munyakazi found out that he was HIV positive, Mariana became the main character in the soap opera to address messages on stigma and discrimination against people living with AIDS. The story of having Munyakazi infected by HIV/AIDS was introduced in the soap to show that anyone can be infected. Even though Munyakazi was a role model in Nyarurembo, one day he cheated on his wife and got HIV.

This storyline made a very big impact on the audience, who learned that you can get HIV even through one unprotected sexual intercourse. Messages on stigma and discrimination were also introduced in this storyline, when Munyakazi developed AIDS and when Mariana took care of him until his death. During one community outreach session, a listener said. "I used to over-charge clients I suspected being HIV positive and sent them away, but after listening to Urunana programs on stigma I abandoned the habit. I now take them as normal people" (a young barber in Gisenyi province).

This stigma against people living with AIDS was mostly due to the fact that these listeners did not have enough information on how HIV is transmitted. These role model characters are being used in *Urunana* as an instrument of behavior change in the target audience.

Another listener said, "Urunana program came at the right time. It helps the young and old, literate and illiterate. It talks about our daily life. It makes us think about our future: being real people, giving our lives a direction and objective" (a student in secondary school). Following this impact made by the program on the target audience through realistic stories developed in the soap, there is a kind of confusion; there is a loss of a distinction between the actors and characters they are portraying. Josephine Mukamusoni, an actress playing Mariana, a health adviser in Nyarurembo confided,

> being a role model in the soap opera has attracted many people who come to me for advice. Playing a health adviser in the soap made me an adviser in my village. I also personally receive letters and calls from people seeking advice from me. The latest letter was received from a Rwandese young girl living in Belgium.

b. Negative role model characters

These characters stand out to reject and act against positive values upheld in the soap. Characters in this group get penalized for their actions. Stefano, a man in his late 40s, proves to be the most mischievous in the village, an irresponsible guy who does not take care of his family and who beats his wife. At the insistence of his wife, Nyiramariza, recalling him to his responsibilities to provide for the family, Stefano bumps into another woman who "will give him peace of mind." It does not take long before the relationship ends in a pregnancy. Stefano denies his responsibility and fears Nyiramariza will turn roughly against him if she happens to know. He contracts gonorrhoea as a result of his infidelity.

Pressed hard by threats from his mistress to bring him to justice, Stefano eventually resolves to flee from the village. After meeting total failure in town, he returns to the village miserable, to face the consequences of his actions. First of all, he is not welcomed by his wife, for whom he failed in his promise to change. His wife accepts him back in the home but refuses to have sex with him. She recalls the health adviser's advice that "if you suspect that your partner has had other sexual partners, it is possible he/she has contracted HIV/STDs, suggest using condom all the time until you get tested, to prevent yourself from getting HIV/STDs."

Nyiramariza is sticking to this advice to protect herself from being infected.

c. The doubters

These characters are unsure which side to take; but as the plot develops, they realize they need to belong to the group that best serves their interests. They are easily "manipulated" by either side. They get rewarded or punished depending on the side or friends they choose.

Bushombe, *Urunana's* funniest character, is one of the doubters. After long years of a childless relationship with his wife, going to witch doctors, and pushed by his fellow men, he decided "to try outside" to prove his "manhood." But after some time of an extra-marital relationship that also does not result in pregnancy, he has to accept that the infertility problem could possibly lie with him, and not his wife. Subsequently, the couple seeks medical consultation at the referral hospital in town where Bushombe's hormone level is boosted, and finally the couple gives birth to a baby girl.

These three categories of characters are used to portray both negative and positive attitudes. The audience moves along with the characters and they are encouraged to make decisions in relation to the messages addressed in the soap opera and the consequences their favorite characters experience after they fail to change their negative behavior.

For instance, for the last two years the program has addressed the issue of teenage pregnancies. Agnes, a young school girl in the story, was impregnated by her classmate Semana. She is then shown to go through a variety of difficulties after the birth of her baby, including dropping out of school for one year, frustrations caused by her family, and loss of hope. By illustrating the negative impact of the teenagers' behavior, school girls and boys in Rwanda are encouraged to make the decision to avoid unplanned pregnancies and not have sex before marriage. In turn, parents have also been encouraged to allow their teenage daughters to return and complete school after giving birth.

Appealing to the Core Values of the Target Audience

For any project that is community based or dealing with sensitive issues to be successful, respecting the core values of the target audience or the community it works with is essential. Failure to take these into consideration during the designing or implementation of a program risks hitting a brick wall and failing to achieve the desired results.

The target audience will regard the program to be foreign or an intruder who has come to destroy their values and lose interest in it, leading to stiff rejection, when the core values of the target audience are not given due respect and attention.

The method that is used most often in *Urunana* to promote behavior change by appealing to compelling target audience core values is the information education communication principle of Persuade, Encourage, and Enable. Individuals' or communities' negative behavior is exposed and consequences that can occur as a result of that particular behavior or practice are put into the spotlight. After the exposure of the negative behavior and possible consequences, the target audience is persuaded to take on the alternative behavior by showing the benefits of adopting it. Enabling the target audience to achieve the desired change follows persuasion. This is done by showing or providing means by which the audience can adopt the desired change.

In order to be successful, *Urunana* has taken the core values of the target audience into consideration and this has most contributed to the production of realistic and believable programs, which have always reflected the knowledge, practices, beliefs, and attitudes of the target audience. Most of the target audience identify themselves with situations and stories in the soap opera and the characters, as well as with some similar people in their communities. Appreciation of the program culturally has given *Urunana* a chance to successfully address even several issues considered taboo within Rwandan culture. Much attention and respect was given to the language used and to the traditional practices of the Rwandan culture. This has been achieved by using an entire local production team that has strong knowledge and understanding of the culture.

Language

In Rwandan culture, the value attached to sexual and reproductive health is that it can only be talked about by adults, and only in their bedroom or other private places. Discussions between parents and children about sexual and reproductive health are almost non-existent; children are left to get any information from peers who also have insufficient information about sexual and reproductive health (Ministry of Gender and Women, 2002).

One of the main challenges for the project was to bring what were considered "dark bedroom discussions" to radio airwaves and to highlight the importance of open discussions between parents and their children, and between peers, without offending the cultural values attached to sexual and reproductive health among the target audience.

Appropriate use of language has been fundamental throughout the production of *Urunana*. Words have been carefully selected and used in the drama. Very offensive words have been avoided and efforts made to find appropriate metaphors. In most cases, the production team has used humor to correct bad manners, *"ridendo castigare mores."* At the beginning it was very hard to broadcast messages on condom use, but slowly listeners understood the importance of discussing ways of preventing unplanned pregnancies, sexually transmitted infections and HIV/AIDS. Asked during a listenership survey whether they are offended by the messages, language, and topics addressed in Urunana, , 86.6% of the listeners did not report being offended by the topics and the language used, with only 6.2% reporting being "offended" and 7.2% stating that they are "sometimes offended." These findings differ from earlier listeners' complaints reported in 2000, which revealed significantly more discomfort over the sexual and reproductive health messages broadcast in Urunana, even though the public health topics are similar.

It is often difficult to address certain issues since it could be considered going too deeply into private issues, which would conflict with the values of the target audience. However, *Urunana* builds up the stories, thus creating a need to talk about particular issues, as well as stirring anxiety within the audience who want to know what is going to happen next to the character to get out of such a situation. With careful attention to balancing language, values, humor, and the objectives of the project, parents and children can now sit together to listen to the program, even as it addresses some very sensitive issues.

Settings of Actions

Settings in the *Urunana* soap opera have been carefully chosen in the development of stories to address health and other issues that affect the Rwandan society. Consideration is given to using places that are valued to be social gathering places for men and women or for children and young people. For instance, it would be unconvincing, if not insulting, to have men meet at a place that is traditionally a women's meeting place, such as the river bank, to fetch water and have them talk about issues affecting their homes, wives, or village. The *Urunana* production team instead chooses a more realistic and appropriate setting where men tend to meet, such as a bar, home, or somewhere sitting around sharing a drink and discussing issues.

This is not to say that *Urunana* does not promote breaking gender barriers. For instance, in *Urunana,* women also meet in the "Women Association activities," to share ideas regarding their health concerns, something which many "traditional men" have difficulty accepting. However, this is done carefully, and with attention to the perceived credibility of the program. For instance, traditionally in Rwandan culture men will not enter the kitchen or cook as cooking is usually a task for women. So, in most storylines, a scene will not be set in a kitchen with a man cooking as it would not be perceived as credible. However, when the message is one on gender equity and the producers want to encourage a culture in which men support women in all home activities and share responsibilities, they can introduce a man helping his wife to prepare food for the children. This way, the man's actions (i.e., doing a nontraditional man's task) are used to educate the audience on gender equity and sharing of responsibilities.

Traditional Practices

There are several traditional practices that are valued by the Rwandan society. As program makers, there is a need to respect these values so as to increase a feeling of ownership of the program and relevance to the target group. In Rwandan culture, for example, it is important that after a baby is born, friends and relatives visit to congratulate the parents on their newborn and also to perform a naming ceremony which brings together many people. Traditional practices like this are promoted in the program. They help to create variety and bring about dynamics in the soap opera. Other unharmful and valued traditional practices referred to in the soap opera include traditional wedding ceremonies and burial ceremonies.

However, there are some other traditional practices that are harmful. These practices are addressed in the soap opera to discourage the target audience from practicing them. For example, there is a belief in Rwanda that if a man doesn't have sex with his wife eight days after giving birth, it will take very long for a woman to recover from delivery. The practice is referred to in Kinyarwanda as "*komora*." However, from a medical perspective, this practice does not help the woman recover from any painful side effects of the delivery; instead, it can cause infections and further complications for the mother. Another example is the belief of children having "false teeth" which should be extracted by a witchdoctor, known as "*Ibyinyo*," when extracting the child's teeth is harmful, unnecessary, and risky when done by unqualified doctors. These and other common harmful traditional practices have been discouraged in the program without offending the culture. Different strategies have been put in place to address these traditional practices on air without offending our listeners and our culture such as mixing education and entertainment, or using humor.

Creating a Brand for Urunana

Urunana, like any other product in the marketplace, needs to be well positioned in the minds of the audience in order to effectively achieve its objectives (Kapferer, 1992). The mammoth task of a mass communication intervention is to capture and maintain the audience's attention about the program within a competitive environment. The target audience must be convinced before hand why they should listen to it and listen regularly, and in which way this particular program is different from others.

The preliminary survey carried out before the actual launching of *Urunana* shows that drama ranked among the three most popular programs. In Rwanda, drama had always consisted of on-off traditional radio plays. Serial drama was still new. By its relentless nature, being long running with interweaving stories and with a stock of characters, a soap opera needs time to position itself correctly in the minds of listeners. But it is well-poised to do so.

In order to "hook" the audience, *Urunana* had to start with the most immediate thing: its name. *Urunana* in the vernacular Kinyarwanda means "hand in hand." In the Rwandan post-conflict and genocide, "hand-in-hand" seemed almost too enterprising when the project started. The Rwandan society was torn apart by the genocide and suspicion was rife in the communities. The name suggested that people irrespective of their ethnic or family affiliation should come together to talk about the common health issues facing them. Yet, this is exactly what the program has achieved: bringing people together and emphasizing their similarities, rather than their perceived differences.

The *Urunana* soap opera signature tune adds strength to the attributes the name embodies; "this is Urunana which entrenches dialogue of those who share the walk. Let's come together, sit down on the grass to talk about issues." *Urunana* proposes to provide a forum where issues are discussed and solutions are mutually suggested. Internally, staff have gone a long way to understand that the program needs to be audience driven, that in order for *Urunana* to properly serve its target audience, there is a need to be close to them.

Providing accurate messages is one of the strengths of *Urunana* as a behavior change communication strategy in Rwanda. The accuracy stems from wide range consultations with all the stakeholders and this increases ownership and credibility. In order to ensure this, *Urunana* also uses the services of an independent medical expert to crosscheck the messages after scripts are developed and before the final stage in the production cycle studio production.

Respect of the culture of the wider audience in general and that of the target audience in particular is the best way for the program to rally acceptance of the listeners. Addressing culturally sensitive issues while trying to change people's behaviors proves to be very demanding. The biggest problem has been how to talk about sexual and reproductive health related issues to an audience composed of women, men, young boys and girls and small children. The recent story about a young couple where a man had a problem of premature ejaculation caught the audience by surprise. In the Rwandan culture, like many other traditional cultures, talking about men's sexual problems equals attacking men's self-esteem. The language to talk about this does not come easily. After much pre-testing of various potential ways of talking about premature ejaculation, it was decided to describe the problem in one simple way: "to leave a cup of milk unfinished." Adults understood the plot and the message and never felt discomfort listening to the story in the presence of children.

The biggest promise of *Urunana* is to deliver a good balance between education and entertainment. The impact of *Urunana* educational messages has been expanded through the use of the soap opera in schools and youth centers. Questions about *Urunana* messages and stories have been used by the Rwandan National Examination Council for the primary and secondary school leavers. They are also used in youth centers as case studies and as discussion starters. In Rwanda, when *Urunana* is mentioned, names of humorous characters are immediately singled out. In order to produce a humor that will make the audience "titillate," the production team needs to know the audience inside out.

The pyramid in **Figure 7-1** shows the promises *Urunana* is set out to deliver to the audience. On the top of the pyramid is *Urunana* beliefs and values: "Needs-based programs." If listeners perceive that the program talks about people like themselves, there is no doubt that they will become loyal to the program and develop trust in the messages and modeling of intended behaviors. This puts the target audience at the heart of production right from the conception. Sexual and reproductive health

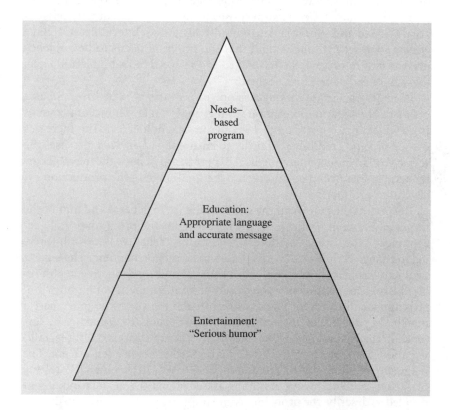

Figure 7-1 Distinctive Symbols of Urunana

issues of youth as they are perceived differently from adults needed to be reflected upon in a particular way. The magic of soap opera does this in interweaving different plots at the same time. For example, the issue of Budensiana whose father wants her to marry a wealthy man of the village against her will runs concurrently with the story of the Shyaka couple going to the hospital in the city for their infertility problems. The relevance of the programmatic issues to the target audience stimulates listeners to sympathize with characters and emulate their good examples.

The middle level reflects benefits that *Urunana* confers to its listeners. Accurate messages in "non-scandalizing" language mean people will develop a listening habit. The long running stories keep listeners interested to know the outcome of a situation their role models are struggling with; how they are getting punished for performing socially unaccepted behaviors and how they are rewarded for performing a socially desirable behavior. In the process, listeners will easily follow messages being passed along and learn from their models' experiences. The tribulations of the doubter Bushombe and his wife Kankwanzi in trying to get a child will linger in the memory of listeners. Messages are given naturally, through true-to-life experiences and in real time; for example, it takes nine months for a pregnant woman to give birth, so in the drama we stay within the real time frame. The effect of stories like this one is in the recognition of the program and the fact that people associate easily with the characters and the messages they convey. For example, when one talks of 'Nyiramariza,' the image of a strong willed, hardworking and enterprising woman comes to mind, and how she resisted having unprotected sex with her wayward husband Stefano.

The third dimension of the *Urunana* symbol is entertainment. Humor is instrumental in keeping the audience tuned in as most people under normal circumstances will not resist a good laugh and "the essential rhythm of human experience contains a balance of tension and humor. Humor is the survival mechanism of the tragic experience. I would recommend that the emotional rhythm of the play dances on the listener's heart and mind: tension, humor, tension, humor, charm and alarm" (Kotler, 2003). The popularity of comic characters has the potential to attract and maintain listeners for a long time. As listeners wait to be entertained wittingly by their cherished humorous characters, they simultaneously get educated.

Because of the great concern given to the values of the target audience, the program has achieved a high level of perceived relevance in the lives of the target audience. Of 965 persons surveyed between 2002 and 2005 about the relevance of *Urunana* messages, 91% confirmed that the messages were relevant to them (Health Unlimited Rwanda Well Women Media Project, 2005).

■ CONCLUSION

In Rwanda, *Urunana* is now the most popular radio program with up to 74% of the Rwandan population listening to the program (Health Unlimited Rwanda, 2005). More and more organizations seek partnership with *Urunana* for message insertion in the drama as it has a big outreach and listenership, particularly in rural areas of the country.

The involvement of the target population in designing and implementing the program and the combination of humor and education in addressing sensitive issues of sexual and reproductive health are the main ingredients which have led to the success of *Urunana*. It is upon this success that Health Unlimited is building a local independent organization that will have the name of the program: *Urunana Development Communication*.

The *Urunana* soap opera produced in Rwanda is proving that the combination of humor and education is an effective communication strategy to address culturally sensitive health and social issues considered to be taboo in rural areas.

The success of *Urunana* stems from a mix of communication and marketing principles linked to formative research to identify and understand the sexual and reproductive health behavior and core values of the target audience.

By using radio, which is accessible to the mainly non-literate target audience, *Urunana* listeners identify with stories and characters who serve as models to adopt promoted behaviors. The project continually promotes, in an integrated manner, key sexual and reproductive health issues, and also contributes to national and regional campaigns on public health.

■ ACKNOWLEDGMENTS

The authors wish to thank the following persons for their invaluable editorial support in the writing of this chapter (in alphabetical order): J. Gathogo, M. Mwangi, and A. Sharma.

This chapter was contributed by:

Health Unlimited Rwanda
P.O. Box 4720
Kigali, Rwanda
www.healthunlimited.org
UK Charity No. 290535

References

Adam, G. & Harford, N. (1998). *Health On Air*. London: Health Unlimited.

Bandura, A. (1986). *Social foundations of thought and action: A social cognitive theory*. Englewood Cliffs, NJ: Prentice Hall.

Crook, T. (1999). *Radio drama: Theory and practice*. Oxford (UK): Routledge.

DeFossard, E. (1997). *How to write a radio soap serial drama for social development: A script-writer's manual*. Baltimore, MD: The Johns Hopkins University School of Public Health, Center for Communication Programs, Population Communication Services.

Health Unlimited Rwanda. (2005). *Baseline survey report of the Urunana/Umuhoza rural extension project-2005–2008*. Kigali, Rwanda: Author.

Health Unlimited Rwanda Well Women Media Project. (1999). *Gaps analysis of KAPB research*. Kigali, Rwanda: Author.

———. (2005). *Preliminary evaluation of the Urunana KAP monitoring data. Statement of major findings (September 2002–July 2005)*. Kigali, Rwanda: Author.

Institute for Reproductive Health. (2004). *Mid-term assessment of the Standard Days Method (SDM) introduction in Rwanda*. Washington, DC: Institute for Reproductive Health, Georgetown University.

Kapferer, J.N. (1992). *Strategic brand management: New approaches to creating and evaluating brand equity*. London: Kogan Page.

Kotler, P. (2003). *Marketing management (11th edition. International edition)*. Englewood Cliffs, NJ: Prentice Hall.

Ministry of Finance and Economic Planning. (2002a). *Rwanda national census*. Kigali, Rwanda: Author.

———. (2002b). *Rwanda poverty reduction strategy paper (PRSP)*. Kigali, Rwanda: Author.

Ministry of Gender and Women in Development & United Nations Population Fund. (2002). *A study on beliefs, attitudes and socio-cultural practices related to gender in Rwanda*. Kigali, Rwanda: Author.

Ministry of Health. (2001). *Demographic and health survey*. Kigali, Rwanda: Author.

———. (2004). *Health sector strategic plan 2005–2009*. Kigali, Rwanda: Author.

United States Agency for International Development (USAID) (2000). *Aftermath: Women and women's organizations in postgenocide Rwanda* (USAID Evaluation Highlights No. 69, December 2000). Washington, DC: Author. Available at: http://www.peacewomen.org/resources/Rwanda/usaid2.pdf).

CHAPTER

8

Marketing Public Health as an Institution: A Case Study

Erin K. Fortunato, MPH

Social and Behavioral Sciences Department
Boston University School of Public Health

Public health practitioners must market public health itself as a fundamental societal institution. Despite several ongoing efforts to study the ways in which public health can be effectively marketed and framed, the research literature on this topic is limited. There is a clear need to study framing of public health as an institution. This chapter identifies and analyzes the current frames of public health and formulates improved frames for the future.

The dominant frame of public health as an institution is one of health promotion, using the relatively weak core value of health and equating public health with medical care for the poor. To be successful, public health must be re-framed so that it reinforces the most compelling core values of American citizens and policy makers. Framing public health as security, a very strong core value shared by nearly all Americans regardless of social class and a top priority of policy makers, is a very promising option. In the wake of 9/11, gaps in security are perceived to be significant, universal threats to the public's freedom, independence, autonomy, and control. Appealing to Congress for funding to protect the nation's security and the security, survival, and freedom of our people, is much more likely to result in approved funding than appealing to Congress for funding to promote health. There is a great opportunity to frame public health as freedom from the unknown, control over threats to our economic and physical survival, and ultimately security against natural and man-made disasters.

Public health practitioners must not only market changes in health behavior, adoption of public health policies, and funding of specific public health programs, they also must market public health itself as a fundamental societal institution. With the threats of managed care, budget cuts, low demand for public health, and other factors discussed in Chapter 4, public health practitioners must often compete to obtain funding for their agencies, independent of promoting health behavior change and specific public policies.

There are several ongoing efforts to study the ways in which public health can be marketed and framed more effectively. The Office of Communication at the Centers for Disease Control and Prevention (CDC) has a Social Marketing Practice Area dedicated to applying the tenets of social marketing to public health interventions (Communication at CDC, 2006). A frequently cited definition of social marketing was formulated by Alan Andreson in 1995:

> Social marketing is the application of commercial marketing technologies to the analysis, planning, execution, and evaluation of programs designed to influence the voluntary behavior of target audiences in order to improve their personal welfare and that of their society. (p. 7)

CDC has embraced social marketing so fully that it created its own brand of social marketing called Prevention Marketing, which augments social marketing with a strong emphasis on behavioral science and community involvement (National Center, 2006). Born out of HIV prevention efforts, Prevention Marketing can be applied to many areas of public health marketing.

CDC is also involved with Turning Point, an initiative working to transform and improve the U.S. public health system by increasing community involvement and collaboration (Turning Point, 2006). Because the multifaceted social issues that form the basis of poor health are too complex to be understood and solved using traditional medically-based disease models, Turning Point's strategy is to link public health agencies with professionals and organizations in other fields beyond health care. Turning Point's marketing efforts are concentrated in its Social Marketing National Excellence Collaborative. Through this Collaborative, Turning Point works with partners, including CDC, to use social marketing techniques to improve the delivery of public health services. As part of this effort, they have created an array of web-based trainings and electronic and print-based products designed to assist public health professionals in creating, implementing, and evaluating social marketing programs to address health problems.

A major challenge in marketing and framing public health is the lack of a commonly understood language to accurately describe public health.

The public's low demand for public health may lead to the incorrect belief that Americans do not value public health. In fact, Americans do value public health and believe more should be done to protect it (CDC, 2000). This disconnect arises because the language to express the mission and values of public health is not the dominant language in our culture and, therefore, has not been sufficiently cultivated (Wallack and Lawrence, 2005). Wallack and Lawrence describe the primary language of American culture as one rooted in individualism with a strong emphasis on freedom, individual responsibility, self-discipline, and minimal government interference. Conversely, the mission of public health is more accurately described by a second language of American culture, which is rooted in values such as egalitarianism, humanitarianism, interdependence, and community. Though many Americans share these values, they often struggle to express them because this second language is not fully developed.

Under the leadership of cognitive linguistics expert George Lakoff, whose work strongly informs Wallack and Lawrence's work, the Rockridge Institute is exposing and analyzing the frames and assumptions that structure political discourse in the U.S. The Rockridge Institute is a progressive think tank that is reframing the public debate around a variety of issues to ultimately change public policy. Much of the Institute's work centers on defining and strategically framing progressive ideas and values to advance progressive policies (Rockridge Institute, 2004, 2005). While not specifically focused on public health as an institution, many of the policies the Rockridge Institute seeks to advance directly support the mission of public health. The Longview Institute is a non-profit research center and educational institution that evolved out of the Rockridge Institute. The Longview Institute is working to create a progressive vision for the future of our nation that includes social justice and a "moral economy," defined as one that is consistent with our nation's most fundamental values (Block, 2006; Longview Institute, 2006). The Longview Institute also focuses on gender, reproductive rights, and health. Much of their work, while not specifically on the institution of public health, furthers the mission of public health and shares public health's commitment to social justice and the delicate balance that must be achieved between individual liberty and collective responsibility. The work of both Institutes can and should be used to more effectively market and frame public health as an institution.

Despite these active efforts to successfully market and frame public health, a literature search revealed relatively few articles focused on framing specific public health issues (Brown et al., 2004; Coleman & Thorson, 2002; Connor & Wesolowski, 2004; Driedger et al., 2002; Flick, 1999; Fox, 2005; Garvin & Eyles, 2001; Kolker, 2004; Korn, Gibbins & Azmier, 2003; Lima & Siegel, 1999; Lollar, 2002; Menashe & Siegel, 1998; Myhre et al., 2002; Rodgers & Thorson, 2001; Roth, Dunsby & Bero, 2003; Smith

& Wakefield, 2005) and almost none on framing public health as an institution (Devlin, 2005; Dorfman, Wallack & Woodruff, 2005; Schutchfield, Ireson & Hall, 2004). There is a clear need to study framing of public health as an institution and to use the dominant language of our culture to appeal to broadly held values to improve framing of public health. This chapter will identify and analyze the current frames of public health as an institution and formulate improved frames for the future.

■ METHODS

In order to identify the current frames of public health, we examined the Congressional debate over the final Department of Health and Human Services budget for Fiscal Year 2006 and thirty-eight newspaper articles from U.S. regional sources from 2/1/05 to 8/1/05 using the search terms "public health" and "budget cuts."

■ RESULTS: CURRENT FRAMING OF PUBLIC HEALTH AS AN INSTITUTION

Based on the analysis of the *Congressional Record* and newspaper articles, it appears that the dominant frame of public health as an institution is one of health promotion using health as the core value. For example, the executive director of the American Public Health Association, Georges Benjamin, MD, FACP, responded to cuts to the Medicaid budget by saying, "This program [Medicaid] provides invaluable security for more than 50 million Americans, giving them access to primary and preventive health services that are essential to their well-being and, in many cases, their survival. We are deeply disappointed that Congress . . . chose not to protect the health of Americans" (American Public Health Association, 2005). While Benjamin alludes to security, health is clearly the core value in his statement. As already discussed, health is not a very strong core value. Historically, concerns about health have not led to government support and funding for public health programs and organizations. Compelling core values, such as freedom, autonomy, control, and security, resonate with and more effectively motivate action among policy makers and citizens.

Benjamin's statement also alludes to a common premise of the health promotion frame, which equates public health with medical care for the poor. In the *Congressional Record*, Representative Solis of California clearly equated Medicaid with public health when she said, "Medicaid cuts would shut the neediest individuals out of the public health insurance system . . ." (Solis, 2005). As illustrated by these two statements, above, discussions about public health often become discussions about health care and therefore become discussions about Medicaid, which is described by California's Senator Boxer (2005) as ". . . the health care program for the poor and disabled. . . ." Equating public health with medical care for the poor perpetuates two common misperceptions: that the role of public health is purely to provide medical treatment for the poor and disabled, and that individual medical treatment is more valuable than preventive public health measures in improving the health status of a population. As discussed in Chapter 4, there is much evidence to suggest that public health measures have had a greater impact on improving the health of populations than medical treatment.

The visual image of a safety net, frequently used throughout the *Congressional Record* and in news articles to describe public health, reinforces the erroneous belief that public health only benefits the poor, who need a safety net, while providing no benefit to other individuals and society as a whole. This belief is perpetuated by the public health community, as evidenced by the response of a Health Department Director in Erie County, New York, to budget cuts. "I'm horrified. We're supposed to be the safety net. I think what we've eliminated are some of the last vestiges available to populations that rely upon public health to be the providers of health care" (Sommer, 2005). The headline of the article in which this quote appears, "Health Dept. Cuts Hurt Most Needy, Official Says," highlights the message that cutting public health only hurts the poor and therefore, clearly implies that supporting public health only benefits the poor. This type of messaging does not appeal to the wealthy and powerful and will not generate broad support for public health.

Another example of how the current framing of public health sustains the misperception that public health only benefits the poor is found in a quote issued by Charleston, West Virginia Mayor Danny Jones in March of 2005. "You can't pull a lot of money out of the community and expect that we can keep providing services and housing and retaining walls like we have been. And it's going to be the poorest people who get hurt most" (Long, 2005). In the aftermath of Hurricane Katrina, which ravaged the Gulf Coast of the United States. in August of 2005, parts of Mayor Jones' statement seem prophetic. Tragically, this type of messaging did not galvanize the support necessary to prepare retaining walls and other emergency plans along the Gulf Coast. And, as Hurricane Katrina made very clear, it was not just the poor who suffered. The entire nation suffered. Our economy, freedom, and security were all compromised.

■ EVALUATION OF CURRENT FRAMING OF PUBLIC HEALTH AS AN INSTITUTION

There is a major problem with the dominant health promotion frame of public health as medical treatment for the poor: it inherently requires someone to sacrifice. Currently in this frame, the poor are being forced to sacrifice because the wealthy will not finance their medical treatment. Many supporters of public health in Congress reinforce this sacrifice theme when they talk about the poor being forced to sacrifice so that the wealthy can enjoy prolific tax cuts. The sacrifice theme, found throughout the *Congressional Record*, is illustrated by a quote from Representative Langevin, a Democrat from Rhode Island. "The Republican budget asks the mothers and grandmothers in the nursing home, the disabled children, the poor, those with Alzheimer's and Parkinson's disease, to sacrifice their health and dignity in order to finance the tax cuts of the wealthiest one percent in this country. It asks those who have nothing to sacrifice everything, and those who have everything to sacrifice nothing" (Langevin, 2005). While Langevin's statement may be accurate, using the frame of sacrifice is unlikely to be effective in securing funding for public health for several reasons.

First, because the current frame requires the poor to sacrifice, it also implies that the wealthy should sacrifice to help the poor. However, no one wants to sacrifice. People are primarily concerned with providing for themselves and their own families, and they generally need a very compelling reason to sacrifice anything for others. An article in *The Buffalo News* depicts the common problem of public health professionals misguidedly expecting the wealthy and powerful to champion the needs of the poor and vulnerable. "Zimmerman . . . said he got into public health to help vulnerable populations. He described himself as deeply troubled by the [budget] cutbacks and said he wonders why they have not sparked a public uproar. 'It is the poor that get the shaft, and right now I'm not seeing anybody stepping forward as their advocate,' he said" (Sommer, 2005). Rather than implying that the wealthy should feel obligated to help and sacrifice, it would be much more effective in rousing support and inspiring action to frame public health so that everyone clearly benefits.

Second, instead of bringing the wealthy and powerful onto the side of public health, the current framing pits them against the poor and vulnerable who are seen as needing public health. In a competition with the wealthy and powerful against the poor and vulnerable, it is obvious who will win; this frame positions public health on the losing side.

Third, there appears to be a conflict of interest when Congressional members suggest that the wealthy should sacrifice. In many cases, members of Congress have campaigns funded primarily by the wealthy people and corporations who they proclaim to be asking to sacrifice. It is reasonable to question how members of Congress can truly dedicate themselves to the poor and vulnerable of society, or even to average Americans, at the expense of the wealthy to whom they are beholden. Due to this clear conflict of interest, it seems that they cannot legitimately ask the wealthy to sacrifice.

Fourth, from a marketing perspective, the sacrifice theme is a failure. Successful charitable organizations that regularly appeal to wealthy individuals never attempt to get donations by telling people that they should sacrifice to benefit others. Charities focus on how giving makes the giver feel good. While we do not want to market public health as charity, even if we wanted to equate supporting public health with supporting charity, this is not the way to do it.

Finally, the sacrifice theme is historically ineffective. While there is a traditional argument in public health that the upper classes should want to help the poor, even if they have to sacrifice to do it, history demonstrates that widespread support for public health does not occur until the upper classes either are or feel threatened. A brief review of some highlights in public health history reveals the longstanding ineffectiveness of the sacrifice theme in facilitating government support of public health programs and organizations.

During the eighteenth century, pervasive opposition to the use of a smallpox vaccine, which was regarded as safe and effective, continued in Europe until 1774, when Louis XV died from the disease (McNeill, 1989). Likewise, in the U.S., the early outbreaks of cholera in the nineteenth century resulted in paltry interventions such as cleaning streets, nursing the sick, and removing the dead (Duffy, 1992). In the middle of the nineteenth century, public health advocates called for comprehensive sanitary reforms to deal with a recurrence of cholera outbreaks. Despite numerous reports recommending infrastructure reforms, such as creation of water and sewer systems, proper collection of waste, establishment of authoritative health departments, and other sanitary measures, the government, at every level, did not authorize or fund significant infrastructure changes until the mid-1860s when the nation was faced with the threat of another outbreak of epidemic proportions (Duffy, 1992).

One significant reason for incomplete and delayed adoption of sanitary reforms was that the initial cholera outbreaks mainly affected the poor and were therefore viewed as a result of foul surroundings and habits. As Duffy (1992) pointed out, "In New Orleans, where civic leaders insisted that only strangers and the intemperate poor fell prey to pestilential disorders, the city's experience with cholera merely reinforced their belief" (p. 84). Further, financing sanitary infrastructure improvements would have required increasing taxes for the wealthy. Duffy explained that "the upper classes in general had no desire to tax themselves for the welfare of the poor" (p. 100). The public, in general, and government, in particular, were relatively apathetic to the welfare of the poor. "Health and social reformers inveighed against the prevailing social injustices and unsanitary conditions of the times, but the propertied classes had little concern for the welfare of the poor, and without their support little could be done" (Duffy, 1992, p. 118).

Clearly, the sacrifice theme failed to yield support and funding for public health in the past, and it is still failing today. Abandoning this failed theme and adopting a frame of public health that clearly conveys the many benefits to all, especially to the wealthy and powerful, is critical to gaining the support and funding necessary to effectively serve all members of society and fulfill the mission of public health.

■ RECOMMENDATIONS FOR FRAMING OF PUBLIC HEALTH AS AN INSTITUTION IN THE FUTURE

Following the terrorist attacks of September 11, 2001, and the subsequent anthrax scares, the focus of the government and the public in regards to public health was almost exclusively on bioterrorism and emergency preparedness. The result was a massive infusion of federal money into state public health departments for combating bioterrorism and preparing for emergencies (Trust for America's Health, 2003). A portion of the funding supported an unprecedented and controversial smallpox vaccination program, which initially aimed to vaccinate 500,000 members of the armed forces and 500,000 health care workers (Cohen, Gould, & Sidel, 2004). Due to safety and political concerns, the initiative was met with broad resistance and fewer than 8% of the targeted health care workers were vaccinated. Tragically, in the absence of any actual smallpox cases globally, the vaccinations caused the deaths of at least three civilians.

The commitment to preventing unlikely biological attacks continues. In 2004, President Bush signed legislation known as Project Bioshield to authorize billions of dollars to fight potential bioterror agents (Williams, 2006). More than $1 billion of the funding is specifically earmarked for the development, purchase, and storage of anthrax vaccines. While anthrax is a deadly health threat that killed five people in 2001, it has never been deployed as a weapon of mass destruction, and there is a conspicuous absence of evidence indicating a true threat (Cohen, Gould, & Sidel, 2004).

With no smallpox cases anywhere in the world and with the federal, state, and local budget crises that followed 9/11, how is it possible that so much effort and money could have been dedicated to a smallpox vaccination program? Furthermore, why does the government continue to spend billions of dollars to prevent improbable biological attacks while slashing funding for health issues that claim millions of American lives every year? Clearly if public health dollars were allocated to health issues based on the number of lives lost or based on the actual risk of specific health threats, funding to combat smallpox, anthrax, and other potential bioterror agents would be infinitesimal, while programs focused on chronic disease prevention and injury control would be fully funded.

The reason this funding scheme continues is that the perceived threat of bioterrorism fuels a fundamental fear and ignites a survival instinct within every person. By tapping into this fear and the human need for survival, the framing of the fight against bioterrorism rests on the core value of security. Security is a very strong core value shared by nearly all Americans regardless of social class and is a top priority of both the public and the government. Public health as an institution must be framed so that it reinforces the most compelling core values of American citizens and policy makers. Framing public health as security is a very promising option.

In the wake of 9/11 and with the continuing War on Terror, gaps in security are perceived to be significant, universal threats to the public's freedom, independence, autonomy, and control. Unlike health problems, which can easily be dismissed by many as affecting only "other people," problems with our nation's security are perceived to threaten everyone in society regardless of social class. The terror of 9/11 proved that everyone, rich and poor alike, is susceptible to security threats. Though the reality may be that more lives will be cut short by common health problems, such as chronic disease and injury, than by the results of security breaches, security is a top priority while health is not.

Because health is not a very strong core value, health only becomes a key concern when it threatens security. Among individuals, disease and injury cause significant suffering and loss. At a societal level, disease and injury are viewed as problems not because of the suffering they cause, but because they may restrict the freedom, autonomy, and security of individuals, groups, and institutions. Individual suffering, even extreme suffering, does not typically motivate government action. Rather, government action ensues when the cause of the suffering is perceived to threaten society's freedom, autonomy, and security. Therefore, when public health is framed as health, it is a low priority; however, when it is framed as security, public health becomes a top priority.

An example of the effect of this change in priority status can be found in the aftermath of Hurricane Katrina. Before Hurricane Katrina, bird flu was framed as just another disease that could possibly threaten health, and there were very few references to it in the *Congressional Record* and news coverage. However, once the disastrous aftermath of Hurricane Katrina exhibited the devastation and security risks that result from disregarding public health needs, bird flu came to be viewed not just as a potential health threat but a threat to the autonomy, freedom, and security of individuals and the nation as a whole. Consequently, bird flu is now a top priority. Perhaps this lesson will be one of the few positive effects of Hurricane Katrina.

Framing public health as security incorporates the lessons of history. As described earlier, it was not simply the risk of disease in the nineteenth century that led to government action and support for public health measures, but rather the threat of disease that could affect members of all classes of society. This universal threat to freedom, autonomy, control, and security ultimately motivated policy makers to take action. During the 1960s, the need for a healthy pool of military draftees to protect the country resulted in the inclusion of children in the Medicaid program (Kennedy, 2005). Now, as much of our nation's focus on defense shifts to homeland security, we must frame all of public health, not just access to medical care, as essential to providing security for the nation.

Further, the current political climate is much more hospitable to security than health. While policy makers and the public frequently reject any infringement on individual rights in the name of health, we are all accustomed to giving up some liberties in the name of security. And public health truly is the way to protect our security. Public health protects us by countering bioterrorism, preparing for and responding to attacks and disasters, and reducing vulnerabilities. Public health empowers individuals to maintain control over their own lives, guarantees our freedom to travel without restraint through the nation, enables citizens to work productively and fuel the economy, and ensures that our troops are strong and therefore able to protect the country. Public health is a critical part of the nation's security infrastructure.

Finally, because security is such a strong core value and a top priority of policy makers, it is well funded by the President and Congress. "The budget fully accommodates the President's request for defense and homeland security. This is our number one job. None of the rest of the discussion matters if we do not protect the country" (Nussle, 2005). Appealing to Congress for funding to protect the nation's security and the security, survival, and freedom of our people is much more likely to result in approved funding than appealing to Congress for funding to promote health.

Though the security frame has strong potential to garner the widespread support and significant funding needed for public health to fulfill its mission, some public health professionals are currently framing public health so that it is opposed to security. "With its passage last night of a budget resolution that cuts public health by billions of dollars over five years, Congress has shown the dismally low priority it has placed on protecting the health of Americans. The approved budget resolution will add millions of dollars in defense and security spending and expand and preserve tax cuts for wealthier Americans. At the same time, the measure will usher in huge reductions to the Medicaid program and to our nation's public health system" (American Public Health Association, 2005). This type of framing—using health as the core value, requiring sacrifice, pitting public health against security, and positioning public health on the losing side—is not likely to be effective and should be avoided.

While shifting the core value of public health from health to security may seem like a minor change, it is actually quite significant because security is such a strong core value. There is a great opportunity to frame public health not just as health but as freedom from the unknown, control over threats to our economic and physical survival, and ultimately security against natural and man-made disasters.

■ CONCLUSION

It is critical that public health practitioners market not only changes in health behavior, adoption of public health policies, and funding of specific public health programs, but that they also successfully market public health itself as a fundamental societal institution. Currently, public health as an institution is ineffectively framed as health promotion using the relatively weak core value of health and erroneously equating public health with medical care for the poor. This frame is unlikely to be effective in securing funding and support for public health.

Public health as an institution must be framed so that it reinforces the most compelling core values of American citizens and policy makers. Security is a very strong core value shared by nearly all Americans regardless of social class and is a top priority of both the public and the government. Therefore, it is expected that framing public health as security will be very effective. Because security is such a strong core value and a top priority of policy makers, appealing to Congress for funding to protect the nation's security and the security, survival, and freedom of our people, is much more likely to result in approved funding than appealing to Congress for funding to protect health. This seemingly simple shift in core values from health to security provides a great opportunity to frame public health as freedom from the unknown, control over threats to our economic and physical survival, and ultimately security against natural and man-made disasters.

References

Andreason, A.R. (1995). Marketing social change: *Changing behavior to promote health, social development, and the environment.* San Francisco: Jossey-Bass.

American Public Health Association. (2005). American Public Health Association chides congress for its passage of billions of cuts to Medicaid and inadequate investment in public health programs (April 29 ed.): U.S. Newswire.

Block, F. (2006). *Reframing the political battle: Market fundamentalism vs. moral economy.* Berkeley, CA: Longview Institute. Available at http://www.longviewinstitute.org/projects/moral/sorcerersapprentice.

Boxer, Sen. [CA]. (2005, April 28). "Concurrent Resolution on the Budget for fiscal year 2006—Conference Report." *Congressional Record.*

Brown, P., Mayer, B., Zavestoski, S., Luebke, T., Mandelbaum, J., & McCormick, S. (2004). Clearing the air and breathing freely: the health politics of air pollution and asthma. *International Journal of Health Services, 34*(1), 39–63.

Centers for Disease Control and Prevention. (2000). Public opinion about public health—United States, 1999. *Morbidity and Mortality Weekly Report, 49,* 258–260.

Communication at CDC. (2006). Practice Areas Social Marketing. Atlanta, GA: Centers for Disease Control and Prevention, Communication at CDC. Available at: http://www.cdc.gov/communication/practice/socialmarketing.htm

Cohen, H.W., Gould, R.M., & Sidel, V.W. (2004) The pitfalls of bioterrorism preparedness: The anthrax and smallpox experiences. *American Journal of Public Health,* 94, 1667–1671.

Coleman, R., & Thorson, E. (2002). The effects of news stories that put crime and violence into context: Testing the public health model of reporting. *Journal of Health Communication,* 7, 401–425.

Connor, S.M., & Wesolowski, K. (2004). Newspaper framing of fatal motor vehicle crashes in four Midwestern cities in the United States, 1999–2000. *Injury Prevention,* 10, 149–153.

Devlin, L. (2005). Behold the turtle: Positioning public health for the 21st century. *Journal of Public Health Management & Practice,* 11, 168–169.

Dorfman, L., Wallack, L., & Woodruff, K. (2005). More than a message: Framing public health advocacy to change corporate practices. *Health Education & Behavior,* 32, 320–336.

Driedger, S.M., Eyles, J., Elliott, S.D., & Cole, D.C. (2002). Constructing scientific authorities: Issue framing of chlorinated disinfection byproducts in public health. *Risk Analysis,* 22, 789–802.

Duffy, J. (1992). *The sanitarians: A history of American public health.* Urbana, IL: University of Illinois Press.

Flick, W.G. (1999). The third molar controversy: Framing the controversy as a public health policy issue. *Journal of Oral and Maxillofacial Surgery,* 57, 438–444.

Fox, B.J. (2005). Framing tobacco control efforts within an ethical context. *Tobacco Control,* 14(Suppl 2), ii38–44.

Garvin, T., & Eyles, J. (2001). Public health responses for skin cancer prevention: The policy framing of Sun Safety in Australia, Canada and England. *Social Science & Medicine,* 53, 1175–1189.

Kennedy, Sen. [MA]. (2005, April 28). "Concurrent Resolution on the Budget for fiscal year 2006—Conference Report." *Congressional Record.*

Kolker, E. (2004). Framing as a cultural resource in health social movements: Funding activism and the breast cancer movement in the U.S. 1990–1993. *Sociology of Health & Illness,* 26, 820–844.

Korn, D., Gibbins, R., & Azmier, J. (2003). Framing public policy towards a public health paradigm for gambling. *Journal of Gambling Studies,* 19, 235–256.

Langevin, Rep. [RI]. (2005, April 28). "Conference report on H. Con. Res. 95, Concurrent resolution on the budget for fiscal year 2006." *Congressional Record.*

Lima, J.C., & Siegel, M. (1999). The tobacco settlement: An analysis of newspaper coverage of a national policy debate, 1997–98. *Tobacco Control,* 8, 247–253.

Lollar, D.J. (2002). Framing and using measures of chronic conditions in childhood: A public health perspective. *Ambulatory Pediatrics,* 2, 24–25.

Long, K. (2005, March 07). Exporting the deficit. *The Charleston Gazette,* p.1F.

Longview Institute. (2006). Moral Economy Overview. Berkeley, CA: Longview Institute. Available at http://www.longviewinstitute.org/projects/moral/over.

McNeil, W.H. (1989). *Plagues and peoples*. New York: Anchor Books.

Menashe, C.L., & Siegel, M. (1998). The power of a frame: An analysis of newspaper coverage of tobacco issues—United States, 1985–1996. *Journal of Health Communication, 3,* 307–325.

Myhre, S.L., Saphir, M.N., Flora, J.A., Howard, K.A., & Gonzalez, E.M. (2002). Alcohol coverage in California newspapers: Frequency, prominence, and framing. *Journal of Public Health Policy, 23,* 172–190.

National Center for HIV, STD and TB Prevention Divisions of HIV/AIDS Prevention. (2006). The Prevention Marketing Initiative. Atlanta, GA: Centers for Disease Control and Prevention, National Center for HIV, STD and TB Prevention Divisions of HIV/AIDS Prevention. Available at: *http://www.cdc.gov /hiv/projects/pmi.*

Nussle, Rep. [IA]. (2005, April 28). "Conference report on H. Con. Res. 95, Concurrent resolution on the budget for fiscal year 2006." *Congressional Record.*

Rockridge Institute. (2004). The strategic framing overview. Berkeley, CA: Rockridge Institute. Available at http://www.rockridgeinstitute.org/ projects/strategic/framing.

———. (2005). Creating a progressive values movement. Berkeley, CA: Rockridge Institute. Available at http://www.rockridgeinstitute.org/research/ rockridge/valuesmovement.

Rodgers, S., & Thorson, E. (2001). The reporting of crime and violence in the Los Angeles Times: Is there a public health perspective? *Journal of Health Communication, 6,* 169–182.

Roth, A.L., Dunsby, J., & Bero, L. A. (2003). Framing processes in public commentary on US federal tobacco control regulation. *Social Studies of Science, 33,* 7–44.

Scutchfield, F.D., Ireson, C., & Hall, L. (2004). The voice of the public in public health policy and planning: The role of public judgment. *Journal of Public Health Policy, 25,* 197–205.

Smith, K.C., & Wakefield, M. (2005). Textual analysis of tobacco editorials: How are key media gatekeepers framing the issues? *American Journal of Health Promotion, 19,* 361–368.

Solis, Rep. [CA] (2005, April 28). "Waiving requirement of Clause 6(a) of Rule XIII with respect to consideration of certain resolutions." *Congressional Record.*

Sommer, M. (2005, May 02). Health dept. cuts hurt most needy, official says. *Buffalo News,* p. B1.

Trust for America's Health. (2003, September) *Ready or not? Protecting the public's health in the age of bioterrorism.* Washington, DC: Author. Available at *http://healthyamericans.org/state/bioterror/Bioterror.pdf.*

Turning Point. (2006). About Turning Point. Seattle, WA: Turning Point. Available at: http://www.turningpointprogram.org/Pages/about.html.

Wallack, L., & Lawrence, R. (2005). Talking about public health: Developing America's "second language." *American Journal of Public Health, 95,* 567.

Williams, T.D. (2006, April 10). At odds over anthrax: The federal government wants to stockpile anthrax vaccines to protect Americans from a biological attack; critics question costs, wonder if effort is even necessary. *Harford Courant,* p. A1.

II

Using Marketing Principles To Design, Implement, and Evaluate Public Health Interventions

SECTION

I

Planning

Adequate planning is at the heart of all marketing—whether for a commercial product or service, a social change, or public health. It is during this stage that the types of changes needed to address a specific problem are identified and prioritized. These changes might include modifications in individual behaviors and lifestyles, reforms to social or organizational policies and/or other improvements in social and economic conditions. Once changes have been identified and prioritized, a strategic plan for addressing them is developed.

The first two chapters in this section review the major marketing concepts and present a strategic planning process. The last two chapters cover activities that are used to support the strategic planning process: conducting formative research and developing strategies to frame messages about the public health offering.

CHAPTER

9

Applying Marketing Principles To Public Health

The principles of marketing provide a disciplined, audience-focused, research-based process to plan, develop, implement, and assess many different types of initiatives designed to improve the public's health or use and appreciation of public health institutions. Marketing can be used to change personal health behaviors directly or to change the environment in which such behaviors take place. Although marketing public health changes and institutions is different from and often more difficult than marketing commercial products and services, the basic goals should be the same: Create, communicate and deliver value. Marketers and social marketers accomplish this goal by understanding the needs, wants, and values of target audience members, and use that understanding to build relationships with audiences and address the traditional marketing concepts of product, price, place, and promotion. Social marketers must adjust these concepts to the environment in which social change takes place.

■ THE EVOLUTION OF MARKETING SOCIAL CHANGE

The idea of using marketing principles to "sell" social changes as diverse as health practices, recycling, volunteerism, and voting has been around for a long time. In an oft-cited article, Weibe noted in the early 1950s that nonbusiness managers see private-sector marketing communications and ask, "Why can't you sell brotherhood like soap?" In 1971, Kotler and Zaltman published their landmark article, "Social Marketing: An Approach to Planned Social Change," in which they defined social marketing as "the design, implementation, and control of programs calculated to influence the acceptability of social ideas and involving considerations of product planning, pricing, communication, distribution, and marketing research" (p. 5).

The first practical public health applications of social marketing took an advertising approach, providing informational, or "what to do" messages, such as "stop smoking—it might kill you" but not "here's how to do it" information directed at overcoming barriers or building skills based on research with the audience, as Fox and Kotler observed in a 1980 retrospective. They noted that the social advertising approach then evolved to social communication (making greater use of personal selling and editorial support in addition to mass advertising), and finally, a true marketing approach characterized by (1) marketing research—what we refer to in this book as formative research—to understand the potential size of the market, the major groups or segments within it, and their corresponding behavioral characteristics; (2) product development, in terms of searching for the best product to meet the need, rather than using a sales approach of trying to sell an existing product; (3) using incentives; and (4) facilitating behavior change by considering ways to make adoption of the behavior easier.

To effectively change individual health behaviors, it is necessary to consider the historical, cultural, political, and social environments in which change will take place. Often it is necessary to change aspects of those environments as well; sometimes widespread social change will not or cannot occur until laws, regulations, or other governmental and nongovernmental policies either change to facilitate a particular behavior or add a measure of enforceable behavior change. For example, seat belt use in the United States did not increase significantly until a large number of states passed laws mandating their use. In 1983, seat belt use prevalence was only 15%; by 1995, all but two states had seat belt laws in effect and use prevalence had increased to 67% in 1994 (Nelson, Bolen, & Kresnow, 1998). Similarly, nonsmokers had no real way of escaping cigarette smoke until regulatory changes were widespread, such as bans on smoking on domestic flights and mandates for smoke-free workplaces.

Scholars of social marketing have always recognized the frequent need to address the environment in which an individual's behavior occurs as well as the behavior itself. In 1980, Fox and Kotler outlined four broad approaches to producing social change: legal, technological, economic, and informational. More recently, Rothschild (1999) described three primary classes of strategic tools available to public health: marketing, education and law. He noted, "Current public health behavior management relies heavily on education and law while neglecting the underlying philosophy of marketing and exchange" (p. 24). He conceptualized each domain as follows:

- Marketing: "attempts to manage behavior by offering reinforcing incentives and/or consequences in an environment that invites voluntary exchange. The environment is made favorable for appropriate behavior through the development of choices with comparative advantage (products and services), favorable cost-benefit relationships (pricing), and time and place utility enhancement (channels of distribution). Positive reinforcement is provided when a transaction is completed" (p. 25)

- Education: "messages of any type that attempt to inform and/or persuade a target to behave voluntarily in a particular manner but do not provide, on their own, direct and/or immediate reward or punishment" (p. 25).

- Law: "the use of coercion to achieve behavior in a nonvoluntary manner or to threaten with punishment for noncompliance or inappropriate behavior" (p. 25). Rothschild also noted that law can be used to increase—through price subsidies—or decrease—through taxes—the probability of transactions that might not develop as desired through free-market mechanisms.

Often those working to improve public health may need to use all of these strategic tools—marketing, education and law—in combination. To illustrate, consider the problem of automobile child safety seats in the United States. In 1996, almost 80% of child safety seats were used improperly (National Highway Traffic Safety Administration [NHTSA], 1996). Many were not properly secured with seat belts, and many were put in the wrong position in the car (for example, in an airbag-equipped passenger seat). Solving the problem involves a combination of approaches. Education provides parents and other caregivers with information on how to install the seats properly; directions are included with the seat itself and with the car, and many federal, state, and local agencies make information available. Many communities also demonstrate proper installation by publicizing days on which police officers will be available to check, and, if necessary, correct installation.

However, technological changes to cars and child safety seats were necessary to address the underlying problem of the seats being excessively difficult to install properly. Bringing about such changes required marketing research: NHTSA and the manufacturers investigated a variety of alternative installation systems and explored which ones consumers could use with the greatest success. They also weighed the costs of various types of systems. The force of law was then used to both allow and require a new installation system: NHTSA issued a new federal regulation that required specific standardized installation components in vehicles and on child safety seats (NHTSA, 1997).

Even with improved anchorage systems available and laws mandating the use of child restraint systems, ongoing marketing activities will always be necessary to inform and persuade new parents and other caregivers to use them, and ongoing educational activities will be necessary to teach them how to properly install and use the restraints.

■ USING MARKETING IN PUBLIC HEALTH TODAY

Today, many individuals and organizations interested in public health are working hard to become more marketing driven and are harnessing the power of the marketing mindset to bring about change, both in personal health behaviors and in the environmental facilitators of and barriers to those behaviors. At the most basic level, any type of change involves an individual taking an action: a member of the public choosing more low-fat foods or getting an immunization; a restaurant chef ensuring plenty of appealing, healthful menu items; a school administrator introducing a policy that increases student and/or staff opportunities for physical activity; a legislator voting for a bill that includes adequate public health funding. To convince any of these audiences to take the desired action, the one doing the convincing will need to build a relationship with that audience and create, communicate, and deliver value to the audience, which is the definition of marketing, according to the American Marketing Association [AMA] (2005). Therefore, marketing can help bring about any of these types of changes.

■ KEY CONCEPTS FROM COMMERCIAL MARKETING

Marketing principles can be used to directly influence individuals' personal health behavior or to reduce barriers to or increase benefits of those behaviors in the environments in which the behaviors occur. To successfully apply marketing principles to public health programs, one must first understand the key concepts underlying commercial marketing and distinguishing it from other approaches to social change:

- Exchange
- Self-interest
- Behavior change
- Competition
- Audience orientation and segmentation
- Product, price, place and promotion—the marketing mix
- Building relationships

Exchange

As discussed in Chapter 2, marketers believe that the notion of exchange plays a central role in the choices people make: a person gives something in order to get something in exchange. Hastings and Saren (2003) note that exchange theory "assumes we are need-directed beings with a natural inclination to try and improve our lot" (p. 309) and list five prerequisites for a marketing exchange (citing Kotler, 2000):

- There are at least two parties.
- Each party has something that might be of value to the other party.
- Each party is capable of communication and delivery.
- Each party is free to accept or reject the offer.
- Each party believes it is appropriate or desirable to deal with the other party.

Hastings and Saren also note, "central to these assumptions is the notion that the exchange must be mutually beneficial" (p. 309). For example, if you are walking down the street on a hot day and you pass someone with a lemonade stand, you might decide to pay $1 and get a glass of lemonade. Each party benefits from the transaction in obvious ways: the stand owner makes money and you get a glass of lemonade. But each of you may also accrue other benefits, and it is those other consumer benefits that are critical to understand, because they often differentiate one offering from another. When you engage in the lemonade transaction, you are actually "buying" a way of quenching thirst—and you determine that is worth $1. The good or service is often merely a means of obtaining the desired benefit.

To illustrate further, let's change our example a bit. You're still walking down the street on that hot day, but instead of a lemonade stand, you encounter a convenience store with many types of drinks. When deciding which drink to purchase, you weigh the costs of each against the benefits of each. The costs may be more than financial; for example, calories are a cost if you are watching your weight; therefore, water or a diet soft drink would be a low-cost choice. And benefits beyond thirst-quenching ability are likely to come into play. Perhaps one is a childhood favorite and thus brings to mind many happy memories, but another is 100% fruit juice and therefore has the added benefit of higher nutrient value. But perhaps the 100% fruit juice is also more expensive. Now you must compare the choices and decide what is most important to you.

As these examples illustrate, regardless of the type of exchange, people go through a process of weighing the benefits they attach to a product or service (tangible and intangible) against the costs (again, costs may be tangible, such as money, and intangible, such as time or status) before making an exchange. The benefits must outweigh the costs for a person to complete the transaction. These mental transactions can become quite complex, particularly when (as is often the case) people are being asked to replace an existing behavior. In such cases, they must calculate the costs and benefits associated with their existing behavior and the costs and benefits associated with the new behavior, and then compare the two before making a decision. Chapters 3 and 6 discussed the important role that core values—such as freedom, independence, autonomy, and control—play in how people perceive and evaluate costs and benefits. The field of behavioral economics provides insights into how factors such as self-control, impulsiveness, and temporal discounting (e.g., valuing a future consequence less than an immediate consequence) can impact the cost-benefit equations people construct, and therefore their behavior (see, in particular, Bickel & Vuchinich, 2000).

This notion of trading off benefits and costs is not unique to the marketing approach; many commonly used models and theories of health behavior change incorporate similar concepts. For example, one of the most widely used models of health behavior, the health belief model (Janz, Champion & Strecher, 2002) posits that individuals

> Will take action to ward off, to screen for, or to control ill-health conditions if they regard themselves as susceptible to the condition, if they believe it would have potentially serious consequences, if they believe that a course of action available to them would be beneficial in reducing either their susceptibility to or the severity of the condition, and *if they believe that the anticipated barriers to (or costs of) taking the action are outweighed by its benefits* [italics added]. (pp. 47–48)

Similarly, the transtheoretical model of stages of change includes a decisional balance construct described as the pros and cons, or benefits and costs, of changing a behavior (Prochaska, Redding, & Evers, 2002). The model is described in greater detail in Chapter 18. The basic premise is that individuals go through a series of stages in making a behavior change (precontemplation to contemplation to preparation to action to maintenance and, for some behaviors, finally to termination). After studying 12 problem behaviors, Prochaska concluded that progression through the stages—to the point of taking action—is related to quantifiable changes in the cost benefit equation. More specifically, progressing from precontemplation to action involves approximately a .5 standard deviation decrease in the cons, or costs, of changing; progressing from contemplation to action involves approximately one standard deviation increase in the pros of changing (Prochaska, 1994; Prochaska et al., 2002). Discussing these changes, Prochaska (1994) noted that the pros and cons of behavior change are likely to be crucial for progress across the first four stages of change, in part because they represent an interaction of individual psychology and public health policy. The pros and cons for the 12 behaviors [studied] are assumed to assess the individual's internal representations of the actual consequences of changing high-risk behaviors. Those representations are clearly related to the individual's stage of change. The internal presentations are probably also related to the society's readiness to change public policies, to increase the pros of healthy behavior changes and the cons of not changing. (pp. 50–51)

Social cognitive theory (SCT), which is often used to shape public health interventions, also includes the concept of costs and benefits. Its basic premise is that behavior is determined by a series of reciprocal interactions among behavior, personal factors, and environmental influences (Bandura, 1986). SCT is discussed in more detail in Chapter 18; one of the concepts incorporated in the theory is the notion of outcome expectancies (or what Bandura called *incentives*), which are defined as "the *values* that a person places on a particular behavior. . . . Expectancies influence behavior according to the hedonic principle; that is, if all other things are equal, a person will choose to perform an activity that maximizes a positive outcome or minimizes a negative outcome" (Baranowski, Perry, & Parcel, 2002, pp. 172–173).

Self-Interest

People act in their own self-interest. From both a marketing standpoint and from the standpoint of the health behavior models described above, the only relevant costs and benefits are those that are important to the person. In some instances, one person's cost might be another's benefit. In our earlier beverage example, calories were considered a cost by our hypothetical consumer. Another consumer might consider calories a benefit, and a third might not think of them at all when assessing the costs and benefits of different beverages. Failing to consider self-interest can result in mistakenly assuming that benefits to the public's health will be perceived as benefits by individuals being asked to make a change. Often they are not—or are not important enough to affect the balance of a transaction. As Rothschild (1999) observed:

In commercial marketing, this self-interest clearly and consistently is acknowledged and pursued. . . . In public health and social issues, managers often ask members of the target market to behave in ways that appear to be opposite of that member's perception of self-interest and are often the opposite of the current manifestation of that self-interest as observed through the member's current behavior. People choose to eat junk food, not exercise, smoke and drink to excess, or engage in unsafe sex because they have evaluated their own situation and environment and made a self-interested decision to behave as they do. (p. 26)

The marketing process is designed to identify the audience's self-interest and then construct an exchange that appeals to and fulfills that self-interest. Marketers

1. Get to know the potential audience, to find out what their current behaviors are and what benefits and costs they attach to a particular exchange.
2. Make any needed adjustments to the product, its price, or where customers can obtain it, so as to maximize the benefits important to the customer and minimize the costs.
3. Promote the exchange to audiences by emphasizing perceived benefits and when necessary illustrating how to minimize or overcome perceived costs.

As Kotler and Andreasen (1996) phrase it, "for the marketer to be successful, the customer must believe that the exchange that the marketer is promoting is better than any reasonable alternative—including doing nothing" (p. 111).

Chapter 8 discussed how a failure to consider self-interest leads to inappropriately framing public health as an institution. When cuts in public health funding are framed as requiring the poor to sacrifice, the frame inherently implies that instead the wealthy should sacrifice to help the poor. But, as the chapter noted, no one wants to sacrifice. Setting up a "wealthy versus poor" frame may appear to appeal to the core value of fairness, but because it ignores the wealthy's self-interest, in fact it merely says it would be more fair if they were the ones making the sacrifice—a point of view they are unlikely to share. While no one would argue that the wealthy can better afford the cost, they are unlikely to agree to afford it if it is presented to them as a cost with no offsetting personal benefits, as this frame does. As noted earlier, exchanges need to be mutually beneficial: emphasizing the benefits everyone, including the wealthy, receives from public health funding should go a long way toward encouraging them to embrace the exchange.

Emphasis on Behavior Change

Kotler and Andreasen (1996) noted that "in our view, the bottom line of all marketing strategy and tactics is to influence behavior. Sometimes this necessitates changing ideas and thoughts first, but in the end, it is behavior change we are after. This is an absolutely crucial point. Some nonprofit marketers may think they are in the 'business' of changing *ideas*, but it can legitimately be asked why they should bother if such changes do not lead to action" (p. 110). Likewise, improving public health requires focusing on behavior change. Sometimes individuals need to change personal behaviors; at other times, "upstream" individuals need to make changes to improve the environment in which the personal behavior takes place. For example, a public health initiative can be directed to children, to help them make healthier food choices. But such an initiative can also be directed to the many people who can increase the child's ability or willingness to do so: parents can send nutrient-rich snacks to school, cafeteria managers can move fruits, vegetables, and other nutrient-rich choices so they are at the front of the lunch line and easily reached; classroom teachers can refrain from giving candy as rewards; principals can mandate the availability of healthful foods at all gatherings where food is served; district policy makers can require healthy choices in vending machines and a la carte offerings, etc.

Commercial marketers have an obvious reason for wanting to influence behavior—and a singular goal: to increase sales. Typically the behavior they want to influence is what brand of product or service the consumer buys. Public health goals and objectives often are not so clearcut. There may be a variety of behavior changes that people could make that would lead to reduced morbidity and mortality. In addition, there often is not a direct relationship between the action of an individual and reductions in incidence or death; rather, the aggregate actions of a group will lead to morbidity and mortality improvements for the group that may or may not accrue to any particular individual in it. Choosing behavior-focused goals and objectives can also be difficult if sponsoring institutions see their role as "disseminating information" or "educating." Similarly, staff within an organization may have been trained in the knowledge-attitudes-behavior (KAB) paradigm and believe that by increasing people's knowledge or changing their attitudes, behavior change will follow. Noting that interventions changing knowledge or attitudes do not usually result in behavior change, some researchers argue that the KAB paradigm is too simplistic and does not reflect our best understanding of how to influence behavior (Baranowski, 1997).

This is not to say that social change programs should never make an effort to increase knowledge or change attitudes. Rather, behavior change should be the end goal. Sometimes more knowledge is necessary before behavior can change—for example, parents are unlikely to immunize their children unless they know that they need to. However, the information needs to be related to the behavioral goal and tailored to the target audience's needs based on how ready they are to change their behavior. For example, in a review of nutrition education interventions, Contento and colleagues (1995) found that many of the interventions emphasized "how-to" knowledge or skills information, when the audience members were not yet ready for such information. They needed motivational information about personally relevant positive or negative consequences of behavior or other motivators of change before they were ready for "how-to" information.

For these reasons, one challenge public health practitioners face is selecting a specific behavior to change. If a variety of behaviors could be changed, they usually can be prioritized according to most significant public health benefits or audience willingness to make the changes. If an organization's mission is to "disseminate information" or "educate," why is that the mission? What do the organization's mission-writers think will change if people have the information or become more educated? These answers usually will reveal a link to a behavior. Using appropriate models and theories of behavior change can help practitioners focus on realistic behavior changes. This process will be discussed in greater detail in Chapter 10.

Competition

To craft an acceptable exchange, one must understand the competition: alternative behaviors (in particular, the individual's current behavior) and the benefits they deliver. As discussed earlier, people act in their own self interest and generally choose the behavior that offers what they perceive to be the most desired benefits. *Every* proposed behavior change has competition: the existing behavior. Target audiences often have very good reasons for maintaining their behavior patterns. The benefits they receive from their current behavior—or the drawbacks associated with a new behavior—may outweigh the benefits associated with the new behavior. Part of the marketer's challenge is to develop and deliver a bundle of benefits that target audience members perceive to be superior to the benefits they will receive from engaging in any alternative behavior.

Competition can take many forms. When the desired behavior is supporting a public health program or policy, the competition may have to do with resources (other funding needs are more of a priority to the policy maker), philosophy (such as a belief that there are too many government programs already or that government should not intervene in personal decisions), or pressure from interests that are not related to health (i.e., businesses saying increased regulations to safeguard the public's health would be "bad for business"). Sometimes it is necessary to restructure the public health offering in order to overcome problems related to competition.

Audience Orientation and Segmentation

To influence an audience, one must first understand the audience and the determinants of their behavior. Therefore, marketers make customers the focal point of their efforts and analyze all aspects of the exchange transaction from the customer's viewpoint. Commercial marketers place enormous emphasis on learning all they can about their customers and potential customers. Their mission in life is to know who their customers are, what they want and need, and where and how to reach them.

Marketing is often described as being *consumer driven*. In commercial marketing, that usually means identifying a consumer need and then developing or positioning a product or service to fulfill that need, although there are instances when a product has been developed or discovered and then a "need" is identified. In public health, we usually have to "create" need, but we often have a harder job: We start with a product people perceive as contrary to their self-interest and therefore don't want ("negative demand") and must then ferret out benefits they can or do associate with it in order to find a way to position it as superior to competing products. This makes solid research—especially in terms of core values and benefits the people can associate with a product or behavior change—even more important for public health practitioners than it is for commercial marketers. Chapter 2 discussed negative demand in more detail.

Public health organizations using a marketing approach often have difficulty being truly customer driven. A number of factors contribute to this difficulty. First, the structure of most public health organizations is not conducive to the marketing mind-set. Public health institutions typically are not run by individuals with a marketing background, and priorities are not set from within a marketing or behavior change framework. Unlike commercial marketers, who develop products and services based on what customers are most likely to purchase, public health institutions often allocate resources based on legislative priorities as reflected in mandates or current funding streams (i.e., if tax money or grants are available for tobacco control, then the institution focuses on tobacco control), rather than on an analysis of what changes might best impact a population's health—let alone what changes are most likely to be made by the population served. Rather than driving the effort, marketing is usually only one component of it.

The position of staff within the organization attempting to develop a marketing-based effort leads to the second factor that affects a public health institution's ability to be customer driven: Because staff are often part of communication or public information departments, they often have little or no ability to influence priorities or institute other changes needed to support a marketing approach. While Andreasen (1995), among others, has criticized many social change marketers for effectively defining marketing as communications, it is not surprising that social change efforts often center around communication activities, given the background and organizational position of the staff. For example, a governor announces a new campaign to improve mammography rates among women age 50 and older. The public information staff can use marketing principles to develop the campaign: They can conduct formative research to identify appropriate audiences, learn the benefits and barriers the audiences associate with mammography, and learn the ideal places to deliver mammograms and messages about them. They can develop, pretest, and produce a thorough promotional effort to be delivered through mass media and health care facilities. But most likely the public information staff will be able to do almost nothing about the financial cost of a mammogram, and/or about the extent to which insurers will cover the cost. Similarly, they will be unable to overcome accessibility barriers, such as those faced by women who live far from the nearest mammography facility or who cannot afford to take time off from work to visit such a facility during business hours. Addressing these barriers would require working in partnership with local providers, something that may not be encouraged under the staff's organizational structure.

The third factor that affects many public health institutions' ability to be customer driven is a hesitancy to focus on specific groups of customers because of a mandate to serve "everyone." Trying to appeal to everyone is problematic for a number of reasons. It wastes resources because not everyone needs a particular intervention. Often, particular subgroups of the population are reached by other entities, have a very low incidence of the problem the intervention addresses, or have already embraced the behavior being promoted. Furthermore, key to being customer driven is identifying and understanding the customer in question. Even if "everyone" needs a particular intervention, some subgroups are likely to be closer to actually changing their behavior (perhaps they have even tried to change) while others are not nearly ready (maybe they have not even thought about it). Or the public health offerings may be more easily accessed by some groups. And different groups will associate different costs and benefits with the behavior in question. An intervention designed for "everyone" will likely either

- persuade no one because it is too scattered and resources are wasted promoting costs and benefits to audiences who do not perceive them as the most important costs and benefits, or
- focus on specific costs and benefits and therefore be relevant to only particular segments of the population (in other words, targeted by default rather than by intention).

Finally, public health resources are often extremely limited. By trying to stretch them to include "everyone," no audience group will be reached with any intensity. Consider a commercial sector analogy: What would happen if an automobile manufacturer decided that the target audience for a new car was everyone? Using a targeted approach, the communication firm(s) would develop a profile of people most likely to buy that brand and type of car and the best times, places, and media to reach them. They would then use that information to develop a campaign that promises the target audience specific benefits they desire, and place ads using a media plan that reaches as many members of the target audience as possible as frequently as possible without going over budget. They would also try to generate news and feature stories about the car in appropriate media. Using the "everyone" approach, the communication firm would have difficulty deciding what benefits to convey in the ads and, when developing a media plan, would have to strive for reaching the most people, in all likelihood sacrificing frequency. Given the number of media vehicles and the fact that few reach a large proportion of the entire population, most people might be exposed to information about the car only once or twice, if at all. By contrast, targeted consumers are likely to encounter information about the car quite a few times. The next time they shop for a car, they are much more likely to think of the new car if the advertising resonated with them, and if they were exposed to information about it multiple times and not just once.

The Four Ps: The Marketing Mix

In commercial marketing, *product, price, place,* and *promotion* are referred to as "the four Ps" and constitute what is termed the marketing mix—the group of independent variables that a marketer can alter to influence behavior. Together, these four form the core building blocks of marketing strategy. There has been substantial debate as to how well the four Ps apply to social marketing (see, for example, Peattie & Peattie, 2003) and, even within the marketing literature, efforts to supplant them with other conceptual schema. However, the four Ps terminology continues to be widely used and, in addition to providing a common vocabulary for public health and other social marketers to use when communicating with other types of marketers, it remains a useful framework for thinking through the major variables available to marketers regardless of the type of marketing in which they engage.

As we noted earlier in this chapter, people must believe benefits outweigh costs before they are willing to engage in an exchange. As marketers, we can increase the likelihood that people will choose our behavior by increasing benefits, decreasing costs, or both, as **Figure 9-1** illustrates. The four Ps give us a framework for affecting this balance. A brief description of each variable and some of the issues surrounding its conceptualization in social marketing is presented. Chapter 10 will describe how a program's strategic planning process can address the marketing mix variables.

Product

Product is often conceptualized as a tangible good, service, or behavior. However, it is most useful to think of product as the *bundle of benefits* that is exchanged with the target audience for a price. As noted earlier, the bundle of benefits is what the audience actually seeks to obtain when they

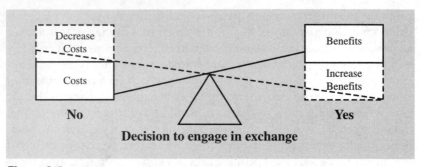

Figure 9-1 Changing the Balance of the Cost-Benefit Analysis

engage in the exchange. The bundle of benefits will be linked to a specific behavior but may or may not be linked to a tangible product or service. For example, in a family planning program the desired behavior may be to space pregnancies out, rather than having one birth immediately after another. Contraceptives are an obvious tangible product likely to be involved in this exchange—even though spacing is what is actually being sold. Similarly, some efforts to improve eating habits encourage increased consumption of particular products, such as fruits and vegetables or whole grains. Other programs, such as those promoting increased physical activity, decreased fat consumption, or violence prevention, often cannot easily tie their behavior changes to a particular product or service.

Sometimes the lack of a tangible product or service causes program planners to get caught up in defining the social change product. Asking the following questions can help:

- What are the benefits of the behavior change that members of the target audience will value? What needs or wants do they have that our behavior change can fulfill?
- What is the competition for the behavior? What other behaviors can provide benefits the target audience perceives to be equal or superior?

It is vital to define the product in terms of the benefit it will provide to target audience members. How will it satisfy an existing need or want? The benefit delivered must be something the person values enough to engage in the behavior. Some public health programs try to sell the long-term public health benefit (e.g., reduced risk of cancer, lives saved from seat belt use, etc.), rather than short-term individual benefits. While some people will change a behavior to benefit society if it is at very low cost to them, many will not be sufficiently motivated to change health-related behaviors because society might derive a benefit or because they may derive a benefit in the distant future. They are more likely to change their behavior because they will achieve a short-term benefit for doing so (Backer, Rogers, & Sopory, 1992; Baranowski et al., 2002). Behavioral economists assert that short-term benefits are more likely to be chosen because "all behavior occurs in an economic context in which concurrent reinforcers vie for the resources of the consumer" (Madden, 2000, p. 23) and people discount delayed consequences—positive ("reinforcers") or negative ("punishers"). In marketing language, at any moment in time a person can choose from a variety of competing benefits. The person is more likely to choose a benefit he or she will obtain immediately, even if the immediate benefit is smaller than that they could obtain by waiting. The delay associated with the long-term benefit results in the person "discounting" that benefit's value.

Price

Price is the cost to the target audience of making an exchange. In commercial marketing, price almost always has a financial component; if consumers are considering trying a new product or service, the associated risk of change creates a psychological component as well. With health and other social changes, the price may have a financial component but is more likely to be time, effort, lifestyle, or psychological cost. For example, insisting that a sexual partner use a condom has a high potential psychological cost: The partner may reject the one insisting or make assumptions about promiscuous behavior or lack of trust. Being the first policy maker to change from opposing to supporting a policy can create a high psychological or social cost. Many individuals perceive various health behaviors, such as increasing physical activity, as costing a great deal of time. And some behaviors require effort, such as obtaining more nutritious foods if they are not readily accessible. Rothschild (1979) argued that these nonmonetary costs "may be perceived as greater than monetary costs which dominate the price of consumer products" (p. 13).

When the product is a public health program or policy, the perceived psychological price may include an infringement on basic values, such as that resulting from government interference or limitations on freedom. Laws mandating seat belt use and restrictions on smoking are two examples that fit both categories.

Costs, then, are barriers between the target audience and the action we wish them to take. Sometimes they can be easily reduced or eliminated (often by improving *place*, another marketing variable); at other times they are more challenging. Asking the following questions may help program planners work through the price of their social marketing product:

- What will the behavior change "cost" each target audience member in money, time, effort, and psyche?
- Do target audience members perceive the costs to be a fair exchange for the benefit we are promising in exchange?
- How can our marketing effort reduce costs?

Usually, the only way to answer these questions is through careful formative research as will be outlined in Chapter 11.

Place

Place equates to marketing or distribution channels, "a set of interdependent organizations involved in the process of making a product or service available for use or consumption by the consumer or business user" (Kotler & Armstrong, 2004, p. 400). Depending upon how they are constructed, distribution channels can allow a marketer to lower an audience's barriers to access, increase utility, or deliver a bundle of benefits to the target audience (Strand, Rothschild & Nevin, 2004).

Place is often the most difficult commercial marketing "P" to conceptualize in social programs—and the one that can be most difficult to control. Behaviors that involve a tangible product usually have obvious channels of distribution. For example, if the goal is to increase usage of services provided by a health clinic, marketing research can help assess various aspects of the clinic that might create barriers and/or affect the bundle of benefits delivered, such as accessibility (What are the hours? How can people get there? Do they have access to those modes of transportation? How difficult is it to make an appointment?), cost of services, staff behavior, waiting times, crowding, temperature, cleanliness, and provisions for child care or for activities for children while they wait. Other behaviors, such as increasing consumption of certain foods, also have clear distribution channels associated with them. However, unlike their commercial counterparts, social marketers have to consider all distribution channels (e.g., everywhere a target audience member could obtain the food), not just those channels that distribute a specific brand of a specific product.

For other behavioral interventions, place is not as obvious or clearly delineated. For example, consider the many public health programs that encourage lifestyle changes, such as increased physical activity or reducing the risk of acquiring or transmitting a communicable disease. In these instances, no one physical place is associated with the behavior.

In social change programs, "place" often winds up being conceptualized as message delivery channels. It is more useful to define "place" as the situations in which the behavior does or can occur. Thinking about such situations and their associated channels of distribution can allow the public health marketer to identify opportunities to lower barriers, deliver benefits, or differentiate public health offerings from competitors. Commercial marketers often use place to differentiate their offerings; for example, consider getting a cup of coffee at McDonald's versus Starbucks. Both strive to provide coffee of consistent quality across outlets. But the experience of going to each one is quite different: McDonald's is relatively inexpensive, provides few coffee choices, and is fast, bright, utilitarian and geared to people in a hurry. Starbucks is relatively expensive, offers so many choices that the company has run campaigns to increase people's ordering self-efficacy, and, though drinks are delivered quickly, the lighting, comfortable seating, and provision of power outlets encourages lingering.

The following questions can help you think through the opportunities place can provide:

- What are target audience members' perceptions of the situations in which the behavior can take place?
- How can channels of distribution reduce or minimize barriers to the behavior?
- How can we use channels of distribution to create or improve situations so they deliver the benefits target audience members value most?
- How can channels of distribution differentiate the public health offering from competitors?
- How can we access the best channels of distribution for our product and audience?

As an intervention is developed and specific behavior changes are selected, formative research can help identify situations in which the desired activities do or can take place. Armed with this knowledge, public health marketers can work to change the characteristics of these places and/or, through promotional activities and materials, to provide target audiences with ideas for making their own changes. As the definition at the beginning of this section emphasizes, channels of distribution typically involve multiple interdependent organizations, so creating or improving channels involves identifying and working with the organizations that form or provide the best channels—those that provide access to the audience(s); add value, credibility and sustainability to the public health offering; deliver immediate and relevant benefits; help overcome the biggest barriers; and counter competition (Strand et al., 2004). Chapter 14 discusses how to form and manage such relationships.

Changing place characteristics often necessitates approaches beyond marketing, such as changes in policy or regulations. For example, widespread smoke-free public places would not have been obtained without changes in local ordinances. Providing children with adequate time to eat a healthful lunch or including sufficient instructional time for health education also requires policy changes at the school level and often at the district or state level. In situations such as these, a marketing approach can help identify the characteristics of the ideal place, and promotional activities often can support the need for such characteristics. However, techniques other than promotion are necessary to bring about such changes.

An example of using promotional activities and materials to help audiences modify their own "places" can be found in the early days of the U.S. 5 A Day for Better Health program. Formative research conducted for the program revealed that two reasons people were not eating more fruits and vegetables was that they were not accessible (because vending machines often don't contain them, for example) and that people did not think of them (because the fruits and vegetables were at the bottom of the refrigerator in a dark bin). Although the program planners could not control every place that someone might obtain fruits and vegetables, they incorporated simple ideas into promotional activities and materials to help consumers improve their fruit and vegetables "places." For example, they included suggestions such as making fruits and vegetables accessible during the day by putting them into briefcases and packed lunches, and putting them out in a bowl or on a higher shelf in the refrigerator so that people could see them more easily when hunting for something to eat (Lefebvre et al., 1995). More recently, the Produce for Better Health Foundation compiled a National Action Plan that included many ideas for increasing the availability and accessibility of fruits and vegetables by modifying place, from changing federal, state and local policies to changing food offerings at restaurants, grocery stores, workplaces, schools and camps (Produce for Better Health Foundation, 2005). More detail on the plan and its approaches is provided in Appendix 9-A.

Promotion

Traditional *promotion*—for commercial or social marketing—consists of communicating the exchange being offered to the target audience through some combination of advertising, media relations, events, personal selling, and entertainment. When policy change is the goal, promotion often includes techniques such as grass-roots advocacy, media advocacy, and lobbying. Some of these techniques use many of the same promotional tools but in a different way. For example, the media advocacy approach is fundamentally a promotional approach: It relies on media relations and, often, paid advertising. But the purpose is different from using these tools to reach individuals and convince them to change their personal health behaviors:

> The purpose of media advocacy is to promote public health goals by using the media to strategically apply pressure for policy change. It provides a framework for moving the public health discussion from a primary focus on the health behavior of individuals to the behavior of the policymakers whose decisions structure the environment in which people act. It addresses the power gap rather than just the information gap. (Wallack & Dorfman, 1996, p. 293)

All promotional activities have a common goal: to maximize the likelihood that target audience members will take the desired action by reaching them with messages highlighting the exchange's benefits to them and, when necessary, providing methods to overcome the costs. Advertisements are perhaps the most visible form of marketing promotion. Examples of other types of promotion activities include

- framing media coverage through media relations efforts, such as print, audio, and/or video news releases, press conferences, and reporter briefings;

- community events, such as health fairs;
- personal selling, such as having physicians or nurses "talk up" a particular behavior related to family planning or the availability of new vaccine; and
- entertainment, such as integrating public health messages into television series' story lines or producing popular entertainment with a public health message, such as the top-10 Latin American music hits written and produced as part of a U.S. Agency for International Development project (Braus, 1995).

To develop the promotion component of a public health effort, it is necessary to fully understand product, price, and place and then use that information to develop a communication strategy for each primary and secondary audience. (Chapter 12 presents a process for developing a communication strategy.) The communication strategy helps managers frame and deliver promotional messages by describing

- The action the target audience should take as a result of the communication.
- The barriers to the action.
- The benefit to be promised in exchange for the action.
- The support for the benefit.
- The tone communications should use.
- The openings through which target audiences can be reached with the communication.

The communication strategy then guides development of the promotion plan. This plan spells out the materials and activities that will form the promotion, as well as the timeline for development and implementation. Key questions that guide development of the communication strategy and promotion plan include the following:

- What action do we want the audience to take, and what are they doing now?
- What benefit can we promise in exchange for taking that action, and how do we support it?
- What are the times, places and states of mind when target audiences can best be reached with materials and activities?
- What promotional materials and activities are appropriate for the message and the openings through which it will be delivered?
- Given our resources, how can those materials and activities best be delivered to target audience members?

Chapters 13 through 15 provide a more detailed analysis of some issues to consider and steps to take when developing and implementing promotional activities.

An Additional P: Partners

Beyond the traditional marketing mix of product, price, place, and promotion, public health efforts often have to consider an additional P: *partners*.

Social change efforts typically gather speed when there is scientific consensus that a particular change will benefit the individual and society. By the time such consensus is reached, many organizations (often both public and private) may have an interest in promoting the behavior and, if necessary, in developing technological, educational and policy changes to facilitate such behavior change. Unfortunately, what often happens is that each organization has different ideas about how to proceed and does not coordinate efforts with the other organizations. Completely separate programs can jeopardize success in a number of ways. First, they can lead to framing the issue in multiple and sometimes counter-productive ways. The public and policy makers may become confused or uncertain as to the actions they should take. Second, resources can be wasted working at cross purposes.

Often, a better solution is for organizations to recognize that others are also interested in bringing about the social change. By combining or coordinating efforts, members of the public, healthcare providers, policy makers and other audiences are reached by sources they trust with a consistent, clear message—and resources are maximized. Each organization can perform the activity for which it is best suited. Unfortunately, these types of partnerships and alliances are all too rare. At the conceptual level, they can be difficult because each organization has its own wants and needs. At the operational level, a host of practical difficulties can prohibit progress, including different fiscal years and institutional timetables, restrictions on government agencies working with private sector organizations, and organizational cultures.

Even if strong alliances or perfect partnerships cannot be formed, it is important to know the other organizations addressing the same issue and to coordinate activities with them when possible. At a minimum, doing so allows your organization's efforts to complement, rather than compete with, the efforts of other entities. Often, judicious alliances or partnerships can provide much more, such as access to or added credibility with key target audience segments. The case study in Appendix 9-A provides an example of how many organizations—national, state and local, commercial, non-profit and government—could work together and in parallel to address a social problem.

During the planning process, addressing the following questions should provide a starting point for ensuring that social change efforts are planned with potential partners, alliances and intermediaries in mind:

- What other organizations are addressing the social change?
- What organizations could or do provide something we do not, or provide it better—access to an audience, delivery of key benefits, reduction or elimination of critical barriers?

- What are the opportunities to work together with or complement other organizations?

Chapter 14 provides additional information on forming and managing relationships with other organizations. **Exhibit 9-1** summarizes all of the *Ps*.

Building Relationships

In recent years, marketers have come to realize that the best way to influence behavior is not through one-time transactions, but by building ongoing relationships with their customers. (Hastings, 2003, p. 15)

The need to build relationships is deemed so important to successful marketing that it has become part of the American Marketing Association's definition of marketing as "an organizational function and a set of

---

Exhibit 9-1 The Social Marketing Mix

Product

The bundle of benefits exchanged with the audience for a price.

- What are the benefits of the behavior change to members of the target audience—what needs or wants do they have that our behavior can fulfill?

Price

The total cost (financial and other) to the target audience member of engaging in the behavior.

- What will the behavior change "cost" each target audience member in money, time, effort, lifestyle, and psyche?
- Do target audience members perceive the cost to be a fair exchange for the benefit we are promising in exchange?
- How can our marketing efforts reduce audience costs?

Place

The channel(s) through which products are distributed—or situations in which the behavior of interest can or does occur.

- What are target audience members' perceptions of the situations in which the behavior can take place?
- How can channels of distribution reduce or minimize barriers to the behavior?
- How can we use channels of distribution to create or improve situations so they deliver the benefits target audience members value?
- How can channels of distribution differentiate the public health offering from competitors?
- How can we access the best channels of distribution for our product and audience?

(continues)

Exhibit 9-1 The Social Marketing Mix (continued)

Promotion

A combination of advertising, media relations, promotional events, personal selling, and entertainment to communicate with the target audience about the exchange being offered.

- What action do we want the audience to take, and what are they doing now?
- What benefit can we promise in exchange for taking the action, and how do we make it compelling?
- What promotional materials and activities are appropriate for the message and the openings through which it will be delivered?
- Given our resources, how can those materials and activities best be delivered to target audience members?

Partners

Other organizations involved with a social change effort or providing channels of distribution.

- What other organizations are conducting activities addressing the social change?
- What organizations could or do provide something we do not, or provide it better—access to an audience, delivery of key benefits, reduction or elimination of critical barriers, differentiation?
- What benefits can we offer other organizations?

processes for creating, communicating and delivering value to customers and for managing customer relationships in ways that benefit the organization and its stakeholders (AMA, 2005). Thinking beyond a specific transaction, campaign, or program to building relationships with the audiences whose behavior we want to change can also have profound implications for public health.

> First, social marketers . . . frequently deal with behaviors that require long-term effort to change. Giving up an addictive behavior like smoking, for example, typically takes five or six attempts. . . . Similarly, responding to good dietary and exercise advice typically involves lifestyle changes rather than one-off adoption of specific offerings. Such behaviors are likely to be much more susceptible to strategic relationship marketing than traditional transactional thinking.
>
> Second, relational marketing is also vital when social marketers consider the social context and the need to make this conducive to individual healthy behavior. . . . On a general level, critical theory emphasizes the importance of 'altering institutions that form the social system within which the individual operates' (Goldberg, 1994). Wallack et al. argue that the media advocacy approach should be

seeking to address flaws, not in "the loose threads of the individual," but in the "fabric of society" (Wallack et al., 1993). Similarly, "social cognitive theory" begins to reconcile the conflicts between the individual and collective view. It sees behavior as "being reciprocally determined by internal personal factors and the environment in which the person lives" (Maibach and Cotton, 1995). All this, of course, gels with marketing theory which makes an important distinction between the immediate environment and the wider social context (Hastings and Heywood, 1991).

Third, relationship building in social marketing can benefit from its noncommercial nature. If, as Morgan and Hunt's (1994) work suggests, commitment and trust are the bedrocks of successful relationship marketing, these could be built more easily when neither party stands to make monetary gains. (Hasting & Saren, 2003, pp. 311–312)

Any encounter a person has with an organization—its physical spaces, its offerings, its communications, its employees—can contribute to building or destroying a relationship. Savvy, successful organizations recognize this simple fact and work to ensure that every encounter is positive. When they ask someone to engage in an exchange, they look beyond the exchange to make sure every aspect of it contributes to building and supporting that relationship. Can the person easily engage in the behavior? Are unnecessary costs (time, social, psychological, dealing with unpleasantness, etc.) eliminated or minimized? Does the person have whatever supports may be needed (information, demonstration of behavior, etc.)?

Organizations also use branding to help them build relationships by differentiating their offerings from competitors and conveying a consistent identity.

Everything that a company does—from the way it paints its trucks, to how long it takes to answer your telephones, to what people in your factories tell their friends—communicates with the public.

Strategies beget brands, and brands in today's marketplace transcend products. Brands are much more than what you eat or drink or brush your teeth with. Brand strategy is the summation of all your communications. (Zyman, 1999, p. 41)

On the surface, a brand is "a name, term, sign, symbol, or design, or some combinations of these, which identifies [the goods or services] as the marketer's and differentiates them from competitor's offerings" (Kotler & Andreasen, 1996, p. 374). Initially, brands were used to distinguish products that otherwise could not be differentiated easily. Over time, organizations discovered that a brand has far more powerful functions than simply allowing customers to identify their products. A brand also forms the relationship between the organization or product and its consumer; it has been characterized as a repository, not merely of functional characteristics, but of meaning and value (Mark & Pearson, 2001; McDivitt et al., 2003).

> A brand is more than a name and a means of identification. It is a set of added values that offer functional and psychological benefits to the consumer, values signaled in consumer products by packaging, price, color, taste, smell, or shape. (Roman et al., 2003, p. 13)

Brands can be positioned on product attributes (not advisable because attributes are easily copied), desirable benefits (e.g., Volvo: safety; FedEx: guaranteed overnight delivery; Nike: performance; Lexus: quality), or beliefs and values. The strongest brands are positioned on strong beliefs and values (Kotler & Armstrong, 2004).

The notion of deliberately attempting to build a brand identity makes many in public health uncomfortable, perhaps because doing so seems too commercial or likely to lead to accusations of wasted resources. However, public health institutions have brand identities, whether or not they want to, and unfamiliarity with brand management can lead to mistakes and missed opportunities. Every public health institution has an identity in the mind of funding agencies, potential partners, the media, and target audiences. The identity may be fuzzy or clear, positive, neutral or negative; but it exists.

> A brand is the company's promise to deliver a specific set of features, benefits, services, and experiences consistently to the buyers. It can be thought of as a contract to the customer regarding how the product or service will deliver value and satisfaction. The brand contract must be simple and honest. (Kotler & Armstrong, 2004, p. 293)

Working through branding exercises can help an organization clarify its core mission, prioritize institutional goals, and reconcile internal versus external perceptions. Actively projecting a clear, consistent and compelling organizational identity can help a public health institution accomplish its mission by building relationships with supporters, partners, and target audiences. For organizations involved in direct product or service delivery, a customer's every experience with the organization provides an opportunity to strengthen the relationship. Using brand management techniques to ensure that each interaction communicates a consistent identity and delivers the benefits those customers value can help organizations build stronger relationships. Brand management techniques can be used in similar ways to manage relationships with other organizations.

There has been considerable discussion about whether a particular health behavior can or should be branded in the same way that a commercial product or service is (McDivitt et al., 2003; Lefebvre et al., 2003). At a minimum, understanding how commercial marketers use brands to build relationships with audiences can help practitioners design effective interventions. Reflecting on a conference session on using branding in social marketing, Bill Novelli observed that we need to think about the brand-related questions in the minds of target audience members, such as "What can you give me that I can't get elsewhere?" and "If I didn't have this brand, I would _____" (Lefebvre et al., 2003). Carol Bryant observed that branding can help us move away from focusing too much on the individual and persuasion and instead take a more expansive view, addressing the values, dreams, needs and aspirations of our audiences; in addition, branding reminds us to take time and stick with it rather than constantly changing things (Lefebvre et al., 2003).

At times, creating a public health brand may make sense if it is appropriate for the situation and sufficient resources are available. In the United States the Florida *truth*® campaign worked to destabilize tobacco companies' relationships with their youth customers by offering youth a replacement brand. Branding also helped the intervention through accumulated awareness: all marketing components built on awareness created by their predecessors (Hicks, 2001). This aspect of branding—making sure all components of an intervention communicate the same identity and therefore build on each other—is always good marketing practice. Chapters 10 and 12 discuss integrating aspects of branding into planning interventions and communication strategies.

■ CONCLUSION

Marketing principles can be used to guide the process of developing, implementing, and refining efforts to improve public health. As is also true in many theories of behavior, in marketing the cost/benefit exchange is essential to the choices people make: a person gives something (cost) in the expectation of receiving something (benefits). Public health, commercial, and other marketers can influence this exchange by altering the marketing mix: the *product* (benefits), the *price* (costs), the *place* (channels of distribution, which can in turn decrease barriers or costs, or increase benefits) and *promotion* (communications about the cost/benefit exchange).

To successfully influence behavior, all types of marketers must take into account a number of factors, particularly (a) people act in their own self-interest to satisfy wants and needs, so promised benefits must provide something they value, and (b) all proposed behaviors have competition, either from current behaviors or other alternatives. To be successful, the cost/benefit exchange of the public health behavior must be more appealing than that associated with any alternative behavior, including doing nothing.

Because the cost/benefit exchange can vary significantly for different groups of people, careful segmentation and selection of target audiences is crucial, so as to design and communicate cost/benefit exchanges that are relevant to and valued by the target audience and that can be cost-effectively delivered by the marketer, either directly or through alliances, partners, and/or intermediaries.

The marketing framework can be used to design interventions to directly influence individuals' personal health behaviors or to improve the larger environment in which those behaviors occur so that individuals can more easily engage in the behavior and obtain desired benefits. Marketing principles can help select specific behavior or policy changes on which to focus by first identifying the wants, needs, and values of a target audience— whether that target audience is a member of the public or a policy maker— and then creating and delivering a bundle of benefits to satisfy those wants, needs, and values. Branding and brand management techniques can help ensure that a consistent identity is communicated and delivered to supporters, partners, and target audiences, thereby enabling public health marketers to build strong relationships with all these groups.

References

American Marketing Association. (2005). Definition of marketing. Retrieved November 10, 2005 from http://www.marketingpower.com/content4620.php

Andreasen, A.R. (1995). *Marketing social change: Changing behavior to promote health, social development and the environment.* San Francisco: Jossey-Bass.

Backer, T.E., Rogers, E.M., & Sopory, P. (1992). *Designing health communication campaigns: What works?* Thousand Oaks, CA: Sage.

Bandura, A. (1986). *Social foundations of thought and action.* Englewood Cliffs, NJ: Prentice-Hall.

Baranowski, T. (1997). The knowledge-attitudes-behavior model and defining "behavior changes." In L. Doner (Ed.), *Charting the course for evaluation: How do we measure the success of nutrition education and promotion in food assistance programs? Summary of proceedings* (pp. 26–27). Alexandria, VA: U.S. Department of Agriculture.

Baranowski, T., Perry, C.L., & Parcel, G.S. (2002). How individuals, environments, and health behavior interact: Social cognitive theory. In K. Glanz, B.K. Rimer, & F.M. Lewis (Eds.), *Health behavior and health education: Theory, research and practice* (3rd ed., pp. 165–184). San Francisco: Jossey-Bass.

Bickel, W.K. & Vuchinich, R.E. (Eds.) (2000). *Reframing health behavior change with behavioral economics.* Mahway, NJ: Lawrence Erlbaum Associates.

Braus, P. (1995). Selling good behavior. *American Demographics,* 60–64.

Contento, I., Balch, G.I., Bronner, Y.L., Lytle, L.A., Maloney, S.K., White, S.L., Olson, C.M., & Swadener, S.S. (1995). The effectiveness of nutrition education and implications for nutrition education policy, programs, and research [Special issue]. *Journal of Nutrition Education,* 27(6).

Fox, K.F.A., & Kotler, P. (1980). The marketing of social causes: The first 10 years. *Journal of Marketing,* 44(4), 24–33.

Goldberg, M.R. (1994). Social marketing: Are we fiddling while Rome burns? Presidential Address, *Society for Consumer Psychology,* February 19.

Hastings, G. (2003). Social marketers of the world unite, you have nothing to lose but your shame. *Social Marketing Quarterly,* 9(4), 14–21.

Hastings, G. & Saren, M. (2003). The critical contribution of social marketing. *Marketing Theory,* 3(3), 305–322.

Hastings, G.B. & Haywood, A.J. (1991). Social marketing and communication in health promotion, *Health Promotion International,* 6(2), 135–45.

Hicks, J.J. (2001). The strategy behind Florida's *truth* campaign, *Tobacco Control* 10, 3–5.

Janz, N.K., Champion, V.L., & Strecher, V.J. (2002). The health belief model. In K. Glanz, B.K. Rimer & F.M. Lewis (Eds.), *Health behavior and health education: Theory, research and practice* (3rd ed., pp. 45–66). San Francisco: Jossey-Bass.

Kotler, P. (2000). *Marketing management* (Millenium ed.). Upper Saddle River, NJ: Prentice Hall International.

Kotler, P., & Andreasen, A.R. (1996). *Strategic marketing for non-profit organizations* (2nd ed.). Upper Saddle River, NJ: Prentice-Hall.

Kotler, P., & Armstrong, G. (2004). *Principles of marketing* (10th ed.). Upper Saddle River, NJ: Prentice-Hall.

Kotler, P., & Zaltman, G. (1971). Social marketing: An approach to planned social change. *Journal of Marketing,* 35, 3–12.

Lefebvre, R.C., Bloom, P., Bryant, C. & Novelli, W. (2003). Emerging innovations: What have we learned? *Social Marketing Quarterly,* 9(3), 33–38.

Lefebvre, R.C., Doner, L.D., Jonston, C., Loughrey, K., Balch, G., & Sutton, S.M. (1995). Use of database marketing and consumer-based health communications in message design: An example from the Office of Cancer Communications' "5 A Day for Better Health" program. In E. Maibach & R. Parrott (Eds.), *Designing health messages: Approaches from communication theory and public health practice* (pp. 217–246). Thousand Oaks, CA: Sage.

Madden, G.J. (2000). A behavioral economics primer. In W.K. Bickel & R.E. Vuchinich, (Eds.) *Reframing health behavior change with behavioral economics* (pp. 3–26). Mahway, NJ: Lawrence Erlbaum Associates.

Maibach, E.W., & Cotton, D. (1995). Moving people to behavior change: A staged social cognitive approach in message design. In E. Maibach & R.L. Parott (Eds.), *Designing health messages: Approaches from communication theory and public health practice* (pp. 41–64). Thousand Oaks, CA: Sage.

Mark, M. & Pearson, C.S. (2001). *The hero and the outlaw: Building extraordinary brands through the power of archetypes.* New York: McGraw-Hill.

McDivitt, J. Schwartz, B., Round, C, Young, E., & Lefebvre, R.C. (2003). Innovations in social marketing conference proceedings session II: Is there a role for branding in social marketing? *Social Marketing Quarterly,* 9 (3), 11–17.

Morgan, R.M. & Hunt, S.D. (1994). The commitment-trust theory of relationship marketing. *Journal of Marketing* 58, 20–38.

National Highway Traffic Safety Administration, (1996). *Patterns of misuse of child safety seats: Final report* (Rep. No. DOT HS 808-440). Washington, DC: Author.

————. (1997). *Tether anchorages for child restraint systems; Child restraint anchorage system,* 62 Fed. Reg. 7858.

Nelson, D.E., Bolen, J., & Kresnow, M. (1998). Trends in safety belt use by demographics and by type of state safety belt law, 1987–1993. *American Journal of Public Health,* 88, 245–249.

Peattie, S. & Peattie, K. (2003). Ready to fly solo? Reducing social marketing's dependence on commercial marketing theory. *Marketing Theory,* 3(3), 365–385.

Prochaska, J.O. (1994). Strong and weak principles for progressing from precontemplation to action on the basis of twelve problem behaviors. *Health Psychology,* 13(1), 47–51.

Prochaska, J.O., Redding, C.A., & Evers, K.E. (2002). The transtheoretical model and stages of change. In K. Glanz, B.K. Rimer & F.M. Lewis (Eds.), *Health behavior and health education: Theory, research and practice* (3rd ed., pp. 99–120). San Francisco: Jossey-Bass.

Produce for Better Health Foundation. (2005). *National action plan to promote health through increased fruit and vegetable consumption.* Wilmington, DE: Author. Retrieved April 4, 2006 from http://www.pbhfoundation.org/pdfs/pulse/action/pbh_nap_book041905.pdf

Roman, K., Maas, J. & Nisenholtz, M. (2003). *How to advertise* (3rd ed.). New York: St. Martin's Press.

Rothschild, M.L. (1979, Spring). Marketing communications in nonbusiness situations or why it's so hard to sell brotherhood like soap. *Journal of Marketing,* 43, 11–20.

————. (1999). Carrots, sticks and promises: A conceptual framework for the behavior management of public health and social issues. *Journal of Marketing,* 63, 24–37.

Strand, J., Rothschild, M. L. & Nevin, J. R. (2004). Session I: "Place" and Channels of Distribution. *Social Marketing Quarterly* 10 (3–4), 7–13.

Wallack, L., & Dorfman, L. (1996). Media advocacy: A strategy for advancing policy and promoting health. *Health Edcation Quarterly,* 23, 293–317.

Wallack, L. Dorfman, L., Jernigan, D., & Themba, M. (1993). *Media advocacy and public health.* Newbury Park, CA: Sage.

Weibe, G.D. ([1951] 1952). Merchandising commodities and citizenship on television. *Public Opinion Quarterly,* 15, 679–691.

Zyman, S. (1999). *The end of marketing as we know it.* New York: HarperCollins.

APPENDIX

9-A

Using Marketing Principles To Craft a National Action Plan

In 2005, the Produce for Better Health Foundation released a national action plan to increase U.S. fruit and vegetable consumption (Produce for Better Health Foundation, 2005). Impetus for the plan included the 2005 Dietary Guidelines for Americans, which increased recommended fruits and vegetable intake to 5 to 13 daily servings (USDHHS and USDA, 2005)—in a country where, despite numerous marketing and educational efforts, just one in five adults manages even the bare minimum of five daily servings (Produce for Better Health Foundation, 2003). In releasing the plan, PBH's goal was to outline the multifaceted approach it would take to truly increase fruit and vegetable consumption and to provide concrete ideas for many types of organizations looking to get involved. The plan illustrates many of the marketing principles and approaches to improving health behaviors outlined in Chapters 9 and 10. In the table below, excerpts from the plan appear in the left column, with discussion in the right.

Table 9A-1   Use of Marketing Principles in the National Action Plan to Promote Health Through Increased Fruit and Vegetable Consumption

Excerpts from Plan Discussion	Discussion
Development of Plan	
The National Action Plan proposes an integrated framework of policy[1], marketing and communication strategies that all entities—large and small—that produce, serve, or regulate food can use to help Americans obtain, prepare and consume fruits and vegetables—and in so doing achieve good health.	Using the motivation-opportunity-ability (MOA) framework introduced in Chapter 10, the plan's strategies place a great deal of emphasis on environmental changes to improve people's *opportunities* to eat fruits and vegetables by making them more available and easier to obtain, prepare, and consume.
Produce for Better Health Foundation developed this plan with input from a variety of food, nutrition, marketing, communications and policy leaders and conducted a thorough assessment of the scientific literature. Over 75 strategies, organized in nine different settings, have been identified to more aggressively create an environment where Americans can increase their fruit and vegetable consumption.	In addition, the plan envisions using education and marketing strategies to increase *abilities*, such as to prepare foods or put together meals with adequate fruits and vegetables. Marketing strategies can also be used to increase *motivation*, or willingness, to consume fruits and vegetables.
Goal	
Put into action at the national, state and local levels a set of policy, marketing, business, public health, and communication strategies that can close the gap between actual and recommended fruit and vegetable consumption.	

---

[1] "Policy" is broadly defined to include public- and private-sector plans of action designed to facilitate increasing consumption of fruits and vegetables in the United States. It is not limited to public policy actions undertaken by the U.S. government.

(continues)

Table 9A-1   Use of Marketing Principles in the National Action Plan to Promote Health Through Increased Fruit and Vegetable Consumption (continued)

Excerpts from Plan	Discussion
Objectives of the National Action Plan	
1. Increase the accessibility and desirability of fruits and vegetables, by making them tasty, attractive, convenient, affordable, plentiful, and easily available at all eating and snacking occasions.	This marketing objective emphasizes improving the tangible goods needed to engage in the health behavior. It addresses three marketing mix variables: • *Product:* "making [fruits and vegetables] tasty, attractive, convenient" • *Price:* "affordable" addresses financial cost; "convenient" addresses preparation time and mess • *Place:* "easily available at all eating and snacking occasions" addresses availability.
2. Offer practical strategies to help increase individuals' ability to obtain and prepare meals and snacks rich in fruits and vegetables. The single strongest independent predictor of fruit and vegetable intake is self-efficacy (confidence in one's ability to eat fruits and vegetables in a variety of settings), followed by knowledge of dietary recommendations and taste preferences. (Potter, et al., 2000)	This is an educational objective, designed to increase skills people can use to increase their consumption of fruits and vegetables.
3. Change Americans' attitudes and habits so that they include fruits and vegetables at every eating occasion. Key to making this change is identifying, communicating and delivering the benefits of fruits and vegetables that consumers find most important, in a way that is exciting, enticing, and produces positive behavior change.	This marketing objective addresses the desired health behavior, which is what Chapter 10 would categorize as a continuous or frequent behavior: asking people to include fruits at vegetables at all eating occasions. Note that the second sentence implicitly addresses the importance of considering people's self-interest in creating, communicating and delivering the public health offering.

(continues)

Table 9A-1 Use of Marketing Principles in the National Action Plan to Promote Health Through Increased Fruit and Vegetable Consumption (continued)

Excerpts from Plan	Discussion
Approach to Behavior Change	
To increase consumption of fruits and vegetables, people need *motivation, opportunity*, and *ability*. (Rothschild, 1999). Appropriate communication efforts often can provide motivation and sometimes improve a person's ability to increase fruit and vegetable consumption, but marketing and policy are necessary to change the environment to one that offers increased *opportunities* for fruit and vegetable consumption—an environment where the healthy choice is the easy choice.	This section of the plan explicitly references the MOA framework (discussed in more detail in Chapter 10) to describe how behavior change is expected to occur if plan strategies are implemented.
Environmental and policy approaches designed to make it easier for people to make healthy food choices are a critical component of population-wide behavior change (Seymour et al., 2004). When compared to individual nutrition behavior change strategies, environmental and policy changes are also less expensive and less labor-intensive relative to the number of people they affect (Ammerman et al., 2002).	The second paragraph provides additional rationale for emphasizing trying to change environments so that people have more opportunities to obtain and consume fruits and vegetables, rather than focusing exclusively on trying to persuade people to eat more of them.
Timeline for Implementation of Plan	
The strategies presented in this plan span a wide range of actions that can be taken by an equally broad array of entities. Individuals can take personal responsibility for making better choices; places serving food (cafeterias, restaurants, schools, worksites, entertainment venues and others) and government agencies can make a myriad of changes to increase the availability and accessibility of fruits and vegetables. Some of the strategies presented here include changes that can take effect within days, weeks, or months; others will take years to	This section emphasizes the broad vision of the plan and describes some of the roles that different entities can play in addressing the public health problem. It also discusses the amount of time change is expected to take, and outlines a general approach to evaluating progress.

(continues)

Table 9A-1 Use of Marketing Principles in the National Action Plan to Promote Health Through Increased Fruit and Vegetable Consumption (continued)

Excerpts from Plan	Discussion

craft and implement. To gauge progress, Produce for Better Health Foundation will regularly scan the environment, examining fruit and vegetables consumption figures and indicators of progress, from the frequency of restaurants incorporating fruits and vegetables on menus to federal efforts to increase funding for fruit and vegetable promotion. In addition, entities implementing strategies to increase consumption can evaluate their outcomes with appropriate measures and ideally share their results to develop an inventory of model programs.

Strategies to Increase Fruit and Vegetable Intake

Strategies are included for the following settings:
- Marketing to children
- Supermarkets and retailers
- Fruit and vegetables growers, processors and shippers
- Cafeterias, restaurants and food establishments
- Schools, daycare centers and youth camps
- Worksites
- Health care industry and health organizations
- Communities
- Research entities
- Federal policies

The plan encompasses strategies for:
- Improving *access* to fruits and vegetables every place where an adult or child might obtain food
- Improving fruit and vegetable *products* (and their competitive positioning) by improving taste and making them more convenient and portable
- Increasing *motivation* and *skills* to select and prepare fruit and vegetable dishes or meals containing them

For each setting, the plan leads with a description of the role entities that are part of the setting can play in increasing fruit and vegetable consumption—and the benefits they can accrue by doing so. It then lists specific strategies they can develop and implement.

(continues)

Table 9A-1 Use of Marketing Principles in the National Action Plan to Promote Health Through Increased Fruit and Vegetable Consumption (continued)

Excerpts from Plan	Discussion
Conclusion	
This National Action Plan identifies many strategies to help Americans of all ages eat and drink more fruits and vegetables by increasing the accessibility and desirability of fruits and vegetables, providing practical tips for increasing consumption, and getting Americans in the habit of including fruits and vegetables at every eating occasion. From effective nutrition education and promotion efforts that give consumers the skills and motivation they need to make better choices, to producing and retailing more tasty, convenience-oriented and portable fruits and vegetables, to offering more fruits and vegetables in restaurants, fast food establishments, schools and worksites, to better aligning federal policy with dietary guidelines, this plan provides short and long range initiatives that together will create an environment where the healthy choice is the easy choice, and fruits and vegetables are center stage in producing a healthier America.	The plan's concluding paragraph summarizes how change is expected to occur and reiterates the overall vision: making fruits and vegetables available everywhere all the time, ideally so that it is easier and more appealing to choose a fruit or vegetable than to choose any competitive food.

Source: Reprinted with permission from *National Action Plan to Promote Health Through Increased Fruit and Vegetable Consumption* © 2005 Produce for Better Health Foundation.

References

Ammerman, A.S., Lindquist, C.H., Lohr, K.N., Hersey, J. (2002). The efficacy of behavioral intentions to modify dietary fat and fruit and vegetable intake: a few view of the evidence. *Preventive Medicine*, 35, 25–41.

Potter, J.D., Finnegan, J.R., Guinard, J-X., et al. (2000). 5 A Day for better health program evaluation report. Bethesda, MD: National Institutes of Health, National Cancer Institute. NIH Publication No. 01-4904.

Produce for Better Health Foundation. (2005). *National action plan to promote health through increased fruit and vegetable consumption* Wilmington, DE: Author. (Available online at http://www.pbhfoundation.org/pdfs/pulse/action/pbh_nap_book041905.pdf)

Rothschild, M.L. (1999). Carrots, sticks and promises: A conceptual framework for the behavior management of public health and social issues. *Journal of Marketing*, 63, 24–37.

Seymour, J.D., Yaroch, A.L., Serdula, M., Blanck, H.M., & Khan, L.K. (2004). Impact of nutrition environmental interventions on point-of-purchase behavior in adults: A review. *Preventive Medicine*, 39 (Supplement 2), S108–S136.

U.S. Department of Health and Human Services and U.S. Department of Agriculture (2005). *Dietary Guidelines for Americans, 2005* (6th ed.) Washington, DC: U.S. Government Printing Office. (Available online at http://www.health.gov/dietaryguidelines/dga2005/document/pdf/DGA2005.pdf)

CHAPTER

10

The Planning Process

Adequate planning is essential to the marketing approach—and essential to successfully achieving social change or the adoption of new public health programs and initiatives. Planning begins with conducting a thorough analysis of the situation at hand: identifying the problems and populations affected, determining the types of changes they can make and the environmental changes needed to help them do so, and determining the types of interventions most likely to be effective given the type of problem, the environment for change, and the organization's expertise and resources. The next step is to set goals and objectives by specifying target audiences and the behaviors, conditions, or policies to be changed. Then planners must develop public health offerings that provide audiences with benefits they value enough to choose to take the public health actions and, if necessary, reduce or overcome barriers to the actions. This is done by addressing all aspects of the marketing mix—product, price, place, and promotion.

■ THE MARKETING PROCESS

Developing a strong, effective marketing effort is an iterative process. To facilitate understanding, this book presents the process as a series of discrete, sequential activities (**Figure 10-1** and **Exhibit 10-1**), but in reality, the steps often overlap or repeat based on new information or changing conditions. This iteration is a defining characteristic of the marketing approach, providing the flexibility to adapt to different issues, environments, resource levels, and conditions.

As is evident from the number of activities shown in **Exhibit 10-1** for each stage (and the number of chapters in this book devoted to aspects of planning), adequate planning is vital to successfully marketing a policy, a health behavior, or wider social change. Audience and market

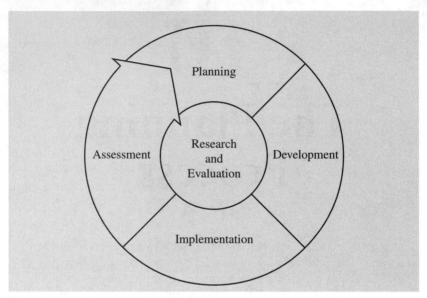

Figure 10-1 Stages of the Marketing Process

research are integral parts of the planning process. Allocating sufficient resources to ensure adequate planning and development can prevent costly mistakes and will result in a stronger, more effective initiative.

■ THE PLANNING PROCESS

The planning process is designed to give project staff the information they need to develop a comprehensive model of the problem, the environment in which it is occurring, and the components of solutions to the problem. This model provides a framework in which to identify how marketing can help bring about those solutions. With that knowledge, we can construct marketing strategies designed to create, communicate, and deliver an offering of sufficient value to target audiences that they engage in behaviors that lead to the solutions outlined in the model.

Although many activities occur along the way, the results of the planning process are summarized into a strategic plan that provides overall guidance for the program. This plan is sometimes called a marketing plan or strategy statement. **Exhibit 10-2** provides a sample outline of a strategic plan. There are probably as many ways of constructing a strategic plan as there are people who write them; the approach presented in this chapter closely follows the planning process outlined here.

The strategic plan should outline how the intervention is expected to work: the audiences it should reach, the actions they are expected to take as a result of the intervention, the exchanges that will be constructed,

Exhibit 10-1 Activities During Each Stage of the Marketing Process

Planning
- Step 1: Analyze the situation:
  - Identify problems and populations affected.
  - Analyze current and possible replacement behaviors.
  - Outline all components of a solution (education, law, marketing).
  - Assess the environment in which change will occur.

- Step 2: Select approaches and determine the role of marketing.
- Step 3: Set goals and objectives: Specify behaviors, conditions, or policies to be changed.
- Step 4: Segment and select target audiences:
  - Determine the target populations for each desired change, and within each population, the audience segment(s) on which you will focus.
  - Identify current and competitive behaviors and how they satisfy needs, desires, and values.
  - Identify barriers to the public health behavior.

- Step 5: Design public health offering(s).
  - Product: Identify and develop a bundle of benefits that you can deliver that differentiates the desired behavior from competitors. Develop any necessary supporting goods and services.
  - Price: Determine how to make costs manageable for target audience members.
  - Place: Determine how you will access channels that deliver the product so that it is easily available to target audience members at prices (financial, time, psyche, social, etc.) they are willing and able to pay.
  - Promotion: Develop communication strategy to position the public health offering as something consistent with the audience's core values that delivers a key benefit.

- Step 6: Plan evaluation.

Development
- Develop budgets and distribution and promotion plans.
- Develop prototype products, services and/or communication materials.
- Pretest with target audience members.
- Refine as necessary.
- Build in process evaluation measures.

Implementation
- Produce offerings and materials.
- Coordinate with partners.
- Implement intervention.
- Use process evaluation to monitor implementation.
- Refine offerings, promotions, and distribution channels as needed.

Assessment
- Conduct outcome evaluation.
- Refine intervention as needed.

Exhibit 10-2 Outline of the Strategic Plan

Executive Summary
Background and Mission
Challenges and Opportunities
Goals
Objectives (Measurable Outcomes)
Target Audiences
Strategies
    Developing the Offering (Product)
    Managing Perceived Price
    Improving Access (Place)
    Promotion
Evaluation Design

---

and how the strategies are expected to bring this action about. Once the strategic plan has been completed, it is used as a guide to develop implementation plans for each strategy and evaluation plans. The plan serves not only as a blueprint for the program, but as an organization's memory, reminding managers (or informing new staff or partners) of the history and rationale underlying the approaches selected. Strategic plans should be dynamic living documents, revised to reflect changing audiences and environments. The next few sections of this chapter outline the activities that culminate in the strategic plan. The activities outlined in Chapters 11 and 12 support strategic planning efforts.

■ STEP 1: ANALYZE THE SITUATION

The first step of planning is to collect and analyze information that will provide an understanding of the problem to be addressed, the environment in which the program will operate, and how marketing activities can contribute to solutions. This process is referred to by various names, including "background review," "market survey," "market audit," "environmental scan," and "situation analysis," the term we use here.

A situation analysis can vary in its level of detail, depending on the resources available, time allotted, and scope of the problem. Constructing it is a two-step process: first, information must be collected, and then it must be analyzed and turned into conclusions and recommendations about how the problem can best be addressed. The starting point of the analysis may be the public health burden or the social environment; this depends on whether one is trying to prioritize the order in which public health problems are addressed or developing an initiative to address a particular problem (e.g., cancer, nutrition, drug abuse). If the goal is to determine the problem an initiative (or initiatives) should address, it is best to begin with the social environment and prioritize the problems in that context (e.g., what problems are contributing to the worst, or most pernicious, social problems?). Green and Kreuter (1991) called this the *reductionist* approach. If instead the goal is to understand the social environment in which a particular initiative will be put into place, it is best to begin by looking at the public health burden associated with that problem and then work outward toward understanding the environment around the problem. Green and Kreuter (1991) referred to this as the *expansionist* approach.

Identify Problems and Populations Affected

Typically, one starts by reviewing existing data defining the problem to identify populations affected by it (or sometimes causing it), beginning to identify potential solutions and the changes needed to bring them about, and beginning to develop a list of additional information needed. For improvements in individual health behaviors, data reviewed typically include:

- Morbidity and mortality data: These include recent trends in the quantities and types of people who already have the condition or are most likely to develop or die from it.
- Known risk factors and, if possible, information on the quantities and types of people most like to be affected by these risk factors.
- Current behaviors that result in or are associated with the public health problem.
- Recommended behaviors: What should people do, and what is the likely impact if they do it? Recommended behaviors may involve treatment regimens for existing conditions, screening for early detection of disease, or lifestyle changes or other action to prevent disease or injury. Much of this information often comes from the institution sponsoring the program. In the United States, supplementary sources include state and local health department data, epidemiological and surveillance data collected by the Centers for Disease Control and Prevention (CDC), and other large federal studies, some of which are discussed in more detail in Chapter 11. In addition, the major health professional organizations and health voluntary agencies often provide information on risk factors, treatment guidelines and the like.

When marketing public health as an institution, it is more likely that the starting point will be assessing the environment in which marketing efforts will take place, a process discussed later in this section under "Assessing the Intervention Environment."

Analyze Current and Possible Replacement Behaviors

Once you have a sense of the dimensions and determinants of the problem and who is affected by it, you can begin to construct a map of current behavior. The goal is to outline the steps involved in the current behavior and—equally importantly—describes the physical, social, and economic environment in which the behavior takes place. Capturing the benefits and barriers audience members associate with their current behavior also is important. Obviously, formative research often is necessary to complete accurate and complete behavioral maps.

It is helpful to start the behavior mapping process by considering the type of behavior. In general, behaviors can be categorized along two dimensions, as shown in **Exhibit 10-3**. One dimension reflects frequency: some behaviors are "one-time" or at most periodic. For these behaviors, people generally make a conscious decision to engage in the behavior and then take the steps necessary to perform it or have it performed. In contrast, for behaviors that occur continuously or very frequently, people often do not make conscious decisions in advance and then take the steps necessary to implement the decision. For some frequent behaviors, individuals may be confronted with situations that do or could involve the behavior as often as multiple times per day (eating, wearing seat belts). This frequency can lead to a certain level of automaticity and so people act without making a thoughtful decision to act in a particular way. Other behaviors require certain pre-planning actions which a person may be unable or unwilling to take if the situation arises unexpectedly (e.g., having a condom or exercise clothing available, getting home after drinking).

Exhibit 10-3 Dimensions of Behavior

	One-Time or Episodic	Continuous or Frequent
Simple	Getting a flu shot Getting screening tests performed at routine exams	Using condoms Not smoking Not driving after drinking Fastening safety belts
Complex	Getting a colonoscopy Preparing a household for natural disasters and other community emergencies Obtaining and installing a child restraint system in a car	Changing eating habits Engaging in physical activity Lowering risk of contracting communicable diseases

The other dimension is complexity. Some behaviors require one simple action to be taken in a specific situation. Others require a series of actions, usually over time and often across a variety of settings. As a result, your task can range from providing a person with the motivation, opportunity and ability to engage in one transaction one time to helping a person integrate motivation, opportunity and ability into his or her life processes every day. Obviously the interventions required across this spectrum differ dramatically. While these dimensions apply most readily to individual health behaviors, they can be applied to efforts to bring about policy change as well.

After determining the type of behavior, you can list the steps involved in it, benefits associated with the behavior, and any obvious barriers to it. Common barriers can include self-interest (e.g., another behavior provides benefits valued more highly), beliefs, pressures, misinformation, competing ways of framing the public health issue, and lack of ability or opportunity to engage in the behavior, such as lack of knowledge or lack of physical or financial access.

To prepare a behavior "map" for simple one-time behaviors, it may be enough to list out the steps involved in the behavior in one column with corresponding columns assessing benefits and barriers. (See Appendix 10-A for an example). For complex frequent behaviors it may be more useful to diagram the common situations the person would encounter. Whether listing steps or diagramming the behavior, it is important to capture the barriers that might affect opportunity or ability and the competition that might affect motivation. Remember that competition can include apathy and inertia as well as alternative behaviors.

Creating a map of current behavior and the physical, social, economic or cultural environmental factors influencing it also allows you to begin identifying the steps people would have to take to engage in replacement behaviors that would improve health outcomes—and the many factors that may affect whether they are willing and able to do so. Beginning with the individual, a person may be receptive to the behavior or resistant to it. Regardless of the individual's receptivity, external factors influence whether he or she can engage in the behavior. Rothschild (1999), building on a model of information processing developed by MacInnis, Moorman and Jaworski (1991), suggests determining whether the person has motivation, opportunity, and ability to engage in the behavior.

- *Motivation* is a person's willingness to engage in the behavior; generally, people are motivated to engage in a behavior when they discern their self-interest will be served by doing so.
- *Ability* reflects a person's skill or proficiency and self-efficacy (confidence in their ability) regarding the behavior.
- *Opportunity* is provided or prohibited by the person's environment.

Thinking about replacement behaviors in terms of motivation, ability and opportunity can help identify solutions that will lead to the greatest progress toward public health goals. Often that progress comes from addressing an external factor, such as opportunity, rather than trying to persuade people to change a behavior when they lack the opportunity or ability to do so.

Choosing a Replacement Behavior

Sometimes there are a number of actions that the target audience could take and you must choose one on which to focus. Graeff, Elder, and Booth (1993) suggested first developing a list of "ideal" behaviors. In the context of changing individual health behaviors, they defined ideal behaviors as "the medically prescribed behavioral steps that the target audience should perform in order to prevent or treat the health problem" (p. 65). From this list, they recommended selecting target behaviors, which they defined as "the minimum number of behavioral steps essential for the health practice to be effective" (p. 65). **Exhibit 10-4** lists some questions they suggested asking to help with choosing a recommended behavior. Although Graeff and colleagues developed these questions to assess

---

Exhibit 10-4   Questions To Select Target Behaviors

1. *Does the ideal behavior have a demonstrated impact on this specific health problem?* If not, it should not be selected as a target behavior.

2. *Is the ideal behavior feasible for the audience to perform?* An in-depth understanding of the target audience is essential if one is to understand the environmental constraints that will affect adoption.
   - Does the ideal behavior produce negative consequences for the person performing it?
   - Is the ideal behavior incompatible with the person's current behavior or with socio-cultural norms or acceptable practices?
   - Does the ideal behavior require an unrealistic rate of frequency?
   - Does the ideal behavior require an unrealistic duration?
   - Does the ideal behavior have too high a cost in time, energy, social status, money, or materials?
   - Is the ideal behavior too complex and not easily divided into a small number of elements or steps?

3. *Are any existing behaviors approximations to the ideal behavior?* Can these behaviors be shaped into an effective health practice through training and skill development? Communication programs are more likely to achieve behavior change if they build on what people are already doing correctly. If existing behaviors are similar to any of the remaining ideal behaviors, they should be included in the list of target behaviors.

Source: Reprinted with permission from J. A. Graeff, J. P. Elder, and E.M. Booth, *Communication for Health and Behavior Change: A Developing Country Perspective*, p. 67, © 1993, Jossey-Bass Inc., Publishers.

behaviors related to individual health practices, they can be modified easily to address other types of social changes.

For example, consider reducing drunk driving, the health problem discussed in Appendix 10-A. A typical approach is to try to convince people not to get drunk if they are going to drive. This approach meets the first criterion in **Exhibit 10-4**: if people who planned to drive did not get drunk, there would be fewer drunk drivers. However, the behavioral analysis revealed this replacement behavior—not drinking before driving—did not meet the second criterion of being feasible to perform, primarily because it was incompatible with the target audience's sociocultural norms. Another alternative behavior, not driving home, was compatible with criterion one but it too failed criterion two. However, it failed for a different reason: not driving home was not feasible because there was no alternative means of transportation. That is a problem that marketing could fix: a new product offering was developed that made not driving home feasible.

The third point in **Exhibit 10-4** is particularly important and often not given adequate consideration by program planners. Some words of advice given to commercial marketers are useful here:

> Overambition is the pitfall of most strategies. Don't ask people to change deeply ingrained habits. Behavior can be changed—consumers go to self-service gas stations and many have learned to bank online, but it's generally easier to get people to change brands. (Roman, Maas, & Nisenholtz, 2003, p. 22)

Those trying to improve the public's health are often in the unenviable position of having to do what our commercial-sector counterparts are told to avoid: change deeply ingrained behaviors. Offering replacement behaviors that are close to existing behaviors makes it easier for target audiences to fit our replacements into their daily lives, and thus makes it more likely that they will agree to do so.

Once the list of possible replacement behaviors is narrowed to target behaviors, you can map the steps a typical person will have to take to engage in the behavior and then compare it to a map of their current behavior.

> A consumer map can help to identify those points in the process where consumers pull away from the recommended health behavior and toward another behavior. . . . What are they doing now, instead of the desired behavior? That action is the competition—the behavior we want to replace. Answers help formulate the intermediate steps that stand between where the consumer currently is and where the science recommends him or her to be. (Sutton et al., 1995, p. 729)

More than likely the initial maps of recommended and current behaviors will have some question marks. Formative research—previously conducted or commissioned specifically for this planning process—can help fill in these blanks. Chapter 11 discusses some approaches and Chapter 18 provides more detail on methodologies.

The Role of Theory and Models of Behavior

The role of theory is to help envision how change will occur and the role that an intervention can play in facilitating that change. In the early stages of planning, theory can help you understand current behavior and likely reactions to recommended behaviors—and, therefore, whether education, law, marketing, or a combination would be most useful. Later, theory can help select specific audience segments, determine actions they can take, and develop offerings most likely to reach and motivate those audience segments to take the desired action. Theory can also help planners set reasonable objectives; if one expects change to occur very quickly and easily, objectives are likely to be quite different than if one expects change to be gradual and difficult.

There is no one theory or model that will work for every situation. It is not unusual for interventions to be guided by the constructs of a number of different models; examples occur throughout this book. Some theories and models are intended to predict or understand individual health behaviors, others interpersonal health behaviors, and others how a health behavior moves through a community or group. Chapter 18 introduces some of the theories and models commonly used in public health; Glanz, Rimer, and Lewis's *Health Behavior and Health Education* (2002) is a good starting point for more information.

Outline all Components of a Solution

Now that you have mapped current and potential replacement behaviors and identified the internal and/or external factors that lead individuals to their current behavior instead of the replacement behaviors, you can create a model of how the problem needs to be addressed. This model will help everyone involved clearly see what types of changes will be necessary in order to lessen or control the problem and what types of tools—education, law, marketing—can bring them about. If you are working with other organizations, for example in a coalition, it is usually wise to work together on this process. Chapter 14's **Exhibit 14-2** provides suggestions on how to usefully convene representatives of multiple organizations, and **Exhibit 14-4** presents a brief case study of using an integrated, collaborative approach to implementing countrywide technological, infrastructure, and behavior changes.

Figure 10-2 contains the beginning of a model of change; in this case, the goal is to increase the percentage of child safety seats that are properly installed in passenger cars. It was developed from information presented in **Exhibit 10-5**.

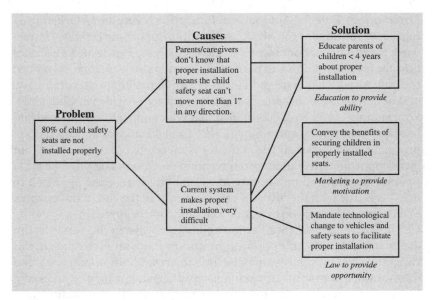

Figure 10-2 Modeling the Child Safety Seat Initiative

Exhibit 10-5 Key Aspects of the Child Restraint System Situation Analysis

Problem

- Child restraints are 71% effective in reducing the likelihood of death in motor vehicle crashes. However, actual average effectiveness of restraints in use is 59%, due to
  - Incorrect use, and/or
  - Vehicle seat and/or seat belt incompatibility issues
- Consumer frustration with installation and compatibility may lead to eroding confidence in the safety of child restraint systems and decreased usage of the systems.

Causes

- Incorrect use. A 1996 four-state study found that 80% of participants made at least one significant error in installation. 72% did not use a locking clip when necessary, or used it incorrectly; 17% used the vehicle seat belt incorrectly.

- Vehicle seat and seat belt incompatibility. Advances in seat and seat belt design features to protect older children and adults have led to increased difficulty with child restraint installation. In consumer clinics (somewhat similar to focus groups) conducted in the United States and Canada, virtually all participants expressed high levels of dissatisfaction with conventional means of attaching child restraints in vehicles.

Source: Reprinted from L. Doner and M. Siegel, *Using Marketing in Public Health*. In L. Novick & G. Mays (Eds.), *Public Health Administration*, p. 489, © 2001, Aspen Publishers. Data from *Federal Motor Vehicle Safety Standards: Child Restraint Systems: Child Restraint Anchorage Systems*, 64 Fed. Reg. 10785, 1999, National Highway Traffic Safety Administration.

Determining Types of Approaches: Education, Law, and Marketing
Earlier we introduced the MOA (motivation, opportunity, ability) framework for thinking about recommended behaviors. **Figure 10-3** illustrates how the framework can also be used to determine the types of tools needed to bring about change in individual health behaviors—education, law and/or marketing (conceptualizations of each are provided in Chapter 9). For example, if you have determined that your audience is motivated and has both opportunity and ability (Cell 1), an educational approach is appropriate. In contrast, if the audience is motivated and has ability but lacks opportunity, a marketing intervention that focuses on providing that opportunity and communicating its availability will be the approach to use—as is true with the "Road Crew" example at the end of this chapter. With other problems, you may need a combination of approaches. Consider Cell 4, where the audience has the ability to engage in the public health action but has neither the opportunity nor the motivation to do so. In this case, a marketing offering may be able to create both opportunity and motivation, but if motivation remains insufficient, law may be necessary.

This framework can be used first to identify whether education, law, marketing, or a combination should be used *with the population whose individual health behaviors you wish to change.* A second level of analysis may be needed to identify the marketing, law, or education needed to enable or force some other group to make a change that will result in increased motivation, opportunity or ability for the population whose behavior

MOTIVATION		Yes		No	
OPPORTUNITY		Yes	No	Yes	No
ABILITY		1	2	3	4
	Yes	Prone to behave	Unable to behave	Resistant to behave	Resistant to behave
		Education	Marketing	Law	Marketing, Law
		5	6	7	8
	No	Unable to behave	Unable to behave	Resistant to behave	Resistant to behave
		Education, Marketing	Education, Marketing	Education, Marketing, Law	Education, Marketing, Law

Source: Rothschild, M.L. (1999). Carrots, sticks and promises: A conceptual framework for the behavior management of public health and social issues. *Journal of Marketing,* 63, 24–37.

Figure 10-3 Application of Education, Marketing, and Law

you wish to manage. To illustrate, in the child safety seat example, some parents and other caregivers had motivation but did not have opportunity or ability; they would be in Cell 6. Education could be used to improve skills for installing existing seats in existing cars. However, before marketing could be used to provide an improved product and therefore opportunity, legal changes were necessary: the regulations had to be changed to both enable and require manufacturers of child safety seats and automobiles to use a different installation system.

Factors to Consider

Sometimes a variety of possible solutions could be used or are needed to address a particular problem. Thinking about these approaches from a number of different perspectives may help prioritize them and narrow them down to the ones that will be the best fit for the problem, the organizations seeking to address it, and currently available resources. Considering the following questions may help.

Should we increase demand, adjust supply, or do both? When the focus is trying to get individuals to take an action that improves their personal health, we are trying to increase demand for that behavior. Sometimes, progress toward health objectives will be achieved much more quickly by adjusting supply: Rather than (or in addition to) trying to persuade the people who need to improve their health to change, we can use marketing to persuade (or, in some instances, legal approaches to mandate) suppliers of a product or service necessary for the health behavior to make a change. For example, adding folate to grain products is a regulatory approach to reducing birth defects: rather than focusing solely on persuading women who are or might become pregnant to increase their folic acid intake (to decrease neural tube defects), requiring that food processors fortify certain grain products with folate allows women to easily increase their intake, in some instances without even realizing they are doing so. Supply-side adjustments can also be brought about through marketing voluntary changes, such as persuading restaurants and other food outlets to decrease portion sizes or the amount of fat or sodium in their foods and convincing fast food restaurants to offer fruit as an alternative to French fries or milk or juice as alternatives to soft drinks.

What type of demand exists? Kotler and Roberto (1989) divided social changes into the type of product or service that must be developed—new, superior, and substitute—depending on the state of demand. New products fill a latent demand; target adopters have an unfilled need that the product addresses. In contrast, superior products are appropriate when there is underfilled demand—the current product or its accessibility does not satisfy target adopters' needs. Their example is rural areas where physicians are too few and too far away. Finally, substitute products or behaviors must be developed to address the *unwholesome* demand that occurs when target adopters are engaging in harmful behaviors, such as drug abuse. The challenge is to "de-market" the existing behavior and provide a substitute that the target adopters will accept. An example is the "Road Crew" ride service discussed in Appendix 10-A.

Is a tangible good or service tied to the product? Kotler and Roberto (1989) divided behavior changes into those tied to a tangible product, such as family planning and contraceptives, versus those that involve the behavior change alone. They argued that if a behavior is tied to a tangible good, the marketer must market both the behavior and the product, a situation they characterize as *dual demand*. They noted that dual demand can take a number of forms, each requiring a different strategy: (1) The tangible good may already be embraced by the target adopters for reasons other than the behavior change on which the program is focusing (e.g., condoms may be used to prevent disease but not as a method of family planning). (2) The behavior change may have been adopted but the particular good or service has not been. (3) Both good or service and behavior change are at the same stage of adoption.

Are we addressing a one-time or frequent behavior? We encouraged consideration of this issue at the beginning of the behavior mapping process. For one-time or periodic behavior changes, such as getting a flu shot or donating blood, Kotler and Roberto (1989) note that demand is *irregular*—the change only needs to happen at certain times or under certain conditions. Therefore, the marketing task is to convince people to do something once. Community tragedies sometimes create a different sort of irregular demand: The public and policy makers suddenly clamor for a public health program previously though to be unimportant. In contrast, with continuous or frequent behaviors, the marketing task is to help individuals fit the behavior into their daily life processes. Building and maintaining a relationship with target audience members is likely to be critical to success. With sustained behavior changes, marketers who have successfully convinced target adopters to try the behavior will eventually face a *faltering* demand situation when compliance with the behavior drops. This situation can occur with individual health behaviors and with the policies that facilitate those behaviors. Those marketing disease or injury prevention frequently experience the ramification of faltering demand among policymakers: When prevention programs are successful, the attention-grabbing poor outcomes stop occurring and policymakers are often tempted to reallocate the prevention resources to burgeoning crises.

Do the "solutions" need to occur in a particular order, or can they happen simultaneously or in any order? Sometimes, changes must be made to product, price, or place so that people have sufficient opportunity before any significant behavior change can occur. And sometimes legal or educational approaches are required to make these changes before marketing can be of use. At other times, two "solutions" can move forward in tandem, as was true with the child safety seats example discussed earlier. Education to tell people how to safely install existing child safety seats and marketing to persuade them to do so took place while a regulatory approach was pursued. Then, once new child restraints and new anchorage systems were available, education and marketing efforts were modified to address the new systems as well.

Which focus would benefit the largest number of people? While sometimes it is important to address those most "in need," regardless of whether they are the largest group, at other times choosing the approaches that would benefit the greatest numbers is the ethical and appropriate decision.

Which focus is the best match for the sponsoring organization? Based on the organization's mission, expertise, and resources, some approaches may be a better fit than others.

If outside funds will have to be raised, which approach has the greatest funding potential? Assuming likely contributions to the public health problem are equal, success is more likely with an approach that will attract more funding.

When analyses are complete, planners can then consider the mandate, resources, and restrictions of the organization(s) and make an objective assessment of what roles the organization(s) can play in the solutions and what roles will have to be played by others. If an organization cannot implement all necessary approaches, the environmental assessment (next section) should provide sufficient information to determine if other approaches are or can be implemented by organizations working in partnership or parallel with your organization.

> The best focus would then have a high potential for behavior change, fill a significant need and void in the marketplace, match the organization's capabilities, and have a high funding potential. (Kotler, Robert, & Lee, 2002, p. 97)

Assessing the Intervention Environment

Once you have determined education, law, and marketing approaches appropriate for the public health problem and identified some possibilities for your organization, reviewing the environment in which the intervention will be implemented can provide further guidance on how to focus an organization's efforts. An environmental assessment will likely encompass reviewing past attempts to address the problem and their results and identifying current complementary and competing activities. It also may include analyzing how the problem or potential solutions to it are currently framed in the media, thereby providing insight into the public and policy agendas.

Reviewing Past Activities and Results

Information can be collected on what has been done before and what the results have been. Identifying approaches from the current program or others that have and have not worked well, and environments in which they were used, can help focus current efforts on solutions more likely to be effective. Ideally, past approaches will have included sufficient process and outcome evaluation measures to provide such information. If not, insight can be gleaned by talking to people involved with implementing the program. Try to identify the target audience(s); goals and objectives; specific products or services, distribution channels, and promotional approaches; and results.

Identifying Complementary and Competing Activities

"Competition" for a public health initiative is anything that limits its resources, diverts attention from the subject of the initiative, or calls for contrary behaviors. There are three main sources of competition: other organizations conducting programs on the same subject, other social changes, and commercial sources. Why view the first two as competition? Because social issues compete for limited resources, space, time, and audience attention. And in some instances a group may be promoting a product, message, or practice in conflict with your organization's goals or solutions to the problem. Identifying "competition" allows planners to position and focus a program appropriately and differentiate its offerings from others.

Often other organizations are addressing the same public health issue or problem. Identifying their activities can facilitate cooperation instead of competition by promoting synergy and preventing duplication of effort. If other organizations are doing a sufficient job of addressing a problem, there may be no need for your organization to get involved at all. In other instances, another group will already have a particular target audience adequately covered or working with them to address the same audience may maximize both groups' resources. Perhaps materials can be shared or responsibilities can be divided up among the partners.

While many commercial entities promote healthy behaviors, some public health activities, such as preventing or stopping tobacco use, have a direct commercial opponent encouraging the very behavior that public health practitioners are trying to stop. More often, there are commercial institutions that emphasize behaviors or choices that are detrimental if not moderated or balanced by other behaviors. For example, a glance at commercial children's television or the cereal aisle from a child's height will reveal far more products containing "added fats and sugars" than the whole grains, fruits, and vegetables that form the base of healthful eating. Similarly, the popular media tend to focus on violence and positively portray characters engaging in risky behaviors, such as smoking and nonmonogamous sexual activity. With the possible exception of physical activity, the media rarely picture everyday healthful behaviors such as using condoms or wearing seat belts.

Identifying "competing" activities helps program planners make informed decisions about how to proceed—whether to compete directly with unfriendly competitors, whether to find a niche among friendly competitors, whether to do nothing (either because other groups are already addressing the problem sufficiently, or because the unfriendly competition is such that progress is exceedingly unlikely without substantially greater resources), etc.

Program planners often know of complementary or competing activities being conducted by other groups. Some activities also can be identified by contacting likely organizations and asking if and how they are addressing a particular issue, through web searches, and through reviews of media coverage. **Exhibit 10-6** illustrates how media coverage of a policy issue can be analyzed; Chapter 17 discusses other approaches to analyzing the content of media coverage.

Analyzing How Public Policy Issues Are Framed

If changes in public policy are likely to be part of the solution to the health problem being addressed, understanding how the issue is currently framed on the media, public, and policy agendas is critical. To help public health practitioners identify and evaluate potential ways of framing an issue, Ryan (1991), adapting previous work done by Gamson & Lasch (1983), developed the framing matrix, which characterizes frames by their core positions, metaphors, images, catch phrases, attribution of responsibility for the problem, and the solution implied by the frame. Ryan and Gamson, through the work of their Media Research and Action Project (MRAP) in the Sociology Department at Boston College, adapted this useful framing matrix from the sociology literature so that it could be used by public health practitioners to identify and outline the frames used by supporters and opponents of public health policy issues (see Ryan, 1991; also see Gamson & Lasch, 1983; Gamson & Modigliani, 1989). Winett, Wallack, and others (Certain Trumpet Program, 1996; Winett, 1995) further adapted these framing matrices, suggesting the idea of a framing memo to list all potential ways an issue could be framed (by opponents and proponents of a policy) and the attributes of each and then provides a strategic analysis based on evaluation of each frame. The framing memo outlines the "arguments, images, and appeals to widely-shared principles that many people use to define and discuss an issue" (Winett, 1995, p. 1). It provides a "map and assessment of the range of arguments on an issue, so advocates may better make their case, and better anticipate what their opponents may say" (Certain Trumpet Program, 1996, p. ii).

To prepare a framing memo, public health practitioners must conduct a systematic search and review of newspaper articles on the public health policy topic of interest. Databases such as Nexis can be used to search and retrieve the text of relevant news articles. Practitioners can then review them to identify how both sides frame, or position, the policy issue. In identifying framing strategies, a matrix is prepared that summarizes, for each strategy,

1. Core position (main argument, summarized in one sentence);
2. Metaphor (the analogy used in the frame, with which the audience is familiar from another policy issue);
3. Catch phrases (phrases used repeatedly to describe the argument);
4. Symbols;
5. Images (visual images evoked by the argument);
6. Source of problem (who the frame implies is the source of the problem); and
7. Appeal to principle (the individual core values to which the frame's arguments appeal).

Once all the framing strategies used in arguing for and against a proposal are outlined, they can be analyzed. Practitioners can compare the strength of frames used by the health advocate and the opposition. In particular, practitioners should evaluate how compelling the metaphors, symbols, catch phrases, and images evoked by the frames are for proponents versus opponents of the policy. What are the core values to which proponent and opponent frames appeal, and how do these core values compare in terms of how salient and influential they are to the target audience?

If influencing public policy is pursued as part of the change effort, the analysis in the framing memo can provide guidance on which frames to emphasize or de-emphasize, which opposition frames need to be specifically countered, and whether it is necessary to develop new proponent frames. The framing memo can guide the development of new issue frames, and it can also help the practitioner to reframe opposition frames so that they support, rather than oppose, the proposed public health policy. Chapter 6 discussed these issues in greater detail. Chapter 12 will discuss using the framing memo to help craft a strategy for communications. **Exhibit 10-6** illustrates how framing memos have been used to evaluate media coverage of the tobacco policy debate.

Exhibit 10-6 The Tobacco Policy Debate

Background

Menashe and Siegel (1997) prepared a framing memo on tobacco policy issues, attempting to identify and analyze the frames used to support and oppose tobacco policy interventions during the past decade. They identified these frames by analyzing all front page articles relating to tobacco that appeared in *The Washington Post, The New York Times, The Los Angeles Times,* and *The Wall Street Journal* from 1985 to 1996. **Table 10-1** outlines the five dominant tobacco industry frames and **Table 10-2** the five dominant tobacco control frames they identified.

In their analysis of how pro-tobacco control and anti-tobacco control groups framed the issue, Siegel and Menashe found that the tobacco industry was much more successful in developing frames that appeal to the most compelling core values of the American public: freedom, independence, civil liberties, individual rights, control, autonomy, equality, fairness, economic opportunity, capitalism, and democracy (**Table 10-1**). In contrast, most of the public health community's frames have been based on the core value of health (**Table 10-2**).

Tobacco Industry Approaches

The tobacco industry has been steadfast in framing tobacco policy in terms of core human values. Their dominant framing strategies—big governmental/civil liberties, moralizing/hostility, accommodation, choice, and health vs. wealth—elicit more of a passionate gut response than those put forth by tobacco control frames. The core frames of the tobacco industry conjure up images of a free America, anti-Big Brother sentiment, freedom of the American citizen, the freedom of choice, strengthening the economic prosperity of America and its citizens, supporting the economic livelihood of the tobacco farmer and the farmer's family, and also concern about America's youth. With the power of these images, it is no wonder that the tobacco industry has been able to remain so supported and successful.

Tobacco Control Approaches

During the late 1980s through mid 1990s, tobacco control advocates increasingly used frames that appeal much more to the most compelling core values. For example, the deceit and manipulation frame (**Table 10-2**) appeals to the core values of fairness, equality, and justice. Its core position is that the tobacco industry intentionally manipulates people to smoke by control of nicotine levels, deceptive advertising, denial of tobacco's harmful health effects, and targeting of specific population subgroups. The core position of the nonsmokers' rights frame is that exposure to secondhand smoke violates people's right to a safe working environment and clean air in public places, and this frame appeals to the values of individual freedom, individual rights, and equality.

In addition, tobacco control frames that have been used most recently tend to attribute responsibility for the problem to society—that is, to the tobacco companies for producing, marketing, and selling an addictive product and to the government for failing to control the sale and marketing of this drug to youth. For example, the smokers at risk frame and illicit drug for minors frame attribute responsibility for the tobacco problem to individual smokers, individual youth, and individual merchants. In contrast, frames such as deceit and manipulation, nonsmokers' rights, and drug delivery device attribute responsibility to the tobacco companies and to the government.

(continues)

Exhibit 10-6   The Tobacco Policy Debate (continued)

Conclusions

The increased use of frames that are based on the most deeply ingrained core values and that shift the attribution of responsibility from the individual to society may, in part, explain the increased success of the tobacco control movement in obtaining unprecedented policy gains at the U.S. federal, state, and local levels. As Wallack, Dorfman et al. (1993) suggest, "one of the great successes of the antitobacco movement has been to win the framing battle with the tobacco companies and erode the credibility and legitimacy of the tobacco interests. As a result of the movement's efforts, the general public increasingly views the tobacco industry as 'merchants of death'" (p. 71).

Now that the dominant tobacco industry and tobacco control frames have been identified and analyzed, tobacco control practitioners can use formative research to test the effectiveness of alternative frames in garnering support for specific tobacco policies. They can also test the effectiveness of new tobacco control frames and attempts to reframe tobacco industry arguments so that they support, rather than oppose, tobacco control policies.

■ STEP 2: SELECT APPROACHES AND DETERMINE THE ROLE OF MARKETING

Once you understand the competitive environment, it is time to make realistic decisions about what solutions to pursue—and, if all critical solutions cannot be pursued, whether it makes sense to devote resources to the problem. The first step is to examine trends and determine the potential opportunities and challenges as well as the types of approaches to change that may be necessary (e.g., education, law and marketing). A common way to do this is to conduct a Strengths, Weaknesses, Opportunities, and Threats (SWOT) analysis. In the SWOT approach, the strengths and weaknesses of both the organization that will sponsor the intervention and of the social change itself are assessed. This information is then used to identify opportunities, or openings, for an intervention to make a difference. At the same time, potential threats to the success of the intervention are identified. This process helps point the intervention in promising directions, rather than wasting time on efforts that are not likely to succeed. Early identification of threats to success allows program managers to proactively address many of these threats or at least factor them in when setting expectations and objectives.

The SWOT analysis can be used to evaluate the solutions previously outlined on the MOA-Approaches to Behavior Management framework (see **Figure 10-3**) and make decisions regarding which approaches will be pursued by the organization. To help think through all of the issues, **Exhibit 10-7** summarizes some challenges to accomplishing social change, particularly when marketing approaches are used. Many of these were discussed in detail in earlier chapters of this book.

Table 10-1 Dominant Tobacco Industry Frames, 1985–1996

Frame	Big Government/ Civil Liberties	Moralizing/Hostility	Accommodation	Choice	Health vs. Wealth
Core position	Big government is interfering with personal lifestyle decisions, taking away smokers' rights.	Antismoking zealots are moralizing to us, discriminating against us, telling us what to do.	We can and should accommodate both smokers and nonsmokers.	Smoking is a matter of choice like any other choice in life.	Business will suffer if tobacco is regulated.
Metaphor	Big Brother Prohibition	Puritanism Holocaust	Accommodation of customers Negotiation Etiquette	Drinking alcohol Sex	Government regulation of small businesses
Images	Prohibition era *1984*	Puritan era Holocaust Prohibition era	Negotiation Hospitality Environments	Prison cell	The Depression Small "mom and pop" stores
Catch phrases	Prohibition, big government, Big Brother, government off our backs, goes too far, red meat, candy, fat	Second-class citizens, cultural war; hostility; accomodation, tolerance, bombarded, antismoking zealots, fascists, health Nazis, attacking smokers, under siege	Accommodation, fair, balances, reasonable, compromise, customers, clientele, hospitality	Choice, mature adults, judgments, clientele, already know the risks	Economic impact, jobs, out of business, tourist, making a living, difficult times, recession, suffering, hardship
Attribution of responsibility for problem	Big government Bureaucracy	Antismoking zealots	Hard-nose, uncompromising antismoking advocates	Individual smokers who make bad choices	Antismoking advocates who don't care about business
Implied solution	Keep government out of tobacco regulation.	Demand tolerance for smokers.	Demand accommodation of smokers and nonsmokers.	Let people decide whether to smoke, where to eat and work.	Let the market operate without intervention.
Core values	Freedom Civil liberties Autonomy Control	Freedom Civil liberties Autonomy Control Democracy	Fairness Equality	Freedom Autonomy Control	Free enterprise Capitalism Economic opportunity

Note: This framing matrix model was adapted from Ryan (1991), following the work of Gamson & Lasch (1983) and Gamson & Modigliani (1989).

Table 10-2 Dominant Tobacco Control Frames, 1985–1996

Frame	Smokers At Risk	Illicit Drug for Minors	Drug Delivery Device	Deceit and Manipulation	Nonsmokers' Rights
Core position	Smokers are putting themselves at great risk by smoking.	Cigarettes are not legal until age 18; thus we must punish merchants who sell them and youth who smoke. Companies manipulate nicotine levels; therefore FDA must regulate the product for consumer safety.	The tobacco industry now manipulates people to smoke through deceptive advertising and lies.		Nonsmokers have a right to be protected from secondhand smoke in workplaces and public places.
Metaphor	Unhealthy habits, like drinking alcohol, eating high-fat foods	Illegal drugs: marijuana, alcohol	Regulation of medical devices and drugs, deceptive packaging, food labeling	Untruthful advertising	Environmental toxins; workplace hazards.
Images	Making love with death; disgusting. dirty habit	Undercover investigations, law enforcement, speeding tickets, fines	Corporate fraud and deceit; painstaking investigation; vultures out to addict people	Secret plans; lying under oath; hiding	Smoke, hazardous workplaces, chemicals, pollution
Catch phrases	Unhealthy habit, discourage smoking	Crack down, sting operations, possession, use, supply, caught, punishment	Manipulation, fraud, deceit, jurisdiction, addictive, consumer watchdog	Lies, deceit, manipulation, targeting, denial, conceal, hide, secret	Nonsmokers' rights, health hazard, protection, danger, secondhand, involuntary, passive, smoke-free
Attribution of responsibility for problem	Individual smokers	Merchants Teenagers	Greedy, sneaky corporations that lie, mislead, and deceive	Tobacco industry	Workplace owners Government
Implied solution	Smokers should quit.	Merchants should not be allowed to sell cigarettes to youth; kids should not smoke.	Public must be protected by federal government.	Advertising and other aspects of tobacco business must be regulated.	Voluntary or legislative policies should restrict smoking in public places.
Core values	Health	Health	Health	Equality Fairness Justice	Freedom Civil liberties Equality Justice

Note: This framing matrix model was adapted from Ryan (1991), following the work of Gamson & Lasch (1983) and Gamson & Modigliani (1989).

Exhibit 10-7 Some Challenges to Social Change

Obstacles associated with using a marketing approach in a noncommercial setting:

- Audience data are more difficult to obtain and often of poorer quality.
- Financial cost may be outside the marketer's control, so managers must rely on changing other costs (i.e., psychological, time, effort, or lifestyle costs).
- Contributions of marketing efforts are often difficult to measure.
- Organizations may not be marketing-savvy and/or control all components of the marketing mix.

Obstacles associated with changing ingrained behaviors:

- Negative demand—the target audience may oppose the change being advocated.
- Legal and regulatory changes may be required to support or facilitate individuals' behavior change.
- The change may involve highly sensitive issues or may conflict with culture.
- The costs of the behavior change often exceed tangible benefits.
- The benefits may accrue to third parties, rather than to the individual making the change.
- Early adopters risk ostracism (for individuals) or losing a competitive standing in the marketplace (for companies).
- Change may take a long time.

■ STEP 3: SET GOALS AND OBJECTIVES

When general approaches have been selected, planners can set measurable goals and objectives for specific target audiences and then proceed to develop market offerings and, if necessary, educational and legal approaches, though our discussion from this point forward is restricted to planning marketing offerings and activities. We have broken "setting goals and objectives" and "selecting target audiences" into two steps for clarity, but in reality these decisions must be made together.

Goals translate a program's mission into specific behavioral outcomes (Andreasen, 1995). For example, the goal of the 5 A Day for Better Health program is to increase Americans' fruit and vegetable consumption. The U.S. Department of Health and Human Services' health objectives for the nation are often used as program goals (as is true for the 5 A Day program).

Objectives quantify the goals and describe the specific intermediate steps to take to make progress toward them. In the private sector, objectives are typically defined in terms of product or service trial, brand awareness, or sales. Public health efforts often include health objectives (such as reductions in morbidity or mortality) and corresponding behavioral objectives that address how the health objective will be achieved.

Objectives should be measurable, solidly linked to a behavioral outcome, associated with a specific target audience, and associated with a specific time period. As Green and Kreuter (1991) noted, "objectives are crucial; they form a fulcrum, converting diagnostic data into program direction" (p. 118). They note that objectives should answer these questions:

1. *Who* will receive the program (health objective) or make the change (behavioral objective)?
2. *What* health benefit should be received or action should be taken?
3. *How* much of that benefit or action should be achieved?
4. *By when* should it be achieved?

Exhibit 10-8 presents some possible behavioral objectives for a mammography program targeting women age 50 and older. The goal of this hypothetical program is to increase the rates of screening mammography among older women, since research has shown that rates decreases with age (Marchant & Sutton, 1990).

In this example, many of the supply side changes necessary to support increased use of mammography had already been implemented in the United States. For example, Medicare and other insurance reimbursements for mammograms had been established. The first objective in **Exhibit 10-8** is actually a product trial objective: Get women who have never had a mammogram to do in once. The second objective is trying to increase population compliance with the recommended schedule of annual mammograms.

The third objective addresses the behavior of a secondary audience: physicians. This objective illustrates one aspect of the iterative nature of the marketing process: how research conducted during the planning phase of a program can result in objectives and audiences that may not have been considered at the outset. In this instance, secondary research had shown that three-fourths of women went for a mammogram because their physician recommended it (Marchant & Sutton, 1990) and that overall visits to physicians increased with age (National Center for Health Statistics, 1990). So if women got mammograms because their physicians recommended them and if older women were more likely to see a physician, why were

---

Exhibit 10-8 Sample Objectives for Mammography Program

1. By 2015, increase by X% the number of women age 50 or older who received their first mammogram in the past year.

2. By 2015, increase by X% the number of women age 50 or older who received a mammogram in the past year.

3. By 2015, increase by X% the number of general practitioners, family practitioners, and internists who discuss mammography at all office visits by female patients over age 50 and provide them with a referral if necessary.

screening rates lower for older women? A survey of women revealed two factors that likely played a role: (1) Obstetricians/gynecologists are more likely to recommend mammograms than are other physicians, but visits to obstetricians/gynecologists are less frequent for older women; and (2) women who went for a checkup were more likely to get mammograms than those who went for a specific problem, which suggests that physicians were less likely to discuss screening tests with women who were there only for a problem (Sutton & Doner, 1992). Therefore, increasing the percentage of physicians who recommend mammograms to all female patients, regardless of whether the office visit is for a checkup or a specific problem, is likely to increase the percentage of women who get them.

To measure progress toward objectives, baseline and follow-up data must be available. In some instances, previously conducted studies can supply baseline data (and help program planners set reasonable objectives by examining current behavior and, with any luck, recent trends over time). In other instances, a custom study must be conducted. When objectives are set, evaluation plans should be developed that spell out how progress will be measured against the objectives.

Green and Kreuter (1991) also outlined a number of other factors that planners should consider when setting objectives, namely that

1. Progress toward meeting objectives should be measurable.
2. Individual objectives should be based on relevant, reasonably accurate data.
3. Objectives should be in harmony across topics and levels.

This third factor is particularly important; occasionally programs will inadvertently establish two objectives that conflict with one another.

When setting behavioral objectives, consider the type of change most likely to result in progress toward a health goal. That is, if the health goal is to reduce by $X\%$ the number of people who die in car accidents each year, a behavioral objective might be to increase by $X\%$ the number of people who wear seat belts. That might be supplemented by a regulatory/legal objective of increasing by $X\%$ the number of states that have primary seat belt laws in effect. It is very important to assess what can be accomplished, given the program's resources, and to refrain from setting objectives that the program cannot possibly address or attain. A thorough situation analysis coupled with a sound theoretical framework for the intervention should help avoid such problems.

In setting objectives to change individual health behaviors, the biggest challenge public health practitioners confront is choosing objectives that are reasonable for the audience to achieve. In general, choose behavioral objectives that are as similar to existing behavior as possible. For example, asking people to engage in more of some behavior they already do is easier than asking them to begin an entirely new behavior.

Asking people to make changes only in some settings can also keep objectives manageable and more likely to be attained. For example, an HIV prevention program might craft an objective such as "Within one year, increase by X% the proportion of men who have sex with men who use a condom the first time they have sex with a new partner," rather than, "Within one year, increase by X% the proportion of men who have sex with men who use a condom every time they have sex." The costs associated with the first behavior (such as occasionally experiencing decreased pleasure) are likely to be less than those associated with the second (chronic decreased pleasure and perceived lack of trust).

Selecting objectives for public health policy audiences can be clear-cut or challenging, depending on the nature of the initiative. When the time frame is clearly defined and the goal is to get the audience to take some specific action now, not to continue taking it for the rest of their lives, the objective is often obvious. For example, the objective for mass media might be to frame an issue in a particular way. The objective for voters might be to get a certain percentage of "undecided" voters to vote for (or against) a referendum, or to call or write a public official to support or oppose a specific policy. The desired action for a food company might be to decrease the amount of salt or fat in its processed foods.

When the time frame is less clearly defined or the behavior changes are more complex or involve more people, the initial action can be difficult to identify and somewhat removed from the ultimate goal. For example, initial efforts to persuade schools to adopt a coordinated approach to school health typically focus to building support among parents and other community members. The action might be asking them to show that support by contacting a school board member. Later efforts might build on that support by forming a school health committee containing parents and school representatives; the committee might then introduce specific changes to the school.

■ STEP 4: SEGMENT AND SELECT PRIMARY AND SECONDARY TARGET AUDIENCES

Identifying population groups who could benefit from a specific health behavior is typically a straightforward process. However, identifying specific audience segments to market to can be nearly as much judgment as science. It also tends to be an iterative process. As additional secondary and primary research is conducted, more is learned and the audiences are refined—or new audiences may be introduced, as the example in the discussion of objectives illustrates.

A program's *primary target audience* is the group that needs to take a specific action. That action might be to engage in a particular health behavior (e.g., add some physical activity each day, eat two more servings of fruits and vegetables, use a condom with a new partner), or the action might be doing something that increases the ability or opportunity of others to engage in the health behavior (e.g., legislators or elected or appointed public officials might be the primary target audience if the goal is public policy change; employers might be the target if the goal is worksite changes; health insurers might be the target if the goal is changes in covered medical services, etc.). There can be more than one primary target audience, although each should form a distinct group. If "everyone" who has certain broad characteristics (e.g., American adults, policy makers) needs to make the change, then program planners need to identify a subset of this group who is either most willing to make the change or will have the most impact on overall public health by making the change. Some of the theories discussed earlier in this chapter can provide guidance in making such choices.

Secondary target audiences are people who can help the primary target audience(s) make the change or influence them to do so. For example, family members of persons with hypertension can help them adhere to treatment regimens. Healthcare providers can counsel patients about various behavioral risk factors or recommend tests for early detection of disease. Health teachers or school food service personnel can help students change their eating habits. Constituents can help policy makers understand the importance of a particular initiative.

Segmentation

Target audience selection usually begins by dividing the population into groups based on some criterion and then looking at the differences between the groups. This process is audience segmentation. The goal of audience segmentation is to identify subgroups whose members are similar to each other and distinct from other groups along dimensions that are meaningful in the context of the marketing effort. Audiences can be segmented on a variety of dimensions, such as demographic, geographic, behavioral, or lifestyle characteristics.

The best starting point for identifying target audiences is to segment the population of interest based on the behavior the program will seek to change. Dividing the population into those who already practice the behavior ("doers") and those who do not ("nondoers") provides some of the information needed to set goals and objectives and to define specific program target audiences. For public audiences, the health statistics reviewed earlier may include this information. For example, planners of an intervention to address youth smoking might divide children and teens into "never smoked," "tried it," and "current smoker." If the audience is policy makers, dividing them into those who have supported similar initiatives and those who have not is a logical starting point. On what characteristics do doers and non-doers differ? Some of these characteristics are the factors that determine each group's behavior. Understanding why, under what circumstances, and how each group engages in their respective behaviors helps us understand the needs, desires, values and barriers that underlie the behavior. Chapter 18 discusses qualitative research techniques that can be used to develop this understanding.

If non-doers are sufficiently homogeneous, a program may target the whole group. More often, non-doers will be further segmented on dimensions such as how close they are to the recommended behavior (e.g., their current amount of physical activity or their current consumption of specific foods, drinks, or other substances), differences in real or perceived barriers to the behavior, or differences in perceived benefits. Chapter 11 discusses approaches to audience segmentation in more detail.

Selection

A number of factors must be considered when choosing audience segments, such as the size of each segment, the extent to which the group needs or would benefit from the behavior change (if the goal is to get them to change individual health behaviors), how well available resources can reach each group, and the extent to which the segment is likely to respond to the marketing offering. These factors and other aspects of the selection process are discussed in Chapter 11.

Profiling

Once audiences have been selected, the task is to learn enough about them to design, communicate and deliver an appealing offering. The behavioral maps constructed in Step 1 provide a good starting point but generally will need augmenting. For segments of the public, public health data sources data may provide some information on knowledge and attitudes, but they almost never include information that helps determine how to reach an audience, such as their media habits and leisure activities. Public health data also usually do not include information on the benefits and barriers people associate with the proposed behavior. When professionals or policy makers are the target audience, even less information is likely to be available. For healthcare providers, sometimes government or academic studies are available on knowledge, attitudes or practices. For public policymakers, obtaining material produced by them, their staff members, or their political parties can help assess how they are likely to think about an issue, as can reviewing media coverage for their comments.

The next step is to identify sources of information that could help further segment the target audience or answer some of these questions once the target audience is refined. Sources of additional information on public and patient target audiences and some professional audiences can include

- Past situation analyses or target audience profiles (prepared for an organization or for others addressing the same topic; federal agencies, voluntary health agencies, professional societies, and trade associations are also possible sources).

- Government data sources. In the United States, these include such as the National Health Interview Survey, the Behavioral Risk Factor Surveillance System, the National Health and Nutrition Examination Survey, and others.

- Syndicated commercial market research studies, for information on demographics, lifestyle, media habits, product purchase behavior, and leisure activities. In the United States, the two largest are conducted by Mediamark Research, Inc. (MRI) and Simmons Market Research Bureau.

- Public opinion polls. Many U.S. polls are archived at The Roper Center for Public Opinion Research at the University of Connecticut.

While many of these sources are national, they can be useful for local programs when no local data are available.

In addition to a demographic description of potential audiences, planners will need detailed information on target audiences' knowledge, attitudes, practices, and behaviors (KAPB) related to the public health problem. They will also need information on target audience members' media habits, lifestyles, leisure activities and general outlook, in order to identify how best to construct and deliver offerings they find appealing and relevant. Chapter 11 discusses this information in more detail.

■ STEP 5: DESIGN PUBLIC HEALTH OFFERING(S)

Once target audiences have been selected and goals and objectives set, it is time to develop the marketing mix strategies. This involves deciding what the product offering will be, determining how price will be managed, identifying the channels through which offerings will be available, and developing a promotion strategy. A strategy is "the broad approach that an organization takes to achieving its objectives" (Andreasen, 1995, p. 69). Strategies are usually long term; they are developed with the intention of using them for 3 to 5 years or more. Once strategies have been determined, the tactics—short-term, detailed steps that will be used to implement each strategy—can be developed for each strategy.

- Strategies are relatively abstract: for example, provide an alternative ride for drunk drivers; reduce embarrassment involved in obtaining condoms; make fruits and vegetables available throughout the day; communicate how to easily add two daily servings of fruits and vegetables;

- Tactics are concrete: create a community ride service; persuade retail outlets to locate condoms where customers do not have to ask for assistance; implement policies requiring fruits and vegetables at all eating occasions (meals, snacks, classroom treats) at school; create and place a subway poster showing easy ways to add two servings of fruits and vegetables during the day.

All four components of the marketing mix must work together to create communicate and deliver a public health offering superior to all alternative behaviors. The product—the benefits one will obtain by engaging in the public health action—is the core of the marketing mix. Pricing and distribution strategies are designed to increase product appeal and accessibility by increasing the benefits or decreasing the costs associated with the product; promotion's role is to make the audience aware of the product and position it in their minds as superior to all alternatives, including doing nothing.

Factors to Consider

There are a number of factors to consider when developing the marketing mix for a public health offering, including maximizing self-interest, the ethics of the intervention, and sustainability.

Maximizing Self-interest

People voluntarily choose to engage in a marketing exchange if they believe it *is* in their self-interest to do so. Therefore, products must be designed and distributed in such a way that it is in the person's best interest to engage in the replacement behavior—and promotions must make a compelling case for how self-interest will be satisfied.

Ethics

Since marketing fundamentally involves trying to persuade someone to do something, it is inherently fraught with ethical decisions. Some think any use of marketing is unethical; some advocates of free choice believe trying to pass laws or regulations that affect the incentives or penalties a person receives as a result of a behavior is, at a minimum, not marketing. In the context of developing a public health offering, the decisions with ethical dimensions include:

- Choosing a replacement behavior
- Designing the marketing mix

Choosing a replacement behavior. In choosing a replacement for an individual health behavior, one must carefully consider the target audience's culture, and the ramifications to its members and others of engaging in the behavior. For example, in the drunk driving program discussed in Appendix 10-A, many public health and community leaders were initially troubled by the focus on providing rides home rather than trying to reduce alcohol consumption. However, planners considered the audience culture and the likelihood of success for each replacement action and concluded that, while excessive drinking can have serious self-destructive consequences, the culture and motivation of the target audience was such that they were very unlikely to be persuaded to drink less. In contrast, providing rides home would better serve the public good by getting intoxicated young men out from behind the wheel and therefore decreasing the societal costs, both of death and injury among innocent bystanders and the financial costs associated with the crashes. In this program, planners also chose a replacement behavior that lent itself to a marketing offer that could become self-sustaining: ride services have a source of income.

Careful consideration should also be given to the length of time the market offering can be provided, or can be provided at a cost target audience members can afford. Particularly when working with extremely vulnerable populations, it is unethical to design a market offering, persuade them to make the behavior change, and then "pull the rug out from under them" by eliminating, or greatly increasing the cost of, supply. One example of this might be demonstration projects that devote considerable resources to providing a good or service but make no effort to create a self-sustaining entity or identify an existing entity that can continue availability can continue after the project ends.

Designing the marketing mix. Often it is not ethical to focus on stimulating demand for a particular behavior, product or service if there are substantial environmental factors inhibiting the target audience's ability to engage in the behavior or access the good or service (such as high cost or distance or lack of availability of tangible goods and services). More ethical would be focusing on improving opportunity or ability. In the child safety seat example discussed earlier in this chapter, would it have been ethical for NHTSA to skip improving the tangible goods involved and focus only on persuading parents and other caregivers to use safety seats and educating them on how to do so properly? Is it ethical to encourage people to seek particular health services without addressing affordability if it is a barrier or travel distances if they are?

Sustainability

Some marketing efforts are inherently short-term and so sustainability is not an issue; for example, efforts to get a particular law or referendum passed or policy implemented are often in this category: once your mission is accomplished, you are done. However, many times public health practitioners are addressing an ongoing public health need, such as immunization, changing lifestyles, or maintaining funding for core programs. In these situations, even if your mandate or funding is short-term (a few months to a couple of years), in planning market offerings, consideration should be given to how the marketing offering will continue to be made available to the target audience, and how they will continue to be aware that it is. Often, involving stakeholders in the design and development of product offerings and making it clear that they are being asked to come up with permanent changes, rather than get involved with a short-term or pilot project, can increase the likelihood that solutions will be available over the longer term because aspects of the solutions become integrated into their normal way of doing business.

Product

> People don't buy products—they buy expectations of benefits. (Roman, Maas, & Nisenholtz, 2003, p. 20).

The product is the bundle of benefits that the target audience receives in exchange for taking the public health action. It may or may not be bundled with a tangible good or service. To craft a successful product, you must understand the benefits a target audience can or does associate with the replacement behavior, and how they are likely to value those benefits, especially in relationship to costs they associate with the behavior. You must then design a product that:

1. The initiative can easily and cost-efficiently deliver.
2. Clearly differentiates the initiative's offering from its behavioral competition.
3. The target audience believes offers more and greater benefits than the ones they associate with their current behavior.

Including the target audience in product development will greatly increase your chance of achieving success. Target audience input should always be sought through formative research, but an advisory group of target audience members also can be helpful in multiple ways. At a minimum, they can suggest and react to ideas for the form, pricing, distribution, and promotion of the product. In some instances, advisory group members can serve as the early adopters and champions, spurring audience adoption of the innovation. In one of the Road Crew communities (Appendix 10-A), bar owners tapped influential, charismatic patrons to serve on their boards, a strategy that helped the product gain rapid acceptance among the tavern's regular patrons.

In deciding what bundle of benefits to offer, the following questions may help.

1. Can we offer benefits that are similar to those the target audience associates with the current behavior? Appendix 10-A provides an example of this approach.

2. Are we offering benefits rather than attributes? Decreasing the likelihood of contracting influenza is an attribute of the flu shot; the benefit is likely to be avoiding suffering or missing work, or, for parents inoculating kids, feeling like they are being responsible parents and caring for their children.

3. Can we link the replacement behavior to core values, such as freedom, independence, autonomy, control, fairness, democracy, or rebellion?

4. What immediate, tangible benefits can we offer? Immediate, tangible benefits are particularly important for continuous/frequent behaviors in which the possibility of a long-term health benefit has to compete with the certainty of a short-term pleasurable benefit.

Behavior patterns that promote long-term health frequently lose the competition with more immediately rewarding choice options. (Simpson & Vuchinich, 2000, p. 194)

Behavioral economics explains this phenomenon is due to opposing short- and long-term preferences and that the value of a specific benefit or cost is influenced by its temporal proximity (Simpson & Vuchinich, 2000). People place greater value on benefits they will obtain immediately and discount those they may attain at some point in the future. As a result, a smaller benefit can be valued more highly than a larger benefit if the smaller benefit is obtained sooner. For example, lottery winners usually take less money in a lump sum up front, rather than more money over an extended period of time. Likewise, people place greater (negative) value on immediate costs and discount those that will occur in the future. This means that the cost/benefit equation associated with a particular behavior changes over time. For many health behaviors, choosing "smaller sooner rewards" (pleasure of fatty foods or watching TV rather than working out) can lead to "larger later costs" (poor health), whereas choosing "larger later rewards" (good health") may mean "smaller sooner costs" (e.g., foregoing the smaller sooner rewards) (Simpson & Vuchinich, 2000).

This competition between the "larger later reward" of good health and the "smaller sooner reward" provided by certain behaviors has been termed "the tyranny of small decisions." This is a "behavioral pattern in which an individual opts to engage in behavior that is desirable at the present time, but is less than desirable and perhaps even harmful at some future point in time" (Bickel & Marsch, 2000, p. 341). In other words, choosing the donut rather than whole-wheat toast, or choosing to sit on the couch and watch TV rather than working out—because at that moment, the poor choice offers immediate benefits that the healthy choice does not. Bickel & Marsch argue that our environment and culture contribute to this problem by selecting for "shortened temporal horizons"—in other words, aspects of our culture promote placing greater value on immediate benefits over longer-term ones (see **Table 10-3**).

In instances where a poor choice's "smaller sooner benefits" trump a healthy choice's "larger later rewards," the public health practitioner must provide some other immediate reward for engaging in the health behavior. Behavioral economists note:

> It would not appear to be necessary, at least initially, that these additional rewards be directly related in any way to health, only that they control behaviors that are necessary for its accrual . . . it would be beneficial to develop a better understanding of the valued non-health rewards to which health behavior maintenance and good health potentially allow access. Interventions that focus relatively less attention on increasing health and relatively more attention on increasing access to the immediately available, tangible activities and rewards to which optimal health allows access potentially will provide the most powerful and lasting interventions. (Simpson & Vuchinich, 2000, p. 211)

Table 10-3 Summary of Temporal Horizon in Modern Society

Factors Promoting Short Temporal Horizon in Modern Society	Related Behavioral Principles
Cultural factors	
Culture of immediate gratification-leisure	High availability of low-cost reinforcers; low effort needed to obtain reinforcer; immediate reinforcement (little delay)
Economic deterioration and destabilization	Unpredictable environments-reinforcers
Community factors	
Erosion of civic-community bonds	Lack of behavioral surveillance with contingencies; high availability of low-cost reinforcers
Erosion of religious or moral training	Lack of behavioral surveillance with contingencies
Family-individual factors	
Erosion of the nuclear family	Lack of behavioral surveillance with contingencies; unpredictable environments-reinforcers

Source: Bickel, W.K. & Marsch, L.A. (2000). The tyranny of small decisions: Origins, outcomes, and proposed solutions. In W.K. Bickel & R.W. Vuchinich (Eds.) Reframing Health Behavior Change with Behavioral Economics. Mahway, NJ: Lawrence Erlbaum. p. 355.

This perspective is validated by experience: Backer, Rogers, and Sopory (1992) found that health campaigns "are more effective if they emphasize current rewards rather than the avoidance of distant negative consequences" (p. 30).

Price

Price is the cost that the target audience associates with taking the public health action. Costs may be monetary or nonmonetary; the latter include time, effort or energy expended; or real or perceived psychological, social, or physical discomforts, risks or losses.

Managing price is a two-step process. First, identify the monetary and nonmonetary costs associated with the public health behavior. The behavioral analysis described in Step 1 and your target audience profile should help identify key costs impeding an audience's willingness, ability, or opportunity to take action. Then, determine whether the initiative should focus on:

1. Decreasing target audience costs
2. Increasing benefits
3. Doing a bit of both

The discussion under "Product" of behavioral economics and the differences in how people value short- and long-term costs and benefits should be helpful in developing a pricing strategy. An anecdote about how the value of perceived costs can change over time:

> A common example of choosing between immediate and delayed costs occurs when deciding whether to go to the dentist. Going to the dentist is hardly pleasant, but the costs associated with dental visits are small relative to the long-term costs of poor dental care and hygiene. Thus, the choice is between seeing the dentist and incurring a little pain and monetary costs now or not seeing the dentist and incurring a lot of pain and monetary costs later. . . . At times distant from both a dental visit and later dental problems, the smaller cost of visiting the dentist is preferred. Thus, the individual will make a dentist appointment. As the time of the appointment approaches, however, the values of the [smaller sooner costs] and the larger later costs change at different rates. Immediately before the appointment, seeing the dentist becomes more aversive than the later dental problems, and the appointment may be canceled. (Simpson & Vuchinich, 2000, p. 198)

It is also helpful to think about the kinds of costs people experience when adopting the replacement behavior. Kotler and colleagues note that there may be *exit costs* associated with abandoning the old behavior and well as *entry costs* associated with adopting the new behavior.

Some public health behaviors involve monetary costs. A variety of tactics can be used to decrease these costs, including discount coupons, cash discounts, quantity discounts, seasonal discounts, promotional pricing (temporary price reductions) and segment pricing (e.g., different pricing for different geographic locations) (Kotler, Robert, & Lee, 2002). Sometimes these costs are within the public health marketer's control (e.g., the public health marketer is responsible for setting the price at which the good or service is sold), but many other times the monetary price is set by an entity or entities other than the public health marketer (e.g., safety equipment, foods, exercise equipment, etc.) and efforts to manage monetary costs may need to be collaborative. In other situations, the goal may be to *increase* monetary costs of undesirable behaviors, as is done through taxes on tobacco products and alcoholic beverages.

A variety of tactics can be used to decrease nonmonetary costs as well. Because nonmonetary costs vary enormously by behavior, it is not possible to list standard ways in which these prices can be managed, but we can offer a few suggestions. For continuous/frequent behaviors, a good start point is examining the costs target audience members encounter and then thinking of how those can be reduced and the behavior can more easily fit into daily life processes. For example, for some behaviors, *time* can be decreased through "embedding" the behavior into present activities, such as suggesting people floss their teeth or exercise while watching TV (Kotler, Robert, & Lee, 2003; citing Fox, 1980).

The following example presents multiple approaches to managing price within one marketing effort. It is drawn from an example of changes in a mammography facility to manage the costs women associated with getting a mammogram that was developed by Kotler and colleagues (2002).

- *Offer new or improved tangible goods or services.* In their example, mammography plates were heated to decrease the physical costs women experienced as a result of cold equipment.

- *Improve distribution of existing goods and services.* Time costs were reduced in two ways: wait time at appointments was decreased and volunteers were used to provide valet parking so that women would not have to arrive early to look for a difficult-to-find parking spot.

- *Lower associated monetary costs.* A sliding fee scale was used for the mammograms themselves and free childcare was provided.

Another approach to managing price is to use incentives, either to increase benefits or increase costs. If they are used to increase benefits, engaging in the behavior earns the incentive. For example, companies that pay part or all of the cost of a fitness club or participating in a weight-reduction program if employees demonstrate a certain level of participation are using an incentive to increase benefits. When an incentive is used to increase costs, changing to the replacement behavior earns the incentive.

For example, health insurance policies that charge more for smokers: people can receive the incentive by stopping smoking. Incentives are most often monetary but can be non-monetary, such as contests, public recognition, or other indications of social approval. McKenzie-Mohr and Smith (1999) outlined the following suggestions for using incentives.

- Closely pair the incentive and the behavior. "Incentives are usually most effective when they are presented at the time the behavior is to occur."
- Use incentives to reward positive behavior.
- Make the incentive visible—an incentive will have little or no impact if people are unaware it exists.
- Be cautious about removing incentives. Incentives are *external* motivations to engage in a behavior. Sometimes incentives replace whatever *internal* motivation some people may have had to engage in the behavior. As a result, when the incentive is discontinued, those who may originally have had an intrinsic internal motivation to engage in the behavior will stop.
- Prepare for people's attempts to avoid incentives that work by raising the costs of not engaging in the behavior. For example, McKenzie-Mohr and Smith described actions solo drivers take in order to use the car pool lane (such as installing a well-dressed mannequin in the passenger seat).

Place

Place refers to the situations in which the target audience does or can perform the health behavior and the outlets through which the target audience does or can obtain any tangible goods or services necessary for the health behavior. The goal of most place strategies is to make engaging in the behavior as convenient as possible for many as many members of the target audience as possible—by putting together the most useful channels of distribution. In some instances, place can be used to differentiate the public health offering from its competitors.

Place is often overlooked as a strategy for social change initiatives. As Mike Rothschild noted during an *Innovations in Social Marketing* conference session on the topic,

> The "good" behavior social marketers promote tend to lose out to "bad" behaviors because we are stuck on messaging while the "bad" products are developing better channels. Availability is a strong competitive advantage. (Strand, Rothschild & Nevin, 2004, p. 10)

Developing a place strategy starts with reviewing the behavioral analyses and looking for ways in which the replacement behavior can be made more accessible or convenient.

- Can you increase the number of locations at which a tangible good or service is available? Ideally, any needed tangible goods or services will be available every time and any time the audience has an opportunity to engage in the behavior—hence attempts to put condoms not only in pharmacies but also in school clinics, 24-hour retail outlets, restrooms in bars and dance clubs, etc.

- For locations that provide a health service, can you move the locations closer to the target audience (mammography vans, for example), better match operating hours to clients' availabilities, address other barriers (e.g., by providing child care during visits), or make the location more appealing?

- Can you help individuals improve their own distribution channels? For example, the 5 A Day for Better Health program suggested that people move fruits and vegetables to a bowl on the counter and move them higher in the refrigerator so when they walk into the kitchen looking for something to eat, they quickly see produce. (National Cancer Institute, 1993).

Place strategies are typically more challenging for public health and other social marketers to implement because, unlike our commercial counterparts, we typically have far less control and power over the organizations that form our channels. This makes it particularly important to identify and deliver meaningful benefits to channel members.

The case study in Appendix 9-A includes many strategies for making fruits and vegetables more convenient and more available; the case study in Appendix 10-A also includes place strategies to increase inebriated drivers' access to rides home.

At times, a place strategy may include making the current behavior *less* accessible or convenient; for example, reducing access to cigarettes by banning cigarette vending machines near places where children gather without supervision, or restricting the hours of opening and quantity and type of alcohol that can be purchased in rural communities (Donovan & Henley, 2003).

Promotion

Promotion is communicating the exchange being offered to the target audience, typically through some combination of advertising, media relations, events, personal selling, and entertainment. Promotional messages should always communicate the product (bundle of benefits) and the action the target audience should take. Messages may also address pricing strategies or convenient places of access to overcome audience barriers or to differentiate a public health offering from its competitors.

Once the public health offering has been designed, it is time to determine the best way to promote it. The first step is to develop a communication strategy that describes the target audience(s), the action they should take and the benefit the will receive for doing so, and how to package and deliver the message so it will reach and motivate them. Messages and promotional materials can then be developed in accordance with the strategy. The process of developing a communication strategy and messages is discussed in detail in Chapter 12.

■ STEP 6: PLAN EVALUATION APPROACHES

Evaluation planning takes place in conjunction with planning interventions. Planning both together can result in early identification of unrealistic objectives and ensures that results of the intervention will be as measurable as possible and as affordable as possible. As objectives are set and strategies are outlined, plans for evaluating progress against those objectives should also be outlined. Typically, process evaluation is used to track when, where, how, and with whom specific tactics were used; the resulting information is used to monitor progress and, most importantly, to make refinements to intervention offerings or implementation. Chapters 13 and 16 discuss approaches to process evaluation in more detail. Outcome evaluation is used to measure progress against objectives. Chapter 17 provides more detail on designing outcome evaluation studies.

■ CONCLUSION

Thorough planning is essential to successfully using strategic marketing in public health. It begins with a systematic analysis of the situation, including defining problems; identifying the populations they affect; analyzing current and possible replacement behaviors in terms of motivation, opportunity and ability; outlining all possible components of a solution, including education, marketing and law; and assessing the environment in which the intervention will compete.

Once a role for marketing has been determined, the next step is to set goals and objectives and select target audience segments based on the specific behaviors, conditions, or policies to be changed; this process should be guided by a theoretical framework or model of how change is expected to occur. To design an effective intervention, target populations must be thoroughly researched. In particular, the needs, desires, values and barriers they associate with their current behavior and the replacement behavior must be understood.

The final step in the planning process is designing the public health offering and marketing mix strategies. The goal is for all four components—product, price, place and promotion—to work together to communicate and deliver a public health offering superior to all alternative behaviors. The product—the benefits one will obtain by engaging in the public health action—is central. Effective products acknowledge self-interest and deliver short-term, tangible benefits. Pricing and distribution strategies are designed to increase product appeal and accessibility by increasing the benefits or decreasing the costs associated with engaging in the behavior; the role of promotion is to make the audience aware of the product and position it in their minds as superior to all alternatives, including doing nothing.

Principles for planning more effective marketing interventions include the following.

Craft an intervention that will impact behavior. Particularly among programs focusing on promotion through the mass media, the focus is too often on building awareness about an issue, rather than on providing target audience members with the tools and motivation to make efficacious behavior changes.

Be theory driven. Using theory wisely is a hallmark of effective marketing practice. Theories and models of behavior change and learning can play important roles in shaping public health interventions. They can help program managers select target audiences, set reasonable objectives, and tailor intervention components to each target audience's unique needs. Many different theories and models can help practitioners structure their interventions.

Understand the target audience. Its members are people, not a bunch of statistics. What are they doing now? How will they react to the action you want them to take? What is motivating? What stands in the way? What goods or services can be developed to aid the behavior change? How can we make it easier or more fun to engage in the behavior change? How can communications be crafted so that they speak to each target audience member and deliver a relevant attention-getting message?

Set realistic expectations. Some public health interventions can have large effects very quickly; more commonly, change is slow and gradual. Be clear about how you expect the program to work (e.g., its model of effect), set expectations accordingly, and capture intermediate progress toward objectives.

Leverage resources and relationships. It is crucial to work aggressively to leverage resources for maximum impact. Both dollars and reach can be stretched through collaborations among government, voluntary, and private sector organizations that share a common goal.

Build in evaluation from the start. A well-thought-out evaluation framework, developed in tandem with the project itself, results in activities that are well targeted, resource efficient, and more likely to result in the desired outcomes. Chapter 11 discusses formative evaluation techniques; Chapters 16 and 17 provide discussions of potential process and outcome evaluation activities.

Appendix 10-B contains worksheets to help you through the planning process.

References

....

Andreasen, A.R. (1995). *Marketing social change: Changing behavior to promote health, social development, and the environment.* San Francisco: Jossey-Bass.

Backer, T.E., Rogers, E., & Sopory, P. (1992). *Designing health communication campaigns: What works?* Thousand Oaks, CA: Sage.

Bandura, A. (1986). *Social foundations of thought and action.* Englewood Cliffs, NJ: Prentice-Hall.

Bickel, W.K.; Marsch L.A. (2001). Toward a behavioral economic understanding of drug dependence: delay discounting processes. *Addiction,* 96(1):73–86.

Certain Trumpet Program. (1996, September). *Framing memo: The affirmative action debate.* Washington, DC: Author.

Donovan, R.J., & Henley, N. (2003). *Social marketing: Principles & practice.* East Hawthorn, Victoria, Australia: IP Communications.

Fox, K.F.A., & Kotler, P. (1980). The marketing of social causes: The first 10 years. *Journal of Marketing,* 44(4), 24–33.

Gamson, W.A., & Lasch, K.E. (1983). The political culture of social welfare policy (pp. 397–415). In: S.E. Spiro & E. Yuchtman-Yaar (eds.) *Evaluating the welfare state: Social and political persepctives.* New York. Academic Press.

Gamson, W.A. & Modigliani, A. (1989). Media discourse and public opinion on nuclear power: A constructionist approach. *American Journal of Sociology,* 95(1), 1–37.

Glanz, K., Rimer, B.K., and Lewis, F.M. (2002). Health Behaviour and Health Education Theory, Research and Practice. San Francisco: Wiley & Sons.

Graeff, J.A., Elder, J.P. and Booth, E.M. (1993). *Communication for health and behavior change: A developing country perspective.* Jossey-Bass Inc., Publishers.

Green, L.W., & Kreuter, M.W. (1991). *Health promotion planning: An educational and environmental approach* (2nd ed.). Mountain View, CA: Mayfield.

Green, L.W., & McAlister, A. (1984). Macro-interventions to support h health behavior: Some theoretical perspectives and practical reflections. *Health Education Quarterly,* 11, 322–339.

Kotler, P., & Roberto, E.L. (1989). *Social marketing: Strategies for changing public behavior.* New York: Free Press.

Kotler, P., Roberto, E.L., and Lee, N. (2002). *Social marketing: Improving the quality of life* (2nd ed). Thousand Oaks, CA: Sage.

MacInnis, D.J., Moorman, C., and Jaworski, B.J. (1991). Enhancing and measuring consumers' ability, motivation, and opportunity to process brand information ads. *Journal of Marketing,* 55, 32–33.

Marchant, D.J., & Sutton, S.M. (1990). Use of mammography: United States, 1990. *Morbidity and Mortality Weekly Report,* 39, 621–630.

McKenzie-Mohr D., and Smith W. (1999). *Fostering sustainable behavior: An introduction to community-based social marketing.* Gabriola Island, British Columbia, Canada: New Society Publishers.

Menashe, C.L., & Siegel, M. (1997). *The power of a frame: An analysis of newspaper coverage of tobacco issues—United States, 1985–1996.* Boston: Boston University School of Public Health.

National Cancer Institute (1993, December) *5 A Day for Better Health: NCI media campaign strategy.* Bethesda, MD: Author.

National Center for Health Statistics. (1990). *Medical care survey*. Unpublished raw data.

National Highway Traffic Safety Administration. (1996). *National drunk and drugged driving prevention month program planner (Rep. No. DOT HS 808-455)*. Washington, DC: Author.

Orlandi, M.A., Landers, C., Weston, R., & Haley, N. (1990). Diffusion of health promotion innovations. In K. Glanz, F.M. Lewis, & B.K. Rimer (Eds.). *Health behavior and health education: Theory, research and practice* (pp. 288–313). San Francisco: Jossey-Bass.

Roman, K., Maas, J., & Nisenholtz, M. (2003). *How to advertise*, (3rd ed.) New York: St. Martin's Press.

Rothschild, M.L. (1999). Carrots, sticks and promises: A conceptual framework for the behavior management of public health and social issues. *Journal of Marketing, 63*, 24–37.

Ryan, C. (1991). *Prime time activism: Media strategies for grassroots organizing*. Boston: South End Press.

Simpson, C.A. & Vuchinich, R.E. (2000). Temporal changes in the value of objects of choice: Discounting, behavior patterns, and health behavior. In Bickel, W. K. & Vuchinich, R. E. (Eds.): *Reframing health behavior change with behavioral economics*, 193–215. New York: Lawrence Erlbaum.

Strand, J., Rothschild, M.L., and Nevin, J.R. (2004). Place and channels of distribution. *Social Marketing Quarterly, 10*:3, 8–13.

Sutton, S.M., & Doner, L.D. (1992). Insights into the physician's role in mammography utilization among older women. *Women's Health Issues, 2*, 175–179.

Sutton, S.M., Balch, G.I., & Lefebvre, R. C. (1995). Strategic questions for consumer-based health communications. *Public Health Reports*, 110.

Wallack, L., Dorfman, L., Jernigan, D., & Themba, M. (1993). *Media advocacy and public health: Power for prevention*. Newbury Park, CA: Sage.

Winnett, L. (1995). *Advocate's guide to developing framing memos*. Berkeley, CA: Berkeley Media Studies Group.

Zaltman, G., & Duncan, R. (1977). *Strategies for planned change*. New York: Wiley.

10-A

Planning a Marketing Initiative to Reduce Alcohol-Related Motor Vehicle Fatalities

The State of Wisconsin's *Road Crew* initiative began as a demonstration project to apply social marketing techniques to community collaborations aimed at reducing drunk driving. The original demonstration project was a collaboration among the Wisconsin Department of Transportation/Bureau of Transportation Safety (using funding from the National Highway Traffic Safety Administration), the University of Wisconsin School of Business, Miller Brewing Company, the Tavern League of Wisconsin, and various community entities. The demonstration project ran from July 1, 2002 to June 30, 2003 in three communities. In its first year, *Road Crew* resulted in a 17% reduction in fatal crashes and obtained the support of community leaders.

Road Crew provides many lessons in planning, developing, implementing and evaluating a public health marketing effort. This case study summarizes the planning phase; Chapters 13 and 17 contain exhibits highlighting other aspects of the initiative. We constructed this case study from information contained in the *Road Crew* final report (Karsten et al., 2003) and Road Crew Social Marketing Toolbox (Rothschild & Karsten, n.d.).

■ STEP 1: ANALYZE THE SITUATION

Problem

Alcohol impairment was responsible for 6.5% of all automobile crashes in the state of Wisconsin in 2000. As **Exhibit 10A-1** illustrates, national data made it clear that 21-to-34-year-old men were the largest contributors to crashes resulting from drunk driving.

In Wisconsin, "a disproportionate share of these impaired drivers was 21-to-34-year-old men living in rural areas where there are few, if any, public transportation options" (Karsten et al., 2003, p. 1).

Analyze Current and Possible Replacement Behaviors

Planners examined the cultural environment in which any effort to change behaviors related to alcohol consumption would take place:

> Among the most difficult of public health issues to address are those rooted in behavior and culture. Drinking and driving in rural Wisconsin is just such an issue. There are deep cultural roots to imbibing linked to the state's northern European immigrant heritage. Over the past century, immigrant brew masters built an economic and cultural force, establishing hundreds of breweries and taverns across the state. Towns centered around two cultural institutions: the church and the tavern. While only a few breweries remain, the Wisconsin tavern culture is alive and well, with taverns lining main streets of hundreds of small towns and rural intersections.
>
> This is where adults mix and mingle. For the small community, taverns are often the center of social life. In the summer, taverns sponsor softball leagues, in the winter dart leagues. Fifty-two weekends a year, taverns offer a place for friends to gather and grab and have a few drinks. (Karsten et al., 2003, p. 6–7)

Exhibit 10A-1   Characteristics of 21-34-year-olds who drive after drinking

- Comprise about half of all drunk drivers involved in alcohol-related fatal crashes;
- Are responsible for more alcohol-related fatal crashes than any other age group;
- Are more likely than any other age group to have been intoxicated at the time of the crash;
- Have the highest blood alcohol concentrations in fatal crashes;
- Are about twice as likely as other drivers to have experienced a prior crash;
- Are four times more likely to have had their licenses suspended or revoked; and
- Are the most resistant to changing their drinking and driving behavior.

Source: Rothschild, M. & Karsten, C. (n.d.). *Road Crew Social Marketing Toolbox*, p. 16 Retrieved April 24, 2006 from http://www.dot.wisconsin.gov/library/publications/topic/safety/roadcrew-toolbox.pdf

Planners looked at the current drinking and driving behaviors of 21-to-34-year-old single men living in rural areas of Wisconsin. They also explored the steps involved and perceived benefits of and barriers to alternative behaviors. **Table 10A-1** summarizes what they learned through a literature review and eleven focus groups with the audience.

Analyzing potential replacement behaviors using the motivation, opportunity and ability framework (Rothschild, 1999), as shown in **Table 10A-2**, identifies types of replacement behaviors most likely to be successful.

Table 10A-1   Perceptions Among Young Men of Benefits of and Barriers to, Behaviors to Reduce Drunk Driving

Behavior	Benefits	Drawbacks/Barriers
Current		
Driving to bars	Few, if any, alternative means of getting there.	Not discussed in report.
Drinking as much as possible	Not discussed in report.	Not discussed in report.
Driving home	*Time and effort:* Their car was available in the morning when they needed it. *Psychological/social:* They proved they could "hold their liquor."	"Nagging concerns about car crashes, the cost of OWI convictions, repercussions on car insurance rates, job security, and the social shame within the extended multi-generational network of their community" (p. 7).
Alternative behaviors		
Leaving car at bar and accepting a ride home	Not having to worry about all the potential drawbacks described above under current behavior.	Vehicle is sacrosanct and source of pride. In a small town, everyone knows who owns what vehicle, leading to potential social consequences: A man's friends might tease him for needing a ride home, or his mom's best friend might mention she often sees his car in the bar parking lot on Sunday morning. Financial: Vehicle might be ticketed or damaged by another drunk driver.

Table 10A-2 Motivation, Opportunity and Ability Associated with Behaviors to Reduce Alcohol-Impaired Driving Among 21-34-year-old Men

Alternative Behavior	Motivation	Opportunity	Ability
Don't drink or drink less	None–they simply aren't willing to do it	Yes	Yes
Designated driver	Unwilling to be the designee	Limited to the least intoxicated person or someone's sober girlfriend driving	Yes
Leaving car and getting cab ride home	Resistant—due to humiliation of being seen as "not being able to hold your liquor" and needing car the next day	Available in some communities and not others	Yes
Ride service for entire evening	Yes, if positioned as (and delivering) providing more and the same types of fun as existing behavior	Would have to be created	Yes, if affordable

Planners concluded that trying to reduce drinking would not be successful because it would go against the prevailing culture and target audience members' free choice: they liked to drink and the benefits they regularly received from the behavior outweighed the costs. Therefore, it made more sense to focus on the specific behavior that was causing the crashes: not drinking, but driving after doing so.

> You might encounter people in the community who say, "Why spend all this time and effort to keep drunks off the road when you should just try to get them to stop drinking altogether?" There is no dispute that excessive drinking is unhealthy and has many negative effects on families, friends and the community. But while excessive drinking itself can be self-destructive, it is drunk driving that threatens the safety of the community at large. This project is about making roads safer for the entire community by decreasing the number of drunk drivers. In addition, by trying to change drinking habits, you may alienate your target ride service customers; they want to drink, but you can help them stay off the roadways after they choose to do so. (Rothschild & Karsten, p. 3)

The second replacement behavior in **Table 10A-2**, designated driver programs, also was of limited use because free choice meant limited opportunity. The relatively low probability of negative consequences (getting arrested for driving under the influence or crashing) caused young men to discount these consequences against the immediate benefit of having fun with their friends. As a result, when designated drivers were used, they tended to be the least drunk among the guys or a sober girlfriend.

Another replacement behavior—getting a cab ride home—was likely to meet with some resistance because the target audience associated the behavior with negative consequences related to leaving their car in a bar parking lot overnight (hassles of getting it the next day, potential social embarrassment).

The most appealing solution was likely to be a ride service to bars and back home—but such a service did not exist in many rural Wisconsin communities.

Outline Components of a Solution

Past efforts to discourage drunk driving and encourage responsible behavior had largely relied on education and law—traffic enforcement and tougher legislation. Yet young men still drove drunk. Planners determined that a marketing intervention could fill a niche not addressed by other approaches, by providing an appealing alternative to driving to and from the bars.

Assess Environment for Intervention

Public health and community leaders were resistant to offering rides due to concerns that doing so would increase alcohol consumption, thereby worsening the overall problem of excessive drinking.

> A major concern amongst the community leaders and the public health community was that a ride program would lead to increased alcohol consumption. In the focus groups done before the program was ever developed, we had asked if a ride program would lead to more consumption; the typical response was "no, we're already drinking as much as we can." (Karsten et al., p. 48)

■ STEP 2: SELECT APPROACHES AND DETERMINE THE ROLE OF MARKETING

State planners decided to move forward with ride programs, believing that such programs could fulfill an unmet need and had the greatest chance of success against the goal (reducing impaired driving).

Most people are aware that they should not be driving after excessive drinking; but often there is no opportunity for them to behave otherwise. *Road Crew* provided such an opportunity. (Karsten et al., p. 3)

In line with their formative research findings and in spite of environmental objections, they explicitly chose *not* to attempt to reduce the target audience's consumption of alcohol. As the report explains:

Understanding that the target's social life often revolves around drinking, communities were convinced that trying to focus on reducing consumption would undermine the goal of increasing highway safety. Using a core marketing principle—selling a positive—the state team understood that if the target group was made to feel badly or shamed about drinking, they would feel humiliated and not buy into using the project's services. This agreement made the initiative more difficult to explain to public health practitioners who work to mitigate a wider range of social ills associated with excess alcohol consumption, but it helped in enlisting the support of local taverns essential to the success of the effort." (Karsten et al., p. 10)

■ STEP 3: SET GOALS AND OBJECTIVES

The program's goals were to decrease alcohol-related crashes by 5% and create self-sustaining ride service programs.
   Objectives included:

* Change the knowledge, attitudes and behavior of the community institution members toward social marketing and the program.
* Change the knowledge, attitudes and behavior of the target group toward the program.
* Reduce the incidence of impaired driving by 5% per year and thereby reduce alcohol-related crashes, injuries and death by the same 5% in each community participating in the project.

■ STEP 4: SEGMENT AND SELECT TARGET AUDIENCE

The marketing target was 21-to-34-year-old single men who live in rural Wisconsin communities. As shown earlier, statistically, single men in this age group account for a disproportionate number of alcohol-related crashes.

The project design is based on empirical evidence of 21-to-34-year-old single men defined in anthropological and psychological terms. Developmentally, psychologists concur that adolescent behavior is prolonged in men not involved in well-developed relationships. These individuals have yet to experience the domesticating influence and responsibilities that accompany wives and children. They engage in riskier behavior than most adults and are influenced to conform to peer norms and expectations, including heavy drinking and driving under the influence. They are more apt to drive home no matter what their blood alcohol level. (Karsten et al., p. 7)

Focus groups enabled planners to profile the typical target audience member and learn enough about him to develop a successful product offering (see **Exhibit 10A-2**).

■ STEP 5: DESIGN PUBLIC HEALTH OFFERING

The overall product and promotion strategies were the same across *Road Crew* communities. However, the services delivering the product offering, the distribution channels used, and the approaches to managing price differed. In each community, leaders built a coalition that included private- and public-sector partners; these coalitions developed the services that delivered the product offering in each community. The *Road Crew* documents stress the importance of this approach, and of including target audience members, ideally as a separate advisory group.

Perhaps most intricate were the partnerships that included tavern owners, young people who often drank to excess, law enforcement, public health workers, and community leaders. Developing the programs required both small business and marketing acumen. In two out of the three communities, the transportation option was completely new and required organizers to put together a business plan. (Karsten et al., 2003, p. 3)

The *Road Crew* reports stress the importance of creating local coalitions that tailor product offerings to the community.

Product

In designing the *Road Crew* product offering, planners started with what the target audience was willing and able to do.

Exhibit 10A-2   Road Crew Target Audience Member

The most likely person to drive after excessive drinking is a 21-to-34-year-old single male, working in a blue collar job, with a high school education or less, who most often drinks beer. He also:

- Drinks heavily with friends in bars
- Feels safe drinking 8 to 12 drinks and then driving
- Often "assigns" the least drunk person to be the designated driver
- Socializes with groups of friends and needs to fit in
- Values masculinity
- Feels immortal

He drinks:

- To socialize
- To overcome inhibitions and develop a different and more exciting personality
- To increase his confidence
- To have a good time
- To get away from the hassles of daily life

His car is important because:

- It gives him a feeling of control
- It keeps the option open of taking a woman home
- It enhances his identity

These single young men like good times, women, sports, their vehicles and activities where alcohol is one part of the action. He drives after drinking excessively:

- To get home
- Because he feels fearless and invincible
- Because he is unaware that his driving skills are impaired
- Because there is social pressure to be like everybody else and fit in
- To relax and have a good time by cranking up music and driving fast
- Because he perceives that there is no other way to get home without a lot of hassle
- Because he is afraid that some other drunk will crash into his car if it is left behind
- Because the perceived risks of actually getting caught or crashing are low

In the mind of the target, disadvantages of driving after excessive drinking are many. His fears include:

- Hurting himself or someone else
- Receiving an OWI [operating a vehicle while intoxicated] citation
- Losing driving privileges
- Losing insurance
- Losing a job
- Embarrassment and loss of respect

Source: Rothschild, M. & Karsten, C. (n.d.). *Road Crew Social Marketing Toolbox,* pp. 16–17. Retrieved April 24, 2006 from http://www.dot.wisconsin.gov/library/publications/topic/safety/roadcrew-toolbox.pdf

Focus group participants said that if you want them to take a ride home, you need to get them to the bar in the first place without their cars. They know that they don't make good decisions at bar closing time so you need to create a situation where they can't make the wrong decision. (Rothschild & Karsten, n.d., p. 20)

Next, they thought hard about self-interest and free choice. Participants *liked* their current behavior, so what could planners offer that would provide a superior ratio of benefits to costs? *Road Crew* was designed to deliver those same benefits: they could still go out, get drunk and have fun with their friends.

Road Crew's core product offering was:

Use *Road Crew* and get a fun, affordable, hassle-free means of getting to and from the bar(s).

Integral to this offering was developing a service that would deliver fun and fit into the spirit of the guys' drinking nights; many existing services (cabs, ride services) were viewed as options. Two communities came up with limousines and other luxury cars. Using these types of vehicles for the ride service allowed the programs to deliver more benefits (Rothschild & Karsten, n.d.):

- Choosing a limo ride was seen as a very cool thing to do and added to the fun of the evening. It was far from the embarrassment of needing a ride home.
- Limo rides offered benefits consistent with those young men obtained from drinking: an opportunity to socialize, increase their confidence, have a good time and get away from the hassles of daily life.
- It was easy to create a party mood by playing music and allowing food and beverage in the vehicles.

However, developing a new limousine service is an endeavor with high start-up costs and ongoing maintenance costs. Other vehicles or existing ride services or taxis can be used to deliver a *Road Crew* program but planners will have to overcome the negative or boring image. Possibilities include music, food and videos, or games and prizes. The *Road Crew Social Marketing Toolkit* discusses the resource requirements of various transportation options and provides discussion questions to help planners work through possibilities.

Price

As outlined in the behavior mapping section, the main prices to be managed were psychological and social, though time, effort, and financial prices also factored in. Because the target audience basically liked their existing behavior, *Road Crew* had to deliver an exchange that provided comparable but greater benefits. It did this largely by reducing price: it provided a means to avoid worrying about the potential negative ramifications of driving while intoxicated. (As discussed above, some implementations also provided additional benefits).

Each implementation of *Road Crew* has a financial cost, though no one is denied a ride due to unwillingness or inability to pay. Ride costs were developed with input from the target audience and adjusted as necessary.

Whether *Road Crew* offsets or eliminates the price the audience associates with leaving their car at a bar (tickets, damage, or embarrassment when someone notices) depends largely on if they pre-plan their evening enough to take advantage of the ride to the bars as well as between them and home.

Place

Part of getting target audience members to accept a ride was providing an alternative means of getting to the bars; most of the implementations incorporated this service. The service itself was available from any bar in the service's market area, although the degree to which individual establishments, bartenders, and wait staff knew this varied.

Promotion

Planners wanted to position *Road Crew* as the only choice to make when considering a night out drinking. They did this by considering the wants, needs, and personality characteristics of the target audience, and then developing promotions to convey *Road Crew* as a brand that resonated with the target audience by offering a "no hassle" theme of fun and convenience. In developing the name, theme, logo, identity and promotional materials for the program, the advertising agency developed a range of ideas and then input was obtained from community leaders and target audience members. *Road Crew, Beats Driving* was the final choice. A print advertisement/poster from the campaign is shown in **Figure 10A-1**.

> While the program would provide a tangible service with tested benefits to capture their minds, an emotional sell was required to capture their hearts. (Karsten et al., 2003 p.2)

■ STEP 6: PLAN EVALUATION

Road Crew was evaluated three ways (Karsten et al., 2003):

1. A quasi-experimental design was used to demonstrate causality. Prior to implementing *Road Crew*, a pre-test survey was conducted with bar patrons in demonstration and control communities to measure

the level of driving after excessive drinking. After the ride services had been operating for a year, a post-test was conducted with the same audience.

2. After the ride services had been operating for a year, a phone survey of the target audience, general population, community leaders, bar owners, and wait staff was conducted to measure awareness of and attitudes toward Road Crew.

3. Rides provided by Road Crew were counted, with each ride representing the prevention of an alcohol-related crash.

Road Crew evaluation results are summarized in Chapter 17.

Figure 10A-1 Road Crew creative

Source: Rothschild, M. & Karsten, C. (n.d.). *Road Crew Social Marketing Toolbox.* Retrieved April 24, 2006 from http://www.dot.wisconsin.gov/library/publications/topic/safety/roadcrew-toolbox.pdf

References

Fox, K.F. (1980). Time as a component of price in social marketing (pp. 464–467). In R.P. Bagozzi et al. (Eds.) *Marketing in the 1980s*. Chicago: American Marketing Association.

Karsten, C., Rothschild, M., Miller Brewing Company, Tavern League of Wisconsin, & MasComm Associates. (2003). *The Road Crew Final Report*. Retrieved April 24, 2006 from http://www.dot.wisconsin.gov/library/publications/topic/safety/roadcrew.pdf

Rothschild, M.L. (1999). Carrots, sticks and promises: A conceptual framework for the behavior management of public health and social issues. *Journal of Marketing*, 63, 24–37.

Rothschild, M. & Karsten, C. (n.d.). *Road Crew Social Marketing Toolbox*. Retrieved April 24, 2006 from http://www.dot.wisconsin.gov/library/publications/topic/safety/roadcrew-toolbox.pdf

Sutton, S.M., Balch, G.I., & Lefebvre, R.C. (1995). Strategic questions for consumer-based communications. *Public Health Reports*, 110, 725–733.

APPENDIX

10-B

Strategic Planning Worksheets

WORKSHEET 1: DESCRIBE PROBLEM, AFFECTED POPULATION GROUPS, AND THEIR CURRENT BEHAVIOR

| Problem | Population affected | Current behavior | Type of behavior
One-time vs. episodic
Continuous vs. frequent | Benefits
(consider self-interest and focus on immediate, tangible) | Costs |
|---|---|---|---|---|---|
| | | | | | |
| | | | | | |
| | | | | | |
| | | | | | |
| | | | | | |
| | | | | | |
| | | | | | |
| | | | | | |
| | | | | | |

■ WORKSHEET 2: ANALYZE REPLACEMENT BEHAVIORS

Possible replacement behavior	Benefits (consider self-interest and focus on immediate, tangible)	Barriers	Does behavior have negative consequences for performing it?	Is behavior compatible with sociocultural norms or acceptable practices?	Does behavior require an unrealistic rate of frequency or duration?	How similar is this behavior to audience's current behavior? (very, somewhat, not at all)

WORKSHEET 3: DETERMINE WHAT TYPE OF INTERVENTION WOULD HAVE GREATEST CHANCE OF SUCCESS

Selected replacement behavior	Barrier	Type of barrier-motivation, opportunity, ability	What type of intervention can overcome or minimize this barrier? (education, law, marketing)	If intervention was successful, would the cost/benefit exchange of the replacement behavior be more favorable than the cost—benefit exchange of the current behavior?

■ WORKSHEET 4: SWOT ANALYSIS

	Strengths	Weaknesses	Opportunities	Threats
Organization				
Intervention Approach				
Intervention Approach				

WORKSHEET 5: DIAGRAM HOW YOU EXPECT THE INTERVENTION TO WORK

Problem

Causes

Solutions

Education to provide ability

Marketing to provide motivation

Law to provide opportunity

■ WORKSHEET 6: SET GOALS AND OBJECTIVES; CHOOSE AND PROFILE TARGET AUDIENCE(S)

Goal(s): _____

Objective	Audience Segment	Profile (key characteristics)

■ WORKSHEET 7: DESIGN PRODUCT OFFERING

Product = Bundle of most immediate, compelling benefits + (if applicable) Tangible good or service	Strategies for managing price	Strategies for managing place, including distribution channels	Promotion strategy

CHAPTER

11

Formative Research

Formative research is at the core of the marketing approach. At the outset, it is used to help define health problems, identify their causes, and identify potential solutions. Next, it helps determine the audiences who can bring about needed changes to the physical, economic or policy environment, and/or segments of the public who can change their individual health behaviors. As audiences are selected, formative research helps create, communicate and deliver exchanges target audiences will value by identifying competition and helping to shape products, pricing strategies, selection or development of distribution channels, and development of promotional strategies and tactics. Depending on the nature of the research questions, quantitative and qualitative research techniques, systematic observations, and experimental and quasi-experimental designs are used.

This chapter begins with a general discussion of the roles of formative research, which provides a foundation for subsequent discussions of how formative research can be used to select audiences for and shape individual health behavior and policy change initiatives. Chapter 18 provides more detail on designing and conducting marketing research studies using various methodologies.

■ THE ROLE OF FORMATIVE RESEARCH

Formative research can be used in many ways during the planning and development stages. At times it is used as a situation analysis tool, to help define the problems an initiative could address, such as lack of motivation, ability or opportunity to engage in a health behavior or ineffective framing of a public health issue. It is essential to identifying the most appropriate audience(s) for a program to reach and understanding their wants and needs. It can also help identify the actions target audience members can and will take that will help them make the most progress toward addressing the public health problem—as well as the benefits and barriers they associate with each action, and the environmental changes, goods, services, distribution channels, or information they may need to take an action. As an intervention begins to take shape, formative research helps shape product offerings, pricing strategies, distribution channels and promotional materials by gathering feedback on possibilities from target audience members.

As an example of how formative research can be used, consider a situation in which immunization rates are lower than recommended for a particular disease. The first thing to do is identify the source(s) of the problem: Why are immunization rates low? Do people have objections to vaccines in general or this specific one? Are target populations aware that they or their children need immunization? Is the vaccine available in sufficient supply? Do target populations have sufficient access to it— e.g., is it affordable and available at an easily-reached location? Armed with this knowledge, we can begin to investigate potential target audiences for a marketing intervention.

Formative research also provides information to help assess what action we can reasonably ask the target audience to take—and the benefits and barriers they associate with possible actions. This in turn can help us design, deliver and communicate offerings that satisfy audience wants and needs. Where are we losing people? What keeps them from engaging in the desired behavior? A useful analogy is that of an interstate highway: The desired behavior is at the end of the highway, but as a person embarks on his or her journey, there may be roadblocks and/or attractive exit ramps before the destination.

Formative research can identify the roadblocks so that we can dismantle them or develop an attractive detour. Continuing our immunization example, we might find that a roadblock is lack of awareness, and all we need to do is tell target audiences about the vaccine and where they can get it. Or we might find that the roadblock is healthcare providers who are averse to the vaccine, so we need to address their concerns. Or perhaps the vaccine is in short supply, only available at distant providers, or too expensive. In these cases, we might work with partners to eliminate roadblocks by increasing supply, decreasing distance, or decreasing price, respectively. Or we might determine that government policy is at the root of all three problems, and work to frame the vaccination issue as threatening a core value or need so that policymakers act.

Formative research can also help us find out who is being led astray and at what exit ramps. Then it can help us to understand why those ramps are more appealing than our destination, so that we can reconfigure the destination accordingly. For behaviors that people engage in frequently (see Chapter 10 for more discussion of these types of behaviors), formative research can help us make a data-based decision about whether to ask target audience members to avoid the exit ramps on every trip, or only under certain conditions. For example, we noted in Chapter 3 that human immunodeficiency virus (HIV) prevention efforts targeting men who have sex with men almost universally choose a risk prevention approach (always avoid the exit ramps): Use a condom every time you have sex. We also noted that many men found it impossible to comply with this guideline. Adequate formative research may have helped program managers realize that a risk reduction approach is more likely to be successful: Use a condom in certain situations, such as with a new partner.

The remaining sections of this chapter discuss

- Formative research to support health behavior change
- Formative research to support non-legislative policy changes
- Formative research to support public health policy initiatives
- Pretesting

■ FORMATIVE RESEARCH TO SUPPORT HEALTH BEHAVIOR CHANGE

Initiatives seeking to change individual health behaviors typically use formative research in three ways. First, it is used to identify one or more target audiences and develop an understanding of their current practices, needs, wants, and values vis-à-vis the public health behavior and any competing behaviors. In this way it can help planners determine if they need to increase motivation, provide more or better opportunities for the behavior, or increase audience members' ability to engage in it. Second, formative research is used to determine what bundle of benefits will be most compelling (e.g., how the behavior change can be positioned as fulfilling the audience's needs or wants and as consistent with their values) and how that bundle of benefits can best be made available. Finally, formative research is used to develop and test product offerings, delivery systems, promotional strategies, messages, and materials designed to support the behavior change.

Segmenting and Selecting Target Audiences

The process of dividing the population into groups based on one or more variables is termed *audience segmentation*. The goal of audience segmentation is to identify subgroups whose members are similar to each other and distinct from members of other groups along dimensions that are meaningful in the context of the behavior to be changed. Target audiences are then selected from these subgroups. Segmentation is a key aspect of effective communication and marketing. As Slater (1995) noted when discussing segmentation for health communication efforts, "success might not be assured by segmentation—there are too many other contingencies regarding resources, quality of implementation, and the inherent difficulty of the task. *Poor or nonexistent segmentation of audiences, on the other hand, is likely to doom public communication or education programs* [italics added]" (p. 186).

Types of Audience Segmentation

Audiences can be segmented on a variety of dimensions, including demographic, geographic, lifestyle, or behavioral characteristics. The goal should be to segment on variables that influence whether people will change the behavior of interest. Slater (1995) notes that these variables can "include attitudinal beliefs and perceptions of relevant social norms (Ajzen & Fishbein, 1980); self-efficacy and presence of behavioral models (Bandura, 1986; Strecher et al., 1986), salience of, and involvement with, the health behavior (Chaffee & Roser, 1986; Grunig & Hunt, 1984); perceived preventability and costs of alternatives (Maiman & Becker, 1974) and constraints regarding the behavior" (p. 189).

Unfortunately, many initiatives rely on what Slater (1995) calls shortcuts to segmentation. These shortcuts are taken for a number of reasons; one is that identifying the antecedents of behavior is a complex process. Even if the antecedents are identified, segmenting based on them often requires an expensive quantitative study and a great deal of time. A third reason may be a lack of behavioral science background among some practitioners.

A popular shortcut is *demographic segmentation*, or grouping people on characteristics such as gender, age, income, education, or race/ethnicity. As Slater (1995) notes, the potential flaw with demographic segmentation is that it often groups people together based on variables that are meaningless in the context of changing the behavior in question: two people can be demographically identical and yet lead totally different lives in terms of health behaviors and the factors that determine them. For example, consider two 23-year-old white males. Both have the same amount of education and income. Both are single and live alone in an apartment. Both have the same type of job. One is straight and regularly practices unprotected sex with a variety of partners. The other is gay and has been in a mutually monogamous relationship for five years. How would a demographic segmentation help a manager identify and understand the target audience member for a new HIV prevention program?

Sometimes *geographic* characteristics (i.e., whether a person lives in an urban, a suburban, or a rural environment; or the region, state/province, postal code, or neighborhood in which he or she resides) are combined with demographic and lifestyle information (i.e., product purchases, leisure activities, media habits, attitudes, interests, and opinions) to identify distinct neighborhood types. This process is referred to as *geodemographic segmentation* or *geoclustering* and is based on the old adage "birds of a feather flock together." That is, people who live near each other have similar attitudes, interests, and behaviors. This type of segmentation strategy can help in planning community outreach activities and services, as well as in delivering targeted messages through the mail. In the United States, commercial geodemographic clustering systems include Claritas Corporation's PRIZM (Potential Rating Index by Zip Markets).

Although there are no hard and fast rules, for many public health programs the population should first be segmented based on current behavior. At a minimum, dividing the population into "doers" and "nondoers"—those who do and do not engage in the desired behavior—allows identification of determinants of behavior and other characteristics that distinguish the two groups. Individual groups can then be further segmented based on readiness to change or psychographic characteristics. **Exhibit 11-1** presents a case study from a 5 A Day for Better Health program describing one application of this type of segmentation.

Exhibit 11-1 Segmenting and Profiling the Audience for the 5 A Day for Better Health Media Campaign

Background

The national 5 A Day for Better Health program helps Americans to increase their consumption of fruits and vegetables in order to decrease their risk of developing certain cancers, heart disease, and other conditions. When the National Cancer Institute (one of the U.S. Department of Health and Human Services' National Institutes of Health) was developing the initial national media campaign, rather than spending their limited resources on a general effort targeting all consumers, planners chose to follow marketing practice and segment the audience to maximize impact. The discussion below is based on the process outlined in NCI's media campaign strategy document (NCI, 1993) and in a chapter reviewing the campaign (Lefebvre et al., 1995).

Method

The first step was to segment based on behavior. A nationally representative baseline survey conducted in 1991 indicated that the average number of servings of fruits and vegetables consumed daily was about 3.5. Since this average intake is a point around which most people cluster, planners looked at this group in selecting a target audience. They then looked to the transtheoretical model of stages of change (reviewed briefly in Chapter 18) for guidance. Planners decided they wanted to first influence the largest number of people possible who would be open to the message (i.e., most ready to increase their fruit and vegetable intake) and who had not yet reached the objective of eating five or more servings daily. Therefore, they defined their target audience as people who were already trying to increase their consumption of fruits and vegetables (those in the contemplation or action stages of the transtheoretical model) but who had not yet achieved the minimum of five servings a day.

Next, they used two different marketing databases to profile the psychographic and demographic characteristics of the target audience. The first database came from MRCA Information Services and linked information on demographics, food consumption (based on food diaries), dietary habits, attitudes, interests, media habits, and other lifestyle characteristics through an annual study of 2,000 households demographically balanced to represent the U.S. population. MRCA data were used to compare two groups. The target audience group was defined as those age 18 or older who reported increasing their consumption of both fruits and

(continues)

Exhibit 11-1   Segmenting and Profiling the Audience for the 5 A Day for Better Health Media Campaign (continued)

vegetables and who currently averaged two servings a day (range of 1.5 to 2.5). This group constituted about 14% of the total population. The comparison group was adults who were already eating 3.5 or more servings of fruits and vegetables per day.

The second database was DDB Needham's 1993 Life Style study, an annual survey of 4,000 consumers who are members of a mail panel. Life Style includes nearly 1,000 questions related to attitudes, opinions, interests, activities, media habits, and demographics. Life Style results are demographically balanced to reflect the U.S. population, but, as with all panel studies, the sample tends to underrepresent the very poor, the very rich, minorities, and transient populations. Two groups were again compared, but they were defined somewhat differently due to differences in the questions asked. The target group was adults who ate or drank two to three servings of fruits and vegetables on the previous day; desire to increase consumption could not be measured because the survey did not include such a question. Thus defined, the target group was about 50% of the population. The comparison group was adults eating five or more servings of fruits and vegetables on the previous day.

Findings from the two studies were consistent overall: The target audience was younger, married with children, employed full time, and generally concerned with good health. The comparison group was older, likely to be retired, and more concerned with a healthier diet. The Life Style profile provided additional insights into the target audience's psychographic profile: Target audience members tended to lead a faster-paced life and had less spare time; were more likely to suffer from stress-related conditions such as headaches, lack of sleep, and indigestion; and tended to be "impulse" buyers. In terms of media habits, target audience members tended to watch local news, news interview shows, and prime-time movies, and listened to soft rock, classic rock, easy listening, and country-western music. They were not as involved in volunteer and community activities as the comparison group.

The target audience profile built from the information in the two databases, coupled with previous qualitative research, was used to answer most of the strategic questions outlined in Chapter 12. However, planners did not know what the image, or personality, of the campaign should be. To find out, they sent a short questionnaire to members of the MRCA consumer panel who met the target audience definition. The questionnaire asked respondents to rate 29 adjectives in terms of how well the adjectives described themselves and then how well the adjectives described someone who eats five fruits and vegetables a day. Target audience members tended to describe themselves as dependable, sensible, concerned, and careful. In contrast, they viewed "5 A Day eaters" as smarter, more disciplined, healthier, and more fit.

Results

Results were used to flesh out and shape the communication strategy for the program. The final strategy is presented in Chapter 12.

Sources of Segmentation Data

Ideally, audience segmentation and profiles would involve a custom quantitative study; however, time and resources often are not available for such endeavors. The usual starting point is to look at existing studies that include data on the health behaviors of interest. In the United States, federal data sources that may help include the National Health Interview Surveys (NHIS), the National Health and Nutrition Examination Surveys (NHANES), the Behavioral Risk Factor Surveillance System (BRFSS), and the Youth Risk Behavior Survey (YRBS).

In addition to measures of health behaviors, these studies include demographic information about respondents. With the exception of NHANES, all of the studies measure self-reported (not observed) behavior. Public-use datasets are available from the National Center for Health Statistics for most of the studies, so custom analyses can be conducted.

Unfortunately, while these sources can provide useful behavioral and demographic data, they often provide very little information on respondents' lifestyles, leisure time activities, and media use habits—the information needed to design effective marketing efforts. In some instances, a commercial marketing study can fill the gap if it contains items that will allow appropriate behavior-based segmentation. In the United States, two well-known commercial marketing studies are the twice-yearly surveys conducted by Mediamark Research, Inc., and Simmons Market Research Bureau. These surveys include hundreds of items assessing what people do with their leisure time: what they read, watch, and listen to—and when they do it; and what products and services they buy—and how much they buy. These studies also contain full demographics for all respondents.

The Audience Segmentation Process

In some instances, other completed studies may allow initial target audience profiling; at other times, it may be necessary to design and conduct one or more studies in order to collect the information needed. The following steps may be involved:

Step 1: Review the literature to identify (1) variables likely to be determinants of the behavior and (2) other studies that may have segmented the population based on these variables.

Step 2: Consider conducting a qualitative study to help identify or explore behavior determinants; even if you have identified likely determinants, there may be determinants affecting behavior in a specific setting or group that past research did not include. For example, a focus group study identified the perceived shortage of available black men as a significant obstacle to HIV prevention among certain black female university students (Slater, 1995).

Step 3: If custom analyses need to be conducted, determine the segmentation approach. As noted earlier, often a good starting point is "doers" versus "non-doers." Will a qualitative or quantitative approach be taken? Often the ideal would be to start with a qualitative study to explore and identify the differences between doers and non-doers, and then follow with a quantitative study to quantify those differences and isolate the most common and presumably most critical. However, budget and timing do not always permit both.

Step 4: Collect—or analyze—the data and segment the audiences. Segmentation is often iterative; it must be revised as necessary until the segments make sense. This process also involves building profiles of each segment—their activities, lifestyles, and personalities. Segments need to be distinct from one another along these dimensions, or it will be impossible to target an intervention to reach them.

Step 5: Select the segment(s) to target with the program. The section below titled "Factors Influencing Target Audience Selection" provides some guidance on this process.

Choosing a Segmentation Strategy

This chapter discusses a number of segmentation strategies; in practice, every segmentation must be "custom fitted" to the problem at hand, and the resulting process is often a combination of approaches. As Slater (1995) noted, "The crucial point here is that it is more efficient, in terms of maximizing impact with given resources, to identify people who are similar in important respects and tailor communication content and delivery to them" (p. 187). To help assess potential segmentation strategies, Kotler and Andreasen (1996) identified six characteristics of an optimal segmentation strategy:

1. *Mutual exclusivity.* That is, each person or organization fits the definition of only one segment.
2. *Exhaustiveness.* Every member of the population is included in a segment (even if not all segments are targeted by the program).
3. *Measurability.* Membership in a segment can be readily measured.
4. *Differential responsiveness*, which, as Kotler and Andreasen noted, is perhaps the most crucial criterion. Each segment should respond to different marketing strategies. If segments respond to the same approaches, then the segmentation strategy is not helping reach a particular audience.
5. *Reachability.* This is the degree to which the segments can be effectively reached and served.
6. *Substantiality*, or size. Segments should be large enough to be worth pursuing.

The last two characteristics apply to making decisions about which segments to target and are discussed in more detail in the next section.

Source: Kotler and Andreasen, *Strategic Marketing for Nonprofit Organizations*, 5/E, © 1996. Adapted by permission of Prentice-Hall, Inc., Upper Saddle River, NJ.

Factors Influencing Target Audience Selection

Once the population has been segmented, it is time to select target audiences. One of two approaches can be used: Interventions can be tailored to each audience segment, or one or more audience segments can be chosen as the target audience(s). The approach used depends on the objectives of the program and on available resources; tailoring interventions for many audiences usually is an expensive proposition. This approach is most often used if most of the intervention will take place one on one; for example, hot line callers might receive different materials depending on the audience segment they come from. Programs taking more of a mass approach, in which aspects of the intervention will be delivered to groups of people, usually select one or two audience segments and develop intervention components specifically for those segments.

When comparing different segments, a number of factors can be used to assess each group's suitability as target audience, as shown in **Exhibit 11-2**.

Audience size. If an overall goal is population-wide improvement, larger audiences will get you there faster—provided that you can provide the motivation, opportunity or ability they need to engage in the behavior. Sometimes program planners select a very small audience—often those most "in need" of a particular change. This decision can make it hard to achieve objectives if an objective is to show population-wide change. In addition, the program may not be able to effect all the environmental changes the audience would need to engage in the behavior. Individuals most "in need" are often defined as those farthest from the recommended behavior; they may be there because they confront the most barriers—some of which you may not have the resources to address. Before choosing a small, most-in-need audience, make sure you can develop an intervention that will adequately address their motivation, opportunity and ability to engage in the behavior.

Extent to which the group needs or would benefit from the behavior change. For some populations, a particular behavior may be a hard sell because the group would derive little benefit from it. For example, it can be difficult to identify the benefits of early detection of breast or prostate cancer for very elderly people. In other instances, the group is already very close to the target behavior and may not see it as different enough from

---

Exhibit 11-2   Factors Influencing Selection of Target Audiences

- Audience size
- Extent to which the group needs or would benefit from the behavior change
- How well available resources can reach the group
- Extent to which the group is likely to respond to the program
- For secondary audiences, the extend to which they influence primary audiences

their current behavior to be worth changing. Appendix 18-A presents an instance where the sponsoring organization chose not to target the most at risk group: the American Dental Association chose to target younger people with a message about the importance of getting oral cancer exams, even though men over 45, and specifically African-American men over 45, have the highest incidence and mortality rates. Their reasoning is that oral cancer incidence is increasing in younger populations (see Appendix 18-A).

How well available resources can reach the group. As Chapter 10 notes, the greatest marketing successes often result from using product, pricing, or distribution strategies to increase an audience's opportunity to engage in the behavior. For each audience segment, consider whether you can implement the changes they need, either directly or through a relationship with other organizations. For promotional strategies, if you are planning to use mass media, do you have sufficient resources to deliver adequate reach and frequency? If materials will need to be produced in six or eight different languages, are sufficient resources available to do that? If the target audience is health professionals, does the program have access to channels that reach them effectively and efficiently? If the behavior change requires access to a good or service, can you deliver it? For example, if you encourage increased fruit and vegetable consumption, are fruits and vegetables available to audience members in the places where they eat throughout the day? If not, can you increase that availability, either by convincing those places to change their policies and provide more fruits and vegetables, or by persuading the audience to travel with fruits and vegetables?

Extent to which the group is likely to respond. If the group has no interest in the behavior change, the program will have to work much harder. Current behavior often can provide some insights into group members' likely interest or level of motivation. For example, if the 5 A day for Better Health program had chosen to target people who currently eat no more than one serving of fruits and vegetables per day, it would have been targeting people who either did not like fruits and vegetables or could not eat them for some specific reason. Instead, the group selected already eats about three servings a day—an indication that they are not averse to the behavior in question.

For secondary audiences, the extent to which they influence primary audiences. Sometimes the best way to convince someone to change his or her behavior is to have someone else do the convincing. This is often true of behavior involving patient interactions with health care providers. Often, people are most likely to get an immunization or screening test or start treating a medical condition when their physician tells them to do so.

Secondary audiences can also form useful bridges to primary audiences for programs promoting the diagnosis of previously undiagnosed conditions or in circumstances when secondary audience members are more motivated to address a health problem than is the person with the problem.

Shaping Intervention Components

Once the audiences have been segmented and selected, managers should know whom they are addressing, what needs to be provided, and how to reach the audience. As they begin to design the components that will constitute the intervention, additional formative research is used to shape each component.

Developing Strategies and Tactics

One of the first tasks for formative research is to identify what *specific* replacement behaviors are likely to be successful. Qualitative techniques can help at this point because they can identify obstacles specific to the behavior. The case study in Appendix 10-A provides an example of this. When possible, the issues identified in qualitative studies can be quantified with surveys.

Formative research can provide similar insights into product development or improving service delivery. For example, focus groups or even informal conversations with clinic users may reveal many reasons why they do not make more use of services: Perhaps they find staff rude, perhaps hours are inconvenient, or perhaps they must travel too far. A training program can address the first problem; clinic hour might be adjusted to address the second problem. The third problem is a more difficult one, but in some instances it might be resolved by adding new locations, perhaps by using a mobile van if services could be delivered appropriately that way.

Framing Messages

The target audience profiles built as part of the segmentation process can be used in developing a communication strategy (see Chapter 12). However, they often do not include sufficient information about exactly what benefit to promise, how to support it, or what image to convey. Qualitative research is often used to explore these topics. Ideally, this research will then be quantified. The case studies in **Exhibit 11-1** (5 A Day) and Appendix 11-A (school health) describe different methods of obtaining some of this information. The moderator's guide (Appendix 11-C) was used for the school health project and provides an example of the type of questions that might be asked to help frame messages. Additional information is included in the section of this chapter on pretesting.

■ FORMATIVE RESEARCH TO SUPPORT NON-LEGISLATIVE POLICY CHANGES

Many entities have policies that can affect public health, largely by making it easier or more difficult for people to take actions that maintain or improve their health. For example:

- Employers can affect employee wellness through how they price and construct health insurance offerings, whether they provide or support on- or off-the-job physical activity and other wellness offerings, etc.
- Schools can impact students' health through their policies on the types of food and beverages available during school meals and other occasions; frequency, duration and content of recess, physical education, and health education; provision of vision and hearing screenings; availability of health services, etc.
- Food establishments can help or hinder their clientele's ability to maintain healthy weight through policies regarding portion size, cooking oils, inclusion of fruits and vegetables as side items, etc.

Formative research can be used to develop a marketing approach to improve these types of policies. First, it can quantify the content and prevalence of various types of policies in the area of interest. Next, qualitative techniques can be used with the policy makers to help uncover the reasoning behind the policies and explore the benefits they do or could associate with changing the policy, as well as identify the barriers that would have to be overcome to implement a change. This information can then be used to craft an exchange the policy makers would value and develop a marketing plan. Formative research may again play a role in pretesting or pilot testing the resulting marketing effort. Many of the techniques discussed in the previous and subsequent sections of this chapter can be used to conduct the formative research necessary for these types of changes.

■ FORMATIVE RESEARCH TO SUPPORT PUBLIC HEALTH POLICY INITIATIVES

Enabling people to improve their health often involves changing an existing public policy or introducing a new program or policy. Formative research plays the same roles in initiatives to promote a public health program or policy as it does in campaigns to promote a change in health behavior. It helps to identify and understand the most appropriate audiences for the initiative to reach, and it helps to develop an initiative that is relevant and motivates the target audience.

Segmenting and Selecting Target Audiences

In most efforts to change or introduce public health policy, there are three target audiences. First, there are the policy makers: those people who have the power to enact the public health program or policy. Policy makers are often elected government officials, such as town selectmen, city council or county board members, or state or federal legislators. At other times, they may be appointed government officials (such as the heads of government agencies and some school boards) or career administrators (such as city managers and school superintendents). Part of the policy-maker audience is the people most likely to influence them: staff members, lobbyists, political party leaders, etc.

Second, there are some members of the general public who can exert a strong influence on policy makers. Third, there are the mass media, which can strongly influence the opinions of policy makers and the general public.

Wallack et al. (1993) explain that the policy agenda (those issues considered important by policy makers) is shaped by both the public agenda (issues important to the general public) and the media agenda (issues covered by the print and electronic news media). The media agenda can influence the policy agenda directly or by first placing an issue on the public agenda. An example of the media agenda directly influencing the policy agenda occurred in 1995 when *The Washington Post* reported that U.S. President Bill Clinton had called for all states to enact legislation that lowered the legal blood alcohol limit for youth drivers to 0.02mg/dL. The issue of more stringent youth drunk-driving laws was directly placed on the policy agenda in all 50 states (Harris, 1995). Policy makers could not ignore the issue once the President had embraced it and the national news media reported on it. In contrast, media coverage of the death of a teenage boy who was killed by a drunk driver in Gloucester, Massachusetts, put the issue of stronger drunk-driving legislation on the public agenda but not on the policy agenda (Langner & Laidler, 1993: Murphy, 1994). Only after a widespread public outcry did state legislators decide to do something about the problem (Wong, 1994a, 1994b).

So in contrast to efforts to change individual health behaviors, in which the target audience usually consists of the people whose health behavior needs to change or those who influence them, the target audience for policy initiatives consists of three diverse groups: (1) policy makers, (2) the public, particularly influentials, and (3) members of the mass media.

Because of the diverse nature of these target audiences, the nature of public health policy initiatives is also diverse. Varying activities are needed to influence each of the audiences. For example, lobbying, making visits to elected officials, and testifying at hearings may all be necessary to directly influence legislative policy makers. Grass-roots educational activities and the effective use of the mass media are necessary to influence the general public. And efforts such as meeting with editorial boards, writing op-ed pieces and staging special events are necessary to influence the media.

For each of these activities, a clear understanding of the audience is necessary to craft messages that will be most effective. But first, careful segmentation within each of these audiences is necessary.

Policy Makers

Policy makers may be segmented based on their likely position on the public health policy or program. For example, one way to segment policy makers is into three groups: those who will definitely support the policy, those who will definitely oppose the policy, and those who are in the middle. It often might be most efficient to focus efforts on the third group. It may not make sense to use limited time and resources on legislators who are unlikely to change their voting positions. For example, in a campaign to promote a mandatory motorcycle helmet law, it may be a waste of time to focus lobbying efforts on a legislator who is a strong civil libertarian who has opposed all health behavior regulations in the past on ideological grounds. It may be equally wasteful to focus on a legislator who has repeatedly sponsored motorcycle helmet legislation in the past.

Formative research can provide several important pieces of background information on legislative policy makers. First, what are the legislators' current positions on the bill in question? How have they voted on similar legislation in the past? What are their ideological views, especially as they relate to the proposed legislation? This includes not only party affiliation, but other aspects of political ideology as well.

Second, it is important to identify elected officials who hold key positions of influence, such as chairpersons of committees to which a bill is likely to be referred. At the state and national levels, the Speaker of the House and Senate Majority Leader are almost always in a position to influence legislation. At the local level, the mayor or first selectman is almost always in a critical position of influence on ordinances. Leaders of the minority party and caucuses of legislators may be important to reach. For example, there is a tobacco caucus in Congress that would be expected to play a critical role in any federal tobacco legislation.

Third, it is important to identify potential sources of influence on critical policy makers. What district does the legislator represent? Who are the most influential individuals, institutions, and other organizations in that district? Could any celebrities or other prominent citizens in the district help influence the legislator? In Fremont, California, for example, the Smoke-Free Fremont coalition enlisted the help of Olympic ice skater Kristi Yamaguchi in convincing city council members to enact an ordinance eliminating smoking in restaurants. Business groups or key businesses in a district may be a particularly valuable source of influence in a public health policy campaign.

Fourth, it may be useful to identify the source of campaign contributions for legislators. For example, in promoting policies to regulate alcohol, tobacco, or firearms, knowledge of campaign contributions to legislators from the alcohol industry, tobacco industry, or the National Rifle Association may help to expose the degree of outside influence on the policy process.

Fifth, at the local level, it may be important to identify friends and family of council members, who may be the most effective liaisons to the policy maker on behalf of the health coalition.

There are many potential sources of this information. In the United States, for state legislatures and Congress, library reference sections have guidebooks that list legislators, describe their districts, outline their committee positions, identify their political party, and provide addresses and telephone numbers. An increasing number of states have detailed information of this type on their websites, as does the U.S. Congress. Voting records and campaign contribution sources are usually available to the public.

Perhaps the best method to obtain information is to meet with each legislator, his or her staff, or both. This approach has the dual purpose of providing campaign representatives with an opportunity to tell the legislator their positions as well as learn about the legislator's. Too often, public health coalitions wait until late in a campaign to meet with legislators. It is usually too late, and important information that could have guided the development of the initiative has been missed.

Andreasen (2006) recommends identifying a set of target policymakers and then preparing a matrix that lists, for each policymaker, the benefits, costs, others who support the initiative or its objectives, and self-assurance issues (BCOS).

Mothers Against Drunk Driving (MADD), in its *How To Compendium* (1991), a policy manual for public health advocates, describes the importance of what it calls community analysis. MADD's description is a useful summary of many important formative research questions for promoting a public health policy.

> Know your community inside out, so that as you set goals and build an action plan, you can gauge the probable reactions of various constituencies, estimate your chances for success and build the power base you need to win. Community analysis means much more than being in command of facts about geography and governmental structures, ethnic and socioeconomic data. It means finding out what the power structure really is, not just what the table of organization says it is. It includes hard information on political make-up and party strength. It looks at the community for residential, business and industry concentrations and asks, "Who really runs which parts of town?" It searches out the ethnic, religious

and organizational alignments, the loyalty groups, formal and in-formal. It finds out who's influential about what and with whom—maybe the local bank president at the state capital, the public works commissioner in the city council, it could even be the rock station disc jockey with his or her devoted listeners. . . . It is imperative to identify the hidden power structure affecting any specific issue you're working on, to line up allies within that power structure but also to spot opposition early in the game. . . . A careful community analysis can help eliminate the surprise and prepare the legislative committee to take the offensive. (p. 138)

The Public and Influential Members of It

It is particularly important to segment the general public, because a small number of individuals or groups usually have a disproportionate amount of influence on public opinion, and, in turn, on legislators.

RoperASW has found that about 10 percent of the adult population of the United States qualifies as Influential Americans®—socially and politically active individuals who are highly engaged and active in their personal lives, their workplaces, and their communities (Keller & Berry, 2003).

> The most engaged Americans, Influentials are conduits of infor-mation for their community and the nation. Their activist bent, many connections, and active minds, as well as the sheer force of their personalities—their clear sense of priorities, belief in growth and change, passionate approach to life, and infectious sense of confidence—make the Influentials natural intersections for intelli-gence. They tend to know more than others, to hear about things first, and to broadcast what they know to many people. (Keller & Berry, 2003, p. 124)

If you reach and convince the Influentials, they will reach other mem-bers of the population and motivate them for you. To get their attention, begin by offering them good, high-quality information. Compared to the total public, they use more information sources. They are particularly likely to value word-of-mouth. They were most likely to say they get in-formation on ways of improving health from other people (32%), mag-azine articles (31%), family (25%), newspaper articles (24%), TV programs (21%) and friends (18%) (Keller & Berry, 2003, p. 124).

One version of RoperASW's questions to define Influentials is shown in **Exhibit 11-3** (the questions are tweaked occasionally). Influential Americans have done three or more of the items on the list other than item h—"signed a petition," which was included to give everyone something to answer af-firmatively to satisfy the human need to say they are doing things they feel they should.

Exhibit 11-3   RoperASW Questions to Identify Influentials

Here is a list of things some people do about government or politics. Have you happened to have done any of these things in the past year? Which ones?

a. Written or called any politician at the state, local, or national level

b. Attended a political rally, speech, or organized protest of any kind

c. Attended a public meeting on town or school affairs

d. Held or run for political office

e. Served on a committee for some local organization

f. Served as an officer for some club or organization

g. Written a letter to the editor of a newspaper or magazine or called a live radio or TV show to express an opinion

h. Signed a petition

i. Worked for a political party

j. Made a speech

k. Written an article for a magazine or newspaper

l. Been an active member of any group that tries to influence public policy or government

Source: Reprinted with the permission of The Free Press, a Division of Simon & Schuster Adult Publishing Group, from *The Influentials: One American in Ten Tells the Other Nine How to Vote, Where to Eat, and What to Buy* by Ed Keller and Jon Berry. Copyright © 2003 by Roper ASW, LLC. All rights reserved.

Another way of thinking about and identifying the type of people most important to reach is provided by Malcolm Gladwell in *The Tipping Point* (2000). He notes "the success of any kind of social epidemic [e.g., when an idea or behavior moves through a population in a manner similar to a disease epidemic] is heavily dependent on the involvement of people with a particular and rare set of social gifts" (p. 33). He identified three types of people who play important roles in social epidemics:

- Connectors—People who know lots of people (often four or five times as many as others) spanning many different social groups. They know who to pass information to, actively do it, and are listened to when they do so.
- Mavens—People who collect detailed information, are socially motivated to share that information, and are viewed by others as expert sources. They "have the knowledge and the social skills to start word-of-mouth epidemics" (Gladwell, 2003, p. 67). For example, market mavens may collect information detailed information on many different products, prices or places and have a strong desire to be of service and influence to others.

- Salesmen—People who are very persuasive, generally through subtle and nonverbal cues that draw people into their physical and conversational rhythms and dictate the terms of the interaction.

Gladwell notes that social epidemics typically involve all three kinds of people.

When trying to move something up on the public and political agendas, it is clear that reaching RoperASW's Influentials or Gladwell's mavens can be important. Both crave information, collect it from many sources, and share it with others. Typically, this will be an easier task if you begin by looking for Influentials or mavens already likely to be interested in your topic. For example, if the goal is to improve Medicare's coverage of prescription drugs, a starting point is to identify Influentials and mavens among senior citizens, and then aim public education and advocacy efforts at this segment of the population.

The general public may also be segmented based on the way they are likely to vote on an issue; those who are undecided or not fully entrenched in their position are often the best group to reach. For example, in opposing a referendum to end affirmative action, it may be important to separately study the opinions of females, persons of color, and liberal and conservative white males. It may be, for example, that liberal white males are the key swing group whose votes will determine the ultimate fate of the referendum. Public education and advocacy efforts could then be conducted most efficiently by focusing on reaching this demographic group. With limited resources, it would not make sense to spend large amounts of money trying to influence the opinions of minority communities, who are likely to support affirmative action anyway.

Mass Media

The mass media should be segmented based on the results of the above formative research, which identifies key policy makers and segments of the general public. The geographic and sociodemographic reach of media outlets can then be studied, and those outlets most likely to reach the target audiences can be selected for media advocacy efforts. In most U.S. states, and at the local level, the majority of the public is reached by one or two major media markets, so efforts can be concentrated on them. It would be inefficient, for example, to run ads on every television station in Massachusetts, when television stations in Boston and Springfield reach the majority of state residents. If a particular legislator is important, then the media market that covers his or her district is essential.

Within a media market, it is important to decide which specific channel(s) is most useful (e.g., newspaper, radio, or television). Within each channel, it is important to identify the specific outlet(s) with the greatest reach and influence. It may be more efficient to meet with editorial boards of the three or four most important outlets than to try to visit every outlet in the media market. Information on the reach and audience composition of various media outlets is available through standard public relations and advertising resources. In the United States, they include online and print media directories, Standard Rate and Data Service (for profiles of all media outlets; www.srds.com), Arbitron (for radio station ratings as well as audience size and composition; www.arbitron.com), and Nielsen Media Research (for similar information on television stations and programs; www.nielsenmedia.com).

To be most effective, public health practitioners should segment their target audience down to the level of the individual reporter. It is important to identify which reporter's beat includes the topic of the public health policy in question and which reporters have taken an interest in this issue in the past. When planning a media event to promote the policy, the press release should be sent specifically to these reporters, and follow-up calls should be made directly to them, rather than to a general news desk. One formative research technique that is very easy, especially since most newspapers now have news archives that can be searched online, is to identify the authors of past news stories on the health topic of interest. Chapter 15 provides more information on working with the media.

Shaping the Policy Initiative

As with initiatives to change individual health behaviors, once audiences have been segmented additional formative research is often needed to understand what actions audiences can take, what barriers need to be overcome, and what benefits to communicate and deliver to persuade them to take action. Sometimes this information can be gathered at the same time as the information used to segment the audiences; at other times it is gathered separately.

Framing Messages
The key to policy initiatives is to frame the message properly. This also is often true with individual health behavior changes. However, it is even more important with policy initiatives, since to bring about policy change the issue must be on the public agenda, and it gets on the public agenda through the mass media.

The formative research process plays three major roles in developing messages for a public health policy campaign: (1) assessing the existing level of support for the policy, (2) assessing the effectiveness of alternative ways of framing the policy issue to garner support for the policy, and (3) assessing the effectiveness of the ways opponents frame the issue to garner opposition to the policy. Public health practitioners can also use formative research to assess variation in support for a policy and the effectiveness of alternative issue-framing strategies by demographic characteristics.

For example, in the United States successful campaigns to promote cigarette tax increase ballot initiatives all used formative research early and often throughout the campaign. Support for proposed cigarette tax increases was assessed long before campaigns were initiated, and in some cases, before the language of the initiative was even drafted. But the level of public support for these policy initiatives was also assessed periodically throughout the campaign, allowing practitioners to refine their campaign strategies. Moreover, the health coalitions used public polling not only to assess the level of support for the initiatives, but to test various strategies for framing the initiative. These polls helped to identify what campaign themes, messages, and arguments would be most salient and influential on the voters.

Detailed examination of the framing of issues may be more valuable in strategic planning than simple data on public opinion about policies. Thus, public opinion polls should assess not only the general level of public support for specific policies and programs, but the degree to which various arguments for and against the policy or program resonate with voters. Chapter 10 discusses how to assess the way the issue is currently being framed by public health advocates and opponents. Once this assessment is available, existing and alternative approaches to framing the issue can be explored through public opinion polls. Practitioners must keep in mind that arguments that appeal to the core principle of health may not be as effective as those that appeal to more compelling core values, such as freedom, independence, autonomy and control (see Chapter 6). Thus, practitioners should be receptive to many alternative frames.

There is no one formative research technique that is best for use in developing a public health policy campaign. For example, focus groups can serve as a valuable tool to explore a wide variety of potential frames, which can then be narrowed down and tested with the population as a whole in a survey. Ideally, formative research methods will be used in concert to achieve the three primary goals of assessing the level of support for a policy and the effectiveness of various ways of framing arguments for and against the policy.

Exhibit 11-4 describes how formative research was used to shape a campaign against a ballot initiative in California. Appendix 11-A provides a description of a very different type of policy initiative: how formative research was used to develop products designed to build community support for coordinated school health programs.

■ PRETESTING

Pretesting takes place as part of developing components that will form the initiative. Pretesting involves assessing how target audiences react—to proposed goods, services, distribution channels, packaging, messages and/or materials. It can help identify what needs to be changed before final production or implementation, or it can help determine which of a number of alternatives is likely to work best, as was done in the initiative

Exhibit 11-4 Using Formative Research To Frame Messages against a Ballot Initiative

Background

The use of formative research in developing a policy campaign was illustrated by the California coalition that successfully defeated Proposition 188 in 1994. Proposition 188 was a ballot initiative sponsored by Philip Morris that would have repealed all 270 local antismoking ordinances in California, as well as the state's new law eliminating smoking restrictions (Macdonald, Aguinaga, & Glantz, 1997). Most damaging, the initiative would have preempted the ability of cities and towns to enact more stringent regulation of smoking in the workplace in the future. Although the initiative was sponsored and promoted by the tobacco industry, the industry hid its involvement in the campaign from the public. Philip Morris used a public relations firm—the Dolphin Group—to run the campaign and formed a front group, Californians for Statewide Smoking Restrictions, to disguise its involvement and to mislead the public into thinking that this was an antismoking referendum. Using deceptive billboards that read "Yes on 188-Tough Statewide Smoking Restrictions—The Right Choice," the industry gathered enough signatures to qualify Proposition 188 for the California ballot in November 1994.

The public health community was in a difficult position. The anti-Proposition 188 coalition had only about $1.2 million to spend, compared to the $18 million spent by the tobacco industry to promote the referendum (Macdonald et. al., 1997). The health coalition needed to be extraordinarily efficient in its campaign: It had to find the single most effective argument that would sway the most crucial voters. The coalition turned to basic marketing principles—and to formative research.

Method

The coalition conducted a public opinion poll to determine the baseline level of support for Proposition 188 and to test the effectiveness of various framing strategies for and against the initiative. The choice of a framing strategy to defeat the initiative was not intuitive. Many arguments could be made in opposition to the proposal: (1) It would set back public health by repealing local antismoking ordinances (2) It would create weak statewide standards that were not adequate to protect nonsmokers from secondhand smoke. (3) It would prevent cities and counties from enacting more stringent secondhand smoke regulations in the future. (4) It would help the tobacco industry protect its profits.

The anti-188 coalition could have simply chosen one or more of the arguments to use as the basis of a campaign. But would such a theme have resonated widely with voters? The tobacco-industry-funded front groups promoting the initiative were making three arguments that could have swayed voters, even in light of the above arguments against the initiative: (1) Proposition 188 completely prohibits smoking in workplaces and restaurants unless strict ventilation requirements are met; (2) Proposition 188 replaces the crazy patchwork quilt of local ordinances throughout the state and replaces them with one tough uniform state law, and (3) The uniform restrictions are stronger than 90% of the local ordinances currently in place—90% of

(continues)

Exhibit 11-4   Using Formative Research To Frame Messages against a Ballot Initiative (continued)

communities in California would see an immediate increase in secondhand smoke protection as a result of passage of Proposition 188 (Macdonald et al., 1997).

Instead of relying on intuition to choose its campaign theme, the anti-188 coalition conducted extensive formative research. Public opinion polls were conducted to assess the reaction of voters to many alternative ways of framing the debate over Proposition 188 (Hypotenuse Inc., 1994; Marttila & Kiley, Inc., 1994). The results were striking. The initial support for the initiative was strong: about 60% of California voters supported Proposition 188. Although specific arguments about the negative impact of the initiative on protections against secondhand smoke did sway some voters, they did not change enough votes to predict defeat of the initiative. However, the poll revealed that simply mentioning that the initiative was sponsored by Philip Morris was enough to turn the vote around completely. In fact, when told that Philip Morris was behind the initiative, 70% of California voters stated that they would vote against it.

Results

The coalition chose "Stop Philip Morris" as its campaign theme. It then conducted a coordinated campaign that included grass-roots advocacy, media advocacy, and paid advertising focused on this single theme. The goal was simply to educate voters about who was really behind Proposition 188, not to worry about making detailed arguments about why the initiative was bad for public health.

The coalition conducted periodic public opinion polls throughout the 3-month campaign period to assess how well its approach was working. By mid-July, the initiative was ahead 52% to 38% (Macdonald et al., 1997). By mid-September, voters were about equally divided on Proposition 188. Seeing the dangerous level of support for Proposition 188, the health coalition stepped up its efforts to educate the public about the initiative's sponsor. The coalition hired Jack Nicholl to produce television advertisements using former Surgeon General C. Everett Koop as a spokesperson and paid to air these ads in the major California media markets during the last week of the campaign. The ads highlighted the deceptive nature of the pro-188 campaign, exposing that Philip Morris was behind the initiative and how Californians for Statewide Smoking Restrictions was trying to cover up this important fact. It was, in fact, the discouraging September poll results that convinced the national American Cancer Society and American Heart Association to make substantial contributions to the anti-188 campaign that allowed the Koop spots to be aired (Macdonald et al., 1997).

On November 8, Proposition 188 was defeated by an overwhelming margin of 71% to 29%. The coalition's strategy had succeeded. Careful formative research and subsequent tracking allowed the coalition to develop an effective campaign, to monitor its progress, and to make necessary refinements along the way to increase the campaign's effectiveness.

discussed in **Exhibit 11-4**. Common methodologies for pretesting include central-site interviews, in-depth interviews, and telephone or web surveys. When possible, it is best to use a quantitative method. More detail on designing and conducting these types of studies is provided in Chapter 18.

Answering the following questions will help you design and conduct a successful pretest.

- *What is being tested?* For example, if an ad is being tested, a focus group setting is unrealistic. People usually do not see an ad and then spend two hours discussing it with a group of people. A one-on-one interview provides a more realistic setting: The interviewer (or web survey) can show the material to the participant for a fixed amount of time (e.g., take back a printed piece after one minute or play a video or audiotape once) and then ask him or her a series of questions about it. Although this situation is still unrealistic because it forces participants to think more about the material than they otherwise might, it is less unrealistic than forcing them to discuss it with others.

- *Why is it being tested?* Do you want an overall assessment, or are there concerns about particular aspects, such as the hours of a new clinic, ease of completing an application form for a new service or navigating a website, the packaging for a new product, or the executional details—voices, music, actors—of a new video? Is it important to know how audience members will obtain, use, or distribute the product, service or material as well as how they react to it? The answers to all of these questions help shape the methodology.

- *With whom does it need to be tested?* Are you interested in target audience reactions? Reactions of intermediaries or community Influentials (in which case, see "Professional Review" later in this chapter)? Is your audience a group that can easily be recruited at a central location, such as a shopping mall? Or is it a low-incidence population that will have to be reached some other way?

- *In what geographic locations does it need to be tested?* If your initiative is local, this question may not arise. For regional or national programs, sometimes it is important to obtain reactions from people in different parts of a state or the country. This may affect your choice of methodology or your choice of vendors.

- *When are results needed?* Obtaining results by mail usually takes the longest amount of time, particularly if packages are sent and returned via regular mail rather than by express services or fax. Individual in-depth interviews can also take a long time: Once the topic guide has been developed and potential participants have been identified, interviews usually take at least two to three weeks to schedule and conduct, and analysis can easily take an additional two weeks or more.

Results from mall-intercept interviews can be available as quickly as a week after the questionnaire and materials are ready if the population is relatively large, although mall-intercept firms usually prefer to have at least two weekends to field a questionnaire and may need longer depending on the population. Results from telephone or web surveys can be available within a week if omnibus studies are used.

- *What decisions will be made with the results?* If you will need to go through a formal clearance process subsequent to the pretesting, is there particular information you can include in the pretest to facilitate clearance? For example, have others raised concerns that you can address through questions in the pretest? Have you included questions that address the types of refinements you could make? If you are going to develop a distribution plan, could the pretest participants provide you with helpful information on where and how to distribute the final products?

Pretesting Messages: A Continuation of Communication Strategy Development

Once a communication strategy has been developed (see Chapter 12), messages using that strategy are developed and explored. Sometimes the testing is to validate the communication strategy; at other times aspects of it are not yet finalized, so prospective messages may use different types of appeals, frames, or core values, or vary in some other way. Sometimes reactions are explored using qualitative research techniques, messages are refined, and then tested using central-site interviews or a telephone or web survey. It is unwise to explore reactions to messages and test promotional materials containing the message at the same time, because it is extremely difficult (and often impossible) to determine what the participants are reacting to—the message or the execution of it.

Regardless of methodology, the goal of pretesting messages and materials is to assess message appeal, recall and comprehension, sources of confusion or offense, and motivation to act. When messages are tested, they are usually presented as statements. Audience members' reactions can be assessed a number of ways:

- Ask them to sort the messages from most compelling to least compelling. (This approach works best if the respondents are interviewed in person.)
- Ask them to indicate how much they agree or disagree with each statement (using a scale of responses).
- Ask them to rate each statement on dimensions such as believability, relevance, and importance to them (again, using scaled responses).

One useful way to pretest messages is to prepare each message as a separate title or headline and ask participants which they would be most likely to pick up and why. If such a process is used, everything should be identical except the message—the same type, colors, graphics, and so on, should be used.

Pretesting Materials

Once a message approach has been selected, materials that will deliver it can be tested. Materials that are often pretested include advertisements, brochures, booklets, audiotapes, videotapes and websites. Sometimes only one version of the material will be tested: at other times, different approaches that convey the same basic message may be tested against each other. Although materials pretests will not tell us exactly how materials will perform, they will identify any "red flags" in terms of unintended interpretations and executional details that need changing (typeface, type size, colors, music, voices, timing, etc.). Pretesting also can help "sell" the materials internally by providing information on target audience reactions to counter criticism from non-target audience members.

Materials being pretested can be in various stages of readiness; the most common formats are discussed here. **Exhibit 11-5** lists some topics commonly covered in pretests; the exact wording of questions addressing each topic depends on the method used for the pretest. For example, see Appendix 11-D, which provides a sample mall-intercept questionnaire covering many of these topics. The *Handbook of Marketing Scales* provides examples of scales that have been developed to measure specific areas of reactions to ads (Bearden & Netemeyer, 1999).

With today's desktop publishing capabilities, *print materials* are most often tested in a form that looks final. Headlines and text are final (unless changes need to be made as a result of the pretest), and the layout and typeface(s) used are those planned for the final product. Stock photos that are similar to those planned for the final version are generally used. If different headlines or tag lines are being tested against each other, all other elements of the ad, poster, or brochure (layout, typeface, type size, etc.) should be identical if possible.

Radio ads and other audio products are most often recorded by program or agency staff, rather than by the talent that will be used in the final version. They do not have music or sound effects included unless they are critical to comprehension.

Videos and television ads can be represented as *storyboards* (similar to a cartoon strip, with separate frames depicting each scene and the script typed or written underneath), *animatics* (basically the storyboard is videotaped; the dialogue is also taped, and each scene changes to match the dialogue), or *prefinished* products (scenes are videotaped and the actual audio track is included, although final music may not be included).

Exhibit 11-5 Topics Commonly Included in Materials Pretests

General Topics

- What is the main idea of the (ad, booklet, etc.)?
- What, if anything, was particularly liked?
- What, if anything, was particularly disliked?
- Was anything offensive? (What? Who would it offend?)
- Was anything hard to understand? (What?)
- Was anything hard to believe? (What? Why?)
- Who is this (ad, booklet, publication, etc.) for? Who would get the most out of it?
- What, if anything, should be changed, added, or deleted?
- Which option would be most likely to induce the desired action?

Topics for Long Publications and Websites

- How was the amount of information—was it too much, about right, or too little? Are there particular sections that should be longer or shorter?
- Were there topics you expected to see covered that were not? Were topics covered that you think are unnecessary?
- Do you have any additional questions about the subject that were not answered?
- What do you think about the layout? How easy or hard was it to find information? What do you think about the amount of white space used?
- What do you think about the type? Was it too large, about right, or too small? How easy or hard was it to read?
- What do you think about the language used? How easy or hard was it to understand?
- What do you think about the (photos or style of illustration)? How easy or hard was it to understand the diagrams? Are there places where diagrams or illustrations would clarify the text? Are there places where they are unnecessary?
- What do you think about the use of color? What types of people do these colors appeal to? (Certain colors have different meanings in different cultures; probe for cultural sensitivity if necessary.)
- Are there any other changes that you would make?
- Where would you expect to find the publication/find out about the website?
- For professional audiences: How would you use this information in your work?

The form in which video products are tested depends largely on the available budget and, to a lesser degree, on the characteristics of the final product. Each format is progressively more expensive. Storyboards almost always test much worse than the other versions because they are not as visually interesting and are often more difficult to follow. Additionally, if the interviewers read the script, each will read it differently, resulting in a less consistent test. Animatics are often used if the visuals include text, because it is difficult for someone to read the type and the script at the same time.

Prefinished products are obviously the best format to test because they are closer to what the final version will be like, but they are prohibitively expensive and rarely tested unless there is some reason they must be tested in that format (i.e., if there is no other way to truly communicate what the final product will be like). If a prefinished version is tested, one way to assess memorability of and attention to ads is to embed the material being tested in a few minutes of other advertising and then begin the test by asking the respondents what ads they remember seeing.

Pilot Tests

Sometimes the best way to test a new material, service, or policy is to implement it, or a number of possible versions, and study what happens. For example, advertisers can do this through split runs in publications, cable systems, or web advertising. A health clinic could try adding a new service or adjusting an existing one for a few months, such as evening hours one night a week, and then assess usage versus cost. Or a school system might implement a new recess policy, different food offerings, or wellness activities open to the public at a few schools for a few months or a school year, and then examine the reactions among students, faculty and staff, and, if appropriate, the community. Policy makers can then decide whether and how to continue the new policy. Appendix 10-A discusses the pilot of a ride service to reduce drunk driving; evaluation of it is discussed in Chapter 17.

Pilot tests most often use an experimental or quasi-experimental design; the basics of such designs are discussed in Chapters 17 and 18.

Professional Review

For many public health organizations, another important component of pretesting is professional review. Asking community leaders and other professionals in your organization, in partner and intermediary organizations, and in the field to review proposed goods, services, messages, promotional materials, or distribution channels serves a number of purposes. First, the process can identify potential problems that planners may not have considered. Second, it provides an opportunity to obtain buy-in early on. Third, it can identify potential objections to the content or structure of program components—and allow you to specifically look for these objections when conducting audience pretests. If the objections are raised by audience members, you will be able to address them; if they are not, you will be able to explain to reviewers that in fact such concerns were not raised by the audience. For messages and materials, professional review helps to ensure that the information presented is sound and can enhance the credibility of messages or materials with other stakeholders.

Professional reviews can be obtained a number of ways. Two common ones are to mail or e-mail a questionnaire and prototypes (or representations of prototypes) to reviewers, or to conduct review in conjunction with an already-scheduled meeting. The latter approach increases the likelihood that reviews will be completed and returned to you.

■ CONCLUSION

Formative research is central to the marketing approach. It is critical to building strong relationships with targeted audiences and other constituencies because it helps create, communicate and deliver the value that forms the cornerstone of those relationships. As Lefebvre and Flora (1988) noted, "in an arena characterized by lower levels of funding, the importance of formative research cannot be overemphasized. Although budget-minded persons might view the additional costs of such research as frivolous, it will prove to be money well spent. Not only can such research suggest changes in program content or delivery that will enhance its reach and/or effectiveness, but it can also circumvent a costly and ill-fated intervention before it receives broad exposure" (p. 305).

The formative research activities discussed in this chapter and in Chapters 3 and 6 will help proponents of public health develop and use a marketing mindset. This mindset—improving customer satisfaction, identifying unmet needs, and creating products to fulfill them—can be used to improve public health offerings and policies, thereby building stronger relationships with beneficiaries of those offerings and allowing the institutions to demonstrate greater value to all constituencies, such as taxpayers, community leaders and elected officials. The marketing mindset also helps public health proponents compete with marketing-driven industry efforts that are detrimental to public health.

References

Ajzen, I., & Fishbein, M. (1980). *Understanding attitudes and predicting social behavior.* Englewood Cliffs, NJ: Prentice-Hall.

Andreasen, A.R. (2006). *Social marketing in the 21st century.* Thousand Oaks, CA: Sage.

Bandura, A. (1986). *Social foundations of thought and action.* Englewood Cliffs, NJ: Prentice-Hall.

Bearden, W.O. & Netemeyer, R.G. (1999). *Handbook of marketing scales,* (2nd ed.) Thousand Oaks, CA: Sage.

Chaffee, S.H., & Roser, C. (1986). Involvement and the consistency of knowledge, attitudes, and behaviors. *Communication Research,* 13, 373–399.

Gladwell, M. (2000). *The Tipping Point.* Boston: Little Brown.

Green, L.W. & McAlister, A. (1984). Macro-interventions to support health behavior: some theoretical perspectives and practical reflections. *Health Education Quarterly,* 11, 332–339.

Grunig, J.E., & Hunt, T. (1984). *Managing public relations.* New York: Holt, Rinehart & Winston.

Harris, J.F. (1995, June 11). Clinton urges "zero tolerance" for young drinking drivers. *The Washington Post,* p. A6.

Hypotenuse Inc. (1994). *Bullet poll: California smoking research.* Verona, NJ: Author.

Keller, E. & Berry, J. (2003). *The Influentials.* New York: The Free Press.

Kotler, P., & Andreasen, A.R. (1996). *Strategic marketing for non-profit organizations* (5th ed.). Upper Saddle River, NJ: Prentice-Hall.

Langner, P., & Laidler, J. (1993, December 14). Traffic deaths restart debate: 3 fatalities fuel push for new laws. *The Boston Globe,* pp. 37, 38.

Lefebvre, R.C., Doner, L.D., Johnson, C., Loughrey, K., Balch, G., & Sutton, S.M. (1995). Use of database marketing and consumer-based health communications in message design: An example from the Office of Cancer Communications' "5 A Day for Better Health" program. In E. Maibach & R.L. Parrott (Eds.), *Designing health messages: Approaches from communication theory and public health practice* (pp. 217–246). Thousand Oaks, CA: Sage.

Lefebvre, R.C., & Flora, J.A. (1988). Social marketing and public health intervention. *Health Education Quarterly,* 15, 299–315.

Macdonald, H., Aguinaga, S., & Glantz, S.A. (1997). The defeat of Philip Morris' "California Uniform Tobacco Control Act." *American Journal of Public Health,* 87, 1989–1996.

Maiman, L.A., & Becker, M.H. (1974). The health belief model: Origins and correlates in psychological theory. *Health Education Monographs,* 2, 384–408.

Marttila & Kiley, Inc. (1994). *A survey of voter attitudes in California.* Boston: Author.

Morgan, D.L., & Krueger, R.A. (1998). *The focus group kit* (Vols. 1–6). Thousand Oaks, CA: Sage.

Mothers Against Drunk Driving. (1991, April 1). *How to compendium.* Irving, TX: Author.

Murphy, S.P. (1994, January 21). Gloucester couple seeks tougher drunken driving law. *The Boston Globe,* pp. 17, 25.

National Cancer Institute (1993, December). *5 A Day for Better Health: NCI media campaign strategy.* Bethesda, MD: Author.

Slater, M.D. (1995). Choosing audience segmentation strategies and methods for health communication. In E. Maibach & R.L. Parrott (Eds.), *Designing health messages: Approaches from communication theory and public health practice* (pp. 186–198). Thousand Oaks, CA: Sage.

Strecher, V.S., DeVellis, B.M., Becker, M.H., & Rosenstock, I.M. (1986). The role of self-efficacy in achieving health behavior change. *Health Education Quarterly,* 13, 73–91.

Wallack, L., Dorfman, L., Jernigan, D., & Themba, M. (1993). *Media advocacy and public health: Power for prevention.* Newbury Park, CA: Sage.

Wong, D.S. (1994a, March 25). Drunken driving bill OK'd by House: Tough rule could allow cars to be forfeited. *The Boston Globe,* pp. 29, 34.

Wong, D.S. (1994b, May 26). Tough bill on drunken driving OK'd: Blood alcohol limit lowered; Weld expected to sign package. *The Boston Globe,* pp. 1, 34.

APPENDIX

11-A

Building Support for Coordinated School Health: Using Multiple Formative Research Techniques to Shape an Initiative

■ BACKGROUND

The Council of Chief State School Officers (CCSSO) and the Association of State and Territorial Health Officials (ASTHO) represent, respectively, the top education official and top health official in each U.S. state and territory. The two organizations came together to develop joint materials that their respective constituents can use to help build support for coordinated school health programs. Such programs link, or coordinate, eight components of school health: health education, physical education, nutrition, health services, counseling, psychological and social services, staff wellness, and partnerships between the school and the community and/or parents.

■ CHALLENGES AND OPPORTUNITIES

A coordinated school health program is a complicated product to market because of the nature of the product and the way it is distributed and implemented. Despite the name, it is not a clearly defined program. Rather, it is a philosophy of ensuring that each aspect of a school contributes to a child's physical, mental and emotional well-being in a coordinated, reinforcing way. As a result, a coordinated approach can be implemented differently in every school. This is an advantage because it allows schools to customize the approach to suit their local needs, but presents a challenge in that it is complex to explain, obtain resources for, and implement.

Source: Copyright © 1998 Lynne Doner Lotenberg and Beverly Schwartz.

Getting the product to the consumer is also complex. Products that require organizational change rather than individual change are inherently more difficult to implement successfully. Changes to school health programs can be particularly difficult because they may not be supported and require many different individuals and departments within an organization to change, and because approval to implement them may require changes at the state, school district, and individual school levels.

An additional challenge for the CCSSO/ASTHO initiative is the broad geographic target audience. Products developed as part of this initiative will be distributed nationally; however, the political, social, and economic environments in which changes are made are different in every state and locality. Indeed, it is sometimes different in every school. Materials developed for national use cannot possibly capture the needs of each community. Therefore, final products need to be customizable.

■ TARGET AUDIENCES

Although the CCSSO/ASTHO materials are for the chief education and health officials or their designees, the initiative's ultimate target audiences are "easy-to-reach" administrators, teachers, school staff, and parents. "Easy to reach" is defined as being supportive of school health programs and, for parents, being active in activities related to school (e.g., a member or officer of a parent-teacher organization, a volunteer or aide at school, or someone who attends school board meetings).

The rationale for these target audiences is rooted in two complementary theoretical frameworks: diffusion of innovations and stages of change. Both were discussed in more detail in Chapter 18. From a diffusion of innovations perspective, the target audience is parents, teachers, and administrators who are already trying to improve their schools and who are innovators and early adopters—the first people to embrace a new idea. Once members of these groups begin coordinating their schools' approach to health, others are more likely to attempt similar changes. In stages-of-change terms, the target audience encompasses those in contemplation (i.e., they are receptive to the idea of a stronger approach to health and may have considered trying to change aspects of their school's approach, but have no specific plans) and preparation/action (i.e., they may have made a decision to try to change the school's approach and may have taken some steps toward trying to make changes or build support for changes).

■ ROLE OF FORMATIVE RESEARCH

Formative research was integrated throughout the process of planning and developing the CCSSO/ASTHO materials. The research activities and their major objectives were as follows:

1. Secondary review of other relevant projects and literature: To identify target audiences' likely perceptions of benefits of and barriers to the comprehensive or coordinated approach and to identify striking linkages between children's health and their school performance to support messages about the importance of a strong, coordinated approach to school health.

2. In-depth interviews with administrators, teachers, and parents in school districts that use a coordinated approach to school health: To explore preliminary message concepts, how they define comprehensive or coordinated school health (CSH) and the language they use when they talk about it, benefits of and barriers to approach, and how they would implement CSH elsewhere.

3. Focus groups with administrators, teachers, and parents in districts that do and do not use a coordinated approach to school health: To explore refined message concepts, definitions of CSH and language used, perceived benefits and barriers, and the first steps they would take in trying to implement it. (A sample recruitment screener and moderator's guide are provided in Appendixes 11-B and 11-C.)

4. Nationally representative survey of American adults: To quantify reactions to concepts in the messages.

5. Focus groups with administrators, teachers, and parents: To pretest prototype materials.

The final materials will be pilot-tested in six states for one year.

Major Findings

The first round of formative research helped CCSSO and ASTHO to understand how school health programs are currently defined and positioned in the minds of target audience members and provided insights into the types of messages that would frame the need to move toward a coordinated approach to school health in a compelling, relevant way. After initial materials were developed, research helped the project team revise the content of those materials to better meet the needs of the target audience.

The following sections present some of the major findings in chronological order to provide a sense of how research at each stage was used to shape and then refine the messages about comprehensive school health and the materials developed to deliver those messages.

Definitions of School Health

Target audience members tended to have a narrower definition of school health than that used in the eight-component model. Furthermore, there was no common definition of what school health encompassed. Health education was mentioned most often; physical education, school meals, and on-site health services (particularly among participants whose schools had them) also came up quite a bit. A fair number of focus group participants asked if mental health was included in the definition of health.

Parents often spoke about an approach to health education, saying they would like to see their children learn more practical skills. After seeing a list of the eight components, research participants generally thought that all were part of a school's approach to health; however, they did not think their schools had all eight, or thought they needed to work on strengthening some of them.

Benefits of a Coordinated Approach to School Health

People from schools that have implemented coordinated school health associated a number of benefits with the approach, including

- Impact on important numbers, such as reduced absenteeism and fewer behavior problems. All groups—parents, teachers, and administrators—said it would be easier to make the case for coordinated school health programs if they had data showing that such programs would make a difference in the numbers by which school districts and individual schools are evaluated;
- Improved classroom performance, in the form of higher test scores after the program was implemented, as well as more alert students and more positive attitudes among students;
- Teaching real skills students can use rather than rote knowledge;
- Bringing everyone together, either by providing a forum for greater parental and/or community involvement, providing an opportunity for the school and other agencies to collaborate, bringing staff together within the school, or providing a program in which students in all areas can participate; and
- For disadvantaged children in particular, getting them ready to learn by meeting their basic needs.

Barriers to Change

Participants whose schools did not have a coordinated approach mentioned the following barriers to implementation:

- Tremendous pressure to "teach to tests," and health isn't a topic on state-level achievement tests.
- Health teachers aren't "part of the team," sometimes figuratively and sometimes literally.
- Health is not stressed in teaching degree programs.
- Parents are not making it a priority, probably because they do not realize how health issues are (or are not) currently addressed in schools.

Message Development: Lessons Learned

After testing a variety of message concepts in the initial in-depth interviews and focus groups, the project team reached the following conclusions:

1. In general, focusing on an immediate problem and presenting a comprehensive or coordinated approach to school health as part of a solution worked best.

2. Tying school health programs to "numbers" that affect funding or by which schools are rated, such as absenteeism and drop-out rates, provided a compelling message to many administrators and teachers. Parents also thought such linkages would help garner support for health programs.

3. Positioning school health programs as providing support and practical skills was believable and likely to be well received by most administrators, teachers, and parents.

4. A lot of teachers, in particular, reacted well to a "whole child" message, but it may not be the best choice for widespread use because some teachers and administrators thought it was "jargon" and some seemed to anticipate negative community reaction to such a message.

5. Positioning a coordinated school health program as unique by saying that it is the *only* approach to addressing multiple health threats was not credible to the target audiences and was viewed as promising too much. While some teachers, in particular, were strong proponents of the comprehensive or coordinated approach and viewed it as the foundation of a successful school, others—and many administrators—viewed it as one component of strengthening a school, not a complete solution.

6. The phrase *comprehensive school health programs* conjured up "expensive" and "daunting." This may be because the word *programs* is interpreted as a separate line-item on a budget. Given the negative reaction to *comprehensive school health programs*, the phrase *a coordinated approach to school health* may be a better term to use.

Based on the results of the research, the final message concepts were as follows. The first two are for teachers and administrators; the second two are for parents.

1. There's a lot of concern these days about absenteeism, drop-out rates, and discipline problems in our schools. But did you know a lot of these problems are health related? A coordinated approach to school health is about more than keeping kids healthy. It's about improving schools by supporting students' capacity to learn.

2. Keeping kids healthy today means focusing on the complete child, from drug and alcohol use to sexuality and stress. A coordinated approach to school health gives students the essential information and practical skills they need so they can deal with the problems they face in and out of school.

3. Being smart isn't all it takes to succeed in today's world. Kids also need to make smart decisions about sex, alcohol, tobacco, drugs, nutrition, and fitness. School health programs help students learn how to make the right choices—for life.

4. For today's kids to succeed, they need to learn to read, write, and understand math. But how much can they learn if they're using alcohol, tobacco, and other drugs; suffering from stress; or have a baby? A coordinated approach to school health gives kids practical skill to deal with today's problems so they have a better chance for success in and out of school.

■ DEVELOPING AND TESTING INITIAL MATERIALS

The initial materials were designed to broaden target audience members' definition of school health and provide them with information to use when talking with others to build support for a coordinated approach. They used the message concepts above to highlight the importance of changing school health and providing relevant benefits for doing so. The materials included two booklets that illustrated a coordinated approach to school health (one for administrators and teachers and one for parents), a slide presentation, talking points, and a series of questions and answers about school health.

The administrators, teachers, and parents who reviewed the materials thought they were attractive but were pessimistic about being able to make changes and wanted specific advice about how to build support. In addition, they suggested adding case studies and repackaging the information to reduce impressions of coordinated school health as complex and overwhelming.

■ DEVELOPING AND TESTING REVISED MATERIALS

The project team refined the content of the materials and the way in which they were packaged, turning to the literature on diffusing innovations in organizational settings and social cognitive theory (see Chapter 18) for guidance on addressing the concerns raised by target audience members.

In refining the materials, the goal was to emphasize that schools can work toward a coordinated approach, and that a coordinated approach will reinforce the role of the family. The positioning was chosen to increase perceptions that the innovation (a coordinated approach to school health) could be compatible with existing practices and values and could be implemented piecemeal—and, if necessary, discontinued—while decreasing perceptions that it had to be complex and/or resource intensive, and, consequently, was risky to attempt.

The final materials are a school health starter kit (basically a community action kit), a PowerPoint slide presentation, two posters, assessment resources, case studies, and a booklet to give guidance to the chief state school officers and health officials and their staffs on how to use the other materials. The starter kit is packaged as a foldout spiral-bound kit with pockets on each side. Graduated page sizes are used for each section (i.e., the pages get progressively wider) to create a "hyperlink" feel and ensure easy access to relevant information. The writing style (light and a bit whimsical) and packaging work together to reduce the impression that the subject is overwhelming. The kit incorporates many of the types of messages recommended by Maibach and Cotton (1995) in their staged social cognitive approach to message design to be described in Chapter 12. Specifically, the materials

1. *Identify how to effectively overcome barriers to change and encourage people to identify and plan solutions to the obstacles they are most likely to face.* The kit outlines a step-by-step approach to analyzing the current environment, including ways to identify barriers to make changes. It includes questions and answers to prepare people for the objections they are likely to face as they try to build support and a worksheet to help analyze how receptive their environment is to change. Items on the worksheet were drawn from a review of the diffusion of innovations literature (Academy for Educational Development, 1996).

2. *Encourage people to set specific goals and instruct them on appropriate ways to set incremental goals.* The kit encourages people to start slowly (rather than trying to change everything at once) and includes a worksheet they can use to identify needed changes and then prioritize them based on how easy or difficult the changes will be to accomplish. Items on the worksheet operationalize many of the innovation characteristics that are presented in **Table 18-2** in Chapter 18.

3. *Bolster self-efficacy to cope with specific situations that people are likely to encounter in their change efforts.* Formative research indicated that people did not know where or how to start building support for a coordinated approach to school health and consequently had no confidence in their ability to do so. The materials outline an approach that is intended to guide people through the initial steps of building support, allowing them to build their self-efficacy as they go along. Many resources (such as the previously mentioned worksheets, as well as sample letters to the editor, press releases, and a listing of additional sources of information) are included.

4. *Model appropriate behaviors* through a series of case studies from schools, districts, and states that have implemented changes consistent with a coordinated approach to health.

References

Academy for Educational Development. (1996). *Developing the marketing plan: Insights from the diffusion of innovations literature.* Guidelines Diffusion Project. Washington, DC: Author.

Maibach, E.W., & Cotton, D. (1995). Moving people to behavior change: A staged social cognitive approach to message design. In E. Maibach & R.L. Parrott (Eds.), *Designing health messages: Approaches from communication theory and public health practice* (pp. 41–64). Thousand Oaks, CA: Sage.

11-B

Sample Recruitment Screener

Interviewer: _____

Date: _____

Time: _____

Hello, My name is _____ from _____,
a research company in _____. We're putting together a
series of small discussion groups with school administrators, teachers, and
parents from certain school districts. The discussions will focus on health
programs in area schools. The groups are being held for the purpose of
opinion research only. I'd like to ask you a couple of questions.

1. How supportive would you say you are of having health programs
   in schools?

   _____ Very supportive   (CONTINUE. ASK Q2.)

   _____ Somewhat supportive   (CONTINUE. ASK Q2.)

   _____ Not very supportive   (THANK AND TERMINATE.)

2. What is your position in or relationship to the school?

   _____ Teacher   (CONTINUE. ASK Q3.)

   _____ Administrator   (CONTINUE. ASK Q5.)

   _____ Parent   (CONTINUE. ASK Q8.)

   _____ None of the above   (THANK AND TERMINATE.)

3. What grade(s) do you teach presently?
   (RECRUIT A GOOD MIX OF GRADE LEVELS.)

   _____ K through 6th grades   (CONTINUE. ASK Q4.)

   _____ 7th through 8th grades   (CONTINUE. ASK Q4.)

   _____ 9th through 12 grades   (CONTINUE. ASK Q4.)

Courtesy of The Academy for Educational Development, Washington, D.C.

4. What courses do you teach?

_____ Health education/programs only

_____ Health education and physical education

_____ Some health education and some other
(specify: _____)

_____ Other (specify: _____)

GO TO TEACHER INVITATION

5. At which school are you employed? _____

(CHECK QUOTAS. CANNOT HAVE TWO ADMINISTRATIORS
FROM SAME SCHOOL.)

6. What grade levels are you involved with in your present position?

_____ K through 6th grades   (CONTINUE. ASK Q7.)

_____ 7th through 8th grades   (CONTINUE. ASK Q7.)

_____ 9th through 12 grades   (CONTINUE. ASK Q7.)

7. What is your administrative position? (DO NOT READ)

_____ Superintendent

_____ Principal

_____ Vice Principal

_____ Dean

_____ School nurse/health provider

_____ Curriculum coordinator

GO TO ADMINISTRATOR INVITATION.

8. Do you have any children who are currently attending school in
this district?

_____ Yes   (CONTINUE.)

_____ No   (THANK AND TERMINATE.)

9. What grade(s) is/are your child(ren) in currently?

_____ K through 6th grades   (CONTINUE.)

_____ 7th through 8th grades   (CONTINUE.)

_____ 9th through 12 grades   (CONTINUE.)

10. Which school(s) does/do your child(ren) attend?

_____

(CHECK QUOTAS. CANNOT HAVE TWO PARENTS OF KIDS
IN THE SAME GRADE FROM THE SAME SCHOOL.)

11. In what type of school activities do you participate?

_____ PTA/PTO officer   (GO TO PARENT INVITATION.)

_____ PTA/PTO member   (GO TO PARENT INVITATION.)

_____ Teacher's aid/   (GO TO PARENT INVITATION.)
assistant

_____ Volunteer at
school functions   (GO TO PARENT INVITATION.)

_____ Attend school   (GO TO PARENT INVITATION.)
board meetings

_____ Other   (GO TO PARENT INVITATION.)
(Specify: _____)

_____ None   (THANK AND TERMINATE.)

INVITATION

Okay, that's all the questions we have for you. We would like to invite you to participate in our discussion group. The group will take place at _____ (time) on _____ (day of week and date). The discussion will take about an hour and a half. For helping us with this research, each participant will receive _____.

The discussion groups will be held at: (NAME, ADDRESS, & TELEPHONE NUMBER OF FACILITY)

We will send you a letter confirming the date and location of the group. Could I please have your name and address?

Name: _____

Address: _____

City: _____ State: _____ ZIP: _____

We will call you a day or so before the group to confirm the time. What is the best time to reach you? What is the best telephone number to reach you at that time? Is there another time and number we can try if we miss you?

Time: _____

Telephone: _____

2nd time: _____

2nd telephone: _____

If anything comes up and you have to cancel, please give us a call at: _____. Because it is such a small group, it is important that you let us know if we will need to replace you. You can call anytime, and if we are not here, please leave a message. Thank you.

11-C

Sample Focus Group Moderator's Guide

DEVELOPING MESSAGES TO SUPPORT COMPREHENSIVE SCHOOL HEALTH PROGRAMS (CSHP)

FOCUS GROUPS WITH PARENTS: MODERATOR'S GUIDE

I. WARM-UP, EXPLANATIONS, AND INTRODUCTIONS (10 minutes)

   A. Introduction and Purpose

      1. Good afternoon/evening. My name is _____, and I will be facilitating our discussion tonight. We're here to talk about school health.

      2. Thanks for joining us. All of your comments-both positive and negative—are important.

      3. There are no right or wrong answers, and it's important that I hear what everyone thinks. So please speak up, even if you disagree with someone else.

   B. Procedure

      1. Our discussion tonight will be audiotaped so that I don't lose any of your comments. I'll use the tapes to write a report summarizing what was said. However, the report will not identify any of you by name.

      2. (IF APPROPRIATE:) Behind me is a one-way mirror. Some people who are interested in what you have to say may be sitting behind the glass on and off during our discussion. They aren't in the same room with us because they can be distracting.

      3. This is a group discussion, so please don't wait for me to call on you. Please speak one at a time so the tape recorder can pick up everything.

Courtesy of The Academy for Educational Development, Washington, D.C.

4. We have many topics to discuss in a very limited amount of time, so at times I may change the subject or move ahead. I'll try to come back to earlier points at the end of our session if there's time.

C. Self-Introductions
Let's do a quick round of introductions. Please tell us your name, how many children you have, and what grades they're in.

II. DEFINITION OF SCHOOL HEALTH PROGRAMS
(20 minutes)

A. Role of Schools Vis-A-Vis Health

1. Name THE (one) biggest health problem facing students at your child's school today.
2. What role do you think most OTHER *parents* think the school should play relative to health? Do you think the role of a school changes relative to their grade level?
3. How do you think your children's health affects their performance at school? Do you link your children's health to school performance?

B. Think for a minute about the ideal school. What is included in its approach to health? (PROBE: Are there any other components? What about health education? Physical education? Health services? Food service? Counseling? School environment (e.g., caring/supportive, tobacco-free, food sold, violence, safety, indoor air quality)? School, community, or parent/family partnerships? Faculty and staff wellness programs?)

C. All of the components on this list are referred to as a comprehensive or coordinated school health program. (SHOW LIST ON EASEL.) How many of you have children in schools that have all or most of these components?

1. What ones does your school do the best job on? What needs improvement?
2. Of these, which are the most important?
3. Which is the least important?

III. BENEFITS OF AND BARRIERS TO CSHP (20 minutes)

    A. Benefits of CSHP

        1. What do you see as the *major benefits* of an approach like the one on the list?
PROBE: Would you expect to see an impact on classroom performance? Behavior? Attendance?

        2. How about those of you whose children go to schools that use a comprehensive approach? What do you find are the major benefits? (PROBE: What impact, if any, have you seen on academic performance? Behavior? Student health? Interest in health? Has it made a difference in the community? For example, has the interaction between the school and the community changed? In what way?)

    B. Drawbacks

        1. For those of you whose children come from schools without a comprehensive approach, what do you see as the *potential drawbacks* to such an approach?

        2. How about those of you who have programs like we described earlier in place? What drawbacks have you encountered?

IV. STARTING A CSHP (15 minutes)

    A. For those of you whose child attends a school with a comprehensive or coordinated approach in place: Did you help to get your program started? Who asked for your help?

        1. Who are the biggest supporters of the current program? How is support demonstrated?

        2. How about the biggest opponents of the current program? How is opposition demonstrated—and how did you address the opposition?

    B. For those of you who *do not* have a comprehensive approach in place: What are the first changes you would try to make? Why would you start there?

    C. For all of you: There are a variety of steps people can take to foster support for comprehensive school health programs. What actions do you think parents could take? (PROBE: Speak to health teacher? Speak to a principal or school board member? Invite to a meeting or spend time with a knowledgeable school district or state official who supports comprehensive or coordinated health programs to learn what the approach would entail? Discuss at a PTA/PTO meeting?)

V.   MESSAGE CONCEPTS (25 minutes)

We're in the process of developing messages that could be used to promote comprehensive school health programs. I'd like to run a couple of messages by you and see what you think. It's important for you to know that I didn't develop these messages.

A.   READ EACH MESSAGE AS YOU PASS THEM OUT TO PARTICIPANTS. ASK:

1. What comes to mind when you hear this message?
2. Now please number the messages so they are ranked from most compelling to least compelling to you. Use a "1" to indicate most compelling, a "2" to indicate next most compelling, etc.

B.   READ FIRST MESSAGE. ASK HOW MANY PUT IT ON TOP OF STACK, PUT IT SECOND, PUT IT LAST. RECORD ON EASEL BOARD. CONTINUE FOR ALL MESSAGES. ASK FOLLOWING QUESTIONS AS APPROPRIATE FOR EACH MESSAGE.

1. For those of you who put (READ MESSAGE) in first or second place, what was appealing to you about it?
2. Was there anything you disliked about this message? Again, I didn't write these, so please be honest.
3. For those of you who rated this message last, what did you dislike?
4. Have we missed something? Is there something you could think of that would present a stronger, more compelling reason to support CSHP?

VI.   MATERIALS (15 minutes)

A.   What do you usually want to know about health at school? How do you usually find out?

1. Are there any materials that you get from your children's schools that describe their schools' approach to health? Could you describe these materials to me? How helpful are they?
2. Are there any materials that you would like to have, but don't? What would they be?

VII.   CLOSING

A.   That's the end of my questions. Do you have any final comments?

B.   On behalf of the Council of Chief State School Officers and the Association of State and Territorial Health Officials, I'd like to thank you for participating in our discussion today. Your input was extremely valuable. Have a nice day.

11-D

Sample Central-Site Interview Questionnaire

John Killpack and Associates
Public Service Advertising—
Mall Intercept Test

Prepared May 3, 1996

Date: _____
ID: _____
INTERVIEWER: _____
LOCATION: _____

Hello, I'm (NAME) from (FIELD SERVICE). We're conducting a short study with people in the mall today. Do you have a few minutes to answer some questions?

1. What is your age?
   Under 50 1   [THANK AND TERMINATE.]
   50–64 . . . . .2 [CONTINUE—50% OF SAMPLE.]
   65 or older . . . . .3 [CONTINUE—50% OF SAMPLE.]
   Refused 9   [THANK AND TERMINATE.]

2. RECORD GENDER OF RESPONDENT.
   Female 1   [50% OF SAMPLE]
   Male 2   [50% OF SAMPLE]

I'd like to show you some advertisements that have been produced as a public service and get your reaction to them. I'm not trying to sell you anything. As a way of thanking you for your participation, we'll give you $3. Would you please come with me to our viewing room?

Source: Reprinted with permission. Copyright 1996, American Association of Retired Persons.

ROTATE ORDER (CIRCLE ORDER USED):

1 — "Mr. McBride," "Mrs. Miller," 800 number, print
2 — "Mrs. Miller," "Mr. McBride," 800 number, print
3 — Print, "Mr. McBride," "Mrs. Miller," 800 number
4 — Print, "Mrs. Miller," "Mr. McBride," 800 number

TELEVISION ADS

I'd like to show you the first television ad and then ask you a few questions about it.

[SHOW AD.]

I didn't have anything to do with creating the ad, so please be honest in your answers—you don't have to worry about hurting my feelings.

	First mention (Circle only one)	All other mentions (Circle all that apply)
1. What was the main idea the ad was trying to get across? Anything else?		
Fraudulent telemarketers are criminals.	1	1
You can be robbed by a telemarketer.	2	2
Telemarketers who send couriers are fraudulent.	3	3
Prize companies who ask for credit card numbers are fraudulent.	4	4
Other	5	5
Don't know.	8	8
2. What is the ad asking you to do?		
Don't fall for a telephone line.	1	1
Be wary/suspicious of telemarketers.	2	2
Hang up on telemarketers.	3	3
Don't give money to couriers for telemarketers.	4	4
Don't give credit card number out.	5	5
Avoid telephone contests.	6	6
Avoid investment opportunities over the phone.	7	7
Other	8	8
Don't know	9	9

	First mention (Circle only one)	All other mentions (Circle all that apply)
3. What, if anything, about the ad did you especially like? Anything else?		
Everything	1	1
Nothing	2	2
Liked message in general	3	3
New information	4	4
I could relate to ad	5	5
Ad/content was realistic	6	6
Words on screen	7	7
Other	8	8
Don't know	9	9
4. What, if anything, abut the ad did you especially dislike? Anything else?		
Everything	1	1
Nothing	2	2
Message was difficult to follow/understand	3	3
Voices were hard to understand	4	4
Type was hard to read	5	5
Words on screen went too fast	6	6
Words on screen went too slowly	7	7
I could not relate to ad	8	8
Ad/content was not realistic	9	9
Other (specify: _____)	10	10
Don't know	11	11
5. Was there anything confusing or hard to understand? Anything else?		
Nothing	1	1
Don't understand what makes caller/telemarketer a criminal	2	2
Didn't know telemarketers were criminals	3	3
Don't know what's wrong with asking for credit card	4	4
Didn't know sending a courier was wrong	5	5
Didn't understand the "telephone line" pun	6	6
Type was hard to read.	7	7
Hard to read and listen at the same time	8	8
Other (specify: _____)	9	9
Don't know	10	10

6. Which of the following statements best describes what the ad way saying:
   [READ STATEMENTS AND SHOW SCALE.]

   ROTATE:

   All telemarketers are fraudulent. 1
   Some telemarketers are fraudulent. 2
   Don't know [DON'T READ]. 8

7. What does "Don't fall for a telephone line" mean to you?

   Nothing. 1
   Don't be taken in by or lose money to fraudulent
       telemarketers/con artists 2
   Don't trip over the telephone cord 3
   Other 4
   Don't know 8

8. Who was the sponsor of the ad?

   AARP/American Association of Retired Persons 1
   Other 2
   Don't know 3
   Refused 9

9. I'm going to read you a set of statements describing the ad you just saw. For each statement, please tell me whether you strongly agree, agree, neither agree nor disagree, disagree, or strongly disagree with the statement.
   [READ STATEMENTS AND SHOW SCALE.]

   ROTATE:

	Strongly Agree	Agree	Neither Agree nor Disagree	Disagree	Strongly Disagree
The ad was believable.	1	2	3	4	5
The ad was scary.	1	2	3	4	5
The words were hard to read.	1	2	3	4	5
The ad was interesting.	1	2	3	4	5
I learned something from the ad.	1	2	3	4	5
The message was relevant to me.	1	2	3	4	5

10. Is this ad offensive to anyone?

   Yes 1
   No. 2
   Don't know 8

IF 'YES' TO Q. 10:

10a. Who?

```
Everyone.........................................1
Legitimate telemarketers.........................2
Me...............................................3
Other (Specify: _____) ...............4
Don't know.......................................8
```

PRINT ADS

These are ads that might appear in a newspaper or magazine. They are in the process of being developed, so the illustrations aren't final yet and all of the text hasn't been written.

[PLACE ADS IN FRONT OF RESPONDENT.]

1. Please pick up the ad you would be most likely to look at. [INDICATE WHICH AD RESPONDENT PICKED UP; REMOVE OTHER ADS.]

```
A................................................1
B................................................2
C................................................3
```

2. What interested you in this ad? Anything else?

```
Picture/drawing..................................1
Headline.........................................2
Particular information...........................3
Other (specify: _____) ...............4
Don't know.......................................8
```

3. What is the ad asking you to do?

	First mention (Circle only one)	All other mentions (Circle all that apply)
Don't fall for a telephone line.	1	2
Be wary/suspicious of telemarketers.	2	2
Hang up on telemarketers.	3	3
Get the caller's telephone number.	4	4
Call the National Fraud Information Center/the 800 number.	5	5
Other (specify: _____)	6	6
Don't know	8	8

	First mention (Circle only one)	All other mentions (Circle all that apply)

4. [PUT OTHER ADS BACK OUT.] Looking at all of the ads, what, if anything, is confusing or hard to understand? Anything else?

Nothing	1	1
Don't understand what makes caller/telemarketer a criminal	2	2
Didn't know telemarketers were criminals	3	3
Didn't understand "telephone line" pun	4	4
Type was hard to read	5	5
Other	6	6
Don't know	8	8

5. What, if anything, is hard to believe? Anything else?

Nothing	1	1
Telemarketers are fraudulent.	2	2
Fraudulent telemarketers are criminals.	3	3
That there are so many fraudulent telemarketers	4	4
Content is not realistic.	5	5
Other	6	6
Don't know	8	8

6. Which of the following statements best describes what the ads are saying:
   [READ STATEMENTS AND SHOW SCALE.]

   ROTATE:

   All telemarketers are fraudulent. 1
   Some telemarketers are fraudulent. 2
   Don't know [DON'T READ.] 3

7. Are these ads offensive to anyone?

   Yes 1
   No. 2
   Don't know 3

   IF "YES" TO Q.7:

7a. Who?

   Everyone 1
   Legitimate telemarketers 2
   Me 3
   Other (specify: _____) 4
   Don't know 8

8. How likely would you be to call the 800 number in the ad if you get a suspicious telemarketing call? Would you say . . . [READ SCALE.]

Very likely 1
Somewhat likely 2
Not very likely 3
Not at all likely 4
Don't know [DO NOT READ.] 8

DEMOGRAPHICS

These last few questions are for statistical purposes only.

1. What is your marital status?

Married 1
Divorced/separated/Widowed 2
Single (never married) 3
Refused 8

2. Within the past year, about how many times have you responded to offers from organizations you were previously unfamiliar with by sending money or giving your credit card number to purchase something, enter a contest, make an investment, or donate to a charity?

Enter number . . . . _____
Don't know 8

3. Please stop me at the range that includes your annual household income:

Less than $15,000 1
$15,000-$25,000 2
$26,000-$35,000 3
$36,000-$50,000 4
$51,000-$75,000 5
More than $75,000 6
Refused [DO NOT READ.] 8

4. Of the following, which best describes your race/ethnicity? Are you: [READ SCALE.]

African-American 1
Caucasian 2
Hispanic 3
Asian 4
Other 5
Refused [DO NOT READ.] 8

CHAPTER

12

Framing and Delivering the Message: Crafting Communication Strategies

The starting point for effective communications is developing a strong communication strategy. The communication strategy describes how the behavior or issue will be framed and positioned in the minds of target audience members. It describes the target audience(s), the action they should take and how they will benefit, and how to reach them with messages. It is based on a thorough understanding of the audience and their wants, needs, and values coupled with knowledge of the types of appeals likely to work in a given situation. Once a communication strategy has been developed, message concepts are developed to present that positioning to the audience and assess whether it is believable, compelling, and relevant. In addition to determining how to best communicate with an audience about taking a specific action, communication strategies are a cornerstone of building and maintaining a relationship with audiences over time.

People are exposed to a barrage of health information every day. They wake up and hear it on the radio or TV, read it in newspapers or magazines, experience it on the Internet, see it when they are commuting to work, school, or other destinations, and hear more from friends, family members, and health care providers. Many feel overwhelmed by all of the often–conflicting advice and perspectives.

Communication plays a major role in many public health marketing efforts. Communication can be used to inform, educate, and persuade. It can be used to model simple behaviors or reinforce existing ones. It can call on cultural symbols and icons to frame an issue—or an organization, or public health itself—in a variety of ways. The challenge is to develop and implement communication campaigns that address health behavior and policy objectives by breaking through the clutter and reaching target populations with persuasive, actionable messages that convey a consistent identity and are scientifically sound but audience oriented. This chapter outlines a process for crafting a communication strategy and developing message concepts based on it. The strategy provides the foundation for effective communications and relationships with audiences by spelling out who the target audience is, what they should do and how they will benefit, and how to reach them. The message concepts translate the strategy into statements that are presented to members of the intended audience—and assessed to determine whether they are believable, relevant, and compelling.

■ THE COMMUNICATION STRATEGY

A communication strategy frames the issue in a particular way and thus positions the social change in the audience's mind. It must address the following points:

1. Target audience: The people the communication should reach
2. Action: What they should *do* after exposure to the communication
3. Key benefit: What they will gain that they value by taking the action
4. Support: How they will be convinced that they will receive the benefit
5. Openings: When and how the audience can best be reached with the communication
6. Image: The tone and personality conveyed by the communication

The audience member might be a "member of the public," a patient, a health professional, a policy maker, a voter, a reporter, or some other type of individual.

The activities conducted to develop an overall strategic plan (described in Chapter 10) start the development of a solid communication strategy. However, target audiences for various communications may have to be refined and/or may require separate communication strategies depending on the action they should take as a result of exposure to the communication.

The communication strategies developed for public health efforts include the same components as their commercial sector counterparts. The consumer-based health communications (CHC) process outlined by Sutton, Balch, and Lefebvre (1995) is an excellent example of modifying the commercial communication strategy development framework specifically to the needs of public health practitioners. It is used as the basis for the approach outlined here.

The Role of Theory

As with development of the overall intervention, the development of communication strategies should be guided by the theories or models of how change is expected to occur. For example, Maibach and Cotton (1995) developed what they term a "staged social cognitive approach to message design," in which they use the concepts of social cognitive theory to determine the most appropriate types of messages for people in each of the transtheoretical model's stages of change. They recommend the following types of messages to help people move from one stage to the next.

For people in precontemplation (no intention to change behavior in foreseeable future; unaware of risk, will not acknowledge risk, or some other reason):

- Enhance knowledge of and expectations about the consequences—good or bad—of the risk behavior.
- Personalize the risk.
- Emphasize the benefits of the new behavior and encourage a reevaluation of the costs and benefits (or outcome expectancies) that includes the new benefits.

For people in contemplation (considering the need to change behavior but with no specific plan):

- Encourage gaining experience with the new behavior (e.g., through trying the new behavior or trying to refrain from the risk behavior).
- Continue promoting new expectations of positive consequences and reinforce existing positive expectations.
- Consider disputing commonly believed but untrue negative consequences and suggesting ways to minimize bona fide negative consequences, though it is typically easier to promote advantages than to challenge perceived disadvantages.
- Enhance self-efficacy by identifying how to effectively overcome barriers to change.

For people in preparation (making decision to change behavior; may try behavior):

- Encourage people to restructure their environments—and instruct them on how to do so—so that important cues for practicing the new behavior are obvious and supported socially.
- Encourage people to identify and plan solutions to the relevant obstacles they are most likely to face.

- Help people to maintain their motivation by encouraging them to set a long-term goal and instructing them on appropriate ways to set short-term goals to keep them progressing to the long-term goal.
- Increase self-efficacy to cope with specific situations and other obstacles that people are likely to encounter in their change efforts.
- Model social reinforcement of appropriate behaviors.

For people in action (beginning to perform the behavior consistently):

- Encourage refining skills, especially those that will help avoid relapse and that allow productive coping with setbacks to prevent full relapse.
- Bolster self-efficacy for dealing with new obstacles and setbacks in the behavior change process.
- Encourage people to feel good about themselves when they make progress, especially in the face of temptation.
- Make explicit or reiterate the long-term benefits of the behavior change.

Chapter 18 provides introductions to a number of theories often used in developing communication strategies; the appendix to that chapter includes an example of using theory to guide development of message concepts and compares the resulting concepts to some that were developed without a theoretical base.

Strategic Questions

Crafting a communication strategy should begin with collecting data to answer most or all of the questions shown in **Exhibit 12-1**. Much of this information will have been collected when the intervention's strategic plan was prepared, or, if the plan and communication strategy are being developed simultaneously, can also be used for it. The answers to all of the strategic questions must fit together; changing one answer often necessitates changing others. Each of the questions is discussed in more detail below. As answers are developed, consideration should be given to the issues raised in the Message Content and Construction section at the end of this chapter.

Exhibit 12-1   Questions To Guide Communication Strategy Development

- Who should be the target audience, and what are they like?
- What is the action they should take—and what are they doing now?
- What are the barriers that stand between the audience and the action?
- What is the benefit to the audience of engaging in the action?
- What is the support for that benefit—what will make it credible to the audience?
- What are the best openings for reaching the audience—and are the channels available appropriate for conveying the message?
- What image should communications convey?

Who Should Be the Target Audience, and What Are They Like?

While many public health agencies have a mandate to serve the public, decisions to target "the general population" do not make for good communications. As Sutton and colleagues (1995) noted, any communication will appeal to some groups more effectively than others, based on executional details (i.e. language used, type of people portrayed, color, music, etc.) if nothing else. It is a far better use of resources to take a proactive approach, carefully identifying the most appropriate audience(s) and then developing communications specifically to address their needs, perceptions, and values. For example, for initiatives seeking to bring about policy change, there are usually at least three audiences: policy makers, some segment of the public, and members of the media. Chapters 9 and 10 introduced audience segmentation as a tool for selecting audiences, and Chapter 11 provides information on particular segmentation approaches. Some public health initiatives may communicate with segments in each of the three audiences; others may restrict their efforts to one or two, depending on how the initiative is expected to work. The promotion strategy developed as part of the strategic plan (Chapter 10) should outline overall audiences, but additional segmentation may be required in some instances for communication efforts.

Once each audience has been identified, communication planners should get to know its members. Thinking of the audience as one person, rather than as a group, is useful and leads to more focused, relevant communications. One way to do this is to write a profile of the person based on formative research. Some creative teams go as far as drawing a picture of a typical audience member. Demographic characteristics (age, marital status, presence of children, ethnicity, political leanings, etc.), are just a starting point. "What's important to this person? What are his or her feelings, attitudes, and beliefs about the behavior change and its benefits and barriers? What can motivate this person to do something different?" (Sutton et al., 1995, p. 728).

What Is the Action They Should Take—and What Are They Doing Now?

To persuade audience members to take a particular action, communication planners must understand exactly what they are willing and able to do. Until we know what people are doing now, we do not know what we are asking them to change—and how great a change we are asking them to make. The behavior analyses conducted as part of strategic planning (Chapter 10) may provide most of the needed information, though sometimes communication efforts focus on a more narrow audience or slice of time and thus behavior analyses may need to be refined. For example, to address the child safety restraint problem discussed in Chapter 10, the initial action parents and caregivers were asked to take would be related to properly installing care seats with the challenging seat-belt installation systems. Later, when new technology was available, the action might be modified, for example to encourage parents and caregivers to use the new systems if possible.

Selecting an action is a critical—and difficult—decision to make. Planners should strive to avoid the trap of focusing on a very narrow audience and persuading them to make a complicated behavior change. This sometimes happens with individual health behaviors because there is usually a group of people far from the behavior and therefore most "in need." Often a better strategy—from the viewpoint of both communication success and change in health status—is to address the easier changes first. Targeting the group most willing or able to make the change often leads to two accomplishments: First, the population makes progress toward the public health objective. Second, as that group makes the change, members of it may begin communicating about it through their social networks, thereby directly encouraging adoption of the change by others and creating and climate in which others are more willing to (and indeed may feel pressure to) make changes.

What Are the Obstacles that Stand between the Audience and the Action?

Although this question isn't explicitly addressed in many communication strategy frameworks (see, for example, Sutton et al., 1995; Roman, Maas, and Nisenhotlz, 2003), we have included it here because knowing what real or perceived barriers stand in the way of taking action is an invaluable aid to developing communication strategies. Understanding barriers helps communication planners select an action audiences are most likely to take and determine whether communications need to implicitly or explicitly remove or help audiences overcome or circumvent specific barriers. Chapter 10 discusses identifying physical, social, and economic barriers. It also discusses how the value associated with certain costs and benefits may change depending on whether a person is choosing a behavior right now or at some point in the future, and provides a framework for understanding how these values change.

For public health policies and promoting public health as an institution, key to understanding obstacles is identifying how the issue is currently being framed on the public agenda. This can be accomplished by analyzing media coverage of the issue and preparing a framing memo that outlines the various ways the issue has been positioned, or framed, by the media. This process was described in Chapter 10; examples are provided in Chapter 10 and later in this chapter.

What Is the Benefit to the Audience of Taking the Action?

This is a crucial point and an area in which many communication planners make mistakes. The challenge is to promise a benefit that outweighs the costs the audience associates with the action and the benefits the audience might obtain from any alternative behavior. As we have discussed elsewhere in this volume, immediate, high-probability benefits are most compelling, especially those that evoke one of a person's core values. Good health generally is neither an immediate, high-high probability benefit nor a core value.

For example, from a public health standpoint, the major benefit of stopping smoking is decreased risk of developing heart disease, various cancers, and a host of other diseases. But from the standpoint of the person deciding whether to try to quit, "decreased risk" is not a high probability, and all of these benefits are off in an uncertain future. The major immediate (and therefore more highly valued when trying to make the change) benefit may be ceasing to cough in the morning or no longer smelling like smoke all the time. Policy makers may not be motivated by funding programs that mostly benefit the not-politically-powerful poor, or by a possible improvement in the public's health that may not be realized for decades—but they usually do want to be perceived as contributing to their community's or the nation's economic or physical security.

The challenge is to identify and focus on one key benefit from the myriad possibilities. Often people have a number of motivations for engaging in a particular behavior. How do you pick one? As we discussed in Chapter 3, understanding the needs and values underlying the current and desired behaviors is critical. Often the greatest need or strongest value provides the most meaningful, compelling benefit. Getting at those basic values can be accomplished in a number of ways. The laddering exercises discussed in Chapter 18, in which qualitative research participants are asked why particular attributes are important, and then why their response is important, are useful. Another approach that can be used in qualitative or quantitative settings is to ask participants to rate a set of adjectives in terms of how well each describes themselves, and then to rate how well each describes people who engage in the desired behavior. What they do—and don't—put in each list speaks volumes about the values they are looking for, and associate, with each behavior. The Rokeach Value Survey (Rokeach, 1973) is an example of a scale often used to identify values important to a target audience segment. It is important to note that the benefit is "promised" in communications. Often it is never explicitly stated. Rather, it is a conclusion that people draw after exposure to the communication. Sutton and colleagues (1995) recommended using the following sentence to link desired and current behavior with a benefit:

"If I (action) instead of (current behavior), I will (benefit)."

For example, for the early 5 A Day media campaign the action-benefit statement was: "If I add two servings of fruits and vegetables the easy way instead of making it hard, then I will feel relieved and more in control of my life" (Lefebvre et al., 1995; Sutton et al., 1995). An action-benefit statement for California's anti-Proposition 188 campaign (discussed in Chapter 11) might have been: "If I oppose Proposition 188 instead of supporting it, I will keep Philip Morris from exerting control over my state." This approach is consistent with our discussion in Chapter 3 about positioning the new behavior as superior to the old by showing (implicitly) that maintaining the old behavior will conflict with basic needs and desires.

What Is the Support for That Benefit—What Will Make It Credible to the Audience?

The support convinces the audience that the benefit outweighs the obstacles. Support is provided through aspects of the message's execution. It can take many forms, such as hard data, demonstrations of how to perform the action, or demonstrations of the valued benefits to the action (e.g., a person feeling more in control after taking steps to improve eating habits). It can be emotional, factual, or both. Aspects of the execution that influence credibility, such as the degree to which models are like target audience members and how they look, talk, dress, and behave, as well as music, colors, background, design, typeface, and paper stock, can all support or detract from the promised benefit (Sutton et al., 1995). In the terms of the action-benefit statement introduced above, support is the "because" (Sutton et al., 1995).

> "If I (action) instead of (current behavior), I will (benefit) because (support)."

Signorielli (1993) criticized the antidrug "Just say no" campaign that ran in the United States in the 1980s, in part, because it lacked support:

> This campaign is problematic because it fails to take the basic principles of adolescent psychology and functioning into consideration. This campaign preaches and tells young people (and the rest of society for that matter) what to do. It does not provide information about why or even how teens, in the face of strong (or not so strong) peer pressure, can "just say no." (p. 155)

Public health communicators often are tempted to use scientific facts as support. They should proceed with caution. Hard data can work, provided they are understandable, relevant, and believable to the target audience. However, practitioners should bear in mind that many members of the public place little credence in scientific data. They recall too many instances when those data later changed or were debunked by yet another new study. In addition, people often do not understand science, particularly intangible concepts such as relative risk, and so personal decisions may be based on faulty reasoning (National Cancer Institute, 1989). Furthermore, it can be difficult for hard data to compete with an emotional appeal to core human values. This problem is illustrated in the case study on affirmative action presented later in this chapter.

What Are the Best Openings for Reaching the Audience—and Are the Channels Available Appropriate for Conveying the Message?

First, planners must determine the times, places, and situations when the audience will be most attentive to, and able to act on, the message. Then they must assess (1) whether the message lends itself to delivery via the channels that can be used to reach that time and place, and (2) whether the program has access to or can reasonably afford those channels.

For example, most mass media are best suited to providing simple information. With the exception of print media and some interactive Internet applications, they cannot be used effectively to convey complex information—and cannot take the place of one-on-one education and monitoring. Used alone, they can induce behavior change only under limited circumstances. However, they can frame a public health issue, raise awareness of a behavior change, provide cost-effective support and reinforcement for the change, and stimulate discussions of more complex information in the appropriate setting. Chapter 15 includes a discussion of some of the pros and cons of various types of mass media. Bellicha and McGrath (1990) provide examples of how mass media can be put to effective use within a larger social change initiative. They discuss how mass media are used to help educate patients, health professionals, and the public about high blood pressure and cholesterol as part of efforts to reduce morbidity and mortality caused by heart disease.

Thorough target audience research is critical to identifying the best openings. The ideal opening allows the target audience to hear or see the message and immediately take the action. A useful approach is for researchers to try to walk through a day in the audience's shoes. When would they be most receptive to and most able to act on messages about the behavior? "Times" may be parts of the day, week, or year. Or they could be wake-up time, exercise time, mealtime, commuting time, or office time. "Situations" may be times when a target is thinking about the benefit ("How can I make a positive impact?" "How can I make my community a better place to live?" "What am I going to have for dinner tonight?").

Once planners identify the best openings, they must assess the channels available to the intervention. Which are best at reaching these openings? Likewise, the channels must be assessed against the type of message. Which will be able to deliver the message in the most compelling, understandable manner? **Figure 12-1** depicts this balancing act. In general, a combination of intepersonal and mass communications channels leads to a more effective campaign (Backer, Rogers, and Sopory 1992).

If there is a conflict between the best channels for the message and the best channels for the audience, the preferable resolution is to examine the message and see if it can be modified to better suit the channels. Likewise, if there is a conflict between the channels that will best reach the audience and the channels an initiative can access, is there a way to access the other channels, perhaps through a partner or intermediary?

What Image Should Communications Convey?

Image is often thought of as the personality of the communication and the action. Image is what makes the communication speak to the target audience. It is also critical to developing brand identity and relationships

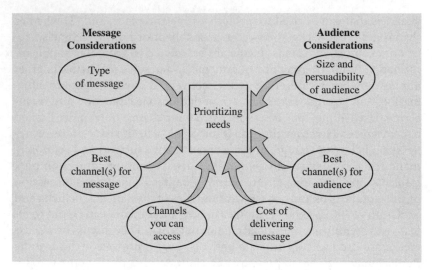

Figure 12-1 Balancing Message, Audience, and Resource Considerations to Select Channels

with audiences, and so should be carefully selected and then remain stable over time. Members must think the communication—and by extension, the action—is designed for "someone like them" or like the people they want to be. The goal is to portray the behavior as something target audience members can see themselves doing and something consistent with their core values. "All but the newest behaviors already have an image—a set of expectations and associated feelings among consumers. . . . Developing or changing an action's image involves creating a look and feel for the action that makes it accessible, inviting, distinctive, and compelling" (Sutton et al., 1995, p. 732).

Image is largely conveyed through how the communication is packaged. The symbols, metaphors, and visuals linked to the behavior or positioning of an issue convey image, as do the types of actors, language, and/or music used. Image taps into what has been termed our *cultural code,* or cultural frame of reference—the associations, expectations, and strategies of interpretation that are shared throughout a culture (Hirschman & Thompson, 1997).

> The cultural code provides a shared understanding of how to read the symbolic meaning embedded in mass media images. From early childhood, individuals are socialized into a deep knowledge of what meanings specific products embody. For example, in U.S. culture, pickup trucks are generally understood to represent rural, blue-collar transportation, whereas chauffeured limousines are seen as representing urban, affluent transportation. Most consumers within the culture are fluent in reading multiple forms of this code. (Hirschman & Thompson, 1997, p. 45)

Hence, communicators can use a variety of symbols and images as a sort of shorthand and, as Hirschman and Thompson (1997) noted, "can use shared understanding of the code to entice consumers to form certain types of interpretations" (p. 45). **Table 12-1** contains a scale that is used in commercial marketing to discern and compare brand personalities—"the set of human values associated with a brand" (Aaker, 1997, p. 347). The section "Using Branding Effectively" later in this chapter provides additional discussion relevant to communicating an image.

As we have discussed in previous chapters, symbols and metaphors are used extensively when public health issues are framed; identifying the exact symbols and images used to frame a public health issue is key to properly positioning the public health perspective. **Exhibit 12-2** illustrates how a framing memo can provide a useful framework to evaluate the metaphors, symbols, and images used to package the offer, as well as the benefits being offered to the target audience by proponents and opponents of a policy, the support used to back up the benefit, and the strength of the core values to which the promised benefit appeals.

Process for Communication Strategy Development

The following steps provide a systematic way of developing the communication strategy and obtaining buy-in from key stakeholders at the same time. The case studies included in Chapter 11 provide examples of the process in action. **Exhibit 12-3** summarizes some potential problems to watch for when developing communication strategies.

1. Develop preliminary answers to the communication strategy questions using the information gathered for the situation analysis. Four worksheets are provided at the end of this chapter to facilitate this process. (See Appendix 12-A.) For public health policy initiatives, the framing memo is a key part of developing a preliminary strategy. Preparing the memo was discussed in Chapter 10; examples are provided in **Exhibit 12-2** and Chapter 10.

2. Convene a workshop of experts in the public health issue (often internal and external to the sponsoring organization) and expert communication practitioners. There should be no more than about 10 people total, including internal and external people. During the workshop, work through the strategic questions and determine what additional information is needed to develop answers that work together.

3. Obtain additional information needed by locating additional sources of secondary research and/or conducting primary research. (See Chapter 11 for details.)

4. Revise the answers to the strategic questions based on research results.

5. Reconvene the group to review the answers. This is best done interactively and, ideally, in person.

Table 12-1 Brand Personality

Trait (item)	Facet	Dimension
Down-to-earth	Down-to-earth	Sincerity
Family-oriented		
Small-town		
Honest	Honest	
Sincere		
Real		
Wholesome	Wholesome	
Original		
Cheerful	Cheerful	
Sentimental		
Friendly		
Daring	Daring	Excitement
Trendy		
Exciting		
Spirited	Spirited	
Cool		
Young		
Imaginative	Imaginative	
Unique		
Up-to-date	Up-to-date	
Independent		
Contemporary		
Reliable	Reliable	Competence
Hard-working		
Secure		
Intelligent	Intelligent	
Technical		
Corporate		
Successful	Successful	
Leader		
Confident		
Upper-class	Upper-class	Sophistication
Glamorous		
Good looking		
Charming	Charming	
Feminine		
Smooth		
Outdoorsy	Outdoorsy	Ruggedness
Masculine		
Western		
Tough	Tough	
Rugged		

Source: From Dimensions of brand personality, bu J. Aaker, 1997, *Journal of Marketing Research*, 34, 354. © 1997 by the American Marketing Association. Reprinted with permission.

"The brand personality scale has five dimensions and 15 facets that encompass 42 items. Items are scored on 5-point Likert-type scales ranging from *not at all descriptive* (1) to *extremely descriptive* (5) for each brand rated. Item scores are summed within each dimension, and then divided by the number of items within a dimension, to form scores for each dimension that can theoretically range from 1 to 5." (Bearden & Netemeyer, 1999, p. 232).

Exhibit 12-2 Framing the Affirmative Action Debate

Background

Woodruff, Wallack, and Wallis prepared a framing memo to guide the development of more effective strategies for promoting affirmative action programs (Certain Trumpet Program, 1996). They used the Lexis/Nexis database to search nine major newspapers for mention of "affirmative action," "racial preference," "California Civil Rights Initiative," or "CCRI" in the first three paragraphs of articles. They identified 221 placements that included news articles, editorials, op-ed pieces, and letters to the editor. Each item was coded for its news type, subject matter, and position(s) on affirmative action. From the articles, the authors identified frames in support of and in opposition to affirmative action. They analyzed each frame for its core position, metaphor, symbols, catch phrases, images, and appeal to principle.

The analysis revealed 11 distinct frames on the issue of affirmative action: five pro-affirmative action (**Table 12-2**) and six anti-affirmative action (**Table 12-3**).

Results

The analysis revealed that "those seeking to eliminate affirmative action have done an excellent job of using drama to capture and frame the news coverage. They are very adept at personalizing their argument by putting a face on it. A highly qualified young white girl is turned away from a selective public high school; her father leaves a prestigious law practice to seek justice for her. This is the stuff of high news drama" (Certain Trumpet Program, 1996, p. 11). In contrast, "the pro-affirmative action groups have simply not yet captured the necessary drama to put forth their argument. The benefits of affirmative action tend to be framed not in personal but in social terms, which don't have the same impact. The gentle, gradual progress toward a more just society does not pack the dramatic wallop of a single sympathetic individual denied a deserved opportunity because of affirmative action" (p. 11). "Those supporting affirmative action have some difficulty in putting a face on the benefit. While there are some examples of a woman or person of color acknowledging that affirmative action policies opened a door and gave him or her a fair chance, in the world of aggressive American individualism this is not a very interesting argument. When government helps people, the story is less dramatic and compelling than when someone is shut out because of a government policy gone bad" (p. 12).

Use of Symbols and Images

Woodruff and colleagues found that both sides of the affirmative action debate effectively used symbols and images of the civil rights movement and appealed to the core values of "fairness, justice, equality, and protecting the American dream. . . ."(p. 12). "However, evocative images of discrimination and civil rights are being used in opposition to affirmative action. These symbols resonate because most Americans support the concept of civil rights; it is a strongly held, shared value. . . . Proponents of affirmative action do not effectively highlight the fact that imagery of the civil rights movement is being applied to measures that could undo the gains of the past" (p. 12).

(continues)

Exhibit 12-2   Framing the Affirmative Action Debate (continued)

Woodruff and colleagues also found that proponents of affirmative action failed to invoke the most powerful image of civil justice: Dr. Martin Luther King and his "I have a dream" speech. On the contrary, anti-affirmative action groups adopted Dr. King's message as a call for a color-blind society and as an argument against affirmative action.

Perhaps more problematic, Woodruff and colleagues found that supporters of affirmative action were relying on communitarian rather than individual values, and communitarian values tend to be less salient and influential than individual values:

> Many of the symbols used by the supporters of affirmative action tend to evoke idealistic values that put community above individuals. The call for "open doors" and a "level playing field," the description of affirmative action as "the medicine American must take for the ills of inequality," and the picture of a multicultural "rainbow community" where diverse groups get along: these images all appeal to a concept of the social good that simply may not resonate to the extent that the opposition messages does. On the other hand, the image of individual achievers in formerly white fields—female firefighters, black doctors—may appeal by putting a face on the successes of affirmative action (p. 13).

Message Consistency and Types of Appeals

Two other conclusions of the framing memo were quite revealing. First, anti-affirmative action groups delivered a strong and consistent message by relying on a few simple and consistent arguments: 70% of the anti-affirmative action messages used were either *content of one's character* or *reverse discrimination*. In contrast, the pro-affirmative action groups used many different arguments. No single message accounted for more than 10% of all pro-affirmative action arguments used. The authors concluded that "this argumentative overkill by supporters of affirmative action may dissipate the power of these frames" (p. 13).

Second, the anti-affirmative action frames tended to use more emotional appeals, while the pro-affirmative action frames tended to rely more on facts. In other words, the support for the benefit promised by affirmative action groups tended to be scientific documentation, while the anti-affirmative action groups backed up their promised benefit with stronger and more compelling documentation: human emotion.

Based on their findings, Woodruff and colleagues offered six concrete suggestions to affirmative action advocates. They recommended that advocates (1) "simplify their arguments, focusing on one or two frames that are most likely to sway voters," (2) "create more dramatic stories that put faces on the success of affirmative action efforts;" (3) "counter the 'reverse discrimination' theme by involving white males in message delivery;" (4) "reclaim Dr. Martin Luther King, Jr.'s language and other dramatic symbols of the civil rights movement;" (5) "stress that quotas are already illegal and are not part of current affirmative action programs;" and (6) "emphasize that measures like Prop. 209 are radical approaches that go too far and would eliminate successful, worthwhile programs" (Certain Trumpet Program, 1996, pp. 14, 15).

Exhibit 12-3 Pitfalls To Avoid When Developing Communication Strategies

- Focusing on very small audiences
- Targeting too many or too diverse audiences
- Including multiple actions or framing an issue multiple ways rather than focusing on one
- Focusing on a long-term benefit when a short-term benefit is more compelling
- Focusing on public health benefits when personal benefits are more compelling
- Appealing to noncritical values (e.g., good health) rather than core values (freedom, autonomy, control, independence)
- Supporting the message with facts alone when an emotional appeal would be more compelling
- Using mass media to convey complex messages
- Developing strategies for different audiences that conflict or send mixed messages

6. Develop *message concepts* based on the communication strategy. A message is the thought or feeling audience members should walk away with after they have been exposed to communications, either through the mass media or directly from materials or events. Messages should stimulate action; for example, an audience member should change his or her mind, vote a different way, or substitute one behavior for another as a result of the message. A message is different from a slogan, a theme line, or a sound bite; each of these is a way of packaging a message to make it accessible to the audience. Appendix 18-A provides some examples.

7. Share the message concepts with target audience members to explore whether the positioning is relevant, appealing, and motivating to them. Message concepts are often explored using qualitative research techniques, which provide an opportunity to gather insights into all aspects of the communication strategy. In some situations, message concepts can then be tested through quantitative techniques, such as a public opinion poll. More detail on approaches to message concept exploration and testing is provided in Chapters 11 and 18.

8. Revise the communication strategy if needed based on the research results.

9. Prepare a *creative brief*—a one- or two-page summary of the communication strategy that is given to the creative team to use for guidance when developing the program materials. (See **Exhibit 12-4** for a sample creative brief from the 5 A Day for Better Health media campaign.)

The creative brief should be used by anyone developing promotional materials for the initiative, to ensure that every communication reflects and conveys the strategy. For example, if the program goal is to increase rates among older women, and components include outreach to women and physician education materials or a continuing medical education module,

Table 12-2 Pro-Affirmative Action Frames

Frame	Core Position	Symbol/Metaphor/Visual Image	Catch Phrases and Quotes	Source of Problem	Appeal to Principle
Keep the doors open	We must maintain gains of the civil rights and women's movements to keep opportunities available.	Level playing field Open doors CCRI is a "U-turn toward exclusion" Women in traditionally male jobs Minorities in professional positions Rights are "a valued heirloom women have fought for."	CCRI would take women back to a second-class status. . . . . "We won't go back." "At PG&E, we don't have preferential treatment and never have. We don't have quotas and never have. But we do have affirmative action, that is affirmatively reaching out and assuring equal opportunity for everyone." "We should mend, not end, affirmative action."	White men trying to slam the door on further progress Fearful White men who are insecure	America Dream—the land of opportunity Maintain/protect civil rights gains
Necessary medicine	Affirmative action is a necessary remedy for historical and continuing discrimination.	Legacy of racism and slavery Symbols of continuing racism: Rodney King beating, power and wealth gulf, glass ceiling	"The reality is that without affirmative action, 230 years of official spoils system based on race, ethnicity and the like will continue." "Prejudice against minorities and White women continues to be the single most important barrier to their advancement." "In order to treat some people equally, we must treat them differently."	Historical racism, sexism, and White male privilege Persistent inequality in housing, education, and jobs	Justice Correcting historical inequities

(continues)

Table 12-2 Pro-Affirmative Action Frames (continued)

Frame	Core Position	Symbol/Metaphor/ Visual Image	Catch Phrases and Quotes	Source of Problem	Appeal to Principle
Political football	Anti-affirmative action forces are playing the politics of divisiveness.	Affirmative action as a wedge issue that divides Democrats Building walls Dirty politics Playing the quota card Political bargaining chip	"Anger has become the emotional gold of American politics."	Cynical, manipulative politicians	Common sense to see through political manipulation
Benefits of diversity	Affirmative action recognizes that the diverse community is of value to all. We must recognize a wider definition of "merit" than mere test scores.	Multicultural society Richness of diverse experience	"Diversity is a 'compelling interest' of educational institutions." All students benefit from a diversity of experiences in the classroom. "The issue is not a person's race-based characteristics; it is experience. And any judge who thinks Black Americans have not had a different experience is blind."	Institutions not adequately responding to shift in demographics Fear of difference Failure to understand benefits of diversity	Value of inclusiveness Difference as a strength rather than a weakness
Preference for the privileged	Admissions and hiring processes are already full of preferences for privileged classes.	"Athletics is the largest preferential program in existence." Preferences extended to "musicians and cheerleaders, athletes of questionable academic potential and dull offspring of alumni." Back room admissions "Old boys" network	"I needed all the help I could get. . . . I mean, this is America. It's not what you know, it's who you know." "Does it make sense to give consideration to a African-American man to allow him to cribble a basketball but not to tecome a teacher or doctor?"	Rot at the top Corruption, hypocrisy, influence peddling	Fairness No special privilege for the rich Equality

Source: Adapted with permission from *Framing Memo: The Affirmative Action Debate,* September 1996 Certain Trumpet Program publication, © 1996, The Advocacy Institute.

Note: This framing matrix model was adapted from Rejan (1991), following the work of Gamson & Lasch (1983) and Gamson & Modigliani (1989).

Table 12-3 Anti-Affirmative Action Frames

Frame	Core Position	Symbol/Metaphor/ Visual Image	Catch Phrases and Quotes	Source of Problem	Appeal to Principle
Content of one's character	People should be judged on their character and merit, not the color of their skin or their gender.	MLK Jr. "I have a dream" speech Color-blind society	Treat people as individuals "It's your ability that counts, not your disability." Reward merit, not skin color/gender.	Sense of group entitlement Lack of individual initiative	Equality Merit
Reverse discrimination	You can't solve discrimination with more discrimination. Affirmative action lowers standards by admitting the undeserving.	Color-blind constitution Qualified White males denied opportunities Level playing field Quotas	"Equal right for all, special privilege for none." "Racial discrimination is not the way to end racial discrimination." Government-sponsored discrimination	Unconstitutional preferences Misguided overcompensation for past wrongs	Fairness
Hurts those it intends to help	Affirmative action is demeaning to minorities and women; people internalize low expectations.	The stigma of being an affirmative action recipient Affirmative action infantilizes/coddles minorities Affirmative action squelches ambition	It's wrong to have "every single minority tarred with the notion that they're less qualified." "Affirmative action is . . . instilling in (minorities) a permanent sense of dependency and inferiority." "You don't want people to think you only go in here because you're Black."	People live up—or down—to society's expectations. Reducing expectations squelches human potential.	Respect for all Equal expectations
No longer needed	Affirmative action is unnecessary because discrimination is no longer a barrier.	Connerly, Thomas, and others who overcame adversity and pulled themselves up by their bootstraps without affirmative action The playing field has been leveled.	"Legally sanctioned racism is a thing of the past." "Affirmative action is a strong-arm tactic that has outlived its time." "If I made it, anyone can."	Confusing real racism of the past with isolated slights of today.	Work ethic Honor for the struggles of the past

(continues)

Table 12-3   Anti-Affirmative Action Frames (continued)

Frame	Core Position	Symbol/Metaphor/ Visual Image	Catch Phrases and Quotes	Source of Problem	Appeal to Principle
Divides, doesn't unify	Affirmative action pits groups against each other, and increases racial tension and divisiveness.	Affirmative action leads to the Balkanization of America around racial lines. Voluntary resegregation Black against White	"Americans pitted against Americans" Affirmative action "undermines tolerance and mutual respect."	Lack of primary identity as Americans	National unity Patriotism Community Cohesiveness
Wrong solution	Focusing on affirmative action diverts us from the real problem.	Affirmative action is compared to forced busing as a misguided policy. Racial numbers game	"Affirmative action is an obsession with racial balance as an end in itself." The affirmative action debate is an unfortunate "subterfuge" for a discussion about race, one that "demonizes" African-American men, who have barely benefited from affirmative action programs.	Affirmative action distracts from more effective policies	Courage and commitment to tackle the tough real issues

Source: Adapted with permission from *Framing Memo: The Affirmative Action Debate,* September 1996 Certa n Trumpet Program publication, © 1996, The Advocacy Institute.

Note: This framing matrix model was adapted from Rejan (1991), following the work of Gamson & Lasch (1983) and Gamson & Modigliani (1989).

Exhibit 12-4   Creative Brief for the 5 A Day for Better Health Media Campaign

Target audience:
People increasing their fruit and vegetable consumption, but eating less than the minimum of five or more servings each day (particularly people currently eating two to three servings). Audience members tend to be 25- to 55-year-olds who lead busy, hectic lives and are strongly motivated by the need to be in control. They are anxiety ridden about nutrition but do not feel urgency to eat healthier. They think fruits and vegetables taste good and know they should eat more, but think doing so is not easy because preparation takes time and they don't think about it. They lack the knowledge and skills to fit in more services.

Action:
Add two or more servings of fruits and vegetables a day "the easy way" instead of making it hard.

Benefit:
I will feel more relieved and in control of my life.

Supports:

- Illustrations of how fruits and vegetables can fit into busy lives.
- A great number of studies have shown that a diet rich in fruits and vegetables has a protective effect against cancer.
- Fruits and vegetables taste great.
- People keep hearing the phrase "5 A Day for Better Health."
- This information is coming from the National Cancer Institute, a credible source of health information.

Openings:

- Times when people are preparing shopping lists or shopping, choosing foods at a restaurant or take-out, or are in transition between activities.
- Places such as the dinner table; by the TV; in stores or restaurants; in the car, train, or bus; and in the kitchen.
- Situations when people are hungry, thinking about what to eat, starting to relax, and/or reflecting on their day or planning for tomorrow.

Image:
People who eat five servings of fruit and vegetables each day can be responsible, balanced, and warm.

Source: Data from the National Cancer Institute's *"5 A Day for Better Health"*: *NCI Media Campaign Strategy,* 1993.

---

the individuals developing the physician materials should refer to the creative brief for women and integrate information on the strategies that work best for persuading women to get mammograms into the physician materials. The overall content and approach to the physician materials should be guided by a separate communication strategy to ensure that the materials are meaningful, compelling, and relevant to physicians.

Some organizations prepare longer documents that summarize the communication strategy but also provide the rationale for the communication effort and include more detail on target audience research and specific message points. These documents are useful for partner organizations and coalition members; they provide insights about communicating with the target audience, and they extend the reach of the sponsoring organization by providing an opportunity for others to develop materials using the same communication strategy.

MESSAGE CONTENT AND CONSTRUCTION: ADDITIONAL FACTORS TO CONSIDER

Constructing health messages is a complex art. The final message a target audience member receives is a combination of the communication strategy, how the message is executed in the materials, and how it is processed by the receiver. This section discusses some of the common types of message appeals used in health communications and provides some insights into how to increase the amount of attention people pay to messages.

Common Types of Appeals

Traditionally, messages have been divided into rational and emotional appeals. Using a rational argument rather than emotion to convey a message is said to be using a *rational appeal*. In contrast, *emotional appeals* are those that attempt to elicit some emotional response—feeling good, laughter, fear, etc.—from the message receiver. As Monahan (1995) noted, some "analyses find most messages utilize, or at least are perceived by audiences as utilizing, both rational and affective appeals (Stewart & Furse, 1986)" (p. 83). In fact, most commercial messages probably do contain both types of appeals, because marketers have learned that people make decisions for emotional reasons, but they want rational justifications (the "reason why") for those decisions.

Rational approaches can be further divided into one-sided and two-sided messages. One-sided messages usually present a major benefit, but do not directly address any major drawbacks. Two-sided messages address both drawbacks and benefits. Kotler and Roberto (1989) noted that each type of message is appropriate for different audiences: "Studies have identified that one-sided messages appear to work best with people who are already favorably predisposed to an idea or practice and who have a low level of education but that two-sided messages work best when people are not predisposed to the product and have a higher level of education" (p. 196).

Emotional appeals can be positive or negative. In general, positive appeals are considered to be more effective. Backer and colleagues (1992) concluded that campaigns that emphasize positive behavior change and/or current rewards are more effective than those that emphasize negative consequences of current behavior or avoiding future negative consequences. Behavioral economics, discussed in Chapter 10, provides some insights into why this happens based on how people value short-term versus long-term costs and benefits, and how these values change depending on the temporal proximity of taking the action. In commercial advertising, positive emotional appeals are most often used for a simple reason: "Research consistently shows advertisements that arouse positive emotions result in more positive feelings toward the product and greater intent to comply with the message" (Monahan, 1995, pp. 81–82, citing Thorson & Friestad, 1989, as an example).

Positive Emotional Appeals. Monahan (1995) divides positive emotional appeals into two types. *Emotional benefit appeals* combine emotional and rational appeals to portray the benefits the message recipients will reap by complying with the message. Her example is "a campaign that shows healthy people engaging in 'fun' activities with a message that tells the viewer to 'live longer and live healthier by eating more fruits and vegetables'" (p. 83). *Heuristic appeals* try to make recipients feel good about the product through executional detail rather than describing the benefits they could derive from complying with the message.

In general, public health communicators will find emotional benefits appeals are more useful than rational appeals. Monahan (1995) recommended using such appeals in the form of comparisons, demonstrations, satisfaction, and testimonials when the audience is unfamiliar with an issue, and she noted that emotional benefits appeals are an excellent strategy when the audience is undecided or confused. She also noted that positive appeals can help reframe an issue. She recommended stressing positive rather than negative outcomes and control rather than helplessness as a way to increase compliance.

Monahan (1995) recommended using heuristic appeals when message recipients are familiar with an issue or campaign; however, few public health interventions reach audience members with enough frequency to assume that they attain sufficient familiarity. Finally, Monahan cautioned against using positive appeals in an attempt to change strongly held negative attitudes.

Threat (Fear) Appeals. Public health campaign planners are often tempted to use what are commonly termed "fear appeals" to scare the audience into changing their behavior. There is enormous debate among practitioners and scholars about whether, and under what circumstances, this type of negative appeal is effective.

A number of researchers have suggested that part of the reason for the apparently conflicting evidence about effectiveness is in the definition of a fear appeal, and that these types of appeals might better be called "threat appeals" (Donovan & Henley, 1997; Hale & Dillard, 1995; LaTour

& Rotfeld, 1997; Strong, Anderson, & Dubas, 1993; Witte, 1993). LaTour and Rotfeld (1997) discussed the distinction between threats and fear: "Threats illustrate undesirable consequences from certain behaviors, such as car damage, injury, or death from unsafe driving, or bad health, illness or cancer from cigarette smoking. However, fear is an emotional response to threats, and different people fear different things" (p. 45).

They further explained: "A threat is an appeal to fear, a communication stimulus that *attempts* to evoke a fear response by showing some type of outcome that the audience (it is hoped) wants to avoid. Fear is an actual emotional response that can impel changes in attitude or behavior intentions (e.g., toward auto safety issues or toward the energy crisis) and consumer actions (e.g., cessation of cigarette smoking or more careful driving habits)" (LaTour & Rotfeld, 1997, p. 46, emphasis in original). They noted that some threat appeals (i.e. appeals intended to arouse fear) may in fact arouse other emotions in some audience members.

There are three main independent variables to consider when developing or assessing fear appeals (Witte & Allen, 2000):

- *Fear,* which as noted above is an emotional response
- *Perceived threat,* which has two dimensions:
  - Perceived susceptibility—the degree to which one feels at risk of experiencing the threat
  - *Perceived severity*—magnitude of harm expected from the threat
- *Perceived efficacy,* which also has two dimensions
  - *Perceived self-efficacy*—one's confidence in one's ability to take the recommended action
  - *Perceived response efficacy*—one's belief that the recommended action will in fact avert the threat

Successful appeals to fear communicate both a severe threat and high efficacy (Witte & Allen, 2000; Hale & Dillard, 1995).

Decisions to use a threat appeal should be considered carefully and the appeal should be tested thoroughly before implementation. Hastings and MacFadyen (2002) argue that, at a minimum, using fear appeals can negate an initiative's ability to build a relationship with the audience, and therefore may not be a good solution over the longer term. In their meta-analysis of fear appeals, Witte and Allen note "much more information is needed on how people process fear appeals, as well as what triggers danger control and fear control responses" (2000, p. 604). Their recommendations for practitioners (Witte & Allen, 2000):

1. Increase references to the severity of the threat and the target population's susceptibility to the threat.
2. Messages that make a health threat serious and likely to happen will be the most motivating (i.e., strong severity and susceptibility messages).

3. Strong fear appeals work only when accompanied by equally strong efficacy messages. Strong efficacy messages make the target audience believe:

   a. They are able to perform the recommended response (i.e., strong self-efficacy). To increase self-efficacy, identify barriers-lack of skills, costs, beliefs, emotions, etc.—that inhibit the audience's perceived ability to perform the action, and directly address these barriers in messages.

   b. Recommended responses will work in averting or minimizing a threat. Clearly outline how, why, and, when a recommended response eliminates or decreases the health threat.

4. Individual differences, such as personality traits or demographic characteristics, do not need to be addressed in communications because they do not appear to influence processing of fear messages.

5. Assess danger control responses (attitude, intention, and behavior changes) and fear control responses (denial, defensive avoidance, and reactance) in evaluation. If a campaign fails, this assessment can determine whether the campaign simply had no effect (in which case perceptions of threat may need to be increased to motivate action) or whether it contained insufficient efficacy messages and thus activated fear control responses rather than danger control responses.

Common wisdom is that death threat appeals are ineffective for young people, particularly young men, because they feel immortal. However, Henley & Donovan (2003) exposed smokers in two age groups (16–25 and 40–50) to one of two messages about emphysema, either a premature death message or a disablement message. Finding that younger smokers responded equally to both messages and expressed a higher level of response than older adults to both, they concluded that death threats can be effective with young people and they do not feel immortal. They also found that women in the older age group responded significantly more to non-death threats than did men in that age group. They concluded that "death is not invariably the most effective threat. Non-death threats can be at least as effective for most people and apparently more effective for some" (Henley & Donovan, 2003, p. 12).

Humorous Appeals. Humor is another popular emotional approach that must be used carefully. If used, humor should convey the main message, otherwise people are likely to remember the humor and forget the message. "If you can remove your product, but the joke remains intact, chances are that it has nothing to do with the key benefit" (Roman et al., 2003, p. 104). The advertising literature is littered with examples of very funny, entertaining ads that didn't sell products. And according to Kotler and Roberto (1989), "humorous messages are more effective when the prevailing communications in the field are not humorous. Second, humor becomes stale if it is repeated too frequently, so it needs to varied if it is not to become irritating. Third, humor works well as along as the basic message is simple; it is inappropriate for complex messages" (pp. 198–199).

Breaking through Inattention

Parrott (1995) lays out a number of content and linguistic factors that can increase the attention people give to health messages, based on Louis and Sutton's (1991) model of "switching cognitive gears." The following recommendations are based on Parrott's analysis:

- Use novel messages, settings, and media. Rather than a skin cancer brochure that begins with a standard factual approach, such as, "Know the signs of cancer," try a positive emotional appeal, such as, "Safeguard your health by knowing the signs of skin cancer." Or try explicitly stating a motive to pay attention: "You can avoid a serious health problem by knowing the following signs of skin cancer so you can detect any unusual skin conditions." Another possibility is to invoke a sense of personal responsibility: "You can help friends and family detect skin cancer early by knowing the following signs." (Examples are modifications of Parrott's.)

- Present unexpected content or present it in an unexpected place. New recommendations, particularly if they run contrary to past recommendations, are one form of unexpected content. Parrott's example is the recommendation to stay out of the sun, when for years sunlight was promoted as health enhancing. An unexpected place can be anywhere people do not expect to receive health messages.

- Instruct the audience to pay more attention by using phrases such as "Now hear this," or, less directly, "Is everyone listening for information about. . . ?"

- Use language that conveys immediacy and personal relevance:
  - Use "your" rather than third person or passive constructions.
  - Use *this, these,* and *here* rather than their more spatially distance counterparts *that, those,* and *there.*
  - Use active present-tense verbs.
  - Avoid qualifiers (e.g., perhaps, may, maybe, possible, it could be, it might be).

Using Branding Effectively

Many public health practitioners shy away from learning about brand management, believing that it is too commercial and using it is likely to result in public criticism, or that branding is not relevant to an industry that is often marketing a product category (e.g., fruits and vegetables, whole-grain or low-fat foods, public health) rather than a specific brand within the category, or a behavior not tied to any particular good or service (e.g., physical activity, not driving drunk).

However, branding has much to offer public health practitioners. Harnessing the concepts underlying building a brand can help create more effective communications, differentiate product offerings, and build relationships with target audiences—all of which are arguably *more* important to public health initiatives given the small size of their budgets relative to their commercial counterparts.

As we mentioned in the earlier discussion of image, using symbols, metaphors, and visuals can tap into the cultural code—our shared understanding of how to read symbolic meaning (Hirschman & Thompson, 1997). At its most basic, that is what branding does: it taps the cultural code to communicate meaning and value. Consistent use of the same carefully constructed brand identity allows an organization to build a relationship with its audiences through the characters and stories that are part of that shared cultural code.

A very literal example of this process is presented in Chapter 7. The radio program *Urunana* is a radio soap opera created to disseminate health messages and improve health practices in Rwanda. In creating *Urunana*, planners took great pains to tap into the existing cultural code of Rwanda. They set the story in a fictitious but typical rural Rwandan village, used proverbs and idioms common in rural villages, created archetypal characters that one might encounter in any rural village, and used story lines also common to village life. The result is a *Urunana* brand firmly set in Rwandan culture, with characters with whom target audience members can identify. Creating this culture-based identity for *Urunana* allows its planners to influence health behaviors and social norms by having characters discuss topics that normally would be taboo. However, as Chapter 7 discusses, the program team constantly monitors reactions to *Urunana* episodes and story lines to ensure that they remain believable, and once a year the writers spend four days living in rural villages to immerse themselves in the culture and ensure that the brand identity remains strong.

Communications for other public health initiatives can use branding strategies to harness the same devices that make *Urunana* such a success by using symbols, images and metaphors as shorthand to evoke our shared archetypal characters and the stories that go along with them. **Table 12-1** contains an inventory of items that can assess brand personalities.

Another useful approach is to think about the product offering in terms of archetypes that reflect core values or can fulfill core needs. Archetypes are forms or images of a collective nature which occur practically all over the earth (Marks & Pearson, 2001). Mark & Pearson (2001) present a system for "finding the right stories" for commercial brands through the use of archetypes; **Table 12-4** presents some of their examples. (Our apologies to readers outside the United States who may be unfamiliar with some of the brands mentioned.) **Table 12-5** illustrates how archetypes "mediate between products and customer motivation

Table 12-4 Archetypes and Their Primary Functions in People's Lives

Archetype	Helps People	Brand example
Creator	Craft something new	Williams-Sonoma
Caregiver	Care for others	AT&T (Ma Bell)
Ruler	Exert Control	American Express
Jester	Have a good time	Miller Lite
Regular Guy/Gal	Be OK just as they are	Wendy's
Lover	Find and give love	Hallmark
Hero	Act courageously	Nike
Outlaw	Break the rules	Harley-Davidson
Magician	Affect transformation	Calgon
Innocent	Retain or renew faith	Ivory
Explorer	Maintain independence	Levi's
Sage	Understand their world	Oprah's Book Club

Reprinted with permission of The McGraw-Hill Companies from *The Hero and the Outlaw: Building Extraordinary Brands Through the Power of Archetypes* by M. Mark & C.S. Pearson. Copyright © 2001 by Margaret Mark and Carol S. Pearson.

by providing an intangible experience of meaning" (Mark & Pearson, 2001, p. 17). Identifying a target audience's concerns and values, and then thinking about them in terms of the archetypes, can provide insight into an appropriate image and identity to communicate.

Archetypes can also be useful in helping you understand and position against a behavior or organization's competition. In formative research, audience members can be given brief descriptions of each archetype and asked which best characterizes the people who engage in each behavior, or, for organizations, the archetype that best characterizes each organization or type of organization.

■ CONCLUSION

Crafting a solid communication strategy is critical to properly framing messages and positioning a social change. The strategy describes the target audience, the action they should take and how they will benefit from it, and the details of how to reach them with messages—the times, places, and situations in which they are receptive and the image to use so that they identify the message as relevant to them. The strategy should be based on a theory or model of how change is expected to occur.

Developing a solid communication strategy is an iterative process involving extensive formative research. Two of the most difficult decisions

Table 12-5	Archetypes and Motivation			
Motivation:	Stability & Control	Belonging & Enjoyment	Risk & Mastery	Independence & Fulfillment
	Creator	Jester	Hero	Innocent
	Caregiver	Regular guy/gal	Outlaw	Explorer
	Ruler	Lover	Magician	Sage
Customer Fear	Financial ruin, ill health, uncontrolled chaos	Exile, orphaning, abandonment, engulfment	Ineffectuality, impotence, powerlessness	Entrapment, selling out, emptiness
Helps People	Feel safe	Have love/ community	Achieve	Find happiness

Reprinted with permission of The McGraw-Hill Companies from *The Hero and the Outlaw: Building Extraordinary Brands Through the Power of Archetypes* by M. Mark & C.S. Pearson. Copyright © 2001 by Margaret Mark and Carol S. Pearson.

involve selecting the action that audience members should take as a result of the communication and determining the benefit to promise them for doing so. Knowing what makes the audience "tick" is crucial to crafting persuasive messages. What does the audience value? What are some immediate benefits that they value and that the action can provide? Asking and answering a series of strategic questions can help create a communication strategy that is focused, believable, and compelling to the target audience.

Understanding what types of appeals work best in a given situation is also an important part of successful communication strategy development. Positive emotional benefits appeals—those that cause audiences to connect taking the action with feeling good—have the widest applicability to public health interventions: They can be used when an audience is unfamiliar with, undecided, or confused about an issue and can be an excellent strategy for reframing an issue—unless existing attitudes are extremely negative. Humor can be part of an appeal, but it must be used to deliver the main message or recall will suffer. In general, threat appeals should be used with extreme caution.

Branding strategies can help practitioners identify the best emotion to convey or elicit and can convey meaning and build relationships with audiences by using symbols, images, and metaphors from our shared cultural code.

Once a communication strategy has been developed, using language that conveys immediacy and personal relevance can help increase the amount of attention paid to the message. Presenting a novel message in unusual or unexpected settings also is effective.

References

Aaker, D.A. (1997). Should you take your brand to where the action is? *Harv Bus Rev.* 75(5):135–42.

Backer, T.E., Rogers, E.M., & Sopory, P. (1992). *Designing health communication campaigns: What Works?* Thousand Oaks, CA: Sage.

Bearden, W.O. & Netemeyer, R.G. (1999). *Handbook of marketing scales,* 2nd ed. Thousand Oaks, CA: Sage.

Bellicha, T., & McGrath, J. (1990). Mass media approaches to reducing cardiovascular disease risk. *Public Health Reports,* 105, 245–252.

Boster, F.J., & Mongeau, P. (1984). Fear-arousing persuasive messages. In Bostrom (Ed.), *Communication Yearbook 8* (pp. 330–375). Beverly Hills, CA: Sage.

Certain Trumpet Program. (1996, September). *Framing memo: The affirmative action debate.* Washington, DC: Author.

Donovan, R.J., & Henley, N. (1997). Negative outcomes, threats and threat appeals: widening the conceptual framework for the study of fear and other emotions in social marketing communications. *Social Marketing Quarterly,* 4, 56–67.

Gamson, W.A., & Lasch, K.E. (1983). The political culture of social welfare policy (pp. 397–415). In: S.E. Spiro & E. Yuchtman-Yaar (eds.) *Evaluating the welfare state: Social and political persepctives.* New York: Academic Press.

Gamson, W.A. & Modigliani, A. (1989). Media discourse and public opinion on nuclear power: A constructionist approach. *American Journal of Sociology,* 95(1), 1–37.

Graeff, J.A., Elder, J.P., & Booth, E.M. (1993). Communication for health and behavior change: A developing country perspective. San Francisco: Jossey-Bass.

Hale, J.L., & Dillard, J.P. (1995). Fear appeals in health promotion campaigns: too much, too little, or just right? In E. Maibach & R.I. Parrott (Eds.), *Designing health messages: Approaches from communication theory and public health practice* (pp. 65–80). Thousand Oaks, CA: Sage.

Hastings, G., & MacFadyen, L. (2002). The limitations of fear messages. *Tobacco Control,* 11, 73–75.

Henley, N. & Donovan, R.J. (2003). Young people's response to death threat appeals: do they really feel immortal? *Health Education Research,* 18(1), 1–14.

Hirschman, E.C., & Thompson, C.J. (1997). Why media matter: Toward a richer understanding of consumers' relationships with advertising and mass media. *Journal of Advertising,* 26(1), 43–60.

Job, R.F.S. (1988). Effective and ineffective use of fear in health promotion campaigns. *American Journal of Public Health,* 78, 163–167.

Kotler, P., & Roberto, E.L. (1989). *Social marketing: Strategies for changing public behavior.* New York: Free Press.

LaTour, M.S., & Rotfeld, H.J. (1997). There are threats and (maybe) fear-caused arousal: Theory and confusions of appeals to fear and fear arousal itself. *Journal of Advertising,* 26(3), 45–58.

Lefebvre, R.C., Doner, L.D., Johnston, C., Loughrey, K., Balch, G., & Sutton, S.M. (1995). Use of database marketing and consumer-based health communications in message design: An example from the Office of Cancer Communications' "5 A Day for Better Health" program. In E. Maibach & R.L. Parrott (Eds.), *Designing health messages: Approaches from communication theory and public health practice* (pp. 217–246). Thousand Oaks, CA: Sage.

Louis, M.R., & Sutton, R.I. (1991). Switching cognitive gears: From habits of mind to active thinking. *Human Relations, 44,* 55–76.

Maibach, E.W., & Cotton, D. (1995). Moving people to behavior change: A staged social cognitive approach in message design. In E. Maibach & R.L. Parott (Eds.), *Designing health messages: Approaches from communication theory and public health practice* (pp. 41–64). Thousand Oaks, CA: Sage.

Mark, M. & Pearson, C.S. (2001). *The hero and the outlaw: Building extraordinary brands through the power of archetypes.* New York: McGraw-Hill.

Monahan, J.L. (1995). Using positive affect when designing health messages. In E. Maibach & R.L. Parrott (Eds.), *Designing health messages: Approaches from communication theory and public health practice* (pp. 81–98). Thousand Oaks, CA: Sage.

National Cancer Institute. (1989). *Making health communication programs work: A planner's guide* (NIH Pub. No. 89-1493). Bethesda, MD: Author.

National Heart, Lung, and Blood Institute. (1994). *A communications strategy for public education: The National Cholesterol Education Program* (NIH Pub. No. 94-3292). Bethesda, MD: Author.

Parrott, R.L. (1995). Motivations to attend to health messages: Presentation of content and linguistic considerations. In E. Maibach & R.L. Parrott (Eds.), *Designing health messages: Approaches from communication theory and public health practice* (pp. 7–23). Thousand Oaks, CA: Sage.

Rokeach, M. (1973). *The Nature of Human Values.* New York: Free Press.

Roman, K., Maas, J., & Nisenholtz, M. (2003). *How to advertise,* 3rd ed. New York: St. Martin's Press.

Ryan, C. (1991). *Prime time activism: Media strategies for grassroots organizing.* Boston: South End Press.

Signorielli, N. (1993). *Mass media images and impact on health: A sourcebook.* Westport, CT: Greenwood Press.

Stewart, D.W., & Furse, D.H. (1986). *Effective television advertising: A study of 1,000 commercials.* Lexington, MA: Lexington Books.

Strong, J.T., Anderson, R.E., & Dubas, K.M. (1993). Marketing threat appeals: A conceptual framework and implications for practitioners. *Journal of Managerial Issues, 5,* 532–546.

Sutton, S.R. (1982). Fear-arousing communications: A critical examination of theory and research. In J. R. Eiser (Ed.), *Social psychology and behavioral medicine* (pp. 303–337). New York: John Wiley.

Sutton, S.R. (1982) Shock tactics and the myth of the inverted U. *British Journal of Addiction, 87,* 517–519.

Sutton, S.M., Balch, G.I., & Lefebvre, R.C. (1995). Strategic questions for consumer-based health communications. *Public Health Reports.* 110, 725–733.

Thorson, E., & Friestad, M. (1989). The effects of emotion on episodic memory for television commercials. In P. Cafferata & A. Tybout (Eds.), *Cognitive and affective responses in advertising* (pp. 305–326). Lexington, MA: Lexington Books.

Wine, K. (1993). Message and conceptual confounds in fear appeals: The role of threat, fear and efficacy. *Southern Communication Journal, 58,* 147–155.

Witte, K. & Allen, M. (2000). A meta-analysis of fear appeals: implications for effective public health campaigns. *Health Education & Behavior, 27(5),* 591–615.

12-A

Communication Strategy Development Worksheets

■ WORKSHEET 1: IDENTIFYING POTENTIAL ACTIONS

A clear, specific statement of what the target audience is to do will help much more than a vague reference to a favorable result. Please identify the behavior being replaced by listing the current action and desired action in terms of pointed, specific behavior changes.

Audience	Current Actions	Desired Actions

Source: Copyright © 1998, Lynne Doner.

■ WORKSHEET 2: IDENTIFYING AND ASSESSING COSTS AND BENEFITS ASSOCIATED WITH POTENTIAL ACTIONS

For each audience-action combination, list the likely costs to the audience of taking the action (include monetary, psychological, organizational, social, time, and other costs). Then list the potential benefits they might associate with the action. (Remember that the benefits should be important to the target audience.) Circle the one you think is most important. Finally, assess whether you think the target audience will think the benefit is worth the cost.

Audience and Action	Costs	Benefits	Is Benefit Worth Cost?

■ WORKSHEET 3: IDENTIFYING SUPPORTS AND IMAGE

For each audience's action-benefit combination, list the supports—the ways in which communication will convey that the benefit outweighs the obstacles. Supports can be emotional, factual, or both. They can include demonstrations of how to perform the action (to increase audience self-efficacy) or demonstrations of obtaining the benefit. Then list the image that will make the communication appealing and relevant to the target audience.

Audience Action-Benefit combination (If I _____ instead of _____, I will _____.)	Supports emotional, factual, or both demonstrations, hard data	Image Adjectives/personality

■ WORKSHEET 4: IDENTIFYING OPENINGS AND CHOOSING CHANNELS

For each audience's action-benefit combination, list the openings where they could best be reached. Then list the channels that are appropriate for the message that can be used to access the openings.

Audience Action-Benefit combination (If I _____ instead of _____, I will _____.)	Openings (Times, places, states of mind when target audience is open to hearing about, and ideally able to perform, action)	Channels we can access that address the opening and are appropriate for the message (consider message complexity and what will be necessary to convey supports)

II

Development, Testing, and Implementation

Once a strategic plan has been developed, the components that will comprise the intervention are developed, tested, and implemented. This section discusses that process. Chapter 13 begins with translating the strategic plan into solid tactics and a carefully timed implementation based on how the program is expected to work, the components of it, and the environment in which the program will be put into operation. As components are developed, process evaluation mechanisms (such as those discussed in Chapter 16) should be integrated into them.

Since efforts to effect social change usually involve a number of organizations, Chapter 14 discusses working with partners, allies, and intermediaries. Chapter 15 discusses developing and implementing promotional materials and activities.

CHAPTER
13
Translating Strategy Into Tactics

The cornerstones of successful implementation are strategically driven tactics, careful timing, and constant monitoring and refinement. The strategic plan must be turned into a concrete plan of action that takes into account the environment in which the activities will be implemented, the available resources, and the complementary and competing activities of other organizations. In addition to readying all products, materials, and services, preparation for implementation includes establishing tracking measures (discussed in Chapter 16) and ensuring that all partners, alliance members, intermediaries, and spokespersons are briefed on the endeavor, so that everyone is "on strategy" when they are delivering messages about the program, whether they are addressing internal or external audiences.

"Vision without execution is hallucination."
(Attributed to various famous historical figures.)

Once the strategic plan (discussed in Chapter 10) has been completed and approved, each component in it must be translated into specific tactics. For example, the strategic plan for an effort to curtail public exposure to secondhand smoke through government and workplace policies might include promoting the changes directly to local business owners and legislators, and through a mass media component targeting the public and policy makers. The next steps are to (1) decide exactly what activities will constitute promoting the changes directly to local business owners and legislators and through the mass media, (2) determine what materials or products will be needed to support these activities; and (3) craft a timeline for developing, testing, and implementing these activities.

This chapter discusses the steps to take and the decisions to make as concrete tactics are selected, developed, and implemented based on the strategic plan.

■ OUTLINING TACTICS

The first step in planning tactics is to revisit the strategic plan and the product, price, promotion, and place strategies in it. The expectations of how change will occur and how the initiative will support change have ramifications for the types of tactics likely to be effective and the timing of implementation (e.g., a short-term flurry of activity to apply pressure to stimulate passage of a bill or other policy change, a moderately-paced effort to develop, deliver and promote a new product or service, or a long-term, multi-year effort to change the physical, social, and/or economic environment and promote or reinforce more difficult behavior changes).

■ ASSESSING RESOURCE AND ORGANIZATIONAL ISSUES

The second step in planning tactics is to identify the resources available to support the initiative and the position that it will occupy within the organization. Green and Kreuter (2005) refer to aspects of this process as administrative and policy diagnosis in the PRECEDE-PROCEED framework. Exactly what transpires at this point depends in part on what has gone before. In general, managers must first assess the resources they will need in terms of time, personnel, and budget and compare that assessment to an assessment of the resources they have available. For more detail, Green and Kreuter (2005) elaborated on some of the steps involved in this process.

Often, one or more of the available resources cannot be adjusted. For example, an initiative may need to accomplish something by a particular date, may not be able to add staff, or may have a fixed budget within which to work. When one of these situations exists, the assessment of resources needed should be adjusted to accommodate the "fixed" resource. That is, if something must be accomplished by a particular date, it may require increased staff or budget. If staff cannot be added, budget will have to increase. If the budget cannot be increased, the time frame may have to stretch out or staff may need to be added. A common solution to a resource deficit (which almost every initiative has) is to identify other organizations that can handle part of the work.

Consequently, a key part of this step is determining appropriate roles for other organizations to play. Some roles may be incorporated into the strategic plan; this is a time to flesh out those roles and, if needed, explore the extent to which they are feasible. In addition to determining what roles it makes sense for other organizations to play from a resource perspective, this is also the time to determine what roles they might be better suited to play because of restrictions on your organization's activities (e.g., an inability to lobby or to produce particular kinds of materials) or internal political issues (for example, a mandate to use a particular department for a particular activity, but the people involved do not consider the initiative important or are not as skilled as partner organizations). Chapter 14 discusses assessing appropriate roles for other organizations.

■ PLANNING CHANGES IN PRODUCTS AND SERVICES

The products and services that could be developed as part of a social change initiative are diverse, making it difficult to present a meaningful discussion of the issues to consider when the development of a new product or service—or changes to an existing one—is being planned. However, some issues are common to all products and services in terms of their development, distribution, and pricing.

Product Development

Additional formative research is often key to success. Depending on the nature and depth of the information collected during the strategic planning process, the research may begin with a targeted needs assessment among potential users of the new product or service. Using that information, a concept of the product or service can be developed and presented to potential users for their feedback, then refined before production. The needs assessment also provides an opportunity to get a sense of the demand for new or updated products and services, allowing managers to predict resource requirements.

Managing Distribution

All public health offerings must be distributed in some way to the individuals who will use them. This distribution process can be direct from the provider to the consumer or it can involve some number of intermediaries. When determining how to distribute a public health offering, a manager must assess which channels can best do the job. Factors that feed into this assessment include the type of distribution outlets each possibility provides (target audiences may prefer or trust one type over another), the number and locations of outlets, and differences in target audience costs to access each outlet (monetary costs, including transportation, as well as nonmonetary psychological, time, or social costs).

Initiatives that use interpersonal distribution channels such as physicians, nurses, community groups, or teachers may need to train individuals before distribution can take place successfully. In general, such training is designed to ensure that the people being trained:

- Understand how to best frame the issues in terms of the benefits to target audience members.
- Have the skills required to successfully distribute messages or services.

For example, the U.S. Department of Agriculture's Team Nutrition initiative included training of food service personnel so that they could prepare healthier meals and learn ways to support improving students' nutritional knowledge and behavior by linking the cafeteria to the classroom (i.e., by providing students with an opportunity to practice what they learn in the classroom) and to the home (i.e., by including nutritional analyses of school menus). As another example, health care providers may not bring up certain topics, such as end-of-life care planning, with patients because they are uncomfortable addressing them. Training can address skill deficits and alleviate many of these problems.

Training can take many forms. Sometimes written instruction, for example, in the form of a case study or article that highlights the key points, is sufficient. At other times hands-on practice or role-playing is the best approach.

Pricing

Kotler and Roberto (1989) noted that the financial price of a product or service serves a number of functions. First, the price affects how easy it is for a consumer to obtain the product or service. Low prices make it easy for many people to obtain a product; high prices can be used to "demarket" a product. An example of this is taxes on alcohol and cigarettes designed to increase the cost and therefore decrease demand.

The second function of price is to send a message about a product's quality. As Kotler and Roberto (1989) discussed, "when target adopters have difficulty judging the quality of a social product, they often use price as a standard. A high price may lead target adopters to view the product as having high quality or prestige. . . . Many 'free goods,' such as public health services or legal assistance, do not produce maximum demand because they imply that the product is 'downscale'" (p. 175). The authors provided an example of a new South American hospital that did not charge indigent citizens. Many of the citizens continued to patronize private physicians and street clinics, even though they had to pay for these services. When the hospital started charging a fee, many patients began to use its services.

Setting financial prices involves weighing the provider's cost associated with the product, competitors' prices, and potential consumers' sensitivity to the price (manifest by ability and willingness to purchase at a given price). Kotler and Roberto (1989) noted that if costs are to be recovered, costs serve as a "floor" on price, whereas competitors' prices serve as a ceiling.

In addition to the financial price, managers should try to minimize the time, effort, and psychic costs associated with obtaining a product or service. The most obvious way to do this in terms of distribution is to ensure that the product is nearby and attainable from a source with which the client is comfortable. Promotional strategies can also be used to moderate psychic costs. Kotler and Roberto (1989, citing Gemunden, 1985) provide the following examples:

- Minimize perceived *psychological risk* by providing the product in a way that delivers psychological rewards.
- Minimize perceived *social risk,* such as stigma or embarrassment associated with usage, through endorsements of credible sources.
- Minimize perceived *risk of usage* by providing reassuring information on the product or a free trial so consumers can experience how the product does what it promises.
- Minimize perceptions of *physical risk* by obtaining seals of approval from authoritative institutions.

Promotional Activities

Just about every social change initiative includes some form of promotional activities; Chapter 15 is devoted to discussion of them.

■ THE DEVELOPMENT AND IMPLEMENTATION PROCESS

The following sections outline a systematic process for selecting and developing the specific tactics to implement the program. Please note that some of the activities described in Chapters 11, 14, and 15 take place during this process.

Develop Concepts for Each Program Component

There are usually a million ways to design a program component. Consider a new service. What exactly will the service provide? When and where will it be available? Who will provide it? How will it be priced? How will nonmonetary costs be managed? The case study in Appendix 10-A includes three different ride services, all developed to address the same strategy.

Planners of a mass media component would have an equally extensive list of issues to consider: Will there be an official program launch? If so, when? What form will it take—press materials only, press conference, special event? Media tour? Will efforts focus on editorial placement or also include paid or public service advertising? What news hooks might help get coverage of the issue? What spokespeople are available? What materials will be developed for editorial coverage: audio, video, electronic, or written news releases, story ideas, camera-ready articles? How will new media be used? What advertising media, sizes or lengths, and schedules will be used?

Planners of each prospective component will have to work through questions like these, using the answers to fashion a component that makes sense given the program objectives, target audience(s), communication strategies, budget, and implementation time period.

Assess How Components Will Fit Together and Reinforce Each Other

Once planners have developed concepts for each component, they should meet and look at the component in the context of others. How do they fit together? What time sequencing makes sense? What refinements can be made to each so that they work together better? This is a critical step: Components targeted to the same audiences must complement and reinforce each other—the environmental changes they bring about, new products or services they introduce, and what they say and when and where they say it should work together.

For components targeting different audiences, a particular sequence may be necessary or may make more sense. For example, in a multifaceted program to increase children's consumption of grains, fruits, and vegetables, a logical sequencing is to train food service personnel first, so that they know how to prepare appropriate foods and have ideas for cafeteria promotions to increase consumption of these foods. Next, the classroom and mass media components could take place. The food service changes would be in place so that children could act on what they learned at school and through the media.

Determine General Timing

This step involves looking at the components and drafting a rough timeline. When does it make sense to launch each component? Sometimes it really doesn't matter; components can go into the field as soon as they are ready. But sometimes activities must be coordinated with partners' activities, or certain times of year are more appropriate. For example, social change efforts that include passing or defeating legislation should be timed to correspond with legislative calendars: When the legislature is in session, members can be reached through media in the city where they meet or at their government offices. At other times of the year, members can be approached in their home districts.

Other types of activities may be seasonal for other reasons. For example, in most of the United States, the ideal time to distribute classroom materials is over the summer, so that teachers have time to incorporate them into lesson plans. Summer is often a good time for training sessions involving 12-month school personnel as well. In contrast, late summer is often a bad time to stage special events because many target audience members will be away on vacation.

For media and community events, it is a good idea to check what else is going on during the time period you are considering. Doing so can provide opportunities to "piggyback" onto other events and can help avoid a time period likely to be monopolized by another health issue. Doing a web search on "national health observances" will yield calendars with relevant information. Holding an event—or sending information about it—during a time when a publication already has plans to cover the topic can also be useful. Most magazines will provide their editorial calendars so that you can assess their upcoming content and place ads or pitch feature stories accordingly.

Obtain Stakeholder Buy-In

At some point in the process of developing a specific plan of action, it is wise to obtain buy-in from key stakeholders. These stakeholders include individuals within your organization, allied organizations, intermediaries who will have a hand in its implementation, and individuals whose support is critical to the initiative's success. You can obtain this buy-in by presenting the plan at relevant meetings or by circulating it in written form. It may be more useful to present it, so that you can discuss and clearly understand objections and concerns.

Finalize Budgets and Prepare Detailed Timelines

After laying out the major program components, it is a good idea to develop detailed budgets and prepare timelines that include all the steps necessary for successful completion and delivery of each component. These work plans typically detail the activities to be conducted, whether supporting materials, products and services, exist or need to be created (and in what quantity), and a timeline specifying each step of development, pretesting, preparation, production, and follow-up required to implement the component.

Once detailed budgets are available, it is a good time to step back and reassess what each component will cost (the total cost is often much higher than the original estimates, but sometimes it is lower than expected). Is the cost reasonable given what the component is expected to accomplish? There are no standard definitions of "reasonable," but there are some questions to ask and steps to take to make sure components do not cost more than necessary. An obvious first step is to obtain multiple cost estimates. To ensure that the estimates are comparable, make sure that each is based on identical assumptions. If one vendor suggests one solution and another goes a different route, ask each one why the proposed solution is superior to the other solution (without naming names, of course). This process often helps identify additional issues or less expensive solutions to consider.

One technique for comparing costs of different components can be borrowed from commercial advertisers, who often compare alternative media placement schedules by calculating the cost per thousand (CPM), or how much it costs for each alternative to reach or be delivered to a thousand people (or whatever quantity makes sense for the progam). This calculation can be difficult for new products or services with an unknown level of demand. However, some components have a finite reach (e.g., a training session that includes a specified number of people). In other instances, reach is estimated and implementation will be measured against this estimate to assess success or failure. The same estimate can be used to calculate CPM.

Knowing how much components will cost and how many people they will reach helps you make informed decisions. Will one program component cost much more than another, yet reach far fewer people? If so, is this cost justified? In many instances it may be: The more expensive component may be designed to have a much greater impact on those reached. For example, a 2-hour training session can be expected to have a much more powerful and lasting impact than a 30-second ad. But if impact will be similar, the additional cost may not be justified. Only by taking a broad look at all components can you begin to make these types of assessments.

It is also important to ensure that all components are designed with cost-efficiency in mind. Making sure that whoever is responsible for approving budgets has a thorough understanding of all the costs involved will also help. In addition to limiting costs by trimming those that are unnecessary or suggesting alternatives that are of equal quality but less expensive, such a person helps avoid cost overruns by ensuring that nothing necessary is left out of the initial budgets.

Finally, it is important to assess to what degree (if any) the timeline is driving up costs, or could drive them up if some preliminary activities happen late. For example, at what point will printers start charging rush charges? Do you run the risk of losing deposits by changing dates for events? Are you going to wind up paying overtime for staff or contractors? It is important that timelines be realistic and have some "float" in them, particularly with large, complex programs—a million things can go wrong and at least a thousand probably will. While timelines shouldn't be developed based on worst-case scenarios at every step, it may help you assess the timeline accordingly if you know what those scenarios are. If you are reviewing timelines for a component with which you are relatively inexperienced, ask the people who will handle each stage what delays could occur and how much time they will take to resolve. Then assess the extent to which the timeline can accommodate likely delays.

The timeline should also be realistic in terms of providing sufficient time to obtain the necessary internal approvals. Asking for expedited approvals now and then may be tolerated, but if you need approval in a rush every time, the approvers will quickly lose patience with you and the initiative.

This is also a good time to prepare a master timeline that clearly identifies all "drop dead" dates. Project management software can be a great help in administering complex interventions. It can be set up to automatically shift the dates of all other activities associated with a project if one activity is late, and it can notify you if the change will make it impossible to meet a deadline.

Develop Program Components and Tracking Mechanisms

Once you have determined that the mix of program components and the timeline are reasonable, the components can be developed and, if necessary, pretested. Providing detailed guidance for developing every conceivable component is beyond the scope of this book. However, Chapter 15 provides guidance on developing promotional materials and activities, and Chapter 11 includes a discussion of pretesting.

As components are developed, process evaluation mechanisms should be built into them. It is often much more expensive to retroactively collect monitoring data, and doing so makes it much more difficult to refine and improve the initiative. Chapter 16 provides a range of ideas for process evaluation mechanisms.

Prepare Spokespeople and Other Staff

Anyone who will talk publicly about the initiative is a spokesperson, whether the individual speaks on national television or at an internal meeting. As the time for implementation draws near, it is important to make sure that all spokespeople can frame the issue appropriately and clearly articulate the program's goals, objectives, target audiences, and major activities.

Formal spokespeople should receive thorough briefings and be prepared to deal with questions and criticisms, to minimize the likelihood that they will get blindsided when speaking about the program in a public forum. Two activities can help you prepare spokespeople:

1. Contact other practitioners who have been involved with programs focusing on the same public health problem. Ask them about the usual criticisms or concerns they hear and the responses they provide.

2. Review media coverage in your area and, if possible, attend any gatherings where the topic is likely to be discussed (for example, county or school board meetings). What is the usual angle of attack? How can these statements be defused or (as is sometimes true) shown to be incorrect?

You can use the information gathered from these activities to prepare talking points and "Q&A" (likely questions and their appropriate, on-strategy answers). Spokespersons can better represent the initiative if they review these materials before they speak about it or attend a meeting or event where they are likely to be asked about it. It is a good idea to update the materials regularly as the program evolves and as you develop a better sense of the usual questions about it.

Formal media training can be useful for spokespeople who will speak publicly about the initiative. This process will help them become more comfortable when handling media interviews (or questions from any audience), as well as help them to learn (and, more important, practice) how to make key points, how to respond properly to various types of questions, how to continue to frame the issue appropriately, and how to maintain their composure in stressful situations. Speaking publicly about a program or service can be a minefield, particularly if reporters are present. The bullet points below were drawn from advice to hospital spokespeople who will be interviewed by the media (Lewton, 1991), but they apply equally to any public discussion of a program or service and illustrate a few of the many potential pitfalls.

- Don't answer hypothetical questions.
- Don't accept unfamiliar facts or statistics, or assumptions with which you do not agree. Don't even repeat them—you could end up quoted using exactly those words.
- Don't argue or get angry with a reporter, especially on camera.
- If you need a break to think and regroup, take one. If necessary, have a coughing fit and ask for a glass of water.

Because it is by nature adversarial, it is best if someone from outside your organization conducts media training sessions with spokespeople. Many public relation agencies and some independent practitioners provide media training sessions.

Brief Partners, Intermediaries, and Stakeholders

Prior to rolling out a new campaign or making changes to existing products or services, it is vitally important that all partners, allies, intermediaries, and other stakeholders be briefed on the upcoming activities. Failing to do so can engender bad feelings because it puts people in a position of not knowing what is going on. It can also jeopardize the chances for success.

The form and nature of the briefing can be tailored to each entity's involvement in the program. Partners and allies should know, in a general sense, all of the activities that are taking place and the specifics related to the when, where, and how of any component that might involve them, even if their involvement will be tangential. This knowledge helps them complement your activities and ensures that they can respond to questions about them. For joint activities, such briefings probably will focus on details and may take place at a meeting. For separate activities, briefings can be in the form of a memo, phone call, or face-to-face meeting. If an organization is playing a role in the activity, it is best to provide the briefing in writing, even if it is a conference report or e-mail prepared after the meeting that summarizes the decisions made about logistics.

The extent to which intermediaries are briefed depends on the role they are playing and how closely they are involved with the activity. In general, they need the details of what they are being asked to do, when they should do it, and how their role will contribute to accomplishing change. Updating the intermediary on other aspects of the program provides a framework and context for the role the intermediary is playing.

When briefing intermediaries, consider both those who are directly involved with your initiative and those who may have to deal with its results even if they are not serving as a direct conduit to the target audience. The following is an example of what can go wrong if you neglect the latter. A few years ago, a new drug regimen to combat a deadly disease was so successful in clinical trials that the sponsor discontinued the trials and announced the treatment so that people in the control group and others across the country could benefit. For various reasons, the letter to physicians discussing the treatment was sent out after the news appeared in the popular media. Physicians found themselves besieged by patients asking about a drug therapy they knew nothing about. The delayed notification of this key intermediary—physicians—meant that patients had to wait before they could talk to their physicians about whether the product would work for them. It also alienated the physicians because they were made to seem less knowledgeable than their patients.

It is also important to brief internal and external stakeholders to make sure that they have an accurate picture of the initiative and how it is intended to work. Without a briefing, they may piece together what you are doing based on some informal communiqués from people who are less knowledgeable and provide faulty descriptions—or who deliberately take one real or imaginary element of a program and blow it out of proportion. Internal stakeholders may begin to question the need for your program, subvert its implementation, or consider diverting the resources it requires. External stakeholders may openly oppose the program, pressuring your organization to discontinue it before it is even in place. Upfront briefings can go a long way toward minimizing such problems.

For example, some school districts working to provide comprehensive school health programs deliberately seek out stakeholders who may be concerned about some aspects of health education or health services, such as how sex education will be taught or whether condoms will be available in school clinics. By briefing these stakeholders before a program is put in place—and, ideally, involving them in the planning process—the administration can make sure that they have a clear picture of what the program really involves. While such an approach will not resolve all opposition, an up-front, open discussion can defuse criticism by making sure judgments of reasonable stakeholders are based on facts and providing an opportunity for them to voice concerns—and time for program planners to address many of these concerns prior to implementation.

Implement, Monitor, and Refine as Needed

The quickest route to failure is to promote a new product or service, get people excited and ready to try it, and then fail to deliver it. All program components need to be ready for implementation before you implement. Often, goods, materials or services are delayed. The best alternative at that point is to delay the launch of your program until they are ready.

Once implementation has begun, close monitoring is essential to success. This can be accomplished by regularly reviewing tracking and monitoring data, as discussed in Chapter 16, and comparing progress to what you had planned. What is working? What isn't? What new opportunities are presenting themselves? The review provides an opportunity to plan a course of action and make the changes. The planning, implementation, and refinement cycle is never finished—strong managers always look for, and are open to, ways to improve the initiative.

■ CONCLUSION

We cannot say it better than Green and Kreuter (1991):

> In the final analysis, textbooks can offer little on implementation that will improve upon a good plan, an adequate budget, good organizational and policy support, good training and supervision of staff, and good monitoring in the process evaluation stage, discussed in Chapter [16]. The key to success in implementation beyond these six ingredients is experience, sensitivity to people's needs, flexibility in the face of changing circumstances, an eye fixed on long-term goals, and a sense of humor. (p. 205)

References

Gemunden, H.G. (1985). Perceived risk and information search: A systematic meta-analysis of the empirical evidence. *International Journal of Research in Marketing*, 2, 79–100.

Green, L.W., & Kreuter, M.W. (1991). *Health promotion planning: An educational and environmental approach* (2nd ed.). Mountain View, CA: Mayfield.

Green, L.W. & Kreuter, M.W. (2005). *Health program planning: An educational and ecological approach* (4th ed.). New York: McGraw-Hill

Kotler, P., & Roberto, E.L. (1989). *Social marketing: Strategies for changing public behavior*. New York: Free Press.

Lewton, K.L. (1991). *Public relations in health care: A guide for professionals*. Chicago: American Hospital Publishing.

CHAPTER

14

Working with Partners, Allies, Coalitions, and Intermediaries

Working with other organizations is an important part of most social change efforts. Building and maintaining effective relationships with other organizations takes time, involves compromise, and often is critical to achieving desired outcomes. Types of relationships between organizations include partnerships, in which two or more organizations jointly sponsor an initiative or component of it; alliances, in which two or more organizations with very different goals come together for a specific, usually short-term, common interest; coalitions, which are similar to alliances but typically involve addressing a health problem over the longer term; and networks of intermediaries that form the channels of distribution for products, services, or materials.

■ ROLES OF PARTNERS, ALLIES, AND INTERMEDIARIES

Working with other organizations often is necessary to successfully bring about change. They can provide additional resources, greater credibility with their constituencies, and expertise that your organization does not possess. Some entities can provide channels of distribution that will allow you to lower barriers to access, increase utility, or deliver a bundle of benefits to the target audience (Strand, Rothschild, & Nevin, 2004). As we discussed in Chapter 9, social marketing efforts often are deficient in these areas.

Organizations or individuals working to bring about changes related to public health may have a need to work with

- public agencies
- community-based organizations
- health voluntaries, such as the American Cancer Society, the American Heart Association, or the American Diabetes Association
- foundations, both those specific to particular diseases and those with a more general focus
- associations of, or foundations set up and supported by, producers of particular products
- individual for-profit businesses—local, regional, or national
- professional associations
- other consumer or health organizations, both national and local
- the media: specific networks, stations, publications, or associations, such as the National Association of Broadcasters

Just as the organizations to get involved come in many varieties, relationships among these organizations come in many forms. Sometimes it is desirable to assemble a strategic alliance of organizations with a common goal; generally, each ally makes a contribution to the effort based on the organization's capabilities and resources. At other times, it is enough to gather supporters; this approach is a good way to demonstrate (and obtain) widespread support on a particular set of recommendations or guidelines.

For other situations, two or more organizations may partner for a specific project or a large-scale program. These partnerships can be relatively simple, narrow in scope, and short-lived, or they can be quite elaborate and last for a decade or more

Finally, many public health initiatives work through a number of intermediaries to reach their target audiences. The traditional role of the intermediaries is to deliver messages, materials, products, or services to the target populations. The mass media are an important intermediary that most programs work with from time to time. For some national agencies, state health departments are the key intermediaries. For professional associations, their members become intermediaries because they are the ones who will actually deliver the message to the target audience. And for community interventions, community-based organizations, local businesses, schools, and other nonprofit and public agencies may play important roles. Public health practitioners would be wise to expand this traditional conceptualization of partners and intermediaries to think more broadly about the channels of distribution they can use to deliver benefits and reduce barriers to their desired health behaviors. "Social marketers need to create and deliver value to our target audiences, remove barriers that inhibit audiences' ability to acquire our services, understand and fit with our audiences' daily life processes, and differentiate our offerings from those of our competitors" (Strand, Rothschild, & Nevin, 2004, p. 12).

■ SUGGESTIONS FOR DEVELOPING SUCCESSFUL RELATIONSHIPS

Exhibit 14-1 presents some general suggestions that apply to all types of potential allies, intermediaries, and partners. Each suggestion is described in further detail below.

Identify Benefits to Partners

Understanding the benefit to the other organization is important when an organization is actively seeking partners, but it is also important to keep in mind when working with them. Sometimes the other organization's actions, positions, or requests may not make sense until you step back and think about it from their position and what they are looking for in the relationship. Potential benefits include

- providing a means of furthering their organization's mission to service particular publics;
- enhancing credibility or stature in the community and with target audiences;
- increasing sales (most often for private sector partners).

Consider Impact on Credibility

Other organizations can be critical for establishing credibility with particular audiences, particularly if the sponsoring organization is unknown or not trusted by target audience members. For example, a government agency trying to reach out to intravenous drug users might be far more successful working through a trusted community-based organization than trying to reach the audience directly.

In some instances, a potential partner may have a negative impact on credibility. This issue often arises when a nonprofit organization or government agency is considering working with a private firm. For example, a pharmaceutical company might be interested in sponsoring aspects of a state or local chronic disease initiative, or might want a nonprofit or government agency to partner with it on a particular project. Often such partnerships can proceed without damaging the credibility of the initiative or the nonprofit/government partners, but it is necessary to think through how the partnership—and the motives of each organization—might be perceived.

Exhibit 14-1   Suggestions for Developing Successful Partnerships

- Think of potential partners, allies and intermediaries as target audiences: What is the benefit to them of helping you?

- Consider each organization's impact on the initiative's credibility.

- Find out what your organization can legally and ethically do before embarking on establishing relationships.

    - What organizations are appropriate to work with?

    - What can you ask other organizations to do?

    - What can you do for those organizations in return?

    - What activities can other organizations undertake that your organization cannot?

- Develop clear ideas of the roles you want other organizations to play—and an understanding of what roles they should not have (from your organization's perspective).

- Be flexible—losing prospective partners can limit a program's effectiveness.

- Put agreements in writing.

- Understand the challenges of working with other organizations.

Identify Legal and Ethical Restrictions

It is important to find out what your organization can legally and ethically do before exploring possibilities with partners. For example, public sector organizations often have to follow myriad laws and regulations regarding relationships with other organizations. Nonprofit organizations have some limits on their activities if they receive federal funding, or may have limits on how they can spend certain types of grants. Knowing what you can and cannot do before starting to create relationships helps shape ideas and saves time, headaches, hard feelings, and sometimes money.

What partners are appropriate? It is best to avoid even the appearance of impropriety. Appropriate partners are those with whom your organization can work publicly without appearing to compromise its integrity. Situations in which to be particularly cautious include the following:

- Regulatory agencies must be very careful about working with any organizations they regulate; such relationships can be construed (by the organizations themselves, their competitors, or members of governing bodies) as meaning that the agency will "look the other way" on any regulatory infractions committed by the partner. Worse yet, large agencies can find themselves in the embarrassing position of having one department partnering with an organization that is under severe sanctions by another department.

- Organizations that issue grants and contracts must be careful about partnering with organizations that are or could become recipients of such awards. Competitors or other stakeholders may assume that working with the funding agent provides partners with an unfair advantage for upcoming grants and procurement.

In addition to the advice provided by your organization's legal counsel, ask yourself this question: "If I woke up tomorrow and read about the relationship in the newspaper, what negative angles would the article cover?" The media—and legislators with an ax to grind—can find intrigue and misspent public or nonprofit funds in the most innocuous of relationships. If there are negatives, but you think they are outweighed by the positives, it would be prudent to spend some time planning how the organization would respond to criticism. Writing talking points and questions and answers that address potential criticisms of the partnership in advance of such criticism is good preparation.

What can you ask partners to do? Before exploring any options with partners, it's a good idea to find out if there are any restrictions on the types of things other organizations can do to support the program, and the ways in which they can indicate their involvement. For example, it is usually fine for private companies to print copies of materials for public agencies—but it may not be if the company's sponsorship will be identified by brand name. If you are going to work on a joint project, such as a classroom or community kit, what are the limitations on visible sponsorship? To what extent (if at all) can brand-name products be featured? To what extent can a public agency or nonprofit organization be represented on the materials? Understanding these restrictions is critical, particularly in public-private partnerships. Often, the main benefit to a private company of working with the public agency is publicizing that relationship. If they can't stamp the public agency's name next to theirs, and their name on products developed as part of the partnership, they may have little incentive to be a partner.

Another issue here is how much control each organization can maintain over the other's activities. For example, if a partner is developing a classroom kit that will feature the program logo, can you approve or reject the contents? For public agencies, the legal answer is often no; you can make suggestions and provide technical assistance, but if the partner is developing it, they control it. Be careful about depending on them to do the right thing.

What can you do for partners in return? The answer to this question may vary somewhat depending on the type of entity—public agency, nonprofit, or for-profit organization—and their existing relationship with your organization. Some of the restrictions here are fairly obvious. For example, most public agencies cannot endorse or appear to endorse particular commercial products. As an extension of this, most public officials must be diligent about ensuring that their presence is not construed as an endorsement of the other organization or its products or services.

On the other hand, providing technical assistance is usually fine—unless the partner is going to sell the resulting product for profit. Then it can become a problem. Asking about specific examples, and as many "what ifs?" as you can think of, is the best way to uncover everything you need to know up front, rather than finding out after the materials or products are developed that they cannot be distributed as planned. Joint projects can get tricky, particularly if the organization is asking for you to fund part of its work. However, sometimes this can be accomplished through a cooperative agreement, where the roles and contributions of both partners are spelled out.

What activities can partners undertake that your organization cannot? Most public agencies, particularly federal agencies, have myriad restrictions on how they can spend money. Nonprofits often piece together money from a variety of sources, and each source may impose different restrictions. Sometimes partner organizations have far fewer restrictions on their activities and therefore can accomplish things that your organization cannot—or can accomplish them faster. The possibilities range from relatively simple tasks, such as providing food for a luncheon or producing high-quality printed products in a short time frame, to far more complex ones such as controlling copyrights.

The copyright issue can be an important one, particularly if you envision developing a strong program identity. Many organizations may want to associate with an initiative by featuring the program logo or symbol on their products or materials. You may want to control who uses the logo and how it is used; for example, it would make sense to restrict use of the logo to partners who are making a contribution to the program (either a monetary one or through in-kind services or materials). Or if it is a logo to appear on products, you would want to clearly define guidelines for products on which it could appear and make sure that the logo or symbol did not appear on products not meeting the guidelines. Nongovernmental entities control their logos by copyrighting them.

The Food Guide Pyramid developed by the U. S. Department of Agriculture provides an illustrative example of what can happen when there is no copyright. The pyramid is probably one of the most widely used symbols the government has ever produced. Walk down nearly any aisle in a U.S. supermarket and you are bound to find it on something. You will find the original official version. And you will find dozens of permutations of it. Most manufacturers include it as a way of saying, "The government says you should eat this." Actually, the government has said no such thing. Yet, since the pyramid is not copyrighted, the government has no way to control its use. Federal government agencies can only copyright material under very limited circumstances; most of what they publish enters the public domain and can be used by anyone in any way. From the taxpayers' standpoint, this makes sense: taxpayers paid for the work, so they ought to be able to use it. From the standpoint of the government, inability to copyright makes monitoring the use of program logos and symbols very complicated.

Develop Appropriate Roles

As discussed in Chapter 10, your strategic plan should outline some of the roles you expect other organizations to play. For example, there may be components of the initiative that should be developed by a partner organization because it has greater expertise in the subject matter and/or more credibility with the target audience. Similarly, the work plans developed for specific tactics will usually include concrete recommendations for specific channels of distribution: intermediaries who will take your product, service, or materials to your target audience.

But sometimes the program conceptualization includes the involvement of various types of organizations without specifying exactly who they will be. Having a list of things prepared that other organizations can do—and another list that reminds you of what they cannot do— saves time and keeps you from losing potential partners while you try to figure out what role they could play. It also helps you retain control of the initiative and ensure that it stays on strategy—because, of course, all of the items on the list will be appropriate for the objectives the program is trying to accomplish. Without a list, it is easy to get caught up in the frenzy of developing a new program and approve an idea that sounds really wonderful but will not help accomplish any program objectives.

Ideally the list should be divided into low-, medium-, and high-involvement activities, so that you can tailor suggestions to the level of commitment the other organization wants to make. Major partners may wind up involving themselves in an entirely different way, but the list serves three purposes: (1) It provides them with some initial ideas to work from; (2) it shows them you are organized and ready to go; and (3) it keeps your program on track.

Sometimes the best way to involve other organizations is to invite them in and figure it out together. However, such meetings require structure or everyone can walk away frustrated. **Exhibit 14-2** presents an approach to holding successful, rewarding conversations.

Be Flexible

Partnership opportunities often arise quickly, particularly as an initiative is gaining momentum. Your program should be flexible enough to incorporate new ideas (as long as they are on strategy) or help from

---

Exhibit 14-2 The World Café

World Café is a process for using focused conversations to foster productive relationships, collaborative learning, and collective insight.

Set the context: Articulate the purpose of the discussion (based on your understanding of the current situation and your assumptions), determine the right participants for it, and identify the parameters of the discussion. Though a café conversation is designed to avoid predetermined outcomes, clarifying possible outcomes helps shape the conversation. Think about a meeting, conference or gathering you've attended that went really well. What was it about how the context was set—either prior to or at the event itself—that contributed to its effectiveness?

Create hospitable space: Ensure a welcoming environment and psychological safety that nurtures personal comfort and mutual respect. Use creative ways to make the meeting environment more dynamic and collaborative. Consider ambiance—music, lighting, access to the outdoors. Think about times when you participated in a really great conversation. What was it about the setting or the environment (physical or psychological) that contributed to its success?

Explore questions that matter: Focus collective attention on powerful questions that attract collaborative engagement. Genuine questions—ones for which we don't have answers—are open invitations to innovativeness. What question, if explored thoroughly, could provide the breakthrough possibilities we are seeking?

Encourage everyone's contribution: Enliven the relationship between the "me" and the "we" by inviting full participation and mutual giving. How might you help people evolve from thinking of themselves as meeting participants to thinking of themselves as active contributors to something larger than themselves?

Cross-pollinate and connect diverse perspectives: Use the living-system dynamics of emergence through intentionally increasing the diversity and density of connections among perspectives while retaining a common focus on core questions. For example, group participants at small tables, then have some of them physically move in iterative rounds of conversation that are 20–30 minutes in length (sometimes longer).

Listen together for patterns, insights, and deeper questions: Focus shared attention in ways that nurture coherence of thought without losing individual contributions. Ask members to take a few moments of silence to consider or make notes on a key insight, idea, or discovery. Ask what's taking shape, what's missing, what the next level of discussion should be.

Harvest and share collective discoveries: Make collective knowledge and insight visible and actionable.

---

unexpected quarters. One of the challenges of working with partners is marrying their ideas and their mission with yours. If an idea truly will not fit, try to suggest a modification that will.

Put Agreements in Writing

Agreements can be formal or informal, but they should always be in writing. If an intermediary agrees to include information on your next cancer screening event on its website or in its newsletter, a quick memo or e-mail can confirm the details. Elaborate cosponsored projects or programs normally have a memorandum of understanding outlining the roles and responsibilities of each partner. Some partnerships may be governed by formal cooperative agreements, particularly when funding flows from one partner to the other. Written agreements safeguard against subsequent misunderstandings by providing a record of what was supposed to happen. They serve as memory for current staff and are invaluable in cases of staff turnover. Plus, they help you manage the program by reminding you of who is doing what and when, so that you can ensure that they have everything they need to perform.

Understand the Challenges

As the National Cancer Institute (NCI) (1989) noted, working with other organizations can

- be time consuming—to locate, convince them to work with you, gain internal approvals, and undergo planning and/or training;
- require altering your program—every organization has different priorities and perspectives, and other organizations may want to make minor—or major—program changes to accommodate their structure or needs;
- result in loss of "ownership" and control—because other organizations may change the time schedule, functions, or even the messages, and take credit for their part (or all) of the program.

■ COALITIONS

Coalitions are groups of organizations that come together to address a common goal. They are most often run by a committee comprised of representatives from each (or many) coalition's members. Coalitions are characterized by two-way relationships; each member has a say in how the program or its components are developed, and each makes contributions to the program. Many of these same factors characterize a relationship between two organizations that jointly sponsor a program or project, so this section can be of use for assessing prospective partners as well as prospective coalition members.

Coalitions are often formed at the community level, but the scope of coalitions can be international, national, regional, statewide, or local. Coalitions take an enormous amount of time and energy to establish.

Exhibit 14-3   Questions To Ask before Establishing a Coalition

If your group may take a leading role in establishing a coalition, answer the following questions to determine whether this is the best choice:

• Is there an organization already in place that could effectively and more efficiently address this problem?

• Would this problem be more effectively or permanently solved with the joint ownership and responsibility of others or can our organization be just as effective working on its own?

• Are there gaps in community services that would be best met through collaborative relationships?

• Is this problem perceived as a priority by other organizations?

• Are we willing to relinquish control of the project to a coalition or do we just want advice? (A coalition may be willing to concede lead responsibility to one agency after agreeing on goals and overall strategy.)

• Do funding sources or our own agency constraints make it impossible to give up or share control of the project?

Source: Project LEAN idea kit for state and community programs to reduce dietary fat. Menlo Park, CA: The Henry J. Kaiser Family Foundation. Not dated.

Exhibit 14-3 lists some questions to ask before establishing a coalition, to help ensure that the coalition approach is the best approach to take.

If you have worked through the list of questions and want to proceed with establishing a coalition or partnership, here are some tips for recruiting and selecting coalition members or partners. They are adapted from information provided in the idea kit commissioned by the Henry J. Kaiser Family Foundation[1] to support development of Project LEAN's coalitions.

• Identify the skills and expertise coalition members will need.
• Look for possible members. Potential organizations (or individuals) should possess at least one of the following attributes:
    – Interest in and commitment to the issue
    – Credibility in the community (as formal or informal leaders)
    – Contacts with other potential members or allies
    – Familiarity and experience with the political system
    – Materials or expertise in program development, promotion, implementation, or evaluation

A good way to identify prospective members and make sure that you are not missing anyone important is the "snowball" method: Interview people who represent organizations, factions, or constituencies you know are respected in the community or field in which you are working. Explain why you are creating the coalition and what you expect it

---

[1] Courtesy of Henry J. Kaiser Family Foundation, Menlo Park, CA.

to accomplish. At the end of the interview, ask the person for names of other organizations or individuals who could potentially contribute to solving the problem. If you are putting together a local or statewide coalition, make sure to include grass-roots leadership. You will know you have identified everyone when the people you interview start providing you with the same names you have heard.

- Take time to get to know potential members, and be cautious before issuing invitations. Make sure that there is a good match between their abilities and the needs of the coalition. Make sure they understand that you are recruiting them not as individuals but as representatives of their organization or constituencies. Assess how committed they are to working cooperatively with others. Think about how they will fit into the mix of members and how they will affect the image of the coalition. Members should not consist entirely of agencies, gatekeepers, and political power holders; grass-roots community leaders and people who have time to work on specific projects and other issues are also important.

- When you issue invitations, be very clear about how much organizational involvement you expect, which could range from public endorsement by their board to the contribution of resources or the appointment of a representative to the board of the coalition.

- Put together participation agreements for all members. The agreements should spell out time limits for membership and any other conditions for involvement in the coalition (for example, if membership is organizational rather than individual, if the individual leaves the organization he or she will no longer be a member of the coalition). Depending on your environment, participation agreements could be an informal memo from you to all members about "keeping everyone informed," or a more formal contract for each member.

Once a coalition has been established, the first order of business is to develop a leadership structure and operating procedures. This process should include the following (many of these suggestions also were adapted from information provided in the idea kit commissioned by the Henry J. Kaiser Family Foundation to support development of Project LEAN's coalitions):[2]

- *Leadership.* Who will hold leadership roles and how will these people be selected? The chair needs to have the ability to set agendas and conduct meetings efficiently while fostering communication and a strong sense of the coalition's direction. If the membership will elect a chair, members should have enough time to get acquainted so that people with strong leadership skills can emerge. One way to proceed is to appoint an interim facilitator (preferably one who is not interested in the position of chair).

---

[2] Courtesy of Henry J. Kaiser Family Foundation, Menlo Park, CA.

- *Coalition/staff relationships.* Who has the authority to oversee the project's development and operation? In many coalitions, it is the coalition members, not the staff (who are often provided by the organization that established the coalition). Staff often must balance providing technical assistance to members so that members can best carry out their roles with the members' role of decision making.

- *Bylaws or rules of operation.* How often will the coalition meet? How long will meetings last? How will decisions be made—consensus or majority rule? What constitutes a quorum? How will the work get done—by the full coalition or through task forces or committees? Who has the authority to speak on behalf of the coalition? How are coalition members appointed? What are attendance rules, and what happens to members who do not attend and participate? Establishing procedures to address these issues at the outset, rather than dealing with them reflexively when a situation occurs, will make the coalition run more smoothly and should keep members from feeling that they were treated unfairly when issues arise.

- *Mission statement and goals and objectives.* A clear, agreed-on mission is very important to the success of the coalition; every member should contribute to preparing the mission statement. All members should also be involved in developing goals and objectives that are clear, specific, and attainable, and in creating a work plan that emphasizes collaborative linkages among members. These activities are important in vesting members in the coalition and giving them ownership of it.

- *Coalition versus individual recognition.* The coalition should find ways to publicly recognize individual contributions without losing opportunities to advance the goals of the coalition. Recognition often becomes a sticking point in coalitions, because member organizations want credit for their contributions. One way to deal with the issue is to ensure that press releases mention the organizations taking the lead on any particular activity, another easy way to provide recognition is to include the names of organizations who developed or printed particular materials on those materials (though less prominently than the coalition name).

- *Guidelines for using logos, theme lines, or symbols.* If a coalition has many members or if it plans to allow other organizations to use its logos or symbols in some way, draw up licensing agreements that spell out what can and cannot be done with logos and other program materials. If possible, coalitions should copyright logos, symbols, and these lines so that they can control how they are used.

Coalitions are often created because many different types of entities will be necessary to successfully bring about a social change. Often, they choose to start off with small projects and build on their successes. Sometimes this is the best approach—particularly if they have few resources and lack dedicated staff to oversee larger endeavors. At other times, it makes more sense to tackle everything at once; **Exhibit 14-4** describes a coalition that the Academy for Educational Development has used with great success.

■ INTERMEDIARIES

In contrast to coalitions, which address a common goal, intermediaries are organizations that may have different goals but will help you reach your target audience with tangible goods, services, messages or materials. In commercial marketing, these are termed marketing channels, the "set of interdependent organizations involved in the process of making a product or service available for use or consumption by the consumer or business user" (Kotler & Armstrong, 2004, p. 400). Relationships with intermediaries are often one-way compared with those among coalition members: Intermediaries have a strong voice in how a message, product or service is delivered to their population, but typically they do not shape the overall program goals, objectives, or strategies.

Many types of intermediaries may be involved in your program; common ones include mass media, professional associations, and consumer organizations (who can access their members). Websites, both your initiative's and those of others involved in the initiative, can form another important intermediary.

Marketers use channels to distribute products and services but also to create customer value by improving the customer's experience in terms of the ratio of benefits to costs (Strand, Rothschild, & Nevin, 2004). Thinking of channels as ways to create customer value may help you identify novel intermediaries you had not previously considered. Evaluating intermediaries in the same way that commercial marketers evaluate distribution channels can also help you create the most effective and efficient distribution strategy:

> To evaluate channel alternatives, companies align channels with customer buying behavior (recognizing it changes over time), ensure the channel fits with the set of products or services, and determine which channels offer the most favorable economics. (Strand, Rothschild, & Nevin, 2004, p. 9)

However, because many public health initiatives will not be able to exercise the same amount of control over intermediaries as a commercial marketer can, it is especially critical to identify and deliver meaningful benefits to intermediaries. Generally speaking, intermediaries don't work

Exhibit 14-4 Starting at Scale

Jordan is one of the ten most water-poor nations on earth. When the U.S. Agency for International Development (USAID) conceived the Water Efficiency and Public Information for Action (WEPIA) program, Jordanians already used less water per day than people in most other countries. Still, water from aquifers was being used at unsustainable levels. Millions of liters of water were being lost through antiquated plumbing systems and fixtures. And demand for water was increasing every day.

With Jordan's options for increasing the supply of water running out, WEPIA focused on reducing demand. It was an approach that would require technical advances, engineering-based solutions, and behavior change.

As a key component of the WEPIA approach, the Academy for Educational Development (AED) created a coalition of organizations from across many sectors and disciplines, using a framework called SCALE™ (Systems-based Collaborative Action for Livelihoods and the Environment; see **Figure 14-1**). Social marketers were at the table with ministry officials. Engineers sat down with people from Jordanian Television. NGO staff met with teachers. The organizations these people represented were linked not only to WEPIA but to each other. The goal was not to train these organizations or to have them put their stamp of approval on a plan that had already been developed. The goal was for all of these organizations to collaboratively develop a strategic plan and then act.

(continues)

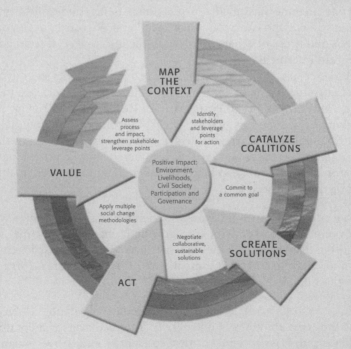

Figure 14-1 Systems-based Collaborative Actions for Livelihoods and the Environment (SCALE™). Copyright 2005 Academy for Educational Development.

Source: Copyright © 2005 by Academy for Educational Development. Reprinted with permission.

Exhibit 14-4 Starting at Scale (continued)

Cross-sector collaboration was enlightening for participating organizations. It gave them a new understanding of how their work fit with that of other entities. As a result, their own work took on new meaning—and they felt a greater impetus to develop collaborative responses to real-world problems. This interdisciplinary, collaborative approach to solving problems is one of the most significant results of WEPIA's work.

This collaborative approach had multiple effects. It energized Jordan's weak nonprofit sector and assisted in strengthening it. It applied social marketing concepts to change individual behaviors, and it helped create the standards and infrastructure needed to make water efficiency a reality.

Perhaps one of WEPIA's greatest achievements is that it did not try to demonstrate efficiency in a small area and then scale up from there. WEPIA, instead, started at scale.

Scale in Jordan meant working nationally in multiple sectors simultaneously. The only way to create change in social and cultural habits was to ensure that, wherever Jordanians turned, they would hear a single message delivered a thousand different ways, whether at school, at worship, in the newspapers or on billboards, at work, or at play. Working at scale became the model with which WEPIA approached all its activities, whether it was with the general public, the universe of large consumers, NGOs, or even the governments of the region.

Today in Jordan, NGOs and CBOs, local government, national agencies, individual consultants, and the private sector are working together to address water-related issues on a scale not previously considered possible—at a fraction of the cost.

In addition, more than half of Jordan's largest water-using facilities have been retrofitted with plumbing fixtures that have reduced their annual water consumption by 18 percent. The National Jordanian Building Codes, which include water conservation, have been modernized, saving 1.4 million cubic meters of water each year. New school curricula are engaging Jordan's youngest citizens to develop the skills they will need as adults to make appropriate decisions about water. Volunteer students and homemakers have worked alongside Ministry of Water and Irrigation staff to provide free water audits to thousands of businesses and homes. Sales of water-saving aerators have skyrocketed. And, illustrating WEPIA's power to create jobs, Jordan now has its first cadre of female plumbers.

Source: Adapted with permission from *From crisis to consensus: A new course for water efficiency in Jordan* by the Academy for Educational Development Center for Environmental Strategies. Copyright © 2005 by Academy for Educational Development.

for the sponsoring organization, typically have other commitments, and may not share the same bottom line (Strand, Rothschild, & Nevin, 2004). Strand and colleagues note that as a result, social marketing channel members may be partners, collaborators, or vendors. Meaningful benefits may include new products or services for the channel member's constituency; helping the channel member build new capacities or improve program effectiveness or efficiency, or providing material rewards, such as equipment, grants, or monetary compensation.

Exhibit 14-5 lists steps to help ensure that your attempts to involve intermediaries in program delivery are successful. Most of these suggestions apply to intermediaries with whom your organization works closely, although some also apply to more distant intermediaries such as the mass media. Chapter 15 provides a thorough discussion of issues to keep in mind when working with the media.

Exhibit 14-5 Steps for Involving Intermediaries in Your Program

1. Choose organizations, agencies, or individuals who can reach and influence your target audience(s).

2. Involve representatives of the organizations you want to work with as early as possible in program planning.

3. Give people at these organizations plenty of advance notice so that they can build their activities into their schedule, and make sure they are comfortable with the role they are to play.

4. Allow them to personalize and adapt program materials to fit their situations, and give them a feeling of "ownership" (as long as they stay on strategy).

5. Ask them what they need to implement their part of the program. Beyond the questions of funding, consider other assistance, training, information, or tools that would enable them to function successfully.

6. If necessary, gently remind them that they have responsibility for their activities, but remember that you may need them more than they need you.

7. Provide them with new local, regional, and/or national contacts or linkages that they will perceive as valuable for their ongoing activities.

8. Provide them with your program rationale, strategies, and messages—in ready-to-use form. Remember that strategic planning, creative messages, and quality production are the most difficult aspects of a communication program to develop, and may be the most valuable product you can offer to some intermediaries, such as community organizations.

9. Don't ask for too much at once. Make requests as small, manageable, and discrete as possible, and provide quick, easy feedback/tracking mechanisms.

10. Assess progress through the feedback/tracking mechanism, and help make adjustments to respond to the organizations' needs and to keep the program on track.

11. Remember to provide moral support, frequent thank-yous, and other rewards (e.g., letters or certificates of appreciation).

12. Provide them with a final report of what was accomplished, and meet to discuss follow-up activities and resources they might find useful. Make sure that they know they are a part of the program's success.

Source: Adapted from *Making Health Communication Programs Work: A Planner's Guide,* 1989, National Cancer Institute, Bethesda, Maryland.

■ CONCLUSION

Other organizations may be involved in public health initiatives as supporters, intermediaries, coalition members, or full partners. They can provide additional resources, expertise that your organization does not possess, and/or channels of distribution for an initiative's tangible goods, services, messages, or materials. Carefully developing distribution channels can allow an initiative to lower barriers to access, increase utility, or deliver a bundle of benefits to the target audience—areas in which many social marketing efforts often are deficient.

The keys to successfully working with other organizations are prior planning, careful consideration, and flexibility. The first step in involving them in an initiative is to assess what type of involvement would best further the initiative's goals. Before approaching other organizations, it is important to clearly understand what roles they can play and what responsibilities you must retain. When they "sign on," carefully articulate—and agree on—the role each will have. Finally, it is good practice to establish procedures governing how the partnership will accomplish its goals at the beginning of the relationship, to ensure smoother and more efficient operations throughout it.

References

Bellicha, T., & McGrath, J. (1990). Mass media approaches to reducing cardiovascular disease risk. *Public Health Reports,* 105(3), 245–252.

Henry J. Kaiser Family Foundation (n.d.). *Project LEAN idea kit for state and community programs to reduce dietary fat.* Menlo Park, CA: Author.

Kotler, P., & Armstrong, G. (2004). *Principles of marketing* (10th ed.). Upper Saddle River, NJ: Prentice-Hall.

National Cancer Institute. (1989). *Making health communication programs work: A planner's guide* (NIH Pub. No. 89-1493). Bethesda, MD: Author.

Strand, J., Rothschild, M. L. & Nevin, J. R. (2004). Session I: "Place" and Channels of Distribution. *Social Marketing Quarterly* 10 (3–4), 7–13.

CHAPTER
15
Promotional Materials and Activities

Most—possibly all—efforts to change individual health behaviors or policies implementing them, or increase support for public health as an institution, include promotional materials and activities. All such activities and materials can build on and reinforce each other and help build relationships with target audience members, if they communicate the strategic positioning and a common identity. They should be easily used or adapted by partners or intermediaries, and provide maximum progress toward achieving objectives for the resources invested.

Once a strategic plan has been developed, the program components most suited for effective implementation of the effort are chosen and developed, as discussed in Chapter 13. All of these components should communicate the initiative's core positioning and reflect its identity or brand. This chapter focuses on some of the most common promotional techniques: news coverage, entertainment education, advertising, websites, print materials, meetings and conferences, and special events. Entire books have been written on how to develop and implement many of the tactics discussed here; our intent is to provide an introduction to some of the practical issues involved with designing and using each type of tactic and some suggestions for assessing potential materials and activities in terms of their utility, cost, and contribution to the initiative's objectives.

■ ESTABLISHING IDENTITY

Establishing a consistent identity helps build recognition and relationships between target audiences and products, services, social change efforts, or public health institutions. Chapter 12 discussed how branding techniques can help develop this identity. To craft promotional materials and activities that convey a common identity and build on each other, the creative team can review the strategic positioning and image developed in Chapter 12 and use the information to develop the content of each activity or material and develop a set of visual and aural standards that will be used on all materials. These standards typically include:

- Campaign or program names, logos, and theme lines, and where and how they will be used.
- Two or three basic colors that are used on websites and all materials—from press releases, packaging and advertisements to t-shirts, sides of trucks, office or event signs, etc.
- Three or four typefaces as well as formats and layout elements for websites, other electronic communications, and printed documents (and paper stocks for the latter).
- Possibly music, if many audio/visual products are produced. For example, radio and television advertisements might use some of the same music.

Standards of this sort are particularly helpful in situations where many organizations may be developing campaign components—for example, as part of an alliance or coalition—or when promotions must be developed very quickly in order to respond to competing information (such as in the heat of a legislative or referendum battle). Establishing standards early on also streamlines the review process by confining it to the content and unique elements of each new item. Those working under tight time deadlines or in committee situations appreciate the ability to avoid new debate about typefaces, color, and where the logo goes each time a new material is presented. In addition, providing creative teams or graphic artists with the standards can help control costs by avoiding situations where they have to start over because the initial concepts were inconsistent with other materials or with the program's image.

When establishing standards, it is helpful to consider other materials and websites developed by your organization and determine if the materials for the new initiative need to be consistent with them. Large organizations may have existing standards (particularly relating to websites or print reproduction costs) that will also apply to your initiative.

■ PLANNING DEVELOPMENT TIME

Campaign planners are often unrealistic about the amount of time required to develop, test, and produce the many elements that comprise a multi-faceted promotional effort. The following outline can be used as a quick check when assessing plans and timelines for completeness and realism.

1. Determine types and quantities of materials to be developed based on the audience, the message, the desired reach and frequency, and the amount of time the campaign is expected to last. Determine how each material will be distributed. For websites, determine the number and complexity of the pages and whether they will form a new site or be added to an existing one.

2. Develop initial concepts (designs and copy points) for each material. For short materials, such as posters or advertisements, often two or three potential concepts are developed.

3. Prepare prototypes.

4. Pretest and submit the prototypes for peer or professional review in accordance with the processes described in Chapter 11.

5. Revise designs and copy to incorporate pretest recommendations.

6. Obtain commitments from directors, talent, photographers, and so forth. If existing artwork, audio, or video material will be incorporated, obtain necessary permissions and releases.

7. If necessary, prepare and submit an approval and/or clearance package that includes all necessary forms, pretest results, and revised prototype materials; revise the designs and copy to address the clearance comments.

8. Obtain final preproduction approval.

9. Produce rough cuts of audio and video materials and camera-ready versions of print materials; obtain approvals. For websites, develop all content and layouts and thoroughly test the site to make sure all links work properly.

10. Make final edits and obtain final approval.

11. Oversee production of the quantities required.

■ ASSESSING PROPOSED MATERIALS AND ACTIVITIES

The following questions can help you assess the utility of any proposed material or activity; subsequent sections of this chapter present issues to consider for specific types of materials and activities.

- *Is the approach and content accurate and on strategy?* The communication strategy (discussed in Chapter 12) was created to ensure that promotional materials and activities contain the appropriate messages, speak to the audience, communicate a relevant and appealing identity, and are delivered through openings likely to reach them. It is good practice to check all materials and activities prior to production to ensure they are scientifically accurate, consistent with public health goals and principles, and consistent with the communication strategy. Especially when materials undergo extensive edits prior to production, accuracy or identity sometimes slips away.
- *Is this the best solution for the least cost?* Public health efforts often have minuscule amounts of funding, so every material and every activity needs to work hard.
- *Does it complement and reinforce other aspects of the social change effort?* Materials and activities that reinforce each other in tone, in look, and in content are more effective because each additional time an audience member is reached, the new contact can build on the identity established before.
- *If it needs to be, is it easily reproducible and customizable by partners or collaborating organizations?* Considering customization and reproduction costs when materials and activities are designed makes it more likely that the final products can be used as intended. For example, if it is likely that intermediaries will photocopy a brochure or classroom materials, printing in dark inks on a standard paper size ensures that copies will be readable. Allowing for customization can increase use of an initiative's materials and enhance their credibility with intended target audiences.

■ MASS MEDIA

Public health initiatives can use mass communication tactics in a variety of ways. Perhaps most important, they can frame public discussion of an issue in terms of core values. They can also be used to increase knowledge, promote specific behaviors, provide sources of tangible goods or direct service delivery, and repeat and reinforce the messages target audience members receive in other forums.

Campaigns that are more effective use multiple media to deliver a single focused message multiple times (Backer, Rogers, & Sopory, 1992; Hornik, 1997; Hornik, 2002). Planners of public health initiatives can use news coverage, advertisements, entertainment programming, or a combination of all three to reach their audiences through the mass media. The mix appropriate for a particular initiative depends on many factors; program goals, communication objectives, the media environment, competition, and available resources all play a part. **Table 15-1** describes some of the major characteristics of mass media channels and the Internet.

The Role of Mass Media

Why are the mass media so important? Because the way they portray the world outside influences the pictures in our heads, to paraphrase Walter Lippmann (1922). What we see in newspapers, magazines, television, and on the Internet—and hear on the radio—can influence us in two ways. First, it can tell us *what* to think about. Second, it can influence *how* to think about it. As we discuss elsewhere in this volume, the media agenda plays a powerful role in setting the public agenda (people's perceptions of what issues are important) and the policy agenda (priorities of legislators, other government officials, and policy influencers such as political parties, lobbyists, think tanks, etc.).

Much of what we know about the media's influence on *what* we think about comes from communication researchers' studies of the way in which the media set the public agenda. Agenda-setting research began in earnest with McCombs and Shaw's (1972) landmark study of the media's role in the 1968 presidential election. They calculated the media agenda by analyzing the content of the main mass media reporting on the election and measured the public agenda by surveying undecided voters—and found an almost perfect correlation in the rankings of issues on the media agenda and the public agenda.

The mass media can influence *how* we think about issues by the way in which they frame their coverage. As Chapter 6 discusses in more detail, the attributes of an issue that are emphasized in media coverage can have a demonstrable impact on public opinion and behavior. McCombs and Shaw (1993) observed that "even when multiple attributes of an issue are included on the news agenda, there is likely to be a perceptible set of priorities" (p. 63). As the authors noted, many studies have demonstrated that this set of priorities is communicated to the public and reflected in what they deem to be important. These media and public agendas can in turn put pressure on the policy agenda—what political leaders are trying to accomplish (Andreasen, 2006).

How are health issues and health behaviors portrayed by the media? Andreasen notes, "Different framing results not only in different interpretations of data but in the ranking of social problems and in the solutions proposed for problems we might care about. Simple labels for social problems can have powerful impacts on the debate about solutions" (Andreasen, 2006, p. 47). His examples include U.S. debates over gun control versus gun safety and "a woman's right to choose" versus "protecting the rights of the unborn."

Wallack and colleagues (Wallack & Dorfman, 1996; Wallack et al., 1993) argue that the media tend to frame health issues in terms of individual health behaviors. Part of the job of social change initiatives is to work to reframe these issues in terms of public policy. However, the way in which media frame health behaviors is problematic as well:

Table 15-1 Characteristics of Mass Media Channels and the Internet

	Television	Radio	Magazines	Newspapers	Out-of-Home	Internet
Reach	Potentially largest, but audiences are increasingly fragmented.	Various formats offer potential for audience targeting.	Can target specific audience segments; audiences are increasingly fragmented.	Can reach broad audiences rapidly. Daily readership in decline. (Sunday readership growing.)	Can target specific neighborhoods; can achieve high frequency with one placement.	Offers many opportunities for targeting.
Openings for messages (other than ads)	News and talk shows; entertainment programming	News and talk shows; disk jockey chatter; letters to editor	Feature stories; regular columns; letters to editor	News stories; feature stories; regular columns	—	Websites; list servers; chat rooms; blogs; emerging formats
Use of public service announcements (PSAs)	Deregulation ended government oversight of PSA use and public affairs content; weak requirements for "educational" broadcast stations.	Deregulation ended government oversight of PSA use and public affairs content.	No requirements for public service/public affairs use; PSAs more difficult to place than on TV or content on radio.	No requirements for use; few larger papers use PSAs.	No requirements for use; limited PSA space available.	No requirements for use; PSA space available on some sites.
Appropriate messages	Primarily short and simple; viewers usually can't refer back to message.	Primarily short and simple; listeners can't refer back to message.	Can be short and simple or can provide more detail on complex health issues and behaviors.	Can be short and simple or can provide more detail on complex health issues and behaviors.	Outdoor: very short, simple. inside trains and buses: can provide more detail.	Ranges from short and simple, to detailed information on complex health behaviors.
Characteristics of medium	Visual and audio make emotional appeals powerful. Easier to demonstrate a behavior.	Opportunity for direct audience involvement via call-in shows.	Audience can clip, reread, and contemplate material and share it with others.	Can convey health news/breakthroughs more thoroughly than radio and faster than magazines.	Frequent viewership; retain control of TV message content.	Permits instantaneous updating; can retain control of message content.

(continues)

Table 15-1 Characteristics of Mass Media Channels and the Internet (continues)

	Television	Radio	Magazines	Newspapers	Out-of-Home	Internet
Type of audience interaction	Mostly passive; active possible with call-in shows.	Generally passive; active interaction possible with call-in shows. Requires attention when aired.	Permits active consultation. May pass on. Read at reader's convenience.	Same as magazines, but short life limits rereading and sharing with others.	Passive; attention may be fragmented or complete.	Permits active interaction; audience can easily search out additional information.
Production costs	Ads and video news releases are expensive.	Live copy: very inexpensive. Produced spots: much cheaper than TV.	Ads are inexpensive. distribution is inexpensive.	Ads are inexpensive.	Costs are higher than with print.	Depends on site design.
Editorial placement issues	Requires contacts and may be time-consuming.	Feature placement requires contacts and may be time-consuming.	Long lead time; relatively little control of timing (often determined by editorial calendar).	Newsworthiness is needed for news-coverage; little control over timing of feature.	—	Varies by format.

Source: Some information adapted from *Making Health Communication Programs Work*, National Cancer Institute, 1989.

Much of the research indicates that many if not most of the images in the media are in serious conflict with realistic guidelines for health, nutrition, and medicine. Research on the contributions of these portrayals to people's conceptions about health and medicine, although scarce, nevertheless indicates that those who spend more time with the media may have beliefs about health-related issues that are in conflict with the things they should do to remain healthy and/or improve the current status of their health. (Signorielli, 1993, p. 153)

Some of Signorielli's (1993) observations include the following:

• Characters in prime-time programming are healthy, relatively safe from accidents, hardly ever need glasses (even in old age), and rarely suffer any form of functional impairment.

• Televised characters rarely take precautions to protect themselves, such as wearing seat belts or using condoms. Nor do they act like good environmental citizens: they rarely recycle or use car pools or public transportation.

• Food, nutrition, and weight messages on television are very unhealthy; the diet portrayed is the opposite of dietary recommendations, but hardly anyone on television is even slightly overweight. Some researchers suspect that bulimia and other eating disorders are an adaptation to the conflicting messages. Food is presented as satisfying emotional or social purposes rather than hunger. Snacking (usually on a sweet) is shown as often as sitting down to a meal.

• Smoking and illegal drug use on television are relatively rare (though smokers abound in print advertisements and are usually portrayed as vibrant, healthy, and beautiful), but drinking is common. Characters drink in response to personal crises or tension and to enhance social interactions, but consequences of drinking too much are rarely presented adequately.

• When illness appears on television it takes center stage, is presented as acute, and is readily cured (except on some daytime serial dramas) with no consideration of the costs involved.

• Mentally ill characters are stigmatized, sinister, often violent, and unable to cope successfully with life.

• "Areas in which the media could provide a real service (e.g., providing full details about the dangers of smoking) often are not addressed because of economic and institutional considerations. It is more important to keep advertisers happy than to provide enough accurate information about health" (Signorielli, 1993, p. 153).

Throughout this book, we have noted that people are most strongly motivated by freedom, independence, autonomy, and control. Part of the reason the public—and policy makers—tend to be complacent about health issues is likely that the media, when they portray health problems at all, do not portray them as threatening any of these values. Sick or injured people either die or have virtually instantaneous recoveries (except, as Signorielli [1993] noted, on some daytime serial dramas, where they may linger in a hospital for months). Have a heart attack and wind up in cardiac arrest? Heroic physicians will fix you and you will walk out the door the next day. Have a cold or any other ailment that can be treated with over-the-counter medication? According to the advertisements, taking a pill will make you instantly better (Signorielli, 1993).

It is difficult to measure exactly how much the media influence people's perceptions of a given issue; many variables undoubtedly come into play. There is some evidence that the media influence perceptions more when other alternative sources of information are not available (e.g., a 1975 study by Tipton, Haney, and Baseheart found that agenda setting is less likely to occur in local than in national campaigns; in 1977, Palmgreen and Clarke reported that less agenda setting occurs when members of the public interact on local issues).

Nonetheless, the combination of the inaccurate way in which media (particularly television) portray health behaviors and issues coupled with the media's ability to set the public's agenda by what is or is not covered (and how it is covered) means that mass media can play an important role in many social change efforts.

Editorial Coverage

We use the phrase *editorial coverage* to refer to any content appearing in traditional media (newspaper, magazine, radio, or television) or on a news organization's website that is not an advertisement and, for television and radio, not an entertainment program—in other words, all the content under the control of an editor, such as news and feature stories, columns, editorials, op-ed pieces, and letters to the editor.

Many mass communication specialists believe that messages embedded in a medium's editorial content (e.g., in a news story) are perceived by target audience members as more credible than advertising. The major drawback of editorial coverage is the loss of control over message content. A few stations and publications will run a news release or suggested story exactly as written, but reporters often alter the material as they see fit. Key messages can easily become distorted or lost in this process. If editorial coverage is compared with paid advertising placement, lost control over reach and frequency is another drawback.

To successfully obtain news coverage of an initiative, it is important to understand

- How to build relationships with members of the media.
- How "newsworthiness" is determined.
- How to frame a topic to increase its newsworthiness and at the same time deliver the public health message.
- The characteristics of the various options for placement in each medium.

Building Relationships with the Media

The first step of effectively using the mass media is building relationships with the reporters, editors, and producers who determine what stories get covered. Many people are understandably uneasy about interacting with members of the media, but learning how to do so effectively can facilitate accomplishment of an initiative's goals. If your organization has a separate press office or public information department (and you are not part of it), a first step in planning media efforts is to determine what contact you can have with the media independent of that office and what support they can provide. This office may not be able to handle all of your media relations needs, either because of other responsibilities or because they have limited experience in "pitching" the media (trying to get them to cover a particular story).

The best way to begin building relationships with the media is by reading current newspapers, magazines, and websites or watching and listening to recent news shows to get a sense of what is covered, how it is covered, and who is covering it. If you are working regionally or nationally, a number of media directories can help you identify media to target. In addition to providing you with reporter and editor names and contact information, the directories provide statistics on circulation and audience size, information on the editorial profiles of publications and programs, editorial calendars, and types of press materials accepted.

One of the goals of building relationships with reporters and producers is to position yourself (and your initiative) as an important, reliable source of information so that reporters will call you when they are running a story on your topic. Once you have developed a media list, you can send a package introducing yourself, your initiative, and why it is important to your community (or region or nation, as appropriate). When reporters call or email, it is important to understand the parameters within which they work. In particular,

- Be ready. Know how you want to frame the topic and have short, pithy "sound bites" developed to support this positioning.
- Be sensitive to deadlines. If reporters want additional information, ask what their deadline is and then make sure you get them whatever they need before then.

- Be available. Make a list of who can talk to the press, and make sure someone on that list is always available—and that everyone else in the office knows who those people are and how to reach them.
- Be aware of the "rules" of talking to reporters: Never say anything to a reporter that you do not want to see in print or broadcast. With some reporters, it is possible to go "off the record" (i.e., say something that cannot be published or cannot be attributed to you as the source), but it is wise to do so only after you are sure you can trust the reporter.

Framing the Topic

In order to successfully gain coverage of a social change initiative, it is important to understand the goals of journalists, producers, and editors. In general, they want to appeal to the broadest number of audience members possible, and they want to tell a compelling story that is relevant to their audience and in the public's interest. Television producers need a visual aspect to the story as well. Therefore, it is incumbent on promoters of social change to frame the issues so that they are easily understood and have broad appeal. One way to ensure the latter is to frame the issue in terms of freedom, autonomy, independence, or control. Chapters 3, 6, and 12 discussed the process of framing an issue in more detail.

The following quote from an interview with Edwin Chen, at the time a science writer for *The Los Angeles Times*, on the role he has played in health communication campaigns illustrates the journalist's perspective:

> The U.S. surgeon general might say that smoking is bad or eating fatty food is detrimental for health, and heart disease prevention might be featured in a campaign by a government agency. But the *L. A. Times* does not see itself involved as a partner with, or part of, such education campaigns for health. The job of the *L. A. Times* is to cover the news. The newspaper might handle campaign press releases and promotional materials or report on the statements of different media campaign officials as long as such material is considered *newsworthy* . . .
>
> Editorial decisions are made to do certain stories, projects, or a series about some specific issue. . . . For example, the paper might write news stories on how to lose weight or measures to reduce the likelihood of AIDS transmission, but it does not see itself as part of a campaign to combat AIDS or other health problems. . . . The newspaper also seeks to inform its readers about what the government and government officials, other agencies, and concerned people are doing or not doing in combating AIDS or other health issues. (As cited in Backer et al., 1992, p. 58, emphasis in original)

Signorielli (1993) described the characteristics that define news:

Timeliness (news must be new); proximity (it happens close by or has psychological proximity); prominence (importance of the people), consequence (something that may have an impact on the lives of people in the audience); conflict (clashing of opposing interests); and human interest (stories that arouse emotion). News also must be inoffensive, fit into existing constructs (typically stereotypes), have a window of credibility, and be able to be packaged in small discrete chunks or bites (the 20-second sound bite) (Dominick, 1990; Meyer, 1990). It also must attract and maintain an audience. (p. xi)

Exhibit 15-1 lists some common questions journalists may ask themselves to determine whether a story is newsworthy.

As Wallack and colleagues (1993) noted, "media attention on health tends to be framed in terms of personal, individual issues that revolve around life-style, disease, and medical breakthroughs" (p. 56). Journalists often frame their stories from the vantage point of the individual's plight. Wallack and colleagues argued that this perspective creates problems when the goal is to stimulate policy changes, because it leads to an emphasis on what *individuals* should do to avoid a problem, rather than a discussion of changes that need to be made to address the *underlying social or environmental conditions*. One of the examples they cited is a crime story that focuses on what individuals can do to improve their safety (in reaction to a woman being kidnapped, raped, and murdered),

---

Exhibit 15-1 Elements of Newsworthy Stories

- Breakthrough—What is new or different about this story?
- Controversy—Are there adversaries or other tensions in this story?
- Injustice—Are there basic inequalities or unfair circumstances?
- Irony—What is ironic, unusual, or inconsistent about this story?
- Local peg—Why is this story important or meaningful to local residents?
- Personal angle—Who is the face of the victim in this story? Who has the authentic voice on the issue?
- Celebrity—Is there a celebrity already involved with or willing to lend his or her name to the issue?
- Milestone—Is this story an important historical marker?
- Anniversary—Can this story be associated with a local, national, or topical historical event?
- Seasonal—Can this story be attached to a holiday or seasonal event?

Source: L. Wallack, L. Dorfman, D. Jernigan, and M. Themba, *Media Advocacy and Public Health*, p. 98, copyright © 1993 by Sage Publications, Inc. Reprinted by permission of Sage Publications, Inc.

rather than on what could be changed to improve the safety of the environment (e.g., better lighting, more security). Chapters 6 and 12 discuss how to work toward framing the content of coverage so that it better addresses the social issues rather than personal problems.

Tactics to Attract News Coverage

Promoters of public health initiatives, issues, policies and institutions can choose from among a range of tactics to generate news coverage and influence how an issue or topic is framed on the public agenda. News releases, press conferences, media tours, editorial briefings, demonstrations, and special events are some of the most common.

News Releases. The heart of many efforts to gain editorial coverage is the news release, sometimes packaged in a press kit that can range from simple to elaborate. A health organization might issue news releases on a variety of newsworthy topics, such as the availability or implementation of infection control measures during a disease outbreak, the release of new study results, the opening of a new facility, or to announce an upcoming special event or award winner. News releases also provide an opportunity to communicate and reinforce your organization's identity through the consistent use of a tagline or descriptive statement.

Traditional written press releases are inexpensive and can be distributed to all types of media; audio and video news releases (ANRs and VNRs) are more expensive to produce—especially VNRs—but can provide the interviews and sound bites (and, for TV, video footage) that radio and television producers need to put together a story.

Written press releases should use the inverted-pyramid structure that journalists normally use: Who, what, where, when, why, and how should be covered, with the most important information at the beginning of the story, followed by progressively less important information. Then if the story needs to be shortened to fit in the available space, key points will not be cut. As with any communication from you or your organization, press releases can help—or hinder—efforts to build a relationship with a particular reporter. Carefully identifying the reporters who cover stories of the type you are releasing, and e-mailing the press release only to them, can pay off by conveying to the reporter that your organization has spent time determining what they cover. When possible, follow up with a short phone call referring to the reporter's recent coverage and explaining why you thought he or she might be interested in this story.

Audio or video news releases are typically about 90 to 120 seconds long and designed as stand-alone news stories, conforming to the broadcast news style conventions of each medium. They frequently include an interview with someone authoritative, such as a physician or researcher, and often a target audience member as well. VNRs can also include footage of the initiative "in action," for example, shots of a new clinic department or an event that took place as part of the initiative. There are a host of technical factors to consider when designing and producing broadcast news releases; the help of a producer skilled in broadcast news production is a must.

Prior to distribution, VNRs can be encoded with an electronic marker so that resulting usage of them can be tracked and their reach and frequency estimated. Chapter 16 discusses in more detail the type of tracking data available.

Press Kits. The contents and format of a press kit are determined in part by how it will be used. If a press kit is distributed in conjunction with or immediately following an event, the kit will generally include the event agenda, a press release, background information on the program, relevant photos, audio, or video, and (if applicable) speaker biographies. If the kit is sent separate from any event, it often includes a news release or cover letter, sample story ideas, and artwork or photographs (or b-roll for television producers).

For print and Internet media, quizzes and "top 10" lists can communicate key messages in a format many editors like and are disinclined to alter. Startling or unusual data presented in a graphically interesting fashion are also useful. Some editors like to include mentions of materials that their readers can order or links to websites with more information.

Press Conferences and Media Tours. Press conferences are usually convened to announce a new initiative or plans for managing a disease outbreak or other public health crisis; unveil study findings or a new product, service, or treatment; or discuss the availability—or unavailability—of a product, service or treatment. Press conferences can be useful for framing an issue through media coverage, as discussed in Chapters 6 and 12. However, they have some potential drawbacks. Most notably, there is a very real risk that no (or few) members of the media will attend—either because they do not consider the issue newsworthy or because some other breaking news story is more important.

If a press conference is held, it should be limited to 30 minutes, be in a location easily accessible to the media, and should include visuals and handouts. Speakers should be the highest level, most visible individuals you can find. To attract television coverage, the conference needs to include something visually interesting. Providing footage (*b-roll*) of activities relevant to the press conference can also help increase television coverage.

An alternative to a press conference is sending spokespeople on a virtual or real media tour, by scheduling interviews with news outlets at predetermined times. Interviews with print and radio reporters can take place over the phone; television interviews can be conducted via satellite uplinks from a local television studio, hotel conference room, convention center, or other location.

Demonstrations are another means of attracting the press. They can take many forms. For example, Wallack and colleagues (1993) discussed how tobacco-control advocates used an embargo on Chilean grapes to gain access to the media. The grapes were embargoed after cyanide was found on them. At press conferences, advocates stacked several bushels of grapes next to a pack of cigarettes to illustrate the quantity of grapes needed to equal the cyanide in one pack of cigarettes and the difference in government policy on fruit versus cigarettes.

Research studies. In addition to releasing results of traditional research studies, another approach is to sponsor a study that frames the issue in a striking way. The Center for Science in the Public Interest (CSPI) has mastered this technique. Its studies often generate enormous media coverage and stimulate product changes because they successfully create news that applies pressure to business leaders. For example, after its analysis of the nutrient content of movie popcorn was reported in the media, many major movie chains began using oils lower in saturated fat or offering air-popped options. The movie popcorn study illustrates the key components of CSPI's approach: Frame a critically important public health issue (the fat content of the American diet) in terms of a product many people use (broad appeal), at least some of whom probably select it because it is supposed to be "healthier" (irony and loss of control) and, instead of presenting numbers that people do not really understand (e.g., percentage of calories from fat or grams of fat), equate the fat to that found in a given number of Big Macs.

The latter part of the CSPI approach is something referred to as *social facts* or *social math*—the art of making numbers, especially large numbers, meaningful. Social math can be a valuable tool. It can help persuade a journalist to cover a story by increasing the perceived news value or providing a new angle, and it can make the story more compelling. Wallack and colleagues (1993), citing Petschuk and Wilbur, described three approaches to making large numbers meaningful: localization, relativity, and effects of public policy. Localization involves taking a large national number (e.g., tobacco causes 400,000 deaths in the United States each year) and applying it to a particular state or community. Relativity is what the members can easily identify. A variation is to make numbers smaller and more familiar. "You might want to remember that $1 billion a year translates into roughly $2.7 million per day, $114,000 per hour, and $1,900 per minute" (Wallack et al., 1993, p. 109).

Another important tactic is to summarize an issue's positioning in compelling sound bites, "short, concise summaries of your issue or position that can be conveyed in a few sentences or less than 10 seconds" (Wallack et al., 1993, p. 112). Sound bites often make their points through ironic analogy, such as CSPI expressing the amount of fat in a food as a quantity of Big Macs.

Coverage Opportunities in Each Medium

Newspapers, magazines, radio, and television all structure their news coverage somewhat differently and hence provide opportunities for different types of coverage. The following sections introduce some of the characteristics to weigh as tactics are planned.

Newspapers and Magazines. "Despite dire predictions that the Internet would kill off magazines and newspapers, Americans continue to read" (Roman, Maas, & Nisenholtz, 2003, p. 112). Mass magazines have declined slightly; special-interest titles—such as magazines about children, teens, and men's health—continue to grow. Daily local newspapers have been losing readers, although weeklies and "alternative titles" (free weekly paper emphasizing local entertainment) have been growing (Roman et al., 2003).

Online and print newspapers and magazines typically offer three main ways of reaching target audience members (other than through advertising): news coverage, a feature story, or a letter to the editor. Newspapers also offer the op-ed (opposite the editorial page) option. Beyond these basic similarities, each medium has important differences in terms of lead times, ratios of news stories to feature stories, and geographic area of interest. For the most part, newspaper reporters are writing tomorrow's story today, and with the exception of some special feature sections, newspapers contain mostly news. In contrast, reporters and editors at monthly magazines may be writing July's story in January, February, or March, according to an editorial calendar determined long before that. The news-to-feature ratios and closing deadlines of weekly news magazines (e.g., *Time*, *Newsweek*, *U.S. News and World Report*) fall between these extremes.

In newspapers, news coverage is often considered the most desirable because the news section of the paper tends to be the most read (especially by policy makers). In contrast, health-related feature stories often appear in the lifestyle or health sections, although there are times when newspapers run feature stories that take more of a social justice perspective in the news section. Letters to the editor and op-ed pieces are useful because the writer retains control over the message (and op-ed pieces are widely read by policy makers), but they are often run in response to previous coverage of a specific issue. Wallack and colleagues (1993) recommended meeting with the newspaper's editorial board as an important way to ensure that the paper at least considers the perspective of the initiative. They noted that sometimes such meetings can result in an editorial supporting an initiative's position; at other times such a meeting may at least moderate the newspaper's criticism of the position.

Radio. Many practitioners think that radio is underutilized by social change initiatives (Backer et al., 1992; Wallack et al., 1993). Americans spend more time with radio than with any other medium—over 20 hours a week—though most are not really listening the whole time (Roman et al., 2003). Radio coverage of an initiative can include news programs, call-in shows, a station's special promotion, or, as Chapter 7 describes, entertainment-education programming. News coverage often results from a written press release or media tour; sometimes audio news releases are used. Some initiatives make their experts available for interviews by station reporters during specific times, often in conjunction with an event.

Call-in shows are a chance to hear community reactions to a proposed social change, but also provide an opportunity for callers (or the host of the show) to disseminate messages that are decidedly off strategy. Before attempting to place a speaker on a call-in show or accepting an invitation to appear, it is wise to listen to a few shows to get a sense of the host and the audience.

Television. Television provides a number of openings to reach audiences with social change messages: news programs, talk shows, and entertainment programming. The latter is discussed in more detail in the Entertainment-Education section of this chapter.

For local television news, there is intense competition for high ratings in most markets; therefore, what gets on the news is usually what producers think will be most shocking or intriguing when used on news promos throughout the day. Because television "wraps every story in pictures" (Wallack et al., 1993, p. 56) and news segments are short, stories must be visually striking and simple.

Television talk shows run the gamut from completely news-oriented to completely entertainment-oriented programs. Morning talk shows can provide a forum to frame an issue or raise awareness of an upcoming special event. Appearing on talk shows requires contact with the producer; a celebrity spokesperson or a very newsworthy development coupled with an articulate, photogenic expert—and luck: The segment will get bumped if a story comes along that the producers think is more likely to attract viewers.

Local Print and E-mail Newsletters. The following non-traditional media can reach some target audiences through unexpected channels:

- Employer newsletters: Some large employers publish periodic newsletters (in print or electronically) that may include a health or wellness column.
- Bulletins and newsletters produced by churches and other religious institutions, community groups, and civic and homeowners' associations: While unlikely to include a health/wellness column, they might include mention of an upcoming event in which members could participate (for example, an immunization or screening drive).
- School system and parent-teacher organization newsletters: Many schools distribute electronic or print newsletters to parents periodically and might include upcoming public health activities that would benefit parents (and especially children). Some also regularly include health and wellness information.

Entertainment-Education

Entertainment-education is the process of embedding social change messages in entertainment media (i.e., movies, television programs other than news, some radio programs, books, novellas, comic books, interactive games); it is sometimes called "edutainment." Backer and colleagues (1992) noted that more effective campaigns utilize educational messages in entertainment contexts. Chapter 7 is a case study of a Rwandan radio program using this approach; it is the most popular radio program in the country and reaches up to 74% of the Rwandan population as well as substantial proportions of people in neighboring countries. Backer and colleagues (1992) provide other examples of how the entertainment-education approach has been used:

- In 1989–90 the Harvard Alcohol Project got the concept of a "designated driver" incorporated into episodes of 35 prime-time television series. A subsequent evaluation by Winston (1990) showed a resulting increased use of the designated driver idea by the U.S. public.
- Johns Hopkins University commissioned songs by popular recording artists in Latin America, the Phillippines, and West Africa to deliver family planning messages. One song was so popular in Mexico that it was played an average of 15 times a day over a period of several months. Backer and colleagues (1992) noted that "this massive, repeated exposure led to knowledge, attitude, and overt behavioral effects concerning sexual abstinence and contraception among the target audience of Mexican teenagers" (p. 169).

As these examples illustrate, the entertainment-education approach can involve developing custom products or working with others who develop programming and materials to incorporate health messages. In the United States, developing custom print and Internet products may be helpful to many initiatives, particularly for some audiences (e.g., comic books or a comic-strip format for young people, novellas when working with Latin American audiences, websites). For television, working with producers and writers of existing programming generally is the most useful and cost efficient approach for most initiatives.

There are a number of reasons to include entertainment-education as part of a social change effort. First, as was discussed earlier in this chapter, the media can influence people's perceptions of reality, and the entertainment media often do not accurately depict health consequences of behaviors or portray responsible behaviors. Second, it is important to reach audience members multiple times through multiple channels—and entertainment vehicles are additional channels and a means of reaching people who might not pay attention to a health program or product. Third, entertainment programming can provide an opportunity to build and maintain a relationship with the audience. This is important for any initiative, but in this context it can have the added benefit of allowing sensitive topics to be addressed that could not be addressed without an established trusted relationship between the audience and the initiative (see Chapter 7).

Entertainment-education approaches can support a social change effort in many different ways. For example, they can

- Model skills and appropriate behaviors. Simple behaviors can be portrayed, such as wearing seat belts, making healthful food choices, engaging in physical activity, taking blood pressure medication, or scheduling a mammogram. Or more complex skills can be illustrated, such as the negotiation or refusal skills needed to manage sexual encounters.

- Educate about realistic consequences of health-related actions and medical conditions. For example, incorporating concern about becoming pregnant or contracting the human immunodeficiency virus (HIV) in story lines that include unprotected sexual encounters or adding characters with chronic conditions such as asthma or more serious illnesses such as breast cancer.

- Influence social norms through highlighting appropriate behavior, commenting on unacceptable behavior, or portraying a range of acceptable options, especially if some of them are likely to be new to the audience. The radio program in chapter 7 is an example. As another example, as part of a large effort to improve end-of-life care in the United States, the Robert Wood Johnson Foundation (RWJF) co-sponsored *On Our Own Terms*, a four-part, six-hour PBS documentary on dying in America that explored the choices people have (or should have) that can lead to a more peaceful death. The foundation also funded the Last Acts Writer's Project, which made end-of-life experts and plot lines available to script writers and producers of television dramas, resulting in story ideas appearing in episodes of ER and other primetime programs (Bronner, 2003).

When approaching writers or producers with suggested story lines, consider the constraints under which they work. First, the ideas have to be consistent with the work's storyline and characters. For example, two episodes of *ER* dealt with the emotional as well as medical needs of a character who was dying—a natural outgrowth of the existing storyline that furthered RWJF's goal of changing expectations about the kind of care seriously ill patients should receive by increasing their knowledge of the possibilities (Bronner, 2003). Second, producers of commercial programming are unlikely to highlight any behavior that will make advertisers unhappy. The Harvard Alcohol Project managed this constraint by addressing drunk driving, not alcohol consumption per se (Backer et al., 1992).

Advertising

> Advertising is not generally the powerful force in moving consumers to act as many people think it is. Rather, it is a subtle force that must be skillfully planned and carefully deployed to maximize its effectiveness. (Tellis, 2004, pp. 16–17)

Compared with editorial placement efforts, advertising allows total control over message content and can include very effective emotional appeals (types of appeals are discussed in Chapter 12). It can be used by a social change initiative in many ways ranging from helping to frame an issue to modeling simple behaviors. However, the brief and fleeting nature of many advertisements (for example, 30-second TV and radio spots) makes them best suited for reminders or simple messages that require little context or explanation. Only print and some out-of-home advertising provide the space to develop ideas in greater detail.

Characteristics of Effective Advertising

In an extensive review of over 50 years of advertising research, Tellis (2004) identified characteristics of effective advertising: *Novelty*—in message, media, target segment, product, and creative—is more likely to result in increased sales than increasing media weight (e.g., running new advertisements, running them in different media, or targeting a new audience is more likely to increase sales than is spending more on advertising in a particular time period); and *emotional appeals* are more likely to be effective than are arguments (using evidence or force of logic) or endorsements (perhaps because emotional appeals are more interesting and thus can more easily cut through clutter and grab attention, because they require less concentration, and/or because they are more vivid and better remembered). In the same review, Tellis reported that:

- Advertising is a subtle force and its effects are not entirely instantaneous (either because consumers take time to think about the ad and become convinced, because they are convinced only after discussing it with someone else, and/or because they may not make the purchase until they are out of stock or feel the need for the product), though carryover effects are generally short, due to noise from competing ads, poor attention to ads, and competition from newer messages.
- Advertising is more effective for new than for mature products.
- Advertising affects loyal users and nonusers differently (loyals need relatively low levels of advertising for brands to which they are loyal, and become saturated with repetitive advertising sooner than nonusers; in contrast, for nonusers heavy repetition is more likely to gain their attention and affect them more positively).
- Advertising is effective early on or never; if effects are not seen in the first few weeks, the campaign is likely to be ineffective.

- Ads reach their peak effectiveness (wearin) almost immediately, and wear out rapidly, perhaps in 6–12 weeks, though wearout may take longer if an ad is complex, uses an emotional appeal, or is run less frequently.

While these findings resulted primarily from the study of consumer packaged-good advertising, they suggest some important considerations when developing and monitoring advertising campaigns to support policy or individual behavior changes. Specifically:

- Frequent change—in creative executions, in media, in audience segments targeted, but not in strategy, is likely to lead to greater success.
- The appropriate level of advertising (media weight) will depend in part on whether the target audience is "loyal"—familiar with and receptive to the policy or behavior, or "nonusers"—unfamiliar with the policy or behavior.
- Desired effects may not occur instantly, but if they are not observed within a few weeks, they are unlikely to occur and the advertising may need to be changed.

Basic Principles of Advertising
There are some basic principles that can be used to guide the development of all advertising, regardless of medium and whether placement will be paid or provided as a public service.

- Advertising messages should be consistent across media and consistent with messages delivered through other channels.
- The goal of advertising should be to sell, not entertain. There is no correlation between entertainment value and sales (Roman & Maas, 1992).
- As the saying goes, "Sell the sizzle, not the steak." The sizzle is the benefit to the consumer, not the product, service, behavior, or sponsoring organization.
- It may be tempting to "scare" the target audience into the desired behavior. Often that is a temptation best resisted. Messages that involve threat appeals are more likely to work with some audiences than others, must provide a resolution that the audience believes they can perform that eliminates or substantially minimizes the threat, and must be carefully tested prior to use. Chapter 12 provides more information.
- Humor can work but should be used carefully. It can relax an audience and make them receptive to a message, distract them from counterarguing, and help attract and retain attention to the ad (Tellis, 2004). Humor should deliver the key benefit, otherwise people may remember the joke but forget the action they are being asked to take. In addition, humorous commercials wear out fast, so you will need more spots than with other approaches. (Roman et al., 2003)

- Celebrity spokespeople should be used with care; generally, it is not a good idea to build an entire campaign around a particular celebrity. Celebrities can be effective if target audience members believe their involvement is authentic (i.e., the topic has personal relevance to them—they actually have the health condition or truly believe the social change is important; they are not just doing it because they are getting paid for it), and for campaigns relying on donated airtime, they can be an effective way to increase airplay. However, celebrities can also overwhelm the message (people remember them but forget the product or service being advertised). Equally important, celebrities can do something embarrassing to your organization, such as hawking an "unhealthy" product or getting arrested.

Suggestions for Assessing Creative

When assessing advertising at any stage of production, first react to the whole message and assess whether it is on strategy. Once you have done so, the following questions may help you examine specific aspects of any ad. **Table 15-2** presents suggestions for assessing advertisements in specific media. It incorporates ideas from Roman and colleagues (2003), who cover each medium in considerably more detail.

1. *"Is the key consumer benefit the central and most compelling idea...?* If it isn't, *turn it down"* (Roman et al., 2003, p. 94).
2. *Is the ad focused and single-minded?* With the exception of some longer print ads, most ads need to make one key point—especially those appearing in media used by people doing more than one thing (e.g., driving, walking, talking, etc.).
3. *Does it reflect your strategic positioning and desired image?*
4. *Does it capture attention early enough?* The first few seconds of a radio or TV ad and the headline and visual of a print ad are critical: The ad must capture the audience's attention then, or it is not going to do so.
5. Is the dramatic approach best for the communication objective? There are four major dramatic approaches (Roman et al., 2003):
   - *Demonstrations* can model a skill or show a product/service/ behavior advantage.
   - *Testimonials*—endorsements from ordinary people, experts, or celebrities—can help make a claim believable and are particularly useful when an advantage cannot be visualized.
   - *Slice-of-life* involves actors telling a story, such as setting up a problem for which the product, service, or behavior is the solution.
   - *Animation* can be especially effective when talking to children, but also can be a solution to other problems, such as simplifying complex ideas (often in demonstrations) or treating abstract (or even distasteful) subjects.

6. *Do the executional details—clothing, jewelry, music, regional accents, props, sets, etc.—convey the image outlined in the communication strategy?* Advertising provides an opportunity to communicate using the powerful cultural frames of reference created by the mass media. But as advertising researchers have noted, "the relative success of an advertisement depends not only on the rational merits of the message being promoted, but also on how well it appropriates desirable mass media images, styles, and cultural icons to its promotional purposes" (Hirschman & Thompson, 1997, p. 44, citing Jhally, 1987; McCracken, 1989; Scott, 1990; Sherry, 1987).

Paid vs. Public Service Placement

The fact that some people refer to PSAs as "people sound asleep" instead of "public service announcements" reflects the concern that they will not be very effective. (Kotler, Roberto & Lee, 2002, p. 312)

Generally it is not a wise use of resources to spend substantial chunks of a budget to produce advertisements but then rely on donated time and space to run them. Most organizations will obtain much greater reach and frequency with their target audiences—and progress toward communication objectives—by paying for placement. There are a number of ways to increase the affordability of paid advertising placement, such as:

- Develop fewer ads or use media with lower production or placement costs. The cost of placing advertising varies enormously by medium; television is most expensive and radio, newspapers, and the Internet are least expensive. Within a medium, cost varies widely depending on such factors as how many people are reached by a particular program, publication, or page, and who is reached (some target audiences are more desirable and thus advertisers are willing to pay more to reach them). If you are considering the use of advertising but are unfamiliar with placement costs, consider inviting a media planner from a local advertising agency to speak.

- Explore media or corporate partners. By cultivating a media partner, an organization can negotiate specific placement in exchange for the partner's exclusive right to sponsor the media component—and garner broader coverage because the media outlet will involve itself in other ways, such as sponsoring contests. Corporate partners can donate some of the advertising space they buy. Because they buy specific spaces (particular television shows, particular times of day on radio, and particular locations within print media), a willing corporate partner can provide a way to execute a particular media placement schedule.

- Negotiate free spots or insertions for certain numbers of paid spots or insertions.

Table 15-2 Suggestions for Assessing Advertisements for Various Media

	Radio	Television	Magazines/Newspapers	Out-of-Home	Internet
Description	Prerecorded spots or announcer-read scripts of 15, 30 or 60 seconds; 60-second lengths most commonly sold in the U.S.	Prerecorded spots of 10, 15, 30, or 60 seconds; 30-second spots are most common in the U.S.	Can range in size from multiple pages to a single page, half-page, quarter-page, or smaller.	"Outdoor" encompasses billboards, posters, dioramas, train stations, exteriors of buses and other vehicles, etc. "Indoor" includes interiors of buses and trains, grocery carts, bathroom stalls, etc.	Banner ads, pop-ups, text presence on relevant search-engine listings.
How to Assess	Play it in your car so you evaluate it the way listeners are likely to hear it.	Look at the pictures first: Do they tell the story? Typically, a storyboard is reviewed first; it looks like a comic strip, with each frame illustrating the action and a written description of what the viewer will see and hear underneath.	Ask to see the ad pasted in a likely editorial environment.	If an ad will be seen in motion, look at it quickly, then look away or put it down.	On a website, as it will appear.
Look for . . . (in addition to the list provided in the text)	Engaging the listener by using voices and sound to evoke pictures. A focus on one idea; radio listeners have too many distractions to grasp or remember more. Conveying to target audience members why the ad is for them early on.	Something that grabs viewers' attention within the first 5–10 seconds. A key visual or one frame that sums up the message. Communicating the message through both senses—sight and hearing. 60-second ads should not add points; they should tell the same story as :30s but with more time, detail, and repetition.	The message in the headline or visual, ideally in both. Whether the reader can "get" the message from the headline alone; often it is all that is read. "Every headline has one job: it must stop the reader with a believable promise." (Roman & Maas, 1992, p. 45) Visuals are often the most important part of the ad.	Outdoor ads need to communicate one very simple message instantly—people are moving when they see them. Copy should be seven words or less. Indoor ads provide the opportunity for more complex messages and can include tear-off pads to deliver coupons, messages, or "send for more information" request forms.	See "magazines and newspapers." If animation is used, is it just to get attention or does it help tell the story? "You cannot annoy the consumer into buying your product or service." (Roman et al., 2003) When the consumer clicks on the ad, does the page that loads deliver on the ad's promise?

(continues)

Table 15-2 Suggestions for Assessing Advertisements for Various Media

	Radio	Television	Magazines/Newspapers	Out-of-Home	Internet
Look for . . . (in addition to the list provided in the text)			Photos usually are more compelling than artwork, and fewer is better: many small pictures lead to cluttered layouts. Appropriate copy length depends on the message and layout; some very successful ads have a lot of copy.		Creating fewer banner ads but increasing their reach and frequency. Banner ads have been shown to be more effective when target audience members are exposed to fewer executions (different ads from the same campaign) across many pages and websites. (Manchanda et al., 2006)
Consider . . .	Radio commercials are inexpensive, quick to produce, and underused in health initiatives. Radio is a very targeted medium; there are over 140 radio formats (all news, all talk, many kinds of music, etc.) in the U.S. Different versions of a spot may need to be made—with different background music or other changes—for different formats.	TV commercials are the most complicated and expensive to produce—and hardest to assess prior to production.	Investing in an advertising copywriter. Writing print ads requires special expertise that other writers are unlikely to have. Whether the ad will be reproduced in a range of sizes and paper stocks. What looks good and is readable on a full page—or on glossy paper—may be lost if the ad is reduced or printed on newsprint. Design ads that will work everywhere or re-design for different environments. For example, crop photos to suggest what appears in the larger version.		

If you wish to pursue public service placement, successfully obtaining it requires (a) building relationships with community affairs staff, who decide what public service ads a station or publication will run, (b) finding media organizations interested in your issue and (c) providing high-quality advertisements (Kotler, Roberto, & Lee, 2002). Newspapers and magazines have no obligation to accept public service advertising. Many newspapers do not; many magazines run them only if they have unfilled advertising space. Because radio and television stations lease the airwaves from the public, they are regulated by the Federal Communications Commission and are supposed to serve the needs of their communities. Broadcasting deregulation in the early 1980s seriously weakened community service requirements, but nonetheless radio and television stations remain the largest users of public service advertising. Part of the job of each station's community affairs director is to determine what public service advertisement to use.

There are services that will handle public service placement for an initiative, but the cost can be high and often it is to an initiative's advantage for staff to build their own relationships with community affairs directors. To do so, it is important to understand the environment in which community affairs directors work. McGrath (1995) outlined the following aspects of the community affairs directors' realities, based on presentations and discussions at four annual meetings of the National Broadcast Association for Community Affairs:

- Their activities are expected to generate or enhance revenues for the station.
- They strive to find a unique position for their station in their market.
- They work in a pressure-cooker environment and are always in a time crunch.
- They are more receptive to people and organizations they know on a personal basis.
- They are committed to their communities and to the organizations working to make these communities a better place to live.

McGrath (1995) made the following recommendations for working with community affairs directors, based on Grunig and Ripper's (1992) situational theory:

1. Help the community affairs director recognize the issue as a problem in the community. For example, provide information on how many people are affected and what the consequences are in terms of individual or family suffering cost, reduced wages or purchasing power in the community, and so forth.
2. Identify and resolve the constraints the community affairs director faces. Three common constraints are a perception that the issue does not affect enough people; a perception that there are other, more

serious issues; or the station is promoting another issue this year. McGrath's (1995) suggestions for resolving the first two constraints are to note, respectively, that although the number of people affected may be small, there is profound impact on individuals and their families; and other, more pressing issues can continue to be addressed while adding this issue into the mix. If a station is focused on promoting a different issue, he suggested identifying similarities between the issues or seeking a portion of time for other issues.

3. Increase the community affairs director's level of involvement with the issue. For example, he or she can be asked to review a script before production, to address a meeting, or to respond to a brief questionnaire about perceptions of conditions in his or her community.

■ MEETINGS AND CONFERENCES

Many social change initiatives develop standard exhibits and presentations to use to communicate their core messages. Establishing a speaker's bureau—a service for placing initiative spokespersons at events—provides an additional way to spread program messages and to increase the visibility of the organization and its contributions. A speaker's bureau can be primarily reactive, responding to requests for speakers, or it can be a proactive component of the initiative, designed to spread program messages by seeking out appropriate venues. The latter form of a speaker's bureau can be designed to address groups within the general public or professional audiences.

To create a smoothly-functioning speaker's bureau, provide both the speaker and the contact person for the group the speaker will address with a form (e-mailed or printed) that includes all details—group name; expected audience size and composition; date, time, location, and directions; audiovisual equipment needed; length, nature, and style of presentation; group's expectation of topic; and names and phone numbers for the group contact person and the speaker (Lewton, 1991). Lewton also advised providing each contact person with a confidential evaluation form. This form allows the performance of individual speakers to be monitored and addressed if necessary and provides an opportunity to improve future talks by assessing how relevant the information was to the group and what additional information they would like to have had presented.

■ SPECIAL EVENTS

Public health initiatives may use special events to generate media coverage or to reach out to target audience members, either to deliver messages or to help them engage in a particular health behavior. Some common events for health topics include conferences for professional audiences, health screenings (often at partner sites, such as a worksite, a shopping mall, or other areas where people congregate), or exhibits in conjunction with events sponsored by partners or intermediaries. If the initiative includes providing some type of service, a tour (for press or for potential users of the service) of new facilities can be a good way to attract attention.

When developing plans or reviewing ideas for a special event, it may be helpful to consider the following questions:

1. Is this event consistent with our positioning and strategy?
2. Is it a cost-effective way of reaching our target audience(s)?
3. What other community, regional, or national activities might impact the attention or attendance the event receives?
4. What date, time and location will best reach our intended audience?
5. Is there a "take-away" we can give attendees to reinforce a behavior or to share with a non-attending target audience member to multiply our reach?
6. Do all of the event details—refreshments, signage, location, etc.— reflect our positioning and image?

■ PRINT MATERIALS

Throughout the life of a social change initiative, many types of print publications and materials may be used. Brochures, newsletters, manuals, and posters often play a role, as well as a host of other collateral materials, such as signs, packaging, folders for meetings or press kits, calendars, letterhead, and envelopes. All provide an opportunity to convey key messages (through the use of a theme line or initiative name if nothing else), and all convey an image. Using the graphics standards discussed earlier in this chapter can help ensure all printed materials communicates the right image for the initiative.

When selecting designs and formats, it is useful to consider the purpose of the piece, the image to be conveyed, how it will be distributed, how it will be reproduced, and how much various choices will cost. For brochures, posters, and other print materials that will deliver messages, review the criteria in the advertising section of this chapter. For all print materials, thinking through the following questions may help.

- *How will the material be used?* If a material will have a short life (i.e., posters to be used in conjunction with a 1-day event), using lightweight (and inexpensive) paper stock probably makes sense. If, on the other hand, it is a booklet or newsletter that people could keep and refer to over a long period, a heavier (but more expensive) stock will ensure that the item holds up over time.

- *Is the image conveyed consistent with the communication strategy?* Many aspects of a printed piece convey image: size, type of paper stock (i.e. matte or glossy, heavy or light, recycled or not), use of color (particularly the number of colors used) and photos, special effects (i.e., die cuts, foil stamping, embossing), and the graphic standards (typeface, layouts) discussed earlier in this chapter.

- *How easy is it to read?* Color, type size and style, and line justification can all affect readability. Black, dark blue, and other dark-colored inks on light backgrounds are easiest to read. Reverse type (light type on a dark background) is very hard to read, as is type that has been printed over a photo or illustration. All capital letters are more difficult to read than a mixture of upper case and lower case. Serif typefaces are easier to read than sans serif. (This sentence, and most of this book, is in a serif typeface; the tables are sans serif.) Ideally, type size should be 12 points or larger and definitely no smaller than 10 points. Type that is set ragged right (ending wherever the words end, rather than adding spaces or hyphenation to fill each line) is easier to read. The way in which the text is laid out on the page also affects readability. Layouts that are simple and open are more inviting than those with densely packed text, as are those that break up large amounts of text with visuals.

- *Is the writing style appropriate for the audience?* In general, text that is as simple, short, and jargon-free as possible is best. However, some professional audiences interpret simple language as an indication that a publication is designed for laypeople, so a balance must be struck.

- *Is sufficient identifying information included?* Date of publication or publication number (in tiny type at the bottom or on the back) can save endless headaches when people call to request a copy of a material; often requests will come years after the publication was first produced. Depending on the design and purpose, most print materials also include some or all of the following: the organization's name, complete mailing address, phone number, and e-mail or website address.

- *How many colors are used, and are they all necessary?* Color can be very powerful, and it can be very expensive. For pieces that are printed rather than photocopied, every additional ink color used increases the cost.

- *Are there any special effects that are increasing cost?* For example, bleeds (printing to the edge of the paper, rather than leaving a margin), die cuts, embossing, and special folding all add costs. Set-up charges for special effects can be substantial and are the same for small or large press runs. If a publication or collateral material (such as poster or tabletop card) is intended to serve as a model that will be customized and printed in relatively small quantities by collaborating organizations, avoiding special effects set-up charges will reduce printing costs significantly.

- *Do the materials make full use of standard size press sheets?* Some odd-sized publications may not take up the whole sheet, resulting in wasted paper.
- *Can the same paper stock be used for several materials so that quantity discounts can be obtained?* Is there a comparable paper stock that is less expensive?
- *What are the mailing cost ramifications of the proposed design?* Lewton (1991) offered a number of suggestions for reducing mailing costs: using standard-size envelopes (odd sizes cost extra postage) or self-mailers (the latter also eliminate the cost associated with purchasing envelopes and assembling their contents) and mailing using bulk-rate permits, rather than first-class postage. Reviewing and updating mailing lists regularly can also help control costs by eliminating duplications and dead wood.
- *How can reproduction costs be minimized?* One of the first steps is to determine whether a particular item should be printed or photocopied. Often if 2,000 or more copies are needed, printing is less expensive (even for black-and-white reproductions). Other methods of stretching a budget include printing lengthy documents such as manuals or reports on both sides of the page (saving paper and mailing costs), or printing newsletter mastheads or folders in color (and in large quantities to reduce the cost per piece) and then printing or photocopying onto them in black or some other single color when they are actually used (Lewton, 1991).

Once a material's design and content have been approved and it is being readied for printing, a few final checks can prevent a lot of headaches. Have someone other than the writer read all copy, checking it for typographical and other errors before it is sent to the printer. Once the printer is ready to go, ordering proofs and checking them carefully often reveals mistakes. When the job is on the press, having someone there to do a press check is a final step that can detect errors and ensure a high-quality product.

■ WEBSITES

Websites can play a number of roles in public health depending on what is to be accomplished and how efforts to bring about change are structured. A website can be any or all of the following:

- A communication medium, delivering news, entertainment, and/or advertisements.
- A distribution channel, augmenting or replacing "brick-and-mortar," telephone, fax, or mail channels.
- A customer-service interface, providing an alternative to telephoning for information.

In all of these roles, an Internet presence should reflect and reinforce an initiative or institution's positioning and communication strategy.

As a communication medium, websites can combine the multi-sensory power of audio and video with the flexibility of print by permitting the user to determine the order in which information will be accessed and the amount of time spent on particular sections of information. Websites can also help people model healthful behaviors and/or take specific actions in a way that is not possible in other media. For example, the website of a group trying to bring about policy change can include a sample letter to policymakers—and the ability for website visitors to quickly customize the letter and send it to the appropriate policymaker(s). This integrated approach avoids many of the usual barriers: the target audience member does not have to compose the letter, identify the appropriate policymaker(s), locate the address(es), find an envelope, find a stamp, and then mail the letter(s).

As a distribution channel or customer service medium, websites allow people to identify the product, service, or information they want and obtain it at a time and place convenient for them. Well-designed sites can provide distribution and customer-service transactions that are faster and of more consistent quality than alternative channels.

However, not all initiatives or institutions need a website. One can be useful if target audience members need information prior to taking an action, have customer service needs that can be addressed on a website (even something as simple as office hours or hours/locations of upcoming flu shot clinics), or can obtain a tangible good or service online.

Website Design

The best websites are designed from the target audience's point of view and make it easy for site visitors to get the information they are looking for or take the action they (or you) want them to take. When planning a site, consider:

- How will people access the site? Through a personal computer, a mobile phone, a PDA? All of the above?
- Where are they likely to be at the time? If they are at work, most will not appreciate background music or other audio that automatically starts playing.
- What are they likely to be looking for?
- How do they want to access or take away information? HTML pages? PDF files? PDA downloads? MP3 files?

Paying upfront attention to site design can improve readability and use, as well as speed approval of site updates.

Color, Fonts, and Backgrounds. Graphic identity can be established by using the same colors, fonts, backgrounds, and signature icons throughout the site; these should be consistent with overall identity standards.

To reduce eye fatigue (which occurs when the eyes have to refocus constantly), experts recommend limiting screens to four nonneutral colors and avoiding complementary colors and red-blue combinations. When assigning colors to various screen elements, keep in mind that users assume objects of the same color are related. Selecting one or two font families and sticking with them provides a consistent, non-cluttered look. As with printed publications, words in all capital letters are more difficult to read. Although background patterns are a way to create unique identity, care should be taken in their use because strong background patterns can render text unreadable.

Site Layout. The best layout for a particular site depends on its content. However, there are some technical aspects of site design that can determine the degree to which the site is friendly (or unfriendly) to use. For example, including a search capability or index on the home page helps users locate the information they want, as does following common conventions, such as having "About us" and "Contact us" pages.

Sites that regularly add menu items run the risk of becoming disorganized and unwieldy over time. A general rule of thumb is to limit lists to seven choices, breaking longer lists into smaller groups. Frequent visitors will appreciate a "last updated" date next to menu items; this feature lets them avoid waiting for a screen to load only to discover there is no new information. Adding hyperlinks to partner sites and resources provides site users with access to more information and increases a site's perceived value.

Including a means to contact the organization sponsoring the site is also important. People may have comments on the site itself (ensuring that each page has a clear, brief title will help them comment and help you understand what they are talking about), or they may have questions about the initiative or want to know if more information is available on a particular topic. It is a good idea to provide both electronic and traditional addresses and telephone numbers, because some people will access the site to find out how to contact the organization through traditional means. Similarly, if the site includes suggestions on actions to take (such as contacting a policy maker), information should be provided on how to contact the appropriate parties (e.g., name, e-mail and mailing address, phone number).

Audio/visual components. Part of a website's appeal is the ability to bring ideas to life and simplify complex information using illustrations, photographs, and streaming audio or video. However, every image added to a page increases the time it takes for the page to appear on someone's screen, and some systems take quite a bit of time to begin playing audio or video. While a target audience member is waiting for your organization's information to load, he or she may get bored and decide to go somewhere else. Use these components moderately and make sure they are optimized to load quickly.

Testing the Site

One of the most important steps in website design is testing the site after it is constructed. Sites are often built and tested using state-of-the art setups: large monitors, the most current versions of software, and, most important, the fastest modes of access. If your site is intended to provide information to members of the public, looking at it through their eyes (and their computers) can help you make sure it does its job as effectively as possible. Some aspects of the site to consider when testing it out include the following:

- *How long do pages take to load using access methods likely to be used by target audience members?* Users are typically unwilling to wait more than 20 or 30 seconds. Some techniques can make the wait seem shorter (because images are materializing on the screen). Putting up brief descriptions that users can click on to proceed before the images load is another way to retain user interest and let them make progress— and to let them know what is on the screen if they have graphics turned off. Some sites give a "text-only" option.

- *What do pages look like when viewed with different browsers, smaller monitors, or lower end graphics settings?* For example, do the pages still make sense if they are viewed with a text-only browser or one with deactivated graphics? What happens if the monitor is set to fewer colors or a lower resolution than that of the screen the site was developed on? How about when the site is viewed over a mobile phone or PDA?

- *How "user-friendly" is the menu structure?* The goal is to strike a balance: If users have to wade through huge lists, they may get frustrated and quit looking before they find what they need. On the other hand, if they have to navigate through a series of menus, each with two or three choices, they may also get frustrated and stop before they reach their destination. Every screen they have to go through increases the chance that they will get bored and go elsewhere.

- *If your pages are part of a larger site, what steps would users have to take find the pages relevant to the initiative?* Most users look for content, not departments, yet many large organizations create websites that are arranged according to their organizational structure. This schema may work for the employees, but it has the effect of burying information on social change initiatives unless a search option is part of the site's home page.

■ CONCLUSION

A broad range of activities can be used to draw attention to a public health initiative, including obtaining coverage in the mass media, establishing a presence on the Internet, speaking at various forums, creating special events, and advertising. Strong promotional efforts use a mix of tactics to maximize the number of target audience members reached, the number of times they are reached, and the number of channels reaching them. The tactics used in a specific situation depend on the communication objectives, the audience(s) to be reached, the message(s) to be delivered, and the available time and resources. All should reflect and reinforce the initiative's identity.

References

Andreasen, A.R. (2006). *Social marketing in the 21st century.* Thousand Oaks, CA: Sage.

Backer, T.E., Rogers, E.M., & Sopory, P. (1992). *Designing health communication campaigns: What works?* Thousand Oaks, CA: Sage.

Bronner, E. (2003). The foundation's end-of-life programs: Changing the American way of death. In S.L. Isaacs & J.R. Knickman (Eds.), *To Improve Health and Healthcare, Volume VI.* San Francisco: Jossey-Bass. Retrieved February 1, 2006 from http://www.rwjf.org/files/publications/books/2003/chapter_04.html.

Cassell, M.M., Jackson, C., & Cheuvront, B. (1998). Health communication on the Internet: An effective channel for health behavior change? *Journal of Health Communication, 3,* 71–79.

Dominick, J.R. (1990). *The dynamics of mass communication* (3rd ed.). New York: McGraw-Hill.

Grunig, J., & Ripper, F. (1992). Strategic management, public, and issues. In J. Grunig (Ed.), *Excellence in public relations and communications management* (pp. 117–157). Hillsdale, NJ: Lawrence Erlbaum Associates.

Hirschman, E.C., & Thompson, C.J. (1997). Why media matter: Toward a richer understanding of consumers' relationships with advertising and mass media. *Journal of Advertising, 26*(1), 43–60.

Hornik, R. (1997). Public health education and communication as policy instruments for bringing about changes in behavior. In M.E. Goldberg, M. Fishbein, & S. E. Middlestadt, *Social marketing: Theoretical and practical perspectives* (pp. 45–58). Mahwah, NJ: Lawrence Erlbaum Associates.

Hornik, R.C. (Ed.) (2002). *Public health communication: Evidence for behavior change.* Mahway, NJ: Lawrence Erlbaum Associates.

Jhally, S. (1987). *The codes of advertising.* New York: St. Martin's Press.

Kotler, P., Roberto, N., & Lee, N. (2002). *Social marketing: Improving the quality of life.* Thousand Oaks, CA: Sage.

Lewton, K.L. (1991). *Public relations in health care: A guide for professionals.* Chicago: American Hospital Publishing.

Lippmann, W. (1922). *Public opinion.* New York: Harcourt Brace.

Manchanda, P., Dubé, J-P. Goh, K. Y., & Chintagunta, P.K. (2006). The effect of banner advertising on internet purchasing. *Journal of Marketing Research,* 43, 98–108.

McCombs, M.E. & Shaw, D.L. (1972). The agenda-setting function of mass media. *Public Opinion Quarterly, 36,* 176–185.

McCombs, M.E., & Shaw, D.L. (1993). The agenda-setting research: Twenty-five years in the marketplace of ideas. *Journal of Communication, 43*(2), 58–67.

McCracken, G. (1989). *Culture and consumption: New approaches to the symbolic character of goods and activities.* Bloomington: Indiana University Press.

McGrath, J. (1995). The gatekeeping process: The right combinations to unlock the gates. In E. Maibach & R.L. Parrott (Eds.), *Designing health messages: Approaches from communication theory and public health practice* (pp. 199–216). Thousand Oaks, CA: Sage.

Meyer, P. (1990). News media responsiveness to public health. In C. Atkin & L. Wallack (Eds.), *Mass communication and public health* (pp. 52–59). Newbury Park, CA: Sage.

National Cancer Institute. (1989). *Making health communication programs work: A planner's guide* (NIH Publication No. 89-1493). Bethesda, MD: Author.

Palmgreen, P., & Clarke, P. (1977). Agenda-setting with local and national issues. *Communication Research, 4,* 435–452.

Roman, K., & Maas, J.M. (1992). *How to advertise* (2nd ed.). New York: St. Martin's Press.

Roman, K., Maas, J., & Nisenholtz, M. (2003). *How to advertise* (3rd ed.). New York: St. Martin's Press.

Scott, L. (1990). Understanding jingles and needledrop: A rhetorical approach to music in advertising. *Journal of Consumer Research, 17,* 223–226.

Sherry, J.F. (1987). Advertising as a magic system. In J. Umiker-Sebeok (Ed.), *Marketing and semiotics: New directions for the study of signs for sale* (pp. 441–452). Berlin: Mouton de Gruyter.

Signorielli, N. (1993). *Mass media images and impact on health: A sourcebook.* Westport, CT: Greenwood Press.

Tellis, G.J. (2004). *Effective advertising: Understanding when, how, and why advertising works.* Thousand Oaks, CA: Sage.

Tipton, L., Haney, R.D., & Baseheart, J.R. (1975). Media agenda-setting in city and state election campaigns. *Journalism Quarterly, 52,* 15–22.

Wallack, L., & Dorfman, L. (1996). Media advocacy: A strategy for advancing policy and promoting health. *Health Education Quarterly, 23,* 293–317.

Wallack, L., Dorfman, L., Jernigan, D., & Themba, M. (1993). *Media advocacy and public health: Power for prevention.* Newbury Park, CA: Sage.

Winston, J.A. (1990). *The designated driver campaign developed nationally by the Harvard Alcohol Project.* Cambridge, MA: Harvard University School of Public Health.

III

Assessing Progress and Making Refinements

Marketers view evaluation as a tool to improve their marketing—and they view marketing as a dynamic set of variables they are constantly adjusting, operating in a dynamic environment full of other variables that also are constantly adjusting. Consequently, they place enormous emphasis on formative and process evaluation and are much less concerned about outcome evaluation. In contrast, the standard emphasis in public health is on outcome evaluation. Often there is an expectation that social change interventions will be evaluated using the same techniques and definitions of success that a clinical scientist uses to evaluate a clinical trial. But social change interventions are messy, complicated affairs that sometimes work directly on the individual who needs to change a health behavior, at other times work through his or her social group, and at still other times work through influencing public norms or policymakers. The randomized experiment can limit the power of the social change initiative (because it has to be constrained to meet the demands of the evaluation design) and sometimes does not adequately address the assumptions underlying how social change occurs.

Process and outcome evaluations can encompass a wide range of activities depending on the complexity of the social change effort. In this section we discuss some of the more common process evaluation activities used in monitoring and refining an initiative. We also highlight the challenges of adequately evaluating social change outcomes and present some approaches that are of use. The last chapter in this section provides information on theories and research methodologies commonly used to support all phases of the marketing process.

CHAPTER

16

Monitoring and Refining Implementation: Process Evaluation Tools

Building process evaluation measures into an initiative provides an important set of management tools. By using process evaluation data to regularly monitor an initiative's progress, timely refinements can be made to programs, products, promotions, and distribution channels. Unfortunately, process evaluation is often overlooked or used solely to document an intervention rather than improve it. This chapter discusses how process evaluation data can be used to monitor and refine implementation, presents a general description of how process evaluation studies fit into program planning and implementation, and gives examples of some common process evaluation techniques and how they are used.

Process evaluation "verifies what the program is and whether or not it is delivered as intended to the targeted recipients" (Scheirer, 1994, quoted in Rossi, Lipsey & Freeman, 2004, p. 171). However, it does not measure the outcomes or impact of the program; that is the role of outcome evaluation, discussed in Chapter 17. Process evaluation typically tracks and documents implementation by quantifying what has been done; when, where, and how it was done; and who was reached.

The monitoring information provided by process evaluation can serve as a powerful management device. As Andreasen (1995) noted, "commercial sector marketers crave data. They want to know how they are doing. They want to correct things before it is too late. . . . The major use of monitoring data is for *control*. In its ideal form, control will be a cybernetic self-correcting system that constantly looks at what is happening, diagnoses why it is happening, and takes corrective action as needed" (p. 128). Thorough process evaluation documents actual implementation and compares it to planned implementation, but for marketers the primary purpose for doing so is to make improvements in the future.

As activities are implemented, process evaluation is used to document implementation and provide feedback on the activity's progress, allowing the individual components and the overall initiative to be refined on an ongoing basis. Process evaluation should begin by capturing characteristics of the environment in which the program is implemented, to provide context for the results. If the program provides services, process evaluation can involve assessing the extent to which the targeted population receives the intended services and their satisfaction with them. For promotional activities, process evaluation provides information on the number of opportunities there were to be exposed to the program messages, and, ideally, characteristics of those who were exposed. For editorial coverage, it can also provide information on the extent to which messages appearing in the coverage were consistent with the communication strategy.

For multifaceted interventions, process evaluation is often piecemeal, because data are gathered separately—often using different techniques—for each component and often each tactic. Process evaluation works when it draws together the results of diverse program activities and provides an opportunity to systematically examine overall performance. It should tie together information on the implementation of different program components, providing managers with an overall picture of the effort and actionable recommendations for refinement. **Exhibit 16-1** provides an example of a range of process evaluation activities conducted for one pilot study.

■ PLANNING AND CONDUCTING PROCESS EVALUATION STUDIES

To be most useful, process evaluation needs to be built into an initiative's activities. It can be much more difficult and expensive to gather data retrospectively, and information collected after the fact is likely to be of little value in managing implementation. The following steps outline the general course of process evaluation activities.

Exhibit 16-1   Process Evaluation of the Team Nutrition Pilot Study

The U.S. Department of Agriculture's School Meals Initiative for Healthy Children, published in 1995, is a comprehensive plan that aims to ensure that children have healthy meals at school. A major part of this plan is an update of nutrition standards that requires school meals to meet the Dietary Guidelines for Americans. Recognizing that simply publishing a regulation is not likely to change children's diets, USDA established Team Nutrition to ensure that schools are able to implement the plan and that students avail themselves of the healthier meals offered.

Team Nutrition supports the School Meals Initiative through two interrelated components: Multifaceted nutrition education, developed in accordance with the tenets of social cognitive theory and social marketing, is delivered through the media, in schools, and at home to build skills and motivate children to make appropriate food choices for a healthful diet. Training and technical assistance is designed to ensure that school nutrition and food service personnel have the education, motivation, training, and skills necessary to provide healthy meals that appeal to children and meet the Dietary Guidelines.

USDA launched a pilot implementation of Team Nutrition in spring and fall of 1996 in seven school districts. In four of the districts, half of the school pairs were randomly assigned to implement Team Nutrition; the others were comparison sites and did not conduct nutrition lessons during the two semesters the evaluation took place. Each school agreed to conduct a set of grade-specific classroom lessons, teacher and food service staff training, at least two schoolwide cafeteria events, at least three parent contact activities, at least two chef activities, and at least one districtwide Team Nutrition event.

The process evaluation was designed to measure the nature and magnitude of the Team Nutrition effort in all seven of the pilot districts. A number of data collection efforts were implemented as part of the basic process evaluation, including:

- Extant data on school and district characteristics including total population, students' racial/ethnic background, and percentage of students receiving free or reduced school meals

- Interviews with school principals at the start of each phase in each implementation school

- Team Nutrition Core Activity Logs filled out by the person responsible for directing each school-based or community activity to document its key features, participation rates, and lessons learned

- Team Nutrition Teacher Activity Logs filled out by all implementing teachers for each scholastic lesson taught, including preparation time, actual classroom time, and which lesson components were utilized

In addition to the above data collection efforts, the teachers implementing Team Nutrition in their classrooms completed surveys that were conducted in group settings before and after the intervention.

Source: R.C. Lefebvre, C. Olander, & E. Levine, "The impact of multiple channel delivery of nutrition messages on student knowledge, motivation and behavior (Part I): Results from the Team Nutrition Pilot Study." In P. Kotler, N. Roberto, & N. Lee, *Social Marketing: Improving the Quality of Life,* 2nd ed, pp. 324–326, copyright © 2002 by Sage Publications, Inc. Reprinted by Permission of Sage Publications, Inc.

Step 1: Set evaluation objectives and design evaluation plans. Data from process evaluation can be used in many ways. Four of the most common are

1. Making decisions about refining the initiative's products (including tangible goods and services), pricing strategies, promotions, channels of distribution, or activities.
2. Documenting and justifying how resources have been spent.
3. Making a compelling case for continued or additional funding.
4. Providing information on what was actually implemented, so that outcome evaluators can avoid a Type III error: evaluating a program that was not adequately implemented and thus drawing incorrect conclusions about its effectiveness (Basch et al., 1985).

Some initiatives will need to address all of these issues and others will not. Determining the ways in which process evaluation data will be used prior to designing the system(s) to collect them can save endless headaches later. However, making these determinations requires thinking about future needs, and this can be difficult, especially for new initiatives. The "backward research" approach developed by Andreasen (1985) can be helpful in identifying the questions that process evaluation data will need to answer. The steps involved in the approach are as follows:[1]

1. Determine what key decisions are to be made using the research results and who will make the decisions.
2. Determine what information will help management make the best decisions.
3. Prepare a prototype report and ask management if this is what will best help them make their decisions.
4. Determine the analysis necessary to fill in the report.
5. Determine what questions must be asked to provide the data required by the analysis.
6. Ascertain whether the needed questions have already been asked.
7. Design sample.
8. Implement research design.
9. Write report.
10. Implement the results.

The key is to identify what decisions will need to be made and justifications prepared and what data will be most helpful in making those decisions. A common pitfall is to collect information that is easy to collect, rather than information that will help manage the initiative. As Andreasen (1995) noted,

---

[1] *Source:* A. R. Andreasen, *Marketing Social Change: Changing Behavior to Promote Health, Social Development, and the Environment*, p. 101. Copyright 1995 by Alan R. Andreasen. Reprinted with permission of John Wiley & Sons, Inc.

thus social marketers may be tempted to keep track of how well they are doing by looking at the number of brochures distributed, the number of advertisements run, the number of people attending various events, or the extent of distribution of the products involved in the behavior. The difficulty with this approach is that the data may or may not bear any relationship to the program's objectives and goals. For example, large numbers of distributed but unread brochures accumulated by illiterate audience members should not be taken as a sign that the program is on target. Nor should television advertisements run at late-night hours with little or no audience. (p. 128)

Tracking the number of brochures distributed or the number of advertisements aired will help document the initiative (which is often necessary), but it will not help manage implementation in any meaningful way (beyond ensuring that the brochures do not run out). To make sure process evaluation data also serve as a management tool, a good starting point is to look at the initiative's objectives and think about how progress against them will be measured and what information will be needed to make improvements. For example, if an objective is to frame the public debate through media coverage, to what extent is that happening? Answering this question involves collecting media coverage on the issue and analyzing its content. If an objective is to persuade audience members to get more information through a hotline, how many are calling and where did they hear about the hotline? If a clinic is trying to increase use of a service, assessing satisfaction with changes in the service may help identify what is working well and what needs additional improvement.

The nature and duration of the initiative will drive the type of process information needed and the frequency with which it will be needed. For example, if a referendum is on a ballot, a bill is coming up for a vote, or a regulatory agency is about to issue a rule, a campaign to impact the policy change will likely be of short duration (often 3 to 6 months and sometimes only a few weeks). In contrast, initiatives to change individual behavior may be in place for years, assuming funding sources continue. The policy change initiative would require constant monitoring and refinement (with reports as often as weekly); the behavior change initiative might be managed very well with monthly or quarterly reports, depending on the level of activity.

Once evaluation objectives have been set and an overall approach has been determined, they should be outlined in a plan that contains:

- The recommended methodological approach and its associated strengths and limitations
- The proposed study design (e.g., sample sizes, sampling procedures, and respondent specifications, if relevant)

- Data collection instruments (and whether they exist or will need to be created)
- An analysis plan
- A timeline (including recommendations for frequency of reports)
- A budget
- Staffing needs

The plan ensures that everyone involved with the activity understands and is in agreement as to what information the evaluation will provide. It also facilitates management of the program by providing information on the timing and amount of upcoming resource needs.

Step 2: Design data collection instruments. The instruments used to collect data will vary depending on the methodological approach employed, but may include:

- Questionnaires, either interviewer- or self-administered. For example, interviewer-administered questionnaires might be used if a telephone survey is used to track public awareness, or by operators answering calls to a toll-free number. Self-administered questionnaires might be used by materials recipients or by visitors to a website.
- Recruitment screeners and topic guides for in-depth interviews or focus group discussions.
- Electronic or paper tracking forms, used to monitor inventory, track aspects of product or service delivery, record the type of requests received or questions asked, or record details of media placements.

Some types of process evaluation do not require a data collection form but do require other types of preparation. For example, tracking airplay of television products (advertisements, video news releases, satellite media tours, etc.) may require encoding the master tapes prior to dubbing and distribution.

Often the data collection instruments will be distributed with particular program components. Instruments that do not need to be distributed with the component should be ready for use prior to its implementation.

Step 3: Implement and report on evaluation activities. Data collection normally begins in tandem with program implementation. Data should be periodically analyzed using suitable techniques, and the research questions and results should be presented in a report format appropriate to the activity. Often, results are summarized in tabular form on a weekly or monthly basis, with a more detailed analysis prepared quarterly, semi-annually, or annually. These more detailed analyses compare planned versus actual implementation, identify strengths and weaknesses in the implementation, and make recommendations for refinement of program components and distribution mechanisms.

■ COMMON PROCESS EVALUATION ACTIVITIES

Process evaluation can be simple or it can be complex, largely depending upon the simplicity or complexity of the intervention. It encompasses an enormous number of activities and methodological approaches, far too many to adequately address in one chapter. The remainder of this chapter provides an overview of some common process evaluation methodologies and how they apply to various program components, particularly those related to tracking reactions to products or services and promotional campaigns. Many of the approaches discussed here can also be used as needs assessment tools when refinements to a program are being planned. For excellent discussions and illustrations of process evaluation applied to public health initiatives (some marketing-based and others not), including lessons learned and instruments from a broad array of interventions, see *Process Evaluation for Public Health Interventions and Research*, edited by Steckler and Linnan (2002).

Tracking Systems

Tracking systems can be paper logs or electronic databases, and they can be used to collect information on activities such as events or trainings, delivery of tangible goods or services, and distribution of materials. For materials or tangible goods, in addition to ensuring the adequate quantities are in stock at all times, inventory tracking provides an opportunity to learn where materials are going, which ones are likely to be reaching the most people, and which ones are the most (and least) popular. A simple way to set up an inventory tracking system is to design a database or log where the following information is recorded each time material is distributed:

- Date of activity, delivery, or distribution
- Name of activity, or good or material distributed
- For activities, numbers of participants; for delivery of products or services or distribution of materials, quantity
- Geographic location

This basic information can be expanded for use in a variety of situations. For activities such as events or trainings, it may be helpful to include items assessing the audience's reactions, what program materials were used and how helpful they were, and suggestions for future activities or revisions to supporting materials. For trainings or facilitated sessions, the tracking form may include items to assess the instructor or facilitator's command of the material, fidelity to the session objectives, interpersonal and presentation skills, ability to stay on time and/or keep group on task, etc.

It may be helpful to include information on the type of requestors (e.g., is the requestor an intermediary or an individual) and how they heard about the activity, service, or item. If requestors call to order the materials, they can be asked how they heard about the material when they call. If requestors complete an order form, a few pertinent questions can be included on the form, or order forms that are printed in other publications can be coded so that the publication can be identified.

Once the inventory tracking system has been established, it can be analyzed to gain insights into a number of aspects of program implementation. For example,

- The number of requests can be plotted by date and compared with when program promotions took place to provide insights into what promotional activities are generating the most requests. Popular activities could be repeated more often or conducted in additional locales. Less popular activities can be examined in more detail. Does it seem likely that these activities are reaching relatively few audience members and therefore should be discontinued? What are the differences between more and less popular activities? Is there a way to alter the latter to increase their utility?

- Geographic locations of requestors can be mapped. Regions where requests are light can be targeted for more intensive program activities.

- If some materials are requested far more often than others (or others are rarely requested), a follow-up study can be conducted by contacting people have requested the materials and asking them what they found appealing (or unappealing) and how they are using the materials.

Product or Service Delivery and Client Satisfaction

For public health programs that include service delivery, monitoring delivery is essential. It can provide information on how to improve the service and can help determine whether delivery is carried out as designed, whether it is reaching the intended target population, the extent to which it meets their needs, and whether the implementation is helping to achieve program objectives as planned. Delivery data can also be important in evaluating the value of a new product or service and whether it should continue to be offered.

The type of data collected depends on the type of product or service. For example, a public health initiative could easily include training sessions or workshops; a new telephone hotline service for referrals or to order information; health services such as screenings or immunizations at sites other than traditional service delivery sites (i.e., health fairs, sporting events, mobile mammography vans, flu shots at the drug store, etc.); or services within a traditional public health setting (i.e., counseling and testing, prenatal care, etc.). Or, as in Appendix 10-A, it could include a ride service for the alcohol impaired.

Monitoring the number and type of people using these services, as well as their satisfaction with them, is an important part of implementation. It facilitates midcourse adjustment, resetting of goals and objectives, administrative planning, and resource utilization. It also "allows program administrators to put into context the implementation of various program components" (Centers for Disease Control and Prevention [CDC], 1993).

The specific service delivery information to be collected needs to be determined based on what is needed to assess whether program objectives are being met and to make necessary refinements. Common information to collect includes:

- Number of people served (or number of visits or calls)
- Characteristics of people served (to assess what percentage are members of the audience the program is trying to reach)
- Quantity of services utilized and characteristics of people using each
- Peak usage times (to assess staffing and adjust if necessary)
- Additional services of interest to clientele (to plan for the future)

In addition to collecting this type of usage information, an invaluable part of assessing service delivery is assessing client satisfaction with the tangible good(s), service(s), facilities, personnel, distribution channels, and pricing (if applicable). **Exhibit 16-2** presents some aspects of each that can be important. Approaches to measuring client satisfaction can be divided into three basic categories:

- *Unsolicited client responses*, such as suggestion or comment boxes. This approach is the least rigorous and, as Lamb and Crompton (1992) noted, is limited by its lack of generalizability (the views of those who comment may be very different from the views of those who do not) and inability to assess degree of satisfaction; provided services meet some minimal satisfaction level, people may not make an effort to complain but may not be highly satisfied either.
- *Observation*, by directly interacting with clients either informally or formally. Informal observation might involve a manager visiting a facility and talking to a few clients about their likes, dislike, and suggestions for improving products or services. More formal observation can be conducted using qualitative research techniques, such as periodic focus groups or in-depth interviews with current and former clients.
- *Surveys*, ideally of both current and former clients. This approach has the advantage of being generalizable to the population served if probability sampling techniques are used and the questionnaire is constructed appropriately.

The last two approaches play an important role in developing a complete picture of client satisfaction: Quantitative methods measure the

---

Exhibit 16-2 Some Components of Client Satisfaction

Services

- Cost

- Waiting time after arrival (how long it takes to be seen)

- Waiting time to make an appointment

Facilities

- Transportation—How is distance? Adequate parking? Convenient to public transportation? Affordable?

- Waiting room—Too crowded? Enough chairs? Enough things to entertain children?

- Exam/counseling rooms—Temperature? Privacy?

- Hours—Convenient?

- Telephone experiences (i.e., amount of time on hold; number of times transferred)

Personnel

- Demeanor (i.e., friendly or rude; rushed or patient)

- Knowledge

- Whether questions are answered

- Whether issues are explained clearly

Tangible goods

- Cost

- Quality

- Packaging

- Value

- Availability

---

percentage of clients who use particular services and are satisfied or dissatisfied with particular aspects of the goods or services themselves, the facilities in which they are delivered, and the personnel who deliver them. They are discussed in more detail in the subsequent section. Qualitative studies can shed light on the reasons underlying usage and satisfaction or dissatisfaction (CDC, 1993). Chapter 18 discusses issues to consider when designing qualitative studies; Chapter 7 includes discussion of how the project team uses qualitative research techniques to monitor how Rwandans are reacting to messages on sensitive health topics conveyed in a radio soap opera.

Designing Client Satisfaction Surveys
Designing, implementing, and analyzing quantitative surveys is a complex endeavor. Chapter 18 provides an overview; a good introduction to

many of the issues involved with sampling, instrumentation, data collection, data processing, and analysis is provided in *The Survey Research Handbook*, by Alreck and Settle (2004). At a minimum, the following five factors warrant consideration.

Questionnaires. Andreasen (1995) and Lamb and Crompton (1992) recommended measuring two dimensions of satisfaction: *how important* each aspect of a program is to the client as well as the typical *how satisfied* the client is with it. First, respondents rate their satisfaction with various aspects of the program on a numeric scale (Andreasen suggested a 10-point scale; Lamb and Crompton used a 7-point scale ranging from *extremely unsatisfactory* to *extremely satisfactory*) and then rate each aspect's importance to them using a similar scale. Andreasen recommended using the resulting information to create a performance-importance matrix by plotting it on a two-dimensional graph. The *Handbook of Marketing Scales* (Bearden & Netemeyer, 1999) contains additional scales that are useful for measuring aspects of customer satisfaction.

Knowing how important various aspects of a product or service are to clients can help managers make more informed decisions about changes to make. For example, if clients are relatively unsatisfied with the waiting room but it is not that important to them, changing it may have little or no effect on clinic usage. In contrast, if their satisfaction with clinic hours is moderate, but the hours are most important to them, changing the hours may result in substantial changes in usage.

Sampling. For some services, such as training sessions, it is relatively easy to ask everyone to fill out an evaluation form. For others, such as clinic services or hotline calls, it would be tremendously burdensome to ask each person to complete an evaluation following each visit or call. The logical option is to sample participants in some way. If a probability sample is used, the results can be assumed to represent the population from which the sample was drawn. A sample is a probability sample if (1) all members of a population have a known (usually equal) chance of being selected and (2) participants are selected randomly. Alternatively, a convenience sample can be used; for example, every person using the service one specific day of the week or week of the month could be sampled. To minimize bias, the day or week should be rotated in case there are differences among people who use the service at different times. Convenience samples are more limited than probability samples but can be considerably easier to construct. Chapter 18 provides more detail.

Data Collection Method. Self-administered questionnaires can be confidential and will work even in situations where identifying information, such as names, is not collected. However, they only work for relatively literate audiences. Alternatively, participants could be interviewed in person immediately after using the service, but they may not be willing to cooperate due to concerns about time or confidentiality. Telephone surveys overcome the literacy hurdle but have problems of their own. Many low-income residents do not have phones, and in order to conduct a phone survey clientele phone numbers are needed. In some instances, calling clients may jeopardize their feelings of confidentiality.

Media Monitoring

Promotional efforts through the mass media may employ efforts to obtain editorial coverage, paid advertising, and/or public service announcements.

Editorial coverage

The term *editorial coverage* refers to all mentions of a topic that appear in the mass media as something other than an advertisement. Tracking and analyzing both the amount and the content of a topic's editorial coverage serves a number of purposes. Specifically, they help

- Calculate how many opportunities there were for people to be exposed to stories containing information about the topic of the initiative.
- Identify which placement tactics are working best.
- Identify what messages are appearing in the media and what ones are not, allowing assessment of the extent to which the issue was framed from a policy perspective and providing guidance for tailoring future content of media outreach efforts.
- Monitor competing messages, again providing guidance for tailoring future efforts to frame the issue.

Analyzing editorial coverage can play important roles during other phases of an initiative. For example, it can be used when an initiative is being planned, to assess how the issue is currently being framed, and to calculate baseline measures of editorial coverage, as discussed in Chapter 10. Its insights into how different reporters and media cover a particular issue can also provide a foundation to use when building relationships with the media, as discussed in Chapter 15.

Terminology

Before attempting to analyze media coverage, it is helpful to understand some of the terms commonly used in conjunction with it.

Circulation and Audience Size. Circulation and audience figures are used to estimate how many people may have seen each story. *Circulation* is the number of copies of a newspaper or magazine that are paid for, either through subscriptions or individual purchases. Because each copy of a newspaper or magazine may have multiple readers (consider the magazines in a physician's office, the many newspapers and magazines that are read by more than one person in a household, or those also available on the Internet), circulation does not equate to number of readers. *Audience* is sometimes used to describe the number of readers. *Audience size* is used in conjunction with television and radio. It can refer to the number of viewers or listeners during an average quarter-hour or the cumulative (*cume*) number of viewers or listeners for the program or part of the day. (Obviously, cume figures are larger.) With television, audience size can be expressed in terms of the number of people or the number of households.

Gross Impressions, Reach, and Frequency. Taking all of the stories on a topic and summing their circulation or audience size figures results in a number the industry terms gross impressions. Gross impressions are not the same thing as the number of people who were "reached" by the coverage. Why not?

1. Gross impressions do not account for frequency, or the number of times a specific individual was reached. Most people are exposed to multiple magazines, radio stations, and television programs, and some newspapers or magazines may run more than one story on the same topic.

2. Not everyone reads every story in every issue, watches every program, or listens to every news item.

Gross impressions provide an estimate of how many opportunities there were for messages to be seen. To know how many people were "reached" (i.e., actually saw the message) requires a survey of the population, and that approach is fraught with measurement difficulties as well, as discussed later in this chapter. Gross impressions are quite useful; for example, if program objectives include generating a certain amount of media coverage, they allow progress to be measured against those objectives. And, perhaps most importantly, they can be used to estimate how much coverage particular tactics generated and track coverage over time. Both types of information help managers determine when tactics should be changed.

Gross impressions are often misinterpreted and used to make statements that are, at best, hyperbole. For example: "We've reached over 350 million people with our message." If that was said of a U.S. campaign, apparently the program in question has gone international, considering that the population of the United States is around 300 million people (225 million adults).

Because newspaper and magazine gross impressions are usually calculated from circulation figures, some practitioners multiply the final number by some amount (2.5 is common). Their rationale for doing so is that circulation figures do not account for pass-along readership (people who read the publication but do not buy it). This is true, but on the other hand not everyone reads every story, and the average number of readers per copy differs greatly from one publication to another. For example, 2006 estimates of U.S. magazines' readers per copy averaged 6.3 but ranged from 1.24 to 44.92 (Mediamark Research, Inc., 2006). Although multiplying circulation by a pass-along readership factor makes the number a lot more impressive, doing so is difficult to defend because it accounts for possible additional impressions without adjusting for people who did not read the stories. Those who want to calculate magazine audience size more exactly can refer to the studies conducted by market research firms such as Mediamark Research, Inc.

Advertising Equivalencies. Advertising equivalencies are used to estimate the value of media coverage by calculating how much comparable amounts of advertising would have cost. Advertising equivalencies have limitations to keep in mind, particularly if part of a program includes paid advertising.

- The dollar amount that the vendor calculates is based on the total length of the story. Particularly in print media, program messages may have occupied a very small amount of the story. Consequently, a one-paragraph discussion of a topic in a two-page story will wind up being valued at what a two-page ad would cost.

- The price of advertising space is extremely variable and volatile, particularly in television and radio. It is like pricing hotel rooms or airline seats: The more unsold space there is close to the deadline, the more the price drops. In advertising placement, location is everything. Different publications or programs cost different amounts; different locations within them also vary enormously in price. Using the standard advertising unit cost (or average) can grossly under- or overestimate the "worth" of various placements.

The Process of Monitoring Editorial Coverage

Tracking news coverage of a public health initiative involves contracting with various vendors, sometimes different ones for each medium. Stories that appear in newspapers and magazines can be obtained through a major national clipping service. However, they do not include trade publications or academic journals; it is best to monitor these publications directly by subscribing to those that are relevant.

Some services also monitor some amount of network, cable, and major local television and radio coverage. Alternatively, such coverage can be obtained by contracting directly with vendors such as Video Monitoring Service. When monitoring television and radio coverage, be aware that the services' coverage of local radio is extremely limited and their television coverage does not include all markets. Television usage of information distributed by your initiative (i.e., video new releases, satellite media tours) can be tracked electronically if the material is encoded before it is distributed to stations.

Print media coverage can also be obtained using electronic services such as Nexis, Dialog, and ProQuest. They often offer coverage of trade publications and academic journals as well (and some coverage of television and radio news programs). Their disadvantage is that they do not include all publications, do not provide information on circulation (or audience size for broadcast media) or comparable advertising cost and generally do not capture any pictures or graphics that accompanied the story. Increasingly, media coverage can be monitored by looking at the websites of the individual media (for campaigns covering a relatively small geographic area) or by using a web search engine.

Construction of the search terms or reading list is a critical part of monitoring editorial coverage. The list needs to be as specific and concrete as possible, which is often quite difficult because it is not as simple as looking for mentions of a specific product or service. The trick is to construct a reading list that is broad enough to capture stories of interest but narrow enough to exclude most of those that are irrelevant. As an example, consider someone managing a cancer prevention and control initiative. Asking for all stories mentioning the word cancer would result in many mailboxes full of obituaries as well as stories of interest.

As with a print clipping service, vendors tracking radio and television coverage work from a topic list and scan all programming to locate appropriate stories and return transcripts or air checks (copies of the segment on tape), accompanied by information on the station and market in which it aired and an estimate of the audience size reached. Additionally, for television materials such as video news releases (VNRs), satellite media tours, and electronic press kits, tracking reports are often provided by the vendor distributing the material. Many vendors use Nielsen Media Research's SIGMA tracking service, which picks up the electronic code of the material each time it is aired. Reports usually indicate, for each time the VNR is used, the station, market, time, date, story length, and estimated cost if an ad of similar length was placed at that time. For an additional fee, air checks or transcripts can be obtained. Transcripts are inexpensive and useful for content analysis; air checks are expensive but useful for documenting implementation and showing others what the program has accomplished.

As an alternative to contracting with a vendor for monitoring, if program staff know that a relevant story appeared during a particular television program, on a particular radio station, or in a particular newspaper or magazine, the resources used by commercial advertisers can be used to determine how many people are likely to have been reached and an approximation of how much the placement would have cost if it had been paid advertising. Some of these resources are listed in **Table 16-1**.

Subscriptions to the services shown in **Table 16-1** can be quite expensive, particularly if only local information is needed. Many advertising agencies and some public relations firms subscribe to some or all of them; provided requests are reasonable, they may be willing to provide information or access to it on a pro bono basis to support the efforts of community organizations or other small nonprofits. In addition, some university libraries carry some of these resources. Alternatively, the information can be gathered by obtaining rate cards from individual stations and publications.

Table 16-1 Selected Sources of Media Information	
Source	**Information Available**
Arbitron (http://www.arbitron.com)	Radio station audience size estimates and profiles
Mediamark Research, Inc. (http://www.mediamark.com)	Magazine audience estimates and profiles
Nielsen Media Research (http://www.nielsenmedia.com)	Television audience size estimates and profiles; SIGMA tracking data
Standard Rate and Data Service (http://www.srds.com)	Newspaper and magazine profiles and ad pricing: television, radio, and outdoor profiles

Analyzing Content

With editorial coverage, it is often desirable to go beyond the information provided by the tracking and clipping services. Because reporters generally use various information sources to prepare their stories, it is necessary to analyze the content of coverage to determine the extent to which the coverage is on strategy (i.e., if it includes key messages and frames the issue as intended) and to identify any areas of confusion or negative coverage. The content analysis process involves reading each clip and coding it according to a previously developed message list, then examining the number of stories and estimated audience reach for each message. This analysis reveals what messages from program materials are being used, what ones are not, and how often conflicting messages appear, providing guidance for future media relations efforts.

Exhibit 16-3 presents an example of media analysis conducted to support the 5 A Day for Better Health program.

Tracking Advertising Placement

If an initiative relies on public service placement of its ads, tracking that placement is the only means of determining who had an opportunity to be reached by a campaign, and the only means of calculating gross impressions, reach, frequency, and what the placement would have cost had it been paid. For initiatives that pay for placement, tracking placement is far less critical; reach and frequency are normally estimated when developing the media plan that lays out where, when, and how often to run the ads. Even if these calculations were not made, they could easily be made using audience estimates supplied by each station or publication. Many commercial advertisers track placement of their own ads to verify that they actually ran as requested, though many social change initiatives may not have such resources available. Advertising tracking services can also be used to keep an eye on competitors' advertising spending and media schedules.

Exhibit 16-3   Analyzing Media Coverage: The 5 A Day for Better Health Campaign

---

Background

The goal of the national 5 A Day for Better Health program, originally cosponsored by the National Cancer Institute (NCI) and the Produce for Better Health Foundation (PBH), is to encourage Americans to eat five or more servings of fruits and vegetables daily to decrease their risk of developing cancer. The program today is a complex web of activities conducted at the national, state, and local levels by government agencies, nonprofit organizations, and the private sector.

Both NCI and PBH have conducted media campaigns to disseminate messages encouraging increased consumption of fruits and vegetables. This case study draws from NCI's initial media analysis report (Eisner, Loughrey, & Davis, 1994) to illustrate how the process works. The report analyzes print media coverage appearing from July 1992 (when NCI's media campaign was launched) through October 1993.

The National Cancer Institute employed a number of tactics to generate media coverage of 5 A Day messages. Regular contact with the media was accomplished through the quarterly distribution of 5 A Day media newsletters to newspaper and magazine food editors. The newsletters contained story ideas, recipes, infographics (**Figure 17-1**), and camera-ready art. The materials were also available on an accompanying disk or could be downloaded through two computer services.

This regular contact was supplemented by a variety of special events and additional media contacts. The 5 A Day media campaign was launched in July 1992 with a press conference featuring U.S. Department of Health and Human Services Secretary Louis Sullivan, M.D., and National Institutes of Health Director Bernadine Healy, M.D.; the launch was also supported by a video news release featuring press conference footage and Olympic swimmer Matt Biondi. In addition, media activities were conducted in conjunction with the launch of 5 A Day week in September 1993, radio, and print public service announcements were produced and distributed periodically, and a magazine media tour was conducted.

Beyond NCI's activities, PBH, produce manufacturers, and retail stores sponsored many additional media activities.

Method of Analysis

To assess the 5 A Day print media coverage, newspaper and magazine placements published from July 1992 through October 1993 were collected by a national clipping service. The clipping service attempted to clip all daily and weekly newspapers in the United States, as well as nearly 7,000 consumer, trade, and professional magazines and newsletters. However, as would be expected with any clipping service, it is doubtful that all stories resulting from the campaign were obtained because no clipping service covers all publications in the United States, and all services inevitably miss some placements. Nonetheless, the clipping service collected 7,625 stories published during the time period.

The first stage of the analysis involved estimating gross impressions by summarizing circulation figures and estimating worth by summarizing advertising dollar equivalencies.

(continues)

Exhibit 16-3 Analyzing Media Coverage: The 5 A Day for Better Health Campaign (continued)

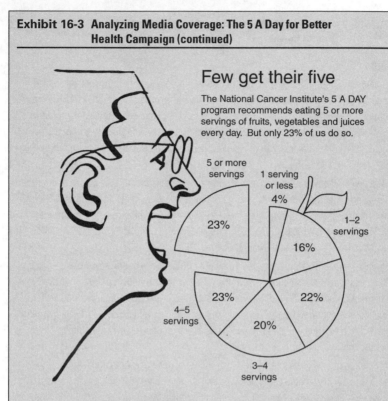

Few get their five

The National Cancer Institute's 5 A DAY program recommends eating 5 or more servings of fruits, vegetables and juices every day. But only 23% of us do so.

5 or more servings — 23%

1 serving or less — 4%

1–2 servings — 16%

4–5 servings — 23%

3–4 servings — 20%

22%

Figure 16-1 Infograph from the 5 A Day Campaign

Source: Reprinted from National Cancer Institute.

To evaluate the content of the coverage in a timely and cost-effective manner, a representative sample was drawn. Sampling was conducted by first grouping the clips by the distribution schedules of their publications—weekly, daily, or monthly. Clips from daily publications were grouped further by the day of the week on which they were published. Proportional samples were drawn based on the percentage of clips in each category (e.g., weekly, monthly, Monday, Tuesday, etc.). The sample included 1,103 clips.

The goal of the content analysis was to improve future media placement efforts by (1) assessing the extent to which media coverage contained NCI's key messages and (2) identifying tactics (in terms of type of information and delivery strategies) that were most successful. To that end, each story was read and coded using a message list that had been constructed with the following objectives:

- Determine the extent to which media coverage reflected NCI's key messages.
- Identify what other story angles were covered.
- Assess what types of statistics and visuals were used most often.
- Assess what sources of information (including spokespeople) were used most often.

(continues)

Exhibit 16-3 Analyzing Media Coverage: The 5 A Day for Better Health Campaign (continued)

Some highlights of the analysis are presented below.

Quantity of Coverage

Circulation of the total 7,625 clips was 396,145,875; based on the size of the clips, the equivalent advertising value was estimated at $5,925,354. Coverage was highest the month the campaign was launched (889 clips with a corresponding circulation of more than 52 million) and the month 5 A Day week was launched (820 clips with a corresponding circulation of more than 40 million).

Content of Coverage

Content analysis of the stories revealed that the vast majority (89% of the 1,100 articles analyzed) contained one or more of NCI's key messages. However, some messages received far more coverage than others. For example, 77% of the articles reported that people should eat a minimum of five servings of fruits and vegetables per day—one of the key messages to increase knowledge. However, only 12% of the stories included another knowledge message—that five servings is a minimum, not a maximum, recommendation.

Messages designed to build skills by focusing on specific actions people could take to increase their consumption of fruits and vegetables received relatively limited coverage, with 28% of the stories including messages such as a suggestion to add two servings each day or more specific actions people could take to add servings (such as having fruit or juice in the morning and having fruit and/or vegetables as a snack).

Messages focusing on the health benefits of eating five or more servings of fruits and vegetables each day received greater coverage: 41% of the placements mentioned a specific health benefit related to this level of consumption, with the association with reduced risk of some forms of cancer being mentioned most often (it appeared in 40% of the stories). Relatively few articles (5%) discussed the barriers to eating 5 A Day, such as seasonality, cost, or preparation time.

The analysis also examined the extent to which the coverage included other story angles of interest to NCI. Just over one-fourth (27%) of the articles discussed 5 A Day in conjunction with food (e.g., recipes, food preparation tips, a specific fruit or vegetable, or a Mediterranean diet). Details and background on the 5 A Day program were mentioned in 16% of the clips; about 5% mentioned an organization or group that had joined the 5 A Day program. About 8% of the articles discussed children and 5 A Day, usually in terms of the value of eating produce. Very few (2%) of the sampled articles mentioned a concern about pesticides used on fruits and vegetables.

Tactics Used

Nearly half (47%) of the sampled articles used materials and/or information that could be identified as coming from the National Cancer Institute. About one-fourth (26%) used information from the July 1992 launch materials, 10 % used information from the media newsletter, and 11% used information from NCI but the precise source could not be identified. About

(continues)

Exhibit 16-3   Analyzing Media Coverage: The 5 A Day for Better Health Campaign (continued)

one-fourth of the articles (26%) mentioned an NCI-provided statistic. Current fruit and vegetable consumption was the most frequent focus; 21% of all stories mentioned that Americans currently eat 3.5 servings of fruits and vegetables daily or that only 23% of American eat 5 or more daily servings. Thirteen percent of the sampled articles used visuals; 5 A Day infographs were used most often, followed by art from the newsletter and photographs.

Source: Data from E. Eisner, K. Loughrey, and K. Davis, 1994, *The National Cancer Institute's 5 A Day for Better Health Program: Analysis of Print Media Placements—July 1992 through October 1993.* Bethesda, MD: National Cancer Institute Office of Cancer Communications.

For initiatives relying on public service placement, tracking data also allow managers to

- Compare ads to determine which ones receive the most play.
- Thank stations that are "heavy users" of materials, and potentially explore the opportunity for station promotions around the issue.
- Refine distribution lists based on who is and is not using program materials.
- Discern any need for follow-up studies with nonusers to identify why they are not using the ads and determine if there is anything that can be done to increase their usage.

Sources of PSA Placement Information. PSAs that appear in magazines or newspapers can be obtained through clipping services. Regional and other specialized editions of magazines make it difficult to obtain all PSA placements (often a PSA will run in one edition that had unsold advertising space but not in all editions). If PSAs are being sent to professional publications, it is often wise to subscribe directly to the publications to ensure PSA placement does not get overlooked.

In the United States, television PSAs can be tracked using SIGMA, Nielsen Media Research's electronic tracking service. To use SIGMA, the sponsoring organization contracts with a service provider that encodes the master tapes prior to duplication and release. This encoding uniquely identifies each PSA and is broadcast with the PSA, but it is not visible to the audience. Nielsen's computers identify this code each time a spot is aired. Airplay reports can be customized but typically include, for each airing of the spot, the station and market in which the spot aired (or network if it ran on a network), the date and time it aired, some basic audience composition information (including estimated audience size), and the approximate cost of the time if it had been purchased for commercial advertising. Because the price of television time is subject to extreme fluctuations, this last item is only a rough estimate. Radio PSA play in major markets can also be tracked electronically; however, doing so is extremely expensive, and many areas of the country are still missed.

Additional information of PSA placement can be obtained through a few different mechanisms:

- Commercial verification reports. Broadcast stations and print publications generally send these to commercial advertisers to verify that their ads ran as requested. Some stations and publications automatically sent these reports for PSAs; others will do so if asked. The reports typically list the name of the program airing when the PSA ran and the date and time it ran.

- Follow-up phone calls with stations and publications. Phoning public service directors to see if they plan to use a particular spot is labor intensive but can be quite useful, particularly if this technique is limited to priority gatekeepers, or those for whom it will be difficult to collect other information, such as radio stations.

- The resources listed in **Table 16-1**. Local initiatives that know when and where their ads ran can consult these sources to estimate gross impressions, reach, and frequency.

- Including phone numbers, websites, or addresses in PSAs. If a PSA includes a hotline number, website, or address, information on who was reached and motivated enough to respond by requesting more information can be collected.

Monitoring Policy Changes

The way in which a policy change can be monitored depends on what type of change it is and who has the power to make it. For example, if a change is taking the form of a referendum, bond issue, or proposition that requires citizens to vote, tracking voter opinion can be critical, as is discussed later in this chapter. If private organizations are being asked to make the change, contact with their public affairs personnel or decision makers within the organizations may be the only way to monitor change. Many policy and funding decisions are made by governments at the local, state, or national level. This section provides some suggestions for monitoring these types of policy changes in the United States.

At the local level, attending city council meetings and maintaining contact with decision makers can be critical in tracking policy changes. Some activities, such as agendas for upcoming meetings and hearings, can also be monitored through contact with local government agencies or through the Internet. Search engines can help identify the websites of local governments, and the Library of Congress THOMAS site (http://www.thomas.loc.gov) provides a number of gateways to local sites.

At the state level, it is increasingly possible to monitor the introduction and progress of bills through legislative websites. Most sites can be accessed from the state's main home page. Additionally, staff of the legislator sponsoring a bill (or legislators opposing it, as appropriate) can provide valuable information on the "behind the scenes" progress. States vary in how regulatory agencies operate, but many states have "government in the sunshine" laws that mandate access to some of the proceedings.

At the federal level, legislation can be monitored through the previously mentioned Library of Congress website (http://www.thomas.loc.gov). This site provides the complete text of bills as well as information on their status, sponsors, referrals to committees, and so forth. It also provides access to the *Congressional Record* (also available through the Government Printing Office [GPO] in hard copy or on its website at http://www.gpo.gov) and to committee reports. Once legislation is passed and signed into law, often an executive branch agency has to issue new regulations to implement the law. At this point, the *Federal Register* can be useful. It is also available in hard copy or on its website. When an agency is planning to issue a rule (regulation), it first publishes the proposed rule in the *Federal Register* and solicits comments; the notice will stipulate where comments should be sent and the length of the comment period. Sometimes it is useful to go back to the Congressional committee reports and compare the proposed rule with the apparent intent of the legislators; many such reports can be accessed through THOMAS. The *Federal Register* also publishes final agency rules prior to their being added to the *Code of Federal Regulations*, as well as a variety of other notices from federal agencies, such as notices of hearings and investigations, committee meetings, agency decisions and rulings, and issuance or revocation of licenses.

■ TRACKING TARGET AUDIENCE AWARENESS AND REACTION

A primary focus of this chapter thus far has been on how to measure messages being sent out by a program, but not how to measure the extent to which those messages are received. There are some practical methods of obtaining information about who was reached by building active response mechanisms into the dissemination effort itself, such as a telephone number or address to write to for more information. Quantitative tracking studies provide a means of monitoring reactions among the population as a whole.

Active Response Mechanisms

Both automated hotlines (those answered by a recording) and live-operator hotlines can provide a wealth of data. Analysis of call volume by date can be compared with other process data, such as dates of media coverage or community events, to craft a more detailed picture of which tactics are having the greatest impact. If the hotline system is more sophisticated and captures area codes and prefixes, or if callers leave their addresses, this information can be mapped and areas of high and low response can be identified. If live operators are available, a profile of who is asking for more information can be obtained by asking callers a few standard questions. For example, asking where callers learned about hotline numbers provides insights into what tactics are generating the greatest response. Learning basic demographics about callers enables program managers to assess the extent to which the callers' profile matches that of the priority population of interest, and may provide insights into how to adjust communication or delivery strategies to better focus them. If the population has been segmented using a stages of change approach, asking callers a few questions can determine what stage they are in. Materials designed for people in that stage can then be sent, if they are available.

Websites also provide an opportunity for collecting data. In addition to analyzing how users navigate a site and which pages are visited more often, websites can include a pop-up customer satisfaction survey. Or, if the site provides individually-tailored information (for example, personal health assessments) such that people have to register to use the site, basic demographic and behavioral data (within ethical confines) can be collected during registration.

Coupons/"E-mail for More Information"
Including a coupon with print advertisements or on websites, or a website or e-mail address on press releases, story ideas, and TV and radio PSAs can provide additional opportunities to learn who is being motivated by the message. Although this approach does not provide information about the participants other than geographic location, it does provide information on the number of people reached. Geographic information also can be useful, as discussed earlier regarding inventory tracking systems.

The coupon idea can be used creatively by public health initiatives that include partnerships with local businesses. For example, if local movie theater owners agree to include a slide about the program or a PSA or video clip in their pre-movie entertainment, viewers could be told on the slide (or video) that ticket stubs from the movie theater could be redeemed for some amount off of a screening test or other product or service. Or they could be redeemed at another partner; for example, at a local grocery store or restaurant for some amount off of a specific healthier food purchase, at a pharmacy for some amount off of a smoking cessation kit, at a health club for one free visit, at a sporting goods store for some amount off of athletic equipment, or at a department store for running or walking shoes or exercise clothes. Collecting and counting the ticket stubs provides information on how many people were reached and, more important, were motivated enough by the message to take action.

Quantitative Tracking Surveys

Quantitative tracking studies, usually in the form of public opinion polls, can be used to support implementation of social change initiatives seeking to bring about changes in individual behavior or policies, or seeking to promote public health as an institution. They provide a means of monitoring levels of knowledge, awareness, and self-reported behavior among the population.

For policy change initiatives, opinion polls provide an excellent way to determine whether the issue has obtained prominence on the public's agenda (Wallack & Dorfman, 1996), monitor public reactions to various ways of framing the issue, and adjust the framing strategies accordingly. The public opinion data can also be used to help persuade journalists to cover a particular aspect of an issue, and to illustrate public support for (or opposition to) a change to policy makers. Most important, they can identify the need for fast action and can be used to rally additional financial support if needed.

An example of how public opinion tracking data were used quite successfully is the 1994 campaign against California's Proposition 188 (described in more detail in Chapter 11). Proposition 188 was a ballot initiative sponsored by Philip Morris that would have repealed all local antismoking ordinances as well as the state's law eliminating smoking in workplaces and replaced them with weak statewide smoking restrictions (Macdonald, Aguinaga, & Glantz, 1997). The anti-188 campaign coordinated grass-roots advocacy, media advocacy, and paid advertising to deliver a common message. To monitor progress, the health coalition conducted periodic public opinion polls during the three-month campaign. About two months before the vote, poll results showed voters were about equally divided on the proposition. In response, the coalition produced television ads featuring former U.S. Surgeon General C. Everett Koop and paid to air them in major media markets the last week of the campaign, using contributions provided by the American Cancer Society and American Heart Association (Macdonald et al., 1997).

Initiatives focused on individual behavior change can use tracking data in two ways: to monitor progress and as a news hook to gain additional coverage. In some instances, they may want to "feed back" tracking data illustrating the population's progress in their future media messages, thus providing social reinforcement for the change. In comparison to policy change initiatives, those focusing on individual behavior change are likely to conduct tracking studies less often. Many organizations conduct them once a year, often after their major media push and in time to feed into strategic planning for the coming year. Others have the resources to conduct them more often, perhaps as often as quarterly.

Initiatives that successfully use tracking studies often incorporate one or more of the following approaches into their study designs:

- Collect data periodically, not just at the end when outcomes are assessed. Periodic information is necessary to refine messages and improve delivery.
- Ideally, collect data immediately after major public events; awareness is likely to be highest then and thus easier to detect.
- Include questions that ask where participants learned or heard about the program or its key messages, to help identify what tactics are working best.

Public opinion polls can be too costly for small organizations, but can be extremely cost-effective for larger initiatives. For example, in the United States adding questions to a nationally projectable omnibus poll costs about $1,000 per question (less for closed-ended questions, more for those with open-ended answers); tabulation of the question against demographic information collected as part of the study is included in the cost. (See Chapter 18 for more information.)

As Chapter 18 will discuss in more detail, when public opinion polls are used to track the reach of an initiative's messages, it can be difficult to assess change over time because of the magnitude of difference needed to conclude statistical change. If the issue is very much on the public agenda, changes in awareness and opinion may be easy to track, but if coverage has been relatively limited, it can be much more difficult to detect, either because such a small percentage of the population was exposed to the message or because the change was subtle. A change of 1 or 2 percentage points will be washed out in sampling error. The issues discussed in the client satisfaction section of this chapter are relevant to designing and conducting public opinion polls.

■ CONCLUSION

Adequately tracking and monitoring implementation is a fundamental aspect of the marketing approach. Process evaluation plays a critical role in ensuring that program components are constantly monitored and refined to improve their performance. Unfortunately, it is often overlooked or compromised in favor of outcome evaluation. Appropriate process evaluation mechanisms can be built into every program tactic and provide important information on what was done, when, where and how it was done, and who was reached.

References

Alreck, P.L., & Settle, R.B. (2004). *The survey research handbook* (3rd ed.). New York: McGraw-Hill/Irwin.

Andreasen, A.R. (1985). "Backward" marketing research. *Harvard Business Review,* 63(3), 176–182.

Andreasen, A.R. (1995). *Marketing social change: Changing behavior to promote health, social development, and the environment.* San Francisco: Jossey-Bass.

Basch, C.E., Sliepcevich, E.M., Gold, R.S., Duncan, D.F., & Kolbe, L.J. (1985). Avoiding type III errors in health education program evaluations: A case study. *Health Education Quarterly,* 12, 315–331.

Bearden, W.O. & Netemeyer, R.G. (1999). *Handbook of marketing scales* (2nd ed.). Thousand Oaks, CA: Sage.

Centers for Disease Control and Prevention. (1993). *Planning and evaluating HIV/AIDS prevention programs in state and local health departments: A companion to program announcement #300.* Atlanta, GA: Author.

Eisner, E., Loughrey, K., & Davis, K. (1994). *The National Cancer Institute's 5 A Day for Better Health Program: Analysis of print media placements—July 1992 through October 1993.* Bethesda, MD: National Cancer Institute Office of Cancer Communication.

Lamb, C.W., & Crompton, J.L. (1992). Analyzing marketing performance. In S.H. Fine (Ed.), *Marketing the public sector: Promoting the causes of public and nonprofit agencies* (pp. 173–184). New Brunswick, NJ: Transaction Publishers.

Macdonald H., Aguinaga, S., & Glantz, S.A. (1997). The defeat of Philip Morris' "California Uniform Tobacco Control Act." *American Journal of Public Health,* 87, 1989–1996.

Mediamark Research, Inc. (2006). *Pocketpiece report results—Doublebase 2006.* Retrieved October 6, 2006 from http://www.mriplus.com.

Rossi, P.H., & Freeman, H.E. (1993). *Evaluation: A systematic approach* (5th ed.). Newbury Park, CA: Sage.

Rossi, P.H., Lipsey, M.W. & Freeman, H.E. (2004). *Evaluation: A systematic approach* (7th ed.). Newbury Park, CA: Sage.

Scanlon, J., Horst, P., Nay, J.N., Schmidt, R.E., & Waller, A.E. (1977). Evaluability assessment: Avoiding type III and IV errors. In G.R. Gilbert & P.J. Cronkin (Eds.), *Evaluation management: A sourcebook of readings.* Charlottesville, VA: U.S. Civil Service Commission.

Steckler, A. & Linnan, L. (Eds.). (2002). *Process evaluation for public health interventions and research.* San Francisco: Jossey-Bass.

Stone, E.J., McGraw, S.A., Osganian, S.K., & Elder, J.P. (1994). Process evaluation in the multicenter child and adolescent trial for cardiovascular health (CATCH). *Health Education Quarterly,* (Suppl. 2).

Wallack, L., & Dorfman, L. (1996). Media advocacy: A strategy for advancing policy and promoting health. *Health Education Quarterly,* 23, 293–317.

CHAPTER

17

Outcome Evaluation Issues and Designs

Outcome evaluation of social change initiatives can play a number of roles, depending on the nature of the effort being evaluated and the reason for the evaluation. This chapter introduces some of the ways in which outcome data are used to shape policy and to refine interventions, presents some of the key issues involved with evaluating such initiatives, describes some potentially useful evaluation designs in greater detail, and discusses the limitations of using randomized experiments to evaluate social change initiatives.

■ THE ROLE OF OUTCOME EVALUATION

An outcome evaluation may be conducted for any number of reasons (see **Exhibit 17-1**). At its most basic, outcome evaluation shows whether a project had the effects it was planned to have. Depending on its scope, it can serve as a management tool by helping to identify how objectives, target audiences, strategies, and implementation might be revised and improved. It may also identify any unintended consequences of a program (particularly important with policy changes). Outcome evaluation is often conducted after a project is finished, but may occur periodically throughout the life of a program. To illustrate many of the uses of outcome evaluation, **Exhibit 17-2** presents evaluation results of *Road Crew*, a social marketing intervention to reduce drunk driving that is described in greater detail in Appendix 10-A.

In addition to serving a useful monitoring function, sometimes the results of outcome studies can be a powerful tool for future social change initiatives. A striking example is a study of the sales impact of local

---

Exhibit 17-1   Uses of Outcome Evaluation

- To assess the extent to which a project met its objectives

- To identify improvements or refinements in objectives, target audience, strategies, or implementation

- To assess reactions to a program

- To identify any unintended consequences

- To assess the cost efficiency of the program

- To provide evidence for future social change initiatives

---

ordinances mandating smoke-free bars and restaurants (Glantz & Smith, 1994). The study compared restaurant sales in the 15 cities that first enacted such ordinances with sales in 15 matched cities without ordinances for the period from 1986 to 1993. It found no impact on revenues during the period following enactment of the ordinances. The tobacco industry tried to dismiss the study as "fatally flawed" and tried to sue Glantz's employer, the University of California, on charges of scientific fraud (Susser, 1997). The study was peer-reviewed twice, once before its original publication and again in response to an unpublished critique cited by the National Smokers' Alliance; both times, all reviewers agreed that the work was sound (Susser, 1997). Subsequent evaluations have substantiated the original study's conclusion that laws requiring smoke-free restaurants and bars do not have an adverse economic impact (Scollo et al., 2003).

Sometimes policy outcomes are tracked after the fact, when it appears that a new policy may have inadvertently created a new danger to the public's health. Airbag regulations in the United States are a recent example. As of October 1, 2001, there were 195 confirmed airbag-related deaths; of these, 119 were children (National Highway Traffic Safety Administration [NHSTA], 2001). After the deaths began occurring, the National Highway Traffic Safety Administration (NHTSA) and other organizations responded with widespread efforts to educate the public about steps they could take to lessen the likelihood of airbag injury (e.g., never put a rear-facing child safety seat in the front seat; put children in the back seat when possible; if they or small adults are in the front seat, push the seat back as far as possible). Initially NHTSA issued a rule allowing dealers and other car repair businesses to install manual on-off switches for airbags in vehicles owned by or used by people whose requests for switches are approved by NHTSA (NHTSA, 1997); later, NHTSA modified rules to require advanced airbags—multi-stage systems that inflate the bag fully, partially, or not at all depending on input from occupant sensing devices that detect the presence or absence, relative weight, and seatbelt status of a front seat passenger (NHTSA, 2000).

Exhibit 17-2 Results of Road Crew Evaluation

Road Crew began as a one-year social marketing demonstration project aimed at reducing drunk driving in the state of Wisconsin. The project was evaluated three ways:

1. A quasi-experimental design was used to demonstrate causality. Prior to implementing *Road Crew*, a pre-test survey was conducted with bar patrons in demonstration and control communities to measure the level of driving after excessive drinking. After the ride services had been operating for a year, a post-test was conducted with the same audience.

2. After the ride services had been operating for a year, a phone survey of the target audience, general population, community leaders, bar owners, and wait staff was conducted to measure awareness of and attitudes toward *Road Crew*.

3. Rides provided by *Road Crew* were counted, with each ride representing the prevention of an alcohol-related crash.

Results of the *Road Crew* demonstration project significantly exceeded goals:

- 19,757 rides were given to potential drunk drivers from July 1, 2002 through June 30, 2003. Rides are estimated to have prevented 15 alcohol-related crashes on area roads, a 17% reduction. [The project goal had been a 5% reduction.]

- The average cost of an alcohol-related crash in Wisconsin is approximately $56,000; the cost to avoid a crash in this program was about $15,300.

- There was no decrease in the percent of patrons who admitted to drinking and driving, but there was a significant drop in the frequency of occurrences per person compared with control group behavior.

- Awareness in the general community was 68%; it ranged from 70%–100% in other groups.

- Among those who were aware of the program, over 80% surveyed had positive feelings, and nearly half of those aware perceived a decrease in driving after excessive drinking in the community.

- Among bar patrons, there was no observable increase in consumption compared to control communities. However, there was an increase in the number of bars visited.

- Community leaders felt that the program should continue. The projects are likely to be sustainable, with plans in place to continue the programs for the next year.

Source: Data from *The Road Crew Final Report*, by C. Karsten, M. Rothschild, Miller Brewing Company, Tavern League of Wisconsin, & MasComm Associates. (2003). Retrieved April 24, 2006 from http://www.dot.wisconsin.gov/library/publications/topic/safety/roadcrew.pdf. Reprinted with permission.

■ CONSIDERATIONS WHEN PLANNING EVALUATIONS

Planning the evaluation in tandem with the initiative eliminates some potential problems and often results in a stronger intervention as well as a stronger evaluation. This section outlines some questions to consider when developing outcome evaluation plans. **Exhibit 17-3** illustrates some failures that can be avoided through proper consideration of this issues and careful program and evaluation planning. Although the exhibit was developed for communication interventions, the points apply equally well to marketing interventions.

What Are the Questions the Evaluation Should Answer?

Exhibit 17-1 alludes to some questions an evaluation can answer, such as: To what extent did a program meet its objectives? What improvements or refinements can we make to improve the program? Going forward, can we expect receptivity or opposition to the intervention? Are there any unintended consequences resulting from our efforts that we should address? What return on investment are we getting for this initiative?

How Is the Intervention Expected To Work?

Rossi and Freeman (1993) defined an impact model as "an attempt to translate conceptual ideas regarding the regulation, modification, and control of behavior or conditions into hypotheses on which action can be based" (p. 119). They went on to note that "the absence of a well-specified impact model severely limits opportunities to control a program's quality and effectiveness (Freeman & Sherwood, 1970). . . . Even if a social program is successful in delivering services and achieving the objectives set for it, without an explicitly documented impact model there is no

---

Exhibit 17-3 Four Types of Failure Common to Communication Interventions

1. STRATEGY Failure: Communication is really not the problem. People need better services, and messages are inadequate in themselves to affect change.

2. EXECUTION Failure: Messages are badly needed, but they are poorly constructed, lack adequate exposure, and/or are addressed to the wrong audience.

3. MEASUREMENT Failure: Communication was the right answer; it was well delivered, but poorly evaluated. Either the instruments measured the wrong change, or time was inadequate to permit the change to become detectable.

4. EXPECTATION Failure: The problem is that real change occurred, but did not meet the expectations of planners or funders. A success was declared to be a failure.

Source: From *From Prevention Vaccines to Community Care* (p. 332), by W. Smith. In *Public Health Communication: Evidence for Behavior Change* by R. Hornik (Ed.), 2002, Mahway, NJ: Lawrence Erlbaum Associates. Copyright 2002 by Lawrence Erlbaum Associates. Reprinted with permission.

basis for understanding how and why it worked or for reproducing its effects on a broader scale, in other sites and with other targets" (p. 120).

For public health education interventions targeting individual behavior change, Hornik (2002) observed the following:

> There are three complementary models of behavior change implicit in many public health communication campaigns. The individual effects model focuses on individuals as they improve their knowledge and attitudes and assumes that individual exposure to messages affects individual behavior. The social diffusion model focuses on the process of change in public norms, which leads to behavior change among social groups. The institutional diffusion model focuses on the change in elite opinion, which is translated to institutional behavior, including policy changes, which in turn affects individual behavior. The models contrast the direct effects of seeing mass media materials (one sees a public service announcement, PSA, about the role of condoms in safe sex; one decides to follow the advice) with the indirect effects of the social diffusion model (discussion within a social network is stimulated by PSAs or media coverage of an issue; that discussion may produce changed social norms about appropriate behavior, and affect the likelihood that each member of the social network will adopt the new behavior). In the institutional diffusion model, media coverage of an issue may operate through either one or both of two mechanisms. Media coverage may affect public norms that affect institutional behavior or policymaker actions, or media coverage may lead policymakers to think that an issue is important and requires action, regardless of whether public norms have actually changed. If a social or institutional diffusion process dominates behavior change, then individuals' detailed knowledge about the benefits of a new health behavior may be less important than their belief that it is an expected behavior. (pp. 54–55)

Exhibit 17-4 provides a succinct description of a social change initiative from the viewpoint of a member of the target audience. As Hornik (1997b) said of this example, "this program is effective not because of a PSA or a specific program in physician education. It is successful because the National High Blood Pressure Education Program has changed the professional and public environment as a whole around the issue of hypertension" (p. 50).

Wallack and Dorfman (1996) provided an example of how a policy change initiative using a media advocacy strategy is expected to work. The expectation is that if the issue is appropriately framed in terms of access (to get journalists' attention) and content (telling the story from the policy perspective), it will get on the public agenda through media coverage. Once it is on the public agenda, it will mobilize groups or individuals

---

Exhibit 17-4 Social Change In Action

A person sees some public service announcements and a local TV health reporter's feature telling her about the symptomless disease of hypertension. She checks her blood pressure in a newly-accessible shopping mall machine, and those results suggest a problem. She tells her spouse who has also seen the ads and encourages her to have it checked. She goes to a physician who confirms the presence of hypertension, encourages her to change her diet, and then return for monitoring.

Meanwhile, the physician has become more sensitive to the issue because of a recent article in the *Journal of the American Medical Association*, some recommendations from a specialist society, and a conversation with a drug retailer as well as informal conversations with colleagues and exposure to television discussions of the issue. The patient talks with friends at work about her experience. They also increase their concern and go to have their own pressure checked. She returns for another check-up and her pressure is still elevated although she has reduced her use of cooking salt. The physician decides to treat her with medication. The patient is ready to comply because all the sources around her—personal, professional and mediated—are telling her that she should.

Source: From "Public Health Education and Communication as Policy Instruments for Bringing About Changes in Behavior," (pp. 49-50) by R. Hornik. In *Social Marketing: Theoretical and Practical Perspectives*, 1997, Mahway, NJ: Lawrence Erlbaum Associates, Inc. Copyright 1997 by Lawrence Erlbaum Associates, Inc. Reprinted with permission.

---

who influence policy makers, and they, in turn, will put pressure on the decision makers, resulting in the policy being enacted or the change occurring. The airbag example mentioned earlier in this chapter illustrates large parts of this process. The media started covering the airbag-caused deaths of infants and children, and NHTSA started getting pressure to allow the airbags to be turned off (car dealers and repair shops normally are not legally allowed to override safety equipment) pending a more permanent solution to the problem.

How Fast Is the Intervention Expected to Work?

Most population-based public health interventions targeting individual behaviors can expect small, gradual changes. However, there are some exceptions. Hornik (1997b) argued that "straightforward substitution of behaviors, when possible, may allow more rapid change than attempts to introduce new behaviors" (p. 55), citing as examples interventions to prevent Reye's syndrome (by using an aspirin substitute rather than aspirin) and sudden infant death syndrome (by putting babies to sleep on their backs rather than on their stomachs). He noted that both of these behaviors were very easy to change and adopting the new behavior "sharply reduced the risk of a rare but devastating event" (p. 55). We would add that in both situations, adopting the new behavior was linked to a core human value: caring for children.

Interventions to bring about environmental changes can also be slow and gradual or fast-moving, also largely depending on the type of change. Environmental improvements that require complex changes in multiple policies by multiple entities generally can expect slow, gradual changes. For example, efforts to improve end-of-life care in the United States can range from national and state changes, such as changes in federal regulations (such as services covered under Medicare and Medicaid), state laws, health insurance provided by private insurers, medical school curricula and continuing medical education, to a variety of local changes, such as increasing the availability of hospice care, changing the policies of hospitals, long-term care facilities, and emergency medical services, and/or introducing or expanding services (e.g., palliative care units, hospice care). Similarly, change may be slow and gradual for environmental changes that may meet with substantial resistance (such as trying to implement local smoke-free ordinances across a state).

What Outcomes Can Reasonably Be Expected?

Perhaps more than any other question, this one illustrates the need to develop evaluation plans in tandem with the plans for the initiative. The starting point for determining what outcomes are reasonable should be the initiative's objectives. As Rossi and Freeman (1993) and Kotler and Roberto (1989), among others, noted, objectives should operationalize a program's goals, thereby making them measurable. However, they also noted that program objectives often do not do this, rendering evaluation very difficult because the evaluators cannot tell what they ought to be measuring. Even if the goals are operationalized, the resulting objectives may be changes of unrealistically large magnitude.

There are three questions to consider when thinking about effects sizes for social change initiatives:

1. What outcomes are reasonable to expect, given the structure of the intervention?
2. What magnitude of effect is needed to make a difference to public health?
3. What will be considered successful in this environment?

The first two questions give rise to all sorts of policy debates, but in the end the answer to either may be an effect size far smaller than what most outcome evaluations designs will be able to detect. The answer to the second question, in particular, can make outcome evaluation particularly challenging, because in some instances the magnitude of effect needed to make a difference to public health can be quite small. As Beresford and colleagues (1997) noted in discussing population-wide efforts to change eating habits, "the public health model, or population strategy, consists of shifting the entire distribution of a risk factor, including the mean, down. The diminution in risk for a given individual is typically small and may not even be clinically important. Nevertheless, because the entire distribution is affected, the impact on morbidity and mortality can be substantial" (p. 615). Citing Prentice and Sheppard (1990), they went on to note that "a 1% reduction in dietary calories from fat made populationwide could result in about 10,000 deaths saved in the United States in a year" (Beresford et al., 1997, p. 615). That 1% reduction would not be detectable at the community level using most available evaluation methodologies, and even if it were detected, it could not be said to be statistically significant because of sampling error.

The third question addresses how "success" is defined in the initiative's organizational environment. That is, how much of a change will an initiative need to demonstrate in order to be viewed as successful? Can the intervention be structured so that it is of sufficient intensity and duration to achieve this level of success? Can an evaluation be structured to measure it if it is attained? As discussed above, sometimes a relatively small population-wide change—too small to adequately capture in an evaluation—can have enormous public health consequences. Demonstrating cause and effect can also be problematic. Other factors may influence outcomes, such as activities conducted by complementary or competing organizations. Evaluation may show an association between exposure to program components and increased awareness of, or engagement in, the appropriate health behavior, for example, but may not show definitively that the initiative caused the change.

Beyond looking to the initiative's objectives and likely definitions of success for direction, one must consider how, and how fast, the intervention is expected to work against issues such as the expected duration and intensity of the intervention. It can take years to see the effects of initiatives targeting individual changes in prevention behaviors. For example, the large decreases in smoking rates and deaths due to cardiovascular disease are seen over a decade or more. Reviewing the results of other initiatives addressing the same or similar topics and using similar implementation strategies may provide some guidance.

The expected outcomes can influence evaluation plans in many ways. For example, if expectations are for small gradual change, large sample sizes will be required (and still may not attain the needed precision), and it would be wise to wait a sufficient amount of time before attempting to measure outcomes. In contrast, if large, rapid effects are anticipated, sample sizes can be smaller and outcomes measured more quickly.

How Will Outcomes Be Measured?

Outcome measures should be driven by the theoretical model used to develop the intervention, and they should be consistent with what the intervention was designed to accomplish. For example, if the intervention was designed to tell people how many servings of fruits and vegetables they should eat, and to convince them to add two servings each day, the outcomes to be measured should be whether the number of people who know how many servings to eat is increasing, and whether people are, in fact, adding two servings per day, not how many servings they are eating.

Beyond problems with measuring outcomes that do not reflect intervention objectives, sometimes outcome measures are not as sensitive to a range of possible changes as they might be. As just one example, consider parts of a commentary by Fishbein (1996) on a community intervention designed to increase the likelihood that young men would engage in safer sex:

> Kegeles [with Hays and Coates, 1996] evaluated their intervention by looking for a reduction in the proportion of men who engaged in *any* act of unprotected anal sex. The question that must be asked is whether this measure fully captures the effect of their intervention. Not reflected in this outcome measure would be a person who had reduced the number of unprotected acts of anal intercourse from 50 at baseline to 25 at follow-up or one who went from no condom use to 75% condom use, or who reduced the number of acts of anal sex or the number of partners, or who substituted masturbation or "outercourse" for intercourse. Did the outcome measures selected by the authors ask too much of their intervention? Was it fair to view a person who reduced unprotected sex acts from 100 to 0 as no more of a success than one who reduced such acts from 1 to none? (p. 1076)

In contrast, the evaluation of an initiative to reduce drunk driving reported in **Exhibit 17-1** includes measures sensitive enough to detect that although there was no decrease in the percent of bar patrons who admitted drinking and driving, there was a significant drop in the frequency of drinking and driving compared to the control group.

Other challenges arise related to the types of data that can be collected at reasonable cost. For example, for programs focusing on individual behavior changes, self-reported measures are often all that can be affordably obtained, and these are not always reliable. Sometimes people do not know aspects of their health status (e.g., blood pressure or blood cholesterol levels), and sometimes they do not really know what they do (e.g. how many servings of grains they ate yesterday). At other times, social desirability influences their answer (i.e., they give what they think the answer should be even if it is not what they do). Many researchers attempt to control for this third confounding variable by measuring social desirability traits as part of their studies.

What Was Actually Implemented?

As Orlandi (1986) observed, assessing effectiveness is difficult or impossible without knowing how the program was implemented. Without process evaluation to detail if and how the intervention was implemented, evaluators may make what Scanlon and colleagues (1977) termed a type III error: evaluating a program that has not been adequately implemented or is not measured as implemented (Basch et al., 1985). Before outcome evaluation is initiated, evaluators should review process evaluation data and determine whether any refinements need to be made to the study design or measures to adjust to a different implementation than was initially envisioned.

How can someone not know if or how a program was implemented? Often outside evaluators are brought in solely to evaluate, and they may not have been involved during implementation. Even if the evaluators are on staff, for may large programs evaluation staff are totally separate from program staff, and they would have no reason to know whether a program had been implemented as planned or not. For multisite programs where collaborating organizations are responsible for much of the implementation, it may be difficult for program managers to truly know the degree to which particular program components have been implemented. Ongoing monitoring and process evaluation activities help ensure this problem does not occur.

■ CHOOSING AN EVALUATION DESIGN

Evaluation designs can be divided into three categories:

1. Experimental
2. Quasi-experimental
3. Other

Each category, and, indeed each design within each category, has limitations and underlying assumptions that preclude using it in every setting. Hornik (2002) outlined some broad principles about what makes evaluation designs stronger:

- The evaluation design needs to respect the program's model of effect—including its mechanism of effect (individual learning, social diffusion, and/or institutional diffusion), how much exposure to messages will be achieved, who should be affected, how fast the effects should occur and what their magnitude should be.
- Some design elements are likely to buy better inferences, all else being equal. These include having many measures over time, incorporating treatment comparison groups if they exist, supplementing evidence

about outcomes with evidence that the program operated as it was supposed to, and having larger rather than smaller samples.

- Designs are specific to a context. A pre-post design may be good enough if one can make a strong case that there are no competing activities that could explain the change in behavior (see, for example, **Exhibit 17-2**); similarly, programs that will be considered successful only if they produce large, rapid effects will tolerate a "lesser" design than programs that expect slow, gradual change.

In the following sections we present brief descriptions of each type of design and overviews of some of the issues to consider in using them. Those planning an evaluation would do well to consult standard evaluation texts, such as Rossi, Lipsey, and Freeman (2003), as well as the classic works on experimental and quasi-experimental design (see, in particular, Campbell & Stanley, 1966; Cook & Campbell, 1979) and Hornik's *Public Health Communication: Evidence for Behavior Change* (2002), which discusses evaluation models and analyses appropriate for various types of programs.

Experimental Designs

A randomized experiment is the "gold standard" approach to outcome evaluation. With such an approach, members of the population of interest are randomly assigned to one of two or more groups. One group does not receive the program intervention and is labeled the control group. The other group(s) receive(s) the intervention (or variations of it, if there are multiple groups). Because participants are randomly assigned to the groups, one group should not differ in any significant way from the other group. Therefore, assuming that nothing differentially affected each group during the intervention time period, any observed differences in outcomes can be assumed to be the result of the intervention. Outcomes are assessed by comparing the treatment group(s) scores with those of the control group. Ideally, both groups are measured before and after the intervention.

Program managers often face tremendous pressure to use randomized experiments because when used appropriately they conclusively demonstrate cause and effect, and because they are a familiar methodology. However, although randomized experiments are useful in a wide array of settings, using them to evaluate many public health interventions often fundamentally violates their assumptions.

Limitations of Experimental Designs When Evaluating Social Change
The premise that the intervention is the only thing that could cause a change in the treatment group because it is the only thing that is different between the treatment and control groups works very well when testing a vaccine in a laboratory—however, public health interventions are

not vaccines (Smith, 1997, 2002). Using vaccines and clinical care as metaphors (see **Figure 17-1**), Smith (2002) argues that the typical public health intervention is more like clinical care, and the critical distinction between the two is that the vaccine model of disease prevention is largely characterized by a *develop and deliver* mentality, whereas the clinical care model is characterized by an *assess, intervene, and adjust* mentality. "I believe within the distinction between the vaccine and the care metaphors lies a more realistic approach to develop and evaluate interventions" (Smith, 2002, p. 329).

Common problems with using randomized case-control trials to evaluate social change initiatives are threefold:

1. The intervention cannot be adjusted to changing conditions.
2. Randomized trials are appropriate only if there is a true control group, which secular trends and/or the scope of the initiative often eliminate.
3. The effect sizes required to demonstrate statistical change are often unrealistic.

Inability to Adjust the Intervention. Social change efforts need to be dynamic, responding to changes in the environment and the audience. It is not reasonable to set out to develop a program that will be implemented in exactly the same way over time or at different locations at different times. If the program is used somewhere else, some adjustments will have to be made to delivery mechanisms if nothing else.

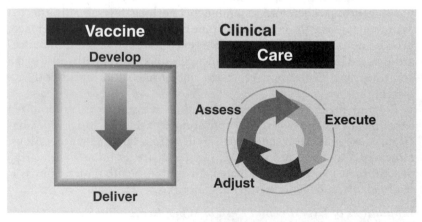

Figure 17-1 Two Metaphors for Intervention Development

Source: From *From Prevention Vaccines to Community Care* (p. 329), by W. Smith. In *Public Health Communication: Evidence for Behavior Change* by R. Hornik (Ed.), 2002, Mahway, NJ: Lawrence Erlbaum Associates. Copyright 2002 by Lawrence Erlbaum Associates. Reprinted with permission.

Let us think of a social change initiative as a plan to replace a roof. The plan is implemented: The new roof is put on. It is supposed to last for 20 years. One year later, the roof starts to leak over the living room. Do the owners leave it that way for the next 19 years, because they put the new roof on according to their original plan and they want to see if it will magically correct itself? Of course not. The answer is obvious: It is not holding up, and it needs to be fixed. In the process of fixing it, the owners probably will ask their roofers to examine what went wrong and fix that same problem elsewhere on the roof, so they do not get more leaks. But by fixing it, they increase the complexity of outcome evaluation. If, after 20 years, they ask the question, "Did it work?" there is no simple answer. From one perspective, it failed: It leaked. But from another perspective, it taught them something very valuable. The got the leak fixed, they applied the same fix elsewhere to prevent future leaks, and no leaks happened. Therefore, to fully assess how the roof performed, one must assess the original plan and subsequent adjustments to it.

Similarly, with social change efforts, it is important to assess what changes were made along the way, and to document why those changes were made—what they were designed to fix or improve—so that we begin to get a sense of the conditions under which combinations of goods and services, message appeals, delivery mechanisms, and so forth, work best. The goal of evaluating a social change program should not be to determine if the program "worked" as initially envisioned or if it is stable enough to use somewhere else. It is not stable, nor is it intended to be. The goals should be to determine how much progress was made toward objectives, and how that progress was made.

As Smith (1997) noted, one of the reasons some of the large community intervention trials may appear to fail is that the interventions are not altered to meet changing conditions. Discussing the 22-community, 4-year Community Intervention Trial for Smoking Cessation (COMMIT), he observed that "because it was a case control program, there were a lot of things that occurred during the four years that the interventionists could have changed because they found out they weren't working as well. But they didn't change them because they were testing a 'vaccine' and the vaccine can't be changed in the middle of the test" (p. 12).

Inadequate Control Groups. Using randomized experiments to evaluate social change often violates one of the assumptions of a randomized design—that there is a control group. With community-based interventions, there rarely is a true control: The control group may not be receiving the program's intervention, but it probably is receiving some intervention, in the form of secular trends if nothing else. Public health initiatives usually do not come into existence until there is a movement within society to make a particular change. "Science does not operate in a vacuum; the forces that operate to justify large, expensive community intervention studies also are operating among the general public to get them to accept the evidence and act on it even before scientific establishment does" (Feinlaub, 1996, p. 1697).

These secular trends can have a devastating impact on an evaluation's ability to accurately measure program contributions. As Rossi, Lipsey and Freeman (2004) noted in their classic evaluation text, "relatively long-term trends in the community, region or country, sometimes termed *secular drift*, may produce changes that enhance or mask the apparent effects of a program" (pp. 272–273). Secular trends combined with the need to keep an intervention "stable" may create a situation in which the control group has access to more state-of-art information and tools than the treatment group over the life of a multiyear program. A number of practitioners and evaluators have argued that secular trends may be why some very large community trials, where interventions take place in one set of communities and other communities are "matched" to those and treated as a control group, fail to show an effect.

Discussing COMMIT, Smith (1997) said "a strong secular trend was affecting both intervention and control communities. Change occurred in both communities; everybody was getting better at decreasing smoking rates. The study showed that the intervention did not produce an effect any stronger than a very strong secular trend. Much of what was going on in the intervention group was going on in the control group as well" (p. 12). Another example comes from the Stanford Five-City Project, a large-scale community-based intervention designed to test whether a comprehensive program of community organization and health education produced favorable changes in cardiovascular disease risk factors, morbidity, and mortality. Authors of one study concluded that "the net intervention efforts were modest. This is due, in part, to the strong secular trends in both health promotion and risk factors" (Winkleby et al., 1996, p. 1778).

Also discussing the effects of secular trends, Hornik (1997a) warned, "local activities build on a spine of national programs that work together. Don't evaluate, don't try to compare treatment and controls that are geographically defined unless there is really going to be a difference in exposure to messages. Don't accept trials as negative evidence until you look hard at the evidence for differences in exposure between the so-called treatment and control areas" (p. 59).

Need for Large Effects. Most public health initiatives do not take place in a lab with 50 participants. They take place in communities and states. Sometimes they take place across the whole country. Unlike the lab, we have little control over exactly who received the intervention and almost no control over exactly how much of it they receive. Yet our field's evaluation standards demand statistically significant change before we can conclude the intervention had an effect. As Fishbein (1996) noted,

Given the nature of our statistical tests and our tendency to use relatively small samples in experimentally controlled studies, this usually means that a public health intervention will be considered a success only if it produces an effect of at least medium size (e.g., a mean difference of at least half of a standard deviation, or about a 20%-to-30% change in a proportion), or, often, an even larger effect size (e.g., a mean difference of a full standard deviation, or a 50%-to-60% change in a proportion). One might ask whether such expectations are either realistic or warranted. That is, can we really expect a usually brief, relatively inexpensive public health intervention to produce medium or large effects? . . . Rightly or wrongly, we appear to be bound by the requirement to demonstrate statistical significance even though we seldom have the resources to evaluate our interventions with sample sizes necessary to detect a small effect. (p. 1075)

To put these effect sizes in context, the Stanford Five-City Project described earlier in this chapter—much more intensive than many population-based public health initiatives—estimated that the adults in the project's treatment communities would have been exposed to around 5 hours of education per year (Farquhar et al., 1990). Is it reasonable to expect even a 20% change—the low end of the range just described—as a result of 5 hours of education over the course of a year? Most public health interventions deliver a much lower dose of exposure.

If we compare social change initiatives with commercial marketing campaigns, which are another type of initiative seeking to induce widespread population change, we see very different standards for measuring achievement. Commercial marketers conclude that their "interventions" are a great success when market share increases 2% or 3%. Writing about this phenomenon Fishbein (1996) remarked, "Thus, while a condom manufacturer would be more than happy if an advertising campaign increased the company's share of the market by 3% or 4%, a public health intervention that increased condom use by the same 3% or 4% probably would be considered a failure" (p. 1075).

Why are the standards for the two fields so different? Although there may be many reasons, two in particular probably play a part. First, expectations about appropriate effect sizes were carried over from expectations about appropriate effect sizes for clinical studies, with no adjustment made for differences in intervention intensity. As Kristal (1997) noted, "the effect size for clinical interventions is large and hopefully fast. In a public health intervention, it's small, and at best, it's gradual" (p. 39). Second, evaluators of many public health initiatives are forced to rely on samples, which are a considerably less exact measure than sales data or many of the measures available in clinical studies. As Kraemer and Winkleby (1997) noted in a response to Fishbein's comments in the preceding paragraph, "if the same condom manufacturers lacked data from the entire population and needed to estimate the market share of the campaign, they might commission a survey research group to sample representative sites within the market area. If the survey research group concluded that the market share was somewhere between 2% and 6%, the condom manufacturers would be uncertain about the effect of the campaign and might be quite dissatisfied with the survey" (p. 1727).

Quasi-Experimental Designs

Experimental designs in this category also compare treatment and control groups; however, assignment to each group is not random (hence the designation quasi-experimental). As with true experiments, outcomes are most commonly assessed by comparing the pre- and post-intervention scores of the groups. A major drawback to quasi-experimental designs is what has been termed "the fantasy of untreated control groups" (Durlak, 1995, p. 76). As discussed earlier in this chapter, social change initiatives are usually developed as a result of strong secular trends; it is unlikely that members of the control group are receiving no aspects of the intervention.

A variety of methods can be used to assign target audience members to treatment and control groups. One popular method of assignment with community interventions is selecting communities that match the communities where the intervention is put into place on key variables. This was the approach used in the COMMIT and Stanford Five-City Project community intervention trials mentioned earlier in this chapter.

An alternative approach that works for some types of interventions is to define different groups within a community. For example, schools could be divided into those that receive program materials and those that do not. For mass media components, some commercial advertising methodologies can be used to divide the overall population into two or more groups. For example, some cable systems can split households, transmitting one ad to half of the households and a different ad to the other half. Some magazines can split press runs in the same way, or they can insert an ad in one edition and not another.

Another technique is to create the control group when outcome data are analyzed, by comparing those who participated in the program (the treatment group) with those who did not (the control group). This approach is rarely an option with community interventions: Because everyone in the community could have been exposed to program messages, even if they do not remember the exposure, there is no way to divide the groups.

Quasi-experimental designs can be used for a number of reasons. They are often used to pilot test an intervention or to evaluate a demonstration project. A true pilot test would normally take place after traditional pretesting but before the planned full-scale implementation. Demonstration projects generally follow the complete program life cycle (e.g., planning, development, implementation, evaluation). The resulting evaluation data can help refine program components and, in some instances, help program planners gauge likely response to or demand for various program elements.

However, expectations of what a pilot test or demonstration project will provide should be carefully considered. Such tests can be expensive because materials and products have to be produced in final form and reproduced in small quantities, and the resources required to adequately evaluate the results can far outweigh the costs of development and implementation. Additionally, expectations often are unrealistic because the pilot implementation is qualitatively or quantitatively different from what the future implementation will be. For example, demonstration sites often receive far more training and technical assistance then will be available to other sites when the program is implemented. Test sites may receive materials for free while other sites will have to pay for them. The small scale may allow proportionally more resources to be expended, increasing both the total number of people reached by the intervention and the frequency with which they are reached, leading to an overstatement of the likely effects.

Quasi-experimental designs are also used for comparison studies in which two or more implementation strategies are tested against each other. The implementations may differ along such dimensions as products or services offered, types of materials (e.g., different advertisements might be tested against each other) or mix of promotional activities (e.g., one implementation uses only mass media, another uses mass media plus community events, and a third uses only community events).

Other Designs
In situations where a randomized experimental design or quasi-experimental design is inappropriate or not feasible, sometimes an alternative design can be used that, while weaker than ideal, respects the way the program is expected to work and adequately considers alternative explanations for any observed outcomes (Hornik, 2002).

The After-Only Design. Evaluators are often asked to evaluate an intervention that has been in place for some time and are limited to a "post-treatment" survey of the target audience. (This is one of the problems that occurs when evaluation is not planned in tandem with the program.) While this is inherently the weakest of evaluation designs, Hornik (2002) offers some suggestions for how it can be useful. His suggestions assume the intervention was a promotional effort, though his logic could be extended to apply to other aspects of the marketing mix. Measuring recall of the messages, knowledge or beliefs those messages might have influenced, and self-reported behavior can allow evaluators to address the following types of questions:

- Does a reasonable amount of the audience report a substantial level of recall?
- Is there an association (in the expected direction) between recall and behavior?
- Is that association robust even when known predictors of the behavior and/or exposure to media are controlled statistically?
- Is there evidence that the intervention worked as expected? For example, if the intervention is presumed to "work" by changing a particular belief which in turn is expected to change behavior, is there evidence that exposure affected behavior through the targeted belief?

Pre-post or Before-After Designs. As with experiments, these involve taking measures before and after an intervention; the difference is that there is no control group so it can be difficult to make a compelling case that the intervention caused the change. Therefore, these designs are appropriate for interventions without competition from complementary efforts to address the issue (for example, the *Road Crew* program discussed in **Exhibit 17-2**). Measures are often collected by surveying representative samples of the target audience before and after an intervention, but other measures appropriate for the intervention can be used, such as sales data (e.g., to measure the impact of a smoke-free regulation on local businesses), number of callers to a crisis prevention hotline, number of children vaccinated, number of people in a cafeteria line including a fruit or vegetable on their tray, etc.

Pre-post designs have a number of variations:

- *Tracking studies* involve taking one measure prior to the intervention and then multiple measures during and after the intervention. For example, self-reported measures of current practice or intent to engage in a behavior (be it increasing physical activity or voting a particular way on an upcoming referendum or bond issue), as well as awareness of the issue and the public health initiative. Tracking studies typically involve independent cross-sectional surveys (in other words, interviewing a new sample of people at each point in time).
- *Time-series analyses*, which involve collecting many repeated measures of the same variables prior to an intervention and then comparing repeated measures postintervention to look for change. Sometimes this can be done using existing datasets; for example, to measure the impact of the U.S. National High Blood Pressure Education Program, trends in awareness, treatment, and control of hypertension were examined using National Health and Nutrition Examination Survey data, and stroke mortality rates were examined using data collected by the National Center for Health Statistics (Rocella, 2002). Time-series analysis can also involve using the pre-intervention measures to project what was expected to occur, and then comparing this projection to the data from the post-intervention time period (see **Figure 17-2**).

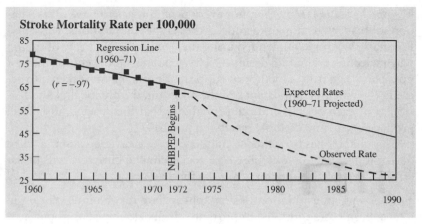

Figure 17-2 Age-adjusted stroke mortality rates: Expected rates from a 1960–1971 regression line of best fit projected to 1990, and observed rates from 1972–1990.

Source: From "Reduction of cardiovascular disease mortality," (p. 83), by C. Roccella. In *Public Health Communication: Evidence for Behavior Change*, by R. Hornik (Ed.), 2002, Mahway, NJ: Lawrence Erlbaum Associates. Copyright 2002 by Lawrence Erlbaum Associates. Reprinted with permission.

- *Panel or cohort studies*, which involve measuring the same people multiple times. In some ways this design is stronger than measuring outcomes with separate cross-sectional studies, as it allows each person's pretest measure to serve as his or her own reflexive control. However, the sample's generalizability may be compromised over time as participants age, leave, or respond to repeated questions on the same subject (NCI, 2002).

■ CONCLUSION

Evaluators and program managers need to work together to ensure that the evaluation design is appropriate for the intervention model and that the outcomes measured are the outcomes the program sought to affect. Outcome evaluations that emphasize the degree to which planned outcomes were achieved and how and with whom they were achieved, rather than whether the program as originally planned achieved the outcomes anticipated, will be more useful and will allow the intervention to be adjusted during implementation in response to changing conditions.

There is no question that researchers need to identify the circumstances under which particular types of program components work best and most cost-efficiently. As Walsh and colleagues (1993) observed, "if (as seems reasonable) the question for funders and program designers is whether and under what conditions socially marketed health interventions produce superior results and are more efficient and effective than common alternatives, almost no useful information is available to answer it" (pp. 115–116). However, not every program has to have an evaluation sophisticated enough to address these types of questions. Rossi and Freeman (1993) recommended using the "good enough" rule of thumb when selecting evaluation designs: "The evaluator should choose the best possible design from a methodological standpoint, having taken into account the potential importance of the program, the practicality and feasibility of each design, and the probability that the design chosen will produce useful and credible results" (pp. 220–221).

This chapter has presented a number of factors to keep in mind when determining how the outcome of a social change initiative will be assessed. Foremost among them are the following:

- Choosing an evaluation design appropriate for the intervention in scope, in cost, and most importantly, in its assumptions about how change will occur. The evaluation should be able to tolerate changes to the program design and implementation.

- Understanding the environment in which the initiative is taking place. Strong secular trends are often present and can mask the effects of an intervention.

- Ensuring that outcome expectations are driven by what is realistic for the intervention and evaluations are designed accordingly.

- Ensuring that the outcomes measured are those the intervention was trying to affect and that the range of possible progress toward those outcomes is adequately captured.

Using traditional randomized designs to assess the outcomes of social change can be problematic in a number of ways. First, the restrictions of the evaluation limit the power of the initiative. As Walsh and colleagues (1993) observed, "the very essence of social marketing is to adapt and change, whereas summative evaluation researchers need a program to stay the course" (p. 115). In other words, traditional outcome evaluation models expect a static, never-changing intervention, but social change initiatives employing marketing principles are designed to be dynamic, constantly adjusting to changing environments and audience needs. Second, large effects may be needed to see statistically significant change, yet sometimes it is not reasonable to expect a large effect, and even a small one may have huge public health implications. Third, the outcome data can be difficult to interpret when strong secular trends are also at work.

References

Basch, C.E., Sliepcevich, E.M., Gold, R.S., Duncan, D.F., & Kolbe, L.J. (1985). Avoiding type III errors in health education program evaluations: A case study. *Health Education Quarterly,* 12, 315–331.

Beresford, S.A.A., Curry, S.J. Kristal, A.R., Lazovich, D., Feng, Z., & Wagner, E.H. (1997). A dietary intervention in primary care practice: The eating patterns study. *American Journal of Public Health,* 87, 610–616.

Campbell, D.T., & Stanley, J.C. (1966). *Experimental and quasi-experimental designs for research.* Boston: Houghton Mifflin.

Cook, T.D., & Campbell, D.T. (1979). *Quasi-experimentation design and analysis issues for field settings.* Skokie, IL:Rand McNally.

Durlak, J.A. (1995). *School-based prevention programs for children and adolescents.* Thousand Oaks, CA:Sage.

Farquhar, J.W., Fortmann, S.P., Flora, J.A., Taylor, C.B., Haskell, W.L., Williams, P.T., Maccoby, N., & Wood, P.D. (1990). Effects of community-wide education on cardiovascular disease risk factors. *Journal of the American Medical Association,* 264, 359–365.

Feinlaub, M. (1996). Editorial: New directions for community intervention studies. *American Journal of Public Health,* 86, 1696–1698.

Fishbein, M. (1996). Editorial: Great expectations, or do we ask too much from community-level interventions? *American Journal of Public Health,* 86, 1075–1076.

Freeman, H.E., & Sherwood, C.C. (1970). *Social research and social policy.* Englewood Cliffs, NJ: Prentice Hall.

Glantz, S., & Smith, L.R.A. (1994). The effect of ordinances requiring smoke-free restaurants on restaurant sales. *American Journal of Public Health,* 84, 1081–1085.

Hornik, R. (1997a). Charting the course from lessons learned. In L. Doner (Ed.), *Charting the course for evaluation: How do we measure the success of nutrition education and promotion in food assistance programs? Summary of proceedings* pp.56–61). Alexandria, VA: USDA Food and Consumer Service.

Hornik, R. (1997b). Public health education and communication as policy instruments for bringing about changes in behavior. In M.E. Goldberg, M. Fishbein, & S.E. Middlestadt, *Social marketing; Theoretical and practical perspectives* (pp. 45–58). Mahwah, NJ: Lawrence Erlbaum Associates.

Hornik, R.C. (Ed.) (2002). *Public health communication: Evidence for behavior Change.* Mahway, NJ: Lawrence Erlbaum Associates.

Kegeles, S.M., Hays, R.B., & Coates, T.J. (1996). The Mpowerment Project: A community-level HIV prevention intervention for young gay men. *American Journal of Public Health,* 86, 1129–1135.

Kotler, P., & Roberto, E.L. (1989). *Social marketing: Strategies for changing public behavior.* New York: Free Press.

Kraemer, H.C., & Winkleby, M.A. (1997). Do we ask too much from community-level interventions or from intervention researchers? *American Journal of Public Health,* 87, 1727.

Kristal, A.R. (1997). Choosing appropriate dietary data collection methods to assess behavior changes. In L. Doner (Eds.), *Charting the course for evaluation: How do we measure the success of nutrition education and promotion in food assistance programs? Summary of proceedings* (pp. 39–41). Alexandria, VA: USDA Food and Consumer Service.

National Highway Traffic Safety Administration. (1997). Air Bag On-Off Switches Rule, 62 Fed. Reg. 62406 (to be codified at 49 C.F.R. § 571 and 595).

National Highway Traffic Safety Administration. (2000). Advanced air bag safety standard. Retrieved October 6, 2006 from http://www.nhtsa.dot.gov/cars/testing/ncap/airbags/pages/FAQsAdvFrontABs.htm

National Highway Traffic Safety Administration. (2001). Counts for air bag related fatalities and seriously injured persons. Unpublished data. Retrieved October 6, 2006 from http://www-nrd.nhtsa.dot.gov/pdf/nrd-30/NCSA/SCI/3Q_2001/ABFSISR.html

Orlandi, M.A. (1986). The diffusion and adoption of worksite health promotion innovations: an analysis of barriers. *Preventive Medicine, 15,* 522–536.

Prentice, R.L, & Sheppard, L. (1990). Dietary fat and cancer: consistency of the epidemiologic data, and disease prevention that may follow from a practical reduction in fat consumption. *Cancer Causes Control, 15,* 522–536.

Roccella, E. (2002). Reduction of cardiovascular disease mortality. In In R. Hornik (Ed.), *Public health communication: Evidence for behavior change* (pp. 73–84). Mahway, NJ: Lawrence Erlbaum Associates.

Rossi, P.H., & Freeman, H.E. (1993). *Evaluation: A systematic approach* (5th ed.). Newbury Park, CA: Sage.

Rossi, P.H., Lipsey, M.W., & Freeman, H.E. (2003). *Evaluation: A systematic approach* (7th ed.). Newbury Park, CA: Sage.

Scanlon, J., Horst, P., Nay, J.N., Schmidt, R.E., & Waller, A.E. (1977). Evaluability assessment: Avoiding type III and IV errors. In G.R. Gilbert & P.J. Cronkin (Eds.), *Evaluation management: A sourcebook of readings.* Charlottesville, VA: U.S. Civil Service Commission.

Scollo, M., Lal, A., Hyland, A., & Glantz, S. (2003). Review of the quality of studies on the economic effects of smoke-free polices on the hospitality industry. *Tobacco Control, 12,* 13–20.

Smith, W. (1997). Confounding issues in evaluations of nutrition interventions. In L. Doner (Ed.), *Charting the course for evaluation: How do we measure the success of nutrition education and promotion in food assistance programs? Summary of proceedings* (pp. 11–13). Alexandria, VA: USDA Food and Consumer Service.

Smith, W. (2002). From Prevention Vaccines to Community Care. In R. Hornik, (Ed.) *Public Health Communication: Evidence for Behavior Change* (pp. 327–356). Mahway, NJ: Lawrence Erlbaum Associates.

Susser, M. (1997). Editorial: Goliath and some Davids in the tobacco wars. *American Journal of Public Health, 87,* 1593–1595.

Wallack, L., & Dorfman, L. (1996). Media advocacy: A strategy for advancing policy and promoting health. *Health Education Quarterly, 23,* 293–317.

Walsh, D.C., Rudd, R.E., Moeykens, B.A., & Maloney, T.W. (1993). Social marketing for public health. *Health Affairs, 105–119.*

Winkleby, M.A., Taylor, C.B., Jatulis, D., & Fortmann, S.P. (1996). The long-term effects of a cardiovascular disease prevention trial: The Stanford Five-City Project. *American Journal of Public Health, 86,* 1773–1779.

CHAPTER

18

Overview of Common Theories and Marketing Research Methods

Theories of behavior change and marketing research methods are used throughout the marketing process. Theories are often critical to understanding how a change will occur, how and with whom we can best intervene to bring it about, and the facilitators or supports our efforts should include. Audience and market research is conducted at every stage of the marketing process using a variety of secondary and primary research methodologies. Qualitative and quantitative studies, quasi and true experiments, surveys and systematic observations can all play a role. This chapter describes some of the theories and methods most often used and some of the situations for which they are appropriate.

■ THEORIES AND MODELS OF BEHAVIOR CHANGE

Theories and models of behavior change are used a number of ways in social change efforts and marketing interventions. In the early stages of planning, theory can help develop an understanding of current behavior and likely reactions to recommended behaviors—and, therefore, whether education, law, marketing, or a combination would be most useful. It can also help determine the intervention's overall model of effect: whether change will be rapid and large or slow and gradual, and, for interventions ultimately seeking to change individual health behaviors, whether the intervention will bring about the change by working directly on the individual, through his or her social systems, through institutional or policy changes, or through a combination of methods. Later, theory can help select specific audience segments, determine actions they can take, and develop offerings most likely to reach, motivate, and enable those audience segments to take the desired action. Theory can also help planners set reasonable objectives; if one expects change to occur very quickly and easily, objectives are likely to be quite different than if one expects change to be gradual and difficult.

No one theory or model will work for every situation. It is not unusual for interventions to be guided by the constructs of a number of different models; examples occur throughout this book. Some theories and models are intended to predict or understand individual health behaviors, others interpersonal health behaviors, and others how a health behavior moves through a community or group. The following sections provide brief overviews of the major constructs in some of the commonly-used theories and models of individual health behavior and how changes move through a social system. Glanz, Rimer, and Lewis's *Health Behavior and Health Education* (2002) is an excellent resource for more in-depth information on those covered here as well as many others.

The Transtheoretical Model of Stages of Change

Researchers from a number of disciplines have developed various models of behavior based on the idea that individuals move through stages of readiness as they change behavior. The transtheoretical model developed by James Prochaska (with Redding and Evers, 2002) is used extensively by practitioners seeking to change health behaviors. The model is based on four core constructs: stages of change, decisional balance, self-efficacy, and processes of change. Descriptions of each of these constructs are provided in **Table 18-1**.

The transtheoretical model has been used to develop interventions targeting smoking cessation and a range of chronic conditions. The model is often used to segment audiences by their stage of change and then to develop interventions tailored to each stage (also called stage-matched interventions). An alternative is to segment audiences by stage, but then select one or two of the stages to target, as was done for the 5 A Day for Better Health program's media campaign discussed in Chapter 11.

As program offerings are developed, the transtheoretical model can provide guidance on the emphasis and content of these components in terms of decisional balance (what marketers would call the cost-benefit equation). Studies of 12 health behaviors have found that for a person to progress from precontemplation to action, pros must increase and cons must decrease—but the pros, or benefits—of changing must increase twice as much as the cons decrease (Prochaska et al., 2002).

Table 18-1 Transtheoretical Model Constructs

Constructs	Description
Stages of change	
Precontemplation	Has no intention to take action within the next 6 months
Contemplation	Intends to take action within the next 6 months
Preparation	Intends to take action within the next 30 days and has taken some behavioral steps in this direction
Action	Has changed overt behavior for less than 6 months
Maintenance	Has changed overt behavior for more than 6 months
Decisional balance	
Pros	The benefits of changing
Cons	The cons of changing
Self-efficacy	
Confidence	Confidence that one can engage in healthy behaviors across different challenging situations
Temptation	Temptation to engage in the unhealthy behavior across different challenging situations
Processes of change	
Consciousness raising	Finding and learning new facts, ideas, and tips that support the healthy behavioral change
Dramatic relief	Experiencing the negative emotions (fear, anxiety, worry) that go along with unhealthy behavioral risks
Self-reevaluation	Realizing that the behavioral change is an important part of one's identity as a person
Environmental reevaluation	Realizing the negative impact of the unhealthy behavior or the positive impact of the healthy behavior on one's proximal social and physical environment
Self-liberation	Making a firm commitment to change
Helping relationships	Seeking and using social support for the healthy behavioral change
Counterconditioning	Substituting healthier alternative behaviors and cognition for the unhealthy behaviors
Reinforcement management	Increasing the rewards for the positive behavioral change and decreasing the rewards of the unhealthy behavior
Stimulus control	Removing reminders or cues to engage in the unhealthy behavior and adding cues or reminders to engage in the healthy behavior
Social liberation	Realizing that the social norms are changing in the direction of supporting the healthy behavioral change

Source: From *Health Behavior and Health Education: Theory, Research and Practice*, 3rd edition (p. 101), by K. Glanz, B.K. Rimer, and F.M. Lewis. Copyright 2002 by John Wiley & Sons, Inc. Reprinted with permission of John Wiley & Sons, Inc.

The transtheoretical model also provides guidance on what type of change process to emphasize based on a person's current stage (Prochaska et al., 2002). Processes such as consciousness raising, dramatic relief, and environmental reevaluation help people more from precontemplation to contemplation. In contrast, self-reevaluation processes are most helpful as people move from contemplation to preparation, when self-liberation processes take over. Once people take action, reinforcement management, helping relationships, counterconditioning, and stimulus control help them make the transition to maintenance.

Health Belief Model

The Health Belief Model (HBM) is another model of individual behavior. It was originally developed in the 1950s to explain why large numbers of people did not participate in disease screening and detection programs even when the programs were conveniently located and free of charge (Hochbaum, 1958). Later, the model was expanded, clarified, and extended to include preventive actions, illness behaviors, and sick-role behavior (Janz, Champion, & Strecher, 2002). The model posits that people will take action to prevent, to screen for, or to control ill-health conditions if:

- they perceive themselves as susceptible to the condition;
- they perceive the medical, clinical, and/or social consequences of the condition will be severe;
- they believe that a course of action is available to them that would be beneficial in reducing either their susceptibility to or the severity of the condition; and
- they believe that the anticipated barriers to (or costs of) taking the action are outweighed by its benefits. (Janz et al. 2002).

More recently, researchers have added self-efficacy (one's confidence in one's ability to take an action) to the model as they attempted to apply it to lifestyle behaviors requiring frequent actions over a long period of time (e.g., to eating habits, quantities of physical activity, safe sexual practices) rather than one-time behaviors, such as immunizations or screening tests (Janz et al., 2002). In addition, the model assumes cues to action (strategies to activate a person's readiness to take action) play a role in health behavior, but their role has not been systematically studied (Janz et al., 2002).

Appendix 18-A provides an example of developing message concepts using the Health Belief Model for guidance.

Social Cognitive Theory

Social cognitive theory (SCT) is the modern incarnation of social learning theory. SCT views behavior as "dynamic, depending on aspects of the environment and the person, all of which influence each other simultaneously" (Baranowski, Perry & Parcel, 2002, p. 168). SCT conceptualizes environment as objective factors that are external to a person but can affect their behavior. Environment encompasses the social environment (family members, friends, classroom or work peers) as well as the physical environment. The term situation is used to describe a person's perception of his or her environment. The interaction among self, environment, and behavior is termed *reciprocal determinism*. The idea is that changes in any one of these three areas influence the other two.

SCT encompasses a number of concepts; the essence of it involves the aforementioned reciprocal determinism, as well as (1) increasing *self-efficacy*, or a person's confidence in his or her ability to perform a particular behavior, (2) *observational learning*—modeling positive outcomes of healthful behavior using credible role models and showing the reinforcements they receive, (3) ensuring *behavioral capability*—both the knowledge and skills to perform a behavior, (4) providing *reinforcement* for the behavior, ideally internal reinforcement (e.g., self-initiated) as it is the most powerful; (5) *expectations*—outcomes a person anticipates as a result of the behavior, and (6) *expectancies* or incentives—the values a person places on a given outcomes: "benefits" in marketing language.

Using SCT to plan an intervention involves identifying appropriate *environmental changes* (similar to what marketers do when they adjust place, price or product) to support the desired behavior change, providing opportunities for *observational learning* by modeling appropriate behaviors for the target audience, and increasing *self-efficacy* by providing audience members with an opportunity to practice small changes and therefore increase their confidence in their ability to engage in the desired behavior. Chapter 12 includes some discussion of how social cognitive theory can be used in conjunction with the transtheoretical model of stages of change to design messages, and the case study in Appendix 11-A illustrates use of these concepts in designing materials.

Diffusion of Innovations

An *innovation* is an idea, practice, or object that is perceived as new by an individual or other unit of adoption, such as an organization or community (Rogers, 1995). *Diffusion* is the process by which an innovation is communicated through certain channels over time among the members of a social system (Rogers, 1995). Diffusion of innovations has been widely studied in a variety of settings and disciplines. Combined, these studies give a clear picture of what happens when an innovation—or a public health "solution"—is introduced to a population. While the basic sequence of events is the same across settings, the amount of time diffusion takes and the ultimate success of a diffusion effort vary widely and depend on factors unique to the type of innovation.

Backer, Rogers, and Sopory (1992) discussed two types of innovations relevant to public health: incremental and preventive. With incremental innovations, an individual takes an action now in order to receive a short-term benefit. With a preventive innovation, an individual takes an action to lower the probability that an undesired event (such as developing heart disease or cancer) will occur over the long term. They note that preventive innovations are more difficult to diffuse successfully. Various authors have identified other characteristics of the innovation that affect its likelihood of being successfully diffused and implemented (Green, Gottlieb, & Parcel, 1991; Kolbe & Iverson, 1981; Orlandi et al., 1990; Leonard-Barton, 1988; Parcel et al., 1989, Rogers, 1995, Smith, Howell, & McCann, 1990; Zaltman & Duncan, 1977). Characteristics affecting the diffusion of many innovations are included in **Table 18-2**.

Classic diffusion theory divides members of a population into five categories based on their rate of adoption: innovators, early adopters, early majority, late majority, and laggards (Rogers, 1995). These six categories are defined mathematically, by plotting time of adoption on a normal curve and dividing it into standard deviations from the mean time of adoption (Rogers, 1995). Green and McAlister (1984) pointed out that some innovations, such as health practices requiring voluntary individual action, typically will not be adopted by the last 50% of the population unless adoption is required by law or by an employer.

■ RESEARCH METHODS

Marketing research is integral to every stage of the marketing process. During the planning and development stages, formative research helps identify audience segments, craft exchanges they will value, and design distribution channels and communications that will reach them effectively and efficiently. When marketing efforts are initiated, research helps monitor and improve implementation. Finally, research helps assess the outcomes of marketing efforts.

Many of the data gathering activities used at each stage employ the same research methods. This chapter describes common methods and discusses how to design and conduct studies using them.

Quantitative versus Qualitative Approaches

Quantitative research provides measures—typically, how many members of a population have particular knowledge or attitudes, or engage in a particular behavior. Quantitative data collection is structured and relatively rigid; the same variables are measured in the same way for each unit being analyzed (e.g., person, transaction, geographic area, etc.). Quantitative research can be analyzed using a broad range of statistical techniques.

Table 18-2 Characteristics Affecting Successful Diffusion of an Innovation	
Compatibility	The degree to which the innovation is congruent with the potential adopters' existing practices, values, and realties
Complexity	The degree to which an innovation is simple or complicated—those that are less complicated usually require fewer changes and are more likely to be implemented
Communicability	The ease with which the innovation can be clearly communicated
Observability	The degree to which the target adopters can watch someone model the innovation before adopting it themselves
Trialability	Also termed divisibility or flexibility—the extent to which an innovation can be divided to allow trial or piecemeal adoption and implementation
Cost efficiency	The degree to which tangible and intangible benefits outweigh cost
Time	The amount of time that must be invested to make the change
Commitment	The quantity of resources that must be invested to make the change
Risk and uncertainty	The amount of vulnerability and doubt associated with adopting the innovation
Reversibility	The ease with which an adopter can discontinue the innovation and revert to previous practice
Modifiability	The innovation's capacity to be changed as updates to it become available
Emergence	The extent to which an innovation is still being developed—those that are still changing may diffuse more slowly due to confusion, concerns about scientific merit, and the need for continual changes or adjustments

Methods to collect quantitative data include surveys, systematic observation, and experiments, sometimes in combination (e.g., an experiment can include a survey or observation). Quantitative surveys use a structured questionnaire in which questions are always asked in the same order, and most questions have a fixed list of responses from which respondents must select their answer. Observational methods involve counting how many people engage in a particular behavior, such as smoking in a public place, fastening their seat belt, voting a particular way on a bill, buying two products together, calling a telephone hot line, or leaving their vegetables uneaten in a worksite, school, or commercial cafeteria. Observational methods can also be used to assess availability of a good or service; for example, to count the number of retail outlets selling cigarettes, condoms, or fresh produce within a mile of a workplace or school. Other types of quantitative measures can include product sales and inventory tracking. Experimental and quasi-experimental designs are most often used in public health marketing research to pilot test materials, products or services, or to assess outcomes.

In contract, qualitative research provides insights into a target audience. The goal is to understand reactions and motivations. Most qualitative research takes the form of a discussion, with an interviewer asking questions that stimulate conversation in a group or one-on-one setting, rather than questions that require the respondent to choose from a fixed number of responses. Compared with quantitative surveys, qualitative approaches are relatively unstructured; the interviewer works from a topic guide, rather than from a questionnaire, and the next question participants are asked often depends on their response to the previous one. Qualitative research usually takes place among a relatively small number of people selected because they have certain characteristics. Qualitative data should not be quantified, subjected to statistical analysis, or projected to the population from which participants were drawn.

Table 18-3 presents distinctions between qualitative and quantitative approaches. Each is appropriate—and inappropriate—for different types of research questions. Thinking about these distinctions when planning a study can help determine what type of approach is needed.

Gaining Insights: The Qualitative Approaches

Qualitative research is exploratory in nature. Rather than trying to measure how many people engage in behavior or hold a particular opinion,

Table 18-3   Distinctions between Qualitative and Quantitative Research

Qualitative	Quantitative
Provides depth of understanding	Measures level of occurrence
Asks "Why?"	Asks "How many?" and "How often?"
Studies motivations	Studies actions
Is subjective	Is objective
Enables discovery	Provides proof
Is exploratory	Is definitive
Allows insights into behavior, trends, and so on	Measures levels of actions, trends, and so on
Interprets	Describes

Source: Reprinted with permission from M. Debus, *Handbook for Excellence in Focus Group Research,* © 1988, The Academy of Educational Development.

qualitative research helps us find out *why*. Qualitative research can be used a number of ways:

- To provide insights into the results of quantitative studies.
- To provide insights for planning and product or service development.
- To help flesh out profiles of the target audience and identify perceived benefits, barriers, and misconceptions that target audience members associate with a behavior.
- To explore changes to the product, price, or distribution channels that will facilitate behavior change.
- To explore how to frame messages.
- To explore the image or identity a product offering should convey

The two major qualitative research methodologies are focus groups and in-depth interviews. **Table 18-4** provides guidance on which method to choose for particular research questions. Each method is described in more detail below.

Focus Groups

Traditional focus group sessions are 1- to 2-hour structured discussions among 6 to 10 participants. They can take place in person or on a telephone conference call; **Table 18-5** presents some of the pros and cons of each setting. They are led by a trained moderator working from a list of topic areas and questions (referred to as a moderator's guide or topic guide). People chosen to participate in the group meet certain criteria designed to ensure that they have the requisite target audience characteristics. Focus group results are by nature more subjective and open to interpretation than methodologies involving more people or one-on-one questioning. Quantitative reporting or analysis, such as reporting the percentage of participants who gave a particular response, is inappropriate.

Focus groups are a valuable technique for addressing many exploratory research questions, such as how an audience feels about a particular health behavior, the barriers, benefits and image they do or could associate with the behavior, the situations under which they do or do not engage in a behavior, etc. They also can be useful when developing and refining concepts for messages, products or services; in these instances, group discussion about reactions can provide insights into underlying motivations or values, or stimulate new ideas. Focus groups tend to be overused for obtaining audience reactions to products or materials that are nearly final, largely because group reactions may be misleading for something that will be experienced individually. For example, most people do not discuss ads that they see with others unless the ads are particularly provocative. By showing ads and then forcing a lengthy discussion, even the best ad is likely to be torn to shreds, and much of the feedback will not be helpful because the group setting and length of discussion is unrealistic.

Table 18-4   Which to Use: Focus Groups or Individual In-Depth Interviews?

Issue to Consider	Use focus groups when . . .	Use individual in-depth interviews when . . .
Group interaction	Interaction of respondents may stimulate a richer response or new and valuable thoughts.	Group interaction is likely to be limited or nonproductive.
Group/peer pressure	Group/peer pressure will be valuable in challenging the thinking of respondents and illuminating conflicting opinions.	Group/peer pressure would inhibit responses and cloud the meaning of results.
Sensitivity of subject matter	Subject matter is not so sensitive that respondents will temper responses or withhold information.	Subject matter is so sensitive that respondents will be unwilling to talk openly in a group.
Depth of individual responses	The topic is such that most respondents can say all that they know in less than 10 minutes.	The topic is such that a greater depth of response per individual is desirable, as with complex subject matter and very knowledgeable respondents.
Interviewer fatigue	It is desirable to have one interviewer conduct the research; several groups will not create interviewer fatigue or boredom.	It is desirable to have numerous interviewers on the project. One interviewer would become fatigued or bored conducting the interviews.
Stimulus materials	The volume of stimulus material is not extensive.	A large amount of stimulus material must be evaluated.
Continuity of information	A single subject area is being examined in depth and strings of behavior are less relevant.	It is necessary to understand how attitudes and behaviors link together on an individual basis.
Experimentation with interviewer guide	Enough is known to establish a meaningful topic guide.	It may be necessary to develop the interview guide by altering it after each of the initial interviews.
Observation	It is possible and desirable for key decision makers to observe "first-hand" consumer information.	"First-hand" consumer information is not critical or observation is not logistically possible.
Cost and timing	Quick turnaround is critical and funds are limited.	Quick turnaround is not critical and budget will permit higher cost.

Source: Adapted with permission from M. Debus, *Handbook for Excellence in Focus Group Research,* © 1988, The Academy for Educational Development.

Composition. Focus group sessions are usually most productive when they are composed of homogenous individuals. A recruitment screener is used to identify people with the desired characteristics (see Appendix 11-B for an example). Participants are often divided into different groups

Table 18-5 In-Person and Telephone Focus Groups: Advantages of Each Setting	
In-person	**Telephone**
Can more easily show stimulus materials—ads, packaging, etc.	Can bring together geographically dispersed populations or populations that have difficulty traveling to a central location.
In-person interaction may be more comfortable for some people.	Can easily include participants from rural areas and smaller communities.
Allows moderator and observers to see body language, though few are sufficiently trained to interpret it accurately.	Provides greater anonymity, which often encourages participants to speak more freely and decreases the likelihood that participants from small geographic or professional communities will recognize each other.
	Participants can react only to information conveyed by the voices of other participants and the moderator—reactions to the appearance, clothing, jewelry, etc. of others are avoided.
	Side conversations are not possible and therefore do not distract other group members.
	Participants who should not have been recruited or who adversely affect group dynamics can be dismissed from the group less obtrusively.
	Moderator and observers do not have to travel.
	Moderator can receive questions or instructions from observers without participants being aware of the delivery.

based on demographic characteristics such as gender, age, and socioeconomic status. The reasons for such divisions are twofold: (1) People are more likely to speak openly in front of other people whom they perceive to be like themselves, and (2) any real or perceived hierarchy among group members will impact group dynamics. For example, if nurses and physicians are combined in one group, it is unlikely that much useful information will be obtained from the nurses. Many will defer to the physicians because physicians are viewed as more expert. If the nurses do participate, they will likely provide socially acceptable responses, describing what they are supposed to do. If in reality they do something differently, they are unlikely to talk about it in front of physicians, and so many valuable insights may be lost.

Most researchers think carefully about topic matter before combining men and women in a group consisting of patients or members of the public, in part because there are many health topics that each gender will discuss more openly if members of the other gender are not present. Similarly, people with divergent educational backgrounds typically are not combined in one group. People with higher education often are more articulate than their counterparts with lower education, causing those with lower education to shut down. Additionally, people tend to use language differently when they are among members of their own "group," whatever group that happens to be, in part as a way of signaling group identity. This phenomenon is perhaps most pronounced with teenagers, but occurs with other groups as well. If one goal of conducting the groups is to learn how to talk to them or how to reference particular behaviors or products, mixing group members may thwart that goal because people may not use their normal word choices or speech patterns.

In addition to natural differences in conversational style, some demographic characteristics, particularly age and socioeconomic status, can lead to lifestyle differences. Depending on the subject matter, these differences may not only make it difficult for participants to relate to each other, but may in turn lead to differences in behavioral determinants and perceived benefits of and barriers to particular behaviors. For example, consider behaviors such as changing food preparation methods or increasing physical activity. In general, retirees can fit such changes into their schedules much more easily than younger people with full-time jobs and children. But retirees may have many health-related barriers to such changes that most younger people do not have. Differences in socioeconomic status can have a similar effect: Among low-income people, product price and availability (for example, of particular foods) are often the number one barriers; among high-income people, they may not be— though, at least in the case of food, not necessarily for the reasons one might think. Paradoxically, food prices are often lower in middle- or high-income area neighborhoods because they are more likely to contain supermarkets, which tend to have lower prices than the convenience stores or small grocery stores often found in lower-income neighborhoods. In addition, because supermarkets are larger than convenience stores or small grocery stores, they tend to stock a wider range of healthier foods.

In general, discussion is more honest if participants do not know each other. However, in some instances it is nearly impossible to convene a group in which no one knows anyone else. This problem often occurs when groups of professionals are assembled, particularly in smaller geographic areas. For example, healthcare professionals are likely to know each other—or to have worked at the same places. Principals and teachers often know each other, as do business or community leaders. Those working regionally or nationally can often overcome this challenge by convening telephone focus groups to widen the pool of participants.

Morgan and Krueger (1998) and Krueger (1994) provide in-depth discussions of planning, developing, implementing, and analyzing focus group studies. **Exhibit 18-1** provides suggestions for developing the topic guide.

Choosing a Moderator. Three types of people can be used to moderate focus groups: professional moderators, untrained staff members, and community volunteers. When deciding on a moderator, be aware that moderating a focus group is not as simple as running a meeting. The moderator must perform a delicate balancing act of being detached in the sense that he or she asks questions but does not offer opinions, yet is able to persuade group members to open up. Moderating focus groups requires substantial background in group dynamics and skill at handling

---

Exhibit 18-1 Suggestions for Developing the Topic Guide

- Open by thanking participants and explaining the process (i.e., there are no right or wrong answers: the goal is to get their opinions; the conversation is being taped). Provide a general description of the topic they will discuss and, if they may be anxious or suspicious, the reason why you convened this particular group.

- Begin by asking participants to introduce themselves; then ask one or two "warm-up" questions that get them talking and ease them into the subject matter.

- Most questions should be open ended. The goal is to stimulate conversation, not tally responses. The transition from writing structured quantitative questionnaires to relatively free-flowing qualitative topic guides is a very difficult one for most researchers to make.

- Build in exercises. They keep the group from getting bored and are a useful way of obtaining and capturing different kinds of information.

  1. Laddering exercises can be used to get at core values. Participants are first asked to name the positive attributes they associate with a behavior. The moderator records each attribute on a flip chart and, as each one is names, asks why that is important. The moderator continues asking why each subsequent attribute is important until the participant can no longer answer. For example:

     – What are the advantages of going for a 20-minute walk each day? It makes me feel good.

     – And why does it make you feel good? Because I have more energy the rest of the day, and I know I'm doing something good for my health.

     – And why is it important to have more energy? Because I can get more work done and feel more in control.

     – And what's good about doing something good for your health? Well, I want to be around for my kids . . . and I feel like I should . . . and I never have any time. There's so many things I don't do, so it makes me feel good when I accomplish taking the walk.

(continues)

Exhibit 18-1 Suggestions for Developing the Topic Guide (continued)

Now we have learned that the walk makes the person feel more in control, is motivated in part by a need to meet family obligations, and increases self-esteem by making the person feel good.

2. Free association is another technique to identify the attributes people attach to particular products or behaviors: "I'm going to say a word (or phrase) and I want you to tell me what comes to mind. The word is ..."

3. Participants can sort message concepts (provided on separate sheets of paper) from most compelling to least compelling (and then explain their rankings to you).

4. Pictures can be used as stimuli in many different ways. For example, you can show participants a picture of someone engaging in the desired action and ask them to describe that person (another way of getting at values). You can also ask them to describe how they are different from, and similar to, the person pictured.

- Ask participants to recount a recent experience involving the behavior. Have them walk you through what happened and their perceptions of various aspects of the experience. For example, if you are trying to improve a health clinic, you might ask: Think about your last visit to the clinic. How did you make your appointment? (Probe for staff promptness and timeliness.) Was the appointment time that you wanted available? What happened when you arrived for your appointment? How were you treated by the front desk staff? What was the waiting room like? (Probes: What was good about it? Bad about it?) How long did you have to wait to be seen? Was the wait longer or shorter than you expected? How was your experience with the nurse? Now tell me about the exam room. What was good and bad about it?

- Close the group by asking whether people have any additional comments about any of the topics discussed. If necessary, address any dangerous misperceptions or inaccurate information that may have been discussed. Then thank them for their participation.

- Before finalizing it, review the guide to make sure the topics flow from one to another in a logical, natural way; jumping around from topic to topic or back to topics previously discussed can be disorienting to participants and therefore interrupt the flow of discussion.

---

a range of personality types. Additionally, an outside moderator's distance from the program is often a plus. Someone on the program staff is vested in how the groups turn out, particularly when ideas are being explored, and may have difficulty remaining unbiased or unintentionally lead the group in the "right" direction.

If you want to hire a professional moderator, the best way to identify a good one is to ask colleagues for recommendations. Alternatively, the Qualitative Research Consultants Association maintains a database of independent moderators and their areas of expertise (www.qrca.org). When you have identified two or three candidates, ask them for tapes (all will have audiotapes; many have videotapes as well) to get a feel for how they run groups. Generally speaking, it is a good idea to match the gender and ethnicity of the moderator to the gender and ethnicity of the group, especially for in-person sessions. Most professional moderators will not have as much health knowledge as program staff, but it is best if they have moderated groups on health topics with similar audiences in the past. In particular, if you are conducting focus groups with children, it is important that you use a moderator who specializes in working with children.

Moderators can have varying amounts of responsibility; most can draft the recruitment screener and topic guide, manage the recruiting, conduct the groups, and prepare a report. However, many moderators' reports are analytically weak; ask for examples of their reports before contracting out this critical aspect of the project. Moderators usually charge per group and may charge separately for writing a guide and report.

Recent trends have been toward greater community participation in the focus group process. There are a number of reasons for this trend; two pragmatic ones are quality of data and cost. As Krueger and King (1998) note, there are many situations in which an outside researcher may be unlikely or unable to collect the in-depth inside information that a community member volunteer can collect. Volunteer moderators can also be appropriate when the required research is not complex or does not demand highly technical skills; when the process of research is more important than its product (i.e., the study can encourage people to think in new ways about a situation); and when the program or situation to be studied is not highly political (Krueger & King, 1998). When none of these conditions is true, Krueger and King recommend using professionals.

Analyzing the groups. There are a number of approaches to analyzing focus group data. Some people present the results of each group separately; that is generally inappropriate for many projects since the point of analysis is to look for trends across groups or to identify and categorize a range of issues. The approach that often works best is to review all the conversations on a particular topic, and then in the report make summary statements and support them with illustrative verbatim comments identified by type of speaker.

In-Depth Interviews

With telephone or in-person in-depth interviews, a trained interviewer talks with one research participant at a time. In-depth interviews (IDI) are commonly used when a group setting would have a chilling effect on discussion or when speaking with one person at a time is appropriate for the research purpose or audience. For example, if the research participants are very young children, a one-on-one format is better suited to their attention span and tendency to become shy in groups of children they do not know.

In-depth telephone interviews typically last 30 minutes to an hour. Interviews conducted in person can last up to about an hour, except with young children, in which case they should be kept to about 30 minutes.

If all objectives cannot be addressed adequately in that amount of time, cut some objectives. As with focus group studies, determining what decisions will be made based on the study can help refine objectives. The conversation should focus on one subject as much as possible; too much bouncing around distracts interviewees.

It is good practice to conduct at least 8 to 10 interviews with each subgroup. As with focus groups, if you are conducting IDIs to understand the benefits and barriers associated with particular behaviors, consider conducting some interviews with "doers" (those who already engage in the desired behavior) and "nondoers." This approach can help you identify the determinants of doers' behavior and then explore what types of marketing strategies would help non-doers change their behavior.

In some instances, it may be desirable to set up the interviews as dyads, in which the interviewer talks to two people at once. For example, dyads can be useful for discussing some behaviors involving couples.

A professional qualitative researcher, staff member, or volunteer with some training can conduct interviews. **Exhibit 18-2** includes information on the characteristics of good interviewers and how to train them. Many focus group moderators also conduct in-depth interviews; other qualitative researchers specialize in interviews. If you contract out for the interviewing, the interviewer will most likely prepare the report (unless you want to read a lot of transcripts or listen to hours and hours of tapes). Asking for sample reports will help ensure that you hire someone who writes the type of report that will be helpful to your initiative.

Measuring: The Quantitative Approaches

Major quantitative research methods are surveys, observational studies, and experiments.

Surveys
Surveys typically consist of a series of predominantly closed-ended (forced-choice) questions. They can be administered by an interviewer, either in person or over the telephone, or they can be self-administered by the respondent, using a paper-and-pencil or electronic questionnaire received through the mail, in person, or over the Internet. A good introduction to many of the issues involved with sampling, instrumentation, data collection, data processing, and analysis is provided in The Survey Research Handbook, by Alreck and Settle (2004).

Sampling. The extent to which survey results are representative of the population surveyed depends upon a number of factors, the most important of which is how interviewees were selected. Since it often is not possible to conduct a census (e.g., question an entire population) unless the population of interest is quite small, members of it must be sampled in some way.

Exhibit 18-2 Tips for Identifying and Training Interviewers

Good interviewers are outgoing enough to be comfortable approaching or calling people they do not know, capable of quickly putting others at ease, and articulate without dominating conversations. They should also be patient enough to let respondents complete their answers but able to gently move a respondent along when necessary. Interviewers for quantitative studies need to be particularly capable of following instructions so that they consistently administer questionnaires exactly as they are written.

To train interviewers:

1. Begin by explaining the project and its purpose.

2. Provide interviewers with a copy of the questionnaire and all supporting materials.

3. Demonstrate an interview.

4. Explain the process, covering details such as:

   • How interviewees should be selected (if the interviewer is doing the selecting)

   • For phone interviews, how callbacks, answering machines, etc. should be handled

   • For materials tests, the number of times (or length of time) respondents should hear or view materials

   • For quantitative studies, the need to read each question exactly as written each time (if interviewers start reciting from "memory" the wording will change significantly over time)

   • For qualitative studies, whether it is OK to ask questions out of order if the conversation goes that way, or whether it is important to keep them in order

   • How to record responses to each question, especially those for which the respondent may have multiple answers

   • For paper questionnaires, the need to review each questionnaire for completeness immediately after the interview

   • For paper questionnaires, what to do with completed questionnaires

5. Have interviewers role play: One administers the questionnaire to the other. The act of administering the questionnaire allows the interviewer to identify questions—and get answers—before they come up during a "live" interview.

6. Discuss any additional questions.

Probability samples give each member of a population an equal, non-zero chance of being included in the sample. Creating a probability sample starts with using an accurate and complete *sampling frame*, which can be thought of as the list from which the sample is drawn. The second step is to select from the list in such a way that each item on it has an equal chance of being selected. For example, to draw a probability sample of conference attendees, you could take a list of all the attendees, write each name on a separate piece of paper, put the papers in a bowl, mix them up, and randomly draw out the desired number of names. That would constitute a *simple random sample*. Alternatively, if you did not wish to spend all that time cutting, you could select every *n*th name on the list, where *n* is an interval that will provide you with the desired number of names.

Obviously, sampling larger populations, such as residents of the city or country, is more complex but it still uses the basic principles of starting with an accurate and complete sampling frame and then randomly selecting units from that frame. The appropriate sample size depends upon how much precision a project requires; smaller samples are subject to greater sampling error and therefore less precise than are larger samples.

Most basic statistical texts will include a chart showing the margin of error for samples of various sizes. For example, the margin of error for a probability sample of 1000 people is ±3.1 percentage points. This means that if 50% of the sample said "yes" to a particular question on the survey, if the survey was repeated with 100 probability samples constructed the same way, between 46.9 and 53.1% of those sampled would say "yes" 95 of those times.

Once a probability sample has been drawn, a potential threat to the representativeness of a survey is nonresponse bias: people who are sampled but do not complete the survey, either because they could not be reached or because they do not wish to comply, may differ in important ways from people who do complete the survey. Researchers are less concerned about nonresponse bias when the survey response rate is high (i.e., a majority of those sampled complete the interview) and more concerned when the response rate is low.

Reliability. If respondents are asked the same question multiple times, their answers should be substantially the same each time. Reliability depends in part on the nature of the questions asked. The more concrete and easy to answer accurately, the more reliable they are likely to be. Other factors that can affect reliability include differences in the situation in which the questionnaire is administered (e.g., consider what might happen if a client was verbally interviewed about satisfaction in a waiting room full of other clients versus privately), differences in how it is administered, and even differences in the mood of the person completing it (Rossi & Freeman, 1993).

Validity. Does a question measure what it is intended to measure, and are the measures accurate? For example, self-reported information on behavior is often inaccurate because people tend to report what they *think* they should do rather than what they actually do. There are many potential threats to validity. Rossi and Freeman (1993) outlined four criteria that social scientists used to assess validity: *consistency with past usage* (a new scale or question should not contradict the usual ways the concept has been used previously), *consistency with other measures* of the same concept (the measure should produce substantially the same results as other measures), *internal consistency* (i.e., if several questions measure the same concept, each should produce similar results, and for measures that attempt to predict future attitudes or behavior, *consequential predictability*—in other words, a measure of "propensity to use clinic services" in fact predicts subsequent usage of clinic services. For a measure to be considered valid, it must meet one of the criteria.

Analysis. Survey analysis can range from simple univariate and bivariate statistics to complex multivariate modeling; what is possible or advisable depends on the degree to which data collected conform to the assumptions underlying the statistical techniques, the research questions, and the available resources. A common starting point for most marketing research is to examine the entire sample's responses to each question by looking at frequency distributions (also called *marginals*) and then creating crosstabulations (also called *stub and banner tables*) in which each question is presented as a separate table. The table rows are the responses for the questions; the columns are responses from different groups of people. Sometimes the columns reflect the entire sample's responses to different questions using the same response scale (to facilitate comparisons; for example, to compare reactions to different advertising executions). Commercial survey suppliers generally include 16 to 20 banner points in the basic price. More sophisticated multivariate analyses typically are conducted by a researcher with statistical training.

The following sections discuss three types of surveys often used in marketing research: central-site interviews, telephone surveys, and Internet surveys.

Central-site interviews are simply interviews conducted in a place where target audience members gather. Because these interviews frequently take place in shopping malls, this methodology is often referred to as *mall-intercept interviews* due to the way interviewers "intercept" shoppers as they walk around the mall and then interview them, either where they were intercepted or at a facility in the mall. With appropriate permission, a central-site interviewing methodology can be used at other places target audience members gather, such as clinics, meetings, schools, fairs or other community events, or exhibit halls.

Central-site interviews are appropriate when you want to know *how* a target audience reacts but do not need great detail on *why* they react that way. The methodology is generally not appropriate for exploratory work that requires probing by highly trained interviewers. Interviews typically last 10 to 20 minutes and are often used to pretest packaging or promotional materials, such as advertising, posters, or brochures. They are generally not a good forum for testing longer print materials because of the length of the interview that would be required. Sometimes only one item is tested; at other times, alternative executions may be tested against each other or executions in different media will be tested at the same time.

While central-site interviews typically use a quantitative questionnaire (e.g., most questions are closed-ended), they usually are not projectable to the population from which the sample is drawn because the sampling methods used do not give each member of the population an equal chance of being interviewed. The methodology usually uses convenience and/or quota sampling. In a convenience sample, the group of people interviewed is composed of those most accessible and willing to participate. At a shopping mall, interviewers usually assume people alone will be more willing to participate because they do not have the distraction of children or companions, and probably will approach those people who look like they fit the criteria and look friendly and likely to comply. Additionally, central-site interviews often involve quotas, or a preset number of interviews completed with people in certain categories. For example, a study might specify 100 men and 100 women, divided equally among predefined low-, middle-, and high-income categories. Once a quota has been reached, no further interviews with participants in those categories will be conducted. However, it is possible to construct a probability sample using shopping malls and some other central sites. For example, malls can be selected so that their probability of selection is proportional to the number of customers they serve, and a procedure can be used to randomly sample individuals within each mall (Andreasen, 2002).

Telephone surveys most often use random-digit-dialing (RDD) samples, in which blocks of numbers the telephone company has put into use are sampled by using random numbers for the last one or two digits. In many countries, constructing an RDD sample of households has become more expensive and more challenging with the advent of overlapping area codes and the proliferation of cell phones, fax lines, and households with multiple voice lines. For example, the pool of possible U.S. residential telephone numbers increased by 89% between 1988 and 1998, while the number of households with telephone increased only 11%—reducing the likelihood of reaching a working residential number through random digit dialing from 21% to 13% (Piekarski, 1999). As a result, many organizations now use two-stage cluster samples; in the first stage, they attempt to eliminate banks of numbers with few residential numbers (Pothoff, 1987). Researchers attempt to improve the representativeness of such studies by asking interviewees how many phone lines are at their location and then weighting their responses accordingly.

Telephone surveys are most often used to gather information on awareness, knowledge, attitudes, practices, and customer satisfaction—information useful in formative research or as part of a process or outcome evaluation. They also can be used to test messages if the messages can be understood when expressed as simple statements with little or no background information. Chapter 11's **Exhibit 11-4** provides an example.

Telephone surveys can be *custom* or *omnibus*. Custom surveys are typically sponsored by one institution and focus on one topic. Omnibus surveys include questions from a number of organizations. They are cheaper and faster then custom surveys: cheaper because the costs of standard demographic questions are shared over many organizations and faster because the research suppliers field them regularly and thus have pre-reserved interviewers and call centers. Omnibus surveys are appropriate if the target audience is a sufficiently large segment of the population surveyed, if you have only a few questions, and if you can live with their response rates (since speed is of the essence, fewer callbacks are done than might be done for a custom survey). For example, omnibus studies can be an ideal way of assessing how people will react to alternative ways of framing a message. In the United States, national omnibus surveys of the adult population are conducted once or twice a week; you can submit questions and have data back within a week. Major commercial suppliers include International Communications Research and Synovate. Many universities and local firms also offer omnibus studies of a state or metropolitan area, typically on a less-frequent basis.

Internet surveys. Internet surveys have a wealth of appealing characteristics: large samples of people can be reached quickly and inexpensively, and the multimedia nature of the Internet permits respondents to react to visual or audio stimuli, including advertisements, video or audio programming, pictures of proposed packaging, etc. However, a major drawback is that no sampling frame exists from which to construct a probability sample: there is no list of all Internet users and no equivalent of RDD technology. Some commercial firms are working to overcome this drawback by compiling large panels of Internet users willing to be surveyed or random panels. (Berrens et al., 2001). For example, Harris Interactive has created a large panel—over 7 million individuals in 2000—through advertisements and sweepstakes, the Harris/Excite poll, telephone surveys, and product registrations (Taylor et al., 2001). Harris Interactive samples the panel for surveys, and uses propensity weights to make the sample representative on selected covariates. It determines the propensity weights by conducting contemporaneous telephone and Internet surveys that include the same attitudinal and behavioral questions, then merging the data and using attitudinal and standard demographic variables to predict the probability of being in one sample or the other; these probabilities are then used to weight the Internet sample so that the attitudinal and behavioral responses match the telephone sample (Berrens et al., 2001). Random panels can be constructed by using RDD to call and recruit people to join a panel; Knowledge Networks has done this with some success (Berrens et al., 2001). A U.S. study comparing responses of a traditional RDD telephone sample, a sample of Harris

Interactive's large panel, and a sample of Knowledge Networks' random panel of Web-TV enabled respondents found that "across a variety of tests on attitudes and voting intentions, the Internet samples produced relational inferences quite similar to the telephone sample" (Berrens et al., 2001, p. 29).

It appears possible to construct representative samples of Internet users. The advisability of using Internet surveys for a particular research question will depend upon the extent to which the population of interest uses the Internet, whether or not a probability sample is necessary for decisions to be made, and if it is, whether a sampling frame is available to construct such a sample or whether an alternative, such as Harris Interactive's propensity weights, can be employed.

As with telephone surveys, Internet surveys can be used to gather information on awareness, knowledge, attitudes, practices, and customer satisfaction—for formative research or as part of a process or outcome evaluation. However, because they can include audio and visual materials, Internet surveys can play a greater role in formative research and pretesting.

Internet surveys can be fielded in a number of ways. They can "pop up" on a web site; many institutions use such surveys to monitor customer satisfaction with site design and content and collect demographic and other information on site users. Links to surveys or surveys themselves can also be e-mailed to respondents, as typically is done when conducting a study using a representative sample. A number of suppliers provide technology for composing and administering Internet surveys; at the time of this writing, Zoomerang and Survey Monkey are two popular choices. Researchers create their surveys on these vendors' sites, then include a link to the survey in an e-mail or on a website. Vendors collect the data which can then be downloaded and analyzed using spreadsheet software (for rudimentary analyses) or statistical software.

Experiments and Quasi-Experiments

These techniques are used most often for pretesting, pilot testing, or process or outcome evaluation. Chapter 17 presents an overview of experimental designs.

■ DESIGNING AND CONDUCTING MARKETING RESEARCH STUDIES

All research studies follow a similar series of steps; **Table 18-6** outlines the steps and decisions to be made or issues to consider during each step for common types of formative marketing research. The first and in many ways most important step of any research project is to set research objectives. They are used to guide methodological choices, study design, analysis, and reporting. Some of the principles of "backward research" advocated by Andreasen (1995, 2002) can help set useful and appropriate objectives. For example, determine what decisions will be made as a result of the study, and outline the research report as a way of coming to agreement on what information the study will provide. This process also helps identify any areas of miscommunication between researchers and program managers and keeps research costs down by separating "nice to know" areas of inquiry from "need to know" questions.

Reviewing past research on the topic and looking to models and theories of behavior can help you set objectives and design studies, data collection instruments and analyses that provide the most useful information for the least cost. Research reports typically contain:

- Introduction or background section describing the program and the objectives of the research
- Methodology, outlining what research techniques were used; how, when, where and with whom the research was conducted; and the strengths and limitations of the research techniques and the particular study
- Findings of the research
- Conclusions and recommendations for the program and/or for further research

Table 18-6 Steps in Planning and Conducting Market Research Studies

	Focus Groups	In-depth Interviews	Quantitative Interviews
Step 1: Set research objectives	Typical objectives are exploratory, seeking to gain insight into how and why an audience thinks, feels and acts or reacts in particular ways. • In a two-hour group of eight participants, each has only 10–15 minutes to talk. What can be covered in that time frame? • Discussion should be focused. If there are many topics, prioritize or conduct multiple studies.	• One-on-one setting allows for more thorough discussion and individual feedback, for example on materials or prototypes.	Typical objectives are to measure what proportion of an audience thinks, feels, acts or reacts in a particular way, or to measure the strength of a relationship between two variables.
Step 2: Select methodology and design study; prepare timeline and budget	Determine: • In-person or telephone groups? • Composition and size (usually 8–10 participants) of each group; total number of groups. Each group should be homogenous; different types of people should be placed in separate groups if combining them is likely to hinder discussion. Sometimes mini-groups (4–5 participants) are useful. • Consider group of "doers" (those who already engage in the desired behavior) and "non-doers" (those who ...) to help identify determinants of doers' behavior Develop recruiting specifications (plan to recruit two more participants than needed to account for no-shows).	Determine: • Telephone or in-person interviews? If in-person, will the interviewees come to a central site or will the interviewers go to them? • Characteristics of the group(s) to be interviewed and the total number of interviews to be conducted (typically 8–10 per audience segment). • Any equipment the interviewee may need (e.g., a computer with access to the Internet to view proposed materials, products or packaging). • Consider "doers" vs. "non-doers." Develop recruiting specifications if necessary (some interviews are conducted with people known to qualify) and determine how potential interviewees will be identified.	Determine: • Type of sampling: Probability, so results are projectable to the entire audience? Convenience? • How questionnaires will be administered—If by an interviewer, over the phone or in person? If by the respondent, will they be mailed? Handed to them (on paper or a handheld computer)? E-mailed? • Sample size. For central-site interviews, at least 60, and ideally 100, interviews should be conducted with each group of interest. For probability surveys, total sample sizes of 600 to 1200 are common. • Sample characteristics. If the audience is low income or the household food shopper, interviewees should have these characteristics. • Study location. Local, regional, national?
Step 3: Arrange logistical details	Set dates for groups and contract with recruiters, teleconference service (use one that specifically offers focus group calls and trains their operators accordingly), focus group facilities and moderators. Useful directories of commercial facilities are the	For interviews conducted at a central site, focus group facilities can recruit and provide an interviewing room. For telephone interviews or those to be conducted at an interviewee's location, some focus group facilities or independent recruiters can	Determine who will conduct the interviews and analyze and report on the data. Your staff? A commercial research vendor? (See focus groups column for directories.) University professors and/or their students? (Their projects typically take longer

(continues)

Table 18-6 Steps in Planning and Conducting Market Research Studies (continued)

	Focus Groups	In-depth Interviews	Quantitative Interviews
Step 3: Arrange logistical Details (continued)	*Blue Book* (www.bluebook.org) and *GreenBook*® (www.greenbook.org). For moderators, the Qualitative Research Consultants Association (www.qrca.org) maintains a database.	recruit interviewees. Interviews can be conducted by a qualitative researcher, a staff member, or a volunteer. **Exhibit 18-2** includes information on identifying and training interviewers.	but are more rigorous than commercial suppliers.) As necessary, obtain permission to conduct interviews in a central site and/or train interviewers.
Step 4: Prepare data collection instruments	Develop recruitment screener (questionnaire to identify qualified participants and exclude those who are too expert in the subject or the method; see Appendix 11-A), moderator's guide (see **Exhibit 18-1** and Appendix 11-B), and stimulus materials.	Develop recruitment screener (if one is needed), topic guide, and stimulus materials.	Develop questionnaire and any needed stimulus materials. The questionnaire should be written by someone with appropriate training; many factors influence wording of survey questions and construction of response scales. The first few questions typically screen for qualified respondents. For materials tests, if multiple materials are being tested the order in which respondents are exposed to them should be rotated to minimize order effects. Pretest the questionnaire with audience members.
Step 5: Collect data	Expect to make revisions to the guide following the first group(s); ensure someone on the project staff attends all or most of the sessions. If you plan to use audio or video from the groups in presentations, get signed releases from participants and be aware that the audio levels for in-person groups are generally too low for this purpose.	After the first two or three interviews, revise topic guide as needed.	Monitor the questionnaire administration as needed.
Step 6: Analyze data	Generally, the goal is to look for trends across groups or to identify and categorize a range of issues. Compile all the information on a specific topic from all the groups and then summarize, noting differences where appropriate. Software	Analytic approaches are similar to those used for focus groups.	If paper questionnaires were used, the initial step is to input and clean the data. For all questionnaires, initial analysis typically involves examining frequency distributions (responses of the entire sample to each question) and creating crosstabs to compare

(continues)

Table 18-6 Steps in Planning and Conducting Market Research Studies (continued)

	Focus Groups	In-depth Interviews	Quantitative Interviews
Step 6: Analyze Data (continued)	programs can be used to organize qualitative data, but they must be used cautiously. Each transcript must be painstakingly coded and results carefully interpreted to ensure the meaning of remarks taken out of context.		responses across groups. Additional analyses may be conducted depending on the research questions, types of data, and resources.
Step 7: Prepare reports	In the written report, findings on each topic are summarized and then supported with additional discussion and illustrative verbatim comments, usually identified by type of participant (e.g., Baltimore primary care physician). Conclusions and recommendations based on the findings are presented separately. Oral presentations often flow better if they are organized around the conclusions and recommendations, with findings presented as support.	Written and oral reports are similar to those used for focus groups.	Each finding is typically discussed, and, where appropriate, illustrated with a table or chart. It is often best to have a trained marketing researcher who is familiar with the initiative review the data and develop conclusions and recommendations.

■ CONCLUSION

Theory and research are important tools used in constructing, managing, and evaluating marketing efforts. Both are central to the marketing approach and play a critical role in shaping public health initiatives. The theories selected should fit the model of how the intervention is expected to work (e.g., directly on the individual, through his or her social system, or through changes in policy).

A variety of research methodologies can be employed depending upon the research question. Quantitative techniques can tell us how many people act or feel a certain way; surveys and observational methods are two common quantitative techniques. Qualitative techniques can tell us why people act or feel a certain way and uncover additional issues. Experiments and quasi-experiments provide an opportunity to test one possibility against another or one implementation against another.

References

Alreck, P. and Settle, R. (2004). *The survey research handbook* (3rd ed.). Boston: McGraw-Hill/Irwin.

Andreasen, A.R. (2002). *Marketing research that won't break the bank*. San Francisco: Jossey-Bass.

Andreasen, A.R. (1995). *Marketing social change: Changing behavior to promote health, social development, and the environment*. San Francisco: Jossey-Bass.

Backer, T.E., Rogers, E. ., & Sopory, P. (1992). *Designing health communication campaigns: What works?* Thousand Oaks, CA: Sage.

Baranowski, T., Perry, C.L. & Parcel, G.S. (2002). How individuals, environments, and health behavior interact: Social cognitive theory. In K. Glanz, B.K. Rimer & F.M. Lewis (Eds.), *Health behavior and health education: Theory, research and practice* (3rd ed., pp. 165–184). San Francisco: Jossey-Bass.

Berrens, R.P., Bohara, A.K., Jenkins-Smith, H., Silva, C., & Weimer, D.L. (2001). The advent of internet surveys for political research: A comparison of telephone and internet samples. *Political Analysis,* 11, 1–22. Accessed April 28, 2006 at http://www.websm.org/uploadi/editor/Berrens_Bohara_2003_Telephone_internet.pdf

Campbell, D.T., & Stanley, J.C. (1966). *Experimental and quasi-experimental designs for research*. Boston: Houghton Mifflin.

Cook, T.D., & Campbell, D.T. (1979). *Quasi-experimentation design and analysis issues for field settings*. Skokie, IL: Rand McNally.

Glanz K., Rimer B.K., Lewis F.M. (Eds.). *Health behavior and health education: Theory, research, and practice* (3rd ed.). San Francisco: Jossey-Bass, Inc. 2002.

Green, L.W., Gottlieb, N.H., & Parcel, G.S. (1991). Diffusion theory extended and applied. In W.B. Ward & F.M. Lewis (Eds.), *Advances in health education and promotion* (3, pp. 91–117). Greenwich, CT: Jessica Kingsley.

Green, L.W., & McAlister, A. (1984). Macro-interventions to support health behavior: Some theoretical perspectives and practical reflections. *Health Education Quarterly,* 11, 322–339.

Hochbaum, G.M. (1958). Public partcipation in medical screening programs: A sociopsychological study. *Public Health Service Publication No. 572.* Washington D.C.: U.S. Government Printing Office.

Janz, N.K., Champion, V.L., & Strecher, V.J. (2002). The health belief model. In K. Glanz, B.K. Rimer, & F.M. Lewis (Eds.), *Health behavior and health education: Theory, research and practice* (3rd ed., pp. 45–66). San Francisco: Jossey-Bass.

Kolbe, L.J. & Iverson, D.C. (1981). Implementing comprehensive health education: Educational innovations and social change. *Health Education Quarterly,* 8, 57–80.

Krueger, R.A. (1994). *Focus groups: A practical guide for applied research* (2nd ed.). Thousand Oaks, CA: Sage.

Krueger, R. A., & King, J.A. (1998*). Involving community members in focus groups.* Thousand Oaks, CA: Sage.

Leonard-Barton, D. (1988). Implementation characteristics of organizational innovations: Limits and opportunities for management strategies. *Communication Research*, 15, 603–631.

Morgan, D.L., & Krueger, R.A. (1998). *The focus group kit* (Vols. 1–6). Thousand Oaks, CA: Sage.

Orlandi, M.A., Landers, C., Weston, R., & Haley, N. (1990). Diffusion of health promotion innovations. In K. Glanz, F.M. Lewis, & B.K. Rimer (Eds.). *Health behavior and health education: Theory, research and practice* (pp. 288–313). San Francisco: Jossey-Bass.

Parcel, G.S., Eriksen, M.P., Lovato, C.Y., Gottlieb, N.H., Brink, S.G., & Green, L.W. (1989). The diffusion of school-based tobacco-use prevention programs: Project description and baseline data. *Health Education Research,* 4(1), 111–124.

Piekarski, L. (1999). Telephony and telephone sampling: The dynamics of change. Paper presented at the International Conference on Survey Nonresponse, Portland, Oregon, October 28–31.

Pothoff, R.F. (1987). Generalizations of the Mitofsky-Waksberg technique for random digit dialing. *Journal of the American Statistical Association,* 82:398, 309–418.

Prochaska, J.O., Redding, C.A., & Evers, K.E. (2002). The transtheoretical model and stages of change. In K. Glanz, B.K. Rimer, & F.M. Lewis (Eds.), *Health behavior and health education: Theory, research and practice* (3rd ed., pp. 99–120). San Francisco: Jossey-Bass.

Rogers, E.M. (1995). *Diffusion of innovations* (4th ed.). New York: Free Press.

Rossi, P.H., & Freeman, H.E. (1993). Evaluation: A systematic approach (5th ed.). Newbury Park, CA: Sage.

Smith, D.W., Howell, K.A., & McCann, K.M. (1990). Evaluation of the coalition index: A guide to school health education materials. *Journal of School Health,* 60(2), 49–52.

Taylor, H., Brenner, J., Overmeyer, G., Siegel, J.W., & Terhanian, G. (2001). Touchdown! Online polling scores big in November 2000, *Public Perspective,* March/April, 38–39.

Zaltman, G., & Duncan, R. (1977). *Strategies for planned change.* New York: Wiley.

18-A

Using Theory and Formative Research To Guide Message Development

Chapters 10 and 12 discuss the importance of using theory and formative research to guide development of marketing interventions and communication strategies. This case study discusses two efforts to promote oral cancer screening. In the first, the National Institute of Dental and Craniofacial Research (NIDCR), part of the U.S. Department of Health and Human Services' National Institutes of Health, used a theory of individual behavior change, qualitative research, and many of the marketing and communication principles outlined in Chapters 9, 10 and 12 to guide development of messages encouraging screening for oral cancer exams. While the study was very small and exploratory and has not yet been validated with additional research, NIDCR's findings about messages most likely to work are particularly interesting when contrasted with results of the second effort, an outdoor advertising campaign promoting oral cancer exams that was conducted by the American Dental Association. Evaluators concluded the limited effectiveness of the ADA campaign may have been due in part to not using theoretical models or principles of effective communication in message development, targeting, and execution.

■ NIDCR MESSAGE DEVELOPMENT [1]

The National Institute of Dental and Craniofacial Research wanted to gain an understanding of how to communicate about oral cancer screenings with an audience at elevated risk of developing and dying from the disease: African American men age 45 or older who smoke and drink. In the United States, oral cancer incidence rates are more than twice as high in men as in women, and the disease disproportionately affects African American men: compared to white men, African American men have a 30% higher incidence rate of oral cancers and a 90% higher death rate (American Cancer Society, 2005). In addition, 75% of oral cancers are related to tobacco use, alcohol use, or using both substances, and most oral cancers occur in people over age 45. Although there have been a number of national and local campaigns in the United States to raise awareness of oral cancer, encourage people to talk to their dentist or dental hygienist, and/or get an oral cancer exam, none of these efforts were designed specifically to reach African American men.

NIDCR conducted two small focus group studies with African American male smokers age 45–65 who live in Washington, D.C., a city with one of the country's highest rates of oral cancer. The first study was conducted with three groups in 2003-2004; the second was conducted with two groups in 2005. Two objectives from the second study are the focus of this discussion:

1. Gain insight into the types of appeals that will and will not work with African American men who smoke and drink (e.g., fear/threat appeals, factual appeals, positive affect appeals)

3. Gain insights into benefits they can or do associate with taking action to reduce risk for or detect oral cancer

Messages

NIDCR's first task was to develop a series of potential messages. As the second objective indicates, one decision they faced was whether to use messages asking people to take an action to *reduce their risk* of developing oral cancer or to use messages asking them to *get screened* for oral cancer. For this study, they decided to explore messages with the latter focus (though they obtained reactions to some risk reduction information later in the focus group sessions). Their reasoning is instructive for many public health topics in addition to oral cancer:

> We chose not to explore messages calling for risk reduction (e.g., stop smoking, limit alcohol consumption, use sunscreen) for a number of reasons. First, we wanted to limit the number of variables participants were reacting to at one time [e.g., they did not want

---

[1] This summary is adapted from *Insights into How African American Men React to Messages about Oral Cancer*, National Institute of Dental and Craniofacial Research, Bethesda, MD, 2005.

to expose participants to a mix of risk reduction and early detection messages]. Second, messages about risk, including risk reduction, are difficult to communicate successfully and little is known about how best to communicate about risk in relation to cancer screening behaviors (Vernon, 1999). Third, many of the behaviors someone would engage in to reduce oral cancer risk—stopping tobacco use, eating more fruits and vegetables, and limiting alcohol consumption—also reduce risk of other cancers and have other health benefits, so it seemed unlikely that participants would find engaging in these behavior to prevent oral cancer particularly compelling. Fourth, many entities with far more resources than NIDCR already bombard the public with messages to change these behaviors. Finally, because using tobacco and/or alcohol is an addictive behavior for many people, stopping or limiting their use requires interventions that extend beyond communications, thereby severely limiting the likely effectiveness of any risk reduction messages NIDCR might promulgate. (NIDCR, 2005, p. 9)

Note that in making their decision, the NIDCR team considered the likelihood of successful communication (second point), the extent to which they could identify benefits that would differentiate their offerings from others (third point), the competitive environment in which their behavior change promotion would occur (fourth point), and the likelihood that the audience could make the behavior changes solely as a result of the type of intervention they could create (last point).

In developing possible early detection messages, NIDCR was guided by the Health Belief Model (see Chapter 18 for an overview) and the components of successful health communication strategies (Sutton, Balch & Lefebvre, 1995). The institute used the same early detection call to action in all messages ("ask a doctor or dentist for an oral cancer exam") but varied message length, type of appeal (factual, positive affect, or threat), benefit promised, support provided, whether and how the message specified who was at risk, and the extent to which each message reflected the constructs of the Health Belief Model. **Table 18A-1** presents the five messages explored in the focus groups.

The NIDCR report describes the messages as varying in:

- The degree to which the messages specify a particular target audience. Messages #1 and #4 do not specify an audience; message #2 identifies an audience by behavior (smoking or drinking), and message #3 and #5 have the most specificity, identifying the audience both behaviorally (smoking, drinking, or doing both) and demographically—African American men over 40. The report notes planners chose to focus on men over 40 so that African American men would be included before they develop oral cancer, which peaks in African American men much earlier than in white men.

Table 18A-1 NIDCR Oral Cancer Screening Messages

1. Do you know the signs of oral cancer? Ask a doctor or dentist for an oral cancer exam.

2. Anyone can get oral cancer. But did you know that people who smoke or drink are at much higher risk? Oral cancer can be treated more successfully if it's found early. If you smoke or drink, ask a doctor or dentist for an oral cancer exam.

3. Among African American men, those over the age of 40 who smoke, drink, or do both have the greatest chance of getting oral cancer. Less than half survive more than five years. Avoid disfiguring surgery or death. Ask a doctor or dentist for an oral cancer exam.

4. Protect your health so you can be there for your loved ones. Ask a doctor or dentist for an oral cancer exam. Oral cancer can be treated more successfully when it's found early.

5. Among African American men, those over the age of 40 who smoke, drink, or do both are at the highest risk for oral cancer. Ask a doctor or dentist for an oral cancer exam. It's quick, painless, and it could save your life.

- The type of appeal used. Messages #1 and #2 are straightforward, fact-based appeals. Message #3 is a threat/fear appeal, whereas message #5 has elements of a threat appeal, but focuses on the positive: ". . . it could save your life." Message #4 emphasizes positive affect.
- The benefit promised. Message #1 does not include a benefit (other than perhaps satisfying curiosity); messages #2 and #4 convey a somewhat vague promise of the possibility of more successful treatment in exchange for an oral cancer exam. Message #3's implicit promise is that getting an oral cancer exam can help one avoid very negative consequences—disfiguring surgery and death. Message #5 promises an easy way to potentially save one's life.
- The way in which they support the promised benefit. Message #1 provides no support; messages #2 and #4 include a general statement that oral cancer can be treated more successfully if found early. Message #3 lays out specific negative consequences—low survival rates, disfiguring surgery or death. Message #5 conveys details of the procedure—quick and painless.

Reactions

NIDCR reported that focus group participants most often chose Message #5 as the one most likely to convince them to get checked for oral cancer; about half of each group chose it. Message #3 was chosen next most often; however, a couple of men said it was the message *least* likely to convince them to have an oral cancer exam. Participants noted Messages #3 and #5 were quite similar and captured their attention by referencing African American men, smoking and drinking, and potential consequences of not acting. However, they seemed more comfortable with the fifth message and divided on whether the third message was too alarming.

Participants described Message #5 as straightforward, believable, and not too alarmist. This message concept most closely reflects key components of the Health Belief model: it clearly specifies the susceptible audience ("Among African American men, those over the age of 40 who smoke, drink, or do both are at the highest risk for oral cancer"), the potentially serious consequences (". . . could save your life"), and the action the susceptible audience could take (get an oral cancer exam) to reduce the severity of those consequences. In addition, it provides information ("it's quick, painless") to increase self-efficacy and reduce potential barriers to getting the exam.

Although Message #3 also clearly specifies the susceptible audience, the potentially serious consequences, and the action that may reduce the severity of those consequences, it uses a strong threat appeal to describe the consequences and does not incorporate information to increase self-efficacy or reduce barriers. In discussion reactions to Message #3, the report noted:

> Health communication researchers urge great caution in using threat appeals, noting that fear appeals are effective only under certain circumstances: they must include a severe threat of physical or social harm, evidence that the target audience member is personally vulnerable to the threat, and solutions that are both easy to perform and effective (Hale & Dillard, 1995). Although messages about the importance of detecting oral cancer early can conform to the first two criteria, early detection messages using a threat appeal inherently do not conform to the third criterion of an effective solution because less than half of African American men with oral cancer survive more than five years. This information helps explain the mixed reaction to [Message #3], which got attention but for some went too far. (NIDCR, 2005, p. 19)

Of the remaining three messages, Message #1 was chosen by almost all participants as the message *least* likely to convince them to have an oral cancer exam, mostly because it was too vague, did not provide enough information (such as the signs of oral cancer), and did not create a sense of urgency. A few participants chose Message #2 as the one most likely to convince them to get checked for oral cancer, saying it spoke to them because they smoke and drink; none rated it least likely to convince them.

Message #4 generated a lukewarm reaction: no participant chose it as most likely to convince him to get an oral cancer exam, but only one person said it was the least likely to do so. This message is notable because it promises a benefit NIDCR's previous focus groups had indicated was valued by African American men: "being there" for loved ones. However, participants' reactions suggested that the benefit was overused in communications to them, did not differentiate the behavior, and did not motivate them.

■ CONCLUSIONS

NIDCR's report concluded that if the focus group participants were typical members of the target audience, it is likely that many African-American men at risk for oral cancer have little awareness of the disease and little or no awareness of their risk for it (parts of the focus group discussions not summarized here revealed that if they think of oral cancer at all, they think of it as something that happens to white residents of the southern United States, baseball players, and others who use smokeless tobacco). As a result, they have little reason to attend to messages about oral cancer unless those messages convey that they are at risk.

NIDCR's report also concluded that their findings were consistent with the principles of the Health Belief Model, in that the message concept most preferred by the focus group members conformed to the model's principles, and the messages that were not preferred did not. The preferred message first tells the target audience that they are at risk for oral cancer by specifying African American men over the age of 40 who smoke, drink or do both. Second, the phrase "and it could save your life" conveys the potentially serious consequences of undetected oral cancer. Third, the message informs target audience members that there is an action they can take (get an oral cancer exam) that can reduce the severity of oral cancer's consequences. Finally, it addresses and reduces anticipated barriers to taking action by stating that the exam is quick and painless.

■ ADA OUTDOOR ADVERTISING CAMPAIGN

In the fall and winter of 2001–2002, the American Dental Association (ADA) sponsored a six-month, 11-city outdoor adverting campaign (billboards, bus boards, taxi tops) to increase awareness of the importance of early detection of oral cancer (ADA, 2003). All advertisements featured one of two images: a Caucasian female in her twenties with a lesion on her tongue or a mouth with a lesion on the tongue, and included the messages,

"It's tiny now. Don't let it grow up to be oral cancer," and
"See your dentist. Testing now is painless."

The campaign's implementation in Miami-Dade County, Florida was evaluated to determine community changes in awareness of the campaign, attitudes, and behavior. A non-equivalent control group design was used in which results from pre- and post-intervention telephone surveys of adults in Miami-Dade County were compared with results from Jacksonville-Duval County in northeastern Florida, where the campaign did not run (Papas, Logan & Tomar, 2004).

Papas and colleagues reported that respondents in Miami-Dade were more likely than those in Jacksonville-Duval to correctly identify the billboard message to get tested for oral cancer. However, Miami-Dade respondents were less likely than those in the Jacksonville-Duval control community to report ever having an oral cancer examination, or to have heard of oral cancer. Evaluators found that oral cancer examinations were significantly more frequent in both counties after the campaign, and there were no significant differences between the two counties on the proportion of individuals who reported having seen the campaign or on any other item measuring awareness or impact of the campaign.

The evaluators concluded, "Results suggest the Florida billboard campaign had limited success in increasing public awareness. Future cancer awareness campaigns should incorporate theoretical models, target high-risk groups and the broader community and provide culturally relevant messages as part of a multi-media campaign." (Papas et al., 2004, p. 121). Papas and colleagues discussed in detail their concerns about how the messages and creative approach used were likely to have been interpreted by high-risk groups:

> Using social cognitive theory to analyze the ADA billboard campaign message depicting a white woman in her 20s, the message conveyed was that oral cancer is a disease of youthful Caucasian women. Because persons at greatest risk for oral cancer are black and white men over age 50 and African American men who smoke or are heavy drinkers are significantly less likely than any other group to see a dentist in a given year, the billboard message may have been inappropriate for reaching the groups at high risk. Blacks constitute the largest proportion of our sample, suggesting the limited effectiveness of the campaign may be associated with the racial dissimilarity of the model and hence the seeming irrelevance of the message (p. 130).

ADA has defended the campaign's focus on younger people and its creative approach. ADA President T. Howard Jones, D.M.D., said, "While those at greatest risk for oral cancer are typically over 40 with a history of smoking and/or alcohol use, we are seeing reports of an increase in populations traditionally considered at lower risk" (ADA, 2003). In addition, an article in the *Journal of the American Dental Association* notes studies have shown "a nearly fivefold increase in the incidence of oral cancer in young oral cancer patients (those younger than 40 years of age), many of whom had no traditional risk factors" (Stahl, Meskin, & Brown,

2004, p. 1266), that incidence of oral cancer in women has increased significantly in the past 40 years, and that "the image used by the ADA oral cancer campaign captured the attention of both the consumer and the dental profession, and it created dialogue about a disease that had been ignored for far too long" (p. 1266). The ADA website relates one anecdote of a 27-year-old man (race not reported) being diagnosed with oral cancer after his girlfriend and roommate saw the billboards and encouraged him to see a dentist. (ADA, 2002).

■ DISCUSSION

Evaluation of the 2001–2002 AMA campaign by Papas and colleagues indicates the campaign was not effective for the audience most at risk of developing oral cancer and therefore its messaging approach would not be a good choice if one's goal was to have the greatest impact on the public's health. The NIDCR study provides an example of how alternative messages can be developed using theory for guidance and then explored with high-risk audiences.

References

American Dental Association. (2002). Oral cancer survivor credits ADA campaign, *ADA News,* January 25. Accessed April 21, 2006, at http://www.ada.org/prof/resources/pubs/adanews/adanewsarticle.asp?articleid=862

American Dental Association. (2003). "Screen your patients early for oral cancer," *ADA Community Brief,* 1(5), 4–5. Accessed April 21, 2006 at http://www.ada.org/prof/resources/pubs/epubs/brief/brief_0306.pdf

American Dental Association. (2004). The American Dental Association's oral cancer campaign: The impact on consumers and dentists. *Journal of the American Dental Association,* 135 (September), 1261–1267. Accessed April 21, 2006 at http://jada.ada.org/cgi/reprint/135/9/1261

Centers for Disease Control and Prevention. (1994). Examinations for oral cancer—United States, 1992. *MMWR, 43,* 198–200.

Hale, J.L., & Dillard, J.P. (1995). Fear appeals in health promotion campaigns: Too much, too little, or just right? In E. Maibach & R.L. Parrott (Eds.), *Designing health messages: Approaches from communication theory and public health practice* (pp. 65–80). Thousand Oaks, CA: Sage.

Horowitz, A.M., Mourjah, P., Gift, H.G. (1995). U.S. adult knowledge of risk factors for and signs of oral cancers: 1990. *Journal of the American Dental Association, 126,* 39–45.

National Institute of Dental and Craniofacial Research. (2004). *Focus group summary report: Oral cancer in african american men.* Bethesda, MD: Author.

National Institute of Dental and Craniofacial Research. (2005). *Insights into how african american men react to messages about oral cancer,* Bethesda, MD: Author.

Papas, R.K., Logan, H.L., & Tomar, S.L. (2004). Effectiveness of a community-based oral cancer awareness campaign (United States). *Cancer Causes and Control,* 15, 121–131.

Stahl S., Meskin L.H., Brown L.J. *J Am Dent Assoc.* 2004 Sep;135(9):1261–1267

Sutton, S.M., Balch, G.I., & Lefebvre, R.C. (1995). Strategic questions for con-sumer-based health communications. *Public Health Reports,* 110, 725–733.

Tomar, S.L. (2000). Oral cancer risk factors and dental visits among U.S. racial/eth-nic groups. [Abstract 3281]. *Journal of Dental Research,* 79 (special issue), 554.

Vernon, S.W. (1999). Risk perception and risk communication for cancer screen-ing behaviors: a review. *Journal of the National Cancer Institute Monographs,* 25, 101–118.

A

Hiring Agencies, Contractors, and Consultants

This appendix is designed to provide guidance on (1) determining when to go outside your organization for assistance in developing, implementing, or assessing marketing interventions; (2) assessing the options to ensure a good fit between the organization and the agency, consultant, or contractor once the decision has been made; and (3) working with outside firms or consultants. Many of the specific examples are oriented toward selecting firms for marketing communication tasks (usually advertising or public relations agencies) because their services are, often used in social change interventions. However, many of the tips would apply when hiring firms for other activities.

■ WHEN IS OUTSIDE ASSISTANCE NEEDED?

Social change interventions can include such diverse components as advertising, continuing medical education modules, grass-roots advocacy, lobbying, media relations or advocacy, special events, train-the-trainer courses, and direct provision of tangible goods or services. Public health organizations turn to outside help for one or more of the following reasons:

- To obtain specialized skills not available internally. For example, few public health organizations employ staff with advertising copywriting and production skills.
- To handle work overflow. Sometimes in-house staff have the necessary skills, but the intervention creates more work than they can handle.
- To obtain an outside viewpoint. Evaluation is most often contracted out for this reason, but outside viewpoints also can be very helpful

with strategic planning and message development. And in some situations, the opinions of "outsiders" may have more credibility than the opinions of staff who are trying to get an intervention funded.

■ TIPS ON SELECTING AGENCIES, CONSULTANTS, AND OTHER CONTRACTORS

Every organization has unique constraints on hiring outside contractors. The process outlined below can be modified to fit your organization's requirements.

1. Determine what in-house staff can do—based on skills and time available—versus what should be contracted out.
2. Group the tasks that must be contracted out based on skills required to perform them—for example, market research, evaluation, advertising, media relations, grass-roots advocacy.
3. Determine how many contractors you will need. Be careful about assuming that one contractor can handle many diverse tasks—or about believing those who say they can. For example, organizing grass-roots advocacy is very different from producing advertising or handling media relations; most firms do not have staff that can handle all of these assignments equally well. At the same time, try to avoid hiring contractors with overlapping expertise or multiple contractors for assignments requiring the same skills. For example, assigning different communication projects to separate contractors may increase costs (representatives from each may need to attend planning meetings, and each firm needs to manage the account) without providing a commensurate increase in quality. If your organization's staff does not have the expertise to assess the types of contractors needed, it may help to convene a search committee that includes in-house staff and outside consultants.
4. Identify potential contractors (firms or independent consultants). Ask colleagues for recommendations, and find out who did work that you think is outstanding. A good next step is to send a short questionnaire to each firm (or consultant) to assess its interest and capabilities. (See **Exhibit A-1** for sample questions for advertising and public relations firms. The list of questions in the exhibit is extensive; some questions could be reserved for the written proposals.)
5. Request written proposals or presentations from the firms of interest to you. Make the request in writing, and be clear about what you want done. Convey, at a minimum,
   - Basic facts about the program, including goals and objectives.
   - Specific services that will be needed.
   - Details regarding compensation.

6. Protect yourself. As part of your initial request or, at the latest, before a contract is signed:

- *Ask about any conflicts of interest.* While "real" conflicts of interest are rare (e.g., the same account team handling both your effort to reduce soft drink consumption and the agency's Coca-Cola account), "perceived" conflicts can result in bad publicity, particularly for non-profit and government agencies. Determine what your organization can tolerate. Many public health organizations will not allow agencies to bid on their business if they also have clients whose products are deemed detrimental to public health, such as tobacco companies. However, in today's world many communication firms are owned by a few behemoth holding companies, so carefully phrase requirements regarding conflicts of interest or you may inadvertently disqualify many firms (it is not unusual for two firms with the same owner to compete against each other for business). For example, you may have legitimate concerns about a 10–20 person firm working on your campaign to reduce drunk driving and a beer company's business, but would not have these same concerns about another unit of a large conglomerate servicing the business. Finally, consider the advice of respected advertising agency veterans Roman, Maas, and Nisenholtz (2003):

  > Conflicts are largely an emotional issue, seldom (if ever) a real one. We've never heard of any trade secrets being stolen—it's hard enough to get people to pay attention to the research and data they have in hand.
  >
  > The real issue is loyalty—whose side are you on? Other professional service firms such as management consultants, lawyers, and accounting firms handle several clients in a product category. Better to look the other way on tangential conflicts than to eliminate a strong agency from consideration by being a hard-liner (p. 224).

- *Ask what percentage of time proposed staff are committed to other projects.* Some contractors are notorious for the "bait and switch": They know their star staff are committed to other projects, but they bid them to increase their chance of winning the business. Then when they have the business, they substitute other, less experienced staff.
- *Include a "key personnel" clause.* This clause states that the contractor cannot remove anyone designated "key personnel" from your project without notifying you first, and that you must approve any "key personnel" replacements.
- *Ask for unit pricing and cost assumptions* (including any additional tasks or materials needed to complete the project that are

Exhibit A-1 Screening Questions To Identify Potential Communication Firms

General Information

1. What were the total annual billings of your firm for each of the last 5 years?
2. List your firm's three largest clients and the percentage of total current agency billings each represents.
3. List three average-sized clients and the percentage of billings each represents.
4. List the accounts your firm has won and lost over the past 2 years and the total billings for each account. Why were the accounts lost or resigned?
5. Describe any experience that your firm and executives have with [SOCIAL CHANGE TOPIC].
6. What experience has your firm had that is pertinent to the marketing, merchandising, and advertising of [SOCIAL CHANGE TOPIC]?
7. (For Advertising Agencies) Approximately what percentage of your last year's billings went into the following media? (List TV, radio, newspaper, magazines, outdoor, Internet, other.)
8. Describe your approach to developing communication messages and materials.

Organization and Personnel

1. What is the total number of people employed full time by your agency? Provide a breakdown by department or function.
2. Describe the organization and philosophy of your creative department. What are the agency's capabilities regarding the creation and production of TV, radio, Internet and print advertising?
3. Who is your creative director, and how long has this individual been employed by you? What other agencies has he or she worked for?
4. (For Advertising Agencies) What is the organization of your media planning staff? Describe how they function.

Research

1. If applicable, describe the organization and capabilities of your research department.
2. How would you describe effective communications?
3. Have you measured the effectiveness of your work for clients?
4. What methods do you use to measure communication effectiveness pre- and post-production?

Additional Information

1. Provide a functional organizational chart of your firm.
2. Furnish biographical information on the people who will work on the account.
3. List your current accounts, approximate billings, and length of time they have been with the firm.
4. Assuming you have no objection, please provide the names, addresses, and telephone numbers of several of your clients and principal contacts, preferably at least one large account and one medium-sized account.
5. List any new products or services you have introduced for clients during the past 3 years.
6. In a paragraph or two, describe the attributes of your agency vis-à-vis other agencies in [NAME OF CITY/STATE].

Source: Adapted with permission from D. Zucker, *The Advertising Agency: Your Partner in Communications,* © 1992, The Academy for Educational Development.

not in the budget). Both pieces of information help you compare contractor costs. Also, sometimes organizations forget to include particular items in their request (or don't realize they should be included). Scrupulous contractors then find themselves in a quandary: Should they include the necessary steps in their budget, thereby increasing their costs (and possibly causing them to lose the business), or should they assume that the organization will handle the other tasks some other way? (Unscrupulous contractors just ignore the other tasks and materials, wait until the contract is signed, and then bring them up as modifications.) If the contract is for materials that could go through many revisions, ask for the number of anticipated revisions to be noted in the assumptions.

- *Ask for budgets in terms of labor hours as well as dollars.* This information will help you (1) assess whether the contractor understands the scope of work and (2) compare the level of effort each contractor is proposing (i.e. the total dollar amount might be the same but might buy you vastly different quantities of professional time).

- *Ask for examples of past work done by proposed staff.* Ask that each example be accompanied by a description of the role each staff member played in it. When you hire a contractor, particularly for creative products, you are really buying the expertise of the individuals who work on your project. Asking for examples of their work (rather than or in addition to the firm's) helps ensure that you get what you think was proposed.

- *Always get multiple bids or proposals for complex scopes of work.* Doing so not only helps you compare prices, it helps you assess how clear you were in your instructions—if all bidders have radically different proposals and prices, your scope of work may not have been clear.

- *Stipulate that the contractor will incorporate your revisions before finalizing the product.* While most contractors want you to be happy with the final product, it is safest to have all approval points written into the contract.

7. Evaluate the prospects. **Exhibit A-2** lists 10 questions to ask any type of contractor or consultant and **Exhibit A-3** lists some specific characteristics to assess in communication firms. Some thoughts to keep in mind as you assess each candidate:

- *Excellent skills are more important than content knowledge in most cases.* Successful contractors get that way by being fast learners. You can teach them what they need to know about your problem, but you can't teach them their discipline. For example, if you have to choose between an advertising agency with great creative abilities but little knowledge of your particular topic and an agency with mediocre creative abilities but lots of content knowledge, go

---

Exhibit A-2   Questions for Potential Contractors

---

1. How would you propose working and communicating with us?
2. Why are you interested in this project?
3. How important would this work be to you firm? Why?
4. Tell us about the most personally satisfying project that you've worked on over the past several years.
5. What makes your firm unique?
6. What is your firm's greatest strength?
7. What is the biggest unexpected problem you've encountered on a recent program, and how did you address it?
8. What would you expect from us as a client?
9. Who will be working on our account?
10. What is your preferred/typical method of compensation?

Source: Copyright © John Killpack.

---

with the former, with one caveat: Agencies that have no experience working with public health organizations often have difficulty working within the scientific constraints imposed by the field and the levels of approval required. Evaluate such agencies carefully to see how willing they are to work within your parameters.

- *Make sure they tell you how they will apply their experience to your problem.* They may have done some great work in the past, but if they can't apply it to your needs, who cares?

- *Did they follow your instructions?* Contractors are on their best behavior when they are pursuing a business opportunity. If they don't listen to you now, they never will.

- *Don't penalize them if they didn't provide something you didn't ask for.* One contractor may include a great idea that goes beyond the services you requested. It is unfair to penalize the others for not proposing something comparable.

- *Make yourself available for questions.* If possible, meet with the candidates before you ask for proposals. You're hiring contractors for their expertise. They may recommend a totally different approach after hearing a little bit about the issue.

- *How's the chemistry?* Do you want to work with them? Contracting relationships are often fraught with tension due to project demands. If you aren't comfortable with the project staff, you won't have a good working relationship with that organization, and the project will suffer.

Exhibit A-3 Evaluating Communication Contractors

Core Capabilities

- **Using research.** It has been clearly demonstrated that the most effective communications programs are based on the ability to understand the true implications of research. Does the firm have a track record of using research to shape effective communication strategies? Does it demonstrate a comfort with research? (Many successful communicators still prefer to go with "gut instincts" or strategies that have worked in the past.)

- **Developing strategy.** Many firms have standardized approaches to developing communication strategies and messages. Does the firm have a specific process it prefers to follow? Is it rigid or flexible? Are the firm's strategies centered on consumer needs or client desires?

- **Innovation.** While traditional approaches to communications and marketing can be comfortably safe and proven, the greatest leaps are often made by those who are willing to take a chance on a new or unproved approach. Can the firm be expected to present fresh approaches? How has it helped other clients become innovators?

- **Execution.** The smartest, most innovative strategy is of course useless if it can't be executed, or isn't executed properly. Does the firm inspire confidence in its ability to get the job done? Can it work "smart" to get the most out of a limited budget?

- **Evaluation.** The success of many communication programs is difficult to measure, particularly when there are no sales figures to examine. How does the firm assess the relative benefit of its work? (Numbers of articles generated or interviews scheduled are not valid measures of success unless those are specific objectives of the program.)

- **Client service.** Every firm will say that its philosophy is to be a "partner" with its client, but what does that really mean? How does it like to work? Working with a committee can be a challenge: How would the firm suggest approaching the project?

- **Fiscal responsibility/terms.** What is the firm's preferred method of compensation? Is it familiar with the billing and accounting procedures necessary to work with government agencies?

Chemistry

One of the primary reasons to have individual interviews is to assess the "chemistry" between the committee and representatives from the candidate firms. Provided that all firms are qualified to handle the project, chemistry may be the most valid basis for making a choice. Would it be enjoyable to work with these people?

Interest

One of the things that will hopefully become clear in candidates' presentations and/or proposals is their level of interest in the project. If they do not answer the question unprompted, a question to pose is: "Why are you interested in working on the project?"

Source: Copyright © John Killpack.

■ TIPS ON WORKING WITH CONTRACTORS

Once you have selected a contractor:

- Make sure you understand how the contractor charges (i.e., hourly, retainer, per project, commission, or some combination) and what the contractor will charge for, including incidentals (such as local travel and phone). Find out how much the contractor charges for services such as photocopying and faxing—these are often moneymakers for the firm and can send your bill higher than you anticipated. Ask if the contractor marks up out-of-pocket costs, and if so, how much (charging 15% or more is not unusual and can add up fast on major expenditures, such as research and production).

- Remember that for most contractors time equals money. Don't waste your money by wasting your contractor's time, and don't expect the contractor to give you lots of time for free. Contract staff who bill hourly face enormous pressure to bill as many hours as possible.

- Make sure everyone involved understands who is responsible for each aspect of the project. Make sure you understand who your point of contact is for each aspect.

- Limit contractor staff at meetings to those who absolutely need to be there (everybody is usually costing you money). But make sure that everyone who needs to be there is.

- Always give as much direction as possible up front, and be consistent. It usually costs you a lot of money if contractors have to go "back to the drawing board," plus it can demoralize them and, if it happens repeatedly, jeopardize the quality of future work.

- Establish a timeline that includes regular meetings and milestones for you to review the work. Waiting to review a project until it is "finished" is almost always a bad idea because there are too many opportunities for the contractor to go off strategy.

- For creative products:
  - Keep the approval process simple and the number of people who must approve small. Good creative product almost never emerges from a committee.
  - "Learn the fine art of conducting a creative meeting. Don't nitpick. Deal with the important issues first—strategy, consumer benefit, brand positioning, personality. State clearly whether the advertisement [or other creative product] succeeds in these areas. And if not, why not. It frustrates a creative team to push themselves hard to come up with a great campaign, only to have the client deal with details. It's okay to tell people they have missed the target. Just don't leave them there guessing" (Roman et al., 2003, pp. 217–218).

- "The best clients are not meddlers. Agencies work harder if someone points out the problems, then lets them find the solution. If
  they expect someone will always tell them what to do, they won't
  try as hard" (Roman et al., 2003, p. 218).

- Ask for estimates of hours for all tasks, and ask for monthly progress
  reports that account for all hours and expenditures. Monitor them
  carefully, and discuss any significant discrepancies between estimated
  and actual costs with the contractor immediately. You don't need to
  find out halfway through a project that you're out of money.

Reference

Roman, K., Maas, J., & Nisenholtz, M. (2003). *How to Advertise*. (3rd ed.).
New York: St. Martin's Press.

APPENDIX

B

Suggested Readings

Andreasen, A.R. (1995). *Marketing social change: Changing behavior to promote health, social development, and the environment.* San Francisco: Jossey-Bass.

Andreasen, A.R. (2006). *Social marketing in the 21st century.* Thousand Oaks, CA: Sage.

Backer, T.E., Rogers, E.M., & Sopory, P. (1992). *Designing health communication campaigns: What works.* Thousand Oaks, CA:Sage.

Bickel, W.K. & Vuchinich, R.E. (Eds.) (2000). *Reframing health behavior change with behavioral economics.* Mahway, NJ: Lawrence Erlbaum Associates.

Bandura, A. (1986). *Social foundations of thought and action.* Englewood Cliffs, NJ:Prentice-Hall.

Grier, S. & Bryant, C. (2005). Social marketing in public health. *Annual Review of Public Health,* 26, 319–39.

Chapman, S., & Lupton, D. (1994). *The fight for public health: Principles and practices of media advocacy.* London: BMJ Publishing Group.

Gladwell, M. (2000). *The tipping point.* Boston: Little, Brown.

Glanz, K., Rimer, B.K. & Lewis, F.M. (Eds.). (2002). *Health behavior and health education: Theory, research and practice* (3rd ed.). San Francisco: Jossey-Bass.

Goldberg, M.E., Fishbein, M., & Middlestadt, S.E. (1997). *Social marketing: Theoretical and practical perspectives.* Mahwah, NJ: Lawrence Erlbaum Associates.

Green, L.W., & Kreuter, M.W. (2005). *Health program planning: An educational and ecological approach* (4th ed.). New York: McGraw-Hill.

Hastings, G. & Saren, M. (2003). The critical contribution of social marketing. *Marketing Theory,* 3(3), 305–322.

Hornik, R.C. (Ed.) (2002). *Public health communication: Evidence for behavior change.* Mahway, NJ: Lawrence Erlbaum Associates.

Kotler, P., & Andreasen, A.R. (2003). *Strategic marketing for non-profit organizations* (6th ed.). Upper Saddle River, NJ: Prentice-Hall.

Kotler, P. & Armstrong, G. (2004). *Principles of marketing* (10th ed.). Upper Saddle River, NJ: Pearson Education.

Kotler, P., Roberto, E.L., & Lee, N. (2002). *Social marketing: Improving the quality of life* (2nd ed.). Thousand Oaks, CA: Sage.

Lefebvre, R.C., & Flora, J.A. (1988). Social marketing and public health intervention. *Health Education Quarterly,* 15, 299–315.

Maibach, E., & Parrott, R.L. (Eds.). (1997). *Designing health messages: Approaches from communication theory and public health practice.* Thousand Oaks, CA: Sage.

Mark, M. & Pearson, C.S. (2001). *The hero and the outlaw: Building extraordinary brands through the power of archetypes.* New York: McGraw-Hill.

McKenzie-Mohr, D. & Smith, W. (1999). *Fostering sustainable behavior: An introduction to community-based social marketing.* Gabriola Island, BC: New Society Publishers.

National Cancer Institute. (2002). *Making health communication programs work: A planner's guide* (NIH Pub. No. 02-5145). Bethesda, MD: Author.

Rogers, E.M. (1995). *Diffusion of innovations* (4TH ed.). New York: Free Press

Roman, K., Maas, J. & Nisenholtz, M. (2003). *How to advertise* (3rd ed.). New York: St. Martin's Press.

Rossi, P.H., Lipsey, M.W. & Freeman, H.E. (2004). *Evaluation: A systematic approach* (7th ed.). Thousand Oaks, CA: Sage.

Rothschild, M.L. (1999). Carrots, sticks and promises: A conceptual framework for the behavior management of public health and social issues. *Journal of Marketing, 63,* 24–37.

Steckler, A. & Linnan, L. (Eds.) (2002). *Process evaluation for public health interventions and research.* San Francisco: Jossey-Bass.

Sutton, S.M., Balch, G.I., & Lefebvre, R.C. (1995). Strategic questions for consumer-based health communications. *Public Health Reports, 110,* 725–733.

Wallack, L., & Dorfman, L. (1996). Media advocacy: A strategy for advancing policy and promoting health. *Health Education Quarterly, 23,* 293–317.

Wallack, L., Dorfman, L., Jernigan, D., & Themba, M. (1993). *Media advocacy and public health.* Newbury Park, CA: Sage.

APPENDIX C

Glossary of Terms

Audience segmentation: Dividing the population into groups with the goal of identifying groups whose members are similar to each other and distinct from other groups along dimensions that are meaningful in the context of the program.

Brand: a name, phrase, sign, symbol or design, or some combination of these, which conveys meaning and value, typically through using our shared cultural code.

Coalition: A group of organizations that come together to address a common goal. Most often run by a committee composed of representatives from each (or many) coalition members.

Communication strategy: How the social change will be positioned in the audience's mind. It describes the target audience, the action they should take as a result of exposure to the communication, the key benefit they will receive in exchange, support for that benefit, the image of the action that the communication should convey, and how target audience members can be reached.

Creative brief: A one- to two-page summary of the communication strategy that is given to the creative team to use for guidance when developing materials.

Diffusion of innovations: Theory of the process by which an innovation (an idea, practice, or object that is perceived as new by an individual or other unit of adoption, such as an organization or community) is communicated through certain channels over time among the members of a social system.

Entertainment-education: Embedding social change messages in entertainment media (i.e., movies, television programs other than news, some radio programs, comic books). Also called edutainment.

Focus groups: A qualitative research technique that involves 1- to 2-hour structured discussions among 6 to 10 participants, led by a trained moderator working from a list of topic areas or questions. Appropriate for exploring and gaining insights into a target audience's behaviors, reactions and motivations.

Formative evaluation: Studies conducted to assess reactions to proposed program components so that they can be refined before they are finalized and implemented.

Framing memo: A document presenting an analysis of the ways an issue is framed by proponents and opponents. Its core is a matrix that summarizes, for each framing strategy, (1) the core position, or main argument; (2) the metaphor used (typically a familiar analogy); (3) catch phrases used to describe the argument; (4) symbols; (5) visual images evoked by the argument; (6) the implied source of the problem; and (7) the principle or core values appealed to.

Frequency: The number of times each target audience member is exposed to a particular message or material.

Gatekeeper: An individual or organization through whom a program's components or materials must pass to reach the target audience.

Goals: Translation(s) of a program's mission into specific behavioral outcomes. Distinct from *objectives*.

Gross impressions: An estimate of how many opportunities there were for messages delivered through the mass media to be seen or heard; calculated by summing the circulation and/or audience size associated with each publication of a story or advertisement. Not a measure of number of people reached.

Intermediary: An organization or individual that can or must be used to reach a target audience; part of a distribution channel.

Marketing: an organizational function and a set of processes for creating, communicating, and delivering value to customers and for managing customer relationships in ways that benefit the organization and its stakeholders.

Marketing mix: Product, price, place, and promotion; the variables that a marketer can change.

Media advocacy: Bringing about policy changes by using the media to put pressure on policy makers. This is accomplished by placing issues on the media agenda through media relations efforts and/or paid advertising, or seeing that issues already on the media agenda are framed from a policy perspective. The belief is that once issues are on the media agenda, they become part of the public agenda and force policy makers to act.

Message concepts: Statements that present key aspects of the communication strategy to members of the target audience.

Objectives: Quantification of goals; objectives describe the specific intermediate steps to be taken to make progress toward goals. For public health efforts, objectives are often changes in audience behavior over time; levels of participation in specific program activities; or measured changes in attitudes, beliefs, or skills associated with prevention practices, with the expectation that change in these factors will facilitate or reflect change in outcome behavior and ultimately morbidity and mortality. Distinct from *goals*.

Offering: The product (bundle of benefits) being offered to an audience.

Outcome evaluation: Research conducted to determine whether an intervention had the intended effects on behavior. Usually conducted after the intervention is finished, but can be conducted periodically during and after the intervention.

Place: Situations in which the target audience does or can perform the health behavior and outlets through which the target audience does or can obtain any tangible goods or services necessary for the health behavior.

Price: Cost to a target audience member, in money, time, effort, lifestyle, or psyche, of engaging in a behavior (or purchasing a product or using a service).

Primary research: Studies that are designed and conducted specifically to answer a current research question (as compared with secondary research).

Process evaluation: Studies conducted during and immediately after implementation to document what program components were delivered and to whom, how, when, and where they were delivered. This information can then be used to assess and refine components and delivery strategies.

Product: Bundle of benefits that the target audience receives in exchange for taking the public health action. May or may not include a tangible good or service.

Promotion: Some combination of advertising, media relations, promotional events, personal selling, and/or entertainment to communicate with target audience members about a product, service, program, or behavior change.

Qualitative research: Provides insights into a target audience; addresses questions of why rather than how many. Results are not quantifiable and not projectable to the population from which participants were drawn.

Quantitative research: Provides measures of *how many* members of a population have particular knowledge or attitudes, or engage in a particular behavior. If conducted with a probability sample and appropriately constructed questions, can be representative of and projectable to the population from which the sample was drawn.

Reach: The total number of people exposed to a message or material.

Secondary research: Studies that were originally conducted for some purpose other than the current research question(s) (as compared with *primary research*).

Social marketing: Application of commercial marketing principles to the analysis, planning, execution, and evaluation of programs designed to directly influence the voluntary behavior of individuals or the environments in which those behaviors occur in order to improve personal and societal welfare.

Strategy: Long-term (usually 3 to 5 years), broad approach(es) that an organization takes to achieving its objectives. Distinct from *tactics*.

Tactics: Short-term detailed steps used to implement a strategy. For example, a community event, a specific training module, or a specific public service advertising campaign are all tactics.

EPILOGUE

What Does the Future Hold?

If the public health field successfully embraces a marketing orientation, its future will be brighter. This is because there exists "a readily stimulated reservoir of appreciation for the services of public health, within the public in general and among elected officials in particular" (Kroger, McKenna, Shepherd, Howze, & Knights, 1997, p. 274). An overwhelming majority of Americans already attach a great deal of importance to the core functions of public health. The challenge is to define and frame the public health product to tap into this reservoir of support. The existence of strong support for public health services makes marketing public health a great opportunity for the practitioner.

Public health practitioners at all levels of training, and public health training institutions, must respond positively to this marketing opportunity. Individual practitioners should take advantage of professional education programs to enhance their knowledge and skills in marketing, communication, and media advocacy. Schools of public health should incorporate these disciplines into their research and training programs, and should provide advanced training in these areas to experienced public health professionals. All public health institutions should seek collaborations with experts in these areas from the private sector, if not incorporate positions in these areas directly into their personnel infrastructure.

The federal government and, in particular, the Centers for Disease Control and Prevention (CDC), should continue to play a lead role in placing an emphasis on marketing public health. The formative research the CDC has conducted provides key strategic insights that will allow public health practitioners across the nation to understand target audiences for marketing public health as an institution. But non-profit and private sector organizations should assist in these research efforts as well, and some level of formative research should be conducted by public health practitioners, even at the local level.

Will public health practitioners abandon the traditional selling orientation and bring a consumer orientation to their work? Will they embrace formative research and learn how to create, communicate, and deliver public health behaviors, programs, and policies in a way that satisfies the needs and wants of their target audiences, reinforces those audiences' core values, and develops a compelling positioning for public health, allowing strong relationships to be built with target audiences? Will public health institutions adequately provide for the professional training of new and continuing personnel in the areas of marketing, communication, and media advocacy?

As the public health practitioners of today and tomorrow the future of public health is entirely in our hands. Capitalizing on our opportunity to shape this future will require three accomplishments. First, we must work to restore a unified vision of the mission of public health in society. Second, we must reassert our fundamental role as advocates for the achievement of this mission. Finally, we must turn to the people from whom our charge derives in the first place-the public-and learn how to create and deliver our programs and policies so that their needs and wants are met. Successfully marketing public health requires that we put the public back in public health.

Reference

Kroger, F., McKenna, J.W., Shepherd, M., Howze, E.H., & Knight, D.S. (1997). Marketing public health: The CDC experience. In M.E. Goldberg, M. Fishbein, & S.E. Middlestadt (Eds.), *Social marketing: Theoretical and practical perspectives* (pp. 267–290). Mahwah, NJ: Lawrence Erlbaum Associates.

INDEX

A

ability, in replacement behaviors,
    245–246, 250, 258
  Road Crew example, 283–284
  worksheets for, 296, 298
academic journals, editorial coverage
    in, 474, 480
Academy for Educational
    Development, 417–418
access
  to health care
    as crisis, 9, 17–18, 86
    managed care impact on, 18,
      87–88
    socioeconomic disparity in, 85,
      88, 194
  to marketing resources, target
    audience selection and, 310
accidents
  behavior-related factors of, 9–10
  death caused by, 6
  poverty associated with, 11
acquired immunodeficiency
    syndrome (AIDS)
  death related to, 21, 73
  entertainment-education on, 441
  heterosexual transmission of, 157
  lack of personal control, 46, 47,
    74–76, 77
  preventive programs for, 73–77,
    122, 140, 156–157, 186, 264
    formative research on, 302–303
  in Rwanda, 164, 166, 173–175
  stigma associated with, 173–174
ACS (American Cancer Society),
    100, 101, 146, 484, 538
action, in social change theory, 209,
    210–211, 217
  barriers to, 221, 301–302
  communication strategies based
    on, 356, 358, 359–361
  marketing example, 220, 231–237

worksheet for identifying
    potential, 386
active response mechanisms, for
    process evaluation, 482–484
  unsolicited *vs.*, 469, 481
activities of daily living, severe
    limitations of. *See* disability
adolescents
  alcohol use by, 49
  MADD impact on, 64–67
  public health products targeting,
    58–60, 61, 63
  tobacco use by, 49–51, 59, 227
advertising, 442–449
  basic principles of, 443–444
  creative, suggestions for assessing,
    444–445, 446–447
  effective characteristics of, 442–443
  monitoring of, 476–481
  outdoor, ADA example, 542–544
  outside agencies for, 547–555
  paid *vs.* public service, 445, 448
  placement of, 442–449, 474
    tracking mechanisms for, 476,
      480–481
  for pretesting, 325–326, 327
    school health program example,
      348–353, 354
  for promotion, 424, 425, 442
  public service, 445, 448
    (*See also* public service
      announcements (PSAs))
  resources for, 319
advertising equivalencies, 474
advocacy, in public health practice,
    39–41
  framing theory and, 133–134,
    148–150
  historical perspectives of, 114, 154
  inadequate emphasis on, 40,
    99–100

Notes

Notes

Notes

Notes